Hindu Law

Hindu Law
Beyond Tradition and Modernity

Werner Menski

OXFORD
UNIVERSITY PRESS

OXFORD
UNIVERSITY PRESS

YMCA Library Building, Jai Singh Road, New Delhi 110 001

Oxford University Press is a department of the University of Oxford. It furthers the University's objective of excellence in research, scholarship, and education by publishing worldwide in

Oxford New York

Auckland Bangkok Buenos Aires Cape Town Chennai
Dar es Salaam Delhi Hong Kong Istanbul Karachi Kolkata
Kuala Lumpur Madrid Melbourne Mexico City Mumbai Nairobi
São Paulo Shanghai Taipei Tokyo Toronto

Oxford is a registered trademark of Oxford University Press
in the UK and in certain other countries

Published in India
By Oxford University Press, New Delhi

ISBN 019 566503 1

Typeset in Le Studio Graphique, Delhi 110 017
Printed at Pauls Press, New Delhi 110 020
Published by Manzar Khan, Oxford University Press
YMCA Library Building, Jai Singh Road, New Delhi 110 001

To

Professor J. Duncan M. Derrett
Formerly Professor of Oriental Laws,
University of London
On his eighty-first birthday
30 August 2003

Contents

PART II

SUBSTANTIVE HINDU LAW BEYOND TRADITION AND MODERNITY

PART III

CONCLUDING ANALYSIS

Abbreviations

AIR	*All India Reporter*
All	Allahabad
AllER	*All England Reports*
A&N	Assam & Nagaland
AnWR	*Andhra Weekly Reporter*
AP	Andhra Pradesh
Art.	Article of the Constitution of India, 1950
ASIL	*Annual Survey of Indian Law*
AV	*Atharvaveda*
BJP	Bharatiya Janata Party
Bom	Bombay
CA	Court of Appeal
CEDAW	Convention on the Elimination of Discrimination Against Women, 1981
Ch.	chapter
CMRA	Child Marriage Restraint Act, 1929
CMRAA	Child Marriage Restraint (Amendment) Act, 1978
CrPC	Criminal Procedure Code, 1898 or 1973
FB	Full Bench
FLR	*Family Law Reports*
Guj	Gujarat
HAMA	Hindu Adoptions and Maintenance Act, 1956
HMA	Hindu Marriage Act, 1955
HMGA	Hindu Minority and Guardianship Act, 1956
HP	Himachal Pradesh
HSA	Hindu Succession Act, 1956
ILI	Indian Law Institute
ILR	*Indian Law Reports*
IPC	Indian Penal Code, 1860
J	Judge, or: Journal section
JJ	Judges

J&K	Jammu and Kashmir
JT	*Judgments Today*
Kant	Karnataka
KLT	*Kerala Law Times*
Mad	Madras
MCHR	*Madras High Court Reports*
MIA	*Moore's Indian Appeals*
MLJ	*Madras Law Journal*
MP	Madhya Pradesh
MWPRDA	Muslim Women (Protection of Rights on Divorce) Act, 1986
Mys	Mysore
n.	note or footnote
NGO	Non-governmental organization
NSLS	Non-state legal system
Or or Ori	Orissa
OUP	Oxford University Press
Pat	Patna (HC of Bihar)
PC	Privy Council
P&H	Panjab and Haryana
Pun or Punj	Panjab
Rs.	Indian Rupees
RV	*Ṛgveda*
S.	section of a statute
SB	Special Bench
SC	Supreme Court
SCC	Supreme Court Cases
SLS	State legal system
SMA	Special Marriage Act, 1954
SN	Short Note
SOAS	School of Oriental and African Studies
UP	Uttar Pradesh
WR	Sutherland's *Weekly Reporter*
ZDMG	*Zeitschrift der Deutschen Morgenländischen Gesellschaft*

Preface

This study should not be read as an attempt to revive classical Hindu law or to promote any sort of *hindutva* agenda that claims universality as well as superiority over all rivals. The internal perspective of 'Hinduism' as a cluster of belief systems has always been marked by vast scope for dissent and disagreement, and the constructed uniformities of Hindu law and culture, whether ancient or current, do not match the complexities of reality, whenever and however perceived. As an academic endeavour to study Hindu law in its complex conceptual and historical dimensions, this book is not a political manifesto for a Hinduized India or the recreation of some Golden Past or ancient indigenous laws, but a case study of applied jurisprudence.

Since I am one of the very few remaining scholars of Hindu law in the world outside India, it appeared to be my professional duty to provide a fresh detailed analysis of Hindu law as it presents itself today. The field has been unduly neglected, largely because of modernist assumptions about the growing irrelevance of 'religious' legal systems such as Hindu law. Developments concerning Muslim law have led to a growing realization that non-Western legal orders are not only relevant, but have also acquired increasing prominence in a plural, global world.

My approach and my findings will not please modernists, who still want to see the whole world governed by one giant uniform, but in reality Western-style, 'rule of law'. Rather, this book points to increasing legal pluralization and the never-ending process of legal interactions at different levels of formality and official standing, correlating with recent theoretical work about different forms of legal pluralism and cultural diversity. Today's Hindu law (and also Indian law as a whole, but that is the subject of another study) contains elements from different layers of the past and the present. This legal reconstruction process never stops, leading today to the emergence of postmodern Hindu law. The present study confirms, therefore, that Hindu law has a temple of its own in the pantheon of comparative jurisprudence and is much more alive and versatile than most observers imagine.

But what is Hindu law? Given the lack of a universally agreed definition of 'Hindu', combined with its increasingly politicized *hindutva* significance, the term 'Hindu law' automatically conjures up many dangerous and dark meanings. In these troubled times, in which the outlook on the twenty-first century remains clouded by a worldwide upsurge of radical religious opposition to 'globalization' and the hegemony of Euro-American values, our understanding of Hindu law and 'Hindu' itself remain more critical and difficult questions than ever before. Yet they raise a whole cluster of poorly understood and hotly contested issues.

It needs to be stressed from the outset that Hindu law is, like African law and Islamic law, a *family* of laws rather than one single unit. There may be something like an essential conceptual core, but in the case of Hindu law, even that core has remained so flexible, diffuse, and internally diverse that we do well to think and speak of 'unity in diversity' rather than imagining a fixed, unified Hindu system. In various senses, thus, there is no such thing as Hindu law, and yet it exists visibly and invisibly, and in manifold manifestations, which now include the postmodern. Since Hindu law cannot ever be regarded as a strictly uniform law—rather it has always been characterized by enormous fluidity and internal plurality—the label 'Hindu law' must be taken to cover a large variety of quite different legal systems. Many of its rules are outrightly contradictory, incorporating not only high-caste Sanskritic elements, but also innumerable subaltern, local, and often less prestigious perspectives.[1] Given that the totality of Hindu law is so complex, it has become tempting for many writers to pick out certain aspects or rules as placative evidence of what Hindu law was or is, ignoring the multi-dimensional internal contests within it and, thus, the situational relativity of any one rule or statement.

It is undeniable that the system of Hindu law has been held together by an identifiable underlying traditional conceptual framework, and in that sense must be seen as sharing sufficient internal coherence to be classified as a single unit, conceptually and historically distinct from other major world legal systems. At the same time, however, as much existing scholarship finds difficult to grasp, Hindu law has also always been a collection of socio-legal systems of parallel complexity, fluidity, and diversity, evading codification and, thus, the control of powerful men in human societies who perennially seek to dictate legal rules to all others. Forever defying such positivist ambitions and asserting against it the inexpressible diversity and sublimity of Hindu consciousness, 'Hindu law' exists and survives, albeit not strongly. In fact, it now predominantly languishes as a minor subject of study, often hidden under the label 'personal law', in the syllabus of Indian law schools. Hindu law also figures prominently in the public mind,[2] but what does it comprise? It seems that various myths exercise a

[1] Guha's (1997) important study would appear to recognize this, but does so only to a limited extent, as we shall see.

[2] One must note here, above all, the wrong but still all too common perception (both in India and in Europe) that Indian law generally is just a copied version of English law, while the level of public knowledge of Hindu law among non-Indians now extends to colourful images of 'arranged' or 'forced' marriages, perhaps to sati, and little else. The complex relationships between Hindu law and Indian law escape a wider public, which enables politicized discourse mongerers to dismiss Hindu law and to denigrate Indian laws as and when they please.

powerful influence in this field and that the subject is not only extremely complex, but also politically loaded.

In planning this book, it became evident that the simple collective label itself would remain useful. An exhaustive study of Hindu law, more so if combined with Indian family law, is impossible to write, even if one were to spend an entire lifetime on it. I hope that the modest result of quite limited endeavours presented here will spark off lively criticism. No doubt, some of the messages in this book will not please the guardians of certain vested academic and political interests, but that should prove no deterrent. Academic censorship needs to be resisted in this age of political correctness. If the textual concepts of ancient Hindu law as well as the realities of postmodern Hindu law are there for all to see and study, it should not be a matter of whether we like what we find or not. The ancient building of 'Hindu law' remains open for inspection and use. Hindu law continues to exist, even if it is distressingly complex for academics who would prefer the world to be simpler, or simply different. What matters above all, however, is what India, and I mean in particular the Indian state, as the major country in which Hindu law plays a central role in society, will make of its legal heritage and its present manifestations in the process of seeking to ensure at least a semblance of justice for well over a billion people—an enormous challenge that no liberal democracy in the history of humankind has ever faced.

This book could not have been written without years of study and the help of many people, including numerous bright students who challenged and probed from all kinds of angles, and thus helped sharpen the central arguments of this book. The novice or ignorant outsider often offers a sharp test for the professed expert's ideas. We scholars do well to listen to our students, more so in applied jurisprudence classes than elsewhere perhaps, as the issues debated in a book of this kind concern most of us in some form, and in a very personal sense they are not merely an arcane subject of 'Oriental' legal studies. The present study on Hindu law thus also contributes to the general legal literature, adding dimensions that tend to be ignored or overlooked in mainstream legal work. To have established legal notions questioned and cross-examined in debates never loses its fascination for a teacher of non-European laws who, like myself, straddles the global community of major legal systems with one leg firmly in Europe and the other in Asia. We may talk a lot about fatwas, the guru's word as law, or the 'rule of law' in various garbs. At the end of the day, however, and perhaps in South Asian family laws more so than elsewhere, what is right or wrong remains a matter of personal choice and individual conscience, within a culture-specific context, informed by awareness of dharma or shariat, however subconscious and inarticulate that may be. As this book argues, the postmodern study of Hindu law, and of Hindu family law in today's India and South Asia, needs to re-focus on the concerns of people as individuals who are not only part of families, large and small, of clans, local societies, and nations, but ultimately the universe in a way that Hindus and those who share their universe perceive it.

But who knows about such perceptions; indeed, who wants to know? Even before publication, a book of this kind faces dismissive condemnation as 'stuff we do not want to know about today'. Given widespread ideological hostility to anything 'Hindu', it is no secret that the ivory tower of formal studies on Hindu law has been in danger of becoming a ghost tower. As one of the few remaining Hindu law scholars, I submit with some urgency that Hindu legal studies remain centrally relevant to South Asian scholarship as well as comparative legal studies. Hindu legal studies and related fields need to be filled with fresh life through vigorous conceptual analysis that wipes the dust off the sheets and layers of Orientalist and colonial constructions and shakes the equally dated modernist cobwebs of scholarly politicking about 'traditional' Hindu concepts and their submission to the supposedly superior authority of the modern secular law. Yet, as indicated, this should not be read as an aggressive advocation of *hindutva* in its loaded political sense; rather it must be regarded as a much-needed push for the acceptance of explicitly postmodern scholarship which, while not claiming to be value-free, aims to interrogate and analyse as fairly and comprehensively as possible the relevance of ancient Indian legal concepts for the contemporary world and its problems. Sadly, writing a book on Hindu law will inevitably be seen as conservative and subversive Hinduizing, but that cannot distract from the need to understand the subject for the very central role that it plays in today's development processes in India, South Asia, and elsewhere. I hope that the present study and its arguments about postmodernity as an ancient as well as contemporary phenomenon in South Asia will inspire others to take up various aspects in the study of Hindu law—for the field is vast, and serious scholarship remains pitifully slow in covering it.

Throughout the book, I have been tempted to say much more than I should about Indian public law and its relation to Hindu concepts, and the role of the state in its various forms in particular. It is necessary to emphasize that the field of Indian public law cannot be properly understood without reference to Hindu law. However, hardly any scholar seems prepared to appreciate that, even if we examine the recent work of prominent Indian intellectuals (Shourie 2001; Sathe 2002). It is certainly not enough to make exaggerated claims about some glorious ancient Hindu age in which all modern institutions were already fully developed (Jois 1990a).

Leading institutions of legal education in India now recognize the dreadful state of Hindu law teaching, of the growing gap between theory and socio-legal reality, between law as taught in Indian law schools and as practised in the courts, or indeed outside them.[3] In explicit recognition of this, the present

[3] I am grateful to Professor Mohan Gopal, then Director of the National Law School of India University in Bangalore, for instructive discussions on this deeply troubling issue, to which there are no easy remedies. The ship of Indian legal education has all too long neglected a holistic course and now floats virtually rudderless near the rocks of unfulfilled positivist dreams about top-down control by the

study of postmodern Hindu laws in India needed to be less state-centred than a standard public law approach would allow for. It had to be more centrally focused on how individual perceptions of private concerns and public interest can be combined, to create viable rule systems that in effect place minimal financial demands and burdens on the state, expecting individual citizens in situations of conflict to work out agreeable informal solutions for themselves. The present study identifies the phenomenon of self-controlled order as a central theme of Hindu law, rather than any positivist principle that depends on rulers, lawmakers, or the state. While such self-controlled ordering will not be totally independent of various forms of state law, it would in my view be a fundamental mistake to start with the presumption that in Hindu law it is the state that is central as a lawmaker, or even law enforcer. By constantly looking for the state and its effects and powers, many scholars who wrote about certain aspects of Hindu law have seriously distorted the entire field of study, to the extent that non-lawyers are now routinely repeating cherished assumptions about fixed ancient rules of 'Hindu law', which do not live up to intense scrutiny, while lawyers themselves have remained too impressed with their own self-flattering, self-legitimizing claims to the 'truth' of positivist axioms.

There is thus a need to explore and develop a different way of looking at Hindu law and of analysing its development.[4] As the present study shows, without essentializing the Hinduness of the phenomenon, from early ancient origins right up to the present day, Hindu law has been a vaguely integrated whole (or an open system) in a holistically conceived universe, not some segregated and specialized Western-style legal system that can be manipulated at will by a few legal professionals. Hindu law has been a matter of concern for everyone at all levels and at all times, even for non-Hindus, who may vigorously attack Hindu concepts, but cannot make them non-existent. It was never just religion or the state (or ancient sages) which regulated people's daily lives in South Asia and other parts of the world that have adapted South Asian models into their own cultures.

The implications of this legal system—unlimited and open-textured legal informality and pluralism—cannot and should not be seen as evidence of 'underdevelopment', but on the contrary must be read as a sophisticated, highly developed legal order that nurtured and enhanced flexibility and creative problem solving. Hindu law and other similar Asian and African legal systems must be regarded as culture-specific forms of legal arrangements, markedly different from the processes of 'laying down the law' as Western-style positivism

---

professional classes, while Indian society, as always, largely continues to ignore professional lawyers and everything they represent.

[4] I must here record my methodological indebtedness to Professor J.D.M. Derrett, whose earlier *Introduction to Modern Hindu Law* (1963c) was found inadequate by the learned author himself (in his *Critique of Modern Hindu Law* (1970) because he realized that to state the official law, however comprehensively, was not really the main point of Hindu legal study.

envisages. No amount of modernization will ever totally modify these ancient patterns, which now reappear more visibly as a manifestation of postmodernism in Hindu law. In fact, in the light of ancient Indian 'legal' evidence, as examined in detail in the present study, it is worth considering whether postmodernism is perhaps not all that new and represents a reinvention of ancient wheels, with a few new elements, rather than the pinnacle of sophistication of human development and understanding.

It remains for me here to thank those institutions and individuals who helped to ensure that the present study eventually saw the light of day. British academic structures these days are not sufficiently conducive to the production of scholarly works that demand deep thought over a long period of time. The present book could, and should, have been written much earlier, but it was not until recently that sabbatical arrangements were made more widely available for such purposes. My first round of thanks therefore go to the Nuffield Foundation for awarding me a Social Science Research Fellowship during part of the 1993–94 session. This seems a long time ago now, but it allowed me to leave most teaching and administrative duties to others and to prepare material for several books on Indian law. Further, I thank the School of Oriental and African Studies (SOAS) for granting me sabbatical leave for part of 2002, and especially the Arts and Humanities Research Board (AHRB) for offering a generous award in early 2002 that enabled me to spend a few much-needed extra months of work on the present manuscript. I am also immensely grateful to the authorities at the Tokyo University of Foreign Studies (TUFS), and in particular Professor Masao Naito and Professor Kazuhiko Machida, for creating such a wonderfully supportive research environment in the new campus of the Research Institute for Languages and Cultures of Asia and Africa at TUFS, where the manuscript was finalized.

Many thanks must go to my former academic teachers, now all retired, who laid the foundations for an intensely interdisciplinary combination of cross-cultural and comparative understanding of Hinduism and Hindu law which allowed me to be drawn into a field that was seemingly on its last leg in the early 1980s. Professor Joachim F. Sprockhoff, first at Kiel (1973–76) and later at Bochum University (1977–80), was a real Germanic guru, a fully dedicated mentor as well as a tough boss with high expectations. His deep academic and personal influence might long have remained as invisible as the key concepts of Hindu law that he, together with Professor Jagdishchandra Jain from Bombay (in 1973–74) first taught me.[5]

As the young Sanskritist's attention was gradually drawn more and more towards socio-legal issues and away from grammar and the philosophical quagmires of the Upaniṣads, the combination of a classically trained indologist with legal expertise emerged, a process greatly propelled by a meeting with Professor Derrett in 1980 (Menski 2000b). The quite unexpected result was that I

[5] On the work of Professor Jain and his influence, see Menski (1993b) and the obituary for Professor Jain in Vol. 146 No. 2 [1996] *ZDMG*, pp. 269–77.

became Derrett's successor at the School of Oriental and African Studies at London University from 1981 onwards.

Professor Derrett must be described as an amazingly prolific polymath, not unlike the other great authority on Hindu law, P.V. Kane from Pune, who died in the early 1970s. Derrett's vast and deeply probing academic work remains influential in a number of fields, but has been neglected by many scholars.[6] In India, he is still seen by many as 'that great rishi on the banks of the Thames', and he is undoubtedly the greatest living authority on Hindu law. Professor Derrett decided to retire early from Hindu law studies in 1981, at a time of immense transformations within the Indian legal system and in Hindu law, some of which he vigorously disagreed with. He alerted me to new trends, but it took time for some of those processes of reconstruction to come out as legal evidence that could eventually be analysed in detail. The phrase that 'law is a process' is amply borne out by developments in ancient as well as postmodern Hindu law. Researching Hindu law is in itself a complex exercise in comparative legal study.

It would be disingenuous to claim that I am not following in the footsteps of Professor Derrett. Rereading his work for the purpose of writing the present book, I was often struck how torn Derrett had been between being a member of the British colonial establishment and someone who very rightly claimed to understand India and Indians. He laboured, to some extent, in a condition of postmodernity—between being a traditionalist and an avid modernizer, between mysogyny and fierce protection of the multiple and often only too rightful interests of women, between wishing to aim for clarity in his writing and the trend to overburden the text with learned footnotes that reflect an amazing versatility and a lifetime of dedicated hard work. I could not possibly have carried on where my illustrious predecessor left, nor could I have carried on in his style. The present work is therefore offered in honour of the master with the sharp pen, but with some trepidation. While all deficiencies of the present study are reflections of my own continuing imperfections, it must be said that but for Professor Derrett's acute sense of detachment, wise foresight, cautious initial guidance, and continuing *āśīrvād*, this particular book would never have been written. I therefore dedicate this book to Professor J. Duncan M. Derrett, former Professor of Oriental Laws at SOAS in the University of London, on the occasion of his eighty-first birthday on 30 August 2003.

Others have contributed much more to this study than they might appreciate. In addition to childcare and her own career, my wife has always been a critical sounding board for ideas about Hindu cultural developments. Our sons have now grown up, experiencing the coexistence of tradition and modernity,

[6] A collection of essays in honour of Professor Derrett (Sontheimer and Aithal 1982), focusing on indology and law, contains a complete bibliography of Derrett's work on India at pp. 413–58. Some later additions can be made to that most instructive list, which does not include Derrett's equally numerous studies on a variety of other subjects.

and have been able to partake deeply in the postmodern discussions on which this book centres. I am also particularly grateful to several learned academic colleagues and a group of enthusiastic students who read parts of the manuscript while it was in the making, offering helpful suggestions for clarification on many points. Thanks in this regard go especially to Professor Upendra Baxi of the University of Warwick, Professor Esin Örücü at Glasgow University, Professor Jörg Fisch at the University of Zürich, Dr Roger Ballard at Manchester University, Dr Prakash Shah at Queen Mary College, University of London, and Dr Ihsan Yilmaz at SOAS. Rajesh Bhavsar, Hiren Mistry, Rishi Handa, Anwesha Arya, Mark Johnson, Makiko Oya, and Kyosuke Adachi all contributed in various ways to the making and completion of this book, and I am grateful to all of them, as well as to the anonymous reviewers of the manuscript.

Professor Peri Bhaskararao of the Information Resources Centre at the Tokyo University of Foreign Studies most helpfully offered some extra fonts for the transliteration of Sanskrit terms. The staff at Oxford University Press in Delhi provided efficient back-up and support at all stages. Of course, all errors and omissions remain the responsibility of the author. I have tried to state the current law of India, where relevant, as it stood in early 2002.

June 2003 WERNER MENSKI

PART I

Historical and Conceptual Background

1

Introduction

Tradition and Modernity in Hindu Law

Despite being an ancient legal system, Hindu law has defied many modernist death wishes, copious predictions of its gradual demise or almost complete displacement (Galanter 1972; repeated in Galanter and Krishnan 2001), and even dramatic proclamations of its death (Derrett 1978a). It holds its position as a major legal system of the world, often despised and largely unrecognized, but massively present in the new millennium. At least 800 million people, roughly a seventh of the world citizenry, remain influenced and formally governed by Hindu law in one form or another.

Despite its numerous traditional and modern elements, Hindu law today must be seen as a postmodern phenomenon, displaying its internal dynamism and perennial capacity for flexibility and realignment in conjunction with the societies to and in which it applies. Hindu law has not remained mired in some distant past, as is often too readily assumed by modernist scholars who would not even know where to start studying this complex phenomenon, or who do not trust Hindu law to develop ameliorative internal mechanisms.[1] In a powerful preface, Ashis Nandy (1983: x) noted that over time, 'the attack on the non-modern cultures has become a threat to their survival' and wrote famously of the colonialism of the mind (ibid.: xi). Nandy (2001: x) also emphasizes the need to remind ourselves that human beings not only kill each other for all sorts of reasons, but also have the capacity to negotiate differences, to support each other, and to resist organized mass violence. Thus, he argues (id.):

> ... we are obliged to stand witness to the many lost worlds of culture and culturally based systems of knowledge that have been proclaimed obsolete and, along with the millions of their living practitioners, exported to the past with a remarkable intellectual slight of hand.

Modernist scholarship has developed a mastery of sorts in denying the positive potential of culture and tradition. Assuming that 'tradition' is singularly bad for women, and refusing to see symbiotic gender relations as a potentially positive element, Rajan (1999: 14) develops her conclusion that 'cultural resources are selectively appropriated to mesh with the post-colonial nation state's

[1] Typically, Rajan (1998: 98) denies Hindu law any capacity for justice-focused growth when she insists that 'tolerance alone is too weak a concept to achieve communal harmony and gender justice in India'.

requirements, in this case the social control of women in the context of "modernisation"'. While this kind of analysis centres on the state's role, some feminist writing focuses on the 'false consciousness' (Sarkar and Butalia 1995: 4) of Hindu women of the right. From a variety of angles, so-called traditional elements in Hindu cultures and societies are challenged as counterproductive to ideals of a good life. Such assumptions would appear to leave no room for recourse to 'Hindu tradition' and 'religion' and deny the capacity of Hindu law and culture to act as vehicles of modernization and tools for social welfare.

However, in India today, 'Hindu tradition' as well as Hindu law have become much more than feeble colonial constructs (another scholarly misrepresentation), waiting to be reformed away by a modernizing process of secularization, as envisaged in the long-proposed uniform civil code for all Indians.[2] That project now looks like a political football, 'shot into space'[3]—and thus out of bounds—by recent political and legal developments, on which this book has much to say. The present study provides detailed evidence of the plurality-conscious, justice-focused reconstruction of postmodern Hindu law in contemporary India and thus challenges the basic assumptions of modernity-fixated scholarship on Indian society and development which continues to denigrate culture and 'tradition' and posits that only rational, secular approaches offer remedies for the ills of the past. Meanwhile, 'Hindu tradition' lives on today, and Hindu law prospers in India and elsewhere. In fact, at least in some areas (and not only in family law, as we shall see) it leads the way for sustainable and replicable legal developments within the wider context of India's much-discussed reconstruction of a 'fractured modernity' (Corbridge and Harriss 2000: 238).

The study of Hindu law has been neglected due to a combination of declining knowledge of its classical foundations and the pressures of modern political correctness, to the effect that studying Hindu law is often seen as a regressive activity, dangerous for minorities and, in particular, for women.[4]

[2] This issue arises because India, like most countries of Asia and Africa, operates a system of concurrent personal laws. The call for a uniform civil code then becomes not only a cry for internal legal reform, but virtually a demand for abolition of the existing formal structure in favour of a purportedly uniform Western model. Various benefits are supposed to flow almost automatically from such a restructuring of the legal system, linked to the issue of secularism. Some insight into modernist scholarly and activist mindsets is provided by Agnes (1995: 153) who finds it 'evident that deep-seated communal biases can be overcome only when secularism becomes an important agenda and a conscious political choice for any progressive movement'.

[3] In terms of traditional Hindu concepts, this is *antarīkṣa*, the space between earth and heaven, a kind of 'no man's land'. Strangely, Austin (2001: 15 and 18) assumes that India already has a uniform civil code, which incorporates Hindu law, but not Muslim law.

[4] For example, the otherwise excellent introduction in the important collection of essays in honour of Lotika Sarkar (Dhanda and Parashar 1999) studiously ignores

For many reasons, the label 'Hindu law' still conjures up images of frightful abuses such as sati, dowry murders, caste discrimination, untouchability, and other atrocities in the name of tradition and religion. Anything 'Hindu' is therefore quickly denigrated in many ways, not only by many followers of monotheistic religions, but also those who imagine and assert that a modern world, by which is often meant a Western-inspired world, can do without so-called primitive religious and cultural traditions. Lawyers (as well as more recently whole cohorts of diasporic Indian scholars), as we shall see, have had specific reasons to argue for modernity.[5] Colonialism added its own ideologies and arguments to subjugate not only Hindus, but also Hindu law, all in the name of universalistic legal constructs.[6] In the complex process of scholarly manipulations, many scholars have engaged (often unwittingly) in misleading and sometimes simply wrong representations of Hindu 'tradition'. As we shall see in abundance, prominent among those misrepresentations is the assumption that ancient Hindu texts 'prescribed' certain rules, which even infects the most intricate subaltern writing.[7]

Some important scholarship points out that modernist assertions are misguided (Nandy 1983; 2001) and are being challenged by the recent history of Hindu law as it plays itself out within the wider framework of the post-Nehruvian Indian state. Arguments about the inherent political incorrectness and modern irrelevance of Hindu law have conveniently forgotten that the so-called modern traditions have their own roots in specific Western cultural and religious traditions. So how could India be called upon to 'modernize', if that simply meant, at one level, shedding the social and cultural concepts that make up the fabric of the various hybrid Indian identities? How can hundreds of millions of Hindus be expected, let alone forced, to abandon Hindu law?

Hindu law. Other studies are more explicitly negative about oppression by the two major religions of India (Sarkar and Sivaramayya 1994: 1) and discrimination against women by the personal laws (Parashar 1992; Sarkar and Butalia 1995; Chatterjee and Jeganathan 2000).

[5] S. Basu (1999: 257) points out that those individuals in the executive and legislature who took on the reins of post-colonial government in India 'had invested in learning the allegedly modern British legal system, and campaigned strongly to retain it'.

[6] Guha (1997: 67) locates such powerful influences in 'the pervasive power of the ideology of law in English political thought' and rightly critiques the concept of 'rule of law'. Some recent legal writing finally admits that the 'rule of law' is actually an empty concept (Tamanaha 2001: 98).

[7] Even Guha (1997: 28) cuts corners a little too fast when he argues that the 'Laws of Manu' may be said to speak for all the traditional texts. This amazingly counterproductive argument, given Guha's deep and insightful analysis of colonial hegemonic monopolies, suggests that scholars apply different methodologies to different historical periods, overlooking key elements of continuity, in this case the very basic fact of internal plurality and perennial dissent.

Modernity,[8] calling on all 'others' to assimilate to the supposedly higher, apparently secular and 'modern' value systems represented by the West, amounted to thinly veiled pressure to abandon various indigenous traditions and convert to the supposedly universal idioms of modernity.[9] In other words, modernity expected and demanded unidirectional assimilation to alien lego-cultural norms and models, and a stepping outside of one's own inherited traditions. It demanded de-Hinduization, abandoning of Hindu customs, habits, and traditions. While modernity was, at one level, not concerned about religion, it expected the modern world citizen to be of a secular disposition, thus seeking to prescribe one particular religious perspective as appropriate for modernity.

There has, however, been a counter-current to such modernist demands and claims, in several forms and at various times, in Indian as well as other Asian and African societies. Muslims worldwide have been reacting to modernist Western pressures to 'assimilate' to the supposedly superior standards by placatively demonstrating their presence and religious identity, asserting their specific socio-religious value systems, often by violent force when deemed necessary. It is taken for granted that Muslims, mainly given the polemical nature of their religion vis-à-vis Christianity, will resist westernizing modernization in various ways (Sayyid 1997). It is less clearly understood that other non-Western people in the world also make their own claims to cultural validity and to the creative maintenance of their own culture-specific social and legal arrangements.[10]

[8] The concept of 'modernity' is widely defined as that body of ideas and practices associated with the Enlightenment ideals of industrialization, a strong nation-state system and identity, progress, rationality, reason, and objectivity which emerged around the mid-eighteenth century in western Europe. It has, of course, many facets, and has been debated from many angles. The literature on modernity is huge, and there are many aspects of it. No attempt is made here to circumscribe its literary manifestations in any particular form. However, it is important to note that modernity in the legal field is generally understood as meaning positivist or centralist law-making, which claims that only the state, as the sovereign, lays down and maintains a body of rules for society to follow. Of course, such claims have long been challenged by other approaches, but legal positivism has been so dominant that the Japanese jurist Chiba (1986) critically referred to it as 'model jurisprudence' and highlighted its Western biases. A reasonable overview of the multi-faceted meaning of modernity in legal study is found in Ashcroft et al. (1998: 144–7). Galanter (1989: 15–36) presents a useful application of the key concepts to Indian laws.

[9] The debates on the universality of modernity and of human rights continue to be lively and there are no easy answers. For critical approaches see Renteln (1990) and Caney and Jones (2001). Much of international legal scholarship still uncritically accepts the claims of Western superiority, which subtly manifest themselves in discourses of 'civil society', compliance with international standards, 'good governance', and adherence to the 'rule of law'.

[10] On Asians in Britain, see Ballard (1994).

It is highly significant that Hindu reactions to modernist Western assimilationist pressures may have been less vociferous in comparison.[11] However, they appear no less evident if one cares to look, and if one knows enough about ancient Hindu culture and tradition in the first place to be able to see what is not immediately visible, but nevertheless exists.[12] These reactions to the stresses of modernist challenges are not all violently and manifestly expressed. The constant readjustment of Hindu cultural responses to new situations has been practised for millennia, leading to subtle forms of cultural and social change that require sensitive and intricate analysis. Political slogans against an assumed resurgence of Hindu-ness (*hindutva*) will not do. Their hidden agenda often is to deny Hindus the right, point blank, to express their points of view. This is where someone like myself, a classical indologist-turned-lawyer, has a professional obligation to say some of the things that others do not want to hear, and to write a book explaining the place of Hindu law today, while most lawyers wish that this law would just go away, making life easier for the professional—and (allegedly) for women and other subalterns—opening all doors to an imagined bright, modern future.

The discourse on modernizing Hindu law and purging it of its tradition, as a means of aiding India's development process, has become so fractured and insular that few connections are made today between legal and other social science research on post-colonial India.[13] This compartmentalization works both ways. There is an enormously important and fascinating literature about the idea of India itself (Inden 1990; Khilnani 1997), its historical and political representations,[14] and its recent and current reinvention (Corbridge and Harriss 2000; Talbot 2000). But Hindu law and the entire legal framework of India curiously do not figure as central or even peripheral parameters of development and modernization in such debates.[15] Conversely, the leading studies on Hindu law focus on their specific subject area and take virtually no notice of

[11] In my view, the events in and after Ayodhya in 1992, and more recently the so-called 'sectarian' killings in some parts of India during 2002, as well as atrocities against Christians, are closely linked to such globalizing pressures and are not just local disturbances between Hindus and non-Hindus.

[12] Outrightly secular studies, such as Burton Stein's (1998) excellent posthumous work on the history of India, not only fail to capture the all-pervasive Hindu elements operative in their field of study, but also avoid comments on law, which does not even figure in the index.

[13] Robb (1993: 2) has noted that, '[a]s scholarship has inevitably become federal, with separate fields and knowledge, it has been necessary to adopt what might be called principles of subsidiarity'.

[14] See in particular Brown (1990); Chatterjee (1997); Kulke and Rothermund (1998); Bose and Jalal (1998); Bayly (1999); Hardgrave and Kochanek (2000). Specifically for an American readership, see now Ayres and Oldenburg (2002).

[15] When they do, as in Guha's sharp analysis of British historiography, the images of 'law' employed by the non-legal scholar disclose amazing oversights, to use Guha's (1997: xi-xii) own critical terminology, which appear due to exaggerated

social science scholarship and the wider environment within which legal developments have been occurring.[16] The results can be miserably inadequate, as scholarly subsidiarity may give rise to strange flowers, sprouting distortions that have a habit of becoming myths in their own right. Two cautionary examples will suffice. The first is provided by statements on Hindu history made by Graham Chapman (2000:17), a leading geographer of South Asia, who paints a very readable, fascinating picture of ancient India:

> The first King of India was Manu Svayambhu (the self-born Manu) born directly from Brahma, the god of all, and (s)he was hermaphroditic. From him there sprang a line of descendants who gave the earth its name .... But the most famous Manu was the tenth ...

Such stories within stories, for that is what they are in their 'old' Puranic context, are then wrapped up for the contemporary reader by the assertion, at p. 18, that '[t]he name Bharat, which is used in India to identify itself ... is said to derive from King Bharat, a descendant [*sic*] of the mythical king and lawgiver Manu Svayambhuva'. Most readers will not notice that they are here being fed positivist assumptions about how Hindu law originated. Drawing on Western cultural ideas and assumptions about 'law', Chapman unconsciously depicts Hindu law as a kind of Napoleonic legal system, rooted in the works of an identifiable human lawmaker, and refers to its divine roots for added exotic effect. Although Chapman rightly concludes that '[a]s a name it therefore evokes explicit cultural and religious origins' (id.), the legal message thus produced is as seriously distorted as the misrepresentations in many Hindu law books about the role of 'Manu' as the dominant Hindu lawgiver, on which much more needs to be said.[17]

The second example concerns legal issues in modern India, which contain many tripwires for scholarly subsidiarity, too. I have noted for many years that in relation to the infamous *Shah Bano* case of 1985 and its aftermath,[18] politically motivated analysis often does violence to legal reality, so that legal

---

focus on the formal and 'official' phenomena in law as well as in politics. Thus, a remarkable positivism informs not only standard 'traditional' scholarship, but also still infuses the critical literature.

[16] Practising lawyers, in particular, seem to prefer books that are classed as 'ready reckoner' and just give the user 'the law', without any context or explanation. For a recent sample of such work, which is frustratingly inadequate even for the purposes of legal practitioners, see Punj (2001).

[17] Dogra and Dogra (2000) also refer throughout to Manu as 'lawgiver'. Derrett (1968b: 316) points out that '[t]he artificial revival of interest in India's cultural heritage from the last quarter of the nineteenth century stimulated a romantic interest in Manu; and it is from there that the continuing interest in the *śāstra* comes which we find in some cultured classes'.

[18] This case is reported as *Mohd. Ahmed Khan v Shah Bano Begum* AIR 1985 SC 945. For analysis of the subsequent case law see Menski (2001, ch. 4).

fact and politicized fiction do not match at all. Even the most experienced scholars may become a little too deeply involved in their own representations of India's legal realities, failing to check up on published primary sources, particularly law reports. Thus, Corbridge and Harriss (2000: 115 and 179) allowed themselves to be misled by the politicized and deliberately constructed chatter of earlier writers, (which is reflected even in serious and important current issues magazines) regarding the anti-women effects of the Muslim Women Protection of Rights on Divorce Act of 1986, when in fact this Act explicitly protects divorced Muslim wives.[19] Certain political arguments peddled by modernist scholars just do not make sense in the light of the actual legal position; they need to be revisited.

It is quite evident that the voice of informed legal scholarship has been missing in the current debates in social science research on Indian legal developments. This has allowed amazingly bold politicized scholarly distortions about the alleged 'enslavement of Muslim women' (Kapoor and Cossman 1995: 104) by the state law in a book that starts off with the questionable assumption of concerted action of a Hindu-dominated Indian state 'against the besieged community of Indian Muslims' (Sarkar and Butalia 1995: 1). In reality, it is such myopic feminist scholarly writing that disadvantages and betrays Indian women and commits violence against the very people whom it purports to protect. Claiming, in this particular case, that Muslim women do not have certain rights to maintenance and financial protection, while the postmodern state law very clearly contains a totally different message, can only be described as dishonest. However, since it does not suit the dominant feminist agenda to find that postmodern Indian state law actually protects the interests of Muslim ex-wives, modernist feminist scholarship ends up colluding with male Muslim leaders to hide the official legal message and thus to deprive a whole class of women of their due entitlements, perpetuating ignorance and false myths. This is certainly not genuine scholarship, but rather devious misappropriation of scholarly privileges. Since a lot depends on such distorted misrepresentations, in this case the claim that the current Indian state cannot be trusted to develop gender-sensitive mechanisms for protecting vulnerable women, the

[19] There are many reported cases under this Act, which have been widely ignored, but are discussed in detail by Menski (2001: 275–5). Even experienced legal writers such as Agnes (1997: 565) have fallen victims to such misrepresentations instead of reporting and analysing the legal position as it stands. See also S. Basu (2001: 103) and various articles in Larson (2001). However, Agnes (2000: 105) finally takes account of the official pro-women verdicts given by various High Courts, but also reports that 'Muslim men are constantly being advised by their advocates that they no longer need to pay maintenance to their wives and it is their religion that says so'. This is confirmed by Vatuk (2001), but this does not mean that this is the correct legal position. Similarly, Sathe (2002: 266) still presents a 'conservative' interpretation that is surely no longer maintainable after *Danial Latifi v Union of India* 2001 [7] SCC 740, a long-awaited decision of the Indian SC, which upholds the 1986 Act and reiterates its purpose of protecting the rights and legal entitlements of Muslim wives.

intellectual efforts expended in such deception are amazingly complex. However, the whole vexed issue of *Shah Bano* and its aftermath is a house of cards that has now collapsed and demands a serious clearing-up operation in the Augean stables of Indian modernist scholarship. Putting the issue like this is not a bad-tempered challenge to feminist or modernist approaches, merely a reminder that 'clean' methodologies are expected even in the most contentious areas of scholarship. The *Shah Bano* affair, often in conjunction with sati (Sarkar and Butalia 1995: 2), presents a most evident example of malodorous hiding of legal evidence. Part II of the present study will demonstrate in rich detail that many other methodological problems of this kind are lurking everywhere.[20]

Apart from ideological myopia, a major problem for scholarship on Hindu law is that 'law' has been treated as a separate field, as though it does not belong to the federation of social sciences. Hindu law is often not even classed as law, but defined away as 'religion' or 'culture'. This happens partly in view of the presumed death of Hindu law some time ago, because it is treated more or less dismissively as religious tradition,[21] and because of resurgent modernist fears that the religious basis of Hindu law might one day be revived in India. Consequently, the view is taken that such religio-cultural roots need to be eradicated, either by scholarly cold-shouldering or by active argument against their relevance and vigilant opposition to anything 'Hindu' that rears its head.[22]

The confused and highly contentious debates about Indian secularism are elaborate testimony to such complex and often hidden agenda,[23] as well as demonstrating, for all to see, that we are neither able to define 'law' nor to

[20] Since it is primarily a matter of Indian Muslim law, a detailed analysis of the *Shah Bano* case and its aftermath has no place in the present study.

[21] This is not only an American and European perspective. The Japanese have their own versions of Orientalism and seem to romanticize India as a mystic place in which more or less everything is religious, while Japan is perceived as secular. Ayres and Oldenburg (2002: 3) claim from a US perspective that, partly because of the visible impact of high-flying, top-earning Indo-Americans, '[t]he *idea* of India has also changed in the past few years .... Gone are the days when India evoked only exotic stereotypes of saints and beggars'. Traditionally, the aggressive common strategy of Western observers to declare Hindu law as 'religious' immediately distinguishes everything 'Hindu' from the 'legal' sphere, but denies it legitimacy and validity. Combined with legal centralist claims that it is 'law' that governs the world, this immediately amounts to dismissing the relevance of Hindu tradition for legal study.

[22] The rallying cry against *hindutva* is, for example, forcefully documented in the various contributions to Sarkar and Butalia (1995).

[23] A useful survey of the major literature on secularism is found in Jahagirdar (2001), who pushes his own agenda and fails to produce a sufficiently clear account of the key issues. Madan (1987; 1998) and Nandy (1990) make significant contributions to the debates on secularism and its various claims in the Indian context. Nandy (1999) provides a sharp critique of secularism and highlights its abuses.

understand 'religion' in universally agreed ways.[24] Even in the postmodern context of legal debates, most scholars do not want to see such basic difficulties. This confirms that the problematic character of the nature of law itself, and our divergent and partisan understandings of it, are not built as firmly into academic analyses as they should be. We remain trapped by analysing Hindu law and wider Indian legal developments solely within the binary axioms of 'tradition' and 'modernity', 'religion' and 'secularism', 'custom' and 'law', 'backwardness' and 'progress'. Indian legal and social science scholarship has generally seemed unable and unwilling to move beyond these constructed dichotomies to develop a critical analytical approach that questions the simplicity and falsity of modernist conceptions of law, and the widespread blind adherence to them. At times, this seems like a case of self-inflicted blindness to reality, for which there appears to be no cure.

There is, then, an urgent need to reconsider the conceptual groundwork for a more effective and accurate engagement with the postmodern realities of Hindu and wider Indian legal developments. In a postmodern world, modernist ideological posturing cannot masquerade any longer as value-free legal scholarship that dominates the field to the exclusion of all other perspectives. The present study demonstrates not only that postmodern Hindu law exists, but explains in detail how and why it has been developing and growing. This development occurred not in a vacuum, but in a rich and fertile conceptual space that remains unexplored by modernist analysts who either cannot see the wood for the trees any more, or simply do not want to accept that Hindu law could ever metamorphose into such postmodern incarnations as we find today.

Towards a Postmodern Legal Analysis

The current fixation of legal and social science scholarship on modernist axioms in the study of India is on the way to becoming outdated and discredited, disclosing the potential for a reinvigorated and more critical analysis of Hindu legal developments. The demands highlighted earlier for Indian state and society to follow modernist, supposedly universal standards of law, and to purge themselves of all traditional elements, are increasingly being recognized by academic and legal practitioners as untenable, heightening the long-established, somewhat fashionable perception of prevailing crisis in the field (Baxi 1982). In a postmodern context of fervent critical scholarship that seeks to deconstruct the meanings, value systems, and culture-specific understandings built into our conceptions of reality, truth, and knowledge, an increasing number of scholars have begun to question the so-called universality, and desirability, of

[24] For law, Roger Cotterell (2000) now speaks of a methodology of 'perspectivism'. This would suggest that within legal scholarship itself, not only ideological partisanship but another kind of federalization has been taking place, with similar consequences for the fragmentation of knowledge as observed by Peter Robb for the wider field of research (see note 13 above).

such Western-inspired axioms of legal modernity and of secularism (Nandy 1990). Indeed, as can be witnessed from the impacts of postmodern theories and analyses on social science generally, the modernist Enlightenment claims of universality and certainty in reason, rationality, human subjectivity, truth, knowledge, and reality are breaking down, both theoretically and sociologically, to the extent that 'modernity' is no longer seen as providing a universal solution or path for human existence and understanding about the world (Doherty et al. 1992).

A brief excursion into explaining what is meant by postmodernism (and its related field, post-colonialism) is necessary at this point to avoid possible misunderstandings about their employment in this study. The term 'postmodern' has been frequently used in a variety of different contexts and ways in an undiscriminating (and discriminatory) fashion in referring to an actually very diverse, heterogeneous set of ideas and practices. This is the case in both the Indian and Euro-American social science contexts, but particularly in the former, where it has often become entangled in, and confused with, the concept of post-colonialism (see below). While the prefix 'post' presupposes a clear break from something that was earlier, i.e. the modern, or its transcendence, the whole term 'postmodern' is much more ambiguous and problematic and does not, unlike the term 'modern', have a clear reference to a single historical origin.[25] Postmodernism challenges the modernist Enlightenment ideal of universal true knowledge achieved through the exercise of human reason. It suggests that truth, knowledge and reality are all culturally relative and that human subjectivity and human rationality are heterogeneous and diverse, i.e. not universal.[26] In turn, it problematizes the modernist idea that the advance of reason with material and scientific progress necessarily makes things better, that humans become more civilized, and that a dispensation with myths, superstitions, and religion automatically follows, or indeed is desirable, as its revelatory light spreads over more topics of human concern.

For our present purposes, the postmodern challenge can be understood at three distinct but interrelated conceptual levels.[27] First, it challenges the

[25] Although postmodernism began with a particular stylistic shift in presenting art from the modern, functionalist approach in the field of visual and written arts, e.g. pastiche, bricolage, multivocality, sensory disruption, juxtaposition, simultaneity (see Jencks 1996; Rushdie 1992), it is grounded in a loosely unified set of theoretical, or epistemological, arguments that have developed over a long period of time, traceable to the late nineteenth century ideas of the 'play of light' among French impressionists.

[26] These 'truth statements' were made by Upaniṣadic thinkers thousands of years ago. It is therefore possible to argue that the ideas of postmodernism are perhaps nothing new in principle, but continue to re-manifest themselves at particular historical times.

[27] For further explanation of the range of its arguments and impact on the social sciences see Barrett (1991), Docherty (1993), Doherty et al. (1992), Said (1978), and Sarup (1993).

modernist claim of ontology that there is a world of objects that exists independent of the way it is presented to be. Postmodernism argues that realities/phenomena depend on how they are represented to be. Second, postmodernism challenges the Descartian argument of human rationality, i.e. that the rational human subject is the universal foundation for knowledge, suggesting that the human subject is decentred, driven by all sorts of unconscious and irrational desires. Third, postmodernism refutes the modernist assertion of epistemology, that true knowledge corresponds to how the world actually is and that observation or writing is theoretically neutral and has no effect on the thing being observed. Postmodernist/poststructuralist thinkers such as Michel Foucault (1970; 1980) have argued that truth is whatever we agree to call and construct it as such; there is no Archimedean point from which to observe the world independently of knowledge and power relationships, which are mutually constituted. Representation, or observation, of phenomena is not transparent, but invariably influences and distorts the thing that is being observed or represented. Jacques Derrida (1978; 1981) suggested that scholars should therefore deconstruct the underlying meanings that were suppressed in the formation of 'texts' that seek to represent reality, and thereby challenge their 'meta-narratives' and claims to foundational, universal truth and knowledge.

This poststructuralist view has led to a shift in many social science fields (e.g. political science, history, geography, sociology) towards deconstructing discourse, that is, those specific ensembles of ideas, concepts, and classifications that evolve in a particular set of practices and through which meaning is given to physical and social realities. As linguistic frames that define the world in certain ways and in the process exclude alternative interpretations, discourses may not emanate exclusively from particular individuals and institutions but constitute the cumulative effect of many practices. In Foucault's (1980) analysis, discourses generate truth-claims, which not only enframe the way in which reality gets talked and thought about, but actually structure the possibility of what gets included or excluded and of what gets done or remains undone. By deconstructing discourses, that is, their epistemological, ontological, and ocular-centric objectifications of reality, postmodernist and poststructuralist thought seeks to reveal the mutually constitutive relationships between power and knowledge production.

Postmodernism does not limit itself to the theoretical sphere, however. Notably, Lyotard (1984) has defined postmodernism sociologically as an epoch, attempting to map out the contours of 'postmodern society'. Lyotard argues that the grand narratives—truth, reason, and progress—underwriting 'modern' society are breaking down. Instead of a single grand unifying science constituting an 'ideal' approach to life, the explosion of knowledge and communication of different ideas and approaches is, according to Lyotard, shattering the confidence of society in a single universal science into many different and less all-encompassing knowledges. Hence, the postmodern condition can be understood as one of widespread social scepticism about grand and self-legitimating knowledge claims (see also Anderson 1998; Connor 1997; Foster 1985; Jameson 1991). This postmodern celebration of a plurality of perspectives and the stipulated impossibility of complete knowledge has engendered nihilism, pessimistic fatalism, and a 'crisis of representation' in some social science subjects (Marcus and Fisher 1986). Yet it has also inversely led to a much deeper, critical, and more insightful analysis of the social construction of knowledge and reason, influencing the way in which scholars, and humans generally, perceive, understand, and construct reality according to socio-culturally specific axioms (Sarup 1993).

A product of, and parallel accompaniment to, this broad theoretical framework of postmodernism has been post-colonialism. A political and ideological discourse focusing on the continuing cultural and political ramifications of colonialism in both colonized and colonizing societies, post-colonialism has similarly diverse roots as postmodernism. As a dialectically constituted, theoretical, and historical hybrid incorporating the legacy of anti-colonial Marxist struggles and emancipatory movements of gender, ethnicity, and class against bourgeois nationalism, post-colonialism is a form of activist writing that is interdisciplinary and trans-cultural in theory (Bhabha 1994; Young 2001). While it is impossible to consider all its aspects here, the relevance of post-colonial thought to the study of Hindu law lies in its challenge to the way in which our knowledge and the realities of Asian and African civilizations, histories, and political, economic, and socio-cultural systems have been constructed during the colonial period and today by scholars and societies. It seeks to follow a Derridean deconstruction of these 'texts' to reveal their underlying structures of power/domination, and in the process aims to show that dominant, supposedly universal, epistemological models, theories, and concepts that have been used in analysing and explaining Asian and African societies are specific to European societies and cultures, i.e. are Eurocentric, and are thus biased and inappropriate tools of analysis (see, e.g. Said 1978; Spivak 1988 and 1990; Bhabha 1994). Post-colonialism, like postmodernism, must be understood as a theoretically and ideologically informed critique of colonialism/modernity as much as a socially experienced condition. Young (2001: 6) locates the emergence of post-colonial discourse and practice during the Second World War, whose effect was:

> not only to show that the imperial powers were militarily vulnerable, particularly to the non-Western power of imperial Japan, but also to cause them to lose the hitherto unquestioned moral superiority of the values of Western civilization, in the name of which much colonization had been justified. The West was relativized: the decline of the West as an ideology was irretrievable. Colonialism may have brought some benefits of modernity, as its apologists continue to argue, but it also caused extraordinary suffering in human terms, and was singularly destructive with regard to the indigenous cultures with which it came into contact.

Post-colonial theory thus seeks to reveal the inherent falsities and contradictions of the 'civilizing mission' of European colonialism, and its continuing presence and claims in academia and cultures all over the world. Often within a Marxist framework of reference, and as an explicitly anti-imperialist, deconstructivist project, post-colonial theory and critique involve an analysis of the history of colonialism, and investigate its contemporary effects in Western and non-Western societies. Post-colonialism in turn problematizes the binaries of 'modernity' and 'tradition', concepts that were constructed and interwoven into the civilizational meta-narratives of colonialism, thereby revealing the postmodern condition of Asian and African countries which, as King (1995: 120–1) explains, has a longer history than that of Europe and North America:

> ... the Eurocentrically defined cultural conditions of a so-called post-modernity—irony, pastiche, the mixing of different histories, intertextuality, schizophrenia, cultural chasms, fragmentation, incoherence, disjunction of supposedly modern and pre-modern cultures—were characteristic of colonial societies, cultures, environments on the global periphery (in Calcutta, Hong Kong, Rio, or Singapore) decades, if not centuries, before they appeared in Europe or the USA.

Post-colonialism, in pursuing its critical, emancipatory agenda, utilizes such 'postmodern' intellectual and cultural traditions of Asia and Africa as a body of knowledge against the political and cultural hegemony of the West. Post-colonial theory is an explicit attempt to undo the ideological heritage of colonialism both in the decolonized and colonizing countries. It involves, in essence, a decentring of the intellectual sovereignty and dominance of Europe and a critique of Eurocentrism and Western ethnocentricity, as embodied in the assumption that the white male Western point of view is the norm and is true (Young 2001). As a critique of European civilization and culture from the perspective of the 'tricontinental' countries and cultures of Asia, Africa, and South America (ibid.: 4–5), post-colonial theory dislocates, provincializes, and challenges Western knowledge as a product of colonialist and racist thought, revealing how the ordered narrative of its history subsumes, and excludes, all other histories of the world (Chakrabarty 2000). In turn, in seeking to extricate non-Western cultures from the history of colonialism, it seeks to strengthen and develop the resources of their histories and political and intellectual traditions.

In the Indian context, post-colonial research over the last three decades has involved dissecting the inherited colonial legacy of viewing Indian society through Eurocentric concepts of class, nation, ethnicity, and state, arguing that such models and meanings were constructed to reflect colonial prejudices and power ambitions rather than actual 'realities' of Indian society perceived and understood by Indian people themselves (Chakrabarty 1992; 2000). In particular, there has been fervent scholarship in deconstructing the political elite-centred meta-narratives of 'bourgeois' Indian nationalism to give a voice to the excluded subaltern groups, whose critical role in the formation and construction of a national identity of 'Indianness' has been largely ignored in historical and political science scholarship (e.g. Guha 1982). Apart from Guha, Gayatri Spivak (1988; 1990) and Homi Bhabha (1994) have pioneered deconstructivist analysis of the thinly imagined dichotomy between 'traditional' Indian society and the 'modern' colonial state, broadly arguing (though in quite different ways) for recognition of 'hybridity', 'plurality', and 'in-between' as conceptual tools for understanding the post-colonial/postmodern realities of Asia and Africa.

It is impossible to provide a more nuanced genealogy of postmodernism and post-colonialism at this point without losing focus. However, many of these themes are drawn upon and developed later in this study on Hindu law and its changing representations. At this stage, however, it is necessary to briefly clarify how these key terms are to be employed. Although originating and developing along quite distinct epistemological paths, postmodernism and post-colonialism share a similar analytical approach, namely to deconstruct dominant discourses—the images, 'truth-claims', and representations of reality that pervade action and thought in society—and to reveal their falsities and historico-geographical specificities. Postmodernism seeks to capture the broader analytical shift towards questioning knowledge formation and production, and the role of underlying power relations, while post-colonialism specifically involves challenging the colonial vestiges of Eurocentrism and Western ethnocentricity in dominant discourses of non-Western societies. To reflect the breadth and depth of the analytical and theoretical locus of this study, therefore, the term 'postmodern' is employed rather than 'post-colonial'. The present analysis engages to some extent in a post-colonial discourse, and adopts much of its ideological and theoretical critique of colonialism, but it also transcends it in a significant way by revealing how current post-colonial writing, based on negligible analysis of actual case law, uncritically draws upon, and perpetuates, false representations and characterizations of Hindu law. Such problems arise not only while researchers continue to locate their analyses within the colonialist binaries of tradition and modernity. In the context of the present study, a more serious methodological difficulty is posed by the often unreflected assumption that pre-colonial elements of Hindu culture and law are virtually irrelevant for post-colonial debate. For example, Young (2001: 6) appears to assume that '[p]ost-colonial theory involves a political analysis of the cultural history of colonialism, and investigates its contemporary effects in Western and tricontinental cultures, making connections between that past and the politics of the present'. What is missing from such analysis is even a peripheral analysis of the rich seam of pre-colonial Hindu traditions. Ancient Hindu law has, indeed, been declared irrelevant for contemporary analysis in the twenty-first century in a variety of ways.

The theoretical developments of postmodernism hold much potential to enrich the study of law, and of Hindu law. However, to infuse a postmodern approach into legal analysis is not a straightforward process of simply applying its theories in modified form, as suggested by the historical development of the study of law. It appears that, viewing themselves as distant relatives of the social sciences, lawyers have generally been slow to catch the postmodern bug. Indeed, '[l]egal scholarship, whether it be academic writing directed at legal academics or texts for law students, exhibits a long-standing intellectual insularity' (Hunt and Wickham 1998: vii). Arguably, legal scholars have quite purposefully been reluctant, if not overly hostile, to accept radical postmodernist ideas that would transform the way in which we understand and study law (see in detail Menski 2000a). This reluctance stems from a widespread ignorance of social science subjects among legal scholars today, most of whom have only studied black-letter law at law school or in practice.[28] It also has links to a perceptible deep-seated unease about the disruption that postmodern ideas of questioning our constructed understanding of law may cause to established power relations, within the academic legal field as well as in the practice of law itself. Postmodernism challenges many of the claims of legal centralism, and is thus perceived as a hostile force by many lawyers.

However, the opportunities of postmodern thinking for the study of law can be constructive and positive (Peters and Schwenke 2000). A postmodern legal analysis encourages scholars to question claimed 'essentialisms' under the law about the universality of human institutions and behaviour and their governance; to identify, deconstruct and examine the power relations that have underpinned the hitherto supposedly universal theoretical claims that 'law' should only be understood as state law, and that all else created by society should be deemed as merely 'custom'; and to question the processes of legitimization, as well as the purpose, of such constructed axioms.[29] A postmodernist approach in legal thinking interrogates the supposedly rational claims to universality of our understandings of law, and enables us to critically self-reflect on whether our analyses actually represent the 'truth' and 'reality' of law. This, in turn, would provide refreshing insights and a critically constructive 'humanist' approach in the jurisprudential study and practice of law.[30] It will not necessarily lead to a 'crisis of representation'. The skilful application of postmodernism by legal scholars can avoid the risk of succumbing to apathetic nihilism. The vast field of legal theory has always accommodated a variety of theoretical approaches to our understandings of law, with some more dominant than others. Postmodern approaches demand no more, and no less,

[28] It remains to be seen what the long-term effects of introducing five-year LLB programmes with two years of pre-law study will have in Indian legal education. Preliminary observation suggests that blinkered positivist thinking is implanted as effectively by social science academics as by lawyers.

[29] See the theoretical and methodological insights created by the development of Foucault's ideas of power/knowledge by Hunt and Wickham (1998) into a 'sociology of law as governance'.

[30] This characteristically self-reflexive, critical awareness created by postmodernist thought has been described as engendering a radical 'humanization' of the social sciences, which were threatening to become too detached, cold, and 'inhuman' through their obsession with establishing 'scientific' theories and using mathematically rigorous, quantitative methods and statistics (see Dosse 1999).

than that the stifling and oppressive domination of legal positivism and related legal centralist axioms should be challenged and treated in comparative perspective.[31] Hunt and Wickham (1998: 39), in drawing on Foucaultian thought, offer a good example of this constructive element of a postmodern legal analysis:

> Law is not and never has been a unitary phenomenon, even though the assumption that it is, has played a central role in most legal discourses and theories of law. We adhere to the view that law is a complex of practices, discourses and institutions. Over this plurality of legal forms 'state law' persistently, but never with complete success, seeks to impose a unity. This approach can be identified by the label 'legal pluralism'.

A postmodern legal analysis thus takes a pluralistic approach to law. It recognizes it as a complex amalgam of state-produced, religious, and social rules which are forever in competition with each other and interact systemically (Chiba 1986). Law is phenomenally experienced and practised differently across time and space, and cannot therefore be understood universally as Western-style law, or as state law, as assumed in modernist, positivistic thought. In the case of India, a fertile ground for incisive post-colonial analysis as we saw, evidence for the germination of postmodern ideas in the study of law appears to be gradually emerging. A recent volume of legal essays from India tackles the methodological problems of legal scholarship in some detail and attempts to produce a postmodern, feminist approach to the study of law that allows for a variety of perspectives. Having noted that post-structuralism permits a diversity of meanings, Archana Parashar (1999: 11) shows that the assertion that law is simply the law of the sovereign state misses a critical point. Since the law obtains its meaning from the intersection of legal norms and various other social systems of conventions, which interact in many different ways, the task of legal analysts must be to unravel how various levels of meaning are constituted institutionally. Parashar (1999: 11–12) argues:

> The single most important point for any legal theory therefore is the acceptance of the idea that meaning—including legal meaning—is constructed rather than pre-existing and simply waiting to be discovered.
>
> I wish to argue that law like any other institution of society is interconnected with other institutions .... The task of legal scholars therefore, is to explicate the connections between the law and social, political, and economic systems .... The interdisciplinary study of law by lawyers must mean that they bring their knowledge of the doctrine and analyse it in the context of the knowledge of other disciplines. In doing so they carry the responsibility to try and realize the highest aspirations of their profession, i.e. to achieve social justice for all.

[31] For a detailed conceptual analysis of Euro-American jurisprudential models and a plurality-focused attempt to explore the complexities of Hindu, Muslim, African, and Chinese laws, see Menski (2000a).

While Hindu law is completely excluded from this edited volume, such prescriptive suggestions are of direct relevance to the present study. The aim is to understand why Hindu law has not died in India despite its more or less complete official reform and purported abolition, and how in fact it reappears in various jurisdictions all over the world, as a conglomeration of transnational Hindu communities develops.[32] In view of such observable facts, the relevance of subsisting Hindu elements of law for social justice in today's world cannot be ignored. Taking a postmodernist perspective, one can no longer uncritically accept the a priori ideological argument that traditional Hindu legal concepts are 'bad' and that modern law, i.e. state law, is 'good' for Hindus—a classic reflection of rampant modernist ideology. Academic analysis needs to go beyond placative assertions concerning Hindu law and its position between tradition and modernity. Recent feminist scholarship from India, as cited above, now suggests that this analysis must eschew the positivist orientation of Indian legal scholarship,[33] and must transcend the shackles of doctrinal legal thinking.[34]

Nobody could claim that this process is going to be easy or simple. The tentacles of modernist indoctrination are so strong that they tend to impede analysis and prevent embracing of postmodernist ideas, allegedly for fear of falling 'back' into 'traditional' modes of thinking. Perhaps scholars are also fearful of the nihilistic conclusions which postmodern thought and methodology suggest, since nothing seems fully 'true' and certain any more. A more explicitly radical postmodern approach is therefore needed than many scholars seem prepared to contemplate. It will not be sufficient to critique the limits of modernism while retaining its cherished ideological underpinnings. For example, in the context of combating the so-called Sītā ideal of the Hindu woman, the submissive wife who will accept all hardship that her husband chooses to throw at her, and who has thus become a classic hate figure among feminists, Kishwar and Vanita (1991: 48) claim:

> Those of us who wish to combat or reject these ideals have ... been largely ineffective because we tend to do so from a totally 'Western, modernist' standpoint. The tendency is to make people feel that they are backward and stupid to hold values that need to be rejected outright. We must learn to begin with more respect for traditions which people hold dear.

[32] While research on this remains underdeveloped, some beginnings have been made. See Menski (1987; 1993a) and Baumann (1998).

[33] Parashar, in Dhanda and Parashar (1999: 2) clearly argues for a theory of law that encompasses interdisciplinary understandings of law and, at p. 3, laments that '[t]he state of contemporary Indian legal scholarship shows an overwhelming reliance on positivist ideas about the law'.

[34] On legal positivism or the analytical school of jurisprudence, see in detail Cotterell (1989). In an instructive essay on legal positivism and Indian democracy, S.P. Sathe (2001: 38) highlights that '[l]egal positivism is a theory which defines law as divorced from morality. It looks to the formal validity of law'. While this is correct, no doubt, another aspect of legal positivist theory, which is somewhat more

A little later, this modernist self-critique is concluded with an admission of failure to take account of the needs of common people. Arguing for the need to identify points of strength within cultural traditions, Kishwar and Vanita (1991: 49) write:

> Our cultural traditions have tremendous potential within them to combat reactionary and anti-women ideas .... The rejection of the harmful is then made much easier than attempts to overthrow traditions totally or to attack them arrogantly from outside, as most of us Westernised modernists tend to do, since we have been completely alienated from our own culture ....

Other writers have been less forthright. While Jethmalani (1995: 129–37) writes generally on feminist legal theory, Dhanda and Parashar (1999: 28) merely complain about the '...' thingification of women:

> For the women, stereotyping has robbed away the attributes of a thinking, feeling and doing human. It is only a thing which does not think, feel and act by her own choice. This process of thingification which extends to her commodification has been severely interrogated by Upendra Baxi. A significant strategy to undermine if not reverse this process of commodification is to give voice to the feelings and desires of women. For a thing may be a desirable object and could be desired but she herself cannot desire.

Whether such carping about the systematic disadvantaging of women is productive at all, or actually increases female objectification through the repetition of stereotypes, should be more vigorously debated. Intelligent word plays by clever academics might indeed be doing more harm than good. More activist strategies than loud complaints are needed to bring about change in this field. In an article recommending the introduction of feminist law teaching for all law students, Archana Parashar (1999: 95–6) cautions that asserting the equality of women might be counterproductive:

> But there is scope for also acknowledging the hierarchy of gender and avoid falling into the trap of formal equality, that is, since both genders are constructs both are to be treated on par. Otherwise it would amount to legal theory being gender neutral once again, only in a new garb.

Such subtle critique of legal modernity shows that leading legal scholars do not trust it to deliver justice for women and children. Such activist doubts seem justified, since merely taking a different approach or perspective does not fundamentally change social realities or gender relations on the ground, it affects merely their perception. Yet it is at least acknowledged that law itself seems everywhere weighted in favour of men, as a tool of governance discursively monopolized by them, and it is rather the law itself that partly stands in the

---

relevant here, is that it does not accept non-state laws as law because of its myopic reliance on the Austinian principle of law as the 'command of the sovereign'. On the plurality of positivism itself, see Menski (2000a: 100–5)

way of gender equality as a colossal hindrance.[35] In Lawyers Collective (2000: xviii) the former Supreme Court Judge V.R. Krishna Iyer states in a message that '[o]f course, the statute book has a masculine bias' and exhorts:

> We need a macro-change in the composition of the infrastructure. The laws themselves seemingly neutral are crypto-partial to men. Not only that, various biased presumptions and assumptions are made to prejudice justice to women on dicta by British judges of yore. Especially in cases of molestation and rape, courts adopt unrealistic attitudes, often against the sister segment of society.

Dr A.S. Anand, the then Chief Justice of India, noted in his inaugural address (Lawyers Collective 2000: xxvii–xxviii) that the question of gender equality or gender equity was until recently merely a topic of theoretical discussion. Observing that '[t]hings are changing but rather slowly. Human rights of women do not appear to be high on the national or international agenda. It is high time that human rights of women are accorded proper priority' (id.), he pinpointed the need for change. In the same address, Dr Anand said that '[i]f necessary, a new social system must evolve. The society must respond and change its attitude. Major surgery is required and not merely cosmetic changes' (p. xxxii).

Similar statements could be cited in abundance, showing that awareness of the problem is present among lawyers, but the solutions are merely thought to lie in further legal intervention in the realm of society. Thus the remedies offered, even by the leading lights of Indian scholarship, judiciary, and bureaucracy, still privilege the state and law reform as the major motors of development and good governance, while acknowledging at the same time that legal processes operate primarily within a social environment. Such statements and the underlying thinking clearly reflect realization that modernist analysis and strategies did not achieve the desired results. Going beyond it in postmodern fashion might of course involve a much deeper critique of the role of law itself.[36] This appears to confirm that the often quite reluctant contemplation of postmodernist views and methodology by legal writers reflects strong resistance, at various levels, among the elite against the anti-authoritarian and chaotic models and consequences of postmodernism. Lawyers, it seems, will hide behind the pseudo-modernist phrase of 'rule of law', and now increasingly seek to rely on international norms (Lawyers' Collective 2000; Anand

[35] As discussed in detail in Part II, Agnes (2000) highlights that the traditional patriarchal framework also infuses colonial and post-colonial legal regimes and was therefore not likely to succumb to legislative intervention.

[36] For current jurisprudential efforts to come to terms with postmodernism and legal pluralism see Tamanaha (2001). Hunt and Wickham (1998), drawing on the Foucaultian concept of governmentality, develop a sociological analysis of law as governance—a tool to establish the dominance of one set of power relations and practices over all other competing sets in society.

2002), to make claims about their ability to order the world in a fashion that is beneficial for all concerned, or human rights arguments which involve an explicit commitment to justice (Young 2001: 7), while tricontinental cultural and legal traditions remain blacklisted. Thus, despite the emergence of a postmodern legal analysis in both India and elsewhere, modernist discourses about the primacy and transformative role of state law in governing society for the better continue to dominate current legal scholarship and practice. It is proposed that this theoretically and ideologically informed position can no longer be maintained in the study of Hindu law in India.

Hindu Law Beyond Tradition and Modernity

Taking account of the above postmodern demands for an open-minded socio-legal analysis, it is argued here that despite the never-ending debates about modernization and secularism in India, Hindu law, as the dominant Indian personal law,[37] governing the social majorities of India's one billion plus people, has continued to play a key role in the development of the state legal apparatus and will continue to do so. It does not matter whether scholars like this or not. The presence of Hindu law is a fact, a legal reality that cannot be ignored, particularly if we want to understand how and why India has been developing the way it has, and if we are serious about improving social justice. The Constitution of India and Hindu law are not as incompatible as most modernists and lawyers posit. Both have been interacting with each other in many ways that this book cannot even begin to analyse.[38]

That Indian developments constantly confound the experts is already widely recognized.[39] Dare one suggest that something must therefore be wrong with the experts? One of the main reasons for the experts' confusion is quite simply that they themselves do not know enough about Hindu traditions and Indian ways of life to take them seriously and incorporate them into their analyses.[40] In that sense, prolonged exposure to modernist constructions has

[37] The much-misunderstood personal law system is not just a prominent feature in South Asian jurisdictions, but is dominant all over Asia and Africa, representing an impressive alternative model to the uniformized legal regulation of the bureaucratic central state that Europeans are familiar with.

[38] Early evidence of harmonization is found in *State of Bombay v Narasu Appa Mali* AIR 1952 Bom 84. More recently, in *Ahmedabad Women Action Group (AWAG) v Union of India* AIR 1997 SC 3614, the Supreme Court of India firmly declined to entertain a number of writ petitions challenging the Indian personal law system and various perceived inequalities within it. Bhagwati (1993) offers a useful overview of the scholarly debates concerning Indian secularism.

[39] For example, Hardgrave and Kochanek (2000: 2–3) provide a neatly argued summary of the development challenges posed in, and by, India.

[40] This critique is levelled here particularly at Indian post-colonial theorists and critics. While their deconstructivist analyses of colonial distortions of Indian society are to be welcomed, they either fail to explore in greater detail, or simply dismiss, analysis of Indian and Hindu social practices in their own right.

deprived many scholars (and readers) of even basic, factual knowledge, which in my experience as an interdisciplinary area specialist remains a necessary tool of the scholar. Hindu traditions involve much more than folkloristic decorations,[41] and Hindu law is a demanding multidisciplinary arena which seems to put researchers off.

To some extent, the reforms within the sphere of Hindu personal law have had a pioneer function. They have led outwardly to protests and accusations by Hindu traditionalists opposed to such reforms, who claim that the majority was made to suffer disproportionately in the name of secularism and modernizing reforms, from which minorities (and especially the Muslims) were somehow exempted.[42] However, as this book shows, the reforms within Hindu law itself have allowed the cultivation of fields of experiments with modernity. Its results suggest that the Indian state would be suicidal to throw away indigenous traditions, just because they are 'traditional', 'religious', or 'Hindu'.[43] Some of the resulting experiences of this extended period of experimentation have shown with utmost clarity that an unconditional commitment to what was meant by modernity is not suitable for a country like India. Modernity, in that respect, is also dead in India, an almost superseded axiom that never really was, yet left enormously important legacies.[44]

[41] In an excellent study of popular Hinduism and society in India, Fuller (1992: 6) emphasises that '[t]he ethnographic record clearly shows that there are enduring structures within Hindu religion and Indian society, at both the institutional and ideological or symbolic levels'.

[42] Prominent examples would be the abolition and criminalization of polygamy in 1955 for Hindus, but not for Muslims, and the introduction of divorce on various fault grounds for Hindus by the same Act, but not for Christians. As shown in detail recently (Menski 2001, Chapters 2, 3, and 6), such arguments might have been correct in the 1960s or 1970s, but Indian legal developments during the 1990s have largely ironed out such divergences between various personal laws in an attempt to construct more socially appropriate legal norms for minority communities, as well as harmonizing all Indian personal laws as much as possible to achieve an alternative form of legal uniformity.

[43] I emphasize here the lessons learnt by the state, since the majority of Indians have either not consciously taken part in this learning process or, it could be argued, had no need for it, since state intervention, viewed from their position, would not bring them any tangible benefits. The centrality of the state and its laws, which lawyers and politicians cultivate so avidly, appears much reduced from the perspective of the common Indian citizen, who in Guha's (1982) terminology would be a 'subaltern'.

[44] For the purposes of the present argument, a commitment to modernity appears to have implied an assumption that whatever was traditional could be neatly superseded through a variety of reformative processes. To that extent modernity feeds on images closely linked to earlier thinking about 'development', which has also become obsolete now, because theory and practice manifestly did not match, and the results were not 'just' enough. The essays collected in Fry and O'Hagan (2000) are useful for the wider debates, in which law is again absent as a voice.

Today, it needs to be recognized by all concerned that Hindu law has survived the formalistic onslaught of modernist legal reformers for a number of good reasons. Asserting its presence as an unchallengeable fact, we must return to the troubling issue of what Hindu law actually is. First of all, as the postmodern analysis of this study reveals, Hindu law has always been much more than a fossilized book law that could be reformed or abolished by the stroke of a pen. It could not simply be reduced to redundancy in Austinian fashion, so often practised during colonial rule that it taught India's post-colonial leadership to embrace legal positivism as a philosophy and top-down law-making as a magic tool of development.

In social reality, all that happened was that the official Indian law changed, while more and more of Hindu law went underground, populating the realm of the unofficial law (Chiba 1986). Taking a postmodern analytical approach that seeks to deconstruct the meta-narrative of official law histories, the present study uncovers this semi-hidden underground existence of Hindu law, which is a methodological possibility only if we move away from modernist, positivist constructions of law. Since Hindu law has always been a reflection of the way of life of millions of very diverse people, the practical effects of formal legal reform need to be shown here in a different light than standard legal text-books suggest. What was abolished by the formal law was manifestly only a fragment of the field, not the entire social reality of Hindu law. The conceptual framework and ideologies underpinning multiple ways of life, and hence the entire customary social edifice of Hindu culture, remained largely immune to the powerful wonder drug of legal modernization which had been administered in measured doses before and after 1947.

Given the impossibility of distinguishing 'religion' from 'law', which the central Hindu concept of righteousness (dharma) recognized by idealistically expecting that everyone should simply be doing the right thing at any moment of life, how could modern Indian law aim or claim to abolish Hindu law? As the deconstructivist approach of this study demonstrates, it seems that this ambition could develop only because dharma was in reductionist fashion defined and constructed as 'law' in a positivist sense by the colonial establishment,[45] and because modernity (emerging as an explicit ideological enframement of legal regulation in late colonial times but pursued fervently during the early post-colonial period) temptingly suggested that 'tradition' was amenable to straightforward legislative reform. In other words, it became possible for India's

Roland Bleiker (2000: 227–41) contributed a fine essay to that volume, discussing the end of modernity. On modernity in relation to South Asian law, see Galanter (1981).

[45] This is documented, for example, by a leading judge of the Supreme Court of India (Gajendragadkar 1963: 18) presenting the subject of Hindu law during the 1960s and equating dharma and law. See in detail chapter 5 below for this modernist construction of dharma as positive law.

post-colonial leadership to dream of a better future by applying the magic remedies of modernity. As Derrett (1957: v) noted early on with evidently mixed feelings,

> ... however repellent the 'Code' may seem at first sight, it is the path to the goal, viz., a Civil Code, and the deliberately-chosen path of a legislature which, however vaguely, realised that it was leading a uniquely complex nation towards a clearly-visualised if seldom-described Garden of Eden.

However, as the present study demonstrates, something as complex as Hindu personal law could not be reformed away and abolished by statute, nor could its influence as a legal normative order that permeates the entire socio-legal Indian field be legislated into oblivion. Hindu law has always been a people's law, whether or not the state wished to see it that way. Despite enormous internal changes, Hindu law as a conceptual entity has remained an integral part of the living and lived experience of all Indians,[46] particularly of those very diverse people who might call themselves Hindus, or whom others refer to as Hindu.[47] Whether we approve of this or not is irrelevant. Indian laws in all their various manifestations are strongly rooted in Hindu concepts, just as English law is culture-specific, or French law is ideationally linked to certain foundational concepts such as the image of Napoleon drafting the French Civil Code by candlelight (Legrand 1996: 235). Just as we must recognize that English or French laws are based on certain cultural concepts and are thus forever culture-specific,[48] although not unchanging, there is no escape from the fact that Indian legal systems and Hindu law are similarly rooted and have been equally subject to constant changes. The universalizing claims of

[46] To the evident discomfort of modernists, and particularly Pakistanis, this may well be said for the whole of South Asia. Such a statement need not be read as an attempt to underwrite so-called Hindu hegemony, for it merely highlights the fact that Hindu concepts have remained interwoven and reflected (even if often in opposition) in virtually all forms of South Asian culture.

[47] The term 'Hindu' has remained ultimately indefinable and no purpose is served in offering what will be seen as essentializing attempts at circumscription. For the legal problems of defining 'Hindu' see Derrett (1966; 1979).

[48] Significantly, the important critique of Western legal claims to universality by Masaji Chiba (1986) challenges the hidden assumption that Western 'model jurisprudence' is somehow value-neutral and universally valid. Chiba's approach also implies a critique of modernity. At a different level of legal analysis, Roger Cotterrell (1989: 231–5) discusses the implications of employing either empirical legal theory or normative legal theory. This, too, is a critique of modernity, as it challenges the underlying assumption that we could really just know anything for sure when it comes to law and legal systems. More recently, Cotterrell (2000) reflects on postmodern legal theory, characterizing various forms of subversive legal theorizing as constructive, and encouraging the use of what he calls the 'Pandora's box' of jurisprudential techniques.

modernity denied this, assuming the inevitability of progression towards purportedly global norms.[49]

Today, the concepts and rules of Hindu law are still in evidence wherever we care to look, provided we can see them in the first place, since Hindu law was never exclusively a book law that could be found in handy form and just taken off the shelf.[50] More or less informally, and indeed often invisibly, concepts of Hindu law continue to govern hundreds of millions of people, not only in India but wherever Hindus, as members of the huge transnational and global Hindu diaspora, have settled. Significantly, many Western lawyers vigorously refuse to accept this, primarily because their modernist assumptions about 'law' differ from the internal categories applied by Hindu law. Intimately linked to modernism, positivist claims about the nature of law, which centre prominently on the blinkered assumption that only state law is properly 'law', have remained so strong that a Hindu living in Britain today, for example, would simply be treated as governed by English law. At best there might be elements of Hindu custom or 'cultural traditions', but not law, which could have some relevance for judging the actions of such an individual.[51]

While positivist lawyers constantly marginalize non-Western laws and thereby also deflate the numbers of people potentially governed by Hindu law, the populations following Hindu law in one form or another are growing rather than declining, raising obvious concerns for the Indian government in terms of demography and the resulting pressures on implementation of social welfare norms and Constitutional guarantees. Outside India, the occasionally expressed chagrin of foreign observers and even governments discloses that modernizing projects and more or less official efforts to assimilate and thus de-Hinduize migrant populations have been frustrated by the more or less subconscious adherence of millions of such people to Hindu law principles, if

[49] Significantly, this is questioned with renewed vigour today in the specialist literature. Caney and Jones (2001: 31) argue that diversity cannot be ignored and that it is profoundly misleading to posit that a global civil society represents the pinnacle of human development (pp. 9–10, 21).

[50] The continuing reluctance to move beyond such misleading myths and models has already been noted. Unduly formalistic focus on the *Manusmṛti*, one particular ancient Hindu cultural text, which is constantly misrepresented as 'the Code of Manu', meant that it is often treated as the major formal source of Hindu law. This entrenched construction of 'Manu's law' underpins the false assumption that Hindu law is based on legal codifications and has developed like a continental European legal system.

[51] In this respect, Poulter (1986) denied the status of 'law' to all ethnic minority customs in England, so that individuals carrying their personal laws with them to the UK would also be legally destatussed. This approach is vigorously criticized in a more recent study (Jones and Welhengama 2000), which emphasizes the importance of legal pluralism. Despite reservations about legal pluralism, Tamanaha (2001: 194) now appears to suggest that people themselves have the agency to define what is law.

not definite rules. Hindu law, wherever Hindus have settled, adapts to new scenarios, defies the selective myopia of doctrinal legal scholarship and reasserts the supremacy of law as a reflection of real life.[52] In this sense, too, Hindu law represents in itself a model case of postmodern reality.

Whether in the communally charged environment of India, or in the racism-plagued countries of Europe and North America, Hindus and their cultural and religious traditions are frequently challenged as backward and 'traditional'. The reaction, apart from widespread stoic silence of the common Hindu, has been a somewhat militant and defensive trend to stand up for Hinduism and all that it represents. If Muslims worldwide have learnt to complain vigorously and often violently against being marginalized and challenged to the point of extinction, so have Hindus.[53] Linked to this, there is much evidence of a resurgence of *hindutva*, whatever that implies in particular contexts, and backlashes to it.[54] A hugely important political science literature has grown up around that term and its meanings, with some comments in virtually all the major recent studies referred to above.

The relevant methodological point for the present study is that in its disdain for any Hindu phenomena, modernist and also much postmodernist political and legal scholarship overlooks and marginalizes the place of Hindu, African, South-east Asian and even East Asian laws in today's world. It appears that we do this at a huge cost, since the power centre of the world has recently been shifting towards Asia. Dismissing phenomena like the postmodern reconstruction of Hindu law, insisting that Indians and others should just learn from the West, rather than vice versa, represents dangerous, self-destructive lingering in the tentacles of modernity. As this study shows, Hindu law now assumes a condition of postmodernity, while sticking to the axioms of modernity has itself become backward and traditional. If that basic truth eludes even most Indian lawyers, this may be because they read too much English law, or they simply do not read enough. It is certainly a reflection of the positivism-fixation of Indian law, and the view shared by most of its specialist personnel, that any legal realism which accords legitimacy to internal subaltern perspectives cannot be healthy for the maintenance of the 'rule of law' and 'order' in Indian society. In this sense, too, the nature of Indian legal scholarship strongly

[52] See on this in detail Menski (2000b). The growing literature on the worldwide spread of Muslim law and the attention recently given to Islamic law as an alternative globalizing force and movement (Glenn 2000: 47–50) also challenge and dispel the modernist assertion that non-Western legal traditions do not have the capacity to develop and modernize by recourse to their own internal methods.

[53] In the context of struggles over reservations for certain communities, Baxi (1990: 215) emphasizes that Gujarat, despite its peaceful Gandhian image, is a very violent society on many counts.

[54] Banerjee (1990: 64) writes of feeding the citizens 'diabolical myths' through Hindu indoctrination and warns of the risks connected to the rapid growth of communalism.

reflects traditional upper caste/class (Brahmin and bourgeoisie) structures and biases.

The present study thus argues for a more critical, postmodern engagement with Hindu law. Research to date within and beyond the field of legal scholarship continues to be shaped by a positivistic, modernist discourse about law and law-making in India, the origins of which can be traced to the establishment and development of colonial governance. The discursive construction of Hindu law as a 'traditional' system requiring 'modern' reform is testimony to the hegemony of colonialist meta-narratives in the current understanding and analysis of Hindu law. Contemporary debates are not only shaped by the presumption that this ancient system is codified and 'lays down the rules' in positivistic fashion, but also by its representation as a uniform, static, outmoded, repressive and patriarchal legal culture eternally bounded to superstitious tradition. It is submitted that these understandings are alien to the spirit and character of Hindu law. They can be traced ultimately to colonialist misreadings and misrepresentations, both intentional and accidental, of this complex, dynamic legal system, while their continuing resonance in the discourse of Hindu law can also be identified as a product of the modernist ideologies that have dominated thinking about law and legal governance in India.

The current discourse of Hindu law as a traditional system in need of modernist reform, if not complete abolition, is thus as much a colonial as a post-colonial construct. It reflects an interweaving of originally colonialist understandings of Hindu law developed by white male professionals—which established a basic epistemological and ontological structure—with post-colonial, modernist ideologies to build an imagined strong, progressive nation state. This is an agenda promoted by both the masculinity of the 'tall me' of India as well as the feminist activism of civil society groups.

It is submitted that this discourse—which for the purposes of this study is termed modernist—as it draws on positivistic understandings about Hindu law and law in general—has in turn excluded serious, rigorous analysis of the development of Hindu law in India. Drawing on Foucault's (1980) understanding of discourse, however, its discursive constraints, i.e. the rules and conventions that have governed thus far what can and cannot be said within the boundaries of this discourse, have not just limited the study of Hindu law. These constraints have also productively stimulated the dynamic development, reinvigoration and reincarnation of Hindu law in contemporary India. Thus, while deconstructing the falsities and contradictions of the modernist discourse of Hindu law, the present study unravels how attempts to suppress and suffocate Hindu law have actively shaped and promoted its evolution.

By moving beyond the stymying conceptual shackles of tradition and modernity, the present study demonstrates through its postmodern analytical approach that certain traditional conceptual elements of Hindu law—though not others—have remained relevant and active in the development of Hindu statutory and case law since colonial times and particularly during the post-independence period, leading to a widely unexpected resuscitation and even growth of Hindu law in India during the reconstruction process of the 1980s and 1990s. Having thereby become integral and stronger components of a revitalizing Hindu law, while facing the challenges of modernity, those same conceptual elements have shown their capacity for reconstruction into forms of postmodern Hindu law that have begun to emerge more clearly during the 1990s. Without essentializing Hinduness, therefore, the present study seeks to identify those traditional key elements in Hindu law which have been active motors for conceptual and practical socio-legal development and highlights their continuing relevance at the centre of postmodern trends in Hindu law today. Compared to classical Indologists and those who studied earlier periods of Hindu historical and conceptual development, we are privileged today in that the implications of legal developments can be observed and analysed within their specific contemporary socio-economic and political context. Particularly from an interdisciplinary socio-legal perspective, it has been possible to observe how ancient key concepts in their contemporary incarnation or *avatār* make themselves felt in the latest developments of Hindu law.

It is argued, therefore, that Hindu law must now be understood as a postmodern phenomenon, and not as some ancient, tradition-bound system close to extinction in a modern world. It is postmodern in the sense that it has not simply embraced modernist, positivistic notions of law and legal governance, nor has it completely abandoned its traditional conceptual roots. Rather, it is a complex hybrid reflecting both a disjunction as well as an interweaving of 'modern' and 'pre-modern' legal cultures. Through a network of state-society interactions, Hindu law has experienced a process of adoption, adaptation, and remoulding of various traditional and modern legal concepts, evolving in the meantime into a legal system that has shifted beyond the binary axioms of 'tradition' and 'modernity' into a condition of postmodernity. The reality of Hindu law can thus no longer be examined, understood or represented through current modernist models that portray a legal system 'struggling' to modernize its traditional elements to come up to imagined ideal standards. Hindu law has matured gradually into a postmodern system of legal regulation that draws upon, interweaves, and integrates both traditional and modern legal concepts. As a result, a postmodern analysis and conception of law are necessary to capture these changing realities. It is argued that such processes of adapting the concepts of traditional and modern Hindu law remain critically relevant as tools for constructing India's postmodern legal system and hold lessons for today's global law-making endeavours to secure justice in human societies worldwide.

The Structure of the Study

The analysis contained in this study as a whole is grouped into three parts and thirteen chapters. The seven chapters of Part I lay out in detail the theoretical and conceptual basis for challenging the prevailing negative modernist approaches to Hindu law and its representation as a defunct legal system. A detailed analysis of the various interlinked processes operating within Hindu legal science over time is provided, from Vedic origins to vigorous debates over Hindu law reform—and law reform per se—in the post-colonial period, and their fallout in the most recent case law from India.

Chapter 2 explores in further detail the themes and issues of postmodern Hindu law and postmodern legal analysis outlined in the present introduction. The evident revival of Hindu law and its postmodern manifestations are analysed before the backdrop of a postmodern, pluralist understanding of law that takes into account social reality and eschews legal centralism. The all too simple assumption that law is what the state says it is has in fact never been fully followed or practically implemented in India, even under colonial rule. As this chapter has begun to show, the conceptual foundations of Hindu law work against such a positivist top-down strategy. Secondly, the awareness of the practical importance of self-controlled ordering and local custom precluded the emergence of state legal systems within traditional Hindu law that could claim to lay down and determine the law for everyone. It is only during medieval times, it appears, that the conceptual transition from dharma to law is made more explicit, but even then any law remains at all times subject to the overriding concerns of dharma. Several examples indicate that this remains true today, despite the overbearing appearance of a formal, modern Western-style legal system.

This deconstruction of hegemonic modernist conceptions of Hindu law is further pursued in Chapter 3, where the premise of dharma as a self-controlled ordering system is explored in a historical, diachronic setting which starts from the Vedic origins of Hindu law. Since the conceptual core element of self-controlled ordering implies the practical impossibility of uniform rules of behaviour for all persons in all situations, the theoretical impossibility of state-made codified law that binds all Hindus, or even all people in a ruler's realm, has to be borne in mind throughout. The absence of a strong political centre for most of Indian history must have further strengthened the trend towards diversity rather than uniformity of laws. In accordance with dharma, the equity of the situation and context-specific justice remained of paramount concern. The ruler's major function, first through exhortation and later explicitly through deterrence, was limited to ensuring that this equilibrium of relativities was not unduly tilted in favour of the more powerful. While in practice this may not have worked, this model of assisted self-control has been popularly visualized in the classic image of 'shark rule', the 'rule of the fish' (*mātsyanyāya*), where the big fish devour all the small ones, ultimately not to the benefit of even the big fish. This symbolic image of ordered chaos which constantly strives towards synergetic symbiosis, relies at all times on the contribution of every Hindu individual as an integral part of the imagined cosmic order. Whether one examines late classical conceptions of punishment (*daṇḍa*) or techniques of dispute resolution under the heading of *vyavahāra*, it is shown throughout that the state, and with it any formal sources of law, only play a peripheral role in classical Hindu law, which remains premised on the supremacy of self-controlled ordering processes and local norms and customary laws. The important point is therefore that it is not the state which determines the rules of human co-existence in traditional Hindu law; rather, it is the social norms as crystallized in the concept of 'good behaviour' (*sadācāra*), tested against dharma and virtually embodying it, which provide the ultimate yardstick—in constant consideration of situational relativity.

Chapter 3 shows that supposedly higher levels of organization, including the Hindu ruler as a final appellate authority, had to respect such self-controlled ordering processes, and no purely secular rule system could thus develop. Chapter 4 continues this examination of periods of Hindu law following the late classical stage, and during the medieval ages. The major aim of this postmodern analysis is to find out how the critical transition from dharma to law in the modernist sense of state law occurred during these periods. Was this a consequence of outside and later colonial intervention, or of internal developments within Hindu law itself? This chapter also incorporates an investigation of any conceptual changes during Muslim rule in vast tracts of the subcontinent and as a result of British rule and colonial administration. It is shown that the Muslim rulers adapted to the Hindu conceptual framework of central governance through local self-control. The British, too, understood the critical importance of self-controlled order as well, albeit not in its Hindu dimensions but as a manifestation of custom, which they then sought to control and partly codify through the emerging case law of the Anglo-Indian legal system. The gradual legalization and professionalization of Hindu law during this period led eventually to the formal Anglo-Hindu law as a typical colonial construct, administered by a class of outsiders who were largely ignorant of the structure and functioning of Hindu law.

Chapters 5, 6, and 7 concentrate on the post-colonial period of developments in Hindu law. Chapters 5 and 6 examine the development of modernist agenda to reform and codify Hindu law, and the emerging discourses that followed and actively shaped them. Chapter 5 concentrates on the origins of modernity in Hindu law, examining the way in which debates and activities surrounding the reform and codification of Hindu law arose, largely as a result of prevailing modernist ideologies at that time as well as modernist misconstructions of what Hindu law was, and should be. Chapter 6 expands this analysis to focus on how these modernist agenda and discourses developed, and yet were also constantly contested, in independent India. It examines the rise and fall of the modernist euphoria and discusses in detail to what extent the new rulers and those who followed them were aware of the need to construct a legal system that remained in tune with the aspirations of the people of India in terms of legal regulation.

Leading on from this, Chapter 7 examines the transition of Hindu law to postmodernity. This metamorphosis of Hindu law is charted through an analysis of various processes of society-state interactions in post-colonial India. It identifies the role of judicial activity as critical in shaping this development, particularly following the constitutional crisis of legitimacy of the modern

Indian state and its desperate and draconian attempts, especially under Indira Gandhi, to readjust the balance between state law and self-controlled ordering, without giving up the claims of the state to be in charge of the law. The various stages of the attempted abolition of Hindu law are examined, demonstrating that everywhere the needs of 'little Indians in large numbers' prevail over the legalistic claims of the modern state. By the late 1980s, at the latest, Indian law had already moved into a phase of silent abandonment of outrightly reformist, modernist agenda. During the 1990s Indian law as a whole, and Hindu law with it, moved decisively beyond modernity into a condition of postmodernity. It is argued that this transcendence of the tradition-modernity dichotomy demonstrates not only that the creative use of tradition and the unacknowledged awareness of the *ṛta*-dharma complex are as strong as ever among the people of India who actively 'live' Hindu law, but also that the Indian state and governments worldwide will do well not to ignore such change in constructing just legal orders in the future.

Part II of the present study comprises Chapters 8–12, each of which examines in turn the legal topics of marriage, child marriage, polygamy, divorce, and maintenance. They demonstrate the powerful hybridity of Hindu law's postmodern reality. Through the analyses produced in these chapters, which are all chronologically structured along the same lines to achieve maximum historical and conceptual depth and cohesion, a recurrent historical pattern seems to become evident. The present analysis first outlines what we seem to know about the various 'traditional' aspects of the respective legal topic and then demonstrates that the various elements of traditional, informal Hindu legal diversity were challenged in a new way during colonial rule, which juxtaposed Hindu dharma and positivist law. Traditional diversities were at some point, often with much delay and more or less inefficiently, replaced with modern uniforming rules. The new formal regulation, however, did not amount to significant and total reform of Hindu law as a whole. Legal intervention turned out to be little more than incomplete and half-hearted minor reforms, tinkering with contentious issues as and when they came about, as the lawmakers were only too aware that drastic top-down legal intervention in the Indian personal law systems would give rise to vociferous opposition and thus endanger the vested interests of the lawmakers and the project of colonialism itself. For similar political reasons, but also as a growing reflection of latent postmodern thinking, legal intervention in the post-colonial period remained fragmented and largely ineffective at the local level.

Thus, the Hindu law of marriage solemnization, as discussed in Chapter 8, is even today firmly anchored in traditional Hindu concepts. The state has not even attempted to take control of this central aspect of Hindu law. But a number of recent suggested reforms have continued to miss this critical point and simply challenge the modern state to intervene from above, regardless of socio-economic consequences.[55] Whether we consider Hindu marriage law,

[55] For a sensible critique of such modernist suggestions, but still within modernist paradigms, see Agnes (2000: 172–82).

the legal restraints placed on child marriages (Chapter 9), or the formal abolition of Hindu polygamy (Chapter 10), the colonial rulers as well as the postcolonial Indian state have evidently had to leave vast scope for the recognition of Hindu traditional concepts, whether through explicit legal exemptions, or by applying surreptitious methods of permitting ineffectiveness of the formally codified legal machinery. Thus, Indian child marriage law has continued to uphold the legal validity of any child marriage in a strangely self-contradictory and yet—from a postmodern perspective—sensible attempt to protect the child's best interests. The Indian dowry abolition law, which is not covered in the present study for a number of reasons (see Menski 1998b), provides in Section 6 of the Dowry Prohibition Act of 1961 that any dowry given in violation of the explicit provisions of the Act shall belong to the woman or her heirs. Thus it seems that the lawmakers even contemplated that the unfortunate woman might be killed, and were more concerned about the property aspects than about the potential victim of female murder.

Massive legal disobedience within society is therefore to some extent programmed into the formal legal framework. Legal modernity is being used as a formal cloak to shelter informal recognition of traditional normative standards that will, as the lawmaker knows, continue to operate in society. In other words, Indian law-making is not what it claims to be: it contains rich evidence of positivist self-doubt and of informal recognition of the 'extra-legal' sphere. It is undoubtedly a significant element of postmodern legal reality that the formal Indian state law recognizes as integral to itself a modicum of ineffectiveness and admits, in this way, the inability of the law to control the social field. In every case, we find today a particular kind of hybridity of old and new, of attempted formal regulation by the positivist paternalistic state. This is uneasily matched with more or less implicit recognition of the fact that modernized formal state law may not be followed by citizens in practice, while innumerable local social norms, as historical and conceptual givens within the Hindu system, continue to remain the dominant guide for human behaviour.[56]

The postmodern manifestations of Hindu divorce law (Chapter 11) and the laws of maintenance (Chapter 12) are also analysed in the present study; they are closely related to the above topics. In both cases, the traditional Hindu law contained important protective mechanisms for women and children. However, these were not socially effective in all socio-economic situations, with the result that formal state law was brought in to provide certain remedies. It appears that in the field of Hindu divorce law, modernist reformative efforts were directed at freeing spouses, particularly women, from an unwanted

[56] The key concept is *sadācāra*, 'model behaviour', as the practically most important source of dharmic order, discussed in detail in Chapters 3 and 4. It will become evident later in this study, in relation to subaltern studies, that there is no one Hindu model behaviour—tradition itself is indeed immeasurably diffuse and diverse. One must wonder why this was ignored and overlooked for so long that Guha (1982) could eventually construct his famous 'subaltern' model, despite the fact that this was not really new.

marriage through making divorce easier to obtain. But it soon transpired that many local customary systems had long provided Hindu spouses a variety of informal methods to end non-functioning or difficult marriages, which the new formal legal regulation now seemed to block. Rather than becoming liberating and modernist, the new law was therefore found to be oppressive and regressive.

More importantly, though, the modernist 'opening up' of divorce and nullity of marriages on all kinds of extra grounds began to disrupt society, as Hindu men learnt to use the modern legal provisions to harass their wives more effectively and to drive them out of the home. As the modern divorce law was increasingly found to be in collusion with male-dominated social norms, it began to dawn on Indian judges that the radical liberalization of Hindu divorce laws in the late 1970s and early 1980s was becoming socially undesirable. Thus, postmodern Hindu divorce law seeks to balance the conflicting expectations of individual fulfilment, marital harmony, social stability, and economic viability. The outcome has been a tightening of the official Hindu law on divorce and a virtual blocking of further reformist expansions, which would have led to increased divorce rates. In particular, abandonment of the full-fledged introduction of the principle of 'irretrievable breakdown' can be observed. This was the legal modernists' flagship project, which already collapsed in Parliament in 1981, while modernist scholars have continued to press for its reinvigoration ever since.

In the case of maintenance, it is shown that economic concerns make a significant contribution to the strengthening of postmodern approaches in Indian law and Hindu law regulation. The traditional cultural expectation that Hindu men have to maintain women and children created customary entitlements of Hindu wives and their offspring.[57] Such arrangements are also reflected in the dominant patriarchal normative orders that allocate direct property rights only to members of an exclusively male group, the Hindu coparcenary (S. Basu 2001). However, already in the ancient Hindu legal periods there must have been frequent problems in this area, since the texts state that the ancient Hindu ruler was advised to protect the socio-economic welfare of women and children in his realm. Similarly, the colonial rulers sought to support the claims of women, children and other dependants by criminal law sanctions in cases of male non-compliance.

Modernist legal reformers and scholars have, however, assumed rather too rashly that the ancient ruler or the modern welfare state should be held directly accountable for remedying vagrancy in society. Given the demographic facts of the subcontinent, it is evident that no Indian government in its right mind could even contemplate this as a viable policy. It thus appears that economic pressures propelled the Hindu law of maintenance, and with it the entire Indian legal regulation in this particular field, into a decidedly postmodern

[57] However, modernist and feminist writing tends to treat this as obnoxious evidence of gender inequality and paternalistic oppression.

scenario, in which the state formally watches over flexible, locally and situationally conditioned solutions, but expects social processes to take care of the welfare of women, children, and elderly people.[58]

The most significant development in this field is not, as politicized scholarship tends to assume, the Shah Bano controversy of 1985, but rather the 'quiet reforms' from as early as 1973, when India's old colonial Criminal Procedure Code of 1898 was reworked. This patriarchal colonial law had protected the maintenance rights of wives only during marriage, so that a devious husband in newly independent India could now simply divorce his wife with ease under the modern provisions of the Hindu Marriage Act, 1955 and then refuse all further responsibility for her. By adding 'divorced wife' to the definition of 'wife', Section 125 of the secular CrPC of 1973 ushered in a postmodern revolution which took time to make itself felt. The present analysis of this particular legal topic confirms that modernist Indian lawmakers may have learnt some crucial lessons during the past few decades, mainly about the limits of law in society, but that may not be good enough.[59] Postmodern Hindu law in this field reflects a realistic recognition of the need for formal state law to rely on social support mechanisms from within the family to make up for the lack of a public welfare state system in India. Individualized modernity, in this field, has simply proved too costly for the state, while the family is being rediscovered as a social support mechanism.

Finally, Part III of the present study contains the concluding analyses in various sections of Chapter 13. I argue that dismissing Hindu law as a traditional religious system of suppression with no relevance to the contemporary world has been a grave mistake. It has fractured and compartmentalized our understanding of Hindu law, and of law generally, in a manner that is not conducive to developing viable legal strategies for good governance. Hindu law is, and will remain, a central element of Indian laws.[60] Within a pattern of plurality of personal law and a culture-specific general law, these various Indian and Hindu family laws have metamorphosed into their own specific postmodern conditions rather than remaining stuck in some distant past or colonial pattern.

[58] Similar developments can be observed in Chinese law, and also in Singapore, where Confucian values of filial piety and correct social behaviour have been invoked for a new law in 1993 regarding the maintenance of parents (Harding 2001: 207).

[59] Such lessons are going to be more difficult to accept in the vast field of Indian constitutional law (but see Menski 1996b). The warning signs have been there since long and Arun Shourie (2001: 198) now identifies 'grievance-mongering' through inflated expectations of the law as a major problem for the postmodern Indian state.

[60] At the same time, Indian law is not just Hindu law, and all one may say is that both have been influencing each other. Firm commitment to the secular constitutional principle of Indian law is expressed by Sathe (2001: 189) to the effect that '[i]f secularism is the basic structure of the Constitution, a Hindu State just cannot exist and a statement promising people to establish a Hindu state violates the basic structure of the Constitution'.

As postmodern legal analysts, we must strive harder to understand this new complexity and the resulting amalgams. Doing so will enable us to read and analyse Hindu law as a reality-conscious postmodern system, with the potential to rely on ancient patterns of flexible adjustment and strong internal control mechanisms to bring about a cost-effective and justice-focused system of self-regulation in the future.[61] An official state legal system can only realistically claim to preside over this in a formal manner, and can no longer assert in the modernist, positivist sense that it is capable of regulating the day-to-day reality of people's lives.[62] Without giving up the formal claims of legal domination, therefore, as embodied above all in the Constitution, recognition of the complex plural realities of postmodern legal conditions in countries such as India will enable legal scholarship to think afresh about the relationship between 'traditional' legal systems of the world and their allegedly 'modern' counterparts. It is hoped that such critical postmodern approaches will in turn provide policy planners and lawmakers in governments around the world with the requisite theoretical and methodological knowledge to administer justice more effectively. These issues are not only of legal relevance to Asian jurisdictions, they concern the entire world, especially after mass migration of non-Europeans to the Euro-American sphere.

[61] Sayyid (1997: 132) notes that the development of a global economy 'does not mean that the world has become [*sic*] a more equitable place: globalization does not alleviate poverty'.

[62] It is highly significant in this context that recent theoretical scholarship vigorously questions the idea that law simply 'mirrors' society. See in detail Tamanaha (2001) as well as Nelken and Feest (2001).

2

Rising from the Ashes: Postmodern Hindu Law

The problematic of Hindu law stems by and large from a postcolonial discourse about the nature and direction of a supposedly tradition-bound legal system in India's modern democracy. The ongoing debates regarding traditional, colonial, modern, and postmodern manifestations of Hindu law, however, have led us deeper into two interconnected jungles, namely conceptual debates about the nature of law generally, on the one hand, and more specific theories and conceptualizations of Hindu law, both classical and modern, on the other.

In my view, the main problem that arises in connection with understanding Hindu law and its transition beyond tradition and modernity has been the persistent attempt—by insiders as well as outsiders—to deny that this important legal system actually may have its own conceptual methods of growth and development, and thus the mechanisms and capacity for internal modernization.[1] Apart from denying that Hindu law could make any meaningful contribution to legal science as a whole, two prominent distortions about the subject have prevailed for too long and need to be analysed here. Many observers suggest—and public opinion largely presumes—that Hindu law looks and functions like a Western-style legal system. Portraying an impression of codified roots, found in ancient texts that were presented as legal codes, Indian legal scholarship embraced the idea that eventually, modernizing reforms could simply be introduced and implemented through a 'rule of law' model. From this perspective, Hindu law simply needed to modernize and secularize, and would thus become a variant of an imagined universalistic legal system. Such assumptions were reinforced by certain religiously motivated beliefs, in particular a monotheistic focus, going back to the notion of a divinely revealed tradition that is allegedly God-given and unchangeable. None of these approaches allows the internal diversity of Hindu law to speak for itself and none brings out fully the culture-specific intellectual contributions that Hindu legal science has made over time. Thus, in an odd alliance, legal positivism and monotheistic doctrine appear to have colluded to marginalize knowledge of the internal vibrancy and dynamism of Hindu law.

[1] In the context of a rich debate on communalism and secularism, Nandy (1999: 413) holds against modernist claims of the irrelevance of religion and tradition that 'the traditional codes of tolerance are the ones that matter, however moth-eaten they may otherwise look'.

The present chapter takes the postmodern perspective that 'law' is much more than state law, and thus explicitly rejects the usefulness of legal positivism as an analytical tool for understanding the inherent conceptual richness and actual complexity of Hindu law. As a result, it is argued that the perceived decline and virtual abolition of Hindu law is nothing but an elaborately constructed myth that has served certain purposes and modernist agenda—and continues to do so with much persuasion—but could ultimately not defeat the socio-legal realities of the now probably close to 800 million Hindus in India. The key arguments of the book, to the effect that Hindu law is alive and well at several conceptual levels, are developed in more detail in this chapter. This leads to a discussion of modern India's creative use of Hindu concepts in seeking to construct a postmodern justice-focused legal system that does not need the crutches of a foreign legal order,[2] but remains open to modification and reform as and when circumstances suggest it.

The Perceived Decline of Hindu Law and its Postmodern Reincarnation

The frequently stated Hindu belief that Hindu law as an eternal ordering system (*sanātanadharma*) is rooted in religion and ultimately based on some form of divine revelation has led to scholarly assumptions that as a religious law, Hindu law could be modernized, secularized, and ultimately deconstructed as a thing of the past. In reality, as a chthonic legal system,[3] Hindu law is much closer to African laws and informal East Asian laws than to the major monotheistic legal traditions coming from the Middle East. But a desire to be grouped with 'advanced' legal systems,[4] and scholarly inability even among Hindus to explain the roots of Hindu law within their culture-specific environment have combined to lead the general public astray when it comes to grasping the essence of Hindu law. Alas, the mere attempt to deal with essentials has been so severely criticized as a scholarly method that much writing now waffles over inessentials without a secure understanding of more fundamental foundations of the subject at hand. A critical analysis of the state of scholarship in Hindu law therefore points to numerous deficiencies of understanding which

[2] Many Indian judges have used this symbol from time to time. For an early example, see *Rattan Lal v Vardesh Chander* (1976) 2 SCC 103, at pp. 114–5.

[3] On the concept of chthonic laws, see Glenn (2000). These are laws that relate closely to nature and the earth, rather than a particular personalized or divine lawmaker. They are a form of natural law, linking the social sphere and the environment, as reflected in much respect for nature's phenomena and even worship of fire, water, the earth, and trees. They are thus often treated as 'primitive' when in fact, in their developed forms, they represent sophisticated holistic systems of thought and practice.

[4] Nandy (1999: 416) perceptively notes the inferiority complex of representatives of *hindutva* in view of the monolithic, well-organized Semitic creeds. This appears to be linked, I would suggest from a legal perspective, to a predilection for positivist top-down law-making.

seriously impede the scope for contemporary postmodern analysis. While in a field like political science it would be unlikely for scholars to advocate the removal of their subject, frequent calls for the abolition of Hindu law, and declarations of its death, have been matched by lawyers' persistent efforts to deny that the subject may have any practical relevance at all in today's world.

It is somewhat sad and surprising that very few academic, let alone practising lawyers, even in India today, seem to be interested in studying, researching, and teaching classical Hindu law.[5] Learning in this field has definitely declined worldwide to a point nearing extinction. This not only reflects problems of scholarship on account of antiquity and the inaccessibility of such concepts from the ancient and complex language of Sanskrit but also signifies the assumed large-scale irrelevance of classical Hindu law for most of the commercial litigation that keeps Indian corporate lawyers in bread. It tells us a number of other things, too. Above all, it is a reflection of the frustratingly complex nature of the traditional Hindu legal system and its tools and concepts, which have led in turn to its formal marginalization and a mixed, tainted reputation among the litigating public. For most observers, such negative tendencies appear to have had the effect that Hindu law has been abandoned, perhaps to be reformed out of existence, or modified and secularized in such a way that it could be made conducive to modern legal practice, or indeed to wither away in the kind of natural process of development that 'modernists' are prone to imagine.

The major reasons for such aversions to studying and dealing with Hindu law have long been known. One suspects that well before British colonial officers, many well-meaning Hindu pandits despaired at the ocean of shastric diversity and threw in the dhoti in resignation. The East India Company officials certainly could not handle this mess on their own. Starting off with imperfect assumptions about the nature of law, and having sought the wrong kind of expert help by asking misconceived questions of their native law officers, as the pandits in their service were called, the British engendered a complex process of distortion. The morass of Hindu law only got deeper and eventually the 'monstrous hybridity' of Anglo-Hindu law was produced.[6] By 1864, when

[5] Baxi (1986b: 2–3) complained that Indian legal researchers 'are heavily preoccupied with normative law and doctrinal research'. A number of authors attempted to revive the study of Hindu law, but these fragmentary efforts have not been sustained. For details see Narang (1988), Singh (1990), Dhavan (1992), and Purohit (1994). Jois (1990b; 2000) and Bhattacharjee (1994) represent more consolidated attempts to come to grips with the subject, but have many shortcomings. Nanavati (1998) openly complains about the inadequate levels of Sanskrit scholarship, on which see also Michaels (2001b).

[6] Derrett (1968b: 298) recounts the history of that perception. Derrett (1978a: xii) emphasizes that '[i]ndeed the Anglo-Hindu law of the family is a travesty of the traditional Hindu law and has long been recognised as such'. On the ambivalent function of the Privy Council as the motor for unifying legal developments, see Derrett (1957: 4–5).

the Hindu pandits were simply abolished as an institution,[7] their mischief had allegedly become famous in its own right,[8] but by then it was too late. The road to the emergence of Anglo-Hindu law as a case-based system of law had been paved, and further distortions inevitably followed.[9]

It appears that after 1864, the British desperately attempted to curtail the use of shastric law. It is evident that they could not make sense of the textual basis, nor of the holistic structure and methodologies of Hindu law (Desai 1998: 65). The impact of the emerging judge-made law and its precedent-focused methodology was eventually experienced as oppressive and was characterized by 'unprecedented rigidity' (Desai 1998: 66), further contributing to the 'bogus' nature of the entire legal construct. Ultimately, the mess became so bad that the only salvation for Hindu law was sought in its unification into a civil code, uniform for all Hindus, which Derrett (1957: v), as cited in Chapter 1, poignantly described at the time as an imagined path to the Garden of Eden.[10]

The British judges during colonial times had also sought to restrict the practical relevance of customs as a source of the official law, despite solemn promises and pious pronouncements to the contrary.[11] Given that the underlying concepts of Hindu law could not just be abolished by new legislation or court precedent, and since custom continued to rear its head, there was no 'final solution' to the place of Hindu law. Whoever dealt with Hindu law issues since that era struggled in much political quicksand. The reformed modern Hindu law of the 1950s finally seemed to emerge as a beacon of light for a better, secular future, in which so-called 'religious' norms might eventually become a legal irrelevance.

[7] It appears that the descendants and successors of this élite class of learned men turned to studying English law as the dominant medium of legal education at the time, rather than subjects related to dharma.

[8] Michaels (2001a: 66) captures the resulting frustrations well. On the parallel complaints about Muslim law officers in Bengal and the reactions of their British employers to the diversity of expert opinions and their apparent unreliability, Malik (1994) provides fascinating detail, based on the study of original sources.

[9] Leading Indian authors such as Desai (1998: 62–6) have tended to be more polite about the British involvement in Hindu law and the resulting distortions.

[10] Desai (1998: 66) argues that '[t]he only remedy was comprehensive legislation in the form of a uniform code'.

[11] For the official position, the case of *Moottoo Ramalinga* is frequently cited as the leading authority. In this case, *Collector of Madura v Moottoo Ramalinga* (1868) 12 MIA 397, it was held that under the Hindu system of law, clear proof of usage will outweigh the written text of the law. However, in practical reality, proof of such customs was made so difficult that only a few customs were able to be recognized within the official law. Dissent in this area was silenced, as Derrett (1961) showed with reference to J.H. Nelson, a socially aware British administrator and judge, who came to south India in 1861. Nelson was manifestly ahead of his time, taking perspectives with a postmodern flavour which were not appreciated by his superiors.

Unsurprisingly, given the negative image attached to Hindu law throughout much of its history, there have been few attempts to protect Hindu law from abolition, and to explain that legal system or provide a remedy for increasing ignorance among lawyers. Derrett's *Religion, Law and the State in India* (1968b) is a priceless, timeless treasure in this field. Earlier, Derrett (1957) had commented in detail on the Hindu law reforms of the 1950s. These also motivated Sunderlal T. Desai to write a general introduction to Hindu law, first published in 1958, which is still found in the most recent edition of Mulla's *Principles of Hindu Law* (Desai 1998: 1–68). This is probably the most widely available treatise on Hindu law today, albeit in need of serious criticism. Derrett's *Introduction to Modern Hindu Law* (1963b) and especially his later analysis, *A Critique of Modern Hindu Law* (1970), have remained unsurpassed, awaiting an update for decades. Similarly, Professor Lingat's excellent study of Hindu law (1973) has long been awaiting some critical comment. More will be said on those important studies in Chapter 3. The present enquiry hopes to fill some of the growing gaps left by these earlier leading studies in the light of recent legal developments.

In updating these earlier works, this study demonstrates that Hindu law, as a conceptual system infusing the entirety of Indian law, as a practically applicable form of Hindu personal law regulation, and in its formal as well as informal manifestations, has risen from the ashes of its supposed death.[12] Despite many pronouncements to the contrary, it has not declined at all in importance. Both in terms of theory and practice, Hindu law is actually experiencing a marked resurgence and revival today, as the formalistic experiments of Western-style legal regulation in India have been running into difficulties that were, to a large extent, entirely predictable.

To take only one most evident example, namely the stalled and failed project to introduce a uniform civil code for well over a billion people of very different backgrounds, this certainly meant aiming too high from the start. Hindu law itself was certainly not totally uniformized by the four hotly disputed major enactments of the 1950s.[13] Nor does India have a uniform civil code today, as envisaged by Article 44 of the Indian Constitution and its curious wording that '[t]he state shall endeavour to secure for the citizens a uniform civil code throughout the territory of India'. In fact, as recent authoritative Indian

[12] Traditional Hindu law has been presumed more or less dead since British colonial times. More recently, Derrett's last major study of Hindu law, *Death of a Marriage Law.* Epitaph for the Rishis (1978a: vii) claimed that, 'for practical purposes, Hindu law died on the 27 May 1976', when the president of India gave his assent to the Marriage Laws (Amendment) Act of 1976, which fully de-Hinduized, so it was argued, the laws of marriage and divorce as applied to Hindus in India.

[13] These were ultimately promulgated in place of a comprehensive code and left many areas to be dealt with by ancient rules, which are still from time to time cited and discussed in Indian courts today. The four enactments are the Hindu Marriage Act of 1955 and three Acts of 1956, the Hindu Succession Act, the Hindu Adoptions and Maintenance Act, and the Hindu Minority and Guardianship Act.

scholarship confirms, '[t]he uniform civil code has been put on the back burner even by the BJP' (Sathe 2002: 193).

This manifest failure of the ideology of uniformity in the changing political scenario of India today is remarkable in itself. It also confirms respect for the realization that no state system of legal regulation would be strong enough to effectively determine from above how such masses of people should conduct their day-to-day affairs. The ancient axiom that various patterns of socio-legal self-regulation would be required to maintain order has remained strong. South Asian legal history shows clearly that, first of all, from ancient times Hindu law never developed the aspiration to 'rule' from above in positivist legal fashion. Instead, it sought to rule from within.[14] Furthermore, the marked indigenous preference for a 'soft' state has been continued in the nineteenth and twentieth centuries, under colonial rule as well as in modern, post-independence India.[15] Any post-colonial project of imposing a strong state on India as a whole would eventually find itself stranded on the rocks of insufficient reach and negative public reaction (Baxi 1986a).

This is not just a more or less direct result of the size of the Indian polity or of some assumed lack of development, as posited by many academic and journalistic writings. A deeper analysis yields a systemic, multifaceted truth inherent in Hindu law as a conceptual system: law is and always remains more than a human construct, it is so multidimensional that no state could ever claim absolute legal control.[16] Legal regulation from above, in the positivist Austinian sense, may be formally prominent, but there are deeper layers of legal regulation which any ruling power would ignore at its peril. Hindu law and its underlying philosophy, so much is clear, do not simply accept the wonderful fiction that the state's 'rule of law' can solve all human problems. In Hindu conceptualizations, law is eternally and intrinsically linked with other spheres of life. In fact, Hindu law does not envisage state law as an independent, separate entity, which is most impressively documented and confirmed by the absence of a parallel term for 'law' in the Sanskrit language and the dominance of the wider term dharma, which is most definitely not just 'law' or 'religion'. In that sense, even ancient Hindu law had perceptions and characteristics that we describe today as 'postmodern'.

[14] Being primarily based on dharma, an idealized self-controlled order system, and not on state law as an external force, Hindu law does not have the same conceptual foundations as Western legal systems with their reliance on 'rule of law'. This does not mean that the concept of state law is unknown to Hindus; the critical point is simply that this form of law is not treated as dominant within Hindu conceptualizations of law-making, as later chapters will demonstrate.

[15] On the concept of the 'segmentary state', which is more of a political image, see Stein (1997).

[16] Desai (1998: 2) cryptically notes that '[m]any of the important points of Hindu law are not to be found in the law reports' but does not explain the consequences of his statement.

Thus, to argue that the ancient Indians did not have 'law' would be plain nonsense. If indeed all human societies have law (Moore 1978), why should ancient Hindu societies be any different?[17] The simple answer is that the ancient Hindus conceived of law differently from Western cultures. Hindu law, as is widely acknowledged, represents a culture-specific form of natural law.[18] In that sense, too, it is an ancient chthonic legal system. At the same time, as a holistic legal system it emphasizes and instrumentalizes the intricate connection between different interlinking elements of the whole experience of human life. Here we see again that Hindu law principles agree with postmodern ideas about the nature of law, but are in opposition to classic positivist theories of law. Hindu law concepts thus fall firmly within the theoretical parameters of the historical school of jurisprudence, which treats legal rules as organically grown and socially tested normative orders and therefore does not accept the domination of legal positivism, encapsulated in the claim of the state to be able to determine and enforce rules in an authoritarian fashion. In the socio-legal model proposed by leading theorists like von Savigny, Ehrlich, and many others, which clearly also underlies Hindu legal concepts, any form of state law is seen as a social bargaining chip, not 'the law' as an absolute normative order.

Without disclosing this in so many words, and thus purportedly not making any contribution to legal theory,[19] ancient Hindus were fully aware of such presumably 'modern' theories of legal science, practising what the historical school of jurisprudence later preached, thousands of years before the theoretical founders of that school. Today, the descendants and successors of those ancient Hindus still maintain their own culture-specific, indigenous concepts of law and still do not lay them on the table explicitly, thus maintaining a generic silence that expert observers have been only too aware of, but tend not to highlight.[20] Everyone knows that Hindu concepts are not borrowed from Western models and have their own indigenous roots, yet nobody seems

[17] This strange question refuses to go away and is raised again by Tamanaha (2001: 201), who asserts that 'it is conceivable that there will be societies without law', but would blame the 'primitive' people concerned, rather than the definitional paradigms of legal centralism.

[18] Based on *mīmāṃsā* reasoning, Olivelle (2000: 15) suggests a theological definition, 'as positive, albeit revealed, law, rather than a cosmic or natural law ...'. This seems too narrow, as Olivelle himself also notes.

[19] The debate on whether non-Western legal systems can make any real contribution to global legal theory has led to outright denials of this possibility, especially for African laws (Menski 2000a: Ch. 5).

[20] Derrett has consistently argued that there is a prominent Hindu technique which consists of communication through purposeful silence. This has had the effect that what is known and taken for granted is not explicitly stated, so that some observers of Hindu law have been misled or have tended to become partly myopic of their subject.

willing to state this.[21] So much for cultural continuity, that tenacious, deep-rooted conceptual enemy of modernization and its advocacy of the cutting of roots.[22] Proof that the debates on Hindu law are deeply embedded in the post-colonial and postmodern discourses on the meaning and nature of the state, legal development, and law itself, will be presented throughout this book.

In contrast to the view taken in the leading practitioners' textbook (Desai 1998) and many other writings, my understanding of classical Hindu law from its Vedic beginnings is not impressed with globally dominant, Austinian notions of state-made law, or Western 'model jurisprudence' in Chiba's (1986) sense. Nor would I simply subscribe to the religiously motivated and ideologically loaded assumption of the basic 'revelation' of Hindu law from some divine authority, of which many Hindu authors are so fond.[23] All of these powerful concepts and notions do not make sense as essential ingredients in the diachronical analysis of Hindu law. There is still something beyond that, which is shrouded in purposeful silence. Partly, this silence reflects the fact that what is beyond Hindu law is not 'legal' in the strict sense, and hence tends to be ignored by most analysts. In my view the study of Hindu law as an open system cannot survive without explicit cross-disciplinary engagement and interdisciplinary effort.

Hindus have manifestly disagreed, since very early times, about the nature of the divine at the helm of the Hindu universe—itself a positivist model, it would appear to many Hindus—for whom there is no commonly accepted, let alone doctrinally prescribed, identifiable Hindu god as the author of 'divine

[21] Derrett (1978a: x) observes in passing that '[t]he public image of Hindu law is, thus, more important than one would think'. The fact that Hindu concepts are now occasionally asserted more openly is then at once simplistically misrepresented and dismissed as evidence of *hindutva*. Thus, it seems wiser for Hindus to remain silent and to pretend diplomatically that Hindu law relates to and perhaps even borrows from Western concepts. For this reason, I am critical of Desai's (1998) learned exposition of Hindu law with its frequent references to European thoughts and models, which do not allow the indigenous evidence to speak for itself.

[22] Significantly, Derrett (1978a) observed that an appropriate form of modernity would be one in which traditional concepts are updated and revised, without losing the essence of tradition and replacing it with the essence of modernity. Derrett (1978a: viii), having asserted that '[t]here is no such thing as conscious rejection of traditional Hindu values', argues more specifically that modern Hindu men have definite problems updating themselves as to the needs of their women, who merely want 'their personal worth and dignity to be respected' (p. ix). Significantly, continues Derrett, the women 'deny that Sita is their model, yet they do not aim to have the casual relationships which they despise in Western woman' (id.).

[23] Many samples could be cited. A fairly typical specimen is Panchamukhi (1999: 207), asserting that the Vedas are eternal and 'repeated without any distortion since they always existed in the *buddhi* of the Lord', thus presenting a theistic, positivist underpinning of Hindu law. At p. 215, it is claimed that Western scholars have distorted knowledge of the Vedas and are basically not qualified to comment.

legislation', despite the assertions of many writers. While this is nothing to be ashamed of, most writers are only too aware that Hindu culture is being challenged (or are indeed themselves challenging it) as primitive, polytheistic, and devoid of firmly documented ancient roots (Nandy 1999). Nor have Hindus ever placed the state at the top of their legal hierarchy, even if it may seem otherwise to many observers, who did not notice that the ancient sources did not always talk about key concepts like dharma because they were well known and in constant operation.[24] Again, this is not a reason to develop inferiority or superiority complexes, but such politicizing has obviously not remained without influence on perceptions of majoritarian Hinduness and of Hindu law.[25]

In fact, Hindus can legitimately question any image of anyone 'at the helm' and still define themselves as faithful practitioners. While centralizing concepts such as a god-in-charge are integral and essential to other faiths, the tempting image of divine revelation, which has tended to give a sense of immutability to the undoubtedly ancient roots of Hindu law, looks too much like a cheap imitation of the 'revealed' religions, mixed with a good dose of legal positivism. This is not a legitimate interpretation of the ancient Hindu concept of *śruti* or *shruti*, relating to knowledge that was 'heard' by ancient sages. These oral texts are unquestionably old, in fact so ancient that they are ultimately of undefinable origin.[26] But Hindu textbook writers more or less subtly reconstruct this into concepts that most common Hindus (and those who are now declared to be Hindus) do not share, creating an elitist scholarly version of Hindu law. Some introduce the notion of ancient human lawgivers,[27] while

[24] The most instructive examples for such misreadings arise from interpretations of the Hindu literature on *artha*, the acquisition of wealth and power. While texts like the famous *Arthaśāstra* appear to emphasize acquisition of such goods as the supreme goal, the internal Hindu perspective takes it for granted, and thus does not see any need to state the fact that dharma remains a higher entity.

[25] Ilaiah (1996: x) protests that '[s]uddenly, since about 1990 the word 'Hindutva' has begun to echo in our ears, day in and day out, as if everyone in India who is not a Muslim, a Christian or a Sikh is a Hindu. Suddenly I am being told that I am a Hindu'.

[26] The standard Sanskrit-English dictionary of Monier-Williams, first published in 1899 (Indian reprint 1976, p. 1101) gives the general meaning of *śruti*, uncontaminated by legal politicking, as follows:

> '... hearing, listening ... the ear, organ or power of hearing ... that which is heard or perceived with the ear, sound, noise ... that which has been heard or communicated from the beginning, sacred knowledge orally transmitted by the Brahmans from generation to generation, the Veda (i.e. sacred eternal sounds or words as eternally heard by certain holy sages called *Rishis*, and so differing from *smriti* or what is only remembered and handed down in writing by human authors ...'.

[27] For example, Kesari (1998: 1) merely refers to the Vedic seers as 'the earlier law givers'.

most writers assert that the Vedas are a form of divine legislation.[28] Does this mean that Hindu law is, like Muslim law, a legal system based on direct divine command? Kuppuswami (1986: 14) follows the carefully phrased assertion of divine revelation, rushing to state that '[t]he Shruti, however, has little, or no legal value', thus making a careful distinction between religious theory and legal practice that other authors do not maintain.[29]

Unlike Islam with its core doctrinal belief in Allah's special position, Hinduism and Hindu law are neither premised on a monotheistic core belief nor on the resultant systemic need to obey God's law to the letter. Islamization of the law, as a forensic process of seeking to ascertain what God meant—most impressively recorded through Pakistani case laws during the 1980s and 1990s—may be a political strategy as much as a religious need. For Hindu law, such systemic need never arose, since the religiously elevated position of the Vedas was not seriously transposed into processes of Hinduization.[30] This is so not only because it was impractical, but because Hindu law developed a more relativistic understanding of law than Islamic law could ever have done.

28 Desai's classic text (1998: 3) states that it was 'an article of belief with the ancient Hindu, that his law was revelation, immutable and eternal. Shruti which strictly means the Vedas ... was the fountainhead of his law. It was supreme to the early Hindu like the Decalogue to the later Christian'. At p. 4, we find the subtle assertion that '[t]he Shruti was accepted as the original utterings of the great power'. Mayne's Treatise on Hindu Law (Kuppuswami 1986: 14) takes the view that '[t]he Shruti (that which has been heard) is in theory the primary and paramount source of Hindu Law and is believed to be the language of divine Revelation'. Paras Diwan (1979: 27) argues that the Vedas 'contain the divine revelation', based very much on his own characteristically authoritative representation of Hindu legal history, with an Arya Samaj colouring:

> Hindu law is considered to be divine law, a revealed law. The theory is that some of the Hindu sages had attained great [sic] spiritual heights, so much so that they could be in direct communication with God. At some such time the sacred law was revealed to them by God Himself. This revelation is contained in *Srutis* or *Vedas*.

The same statement, wrongly suggesting a monotheistic pattern of law-making, is still found in later editions. Diwan and Diwan (1993: 27–8) have only removed the spelling error, but retain the assertions about God's personal attention to revelation of the sacred law. Chadha (1974: 2) similarly states that Shrutis or Vedas 'are believed to contain the very words of God, and are, as stated above, regarded as of supreme authority by all law givers'.

29 Similar claims of limited legal relevance are made about the Koran, giving rise to much anguish among Muslims. For Islamic law, the conundrum seems to be resolved when one takes it that the Koran is God's word, and thereby the basis and primary source of law, but not 'the law' itself. Thus, divine legislation as a religious image can be maintained, but its practical application is quite a different matter, as many recent writings discuss in detail (see Menski 2000a, Chapter 4).

30 I examine this issue further in ch. 3. Here we may note that Sanskritisation rather than Hinduisation has been the relevant key concept, with quite different social and legal agenda.

Such relativisms, however, are not immediately evident from the way in which textbook writers portray the origins and history of Hindu law. Having imagined positivistic forms of law-making in the first place, whether through ancient people or even God, they continue along imagined paths, constructing a text-focused presentation of Hindu law which captures only a minute slice of Hindu social reality. Most critically for our present postmodern analysis, directly arising from such foundations centred on law, we must highlight the distortion of what Hindu law actually is through persistent glorification of a mystical primeval man called Manu, portrayed as the human lawgiver par excellence.[31] This has been followed by the contemporary acquisition of lawmaker status by self-appointed, saffron-clad spokespersons of Hinduism, who claim legal authority in the most illegitimate of ways, supported in their mischief by film-makers who glorify ancient sages as the source of legal guidance.[32] More is to be said about this later.

It should be made quite clear here that classical Hindu law was not brought down from heaven one day and remained the same ever since.[33] The concept of *sanātanadharma* or Hindu understandings of 'eternal order' does not necessarily contradict this, since there can be dynamics within an ancient system, which do not change the system itself, only its external manifestations. This is another aspect of the famed 'unity in diversity' of Hinduism, which has always been an organically grown, immensely complex attempt to understand the intricacies of the world and to maintain and promote a sense of order in the human sphere, always in relation to the wider environment, to which it is subject. It is for that reason, too, that neither the entry nor exit points of 'Hindu' existence can be unambiguously defined.[34] Hinduness has never been just a

[31] Numerous quotes could be adduced here to demonstrate the tenacious strength of that myth. Leading legal luminaries perpetuate it all the time and seem unaware of its distorting effects. Thus, Desai (1998: 18 et al.) refers to 'the original law-giver' as though India had at one point possessed a Napoleonic code. In *Kamal Kumar Basu v Kalyani Basu* AIR 1988 Cal 111, A.M. Bhattacharjee J (as he then was), at p. 114, refers to 'Manu, our ancient law-giver'.

[32] Indeed, I am reliably told, the popular Japanese image of Indian law-making is that old men in strange clothes and long beards simply 'lay down the rules' for everyone. These are obviously reflections of popular media constructs, which in turn flow into the way journalists will portray anything related to Hindus as 'religious' rather than holistic or secular.

[33] Hindus must also learn to accept that the very same argument does not even work for Islamic law, which is constantly misrepresented to them, and in fact often *by* them, as a solidly uniform legal system. In reality, the internal diversity of Muslim understandings of law almost matches that of pluralist Hindu conceptualizations. Both legal systems have had to rely on human processes of finding the law to survive and prosper in rapidly changing sociocultural environments over many centuries and to develop their normative orders in harmony with what their respective societies considered to be in line with dharma or sharia (see in detail Menski 2000a, Ch. 4).

[34] On legal attempts to do so see for example Diwan and Diwan (1993: 1–10).

matter of belief. As in other religions and ways of life, it is a consequence of viewing oneself, with more or less firm commitment, within a particular ideational framework. If enough people do so, as has manifestly occurred in the present case, the result is the emergence of a culture-specific legal system.

It amounts to self-defeating scholarship, therefore, to deny the existence of Hinduness or Hindu law and the pervasive presence of culture-specific Hindu elements. Explaining this legal system should not become a matter of either attacking or defending Hindu law, as we see in current scholarly politics. As one of the few surviving active scholars of Hindu law, I see it as my duty to explore its concepts and manifestations in view of its evident relevance to today's world, and not only in the subcontinent. What is wrong with scholarship that delves into the depths of topics that others may consider politically incorrect? I have never accepted that 'dangerous' topics like sati should not be studied, just because some scholars think that knowledge of atrocities is in itself dangerous.[35] If that were a rule of thumb, all legal studies would be defunct.

In such a politicized environment, how should one define and examine Hindu law? A wider legal readership, especially all those young lawyers in India who think they have studied enough Hindu law to be equipped for practice (until they actually start and find they know virtually nothing), will hopefully gain some helpful and critical insights for reading and interpreting the remarkable developments in postmodern Hindu law today in the light of legal history. It is certainly not sufficient now to study one or two of the old standard textbooks on Hindu law, such as the twelfth edition of Mayne's *Treatise on Hindu Law and Usage* (Kuppuswami 1986) or the seventeenth edition of Mulla's equally famous compilation on Hindu law, now edited by Satyajeet A. Desai (1998), assuming that this prepares the diligent student for practice, let alone for debates on the nature, concepts, and rules of Hindu law. The field of Hindu law continues to be in a confused state and nobody should assume that what 'authoritative' handbooks are presenting, or indeed what the law courts are declaring or relevant statutes appear to suggest, is simply 'the law' itself. The unwary student will be entangled in this sticky web and may never emerge as a competent legal adviser when it comes to Hindu law.

The present study seeks to clarify our mangled conceptual understanding of Hindu law and aims to analyse its historical development and postmodern manifestation. An avowedly interdisciplinary approach and the attempt to eschew simplistic, hollow, legalistic statements, locating instead the social reality of the law—however perceived—should make this book useful reading for anyone wishing to know about the Hindu personal law system

[35] In a review article on sati (Menski 1998a), I defended the scholar's right to research in more depth what the subjects of that scholarship, in this case Hindu women, seem to know but might not express vis-à-vis outsiders. The excellent field-based study by Weinberger-Thomas (1999) follows along that line.

today,[36] as well as the postmodern Indian law that has emerged within and beyond this 'Hindu' framework.

The Key Arguments of the Study

This study highlights and analyses major elements of progressive change in the genesis of postmodern Hindu law in India, thus raising a number of issues for detailed debate. First of all, despite the presence of a constitutionally founded system in India that looks like a fine specimen of the Western 'rule of law' model, with its powerful Constitution of 1950 and all the legal paraphernalia of a strong state, Indian law has, particularly during the 1980s and 1990s, developed along very different lines than was expected by many legal observers. Significantly, this ties in with what experts in other areas of Indian studies, be they historians or political scientists, have asserted in their recent authoritative analyses. For example, Sunil Khilnani (1997: 10–11) has commented with particular reference to various economic interest groups that '[c]ompeting ambitions collided to create this lopsided pattern of economic modernity followed after 1947 ... no single vision triumphed'. Corbridge and Harriss (2000: xviii and xix) circumscribe the entire process of Indian post-colonial development as an ongoing struggle, not a planned process and show in detail how various stages of that continuous process may be identified.

Specifically in the legal field, I demonstrate here that the recent emergence of postmodern Hindu law constitutes an important, interrelated element of the socio-economically and politically sensitive legal reconstruction of the nation. This has, and will continue to have, far-reaching consequences not only for India as a whole and for Indian Hindus, but also for our understanding of what postmodern social, political, and legal change generally may be about. Apart from important lessons about 'law' itself, India's legal development therefore also carries messages for the world as a whole in terms of whether certain developments can or cannot be sustained.[37] In this regard, an important emerging literature talks about the decline of the state and argues, as van Creveld (1999: 365) has done, that with very few exceptions, 'all over the world the news for the welfare state has been almost uniformly bad'.

In the wider context of the role of the state in modern Indian law, I therefore continue the debate begun in my earlier study of the gradual readjustment and ultimate withdrawal of the Indian welfare state's ambitions to provide

[36] A personal law system is not just a prominent feature in Indian law or in South Asian jurisdictions, but is virtually dominant, in its various culture-specific forms, all over Asia and Africa. This represents an impressive alternative to the uniform legal regulation of the bureaucratic central state that Europeans are taking for granted as a universal model.

[37] Hardgrave and Kochanek (2000: 2–3) discuss this aspect well. Significantly, in the literature on the state in modern India, it is similarly argued that Indian developments will inform global debates. Giddens (2000: 167) briefly refers to intense debates on this issue in Asia.

various services in exchange for loyal citizenship (Menski 2001). My specific argument here is that the reduction of the Indian welfare state follows certain patterns that are familiar from ancient Hindu legal models in terms of the peripherality of the state and its control mechanisms for the maintenance of order in society. Apart from a gradual localization of justice and the consequent loss of direct interventionist ambitions of the central state, much else has been leading to the concept of the 'shadow state' now espoused by Corbridge and Harriss (2000: 168). This is really a rephrasing of earlier understandings of the 'fragmented' or 'segmentary' state (Ingalls 1954; Stein 1997). The withdrawal or peripheralization of the central state is not only observable through a detailed analysis from a politicial science perspective, but is also neatly reflected in the law as produced by statutes and court decisions. It has been taking place at three levels: first, in terms of principles and underlying concepts which infuse the entirety of the Indian legal system; second, more specifically at the level of the Hindu personal law in its various manifestations and third, in the forever contested, hugely important grey zone between official law and unofficial law, which researchers either dismiss or dare not traverse.[38]

Further, I argue that this change in the use of law in postmodern India did not come about merely in reaction to some traditional sentimentalities such as a reinvented *hindutva*, as some commentators far too quickly assume, but was of necessity designed for the sustainable development of the whole nation, now more than a billion people. It is therefore more the result of an age-old, ongoing rational process of reconsideration of policies than a pandering to so-called irrational sentiments in a certain historic period, or a romantic return to ancient ideals in an age of disillusionment with the promises of modernity. Viewed from such perspectives, the reinvention of postmodern Hindu law appears like a self-saving project, which the initially overambitious modern Indian state had to undertake to retain its own legitimacy, rather than representing simply an emotional shift of emphasis towards religion and 'tradition'.

I argue, therefore, that postmodern Hindu law and its internal processes of change should not be discussed merely in the context of debates about religion versus secularism.[39] The topic cannot be properly understood in isolation from Indian socio-economic and political developments, such as more

[38] Derrett (1978a: ix) notes that the analysis of divorced Hindu wives by Rama Mehta (1975) 'very naturally' passes over the agricultural classes, 'because they are governed largely by custom and traditional mores and unsuitable to her sociological techniques of investigation along with the élite' (id.). Earlier, Derrett (1963a: 169) had quite clearly concluded that 'the law of customary divorces is a world to itself'.

[39] The contested and confused nature of those debates is evident, for example, from reading Tharamangalam (1995). Some of the essays in Larson (2001) make a useful contribution to the debate, but even here, several confusions have crept in.

explicit focus on gender issues (Dhanda and Parashar 1999), the shifting relations between centre and periphery, or similarly between elites and masses in the context of contested modernities, as noted by Corbridge and Harriss (2000: 139). Such legal reconstruction processes, as one can observe from all over India, form an integral part of a much larger and necessarily complex national picture of development that is in fact remarkably cerebral and conceptually coherent, despite the size and diversity of the country and its legal systems and the many different pulls of ideologies and strongly held views.

Saying this, I am aware of the argument by other observers that India's recent developments represent the failings of a modernizing mission and in particular the failure of the Nehruvian design for India (Corbridge and Harriss 2000: 237). But failure in one respect is likely to represent a gain in another field. How can anyone measure such gains or failures on an absolute scale? Relying on the explicitly legal evidence of judicial pronouncements and the intricate wordings of certain statutes, such as the MWPRDA of 1986,[40] I argue that there appears to be a considered method behind some legal measures that have been widely perceived as failings; that such Acts reflect a planned reorientation of Indian policies and laws, designed in the light of socio-economic realities which no state mechanisms could have undone. Far from failure, this is the kind of sustainability-conscious forward planning that development experts hold up as an ideal.

Such findings corroborate what Corbridge and Harriss (2000: 92) concluded with particular reference to the 1980s when they wrote that 'the founding myths of India as a modern state did start to be called into question'. These scholars have gone on to argue that an outwardly resurgent Hindu nationalism, in particular, led to a 'profound rethinking of state-society relations within India's intellectual and public policy establishments' (Corbridge and Harriss 2000: 193). But there is much more to this than a resurgence of Hindu nationalism, as these two authors also recognize (see also Nandy 1999).

Our specific task here is to analyse those processes of change that could be seen as 'legal' inputs. We know now that India's national scheme for sustainable development has had to be revised in the light of implementation problems that anyone with less strongly developed modernist myopia could

[40] This Act followed on from the famous *Shah Bano* case (*Mohammed Ahmed Khan v Shah Bano Begum* AIR 1985 SC 945) and has been systematically and persistently misinterpreted by political analysts, to the effect that the Indian state has callously let down divorced Muslim wives as well as violating the guiding principles of secular governance. Bose and Jalal (1998: 225) speak of 'a curious and ill-advised attempt to placate 'Muslim' opinion' imagining that Rajiv Gandhi 'railroaded through Parliament a deeply conservative Muslim women's bill'. As noted in Chapter 1, such scholarly representations are far removed from the legal facts, since the 1986 Act actually protects the interests of divorced Muslim wives, as the title says and has been used to force Muslim husbands back into uniformity, but within the framework of a separate Act for them—since that is what the Muslim leadership wanted. Thus, the state may have conceded on form, but not on substance, as the growing

have predicted. Especially after the crises of Indira Gandhi's Emergency during 1975–77 and the resulting *catharsis*, with its deepening doubts over the legitimacy of state law, the Indian law-making machinery has had to be ever more conscious of not turning into a new form of elite rule without concern for the common citizen. We know today that post-colonial Indian governance lacked sufficient control mechanisms and effective accountability, so that the ruling classes and the rich and powerful were free to suppress disadvantaged groups and individuals at liberty.[41] In the ideologically loaded more recent debates on majoritarian abuses and India's perceived shift towards *hindutva* policies, it has at times been overlooked that economic survival for the most disadvantaged, and at least nominal adherence to constitutional ground rules within a public interest framework, have remained most basic challenges. Despite—maybe because of—the wonderful but idealistic assumptions of legal and policy planners, things soon went wrong all over the place in the Republic of India, and various remedies had to be found.[42]

The deep crisis of legitimacy that marred the project of the modernist Indian state is by no means over. In fact I would assert that state-made law, in a Hindu conceptual context, must forever be struggling for legitimacy, since the idealized Hindu model remains that of self-controlled order in which the state remains as dormant as a giant snake that is best left alone. But it appears,[43] at least in comparison with the early decades of the Indian Republic, that independent India has more recently experienced significant shifts of emphasis

---

case law under Section 3 of MWPRDA 1986 demonstrates and *Danial Latifi v Union of India* 2001 [7] SCC 740 has now confirmed. All of this means that the Indian state has purposefully used an Act that applies formally only to Muslims to reinforce a new, postmodern social welfare policy from which ultimately all divorced Indian women and their children should benefit. No divorcing husband in India today can merely cast away an unwanted wife and equally unwanted children without violating the state's social welfare law and making himself liable for maintenance claims (see Menski 2001, Ch. 4 and Ch. 12 below). Although this also goes for Muslim men, even the most recent literature does not disclose the true legal position. Rather, modernist scholarship here colludes with traditional Muslim men to undermine the postmodern Indian legal protection mechanism for all divorced wives.

[41] See Corbridge and Harriss (2000: 205), cited further below. In the context of political economy, Bardhan (1984) provides an insightful analysis of the impact of elitist self-interest.

[42] Abundant complaints are, in particular, voiced over the excesses of police powers and the plain abuse of positions of power in various sensitive situations (Dhagamwar 1992). On atrocities against women, see Agnes (1997). On the problem of police violence generally and relevant cases, see Ahuja (1997 Ch. 2). On women's sense of being an oppressed minority, a whole bookshelf could be cited, but there is also much evidence of silence (John and Nair 2000). Further, this study does not even begin to address the specific problems experienced by Dalits and others who now find themselves classified as 'Hindu' (Ilaiah 1996).

[43] I venture to suggest that this is merely an appearance in view of common historical myopia and lack of research. If we had the resources to investigate in

towards a more people-centred and less cavalier, elite-centred view of governance. As the manifest failings of the paper promises of the Constitution emerged for all to see, especially in some of the early cases brought under public interest litigation,[44] a rethinking of the relationship between law and citizenry had to come about to retain at least a semblance of rule of law.[45] The result, visible with greater clarity today, has been a return, so to speak, to an earlier phase of legal regulation, whereby more attention is paid to sociocultural norms and the self-regulatory potential of society than to top-down legal regulation by the modern state. The courts simply cannot deal with all complaints that might legitimately be brought before them, so self-control mechanisms within society need to be strengthened. To portray this partial withdrawal of the state and its organs as 'postmodern' might actually just be a play with words. The technique of taking people's law more seriously could hardly be declared modern, given the evidence from ancient Hindu law and other traditional legal systems that do not centre on direct state intervention, but rely largely on internal mechanisms of self-controlled ordering. Justice-consciousness is not a new phenomenon at all; what has been changing are the ways in which justice is perceived and put into practice.

Thirdly, therefore, closely related to the first two points, it is my observation that the nature of the earlier post-colonial Indian scheme for sustainable development, which was in fact an intricate compromise between tradition and modernity rather than outright modernism (see to this effect also Corbridge and Harriss 2000: xviii), has changed significantly during the 1990s in particular. Within this field of legal movement, the redirection of change *within* an only superficially uniform Hindu personal law regulation system, pulling towards self-control and local dispute resolution, has now become much more obvious to the trained eye. This aspect needs to be analysed here in detail. The emerging postmodern Indian approach to legal regulation, not only in family law, now relies less on state intervention, and certainly less on financial involvement of the state in the realm of interfamilial relationships.[46] Questions arise immediately as to whether this endangers supposedly hard-won advances

more depth how the state, in earlier periods of Hindu legal history, was involved in matters relating to 'the people', we would find abundant evidence of reinvented wheels, too. For such indications see Smith and Derrett (1975).

[44] For details on the case law see especially Ahuja (1997). Shocking cases like *Rudul Sah v State of Bihar* AIR 1983 SC 1086 disclosed, for example, the illegal detention of a prisoner for over fourteen years despite his acquittal.

[45] Mr Justice Krishna Iyer (as he then was) noted pointedly in *Fertilizer Corporation Kamagar Union (Regd.) Sindri v Union of India* AIR 1981 SC 344, that if the judges did not listen to the common man on the street, there could be no social justice. Thus, it was held, '[w]e have no doubt that in competition between courts and streets as dispenser of justice, the rule of law must win the aggrieved person for the law court and wean him from the lawless street' (p. 355).

[46] Related to this is the observation by Corbridge and Harriss (2000: 166) that 'spending has been switched away from the social sector since 1990'.

in gender justice and minority rights. However, the modernist assumption that only modern state intervention can protect specific group interests and vulnerable individuals is clearly wrong, and is now being subjected to fresh questioning from a variety of angles (Baxi 2002).

This quite dramatic reorientation, analysed in some depth in a recent study of reported cases from the higher courts of India (Menski 2001) was not expected, certainly not in this openly retraditionalized form, by most observers a few decades earlier. Some problems were anticipated by seasoned experts such as Derrett, who apparently had his finger on India's pulse all the time and could to some extent predict what would happen next in the law, especially as he approached retirement and no longer needed protective escorts to enter certain High Courts (Derrett 1970: vii). The learned master of Hindu law indicated early on, for example, that when it came to divorce law in India, some time after he had retired, there would be focal concern on the potential predicaments of divorced wives.[47] Acute awareness of the problems caused to divorced Hindu women is particularly evident from his last major study (Derrett 1978a). Nobody took much notice of such warnings at the time, but a careful rereading of Derrett's work today yields several sage predictions about a reorientation of legal concern towards social welfare issues for millions of people rather than the earlier, more elitist emphasis on fine points of constitutional law, which has characterized most post-independence legal writing in India.

Fourthly, these important recent legal developments in India indicate, through certain aspects of the general legal system,[48] as well as in the field of Hindu law and personal law regulation generally, a more or less open admission of the 'limits of law' (Allott 1980). This phrase refers in our present context to more or less explicit recognition by the modern state that it alone, ultimately, cannot regulate everything its subjects and citizens do in their daily lives. However, the gradually emerging strategy of greater official reliance on self-controlled order among the citizens of India has primarily been read as evidence of lawlessness. If the writ of the criminal law does not run into every village, and age-old official laws like the IPC of 1860 are still subverted by social attitudes and lynch justice (Dhagamwar 1992: 314), what is the point of guaranteeing Indian citizens basic rights such as the right to life in Article 21 of the Constitution?

[47] The words chosen to express this concern are such that they are easily overlooked. Derrett (1957: 99) argued that paying regard to custom and practice may appear as 'distinctly conservative steps. They accord with shastric notions as well as with tradition, which fears to allow a wife to be cast out upon the world without a stable future before her'. This reflects precisely the social welfare concern that has become so central to postmodern Hindu law.

[48] A key example here would be the emergence of public interest litigation, analysed in detail by Ahuja (1997). Menski et al. (2000) provide an overview and research bibliography.

If the state is not able to assert its own presence, so that fieldwork often uncovers massive ignorance of official legal provisions designed for the benefit of citizens,[49] it is not surprising that many observers should complain that the reach of state law is deficient and tenuous. On the other hand, it has been argued that if a weak, incompetent post-colonial state is unwilling to transcend 'traditional' concepts, law-making merely strengthens the state's power (Agnes 1997). From a certain perspective, underpinned by the ambition of modern state law to be universally known to the people whose lives it purports to regulate, such observations constitute a valid critique of the modern state's inefficiency. However, was it in fact ever the ambition of the post-colonial Indian state to control all areas of its citizens' lives once and for all? The evidence, adduced in the major chapters of this study, points towards an intricate compromise between 'strong' modern state control and various techniques of the traditional 'soft' state. The Hindu law on marriage in particular (Chapter 8), confirms the unwillingness and/or inability of the modern state to exercise full control over the social sphere.

In view of the remembered patterns from earlier stages of legal development in India, it appears that it was never really a fullfledged ambition of the modern Indian state to achieve unconditional control. The question as to who represents 'the state' arose at various key stages in the development of India, immediately after independence as well as more recently in the post-liberalization period of negotiated transition. Such struggles over state definition illuminate why, early on, Dr Ambedkar ultimately resigned in despair and disgust when his radically modernist project was not approved by a majority big enough to carry the policies of the day. His views were not represented, as purely as he wanted, by 'the state'. The result was a messy legal compromise that needed to work its way through the system. Today we can observe in more depth that this simmering conflict between 'tradition' and 'modernity' has taken quite a different form than in the early days of the Indian Republic and that the scales have been tipped towards social control rather than legal domination. On the other hand, I found it instructive that Corbridge and Harriss (2000: 205) should write of the Indian state as an entity arrogating powers to itself and thus becoming an instrument of control and suppression, to a point where,

> [i]n large parts of north India the state presents itself to poor men and women not as a patron or guardian, but in the guise of a brutalising police force and a corrupt administration. The state then becomes something to be resisted or at least avoided, and not something that is turned to for justice or as a source of empowerment.

Significantly, such comments are made by the learned authors mainly for north India, pointing to a fact frequently evident from reported cases, namely that the temptations to abuse power and to avoid a proper balance of rights and

[49] Dhagamwar (1987) produced abundant evidence of this problem with regard to rules of family law. See also Dhagamwar (1992) on criminal law matters.

duties of those who are 'in charge' is often seriously disrupted in those parts of the country where the supposedly superior Aryan Hindus hold sway. Much more will have to be said on the north-south divides in Indian law and the different approaches to Hindu law, including so-called subaltern perspectives (Guha 1982) in the substantive chapters later in this book.

The present study is not designed to explore in depth either the theoretical jurisprudential aspects of such legal conflicts, nor indeed the heavily contested debate over whether people's law is on the same footing as law made by the state. We also have no space here to delve into the more specifically political implications of such a restructuring for the postmodern Indian state as a whole.[50] The point about change and its direction is made, that must suffice here in broad outline. Others in related specialist fields, such as Indian political science, have already demonstrated their ability to discuss the implications of such legal changes for their own area of expertise. Guha (1997) has famously highlighted the phenomenon of 'dominance without hegemony', particularly for the colonial period, but not restricted to it. For the purposes of the present study, it has been necessary to restrict the analytical focus to the critical role played in this reforming process, within modernity and the process of modernization itself, by various Hindu aspects of law and by indigenous South Asian cultural and legal concepts.[51]

It is my contention, fifthly, that this particular postmodern methodological and analytical approach, which will probably be somewhat distasteful to many of those who wish to deny any contemporary and future relevance to Hindu legal concepts,[52] offers a plausible way of interpreting the richly embroidered tapestry of postmodern Hindu personal law and the ongoing restructuring of the entire legal system in India today.[53] I shall have to assert here, for the moment,[54] that such evidence of purposeful reconstruction of Hindu family laws and of socio-legal regulation among the various communities supposedly governed by Hindu law suggests the immense legal relevance of the

[50] On this see the excellent overview by Corbridge and Harriss (2000) and the analysis produced in Khilnani (1997).

[51] I venture to suggest that an intricate analysis of South Asian Muslim laws would bring out different shades of legal postmodernity which cannot be fully understood in isolation from developments in Hindu law 'next door'. In particular, Pakistan's parallel operation of two sets of Muslim personal laws offers rich material for such an urgently needed analysis.

[52] In this respect, the concept of 'overlapping consensus' as developed by John Rawls and discussed by Caney and Jones (2001: 34–7) with reference to accommodating apparently different and contradictory doctrines and approaches in terms of human rights appears relevant to the present study.

[53] At the same time, this approach matches remarkably well with the methodological suggestions made by Archana Parashar in Dhanda and Parashar (1999: 1–12).

[54] Detailed evidence is presented later in the substantive chapters of Part II.

officially 'non-legal' realm for the improvement of social justice. This is hardly surprising, because law-making is, within a socio-legal context at any rate, primarily concerned with regulating people's lives. To achieve constructive results within the social realm, however, such legal regulation cannot just be top-down dictation of rules; society and its localized politics must be given a voice. Thus, if we add to our usual conceptual and analytical legal tools a willingness to look in depth at the role of Hindu law models, and to re-examine those models and their place and potential in the reconstruction of Indian and Hindu laws, we are opening many doors for a deeper understanding of the postmodern Indian legal system and the place of Hindu personal law within it.[55] In other words, to drop the positivist blinkers of doctrinal legal scholarship and challenge the elitist and misogynist myths surrounding traditional Hindu law, is definitely to be better equipped for the present task.

A critical example should be given here to illustrate such blinkers and their effects on various debates about Hindu law. While some men, as we saw, are elevated as lawmakers beyond all proportions through positivistic constructs,[56] negative myths about the position of Hindu women (and low-caste Hindus) are constantly repeated, and thus reinforced, by the very people who purport to challenge them, which is hardly a constructive approach in itself. For example, Rani Jethmalani (1995: 14) asserts that '[t]ill today women continue to be dependent on men as wives, mother, sisters, daughters. This is endorsed in the Manusmriti—the ancient religious text'. While at least this writer does not invest 'Manu' with lawmaker status, blaming instead religion as the basis of gender-biased rules, can we be sure that the sociocultural message from this text is actually correctly translated from the Sanskrit original?

Even if women are said in this verse and so many others to be dependent on men, is the equally important (and linguistically unimpeachable) other side

[55] An interesting attempt has been made by Guha (1997: 28ff.) to analyse the Indian idiom of *daṇḍa* as a central element of ancient Indian polity. As discussed later in detail in Chapter 3, this concept has deep-reaching legal implications, but not of the kind that Guha (1997: 29) suggests when he imagines a 'classical form of monarchical absolutism' and a force that goes beyond classic punishment, but does not seem to include deterrence as a basis of self-controlled order.

[56] A significant example is found in Pylee (2000: 7), where we read that 'Ambedkar's contribution to the Constitution is undoubtedly of the highest order. Indeed, he was a modern Manu and deserves to be called the father or the chief architect of the Constitution'. This kind of 'double whammy' would never be granted to a woman, perhaps with the exception of Indira Gandhi, whose hate-figure status as an overly angry 'Mother India' now lies shattered, since postmodern Indians seem to yearn for a strong ruler figure like her (*India Today*, 20 August 2001: 18–26). Interestingly, Gandhi herself (1992: 13–14) indicated that she may have modelled herself on the ancient Emperor Aśoka, not some Euro-American figure, while Sathe (2002: 68) claims that Indira Gandhi re-enacted American history 'by casting herself in the role of Roosevelt'. Here, too, strong modernist, positivistic undercurrents are at work. But whose representations do we believe?

of such a coded message not that men are at all times responsible for women's welfare? If the same Sanskrit words are interpreted to mean that Hindu men are at all times liable for the welfare of their womenfolk, why was that aspect of the message not equally emphasized in the academic literature? It clearly exists in popular consciousness, but represents a subaltern perspective that is often not allowed to speak (see now Spivak 2000 on the New Subaltern). It appears that, first of all, ideologically motivated scholarship has constructed a skewed understanding of gender relations among Hindus, reflecting patriarchal perceptions among the nineteenth century indological pioneers and their colonial forerunners, as Guha (1997) explains with reference to early colonial writing. More recently, such male-focused constructs have been employed to justify and ground modernist feminist activism.[57]

Hence one does not need to take recourse to complex schemes of 'overlapping consensus', the simple old image of the two sides of a coin, or the glass that is either half full or half empty does the trick as well. Within the axiomatically interlinked life patterns of Hindus, the male-female symbiosis has, since ancient times, been treated as a key element of microcosmic ordering. But 'symbiosis' has become a bad word among modernists because of its original location in patriarchal structures of gender inequality, so that the word itself carries rather negative connotations for many feminist writers.[58] But neither female enslavement nor systematic suppression of women would, in the ideal Hindu order of things, be seen as appropriate.[59] The basic problem of evidence, namely that everyone seems to quote statements from ancient texts to 'prove' their point of view, feeds on an inadequate understanding of how 'tradition' operates and what role the ancient texts actually played. Clearly, 'tradition' is much more internally plural than modernist writers would wish to know. Despite definite male biases, it remains dishonest to claim that women are, within Hindu cultural traditions, little else than commercially useful chattels.

Allowing a plurality of perspectives rather than pushing one set agenda, however, is by itself a challenge for which many writers on Indian law are quite frankly not equipped. This is either because they do not know enough about the concepts, principles, and processes underlying traditional Hindu law, or because they imagine—and therefore dismiss as unworthy of their attention—other people's constructions of an inflexible system that is not

[57] The somewhat healthy realization that much of this highly strung academic analysis (e.g. Spivak 1988) does not touch the lives of the common Indian woman is occasionally expressed.

[58] For example, S. Basu (1999: 251) refers specifically to the 'justification of "family values" as the ground of women's continuing subordination' and refuses to acknowledge that a discourse of legal protection could work in favour of women.

[59] Treating gender as a point of crisis, Rajan (1999: 4) introduces a collection of activist essays, many of which would not agree with this particular perspective and vigorously blame the collusion of traditional culture and the post-colonial nation state for the continued subjugation of Indian women.

suitable for supple reform from within. Neither Indians nor Western observers are immune from such deficiencies, which shows that it is not enough to be a Hindu to claim insight into the complexities of Hindu law. Conversely, an outsider perspective might help, but what is the correct distance to achieve proper focus? Significantly, this balancing act itself is a distasteful task for many modernist writers, who have simply asserted that there is no meaningful role for traditional Hindu law concepts, indeed for any Hindu law concepts, in India's future scheme of legal regulation. The faster the whole system is secularized, the better. Such wishful thinking with all its related fallacies used to abound in the literature, and has been duly criticized, but it still appears (Galanter and Krishnan 2001). Arun Shourie (1993: 8) castigates Indian intellectuals for being disparaging about India and anything Indian on account of their own ignorance of the rest of the world. His comments reflect the theme of glorifying the West and its models, which parallels Masaji Chiba's (1986) sharp critique of the inflated claims of Western 'model jurisprudence'.

Moving Towards a Postmodern Condition of Legal Regulation

The Indian state's legal realism in the face of socio-economic adversity, its more or less grudging recognition of the limits of its own state-made laws, coupled with a somewhat faint remembrance of ancient concepts that idealized self-controlled order, have led towards a broad change of policy in recent Indian law-making. This constitutes a hugely significant departure from the perceived pure standard of the 'rule of law' model, forming a central aspect of India's legal postmodernity. This has only gradually become more evident, especially during the 1990s. It was earlier pronounced upon by legal luminaries such as V. R. Krishna Iyer, in elaborate language that few cared to examine for its deeper meanings.[60] The rejection of legal modernism is also manifest in a brief Independence Day message by Prime Minister Atal Bihari Vajpayee (*India Today* 20 August 2001: 26c), which concluded:

> Since time immemorial, Indian society has rested on the three pillars of morals, ethics and values. Modernism does not mean repudiation of what lies at the core of Indian identity. Indeed, a modern India must also be a moral India. It is only when modernity and morality combine that we can have a forward looking, forward moving India, a country whose future would be known for its 'manifold greatness'.

This does not appear as a legal message, but it is evident to the trained eye that the nation's leader, the ruler figure, refers here consciously back to indigenous

[60] A new study on the former SC judge V.R. Krishna Iyer (Krishnaswamy 2000: xv) cites the great man himself who claims that '[a]ny person who had drunk deep of the cultural heritage of ancient Indian vintage, justly called the wonder that was India, gains a vision of the human promise too profound for expression in Western diction and West-bound Eastern thought'.

principles of self-controlled order rather than a formalistic, modern 'rule of law' model. The hidden legal message is clouded by nationalist tinges of 'greatness'. It is therefore easy to dismiss such words as a moralistic appeal to Indian traditions and, in some vague sense, further evidence of *hindutva*.[61] However, the above redefinition of 'modernism', its Indianization and in fact Hinduization, clearly demonstrates that the current Indian leadership, weak as it may appear to be, has grasped the deeper message that Indian law-making and governance have had to move *beyond* simple modernism. This has resulted in a process that involves the recycling of ancient indigenous models of self-regulation which bypass and exonerate state law, rather than relying on it. The above appeal to morality implies a hidden refutation of legal positivism, it is not just a rhetorical gaffe, as unsympathetic observers might assume.

Researchers in any field of Indian studies would expect too much if they were to look for open, official admission of the fact that a new guiding policy of supervening state control for an otherwise largely self-controlled social order had been put in place in post-colonial India, rather than a system in which the state simply laid down the rules and expected citizens to follow them. The above statement by the Indian prime minister is not an odd exception. Painstaking research would uncover many similar statements. At least in the field of family law, but also in the constitutional realm, policies relying on morality rather than positivist law were in fact followed earlier.

Our problems of understanding such complexities appear to lie more in the various partly contradictory scholarly perceptions of the field of law than in socio-legal reality itself.[62] If researchers re-examined their evidence more perceptively and stopped highlighting only certain slices of socio-legal phenomena, some progress in understanding law generally, as well as various aspects of Indian postmodernism and postmodern Hindu law, might be made. The fact that earlier researchers did not look for what seems to strike us now as most significant in contemporary Indian legal developments does not mean that such evidence did not cry out for analysis before. Researchers on Indian law, like everybody else, have their own agenda at specific times,[63] and we should certainly not expect them to indulge in research on the irrelevance of

[61] *India Today* (20 May 2002: 9) quotes A.B. Vajpayee as saying: 'I accept the Hindutva of Swami Vivekananda, but the type of Hindutva being propagated now is wrong and one should be wary of it'.

[62] The complex, neo-Kantian legal philosophy of Rudolf Stammler (1856–1938) with its principle of 'natural law with changing content' is seen as an early attempt to explore the universality of natural law on the one hand, and the time-specific and cultural manifestations and ideals of law and justice on the other. The present study cannot do justice to this debate, but it seems relevant to emphasize the culture-specific nature of all forms of law, also of natural law, and to point out that Chiba's (1986) third level of law, the 'legal postulates', is a phenomenon that seems closely related to Stammler's concerns.

[63] In this context, it is necessary to stress again the doctrinal, positivist bias of Indian legal scholarship.

law. That is a pastime for political scientists, as recent writing shows with great conviction.[64] One should not expect an Indian prime minister, however strongly influenced by Hindu concepts he may be, to dwell explicitly on the peripherality of modern state law.

It is an indisputable and well-documented fact that modern Indian state law (and perhaps all state law) has always been a compromise between the desirable and the possible. The initial design of modern Indian family laws after independence—and of Hindu laws within this field—fits that pattern of constant compromise perfectly, as demonstrated in more detail in subsequent chapters. Postmodern Hindu law has involved a remarkable shift from a modernist, legocentric attitude towards a more traditionalist, socially aware approach. This is therefore no outright victory for tradition. Nor does it signal the defeat of the modern state as an important regulator of norms among citizens. The Constitution still exists as an ultimate focal point for legal claims against the state or fellow citizens. The Supreme Court remains in place as the ultimate arbiter within the formal system, and even though access to the courts has only marginally improved, the *possibility* of access to justice is there, so that justice is within reach, rather than offered on a plate (Menski 1996b).[65]

Thus, my argument here is certainly not that the Indian state has become irrelevant for Hindu law regulation and has handed the field over to traditionalism or, assuming the worst, to some saffron league of old men who claim to be able to tell everyone what 'the law' of Hindus is or should be.[66] The main point is that the multiple discussions of the roots and roles of Hindu law and its place in today's world continue, but that there has been a remarkable shift of emphasis, away from law and the state's claim to rule the roost, towards society and greater recognition of the potentially beneficial role of social norms and obligations, i.e. culture in all its diverse and composite Hinduness. The overarching policy concern in this debate has been quite manifestly the state's need to be seen to secure for all Indians a sustainable legal framework for the

[64] Thus, Corbridge and Harriss (2000) emphasize, through the idiom of the state, various aspects of the limits of state legal control and the ultimate inability of the state to regulate local order.

[65] The Supreme Court of India, faced with an enormous quantity of so-called 'public interest litigation' brought by elite activists who now use various lobbying techniques to approach the highest court, has repeatedly given clear signals that it is not an instrument of the elite, but an institution that has to protect higher forms of public interest. Hiding behind rhetoric of the division of powers, the SC in *Ahmedabad Women Action Group (AWAG) v Union of India* AIR 1997 SC 3614, declined to act as desired by an activist women's group. This is not evidence of judicial conservatism, but confirmation of activist excesses.

[66] Significantly, Corbridge and Harriss (2000: xix) argue that Hindu nationalism will ultimately be constrained by its inordinate, exaggerated emphasis on a constructed uniformity. The legal evidence produced in the present study indicates that such artificial uniformity can neither be maintained in socio-political reality nor in the legal field.

protection of basic justice. In the age of increasingly empty state coffers, this has marked a retreat of the state and its institutions to a vigilant safety-valve position, rather than omnipresent state control. In this respect, the postmodern reconstruction of law-making in India has involved a reduction of the state's presence and greater reliance on self-controlled ordering mechanisms within society. All of this, I argue here, has taken place *within* the ambit of Hindu conceptual models, without stepping totally outside Hindu legal traditions and superseding them in an imagined process of modernization.

This has been possible because Hinduism and Hindu law are not something one can radically change overnight, modify through the stroke of a pen, or even remove through residence abroad. As a personal law, Hindu law is presumed to travel with the individual wherever s/he goes. As Derrett (1957: 2–3) highlighted, there is such a thing as 'cultural heritage' and its consequences are manifest in the ways Hindus live and think:

> There is a reality and a permanence in all Hindus of certain fundamental beliefs about the nature of life, the individual's place in it, his essential relationship to his kindred, his caste-fellows and his neighbours, and the consequent duties which and which alone life can demand of him. Economic conditions may change, new ideas may be welcomed and naturalised, adjustments of many kinds necessarily accompany the alteration, but the psychological background and mental furniture of even a western-educated Hindu will remain, by and large, true to his type and his inheritance. Individuals may not be aware of this, and may be more acutely conscious of the differences between caste and caste, tribe and tribe, community and community; this is because at the moment of consideration, they may be more impressed by the formal than by the substantial, the superficial than the essential. The observer must not allow the outer garb to mislead him as to the nature of the inner spirit.

If this is an appropriate reflection of Hindu reality—and I submit that it is—any legal reform project that assumed the possibility of the eventual abolition of Hindu law in India was entirely hypothetical or fictional and could never be a success. In post-colonial India, Nehru in particular knew this only too well and thus sided with Gandhi's tradition-focused approach rather than with Ambedkar's radical modernism. Today, it seems that the early post-colonial path envisaged for reaching the developmental goals of modernity, namely formalistic legalisation and ultimate secularization along Western lines (culminating in uniformity and de-Hinduization) has had to be abandoned, most evidently with regard to the Indian family law system. Since there is no realistic prospect of eventual de-Hinduization of Indian laws, let alone of Hindu law, the Indian legal system will always remain linked to its many cultural roots. The real question is then whether analysts will be able to trace this strong-rootedness in indigenous normative orders, assuming they have the will in the first place to recognize what is happening.

Whatever observers have been saying, it is manifestly visible in recent Indian legal developments that there has been a movement in favour of secularization, but along Indian lines, aiming for a position in which the separate systems of personal family law are retained, while their respective provisions are being modified to become almost identical in substance.[67] Actually, this strategy represents nothing new in a system marked by 'unity in diversity', but many observers have found it difficult to follow this train of thought and to recognize its practical implications for the law. The acknowledgement that tradition incorporates modernity and may include dynamism rather than stagnation, while modernity may not exclude tradition and conservative adherence to established privileges, is also hardly new, but these seemingly binary pairs have confounded many. As so often, a rereading of Derrett's insightful work (1970: 1) helps to solve such riddles:

> In tackling Hindu law the first thing to remember is the tension between the past and the present, the desire to be traditional and the desire to be up-to-date ... it is too readily forgotten that the tensions to which we allude were present centuries ago, though not always in the same form, and the conflict between 'foreign' manners and ancient ways is endemic in India and has been going on since the Vedic age. Far too few critics of the present order realise that their ancestors were engaged in corresponding if not actually similar complaints centuries ago.

Derrett (1970: 13–14) also noted, towards the end of his Introduction, that the underlying concepts of Hindu law could never be abolished. A symbiotic interaction of various elements, representing internal self-control as well as external control and influence, would therefore be necessary to bring about satisfactory legal development in India:

> Flexibility, diversity, adaptability, and the genius for adjustment without changing one's entity—these are the hallmarks of Hinduism, properly not less a way of life than a religion ... the common denominator of Hinduism is still valid in legal contexts and is equally valid in all of them; ... it is not open to being abolished or otherwise interfered with, whether from above or below; and ... one can safely count on its efficacy in the indefinite future. The Old India, which pops up now and then in our law reports, and which is the submerged six-seventh of India, is not going to melt ... in the warm streams of the world's currents, but is going, positively and even relentlessly, to contribute in its turn something to the world's knowledge of how people should live and let live, should co-exist in a positive and not merely neutral sense and should build a common culture in which all elements, however apparently incompatible, can bring out the best in each other. Certainly the Old India is not something which Indian reformers can expect to disappear in their lifetimes, and if they think that they can count without it, they will be making a big mistake. This does not mean that the "missionary" role of

[67] This is one of the possible strategies for bringing uniformity into Indian personal laws, as discussed in Dhagamwar (1989), but it is not an option favoured by modernists, which confirms that their opposition is as much to personal laws per se as to gender discrimination.

> the higher culture is useless: on the contrary the Old India, with its recidivist tendencies, needs the "missionary" culture, with its deep tinge of Brahminism, like a donkey needs the stick .... A stickless donkey and a donkeyless stick are about equally worthless; the two together, with their unseen driver, can reach some goal, which Indian life persistently presupposes and yearns for.

While Derrett's commitment to pluralism and to the peculiarly Indian form of secularism as a means to protect internal diversity and the resultant hybridity is striking, most relevant for the present analysis is how he employs the image of the donkey and the stick to emphasize the need for continued balancing of conflicting pulls and expectations.

More than thirty years later, we can test for ourselves the sagacity of such comments and predictions. In current Indian legal practice, for all to see, this has meant putting Article 44 and the project of the uniform civil code into the Indian Constitution of 1950, while at the same time leaving it in cold storage, now probably for ever.[68] Meanwhile, not only Hindu law but all Indian personal laws have experienced some reinvigoration especially during the 1980s, not only through their continuing intimate link with social norm systems, but through planned legal processes, designed to harmonize all Indian personal law systems along roughly similar lines to minimize unconstitutional discrimination on the basis of religion. This ongoing process demonstrates that the postmodern Indian state has in no way renounced its function as the ultimate arbiter, a point which judges vigorously assert from time to time. The donkey continues to live and is allowed to roam, but not without a measure of control. While the postmodern Indian state has revised its originally somewhat hostile approach to the personal law system, it has now begun to work constructively within a framework of personal law regulation, instead of seeking to abolish the system as a whole in favour of a secular uniform civil code for all Indians.

The key point for our analysis of postmodern Hindu law becomes, then, an investigation of the extent to which this remodelled and reinvigorated system of personal law can deliver justice, specifically to the hundreds of millions of people presumed to be governed by Hindu law today. That particular formulation of the key issue raises, of course, the further question of what is meant by 'justice'. This book demonstrates, in theory and with practical evidence in the various chapters, that assumptions about 'justice' in Indian law have also been subjected to postmodernist analysis by judges, and to change. This has not been widely noted and sufficiently analysed. To the extent that the state and legal centralism had earlier lost credibility as guarantors of justice in India, while postmodernist, retraditionalized, socially and culturally focused approaches to legal regulation regained more open (rather than merely

[68] Dhavan (2001: 317) notes that the uniform civil code 'has now been trivialized into becoming a tragic farce'.

latent and grudging) acceptance, the entirety of Indian law had to undergo near-revolutionary changes.[69] In the field of family law, the postmodern Hindu personal law that has been developing during the 1980s and 1990s now faces critical examination as to whether it can deliver justice.

Although this will be hotly disputed and, from certain perspectives, simply derided and denied, it appears significant that this kind of examination of justice in India focuses more on whether justice is being achieved in a relativized sense and in terms of dharma, rather than in terms of absolute, modernist, equalizing and purportedly universal assumptions of the law. Whether this allows anyone to redefine the postmodern Indian state law as a new element of dharma is in my view a political question which need not be fully answered by lawyers, since there will always remain an element of dharmic foundation in the legal systems applying to, and being applied by, Hindu people.

In this respect, the traditional relativity of dharma and its constant emphasis on situational specificity militate directly against the constitutional reliance on absolute equality of all citizens (Menski 1996b). Most writers appear to see a commitment to dharmic values and to constitutional norms as incompatible. While formally, therefore, India has to stick to its constitutional framework and ideals, in reality the postmodern Indian legal system has been operating more like a reincarnation of traditional Hindu law, allowing for difference in accordance with circumstances,[70] because the modern system did not result in the promised equality. But this is not the Hindu law preached by misguided scholars, saints and confused foreign observers. It is highly significant that Corbridge and Harriss (2000: 179) bring in the concept of 'a kind of reversed Orientalism' and refer to this reconstruction by a number of thinkers (id.):

> They hold that Hinduism, by contrast with the other great religions, is uniquely and distinctively characterized by pluralism and by 'tolerance'. This was Gandhi's view, not least, and is appealed to by several contemporary writers.

Classical Hindu law, indeed, was not what it is made out to be in most 'Orientalist' treatises on the subject. The *Manusmriti*, that so-called 'Code of Manu', a dreadfully persistent misrepresentation of classical Hindu law, is still simplistically read to lay down strict rules which imposed innate Brahmanic superiority and exclusivity, while disempowering other Hindus, including all women (Agnes 1997), to the point of total subservience.[71] Evidently, such

[69] For constitutional law, these are poignantly captured in an analysis by Professor Sathe (2001) of the role of H.M. Seervai, a leading Indian constitutional lawyer and textbook author, initially an avid legal positivist, whose experience of the Emergency and other illegalities eventually led to changed perspectives.

[70] In this, the law follows old models to the effect that what is right (*sadācāra*) is situation-specific and 'context-sensitive' (Larivière 1976: 101).

[71] Madhu Kishwar (2000) makes fun of this blind belief in old men's sayings, suggesting tongue-in-cheek that her own pronouncements might be read as *Madhusmriti*.

interpretations have always suited those who found themselves privileged, and now justify the activism of those who claim to be disadvantaged or more enlightened than the rest. But the scope for self-supporting subaltern opposition has also always been much wider than scholarship, Orientalist or otherwise, has been willing to admit. As indicated earlier, it is remarkable that even the intelligent subaltern analysis of Guha (1997) remains rather too strongly wedded to dominant notions of 'law' as codified rules that govern everyone. While the relativity of anything that is supposedly 'legal' in the ancient Hindu traditional literature should not be a new conceptual element, traditional indological and modern Indian legal scholarship seem to have their own rules about purposeful distortion. I have at times felt like fighting windmills when emphasizing the need to express the multiplexity of Hindu interpretations, rather than rushing towards expedient stereotypes. My esteemed 'Orientalist' colleagues have assured me that I am wasting my time reminding them that Manu was not a lawmaker, but long after Bühler's pioneering blunder, the 'Laws of Manu' have continued to reappear with depressing regularity.[72]

While it seems pointless, and yet so crucial, to insist on the relativity of law within an indological framework of reference, lawyers clearly have their own problem of recognizing the relativity and limits of law, as discussed earlier in Chapter 1. For the present postmodern analysis of Indian and Hindu laws, it is important to highlight that the consequences of India's recent distancing from the axioms of Western-style modernity are not actually hidden from view. They are there for all to see, openly displayed in some statutes, such as Section 7 of the HMA of 1955 (see Chapter 8). Such evidence needs to be highlighted and subjected to fresh scrutiny. Postmodern examples of guidance for the donkey, as envisaged by Derrett, can be found above all in numerous court decisions, some of which are analysed in Part II of this book. Examples from the centre of Indian constitutional law could be given in abundance, too, proving that within an idiom of equal citizenship, explicit recognition of differential statuses remains not only a conceptual possibility but a fact sustained in socio-legal reality.

Thus, in 1982 the Indian Supreme Court, in *S.P. Gupta v President of India* AIR 1982 SC 149, finally accepted that something was seriously wrong in the state of India, and held that access to the fundamental rights guaranteed by the Constitution, through direct petition to the highest court 'by appropriate proceedings' under Article 32, could mean for certain Indians in certain situations that they may send a postcard from jail or a fax from a remote location, or get someone else to initiate legal proceedings on their behalf through public interest litigation. Promptly, many privileged citizens of India, including

[72] They also reappear in Guha (1997: 29), together with ancient Indian lawgivers (ibid.: 112). See earlier Bühler (1975) and thereafter Doniger (1991). The most recent edition and translation of the dharmasūtras (Olivelle 2000) is presented by the publishers as a collection of law codes, though the author himself quite clearly takes a different view. Here again, as for Doniger (1991), the market seems to dictate.

lawyers and legal textbook writers,[73] were up in arms about the favourable treatment given to impoverished co-citizens, who would now flood the courts with their petty claims.[74] When it comes to the much-debated 'protective discrimination' for historically disadvantaged low-caste groups of Hindus, too, privileged Indians are found to complain vociferously.[75] In a similar vein, some male scholars have complained about undue legal privileges given to women (in particular Mahmood 1986). In a pluralist postmodern legal system faced with competing claims, such complaints represent the essence of an ongoing, animated debate about the direction of legal change. This is the equivalent of the almost proverbial 'white male backlash' in America.

The critical point for our present debate is this. By 1982, the Indian constitutional framework was rethought by the superior judges, and by the late 1980s such revised visions of what was appropriate legal regulation for a billion Indians had also made its mark on the courts' handling of family law disputes. Rather than pretending that husband and wife as co-citizens were equal players in a court battle, Indian courts now began to protect women by discriminating against men, and they continue to do so for good reasons.[76] The howls of dismay from male observers have still not died down, but there is a strange silence from modernists who do not seem to believe what they see, do not trust the state (Agnes 1997), or simply do not want to take note of India's restructured postmodern family law regulation. Because the state applies carrot-and-stick techniques to goad the donkey, many observers seem confused about the direction taken by India's legal developments and seem to tell us only what they want to instead of giving a full report.

It is fair to say that India has so far been cautious not to advertise this postmodern retraditionalization process of its legal system during the 1980s and 1990s too widely, probably because this would inevitably generate some

[73] An early, entirely hostile study is Agrawala (1985). It took some time until academic writing in favour of public interest litigation appeared, but note the early attempt by Upendra Baxi (1986b) to publicize social action litigation.

[74] Meanwhile, this strategy of simple access to the superior courts has been abused in many different ways and has inter alia been diverted for the use of middle-class repeat players who pursue their own 'publicity oriented' and 'private-vengeance' litigation', as described by Shri M.K. Damodaran, advocate-general of Kerala, in a speech in 2001(2) KLT J 5, at p. 6. For details of such abuse see also Menski et al. (2000: 106–32).

[75] On the benefits and costs of this policy see Galanter (1984). A huge literature has been built up on this topic, which remains heavily contested and reflects the resentment of many privileged Indians.

[76] This process continues, at present in the field of Christian personal law, where the opening up of grounds for divorce for women by *Mary Sonia Zachariah v Union of India* 1995(1) KLT 644 (FB), has now led to cases by men seeking easy divorce on the grounds of cruelty. As could have been predicted, given the high level of justice-consciousness in the High Court of Kerala, a Christian husband's claim for easy divorce on the basis of cruelty, as attempted in *Philip v Susan Jacob*

bad publicity abroad and cause further misunderstandings about the country's commitment to human rights and the observance of so-called international standards. The chorus of calls for Indian law to follow modern Western and 'universal' standards, frequently made by legal writers, has become even louder in the context of the bulging literature on human rights.[77]

It is entirely predictable that some modernist readers will reel in horror when they see evidence of what postmodern Hindu law permits: continued legal acceptance of religious marriages as legally binding, of child marriages, even of polygamy, to name just a few bones of contention. But that same postmodern Hindu law system also contains other rules, whose importance cannot be denied and should be rethought by those modernists who only seem to look at some of the evidence, but not the whole picture. Thus, most critically in the absence of state welfare provisions, not only Hindu husbands, but all Indian ex-husbands, have been taken to task in honouring traditional obligations towards any wife, once married.[78] Significantly, in principle but depending of course on circumstances, an Indian wife (and that term now includes divorced wives and wives who are a party to formally invalid marriages),[79] is now legally entitled to various forms of maintenance, firmly a charge on the husband or his family.

Thus, postmodern Hindu law emphasizes again the duties of citizens rather than their rights, and in a patriarchal setting expects of men (who have control of most economic resources) that they should behave responsibly towards women, children, and all others who are dependent upon them. The postmodern state law thus reflects social patterns of gender inequality and their economic consequences and remoulds the family law accordingly, rather than reproducing modernist statements of formal equality and individual rights, which would not match with socio-economic realities on the ground. That methodology and procedure in itself will be seen as highly objectionable by modernist observers, such as Agnes (1997), who apparently still wish to make

---

2001(1) KLT 890, or simple nullity on the basis of fraud, as was tried in *Benny Mathew v Philomina* 2001(1) KLT 597, are not to be allowed. Thus the court actually treats all Indian men equally (see Chapter 11 on divorce law, which shows that Hindu men find it more difficult today than a decade ago to obtain easy divorce or nullity). It appears that the learned judges are strict in order to protect women against being thrown out of marriage by unscrupulous men.

[77] See Lawyers Collective (2000:1–63) for a collection of seminar papers focusing on domestic violence, with specific attention to international law.

[78] As noted, Agnes (1997: 565) remains misguided on this issue with regard to Muslims, and various articles in Larson (2001) are seriously deficient in yet more innovative ways. A discussion of the official legal position is found in Menski (2001: Ch. 4).

[79] This well-established position was recently confirmed in *Mannan Khan v Family Court*, reported as Case No. 99 at 2001(1) KLT SN 81 from the High Court of AP.

axiomatic claims for absolute equality. It is notable in this context that a lot of Indian writing on family law still pushes the agenda of modernization and individualization, despite growing evidence that in the supposedly most modern societies of the world social fragmentation creates more problems than it solves whilst existing problems, such as violence against women, have not receded.[80] Notably, Giddens (2000: 85) emphasises that '[t]here is no future for the 'egalitarianism at all costs' that absorbed leftists for so long' and argues strenuously for a restructuring of welfare systems in view of the 'perverse outcomes to which the welfare state has given rise' (p. 121).

Hindu law has developed along this postmodern 'third way' and has re-discovered the joint family as a social welfare mechanism (see in detail Menski 2001, Chapter 5). It has thus revived an institution that most modernists cannot wait to see disappear, but which has tenaciously survived in its various modified forms. Significantly, regardless of what modernist commentators such as Diwan and Diwan (1993) argued with much persuasion, many Indian judges saw such matters differently and behaved much more as active members of Indian society than passive scholars. Through the undoubtedly well-considered mental efforts of judges, manifested in a wide range of judicial decisions, the postmodern Indian state has discovered that a restructuring of family law along traditional Hindu lines, but not of traditional Hindu law per se, emphasizing today's social obligations rather than tomorrow's individualistic rights, would be most appropriate for the state as well as its people. Thus, the Indian state can today rightfully proclaim its concern for the protection of women and children, while no longer facing the expectations that the needs and resulting social welfare claims of such individuals should be met and honoured by the state itself. The postmodern Indian welfare state, by relying on remodelled Hindu concepts, has saved itself from falling into the trap of inflated welfare promises in which virtually all developed countries now find themselves.

Hence, the superior judges as a collectivity have, it appears, performed a wondrous trick. Operating as spokespersons of the modern state, at least some judges (and in fact the judiciary as an institution) feel no inhibitions in seeking to guarantee indigent individuals social welfare protection through recourse to traditional norms.[81] Judges have relied on moralizing appeals to the

[80] Significantly, Diwan and Diwan (1994: xv) point out that '[d]omestic hooliganism and violence against married women—the wife battering—occur all over the world on a significant and disturbing scale'. This is a far cry from insinuations in much of the literature that Hindu and other 'Asian' traditions are responsible for such atrocities against women. Domestic violence against women seems to be as universal as patriarchy, but also takes specific cultural forms in South Asia, and among South Asians in diaspora, such as dowry murders (Menski 1998b) and disproportionate statistics of 'suicides'.

[81] Of course this can never be foolproof. If the husband himself is impoverished, the wife cannot hope to claim from him, although she has a legal right. It was held in *Sivankutty v S. Komalakumari* AIR 1989 Ker 124, at p. 129, that '[i]n a case

individual's conscience, reminding all citizens of their dharmic duties in society, rather than the letter of the modern law as it applies to every citizen of the state.[82] Thus, within an outwardly modernist legal model of uniformity and equality before the law, the judges operate a reality-focused system of dispute settlement in which ultimately the facts and circumstances of every case in relation to the undefinably open category of 'righteousness' seem to count more than the formal letter of the law. Whichever disputed topic we turn to, postmodern Hindu law represents a continuing compromise, not an end point or conclusion in a contest. Hindu law has overcome the limitations imposed by modernist, positivist understandings of law and justice. It has moved beyond modernity to regain access to its traditional roots, not in the sense of directly applying any rules of hoary antiquity and religious authority, but of remoulding ancient wisdom to solve current socio-legal problems. To that extent, therefore, Hindu law now lies in a truly postmodern condition beyond tradition and modernity.

---

where the husband happens to be an indigent person or becomes an indigent person, it is a misfortune that has to be shared by the wife also'.

[82] Interestingly, Giddens (2000: 50–4), in summarizing the 'third way', echoes this principle of reminding members of society of their obligations towards one another.

3

Antecedents and Concepts of Traditional Hindu Law

The present chapter attempts to consider the history of Hindu law in order to examine why it is that certain perceptions of the origins and history of this important legal system have been so manifestly distorted that today's lawyers can easily take the misguided view that Hindu law has become irrelevant. In an endeavour of this kind, it is necessary to begin with theoretical considerations to explain the scholarly perspectives taken here, and to ground the enquiry in the fertile soil of indological scholarship, as well as the thick layer of legal writing and expertise that exists. However, a mere regurgitation of standard textbooks on Hindu law would not serve any useful purpose. The challenge here is to combine the present conceptual journey into the depths of traditional Hindu law with socio-historical research and recent theoretical work in legal philosophy and legal theory from around the world, in particular the instructive model of Chiba's (1986) 'three-level structure of law'.

This chapter first provides a brief historical overview of Hindu law, offering a consolidated conceptual grounding for the more detailed examination of major technical terms and ideas throughout the remainder of the chapter. Starting from the concept of cosmic order in pre-classical Vedic law, major sections focus on the self-control model of dharma, the conceptualization of punishment as 'assisted self-control' in *daṇḍa*, and the limitations of political and legal domination by rulers through the concepts of *rājadharma and vyavahāra*. Finally, the conceptual examination is completed by a detailed analysis of the central role of custom in Hindu law, which leads to the conclusion that state law must remain conceptually inferior to the various Hindu assumptions and beliefs about what may be appropriate in certain situations. Throughout the classical period of Hindu law, absolutist superiority of state-made law simply had no chance to dominate the field.[1]

As this chapter demonstrates in detail, however, this is not how modern scholarship has understood and portrayed the history and development of classical Hindu law. The many distortions produced by scholars, in particular by lawyers influenced through Anglo-Indian and Anglo-Hindu thought, have

[1] Of course there will have been abuses of power, rather than an imagined golden age of total harmony, but that does not prove that the system as a whole allowed dictatorship and militated against any form of democracy. Hindu law is, in fact, amazingly candid about the need to kill an unjust ruler.

led to a contaminated picture of the nature of classical Hindu law. Blowing away the cobwebs and clearing away much of the debris of Orientalist and modernist scholarship, this chapter aims to reinstate conceptual dimensions of Hindu law that exist in the (sub)consciousness of Hindus rather than on the pages of our textbooks.

Theoretical Considerations: Orientalist Constructions of Hindu Law

While one can indeed speak of 'Hindu law' as a collective term, this placative use raises many problems.[2] Given that all legal systems are complex, culture-specific entities of a piecemeal nature (Moore 1978: 9), it is impossible to discuss details of Hindu law without reference to any particular time, locality, or situation. To reiterate, there is no such thing as one Hindu law, but rather many different manifestations of it. While this makes any attempt to study Hindu law extremely complex, the internal diversity of Hindu law is of such a magnitude that the general term needs to be supplemented with additional words to indicate what particular aspect or period of Hindu law one refers to. Specialist scholars have rightly claimed that Hindu law is 'one of the most complicated in the world' (Derrett 1957: 3) and there is agreement among most writers on this subject that Hindu law 'is acknowledged as having one of the most ancient pedigrees of any known system of jurisprudence'.[3]

Taking a methodological approach similar to that of the historical school of jurisprudence,[4] I envisage and present here a historically rooted analysis of Hindu law in which we find a clearly manifested, earth-focused, and surprisingly rational progression of 'legal' philosophy that can be distilled from the ancient Sanskrit literature. Of course, that does not cover the totality of ancient Hindu law. Parallel to the conceptual debates in the ancient literature, we must assume, occurred a logical elaboration of normative orders and legal rule

[2] On the definition of 'Hindu' for legal purposes see Derrett (1963b: 18–21). Agnes (2000: 26) argues that the construction of a 'Hindu' entity 'was an attempt to impose an alien and higher caste system of law upon a pluralistic society'. Significantly, the fact that the introduction of a uniform civil code in India would have a similar effect, imposing elite concepts, is not often acknowledged by modernist writers, but is discussed in Sheth and Nandy (1996) and other works by Ashis Nandy.

[3] Satyajeet A. Desai in the preface to the seventeenth edition of Mulla's *Principles of Hindu Law* (Desai 1998). His grandfather, Sunderlal T. Desai, in the introduction to the twelfth edition of the same book, written in 1958, asserted at p. 1 that 'Hindu law, as it is now generally agreed, has the most ancient pedigree of any known system of jurisprudence'. Early indological scholarship still wrestled with the 'hopeless uncertainty which characterised the earlier speculations of European scholars concerning the origin of the so-called Indian codes of law' (Bühler 1975: xx).

[4] On details of this school, which in a nutshell emphasizes the organic growth of legal systems and views them as socio-legal entities rather than a rule system imposed by the state, see Cotterrell (1989) and Menski (2000a: 99–110).

systems; but for several good reasons these are not fully recorded in writing. Then as now, most of Hindu law was negotiated at the local level and remained unrecorded.[5] Thus, there is no hope that we should ever be able to reconstruct directly from the original sources what ancient Hindu law actually was like in practice. Further, ancient Hindu law was not recorded in codified form, though many Hindu law textbooks assume that it was. None of the innumerable ancient Sanskrit texts are in the nature of law reports from which one could glean the state of the law at any point in time. In addition, the ancient texts cannot be reliably dated, and '[e]xact chronology is defied by these traditional materials which had so long a working life' (Derrett 1968a: 81).

This amounts to saying that we cannot fully reconstruct traditional Hindu law from the textual sources themselves. But, as I must show here in some detail, this is exactly what most scholarship on the subject has been engaged in, erecting in the process a more or less fictitious, hypothetical, and theoretical structure called 'Hindu law'. These various assertions and inventions have influenced and distorted our understanding of what Hindu law is about, as a legal system as well as a conceptual entity. The resultant complex human construction of Hindu law has become a reality in its own right, even an officially recognized legal fact, and yet it involves a massive distortion of social reality. The internally self-contradictory (not to say schizophrenic) nature of such confused and confusing representations and the resulting manipulations can be shown, for example, through a close reading of the first two pages in one of the leading textbooks on Hindu law. In an important text originally published in 1958, Desai (1998: 1) starts with the recognition that '[l]aw as understood by the Hindus is a branch of Dharma', which neatly reflects the internal Hindu perspective. But the lawyer then takes over from the Hindu when Desai (1998: 2) proceeds a little later with the assertion that Hindu law's 'basic structure was the law of the Smritis', which was then developed further through 'a number of explanatory and critical commentaries and digests [*sic*] ... which had the effect of enlarging and consolidating the law' (id.). Within two sentences, thus, Hindu law's cosmic basis has been refashioned into a legalistic, positivistic code. Most significantly, the ancient recognition that 'law' as a holistic entity is subject to a higher set of parameters has been rendered invisible by this shift towards legal centralism. By taking the view that law, and not any other force, regulates the world, an essentially secular legal scholarship has simply declared the conceptual underpinnings of traditional Hindu culture as legally irrelevant.[6]

It seems that this critical distortion, of which many textual examples will be provided later, arose in three ways. First of all, there is evidence that Hindu authors, in particular, declared Hindu law to be based on divine revelation

[5] On the critical importance of customary law see the heading 'The role of custom in classical Hindu law' in a later section in this chapter.

[6] A modified form of legal centralism is subtly introduced by Derrett (1963b: 2), arguing that the *dharmaśāstra* is, 'in so far as it deals with law, no less characteristically jurisprudential than its coevals, the Roman and the Jewish law; and it would be a great mistake to suppose that it was founded or rooted in theology or philosophy'.

when it is neither clear which god should be responsible for this, nor what that revelation precisely involved.[7] Secondly, we find evidence of an Orientalist construction which has taken literary statements as proof of social fact, overlooking Hindu social reality and the practical impact of the non-textual realm.[8] This approach glorified texts, their translations, and later commentaries as fixed entities that somehow expressed cultural facts which were then taken as absolute truths.[9] Thus, just as the label 'Hindu' was eventually constructed to encompass a plural reality that no single term could hope to capture,[10] the deceptively simple label of 'Hindu law' emerged, suggesting uniformity and certainty where in reality there was very little of either.

Thirdly, in relation to legal scholarship, a unique type of Orientalist-cum-legal reconstruction of Hindu law took place, introducing its own obfuscations. Having created a discourse of Hinduness that tended to overlook and marginalize the internal diversity and complexity of the cosmic Hindu system as a whole, Orientalist legal scholarship simply presented dharma as law (Bühler 1975) and suggested thereby that Hindu legal rules could be found fixed in the type of codes familiar from Roman law and more recent legal codifications, such as the French Civil Code produced by Napoleon. Hence what was internally classified as *dharmaśāstra* became a code of law, and texts like the *Manusmriti* could become the 'Laws of Manu'. It is remarkable that such Orientalist distortions have so uncritically been adopted by modern feminists and other writers who should know better.[11]

[7] See the misleading claim by Diwan and Diwan (1993:18–19) that 'Hindus consider their law as a revealed law' (p. 18) and that the great rishis received it 'in direct communion with God' (p. 19).

[8] On Orientalism, see concisely Ashcroft et al. (1998: 167–169).

[9] See for example Keith (1993: 404). While Desai's general statement, as discussed earlier, is not Orientalist, and Desai (1998: 2) also reflects the role of customary law quite well, many authors have been far less careful. A simple example, critically relevant for Ch. 11 later, is the classic statement that traditional Hindu law does not permit divorce, while everyone knows that divorce, albeit a serious deviation from the shastric ideal, was indeed possible in practice, was mentioned in some texts, and was certainly allowed in many local customary Hindu law systems.

[10] The construction of Hinduism has been widely debated. See Bowen (1998: 1–10) with reference to other authors. The volume of conference papers by Sontheimer and Kulke (1989) is considered a major milestone in this field. Jenkins (2001: 113) notes that '[c]haracterized by historian Robert Frykenberg as "[t]his soft concept, this jumble of inner contradictions", Hinduism is particularly susceptible to open interpretations and porous boundaries'.

[11] Roy (1995: 11) simply describes the *Manusmriti* as 'amongst the most well-known prescriptive texts of early India', thus assuming that such texts 'prescribed' models or forms of behaviour when in reality they merely suggested various options. Hence, while Roy rightly questions the construction of a unified and uniform Vedic-centred past (ibid.: 12), her rhetoric is not matched by culture-sensitive analysis, and she still falls into the same methodological traps of uniforming and law-centred distortion as many other writers.

Evidently, European Orientalist scholars and an emerging literate Hindu elite, who were glad to see themselves accepted as part of a literate tradition and more 'civilised' than other colonial subjects,[12] colluded in this venture. Their writings brought about a massive distortion, embellishing the false scholarly assertion that dharma can be equated to law, which could then be applied in formal courts, first in late medieval India and later under British rule. While a certain formalization of dispute settlement processes is already evident from the post-classical Hindu law itself (see the section on *vyavahāra* etc., later in this chapter), the stultifying process of constructing Anglo-Hindu law was later undoubtedly quickened by the convenient equation of dharma (and also *vyavahāra*) with law. This allowed Orientalists to accept, in principle, that the Hindus had law, and thus pleased the emerging Hindu scholars as well, who liked the idea of their system being recognized as 'legal', and who saw growing professional prospects in its application. At the same time, having been relabelled 'law', the element of dharma lost—at least in the eyes of those who now sought to define it for legal practice—its inherent flexibility and situation-specificity. Above all, the official equation of dharma with law secularised the understanding of Hindu legal processes and marginalized the inherent link of all individual actions with the 'cosmic' system of righteousness as the ultimate arbiter of what was 'the right thing to do' at any given moment.

Once lawyers took hold of this system—first British officers of the East India Company, later servants of the Crown, but most importantly judges and practising lawyers with their growing band of Indian colleagues—Hindu law could simply be reconstructed further and was subsequently modelled into a 'proper' legal system which, to the British, meant some form of common law structure.[13] In this new construct, the ground rules of law would be ascertained from new written sources, rather than the confusing ancient texts which indeed turned out to be unworkable as codes. In this way, Hindu law and its formal administration were brought under increasing state control.[14] Orientalist

[12] Madan (1996: 249) highlights Western scholars' unwillingness to accept that ancient Africans might have possessed cosmological knowledge prior to contact with the West. In his seminal analysis of colonialism of the mind, Nandy (1983: 17) notes that '[n]ewly-discovered Africa, with its strong emphasis on the folk, the oral and the rural could be more easily written off as savage. It was more difficult to do so for India and China ...'.

[13] The pervasive hidden influence of English concepts of law in this process should be brought out more clearly in future research by historians. In addition, it is not often noted that many Scottish people were exceptionally active in the field of law, most significantly Macaulay, the author of the Indian Penal Code (IPC) of 1860. Thus, Anglo-Indian law became a curious amalgam and was most certainly not just 'common law', as is routinely assumed, nor was English law the only influence. On the French handling of law in Pondicherry, frequently disrupted by the British, see now in detail Bonnan (1999).

[14] The earlier attempts by the British to commission 'authoritative' collections of law from Hindu experts illustrate the belief that Hindu law could be fixed on paper. For details see Chapter 4 of this book and Bhattacharyya-Panda (1995).

scholarship and the professional concerns of practising lawyers thus colluded in a redefinition of Hindu law which ultimately excluded everything that was not subservient to positivist control, including most customs and local norms.

In terms of the methodological scheme suggested by the legal theorist Masaji Chiba (1986), with its tripartite division of official law, unofficial law, and legal postulates, 'Hindu law' was thus ultimately whittled down and redesignated to cover just official law, ignoring everything else as practically irrelevant and 'extra-legal'. The professional distortion of Hindu law presents an extremely chronic but entirely typical case of legal myopia, an instructive example of how legal centralism manipulates legal reality through taking the view that formal law dominates the world and is to be treated as the central element in human life. Such blurred images of the total reality of Hindu law then culminate, for example, in the poignant statement by Derrett (1968a: 83) that '[t]hus Hindu law has always been a book law', which reflects the distortion instead of opposing it.[15] This is accompanied by much writing about the important role of 'jurists' (Derrett 1968a: 83–84), 'Hindu jurisprudentes' (Desai 1998: 3), or 'juristheologians' (ibid.: 9) and is liberally mixed with assertions to the effect that '[t]he shrewd practical insight of the Hindu Rishis who were both sages and virtually lawmakers left very little that was undefined' (id.), as though the strength of traditional Hindu law depended on legal certainty and the avoidance of gaps in the law.

Within the grotesque picture of such formalized representations of Hindu law, it appears that a purely secular ruler could now preside over his subjects and effectively rule them through his law,[16] instead of helping to ascertain appropriate solutions with a view to supporting the pre-existing Hindu notions of cosmic order. The gradual secularization and resulting transposition of Hindu law into a positivist legal construct eventually left only one option for modernist reform, namely legislative intervention with consequent further marginalization and ultimate abolition of the 'Hindu' element in Hindu law. By the time of India's independence in 1947, further legislation and de-Hinduization were, within this twisted logic, presented as the only viable method of modernizing Hindu law.

However, such multiple distortions of the nature and concepts of Hindu law and the resulting discourses, as real and manifest as they may be in the

[15] May (1985: 54) stresses that the shastric texts are 'by no means a specimen of book-law'.

[16] Desai (1998: 32) is ambiguously worded and takes the *Arthaśāstra* as 'dealing with matters worldly as distinguished from religious'. Diwan and Diwan (1993: 24) suggest that Hindu rulers had the power to make law and take *daṇḍa* as a form of secular punishment (ibid.: 25 and 33). Desai (1998: 3) assumed that '[t]he minutest rules were laid down for the guidance of the king'. Later, at pp. 33–4, the assertion that the ruler can make law, albeit within limits, and that the ruler's law is supreme is at least presented as a matter of controversy, which shows that the learned author did not entirely ignore the internal Hindu perspective.

existing body of legal 'knowledge', are all highly fictitious constructs in themselves. They do not reflect the totality of Hindu law and its methods, nor the social reality of Hindu beliefs and ways of life. We must therefore note that, even today, Hindu law is much more than the alleged book law of the shastras, the opinions of pandits, case reports which claim to be more or less authoritative precedents, and the words of modern statutes.

Given the outrightly contradictory perspectives that the above discussion has identified, nobody should be surprised that India and her people have continued to defy the predictions of experts. The constructs with which the various experts operate are simply not the same as the structures which underpin traditional as well as contemporary Hindu law and Indian society. Officially underwritten expertise in Hindu law, thus, looks more like deliberate ignorance of, and prudent non-involvement in,[17] those areas of knowledge that are not easily susceptible to scholarly research techniques.[18] In other words, Orientalist scholarship on Hindu law, in intimate collusion with legal specialists and the legal profession, has redefined the field of study to make it digestible for lawyers rather than to bring out the central Hindu legal concern for appropriateness.[19] Such scholarship has thereby gradually built up a funeral pyre for itself and for the notion of Hindu law.

Analysing Hindu Legal History

The foregoing discussion should have cleared at least some of the cobwebs around the Orientalist constructions of Hindu law which have thoroughly misled non-lawyers.[20] Having shown that there is much more to study than legal

[17] Derrett (1978: ix) candidly acknowledges that in her study of divorce, Rama Mehta (1975) was wise not to venture into the legal realm of the rural majority, who 'are governed largely by customs and traditional mores' and are thus declared unsuitable for analysis.

[18] Legal knowledge of African law, which is built on ancient and almost exclusively oral traditions, was even more openly redefined to suit legal scholars, so that the definition of African law became enlarged to include the modern statutory laws (Menski 2000a: 329) and expertise in African laws could henceforth be measured without reference to traditional laws, cultures, and languages.

[19] Non-lawyers, looking for 'proper law', are found to complain that the lawyers have not provided suitable material for them. Baxi (1986b: 5) reports on such criticism by Veena Das, phrased in terms of expecting to see a *corpus iuris*. Leading lawyers remain content to criticize and challenge society and its biases and lack of civilizational standards (Anand 2002).

[20] Numerous examples from older and recent writing could be given. For example, Flood (1998: 30) simply accepts the brahmanical view of Hindu morality, 'thought to be based on the revelation (*śruti*) of the Veda, articulated in various law books, the *Dharmaśāstras*', and describes the *Manusmriti* as '[t]he famous Hindu law book' (ibid.: 32). Friedrich (1993) depicts the *Āpastamba-Dharmasūtra* as one of the oldest Indian legal texts.

textbooks indicate and admit, we must now proceed towards an analysis of traditional Hindu legal concepts and their socio-legal contexts in the light of the published discourse on Hindu law, which is being challenged here.

We know from the textual sources themselves that the complex human construct which was later called 'Hindu law' emerged first, in distant antiquity, from the self-controlled 'religious' orders of *rita* or *ṛta* (pre-existent macrocosmic order) and later dharma (self-controlled microcosmic order).[21] Such foundational conceptualizations led more or less directly to the more explicitly legal concept of 'assisted self-control' by threats of retribution with the ruler's punishing rod (*daṇḍa*), and processes of negotiation or dispute settlement (*vyavahāra*) to extract the thorns of disagreement. These interlinked central concepts of the 'classical' or 'traditional' Hindu law are discussed in turn in the various subsections below, followed by an examination of the role of custom.

Unlike the standard textbook treatment of Hindu law, found for example in Desai (1998: 1–68), my analysis does not divide the history of Hindu law into textual periods, but emphasizes the critical importance of conceptual developments in Hindu law. Relying on either method creates its own problems, since neither the complex Hindu key concepts nor the mass of classical texts can be neatly sorted into strict sequences.[22] Textual layers overlap and interact, and so do the key concepts in their floating historical settings. But there is some internal logic in the genesis of central conceptualizations, while it remains totally impossible to establish firm chronologies for the ancient Hindu texts, which are often collections of material from quite different times and localities.[23] Dealing with concepts also has the advantage, in my view, that the key stages of the interlinked conceptual developments within Hindu law can be made more evident through an analytical, rather than descriptive, approach.

To demystify the confusing diversity within Hindu law, it is useful and in fact necessary to divide the 'traditional' or 'classical' era itself into various periods. These are not so much historical sequences as a number of overlapping building blocks, a series of conceptual steps towards the mature growth of a

[21] Olivelle (2000: 14) reiterates that dharma is 'undoubtedly the most central and ubiquitous concept in the whole of Indian civilization'. On the centrality of social self-regulation, see Rudolph and Rudolph (2001: 59–60).

[22] We have neither a fully documented chronology of the ancient writings, nor definite evidence about the identity of the 'authors' of such ancient texts, often compilations produced over a long period of time and available in many variant readings, which are normally not mistakes, but meaningful in themselves. On details of the history of ancient Indian literature see Winternitz (1968; 1985), Keith (1993), as well as a series of studies, entitled *A History of Indian Literature*, under the editorship of Jan Gonda, especially Gonda (1975). The monumental work of Kane (1968–77) also contains a detailed description of all major textual sources.

[23] Larivière (1989, II: xx) rightly depicts a 'chronological house of cards'.

coherent traditional Hindu legal framework in its gradual transition from dharma to law, as Lingat (1973) saw it.[24] The totality of 'traditional' Hindu law is therefore presented here as an interlinked and chronologically overlapping sequence of sub-systems, a method which emphasizes the inherent dynamisms and dialectics within the various stages of traditional Hindu law and its seemingly unlimited scope for flexibility and internal reform. There is certainly no stuffy stagnant traditionalism here, but an open and vibrant atmosphere of debate, reflection, and gradual emergence of a consensus in favour of virtually unlimited diversity and plurality.

Hindu law, it must always be remembered, had no definite starting point in any doctrinally central event or theory, despite assertions by lawyers and others of the divine revelation of the Vedas.[25] As a chthonic system, Hindu law just began somewhere in the distant past, which has posed huge philosophical questions and given rise to various dogmatized beliefs and religiously tinged myths. Over time, Hindu law inevitably turned into a collection of legal systems, held together by little more than its basic concepts and, perhaps, the 'ethnic' awareness that oneself and one's group are not outsiders to this tradition.[26] At the same time, the internal plurality of Hindu law subjects many insider perspectives to the scrutiny of rival views, turning them into challenged positions that must fight for recognition as proper 'Hindu' perceptions. The tendency for upper-caste or Brahmin views to prevail, and to be presented as dominant, criticized elaborately by Guha (1982; 1997), can only partly be explained by the fact that the textual sources have been composed by a literary élite. Later commentators, including Western scholars, have added their own glosses on the strength and authority of particular views and have thus played a crucial partisan role in the reconstruction and eventual distortion of the nature of 'Hindu law'.

The conceptual history of Hindu law firmly suggests that no one textual statement in the ancient sources can represent 'the law'. The Hindu legal system is not built on codified statements by a human legal authority, to which factual situations are then related, nor is it based on a fixed revelation, which came down from heaven one day and binds all adherents.[27] I suggest, therefore, that in Hindu law the principal conceptual starting point is provided by

[24] On Lingat's interpretation see Baxi (1986b: 5–10).

[25] Again, this is a matter of overlapping consensus. The belief in divine revelation exists, but this does not mean that therefore everything was laid down once and for all by one central authority. It appears that all religious traditions face the same problem in principle, albeit in quite different terms.

[26] On this see Derrett (1968a: 80). Virtually all Hindu law textbooks have sections dealing with the complex question of the applicability of Hindu law. Derrett (1963b: 21) suggested that '[p]erhaps the best test is whether people claim to be Hindus and are acknowledged as Hindus by their immediate contiguous society'.

[27] While not asserting, as most legal writers constantly do, that ancient Hindu law is divinely revealed, Keith (1993: 494) suggests that 'another early development

the somewhat unquestionable awareness of a pre-existent entity, the observable order (and occasional disorder) of nature, conceptually embodied in the *ṛta*/dharma complex. This concept of macrocosmic order, beyond direct human reach, militates against any form of positivistic human law-making. Any questions about human order are therefore first addressed in relation to this pre-existing larger order, and not with primary reference to some human edict. Thus, life and death are primarily seen as cosmically linked, rather than being medically examined—a sign not so much of primitiveness, but of an implied early recognition that ultimate truths will forever remain outside the realm of human knowledge. In other words, what occurs is not some blind belief in certain religious doctrines, but an acceptance that there is something higher than all forms of human rule-making or volition, something that cannot be defined with certainty. Hindus have always been free to speculate as to which god or what power may be 'in charge', or if indeed any one power needs to be seen in this way. Denying that kind of higher power altogether is (as for Muslims) not a conceptual suggestion that makes sense to Hindus, who will therefore tend to maintain some kind of sceptical distance to the secularizing axioms of modernity (see Nandy 1990).

Since the many textual rules about what may be in accordance with *ṛta* and dharma are only a methodological tool in the search for appropriateness, or the justice of the situation, it should be clear that they cannot in themselves be treated as the primary source of law—there is always a higher entity, not manifest in writing but seen to exist in the natural environment. A radical postmodern interrogation of Hindu law, therefore, cannot give the ancient texts themselves primacy of place, but must acknowledge the superiority, in theory and in practice, of their conceptual underpinnings. If the texts themselves cannot be 'the law', they are at best sources of law, potential guidance in solving a problem, but not binding legal rules in the Austinian sense.[28]

While there is clearly no such thing as *one* codified Hindu law embodied in the ancient texts, the idea of a common sociocultural and ultimately legal tradition cannot be denied. What scholars are vigorously arguing about is the extent to which this common core may bind every Hindu. It should be obvious by now that scholarly assumptions about 'prescriptive' legal texts and binding Hindu dogmatics merely reflect what Nandy (1983: xi) incisively refers to as 'colonization of the mind'. Challenging such deeply engrained historical processes of knowledge production, we must always return in the present

---

within the Vedic period was the building up of schools of Law in the wide sense of that term which includes religious and civil and criminal law'. The same passage refers later to 'professional schools' after the time of Manu and claims that '[o]nly slowly and imperfectly within these schools was there developed a separation, never complete, of religious and secular law' (id.).

[28] This is where my analysis differs from the secularized view presented by Bhattacharjee (1994), discussed in a later section on dharma and classical Hindu law.

analysis to niggling general questions about concepts of 'law' and about the nature of Hindu law. This is certainly not the same as 'essentializing', since for the Hindu case it is critical to understand that such fixations on essentials must still reckon with unlimited plurality of internal perspectives. In a sense, Hindu law itself denies the theoretical possibility of a Hindu essentialism that is so often stipulated. All that scholars seem to be doing is to construct and reconstruct their own perceptions of 'Hindu', which are often only remotely related to what many other and perhaps more 'real' Hindus have historically thought and done.

My conceptual analysis now distinguishes four major stages of development within 'traditional' Hindu law, starting from the macrocosmic universal order system (*ṛta*) of the pre-classical or Vedic age.[29] This gradually metamorphosed (but we do not quite know when) into the properly 'classical' Hindu law, the idealised system of self-controlled order (dharma), focused on microcosmic order and encompassing every Hindu individual. Third, because of the admitted limits of self-controlled order, we soon find the deterrence-based stage of punishment (*daṇḍa*), which is a typically Hindu form of 'assisted self-control', still relying on the individual's sense of dharma, but now explicitly recognizing that some external pressure is necessary to ensure that cosmic order is being maintained as much as possible. Here we find evidence of greater importance given to the Hindu ruler (*rājā*) who operates at various levels, from head of family to clan chief, village head, and real king (Desai 1998: 35). Crucially, within the Hindu conceptual system all these ruler figures are not absolutist Napoleonic lawmakers, but guardians and in fact servants of dharma, which remains the unspoken, overriding core element of this idealistic self-maintained order system.

Fourth, the more or less formal methods of negotiation or dispute processing (*vyavahāra*) should in my view also be counted as a separate stage of Hindu legal development, still acknowledging the primacy and desirability of self-controlled order, but now recognizing the scope for formal settlement of contested matters, which may culminate in a royal pronouncement as some kind of final word. That, however, is still not a manifestation of secular law, as most of Hindu legal scholarship has argued,[30] but represents a further confirmation of the overriding concern for self-controlled order. A Hindu royal edict does not represent positive law, but constitutes a visible manifestation of the superiority of the *ṛta*/dharma complex, according to which the Hindu ruler is supposed to position himself and his activities.

Orientalist and legal reconstruction activity is quite evident here, too: if the traditional ruler's verdict merely settled a particular situational conflict in

[29] Until recently (Menski 2000a: 165–9), I envisaged only three stages of classical Hindu law, but it appears to make sense to separate the post-classical developments further on the basis of the two key concepts of *daṇḍa* and *vyavahāra*.

[30] Desai (1998: 33–4) points to a lively controversy on this issue. Even most recent scholarship takes a legalistic approach (Olivelle 2000; Rocher 2002).

view of dharmic considerations, how can one legitimately deduce that such decisions represented secular law-making and established a model or precedent that would thereafter have to be followed by others? Did a ruler's verdict really lay down the law for all times to come? For a lawyer in the common law tradition, the image of 'precedent' suggests itself with great force, but we are analysing traditional Hindu law here, not some form of English law. Assuming the emergence of royal precedent or even legislation, therefore, appears to be another form of Orientalist-cum-legalist construction imported into India by outsiders in the light of their own experiences and assumptions, not based on study of Hindu concepts.

Rather than drowning in the fine details of internal Hindu self-regulation, and its genesis over time, the present analysis needs to focus on the critical interface between non-state law and state law.[31] In this respect, the huge literature on ancient Hindu kings and rulers of all descriptions seems to become directly relevant.[32] However, examining it in much detail may be a waste of time for the contemporary legal analyst, as one becomes embroiled in various specialist debates, such as the internal controversies between Brahmans and Kshatriyas (i.e. the head priests and rulers) over which of them is supreme. These two office bearers were having a familiar debate, therefore, not just over whether royal or priestly power is superior, but more profoundly over whether 'law' or 'religion' takes precedence. In other words, they were also contesting the possibility and extent of secularism. In typically Hindu fashion, involving another overlapping consensus, this debate remained inconclusive, in that both parties would maintain their claims to superiority over the other. However, the unspoken message is that above those two contestants, and all around them, there is still the superior element of cosmic interlinkedness, the basic Hindu 'social cement' (Derrett 1970: 2) that keeps the mass of outwardly conflicting positions and claims under one conceptual 'religious' and 'legal' roof.

Thus, while one may learn much from the ancient Hindu literature generally, and more specifically from the later texts that appear to focus on law and governance, such as the famous *Arthaśāstra*, the interpretation of this body of literature as a source of legal rules must remain contested. Reading such

[31] This might well be the subject of a separate study, but such scholarship faces enormous hurdles in terms of lack of evidence. It remains impossible to determine whether a particular shastric rule was or was not followed in practice, because no records were kept until much later (Smith and Derrett 1975). Thus, we are simply not able to conduct such research for the older periods.

[32] The early leading study by Altekar (1958) seems to have been superseded by much recent work. Kulke (1997) provides a useful conceptual overview for the study of the state in pre-modern India and contains a detailed bibliography. In the same volume, Stein (1997: 135) explains that earlier historical studies were too focused on centralized structures, thus challenging similar positivist assumptions as the present study. There is much writing on this subject by German authors, e.g. Kulke and Rothermund (1998) and the earlier work of Wilhelm Rau (1957).

material through the blinkered secularized lenses of modernity, even leading Hindu writers have been tempted to assign Austinian law-making powers to the ancient Hindu rulers and, as noted before, have imagined ancient learned men such as the mythical Manu as powerful lawmakers. Today the argument appears to be that if Hindus themselves have imbibed such interpretations and understandings, whether or not they are myths, they must be representative of 'the law'.[33]

All of this is deeply problematic. Such interpretations forget or purposely ignore one of the most basic constituents of Hindu law, namely that the cosmic world order in the form of *ṛta* or dharma is always present, even if not explicitly mentioned. Thus, even if a text purports to discuss what looks like 'worldly' affairs, such as marriage, making a contract, or ruling a kingdom, the conceptual level of the superhuman Hindu cosmos is still there, exerting its own invisible influence. The dutiful Hindu ruler will therefore be aware of the limits on his law-making powers, while the unwary analyst or reader risks focusing only on the secular, political element of royal power. It is another matter that a Hindu ruler may in practice choose to ignore such higher concepts and dictate what *he* wants, not what seems best in terms of dharma for the situation in hand. This possibility cannot serve as proof that the underlying Hindu conceptual framework is absent or defunct, it merely confirms that despite all idealism, ancient Hindus had bad and corrupt rulers, too. In this respect, again, Hindu law is no different from other legal systems.

Historians have long tended to focus on 'big' men and their impact and this trend has markedly influenced the perspectives of those specialists who wrote about Hindu law. All along, however, while largely inaccessible to the scholarly grasp, Hindu law has also remained the 'living law' of hundreds of millions of people who never had any contact with the official norm-producing agencies that may have existed, following instead what they assumed to be and knew as their own versions of Hindu law. The complex tensions between textually fixed and locally determined Hindu legal concepts and orders were partly overcome through awareness of the fact that both of these arenas for the development of Hindu normative orders were interlinked by knowledge of, and more or less strict adherence to, the same Hindu concepts. Thus *ṛta*, dharma, *daṇḍa* and *vyavahāra* may not have been technical terms that every Hindu was and is expressly familiar with, but the impact of these foundational concepts appears to have been all-pervasive, in the same way as those concepts have remained present, whether at a conscious or subconscious level, among Hindus today. Guha's (1997) subaltern analysis clearly confirms the huge scope for internal oppositions to dominant Hindu models.

[33] This certainly goes for the understanding of Hindu law in South-east Asia, which is rather too strongly based on positivist elements taken from late classical Hindu law (see Huxley 1996). These are necessarily divorced from the Vedic and classical Hindu conceptual framework because of Buddhist influence, which reworked such ideational foundations without totally rejecting them.

Within our conceptual analysis we must therefore note the explicit, abundantly recorded recognition in the ancient shastras that people's customs and local ways of doing things must in principle be allowed to prevail, irrespective of what certain texts may be stating. There is no one religious, moral, or legal code that binds all Hindus together as a matter of dogmatic belief. This undisputable fact underpins an axiomatic rule that cannot please positivist lawyers (or modern feminists) but will make sense to legal pluralists and adherents of the various historical schools of jurisprudence: Hinduism as a religious tradition has always allowed its followers to pick and choose elements from 'the tradition' for themselves. Thus all individuals are empowered, obviously not without sociocultural limits in most cases, to construct their own personal system of belief and practice within the parameters of this cosmically interlinked system.[34] While this was certainly not a matter of totally free and autonomous choice for all Hindus, there is neither a central religious nor legal authority that could determine for all times what the universally binding rules of Hinduism are. There is simply no room in this conceptualization for a Hindu Pope, nor for a central authority that 'lays down the law' for all Hindus.[35] This does not exclude the possibility of strongly held beliefs and firmly stated convictions, but they are always relativized by awareness that there is a form of higher truth, which encompasses more than any individual could think, believe, or do. Ancient and modern Hindus know or simply accept this, and analysts ignore it at their peril—or are indeed on the road to various forms of Orientalist and legal distortions of Hindu law.[36]

Unquestionably, therefore, this rather sketchy and necessarily broad summary of the essential systemic openness of Hindu belief and practice is of immense and direct relevance to any analysis of Hindu law. The inherent flexibility of Hinduism presents itself in harmonious accordance with the basic Hindu expectation that all beings should be empowered to fulfil their very own and personal dharma, whatever that may be. This axiom, universal in

[34] Recent feminist writing has begun to note, but does not fully incorporate, the realization that '[p]lurality of laws and customs and non-state legal structure were the essential characteristics of the ancient Indian communities' (Agnes 2000: 12). In the context of female property rights, S. Basu (2001: 10) refers to 'pockets of equity that have seldom been utilized by Hindu women'.

[35] Newspapers and magazines all over the world peddle the notion of 'Hindu pontiffs', a varying number of which are given, often four. But see Menski (1996a: 7) on the point that no ultimate moral or legal authority can be exercised by any Hindu authority figure. Hindus need to realize that Muslims, too, despite many assertions to the contrary, have no such living persons of absolute religious authority either. Thus, Hindus and Muslims actually share many dilemmas of law-finding and ascertaining dharma or sharia.

[36] Common people in South Asia seem acutely aware of this, more so than scholars. The former are experiencing this plurality in their everyday lives, while Nandy (1990: 69) critiques scholarly language and especially 'secularism' as 'a cover for the complicity of the modern intellectuals and the modernizing middle classes of South Asia in the new forms of religious violence'.

theory and yet totally individualistic in practice, evidently undermines any form of binding uniform legal regulation imposed on individuals and groups of people from outside or from above. Theoretically speaking, as well as in practice, this stops any Hindu rule-maker from imposing his will absolutely on 'his' people—everyone knows that even the highest ruler is never fully autonomous. A Hindu lawmaker may suggest or recommend certain rules or solutions, but they do not bind others in the same way as positive law.

If the basic Hindu conceptual rule was and is that every individual is unique and different, and that every situational context has its peculiar features, requiring a situation-specific response and solution, an appropriate law must of necessity be something different from positivist state laws that prescribe how all people must act in certain situations. Ancient Hindu conceptualisations are certainly not unaware of the power and potential of legal positivism, but have subjected law-making, as everything else, to the overriding authority of dharmic relativism. Thus, a dutiful dharma-conscious Hindu ruler could not prohibit prostitution, the slaughter of animals for human consumption, or highway robbery, but should seek to monitor such activities in terms of whether everyone concerned followed their dharmic duty properly. It is for these reasons, above all, that my approach to the analysis of Hindu law prefers the techniques of the historical school to those of legal positivism.

Seen from this perspective, Hindu law could never become a uniform codified edifice that one might encapsulate in the few words of a statute or code and that would then determine the actions of large numbers of individuals because it was 'the law'. The label 'Hindu law' does not signify uniformity, it covers almost limitless plurality. Law, within the Hindu conceptual context, would have to be determined from case to case, from situation to situation, and it would also vary at different times, as the post-classical concept of the eras of human existence (*yugas*) demonstrates. In short, the conceptual underpinnings of traditional Hindu law and of legal positivism are like chalk and cheese. The methods of the analytical school of jurisprudence are plainly unsuitable for a reality-conscious analysis of Hindu law.

Choosing to follow the historical school of jurisprudence, as well as a conceptual approach for the analysis of Hindu law, takes fuller account of the tremendous internal dynamism within the Hindu legal system than a mainly chronological approach would allow for. It enables us to record more of the distant, ancient conversations, conflicts and tensions that occurred in the long history of Hindu law, because there is an internal logic to the development of the key Hindu concepts which legal analysis must not ignore. Rather than bringing in external perspectives all the time, as Desai (1998: 1–68) clearly does, the present approach therefore claims to reach deeper layers of internal analysis.

Seen in this light, current attempts to portray Hinduism and Hindu law as uniform bodies of concepts and rules appear politically motivated and therefore quite misguided, even mischievous. In particular, efforts to rewrite Hindu 'scriptures' are doomed to dismal failure. Designed, as were some earlier efforts (see in the colonial context Kane 1968–1977), to show that Hinduism and Hindu law are not inferior, today's ambitious Hindu law scholarship again feeds on revivalist political undertones of Hindu superiority in reaction to the many derogatory comments about Hindus, Hinduism, and Hindu law (Jois 1990a; 1990b; more so Jois 2000). These are distractions from the real task, making Hindu law intelligible to Hindus themselves and to outsiders, in the light of today's knowledge and contemporary concerns. But rewriting the past will never undo it. Simply asserting superiority points to ignorance of deeper concepts in one's own traditions and those of others. Claiming that any legal system automatically offers 'justice' simply will not do.[37] The politicized environment of current debates about the place of Hindu law, as well as the extent of disagreement, confirms that the Orientalist distortions of Hindu law and various other constructs—often produced by Hindus themselves—have added further spice to an ancient debate whose subject remains alive and well.

The Concept of Cosmic Order (*Ṛta*) in Pre-classical Vedic Law

The Vedic age of Hindu civilization (c. 1500 BC to c. 800 BC) is an era which some older European scholars have declared to be of a different culture and religion,[38] while Hindu scholars claim that their civilisation is much older and extends as far as 6000 years back.[39] For the present legal analysis, such ongoing controversies are fruitless. No useful purpose, apart from politico-religious power games, is served in fixing a starting date for an ancient cultural tradition that refuses to be pressed into a dogmatic pattern of belief in a certain origin. It is undisputed that Hindu law has an ancient chthonic base and that, as a religious system, it is not based on a specific divine revelation at a specified, fixed time, notwithstanding general references to divine revelation through the concept of *śruti*.

Examining the conceptual framework from within Hindu traditions,[40] we must above all take account of the basic ancient concept of *ṛta* which later

[37] I hope to have said enough about this particular issue here to oppose and discard the notion that ancient Hindu law was focused on what we now call 'justice' in an egalitarian, human rights sense. Ancient Hindu law necessarily concerned itself with myriads of situational appropriateness, not some simplistic assumptions of equality before the law.

[38] Von Stietencron (1989: 23 n. 8) refers to the older work of Gonda (1960) and discusses the difficulties, indeed the impossibility, of finding a uniform definition of Hinduism.

[39] Diwan and Diwan (1993: 27) take the Vedic period back to about 4000 BC. while Desai (1998: 5) relies on Kane and other pioneers of research, arguing that '[i]t is possible that some Vedic hymns may have been composed at a period earlier than 4000 BC'.

[40] Diwan and Diwan (1993: 11) take a similar approach, emphasizing generally that '[t]he concept of Hindu law is deeply rooted in Hindu philosophy and Hindu religion'.

transformed into dharma.[41] This old Vedic conceptualization reflects and signifies the early awareness of people, who only later came to be known as Hindus,[42] that there is a superhuman, macrocosmic form of order in the world which is not directly subject to human influence, but to which mankind in its quest for a good life should relate and, to an extent, submit. This submission of the individual is not as strictly conceived as in Islam, i.e. having to believe in the identity of one particular God, who alone governs and regulates everything. Hindus, it is well known, agreed to disagree over the identity of 'the Absolute' a very long time ago. Consequently, they split over time into numerous groups and sects, creating the impression that Hinduism is merely a constructed term,[43] perhaps a kind of phantom, little else than a loosely connected grouping of sectarian orientations, confused about the nature of God and the universe.

Hindu reality, viewed from within, is far from confused, but it presents an extremely diverse picture for the outsider, offering many points of challenge. The ruminations of anti-religious, anti-Indian, and ultimately anti-Hindu observers have more or less deliberately ignored the deeper layers of Hinduism that only a few authors seem to have been able to articulate.[44] The most ancient conceptual strands of Hinduism, having been overlaid by numerous other factors, are ultimately just modified and updated versions of the same basic truth, namely that humankind does not know what keeps the world going and can only believe in one or another version of what we call 'religion'. Hindus as a collective appear to assume that one cannot expect one particular named superior God to take care of everything, thus all individual beings—gods, humans, and others—should try their best to partake in this superhuman Order, contributing as much as possible to its sustainability. Hinduism is therefore far more than a technique for personal salvation;[45] it also involves an obligation to live in a particular way for an ultimately indefinable but common good.

We have evidence of Hindu cultural texts, dated at least from c. 1500 BC onwards, in which such basic concepts are not so much debated as put into practice through hugely complex Vedic rituals which were apparently believed

[41] On *ṛta* as *logos* see Chaitanya (2000). May (1985: 18–25) discusses the concept in some detail.

[42] On Hindus as a Persian term denoting the people living on the other side of the river Sindhu, or 'the Indus people', see von Stietencron (1989: 11–12).

[43] See in detail von Stietencron (1989), especially his much-cited assertion that not one of the so-called fundamentals of Hinduism, namely recognition of Vedas, belief in reincarnation and the caste system 'applies to all religions in Hinduism' (p. 15).

[44] See in particular Miller (1985), Menski (1996a), and Menski (2000a: Ch. 3).

[45] That assumption is exaggerated by Diwan and Diwan (1993: 15), who claim that 'throughout the existence of Hinduism, the central theme has been the attainment of salvation'.

to have the potential to support and sustain cosmic order.[46] The large Vedic literature provides much detail about this distant period but contains very little material about the actual legal systems at the time. The Vedas, therefore, as legal authors confirm, were treated as divine revelation, but did by no means 'lay down the law', as some scholars with positivist inclinations have been tempted to assert. While the Vedas have a special place and authority in terms of Hindu religion and as a source of the concepts underlying Hindu law, they could not really serve as a direct source of legal rules, and certainly not as a legal code. However, the major legal textbooks on Hindu law tend to confuse readers, especially since some authors introduced grand assertions and engaged in outright myth-making. Mayne's old text (Kuppuswami 1986: 14) contains a fairly sober and concise passage on the Vedas:

> The Sruti (that which has been heard) is in theory the primary and paramount source of Hindu law and is believed to be the language of divine Revelation .... The Sruti, however, has little, or no legal value. It contains no statements of law as such, though its statements of facts are occasionally referred to in the Smritis and the commentaries as conclusive evidence of legal usage.

Desai (1998: 3–4) also highlights the basic Hindu belief in revelation, on the one hand, and the practical irrelevance of the Vedas for positive law-making on the other:

> It was an article of belief with the ancient Hindu, that his law was revelation, immutable and eternal. Shruti which strictly means the Vedas was in theory the root and original source of Dharma. It was the fountainhead of his law. Shruti means, literally, that which was heard. It was supreme to the early Hindu like the Decalogue to the later Christian. The Vedas, however, do not contain much that alludes to positive or municipal law. The few statements of law that are to be found in the Vedas are mostly incidental.

Pathak (1986: 1) states that two views are generally advanced on the question of origin of Hindu law. The orthodox view is that it is based on revelation and hence asserts divine origin for Hindu law, while the European view is rather that Hindu law relies on immemorial custom. More recent writing has embellished the former. Thus, Diwan and Diwan (1993: 27–8) at once claim divine status for Hindu law and then portray the story of revelation in outrightly monotheistic fashion:

> Hindu law is considered to be divine law, a revealed law. The theory is that some of the Hindu sages had attained great spiritual heights, so much so that they could be in direct communion with God. At some such time the sacred law was revealed to them by God Himself. This revelation is contained in *Sruti* or *Vedas*. The word *Sruti* literally means "what was heard".

[46] The fact that this whole system of Vedic rituals has virtually disappeared does not mean that this tradition died. It was reformed and remodelled into various Hindu ritual practices, observed everywhere today, partly revived by reference to 'Vedic' origins, even where none can be proven.

> The *Vedas*, thus, contain the divine revelation .... Since the *Vedas* are said to contain the voice of God, they are considered to be the fundamental or the primary source of law. The *Vedas* are said to be the source of all *knowledge*. In that view the entire body of Hindu law has emanated from the *Vedas*. And since it has emanated from *Vedas*, Hindu law is divine law, a divine revelation. Thus, in theory, the *Sruti* is considered to be the fundamental source of Hindu law.

Significantly, such circular arguments about Hindu theory play with the word 'law' when dharma is meant. Turning to proper 'law', the next sentence from the quote (at p. 28) seems to take everything back; the ensuing discussion questions the relevance of the Vedas in practice without explaining properly what kind of law is meant:

> However, its importance as a source of positive law is doubtful. One view is that the *Vedas* contain practically no law and are of little value.[47] ... The other view is that though rules of law are not enumerated in any systematic manner in the *Vedas* and they are to be gathered from its entire body, yet it would be wrong to say that the Vedas are totally devoid of law.

In fact, the Vedas are primarily sacrificial hymns, invocations to the pantheon of Vedic gods, and as such contain little evidence of any legal rules other than by coincidence.[48] These difficult Sanskrit texts do not primarily reflect what actually happened. They are not anthropological field reports by participant observers or field researchers. Some portions of these texts are in the nature of mythological account and fiction, while some later parts might constitute a ritual manual, with selective references to real life. Overall, this early literature gives a reasonably clear picture of the world views of the Vedic Hindus, of their ideas about man's place in the world, in particular of the Hindu conceptualization of *ṛta* as macrocosmic order (see in detail Miller 1985). Herein, then, lies the importance of the Vedas as a source of 'law' or rather of dharma. They elucidate the early conceptual underpinnings of Hindu law which are absolutely central for understanding the emerging legal system as a whole. The central point appears to be that 'law' is an entity beyond direct human control. It exists, and yet does not claim institutional loyalty, as a state legal system would do.

The early key concept of *ṛta* metamorphosed gradually into dharma (microcosmic order or duty), the central Hindu legal term, which in one form or another underlies and suffuses all the later texts. Dharma became clearly the core concept of Hinduism, and thus of Hindu law. Its relevance in legal terms

[47] This position relies on a section from Mayne's Hindu law book (Kuppuswami 1986: 14, as quoted on the previous page). No authority is given for the second proposition. Most other Hindu law textbooks are too brief on the subject to warrant specific mention here.

[48] Bowen (1998: 5) argues that 'the Veda is not a credal system of propositions to be believed, but is above all else a text used in ritual which legitimates brahmanical socio-ritual traditions. Vedic mantras are used to this day in initiation rites, weddings, funerals, and for private or personal devotion'.

can be explained quite simply in that life is seen as a complex experience, in which everybody and everything has a role to play and is visibly and invisibly interconnected in a giant systemic network of cosmic dimensions, a kind of universal spider's web. Individual roles and obligations are, of necessity, quite disparate for different people; they depend on contextual factors like gender, age, or place in society. Dharma as a uniform, central concept thus suggests unlimited plurality at the level of social reality within a Hindu systems theory that defies rational deconstruction.

The ideal is envisaged as a fluid ordered universe, in macrocosmic as well as microcosmic dimensions, in which every element of that giant cosmic order simply does what is most appropriate. In other words, the Hindu idealization of order reflects a kind of ecologically sound symbiosis in which every component part plays its proper role. But this is merely the theoretical ideal: real life is a never-ending chain of contradictions, role conflicts, and processes to ascertain specific duties. It can also be viewed as a struggle to find one's path, especially later in the more individualistic contexts of salvation-centred beliefs.[49] More pointedly for a legal analysis, awareness of *ṛta* (or later dharma) involved every Hindu in a continuous process of harmonizing individual expectations with concern for the common good, a constant obligation to ascertain the appropriate balance between I and we, good and bad, right and wrong, the permissible and the prohibited. Hindu law, in other words, is from the start based on a complex and continuous dialectic process (Derrett 1970: 2–3). Much of this remains invisible and internalized, a truth later brought out forcefully in the dramatic illustrations of the great Hindu epics, which can be seen as ancient tools for teaching 'order' in every sense of the word.[50]

The major Vedic concept involved here, *ṛta*, cosmic 'order' or 'truth' (see in detail Lüders 1959; Day 1982: 27–41), has unknown origins, with underlying rules that are not known to man but resemble culture-specific elements of natural law (see also Desai 1998: 5). Vedic Hindus respected the limits of human knowledge and, probably observing the regularities of nature, like sunrise and sunset and different seasons, as well as the sudden force of disaster, came up with an understanding of invisible mechanisms for the maintenance of this superhuman order that involved gods, demons, men, and all created beings.[51] Mankind's major duty was at first to invoke the benign influence of

[49] The Buddha defined all of this as suffering and taught about various methods to free oneself from the entanglement in this cosmic spider web. Hinduism, in turn, adopted certain Buddhist concepts into its own conceptual framework. Other anti-Hindu movements, such as Guha's (1982) subalterns, would seek to assert their separate identities and reject 'Hindu' values, but could not make the Hindu concepts non-existent.

[50] On conflicts concerning sexual morality and ethics, Datta (1979) presents a well-focused study.

[51] Hence in Hindu belief, reincarnation can occur in divine form, or as an animal. Such beliefs then had significant impact on dietary rules, for example, and promoted various shades of vegetarianism.

various gods and other forces through elaborate and solemn Vedic sacrifices.[52] Elaborated in those early Vedic texts, these rituals illustrate and seek to recreate the assumed patterns of cosmic interlinkedness.

Here, then, lies the key to a fuller understanding of Hinduism as well as Hindu law (Menski 1993b; 1996a). While a sense of personalized individuality is not unknown, from a vaguely shared Hindu perspective all individuals are perceived as interlinked in many ways, to family members, one's clan, neighbours, the village, society as a whole, and ultimately the universe. Derrett (1970: 2) portrayed dharma as 'a social cement which ties permanently communities with nothing else in common but their domicile in the subcontinent and their millennia-old committal to living together in competitive co-existence in a multi-cultural super-society'. Nobody expected there to be uniform standards or one Hindu view of any matter. This is radical pluralism in action, but under the cosmic umbrella of the *ṛta*/dharma complex and the 'Hindu' label.[53]

Instead of concentrating on individual religiosity and 'salvation', early and classical Hinduism and Hindu law focused on duties related to the overriding demands and expectations of an ordered universe. As we saw above, in the imagined cosmic spider's web of Hindu systems theory, gods and men, animals and other beings all have their place due to some invisible ordering force to which everyone, by necessity, must relate.[54] It can be argued that there is no choice in this matter, a perspective which underpins the universalistic cosmic claims of Hindu concepts and can so easily be exploited today in communalistic and *hindutva* fashion. Thus Hindu law in its dharmic form went far beyond the immediate socio-political sphere, emphasizing the ultimate human link to cosmic dimensions and perspectives.

It appears from this kind of imaging and its Vedic ritualization that mankind as a whole was never perceived as governing this world, but always remained subject to this higher invisible order. Any human law would always be conceptually inferior. Humans, thus, needed to cooperate and coordinate with the other spheres of existence, both visible and invisible. Vedic people

[52] Only later did appropriate action in every respect become the basic human duty, encapsulated in dharma.

[53] This radical pluralism continues to be misrepresented by modernist authors as evidence of tradition-bound discrimination. Bose and Jalal (1998: 206), for example, distinguish formal and substantive democracy, and later produce an assessment of the alleged failure of the post-colonial Indian state to assure and implement equal citizenship rights (ibid.: 243), assuming silently that Western states have done much better.

[54] This relation could be one of opposition. Individuals could opt out of this system, to some extent or altogether, not just by conversion to another religion, but within Hinduism through ways of life or a choice of lifestyles that deny the centrality of interlinkedness and might entirely focus on individual salvation. On relevant ancient concepts and various forms of renunciation see Sprockhoff (1976) and Olivelle (1993). On subaltern perspectives, see in detail Guha (1982; 1997).

sought to sustain and influence the course of the world, as well as events in their own lives, through sacrifices to those gods that are seen as upholders of *ṛta*, prominently through fire rituals and sacrifices to *Agni*, the god of fire.[55] Hymns addressed to various gods indicate that people might pray for rain or victory in battle, but also for a hundred sons and long life.[56]

We cannot be absolutely sure, but it seems that at this stage not every Hindu took a direct, active part in the ritual maintenance of cosmic order. The major religious activities appear restricted to a small elite class of literate ritual performers and functionaries, mainly Brahmin priests. Such ritual experts presumably acted as representatives of a particular section of the people: families, clans, a village, even a whole kingdom. The involvement of more or less powerful rulers in such rituals gradually strengthened the concept of representation of mankind as a whole. But the continued political fragmentation of ancient India, in contrast to China, quite apparently prevented the institution of Indian kingship from asserting claims to become an important determiner of religious ritual and, through royal patronage and legitimation, of legal rules.[57] In a sense, rulers came *after* the pre-existent basic rules, and remained subservient to them, so a particular legal pattern was set before such power claims could arise. The ancient texts quite clearly assume that any human ruler remains at all times subservient to the all-pervasive macrocosmic force. Thus no king, however powerful, could ever become the master of cosmic order. During this phase of development it is ritual action, and more specifically ritually correct action, that is seen as most conducive to the maintenance and support of macrocosmic order.

Apart from ritual detail, we know quite a lot about the social and political organization of the Vedic people (Ghurye 1979; Kosambi 1992). Ancient Indian societies were mainly organized on patriarchal principles, but matriarchal elements are also strongly in evidence. Whether one should speak of 'primitive communism' or early despotism of the Roman paterfamilias type remains unclear. It is evident that law must have been developing more or less informally and was applied locally. This, too, works against any hope of ever tracing recorded legal evidence from such ancient antiquity.

[55] The place of fire as a central medium of linking humankind with the cosmic sphere is still evident today, even in Section 7(2) of the HMA 1955 which appears to expect that there should be a fire as part of the standard Hindu marriage ritual.

[56] Desai (1998: 5) appropriately emphasizes that the Vedic people were vigorous and full of life, concerned to prosper and develop. A useful summary of such arguments, with textual examples, is found in Kulke and Rothermund (1998: 33–7). This contrasts with constructions of later Hindus as salvation-focused escapists.

[57] Diwan and Diwan (1993: 35) suggest that a succession of powerful rulers after about AD 200 actually had the power to make law that 'overrides even the sacred law and custom'. This is quite clearly a false interpretation, another example of how taking a secular approach and ignoring the continuous and overriding existence of dharma leads to misguided conclusions. This matter is further discussed in a later section in this chapter on the role of custom in classical Hindu law.

According to various schools of thought, the Veda is eternal, self-existent and of absolute authority (Kane 1968–77, III: 1269). The *mīmāṃsā* school of Hindu philosophy, especially, later sought to uphold the supremacy of the Vedas as a source of law, but this has remained a minority view (see Derrett 1968b; Desai 1998: 39–42). The existing Vedic literature does not really discuss legal questions, nor the nature of man-made law. While it is thus not legal literature (Lingat 1973: xii), but focuses on aspects of cosmic law, it is certainly not irrelevant here. The pre-classical stage of Hindu law manifestly provides important insights into the basic conceptual underpinnings for the entirety of what is later called 'Hindu law'.

The envisaged basic human task, namely to establish ritual linkages to the various potent forces, is strongly reflected in the nature of the Vedas as sacrificial manuals, premised on the idea that appropriate rituals and sacrifice will yield desirable results. It seems that this quite simplistic view of ritual efficacy partly explains the gradual demise of the ancient sacrificial system. It is a fact that the hugely complex rituals of the Vedic period fell into virtual oblivion later and were replaced by simpler, more popular forms to make them more accessible to the common person. Thus Vedic society learnt, probably quite fast, that relying on sacrifice alone for the maintenance of Order/order was not good enough; something else may be needed, not only proper ritual action, but appropriate individual action at any point in life. This reasoning leads directly to dharma as the emerging key concept of classical Hindu law.

The result, well reflected in the body of ancient Sanskrit literature, was the emergence of two parallel strands of new ritual literature. One section developed and updated the ancient Vedic rituals, based on *śruti*, and is therefore properly classified as *śrauta* texts.[58] Vedic knowledge, with less clearly defined borders in later Vedic literature, was apparently faithfully preserved and propagated by descendants and pupils of the original sages, partly because the ritual performances were premised on precision. The second, new type of literature began to develop the concept of dharma as a matter of daily domestic practice for Hindus. The technical term *gṛhyasūtra* for this category of literature signifies new guidance on 'house rituals' and now seeks to incorporate the daily actions of all Hindus into the ancient conceptual framework of reference. The attempted Hinduization of daily practice is reflected in these works of great interest to socio-legal studies, as well as in the *dharmasūtras* (Olivelle 2000). Hindu law becomes, in this way, more focused on the microcosmic sphere of the individual and thus properly centred on dharma, the key concept of classical Hindu law.

[58] Even recently, some indological pioneers have continued to work on new translations of these immensely complex texts. They are in my view not directly relevant to legal analysis but illustrate the continuing Hindu concern over human linkages to the superhuman sphere.

DHARMA AND CLASSICAL HINDU LAW

It remains impossible to give clearly defined dates for the transition between Vedic and classical Hindu law because there was no sudden change, but a process of deconstruction and reconfiguration over a long time. One may suggest dates between roughly 800 BC to about 200 AD for the classical period of Hindu law.[59] Within this experimenting and consolidating process, leading to the emergence of full-fledged classical Hindu law, there will have been various stages.[60]

Classical Hindu law built on the conceptual foundations of the Vedic period by developing a number of interrelated ideas into a coherent system of obligations centred around the more individualized concept of dharma. In principle, Hindus were now put under an obligation to contribute to cosmic order through their way of life, including rituals. Dharma is, thus, universalistic in the extreme, and yet it is not an absolute notion of 'good', nor is *adharma* the equivalent of 'bad'. In certain situations, as illustrated by the famous scene in the epic poem *Bhagavadgītā*, when Lord Krishna explains to the warrior-hero Arjuna that he must, however reluctantly, kill his relatives in battle to fulfil his dharma, we are shown that Hindu law, quite realistically, refuses to emphasize generally applicable rules like 'Thou shalt not kill' or an absolute prohibition on lying. Clearly, following dharma may demand killing or lying in certain situations. One-sided emphasis on certain notions, like non-violence (*ahiṃsā*), has distorted the picture of Hindus as soft pacifists without the will to fight.[61] Arjuna's dramatic battle of conscience, and communal violence in modern India, forcefully disprove such notions. At the same time, violence without justification, or untruthfulness per se, are clearly not condoned by dharma. As confirmed in the rich Hindu fable literature, it is the lion's dharma to kill, but senseless murder violates even the predator's code of conduct.

To understand this increasing complexity of expectations and their links with reality, it seems useful to make, first of all, an explicit conceptual distinction between the idealized 'classical' Hindu law proper and what I would call 'late classical' Hindu law, discussed in more detail in the next section. However, the two periods overlap to a large extent and the shastric literature draws no such chronological distinction in explicit terms. This literature is a mass of many different floating, originally oral components, only later put into written

[59] Derrett (1968a: 81) wrote: 'The fundamental rules of law and their spiritual supports are available in texts which are usually dated between 500 BC and AD 200. Exact chronology is defied by these traditional materials which had so long a working life'. Desai (1998: 17) suggests about 800 BC to 300 BC for the *dharmaśāstra* literature. Kuppuswami (1986: 15–21) also discusses chronology in some detail.

[60] There are also various shades of meaning of the key term or rather *topos* (May 1985: 9) of dharma, discussed in some depth by May (ibid.: 12ff.).

[61] During the recent Hindu-Muslim atrocities in Gujarat, I heard expressions of surprise from Muslim victims that the supposedly vegetarian Hindus should have reacted with such brutal force ('*ye dal-sabzi khanewale bhi kamzor nahin hain*').

form and collected into texts with specific labels to suggest a particular authorship. Since the material for both periods is found in the same texts, a text-based chronological analysis would not uncover the absolutely critical distinction between 'self-control' and 'assisted self-control'.

It is instructive to draw this distinction between classical Hindu law proper and late classical Hindu law. The former is clearly based on the rather too idealistic assumption that cosmic order can be sustained simply by following dharma, i.e. through every individual's self-controlled behaviour and conscious subordination of personal desires to higher concerns. The latter approach, based on the more realistic observation that individuals are selfish or simply lazy and need to be reminded of their obligations, implies that some degree of deterrence or even punishment might help to strengthen or assist self-control. Both conceptualizations are, thus, premised on the supremacy of self-controlled action, which remains the hallmark of the classical Hindu law system, but there is a significant shift of emphasis within this paradigm. In social reality, it is recognised that self-controlled action expects too much and thus 'assisted self-control' is the dominant mode of social regulation.[62]

If we were to restrict our definition of classical Hindu law only to the period premised on idealistic, self-controlled order, we might find this a very short period indeed. In fact, the ideal of self-controlled order would not be maintainable in real life, since 'the big fish', as many shastric texts elaborate, would simply take advantage of their might. This sounds all too familiar as a characteristic of power imbalances within any human society (Dahrendorf 1969). In reality, thus, the conceptually sound ideal golden age of Hindu law, where everybody simply did their best to follow dharma, cannot have lasted for long, in fact it probably never existed. We should rather imagine a complex period of 'classical' Hindu law in which the basic idealistic principle of self-controlled order is found in constant need of support by various methods and grades of 'assisted self-control'. It is for this reason, too, that the different categories of texts relating to this period constitute persuasive guidance rather than allowing us to read them as law books with rules for all Hindus, to be followed to the letter. As indicated in Chapter 2 earlier, the legal textbooks of today still fantasize over shastras as codified rule books.[63] Orientalists and legal scholars together have colluded not only in distorting the Vedic roots, but have also managed to construct and sustain an image of classical Hindu law that is outrightly unreal and has itself created many problems.

[62] The textual evidence on this is very clear and is documented in the next section.

[63] See for example Desai (1998: 19) with the claim that the author of the *Manusmriti* 'appears to have compiled an exhaustive code binding on all'. The universal application of the *Manusmriti* is also asserted in Kuppuswami (1986: 15), reinforced by claims that this text is always paramount in case of conflicts between textual sources (ibid.: 18–19, 24). These are typical lawyers' reasonings.

It is certain that already during the Vedic period concern over central domestic ritual events such as solemnization of marriage, birth, and death began to emerge in texts like *Ṛgveda* 10.85 and *Atharvaveda* 14, which contain concentrated evidence about early forms of Hindu marriage rituals and some other rites of passage, notably death rituals.[64] Such clearly still macrocosm-focused and thus Vedic beginnings in the ritual elaboration of the domestic sphere were later followed up and, through particular citation techniques, directly woven into the immensely rich class of literature called *gṛhyasūtra*.[65] Such texts provide specific guidance for the Hindu householder and develop, in particular, elaborate ritual models for the celebration of various rites of passage (Pandey 1969). Simultaneously, we find the development of numerous *dharmasūtras* and the still more complex and detailed *dharmaśāstra* literature, amazingly detailed handbooks on dharma, among which the *Manusmriti* is said to hold such an important place.

The early, but properly 'classical' development of Hindu law can be distinguished from the Vedic stage primarily by placing more emphasis on the individual actions of every Hindu,[66] and by developing a more elaborate rule system which reinforces the processes of individualization and Hinduization. In terms of sacrifice, this would mean that every Hindu should now engage in the various sacrificial rituals as part of dharma, but also that ritual action alone would not suffice to achieve positive cosmic reactions. Eventually, right action and appropriate behaviour at every point of one's life became the core expectation of Hindu law, encapsulated in dharma.[67]

Thus, over time Hinduism has evolved and adapted. It has quite radically changed its gods, its forms of sacrifice, but not its conceptual basis in terms of Order/order, which has merely internalised the shift from macrocosmic to microcosmic emphasis. The basic concept of mutuality between the visible and

[64] These texts were examined and retranslated in my doctoral thesis (Menski 1984). On death rituals, see Firth (1997).

[65] Those texts often introduce a particular ritual action, which may be new, but is accompanied by citation of an ancient Vedic verse (mantra).

[66] Derrett (1970: 2) called this 'an educational "suction" ... peculiar to India' and explained, at p. 3, that the *dharmaśāstra* "applied, as I said, suction, drawing upwards primitive, backward, semi-civilised, and often wild tribes into a society in which behaviour was organised and morality was cultivated".

[67] The key concept of dharma is here linked with karma, which is probably more ancient than much of the literature assumes. It is the basic principle that every action, including therefore non-action, will have some effect. In this sense, karma reinforces the Vedic system of cosmic interlinkage and is now applied to extend this linking network to all individual Hindus. The use of the term in common parlance, speaking of 'good karma' or 'bad karma' seems more influenced by Buddhist notions of the possibility of building up positive or negative accounts with regard to individual salvation. The classical Hindu conceptualization of the term, in contrast, emphasizes the inevitable consequentiality of reaction to all human actions. For details see May (1985: 33–4).

the invisible, between human sphere and universe, remains at the core. During the classical period, these linkages become further elaborated and illustrated with innumerable references to situations of daily life. The general shift from an earlier emphasis on ritual action to the expectation of righteous action at any point of one's life is clearly manifest. Kane (1968–77, I.1: 3) has shown how dharma developed out of *ṛta*, which later fell into oblivion as a technical term:

> The word *dharma* passed through several transitions of meaning and...ultimately its most prominent significance came to be "the privileges, duties and obligations of a man, his standard of conduct as a member of the Aryan community, as a member of one of the castes, as a person in a particular stage of life".

This new emphasis is clearly reflected in the complex system of *varṇāśramadharma*, the understanding that at any one point one can circumscribe the individual's ideal duty according to caste status (*varṇa*) and stage of life (*āśrama*). Linked to this, different kinds of specialized dharma, such as women's duty (*strīdharma*) or the ruler's obligations (*rājadharma*) make an appearance, apart from the individual's duty (*svadharma*). A new field of knowledge, the science of *dharmaśāstra*, developed at this stage, defining other main Hindu aims of life, worldly possessions (*artha*), sensual gratification (*kāma*) and ultimately salvation (*mokṣa*) in terms of (and in relation to) the key concept of dharma. By the time this comprehensive conceptualization of individual duty had been fully developed, it was apparently ready to slip into the Hindu subconscious and became anchored there as a key concept that Hindus seem to imbibe, to varying degrees, with their mother's milk. This awareness of cosmic connection, however fuzzy and hazy it may be, critically marks the difference between Hindus and adherents to other religious traditions, and between Hindu law and other systems.[68]

Ultimately, all of this is a matter of culture-specific belief, as well as practice, hence the religious label and the roots of the subsequent Orientalist-cum-legalist assumption that *ṛta* and later dharma represented something like law. The various forms of Hindu 'religious' practice are basically expressions of the latent awareness of interlinkedness with cosmic levels of existence. This remains central to Hindu life and law. Whether one is trying to obtain favours through devotion or prayer, bargain with a deity for something desirable, protect oneself against evil and damage, or simply ask for enlightenment that will likely never come, the intricacies of Hindu religion are such that in the mass of detail the essence should not be lost. No central authority could tell Hindus how to follow dharma or could guide all Hindus in the same way as the Koran

[68] It is therefore entirely appropriate that a major collection of essays on Hindu law should start with the editors' statement that '[w]e reject the notion held generally in Western legal thought for over 2000 years that law is something universal' (Nanda and Sinha 1996: xi).

would appear to do for all Muslims, for whom at least the identity of the highest authority would be a matter of firm belief.

Hence, despite its undoubtedly ancient roots, Hindu law is somehow rootless nevertheless; its basics are so flexible as to offer no binding guidance beyond the rule of righteousness.[69] A Hindu who seeks guidance as to what is appropriate is at sea, so to say, floating on a bed of conceptual support structures that demand of every individual at all times to actively stay afloat by striving to do the right thing. There is no cosy life raft of simple prescriptions, no rope thrown from heaven that may just be grasped for salvation, no binding rule system that may just be applied more or less unthinkingly to stay afloat in the sea of life. Being a Hindu seems to be hard work, and is full of insecurities in terms of rewards for doing the right thing. But perhaps this is not what counts, anyway, since the key point of dharma is not so much the collection of brownie points for one's own salvation,[70] but awareness of cosmic interlinkage and the individual's obligation towards the universe. This aspect was taken up by Robert Lingat (1973: 4):

> In internal terms, *dharma* signifies the obligation, binding upon every man who desires that his action should bear fruit, to submit himself to the laws which govern the universe and to direct his life in consequence. That obligation constitutes his duty: and that is a further sense of the word.

Thus, dharma now covers the eternal order of the universe (the primary Vedic preserve of *ṛta*) as well as order in any particular present life situation. It comprises all levels of existence, macrocosmic as well as microcosmic, and all gods, humans and other creatures. By thus placing everything into a complex network of cosmic interrelationships, the holistic conceptualization of dharma suggests that any human activity, including inaction, becomes perceived as having potentially wide-reaching consequences. This conceptualization is strengthened by elaborating the notion of action (karma) into 'retribution as a result of action', so that dharma and karma together establish a complex system of moral demands and retributional threats and promises, all designed to elicit ideal 'appropriate' behaviour.

In an integrated society, where the spheres of law, morality, and religion largely overlap (Allott 1980: 25), one may see dharma and its implications as religious, but it operates together with other forces and is neither simply law nor just religion. Lingat (1973: 4) thus wrote that dharma 'is essentially social in

[69] This is reflected in statements like 'Hindu law is the law of the Hindu way of life. Originally developed as "the way of righteousness" by the Brahmins on the basis of traditions reaching back to the Vedic age, it once was a complete system of law' (Derrett and Iyer 1983: 80). Nanda and Sinha (1996: xii) also emphasize the 'way of life' approach and correctly state that '[a]ttribution of precepts to a lawgiver, therefore, has no place here'.

[70] This is more a Buddhist (and later also Islamic) notion, which over time has influenced Hindu concepts. In Hinduism, the expectations of the cosmic realm would appear to override individual interest in personal salvation.

the sense that, in a social order visualised as one with the natural order, the individual who obeys its precepts performs a duty which is as much social as religious'. Lingat did not think so much of the common Hindu as of the 'authors' of texts, stipulating a degree of planned message from the cultural texts of ancient India which may have been quite elusive for the common person, but exercised a strong pull, indicated by Lingat (1973: 5):

> It follows, as a matter of course that, for authors committed to the religious significance of action, society's essential end is realisation of *dharma*, when each individual can put his duties into effect. So their structure of law has *dharma* as its axis.

The above analysis, based primarily on internal conceptual categories of Hindu thought, yields an image of idealized self-controlled order which, as indicated, may never have constituted a social reality. Before a more elaborate discussion of 'assisted self-controlled order', it is necessary to examine what sense the specialist literature on Hindu law has made of the idealistic *smṛti* literature and its legal relevance.

We saw earlier that the authors of Hindu law textbooks did not say much about the most ancient or Vedic layers of the Hindu conceptual framework and literature but supported the common assertion that the Vedas represented 'law' in some divinely grounded and revealed form. The classical body of knowledge, now referred to as *smṛti* or 'remembered truth', could also claim to possess great authority, but is no longer seen as revealed material.[71] In the *smṛti* literature, divine inspiration and authority is not altogether absent, but is hidden behind, and eventually totally overshadowed by, the huge body of knowledge that was gradually amassed and extended by a small literate elite.[72] The function of Indian cultural texts is clearly not that of law books, since these texts are handbooks on dharma and thus first of all cultural documents of a private nature, produced by male persons of a certain class in society.[73] While these texts can at best be seen as an indirect source of classical Hindu law, the tempting conclusion for the authors of Hindu law books has been that the *smṛti* texts are manifestations of human law-making and are virtual

[71] The concept of *smṛti* is much less stringently defined than its functional equivalent in Islam. The sayings of the Holy Prophet, classed as Sunna and published in collections of Hadith, claim and hold a much more authoritative position because the Prophet is unique, at least according to Sunni theory, as the last human carrier of divine revelation.

[72] On *smṛti* see also May (1985: 46ff.), with a useful discussion on the role of experts at p. 54. The mass of *smṛti* literature is so diverse that specialization became more and more necessary. Following the Vedic tradition of 'schools', based on the various sacrificial specializations, more school traditions developed in this period. On the diversity of views and schools see Kuppuswami (1986: 15–16) and Diwan and Diwan (1993: 29).

[73] On this see the excellent introduction in Hoadley and Hooker (1981: 1–9); also Derrett (1968b: 148ff.).

codifications of law. Kuppuswami (1986: 15) saw this as follows, before launching into a list of 'lawgivers':

> Rules, as distinct from instances of conduct are, for the first time, embodied in the Smritis. The Smritis (what is recollected or remembered) are of human origin and refer to what is supposed to have been in the memory of the sages who were the repositories of the Revelation. They are the Dharmasastras.

Desai (1998: 6) relies on those textual statements from the Veda which appear to indicate that Manu was the source of all human law-making, building on the assumption of divine revelation as the primary source of Hindu law, further propounding the myth that Manu was the first Hindu lawmaker:

> The Smritikars are agreed and common traditions have always accepted that the earliest exponent of law was Manu. The Smritis purport to embody one traditional law, namely the pronouncements of Manu. The Rig-Veda enjoins observance of the ancient rules of Manu.

While Desai (id.) admits that '[t]he material of that period available to this day does not render much assistance in collating an authenticated account of that body of original law, traditionally accepted as Manu's law, which indubitably existed', the myth is nevertheless maintained. The discussion of this topic is then wrapped up at p. 7:

> All that is known today is that there existed in the Vedic Epoch rules of Dharma traditionally regarded as promulgated by Manu and Sutra-works containing aphorisms on law. It would be a misnomer, therefore, to call this even a bare outline of the legal literature of that first epoch of Hindu law.

This surprising conclusion, still mixing dharma and law, merely reinforces the primacy of the Manu myth. The subsequent debate is highly instructive and needs to be recounted here. Desai (1998: 8) wrote on the nature of *smṛtis* that 'Hindu jurisprudence regards the Smritis ... as constituting the foundation and important source of law. The term 'sources of law' used in many legal treatises on Hindu law and in decisions of the Privy Council is somewhat ambiguous'. Explaining that the notion of sources of law may have been borrowed by the Privy Council from Roman law, Desai (id.) further discusses the nature of the *dharmaśāstra* literature:

> ... the principal Smritis blend religious, moral, social and legal duties. They contain some metaphysical speculations, matter sacramental and also ordain rules of legal rights and obligations. Ethico-religious obligations were regarded by these exponents of Dharma as more important than legal obligations. The Smritikars were not always punctilious about stressing a clear distinction between the positive or lawyers' law and moral law, but this is not to suggest that they were unmindful of this distinction.

The assertion that the ancient 'authors' of *smṛti* texts were somewhat careless in dealing with the distinction of law and dharma is evidently used to defend Hindu law against the claims of outsiders. Desai (1998: 9) writes:

> The charge levelled by some Western scholars against the authors of the Smritis for a want of precision and discrimination between moral and legal maxim is unreasonable and unfounded but it is unnecessary now to take any serious notice of the same .... A clear perspective of Hindu law is not possible unless it is properly appreciated that the blending of religion and ethics with law by these juristheologians was in a large measure the natural result [*sic*] of a philosophy of life which laid emphasis on the supremacy of inward life over things external.

The interrelated nature of dharma and the reference to the Hindu philosophy of life is irrefutably clear, but precisely how do dharma and law relate? Desai's debate manifestly assumes that the two coexisted as equal categories. This is where something has gone seriously wrong. Desai (1998: 9) continues from the previous quote above, arguing that '[t]he acceptance by a corporate society of the connotation of duty (Dharma) which associated religious and ethical concepts with secular matters was bound to be projected into its codes of positive law'. This introduction of the concept of 'secularism' and the assertion, once again, that we find 'positive law' here are evidently based on the author's understanding of the term *vyavahāra* (dispute settlement or litigation), which he translates simply as 'civil law' (id.). Thus, Desai (id.) comes to the desirable conclusion that Hindus had ancient civil law that compares well with Roman law, in particular:

> The later Smritikars mentioned above have treated rules of *Vyavahara* in separate sections (*Prakaranas*) and exhaustively considered rules of positive law and Narada and some Smritikars have compiled rules only of *Vyavahara*. The shrewd practical insight of the Hindu Rishis who were both sages and virtually lawmakers left very little that was undefined. At a very remote period they laid down rules of law both substantive and adjectival. Founders of their own jurisprudence these philosophical jurists enunciated and expounded a system of law which does not suffer in comparison with Roman law.

Unfortunately, in the rush to glorify and prove the standing of Hindu law in the world community of legal systems through this impressive chain of argumentation, it was not taken into account that dharma would at all times remain superior to *vyavahāra* and that, from a Hindu perspective, the moral law of dharma could not be switched off or made irrelevant when it came to dispute settlement.[74] The learned author, when thinking as a Hindu, was evidently

[74] Such arguments reflect modernist thinking, as exemplified by Anderson (1991: 7) in his discussion of how a nation is imagined, arguing that '[i]t is imagined as *sovereign* because the concept was born in an age in which Enlightenment and Revolution were destroying the legitimacy of the divinely-ordained, hierarchical

aware of this, as the progress of his discussion demonstrates.[75] Since Desai (1998: 9) continued to argue as a lawyer, he had to admit that Hindu law was not structured like Western law because according to the Austinian principles of jurisprudence or theories of Bentham much of the traditional law of ancient India would be termed as 'morality' (id).

Yet, the assertion that Hindu law is proper law was not to be defeated by the undoubted and admitted fact that the *smṛtis* were not codes in the Austinian sense. In a tour de force of jurisprudential creativity, Desai (1998: 9–10) managed to argue that Hindu law is nevertheless 'law' because it depends, ultimately, on a divine author. The first step of the argument contains the admission that *smṛti* texts are not law (id). However, the second limb of the argument claims a Hindu variant of the notion of sovereign command, which is really a hidden reference to the *ṛta*/dharma complex, emphasizing the place of a divine lawmaker: 'What was accepted was the rule-dependent notion of what ought to be done as agreeable to good conscience and in conformity with the cherished article of belief that the fundamental rules of law had been derived from a divine author' (ibid.:10).

Here, then, the circle of legalist distortion closes perfectly, and the argument has become that Hindu dharma can be accepted as law because the conceptual system of Hindu dharma itself depends on a divine lawmaker.[76] I doubt whether this is a view of the matter which matches with common Hindu perceptions of the origins, nature, and application of dharma. What we are being offered here is a lawyers' Hindu law, shorn of the inherent social fluidity and flexibility of the indigenous normative order of dharma and its critical element of situation-specificity. Without a doubt, Desai's positivist reinterpretation of Hindu law shows how the door could be widely opened for subsequent distortions of traditional Hindu law and its eventual reconstruction as a case-based legal system. In fact, Desai's representation of Hindu law relies to such a large extent on early positions taken in the Privy Council that the original voice of Hindu law is not allowed to come through.

Other textbooks are similarly marred by the constant confusion of internal Hindu perspectives and categories and the official legal views that crystallized over time into dogmatic statements on Hindu law. Discussing the early *smṛti* literature, Diwan and Diwan (1993: 29) first of all emphasise the importance of

---

dynastic realm'. Anderson's point, it should be noted, does not go as far as denying the realm of religion itself any relevance.

[75] The categorical superiority of dharma is in fact alluded to during this discussion in the statement (at p. 9) that '[t]he best rule was regarded as that which advanced Dharma'.

[76] The jurisprudential argument produced by Desai (1998: 10) illustrates the fixation of Indian legal authors on positivist theory. It is breathtakingly clever in using the terminology of legal positivism and twisting it to suit his argument. Desai could of course have followed a different school of jurisprudence, but that is manifestly not what Indian legal authors are willing or able to do.

customary law in the period after the Vedas and the complexity of the early written material. Typical for Indian lawyers, this is summed up by reference to the promulgation of the original law (as dharma) by the mythical Manu. But then the lawyers swing into action and come to their proper subject asserting that the *smritis* ushered in the era of the systematic exposition of the rules and principles of law. This is known as the golden age of the Hindus (ibid.: 30):

> In theory the *Smritis* are based on the memory of the sages who were the repositories of the sacred Revelation ... What has happened seems to be thus: immediately after the *Vedic* period the need of expounding the meaning contained in the *Vedas* arose. The *Vedas* were to be understood in the light of the new needs of the society which had made further progress from agro-pastoral society.

The stipulated close links between social and textual development suggested here are not followed up, but the theme recurs when Diwan and Diwan (1993: 30–38) examine the various texts in detail. At p. 30, it is said that '[t]he *Dharmasūtras* deal with the duties of men in their various relations' and are composed by human authors, 'based on the teaching of the *Vedas*, on the decision of those who were acquainted with law, and on the customs of the Aryans'. The text continues (id.):

> Nobody can doubt for a moment that they are manuals written by the teachers of the *Vedic* schools for the guidance of their pupils, that at first they were held to be authoritative in restricted circles, and that later on they were acknowledged as sources of the sacred law.[77] Composed in different parts of the country and at different times, they did not present any anomaly, but tended to slide into each other. Most of the *Dharmashastras* mingled religious and moral precepts with secular law.

The last sentence of this quote again confirms the confusion among legal scholars over how to read the ancient Hindu texts. Diwan and Diwan (1993: 32) also indicate their understanding that the later *dharmaśāstras* were dealing with civil law. Again, *vyavahāra* is thus simply perceived as formal 'civil law', rather than flexible dispute resolution management.

On the *Manusmriti*, Diwan and Diwan (1993: 32–33) present a complex and quite self-contradictory picture. While they simply assert that this text 'has been all along considered to be supreme authority in the entire country' (p. 32), they also admit that the identity of the *Manusmriti*'s author is not known, while the supreme position of Manu was emphasized even in the Vedas (id.). With reference to Kane, they then admit that the ancient mythical Manu could not have composed the text and stipulate that an unknown author must have declared his work to be that of Manu (p. 33). While such reliance on indological

[77] Here the text contains a footnote to Bühler's introduction to *The Laws of Manu*, demonstrating how Orientalist scholarship has continued to influence Indian legal writing.

scholarship leads to the correct finding that the *Manusmriti* was not authored by the mythical Manu himself, the lawyers' perspective again rapidly asserts legal centralist thinking, expressed in terms of an urgent need for a code of Hindu law (id.):

> The *Manusmriti* supplied a long-felt need of a legal treatise which could be a compendium of law .... It is a systematic and cogent collection of rules of law. It is the most authoritative reservoir of law. It recasts in a systematic and easily accessible manner the whole of traditional law which was lying scattered .... The *Manusmriti* is a landmark in the legal history of India .... The *Manusmriti* also gives a vivid idea of the customs of the then society and social and religious observances of the people.

Thus, these authors have redesignated this *smṛti* text as a virtual code of law as well as a handbook on ancient Hindu customs, when in fact it was neither. The *Manusmriti* is first of all a guidebook on dharma, not a code of law, and whether it really provides evidence of customs is a widely debated matter taken up again in a later section in this chapter. However, having presented this text as a code of law, Diwan and Diwan (1993: 33) proceed to argue that the ancient Hindu ruler acquired virtually divine functions under this new law and had the power to rule, embodied in the concept of *daṇḍa*, which is also seen as a secular instrument of rule (see section an assisted self-control, etc. later in this chapter). Recent authors who might provide brief summaries of the ancient law as a preface to discussing questions of modern law, particularly relating to Hindu personal law, have sometimes managed to distil the essence quite well.[78] Pathak (1986: 1) summarizes:

> Law as understood by the Hindu is a branch of *Dharma*. Its ancient framework is the law of the Smritis .... As the Hindu Law was influenced by the theological tenets of the Vedic Aryans and their philosophical theories, therefore, we find in the whole system a mingling of religious and ethical principles with legal precepts. In the system of Hindu Law, it is very difficult to differentiate secular and religious matters because certain questions, as for instance, marriage and adoption had the aspect of both. Therefore, if any punctilious attempt is made to segregate any secular matter from the religious adjuncts, it will cloud the comprehensive idea or proper perspective of the true juridical concepts of Hindu Law ...

Similarly, on the nature of Hindu law, Pathak (1986: 2) emphasizes its religious underpinnings, in that 'Hindu law is not the command of the sovereign, nor of a political community which is binding on that community but it is the command of the Supreme Being, which is binding on the sovereign, as well as his subjects'. Thus here, too, the assertion that Hindu law is based on divine authority is maintained.

[78] A very brief and perfunctory overview is given in Mahmood (1981: xli).

In a radical re-examination of Hindu law that identifies many of the inconsistencies in the literature,[79] but still remains confused about the role of dharma in relation to law, Bhattacharjee (1994) has asserted that the Vedas neither are nor ever were, properly speaking, a source of Hindu law. Highlighting the contradiction between Hindu beliefs about the eternal nature of the Vedas and the absence of legal rules in the Vedic texts, he sought to demolish the argument that Hindu law is based on religious sources, emphasizing instead the secular, legal element of *vyavahāra*, for which he expresses staunch admiration (p. 3). Bhattacharjee (1994: 14 and 17) further argues that the old Hindu law of the *smṛtis* was later superseded by commentaries and digests, and thus claimed, in essence, that the assertions of a divine nature and basis for Hindu law cannot be maintained in the light of the history of Hindu law.

While I would agree with much in this analysis, Bhattacharjee's study commits one critical conceptual blunder that ruins his arguments. Like so many other authors, he claims that the Hindu system of jurisprudence represents a system of positive law, 'a law having the oldest pedigree of any known system of jurisprudence, but yet to have surprisingly modern visions' (p. 3). Envisaging ancient codes, Bhattacharjee (1994: 5) simply introduces positivist fictions and thus distorts our view of the reality of ancient Hindu law in his desire to claim exalted status for it:

> I am yet to know of a set of Law Codes, the *Lex Scripta* whereof started governing people more than 2000 years ago and are governing them still today. This irresistible demonstration and irrefutable proof of the unparalleled vitality of the Laws of the Dharmashastras have made them unique in the world of Laws.

Phrases used in the learned author's further analysis, such as 'the written texts of the Law Codes' (p. 6) reinforce this confusion. Outright contradictions are found in statements that '[t]he *Vedas* and the *Smritis* are obviously neither legislations nor precedents nor agreements' (p. 14) and that 'there can be no doubt that the Smritis contain rules of civil law or Vyavahara' (p. 17), while at p. 19 it is stated that 'these Smritikars never pretended or professed to be makers or givers of the law contained therein'. The absence of a detailed discussion on the underlying conceptual foundations of Hindu law as a system of ordering, replaced by the mere assertion that Hindu law represents an ancient form of positive law, leads the reader astray, although the conclusion (Bhattacharjee 1994: 39) seems appropriate:

> It would, therefore, be entirely wrong to say, as has been said by almost all the leading authorities, that the *Srutis* or the *Smritis* or the *Nibandhas are* the sources of the Hindu Law. And if the expression "legal sources" means, as it does according to Salmond and other authorities, something which makes, creates, originates or generates the laws, then these *Srutis*, *Smritis*

[79] Bhattacharjee (1994: 12ff.) provides details on the arguments in earlier leading textbooks.

> and even the *Nibandhas were not also* such sources of law but, only were the evidence and records thereof and, as such, the sources of our knowledge of law.

Such formalistic arguments rely on formal legal criteria, so that by the standards of legal positivism, the ancient sources of Hindu law cannot be seen as proper legal sources. But what has happened to the author's argument that the ancient texts represented codes and that the later commentaries became the real source of Hindu law? And what about recognition of the fact that Hindu law was from the beginning more than a positivist construct? Bhattacharjee's efforts are undoubtedly intellectually interesting, but this study does not manage to portray the conceptual embeddedness of Hindu law in the *ṛta*/dharma complex.

Even the most recent writing produced by modernist and feminist scholars displays and reflects an understanding of classical Hindu law that seems too uncritically based on such confused distortions as the old indologists and British lawyers together produced at some time in the past. Agnes (2000) interrogates the prevailing picture and image of a strictly patriarchal Hindu normative order, dominated by Manu, portrayed as 'the arch law giver of the Hindu religion' (p. 11), setting out to explore whether 'within these strict dictates, the Hindu law permitted any space for negotiating women's rights' (id.). Emphasising the internal plurality of Hindu law and the diversity of its sources, Agnes indicates that there may be huge scope for asserting women's rights under the amorphous and wide 'Hindu' umbrella, but her critique does not go much beyond the flat observation that the key term 'Hindu' is 'more a legal fiction than a religious entity or a social reality' (p. 26).

Thus we find a familiar phenomenon in the literature on Hindu law: Law and legal scholarship seem inherently focused on tangible sources, primarily on written material, while the less tangible conceptual, religious, and anthropological aspects of legal study and their evidence in real life situations have received comparatively less attention from lawyers and legal scholars. It has been easier for lawyers to study texts than to conduct fieldwork or enter into philosophical or philological debates about complex basic concepts of rights and duties. Non-lawyers, as indicated, simply tend to use certain fragments of the legalistic images of Hindu law and leave the rest to the specialists, with the result that insufficient progress appears to have been made, and old stereotypes of Hindu law continue to be repeated also in the most recent editions of leading textbooks.

All of this reflects badly on the study of Hindu law, but certain deficiencies cannot be easily remedied. First of all, fieldwork on classical Hindu law can obviously not be conducted and our sources on litigation only take us back to courtroom situations in the 17th century (Derrett 1968b; Smith and Derrett 1975). Further, the numerous *smṛti* texts do not cover the actual or 'living law'; at best, they propose ideal models which may or may not have been followed in social reality. Simultaneously—because the texts focus on dharma even if they do not say so—they are important, in their totality and as individual pieces of evidence, to our understanding of classical Hindu law concepts, since they indicate what was considered appropriate in certain situations (Larivière 1993). While an individual text did not create a fixed rule or model, it offered a suggested solution at a particular point of time in a specific situation, no more and no less. In the properly 'classical' period of Hindu law with its emphasis on self-controlled order, there was simply no conceptual legitimation for any positivist law-making and the texts therefore must have been guidebooks on dharma but certainly not codes of Hindu law. As the subsequent section on the role of custom discusses in more detail, the focus of self-controlled ordering ultimately fell on the individual within his or her social environment. Since classical Hindu law proceeded methodologically bottom-up, not top-down, there was only very peripheral scope for external law-making. At the fluid end of the classical period of Hindu law, therefore, with the impending transition to 'assisted self-controlled order', the stage is set for more active involvement by forces outside the individual.

Assisted Self-control and *Daṇḍa* in Late Classical Hindu Law

Within the *ṛta*/dharma complex, the demand on every Hindu to strive for the ideals of self-controlled order simply restricts the state as a rule-maker and does not totally legitimize political and legal interference in the daily life of Hindus. The conceptual expectation of self-controlled order in classical Hindu law would have empowered, in principle if not in practice, all Hindus to determine for themselves, as individuals subject to the highest order, what they should be doing.[80] A ruler's claim to make what Hart (1961) called 'primary rules' could never have developed in such a conceptual climate, since in the classical Hindu system such basic rules were to be cultivated in the social sphere and should then be implemented locally and individually in self-controlled fashion. Thus, according to the ideals of classical Hindu law, there is simply no direct need for state law. Only the limited sphere of law-making that comprises Hart's 'secondary rules', dealing with procedures, methods of hearing evidence and so on, could be made subject to the ruler's law-making authority as a matter of good governance.

Later in the classical period, perhaps more at its tail end,[81] this idealized vision of individualistic ordering through self-control processes appears to have given way to the assumption that self-control is ultimately not effective enough in safeguarding dharma. The reasoning advanced for this prominently blames people for being simply too weak and selfish to exercise philanthropic

[80] This point is argued in detail further in a later section on the role of custom.

[81] It is even more difficult to give dates here, since the texts cover both the classical and the late classical periods. On scriptural continuity, see also Lingat (1973: 107). Much of the *Manusmriti* would seem to belong to the present period.

self-control. Many texts speak of an early golden age, the imagined ideal age of self-controlled order, in which the bull of dharma still had four strong feet. Now, however, in the *kaliyuga*, the era of depravity and decay, dharma only has one foot, and clearly needs outside support (*Manusmriti* 1.81–82). The need for 'law' seems to be expressed in texts like *Nāradasmṛti* 1.1–2, which explains why *vyavahāra*, dispute settlement as well as the threat of punishment, is now considered necessary:

> When mortals were bent on doing nothing but their duty and were habitually veracious, there existed neither lawsuits nor hatred nor selfishness.
>
> Now that the practice of duty has died out among mankind, *vyavahāra* has been introduced; and the king has been appointed to decide suits, because he has the authority to punish.

While statements of this kind are often found there is, to my knowledge, nowhere in the ancient literature an argument that state law is needed because without a state and its positive law there would be anarchy.[82] Interestingly, the recent translation of the above-cited *Nāradasmṛti* verses by Larivière (1989, II: 3) emphasizes the need for legal procedure, rather than litigation as such, hence offering a sophisticated explanation for the focus in that text on procedural rules. In his introduction, Larivière (ibid.: ix) repeats the familiar claim that '[t]he Nāradasmṛti is unique in the corpus of Sanskrit legal literature. It is the only original collection of legal maxims (*mūlasmṛti*) which is purely juridical in nature'. All of this is well and good, but the claim that this text is purely secular goes in my view too far, since it ignores the wider social context within which the compiler(s) of this text operated. All that such ancient texts are saying, even if they *appear* to focus on secular procedure, is that self-controlled order was eventually found insufficient by itself. From this, it seems, lawyers have a little too rapidly drawn the convenient conclusion that positive law is a necessity in itself and that legal procedure will be needed.

In the ideal world of ancient, classical Hindu law, there was no such conceptual justification for legal intervention. The leading expectation remained that all individuals should follow their specific dharma in self-controlled manner. Thus a constant balance of symbiotic coexistence would be sustained, rather like a stable ecosystem. But the dialectics of balance involve imbalance and constant rebalancing and are thus unstable and ambivalent. Further, the invisible rules of this symbiotic interaction model are not known to mankind,

[82] Diwan and Diwan (1993: 24–25) reproduce the argument that in ancient India, 'the theory was that our king did not make law; he merely enforced law' (p. 24). But once one powerful ruler succeeded the other, they argue, 'it was but natural for a king to make laws' (id.) so that eventually, '[t]he king-made law was given overriding effect both over custom and sacred law' (p. 25). Rudolph and Rudolph (2001: 40) note the correct position, to the effect that 'Sanskrit law texts held that the king should oversee the self-regulating society rather than create laws for society'. Here, too, whether it is appropriate to speak of 'law texts' should at least be queried, rather than taken for granted.

so that rituals must forever remain a form of speculative 'hoping for the best'. There must have been a realization that the ideal of self-controlled order required support mechanisms apart from appropriate ritual action; it was simply not a sustainable theory. May (1985: 94) emphasizes in this regard:

> Already the early *smrtis* envisaged that the promotion of *dharma* depended to a great extent on the efficacy of certain provisions addressed to a *rājā* (ruler, king) in order to exercise an all-pervading influence on his behaviour. Neither did the *smṛtis* rely on an ideal promotion of *dharma* nor did they pretend 'abstract' or superior wisdom and sufficiency, yet on the contrary, they attempted to be as realistic and practical as possible with regard to their task.

Thus, the centre of activity in maintaining order shifted still more explicitly from heaven to earth and now began to involve a public agent rather than simply individual self-control. While the individual Hindu still carries major responsibility for the maintenance of dharma, the figurehead of the Hindu ruler would now appear to gain greater prominence as a guardian of dharma. This development is reflected by stressing the supervisory function of rulers in various ways. Ideally, like in ancient China or traditional Islamic law, the ruler should not be called into action, as self-control was supposed to work effectively. Yet where this breaks down, the ruler is to step in through deterrence in the form of harsh and potentially quite gruesome punishments (Day 1982; Menski 1992a; Menski 2000a). These are often elaborated in later texts but really appear everywhere in the *smṛti* texts. Such elements clearly belong, conceptually, to the late classical period of Hindu law.

As various texts candidly admit, human selfishness and greed could play havoc with the ideal of self-controlled order and bring about a state of anarchy.[83] In such circumstances, individuals need to be reminded of their duty to follow dharma. This argument introduces a new concept, the punishing rod (*daṇḍa*), which should be seen as a symbol of 'assisted self-control', not necessarily evidence of actual punishment, but a deterrent threat designed to encourage individuals to follow dharma of their own accord.[84] It would be quite wrong to assume that the traditional, classical reliance on individual and situational self-control was completely abandoned. How this process occurred is again impossible to trace with historical certainty, but the conceptual analysis

[83] The classical Hindu image for this is 'the rule of the big fish', or 'shark rule' (*mātsya-nyāya*), where people can neither enjoy their property nor their wives. For details see May (1985: 106–107) with further references and Derrett (1968b).

[84] Guha (1997: 24–30) portrays *daṇḍa* too narrowly as a political tool of suppression, 'central to ancient Indian polity, based in its classical form on monarchical absolutism, and it extends far beyond "punishment" ... to stand for all that is implied by dominance in that particular historical context' (ibid.: 29). Day (1982: 125) indicates that certain punishments may only be inflicted on repeat offenders, an issue that has also been debated in relation to the extremely strict *hadd* punishments under Islamic law.

tells its own story. Day (1982: 17) rightly begins his important study with the telling observation that concerning the Indian understanding of punishment itself, '[n]owhere is this conception formally defined, as if knowledge of its nature and structure had always been assumed'. Day (1985: 99) suggested:

> Protection does not come about 'eo ipso', it requires due attention to internal and external affairs. Appropriate activities are to be executed as *rājadharma* by means of *danda* (literally: stick, punishment), in a wider sense to be comprehended (and so used in our sources) as imposing 'acknowledged' secular disadvantage on somebody in situations resulting from 'contra-dharmic' activities.

Day (1985: 99-100) emphasised the inescapable nature of *daṇḍa*, at least in theory, and correctly pointed out, at p. 100, that punishment for transgressions is not merely a secular activity and that the principle of karma still operates as well:

> Protection by means of *danda*, however, includes the ruler's care for man's secular *and* religious prosperity, demanding the expiation of a sin and the punishment of an unwanted or forbidden behaviour, since an *adharmic* behaviour having the quality of a 'crime' simultaneously pertains to a sin and a punishable 'crime'. Hence to escape the ruler's *danda* may be not difficult, and is often successfully achieved, "but not that of the eternal law of *karma*".

This demonstrates that *daṇḍa* also became associated with the power to punish various transgressions which were originally treated as sins, but might now be seen as a form of crime. Such threats of punishment are not purely secular, therefore, as most legal commentators have assumed. In other words, transgressions of dharma are also seen as sins, which require penance and/or attract posthumous consequences.[85] But quite where sin ends and crime begins could never be fully determined, and so the obvious happened in terms of positivist legal scholarship, in that specialist legal authors have largely ignored the religious elements of *daṇḍa* theories and seem to envisage merely a secular mode of legal regulation. Diwan and Diwan (1993: 33) again emphasized the role of Manu and wrote, still muddling dharma and law:

> When the *Manusmriti* was compiled, the Hindu concept of law was that 'law is the king of kings'. Manu also subscribes to the notion that the king is subordinate to law and that the king is merely a law-enforcer. But he tries to clothe the king with the divine authority and seems to support the theory of divine right of kings .... With a view to strengthening the hands of the king, the *Manusmriti* tends to endow the king with the divine authority .... As a natural corollary to the strengthening of king's position, Manu, while dealing with the duties of the king, emphasizes the importance of *danda*, the secular instrument in the hands of the king for enforcement of law .... *Danda* connotes the secular power of punishment, which the king, as

[85] On penances see Diwan and Diwan (1993: 25) and in detail Day (1982).

> enforcer of law, possesses to prevent breach of law and to inflict punishment on the wrongdoers. Thus the punitive element behind the enforcement of law is emphasised.

This passage is worded in such a way that the culturally aware reader may read 'law' as either positive law or dharma. In a legal textbook of this nature, the trend among readers will be to pick up only the legal message. The dharmic dimension of the concept has thus been lost.[86] It is also not transparent in Desai (1998: 20), where *daṇḍa* is merely portrayed as 'the sanction behind the power of the king [to] restrain transgressions of law and to inflict punishment on offenders'. While Kuppuswami (1986) does not discuss *daṇḍa* separately, other more recent texts also fail to highlight the complex nature of 'assisted self-control' and engage in purely positivism-centred legalistic discussions. Surprisingly, claiming to discuss ancient Indian jurisprudence, Jois (2000: 53) argues as if dharma as self-controlled order is an irrelevant consideration, claiming that the object of *rājadharma* 'can be achieved only by having laws regulating the conduct of individuals and their enforcement through the officers and servants of the State'. This is the price one pays for arguing that the ancient Hindus had everything in place, well before Western civilizations.

It appears that only a few Indological scholars who have managed to retain some link with legal material, particularly Day (1982) and May (1985), have remained capable of addressing and exploring the interlinkages between dharma, *daṇḍa* and law. Day (1982: 243) clearly emphasizes in his conclusion that it is not adequate to take a narrow, legal perspective:

> A statement that judges ought to punish wrongdoers is not simply a statement about law but also a statement about the nature and the importance of justice and of civil order and of dutifulness in judges as divine concerns related to Order as an ultimate value.

Hindu law scholarship in this field is found in a deeply confused state, not only because of its defective understanding of concepts of Hindu self-controlled order, but also due to the strong positivist notion that criminal law is a matter for the state alone.[87] Textbooks on Hindu law have, therefore, significantly failed to make any sensible contribution to a deeper understanding of Hindu conceptions of punishment and have abandoned this aspect of law more or less entirely to secular considerations.

[86] The same positivist colouring is evident from how Diwan and Diwan (1993: 34) discuss other texts in relation to the ruler's power to use *daṇḍa*, here portrayed as 'the power of *danda* that the king enjoys as the principal law-enforcer', albeit without divine authority.

[87] This is no doubt reinforced by the fact that since 1860, the IPC has officially governed more or less the entire field. For a critical analysis of its limited effectiveness, with particular reference to women, see Dhagamwar (1992). The reality of village-based justice (with obvious question marks over 'justice') is captured well by Chowdhry (2000).

Vyavahāra and Informal Dispute Settlement

Late classical Hindu law displays certain conceptual characteristics that warrant still further separate treatment. During the late classical period of Hindu law, another aspect of a more legally technical orientation developed within Hindu law, relating to the more or less formal negotiation or settlement of disputes. Two key terms arise in this context, *vyavahāra* ('litigation' or dispute settlement),[88] and (probably later) the term *rājaśāsana*, which has been translated as 'royal edict' or more generally as the ruler's verdict on a disputed matter, thus constituting more a judicial statement than legislative authority. It will no longer be surprising to find that both terms have been significantly misrepresented by many legal scholars, who again underplayed or totally ignored the *ṛta*/dharma continuity and imagined formal Western-style legal criteria rather than considering Hindu concepts.[89]

The present section focuses on the assumption that formal litigation processes (*vyavahāra*), developing perhaps a growing authority of their own, became seen as a necessary means to uphold dharmic order. Self-regulated ordering processes would not always take place without some discussion and negotiation, which might be mostly informal, but could involve formal methods of dispute settlement. References to the need for dispute processing strengthen the claims of agents of the formal law, whether rulers, judges, or other functionaries, to increased authority in terms of ascertaining dharma, but still not with regard to law-making in a positivist sense.[90]

In terms of literary evidence, especially the important later *smṛti* texts of Nārada, Bṛhaspati and Kātyāyana,[91] developing earlier concepts and building on the classical foundations, clearly continue to retain the dharmic context, as May (1985: 109ff.) strongly emphasizes. Significantly, however, Hindu lawyers have been blind to this and have only seen secular legal rules about dispute settlement where an Indologist sees much more. In a climate in which the *Manusmriti* has already been unambiguously declared the most authoritative

[88] May (1985: 109ff.) provides an overview of the various nuances of meanings that this term may be given. See also Kane (1968–77, III: 242ff.).

[89] On the law-centred conceptualization of *vyavahāra* as 'civil law', see Diwan and Diwan (1993: 20), probably relying on Kuppuswami (1986: 14 and 22–3). On the more recent interpretation of the term as technical 'legal procedure', see the immediately preceding section. On *rājaśāsana* see Diwan and Diwan (1993: 24) and the next section.

[90] Some textbooks contain disputable claims about law-making in ancient India. Pathak (1986: 6) asserts that '[a] striking feature of the Naradasmriti is the fact that it is the first of the Dharmashastras to accept and record the principle that king-made laws could override any rule of law laid down in the smritis'. The related assertion is repeated at p. 7, a plainly too positivist interpretation of *rājaśāsana* or 'the ruler's decision'.

[91] For details see Jolly (1977). On the *Kātyāyanasmṛti* see in detail Derrett (1968b: 148ff.).

code of Hindu law (see Desai 1998: 19–20), these texts have persistently been presented to legal readers as law books.[92]

The texts in question mainly provide indications of an increased perception of the need for dispute settlement, as we saw in the earlier section from *Nāradasmṛti* 1.1–2, and it is doubtful that these are immediately references to formal 'lawsuits'. Similarly, *Bṛhaspatismṛti* 1.1 declares that '[i]n former times people were strictly virtuous and devoid of mischievous inclinations. Now that avarice and malice have taken possession of them, judicial proceedings have been established' (Jolly 1977: 277). Such texts consistently reflect perceptions about the decline and inefficiency of self-control mechanisms in late classical Hindu law. At the same time, they suggest a potential strengthening of the position of Hindu rulers as administrators of justice and indicate that experts in the shastra now possibly moving into positions as legal advisers, assessors, and even judges, might have become increasingly involved in the administration of justice, which at that time still meant ascertaining dharma, not obedience to the state's legal rules. All of this appears to increase the importance of texts and of textual knowledge as a source of Hindu law, but it does not mean that the centre of gravity has now shifted to rule making by the state.[93] The state-centredness of scholarship is also reflected in unthinking translation of *rājā* as 'ruler'; he could also be a family head or the manager (*kartā*) of a Hindu joint family.

According to the shastric texts, rulers were not infrequently called upon to settle disputes, as well as to punish criminals. The former was the case in disputes between individuals or social groups based on conflicting claims, the latter presumably when grave violations of dharma had occurred. However, it cannot have been the severity of a transgression alone which determined whether a case was dealt with by a ruler. Local fora in India to this day claim and exercise the right to devise appropriate punishments, including the death penalty (Baxi 1986a; Chowdhry 2000). In principle, during the late classical period, order was still maintained at the local level, with the ruler exercising at best a supervisory function. Thus, he remained unlikely to be aware of most disputes unless they affected his rule, or occurred in the capital, where access to the superior court was less difficult. Still, rulers would not want to be involved in trivial matters unless they were corrupt and saw administration of 'justice' as

[92] Kuppuswami (1986: 21) states that 'Narada ... is the first to give us a legal code unhampered by the religious and moral teaching, characteristic of the earlier Dharmashastras'. More recent efforts by Sanskritist legal scholars make no dent in the old distortions. Larivière (1989, II: ix) insists on treating the *Nāradasmṛti* as 'purely juridical in nature' and thus marginalizes the wider context within which dispute processing was and is perceived by Hindus.

[93] Derrett et al. (1979: 14) emphasize that the ancient literature neither supports a finding that ancient Hindu rulers legislated for their people, nor that they took any specific interest in the onerous task of dealing with disputes and hunting down criminals.

a means of exploitation. While this cannot be excluded as a realistic possibility, there are clear indications from many texts that vexatious litigation and litigiousness, in general, were not at all favoured.

The concept of *vyavahāra* is often circumscribed as 'removal of doubts', visualized as the extraction of a thorn or a dart (*Nāradasmṛti* 1.3.17; *Manusmriti* 8.12). Investigation and critical evaluation of evidence become, in this context, a new area of interest for the *smṛti* authors, so that legal scholars, centuries later, again saw further growth of technical legal subjects and expertise. Indeed, and remarkably parallel to early Islamic law, one finds here an important development in procedural rules, particularly an impressive body of rules concerning evidence. Such detailed technical rules may only have limited practical value, however. Many later texts introduce innumerable classifications and hair-splitting distinctions for the sake of completeness (see further later). The overriding concern in practice must have continued to be compliance with the expectations of dharma and the equity of the situation, rather than legal niceties of a theoretical nature. Some texts, indeed, warn against placing adherence to technicalities above concern for justice.[94]

The literary sources from the late classical period begin to contain more evidence of a formalization of processes of ascertaining dharma, but these have been reconstructed and are presented by legal textbook authors simply as formal legal processes. Abundant evidence from the texts illustrates such distortions. For example, Kuppuswami (1986: 20) writes:

> The Code of Manu declares the eighteen heads of legal proceedings which were followed by Yajnavalkya, Narada and Brihaspati. These divisions and their order make no pretensions to a scientific system; they were probably due to the practical needs of society and testify to the greater frequency and intricacy of some kinds of disputes than of others.

Early rulers like the Buddhist king Aśoka (c. 274–232 BC) issued edicts that were clearly moralistic guidelines, phrased in idealistic terms of following dharmic concerns about appropriate behaviour, rather than obeying the ruler's laws (Nikam and McKeon 1962). Later Hindu rulers, it was assumed, felt authorised to stipulate harsher penalties to improve self-control processes, while there will also have been abuses of such power.[95] Contemplating punishment

[94] *Bṛhaspatismṛti* 2.12 states that '[n]o sentence should be passed merely according to the letter of the law. If a decision is arrived at without considering the circumstances of the case, violation of justice will be the result'. This was quoted by the High Court of Kerala in *Kunhikannan v State of Kerala* 1968 KLT 19, at p. 23 to save an innocent victim from police overzealousness.

[95] Guha (1997: 30), claims that relying on such Hindu traditions, 'every landlord could indeed play "maharaj" to his tenants'. Further, 'according to this principle, the use of violence by upper-caste elites against untouchables and adivasis or the instigation of sectarian strife by a dominant local group against the subaltern adherents of a faith other than its own, could pass as a meritorious act modeled on a sovereign's defense of dharma' (id.), and the same would go for the treatment of women.

as a tool of governance, the temptation to lay down fixed rules for everybody may have increased. Indeed, in a supposedly later layer of texts, classified as *arthaśāstra* (guidelines on the science of acquisition of wealth and power) or *nītiśāstra* (handbooks on the science of guiding others) we seem to be told at times that an efficient Hindu ruler should behave like an absolutist monarch and should ruthlessly enforce his will on his people. However, it seems to go beyond credibility, and reflects positivist presuppositions, when it is asserted by Kuppuswami (1986: 21) that '[a]ccording to Narada, laws were proclaimed by Kings, and royal ordinances or proclamations could overrule the Smriti law'. In my view, such statements in the ancient texts have been overinterpreted and have been widely misread by legal scholars, who then introduced their own positivist assumptions of how a legal system grows over time. Some insight into how Indian lawyers have argued this matter is provided by Diwan and Diwan (1993: 24):

> It has been seen earlier that the theory was that our king did not make law; he merely enforced law. Yet we find that the king's power to make law—though to a limited extent—by edicts or ordinances—was recognised. It is not clear at what stage of development of law the *Rajyashasana* became important. Yajnavalkya mentions it. Narada clearly states that the king-made law overrides the sacred law and custom. Kautilya is also to the same effect. According to him *dharma, vyavahara, charitra*, and edicts of the king are the four legs of law. Of these four in order, the latter is superior to the one previously named.

While this *smṛti* needs to be further examined, Diwan and Diwan (1993: 24–25) attach to this kind of textual evidence their own political arguments for why ancient Hindu kings should need to make laws:

> Kautilya's period is the glorious period of Hindu history: the Maurya dynasty came to be established. Ashoka ruled over a vast Empire. One powerful king after another succeeded. At this period of glory and in the need of the governance of the vast empire it was but natural for a king to make laws. In response to the need of the time the king-made law was given overriding effect over sacred law. Narada observed: 'As the king has obtained lordship, he has to be obeyed. Polity depends upon him.' The king as the administrator of justice had, by the compulsion of social needs of time which witnessed remarkable political economic and social progress, to be given power to make law ... within the framework of *Shastras* or even in transgression of them, (when need arose or situation demanded) the king could make law. The king-made law was given overriding effect both over custom and sacred law.

It seems that Diwan and Diwan, writing not for a largely Western readership untutored in the finer concepts of Hindu culture, but for Indian law students, import outrightly positivist notions into their text. Their discussion echoes the same debate found in Desai (1998: 33–4) where it is suggested, quite wrongly in my view, that the *Arthaśāstra* 'was written at a period in the history of India during which law and politics were not accepted as wholly and strictly controlled by ancient rules of Dharma but as matters to be dealt with severally and freed from religious domination'. Thus it could eventually become a purported reality that Hindus had rulers like Western states had Napoleon and other great men, who would habitually lay down the law for their subjects. Such familiar images arose prominently among the early British administrators in the growing Indian Empire, but are manifestly also reflected today in the leading Hindu law textbooks. Indian lawyers, as this problematic scenario confirms, have evidently become keen pupils and eager followers of colonial legal and cultural indoctrination.

In late classical Hindu law, a dutiful Hindu ruler would at all times, in theory, have remained subject to the overarching conceptual demands of dharma, also in his pursuit of wealth and power, and he could never permit himself to act as a secular absolutist ruler without knowingly violating *rājadharma*. The development of *rājadharma*, as a specialized branch of the science of duties, offered further scope for positivist conceptual invasions and distortions. From a political science perspective, it is not illogical that a ruler figure should have some concern for, and control over, what 'his people' could and should not do. The texts do not engage in debates on the comparative virtues of democracy or Maine's patriarchal despotism, on which controversy remains alive (Menski 1995a), but emphasize that the ideal Hindu ruler would now take on the functional characteristics of Varuṇa, the divine Vedic guardian of *ṛta* (RV 10.85; *Manusmriti* 9.245). *Rājadharma* thus becomes an important topic in its own right, but is understood as a manifestation of the old *ṛta*/dharma complex. Consequently, when Hindu rulers, their judicial deputies and various other functionaries are depicted in litigation situations in much of the epic and dramatic literature in Sanskrit and various Prakrit languages, they are still acting within the confines of dharma, but they are also visibly engaged in processes of making law.

But the critical question is what kind of law is thus produced. If a ruler makes a declaration or decides a case, this is an attempt to relate particular facts to the perceived needs of dharma, not a purely secular legal action of 'laying down the law'. In other words, this is not legislation, but the conclusion of a process of ascertaining dharma, valid only for this particular situation. It is similar to judge-made law, but not in the sense of binding precedent, as in the British common law tradition. It is evident that Indian legal scholarship on Hindu law has been thoroughly influenced and virtually derailed by colonial concepts of legal administration.

While rulers and their representatives appear to be given guidance in *smṛti* texts about how best to secure dharma, all Hindus are still taught about the need for self-regulated action through such literature. The ruler's main role, in the classical Hindu law context, is therefore still not to produce or enforce his own law, but to enable everyone to follow their own respective dharma as far as possible. This basic rule confirms that there was not yet an operative concept of positive law or state law in late classical India. While the ruler might act as a facilitator of justice, he was not primarily the creator of the legal rules.

However, if Hindu rulers also acted in more and more cases as an arbiter over competing claims, thereby contributing to the development of more formal litigation patterns, then more explicitly legal, procedural patterns of state law might indeed have developed. It is therefore precisely in the arena of dispute settlement that further important evidence for the conceptual development of Hindu law might be found. Gradually, the functions of ruling and watching over self-controlled order are linked to settling disputes in a variety of local forms, culminating in the ruler's supreme function as final arbiter in disputes. While the ruler's judicial functions were probably often delegated to learned Brahmins and later 'legal' specialists, familiar patterns of society's regulation by the state might begin to emerge. It must also be noted again that later British interventions, familiar with the concept of judge-made 'common law', could effortlessly link into such formal patterns.

The leading legal textbooks send confused signals about the extent of any conceptual development in this field but assert, as shown above, a historical growth of positivist Hindu law. In this context, two types of statements from the classical Sanskrit texts have given rise to further discussions about the extent of state control in dispute settlement processes, and particularly about the degree of authority of any royal declaration or verdict that might conclude a dispute.

Various texts elaborate the four stages of plaint, answer, examination of evidence, and finally judgment, though there is little harmony between individual texts on points of detail (see for example *Bṛhaspatismṛti* 3.1ff.). As texts were increasingly arranged by subject, the topic of 'titles of law' (which are also still aspects of dharma) became more prominent. All major texts contain such a list comprising up to eighteen different titles. While *Manusmriti* 8.4–7 merely listed them in one place, the *Nāradasmṛti*, for example, treated the eighteen subjects in considerable detail, focusing in turn on (1) debt; (2) deposits; (3) partnership; (4) resumption of gifts; (5) breach of a contract of service; (6) non-payment of wages; (7) sales affected by another than the rightful owner; (8) non-delivery of a sold chattel; (9) rescission of purchase; (10) transgression of a compact; (11) boundary disputes; (12) mutual duties of husband and wife; (13) law of inheritance; (14) heinous offences; (15) and (16) abuse and assault; (17) games; and (18) miscellaneous.[96]

Increasing formalization of legal rules and processes in the administration of justice at the highest level seems reflected in verses that appear to give the Hindu ruler the last word in deciding disputes, thus establishing a hierarchy of sources of law (or rather, dharma) that is markedly different from *Manusmriti* 2.6 and 2.12 as discussed in the next section. Such verses suggest an advanced

[96] This list is found in Jolly (1977: vii–viii). The *Bṛhaspatismṛti* produces these topics in a slightly different order, but does not otherwise vary much from the *Nāradasmṛti* (ibid.: ix)

form of discussion about the sources of dharma. There appears to be much confusion over their meaning.[97] As a sample, *Nāradasmṛti* 1.10 (Jolly 1977: 7) is useful:

> Virtue [dharma], a judicial proceeding [*vyavahāra*], documentary evidence [*caritra*], and an edict from the king [*rājaśāsana*] are the four feet of a lawsuit. Each following one is superior to the one previously named.

In the translation offered by Larivière (1989, II: 5) the same verse reads: 'The four feet of legal procedure are dharma, legal procedure,[98] custom and the king's decree; each latter one overrules the former'. Jolly (1977: 7) had earlier tried to explain the meaning of this verse, especially the four-fold hierarchy, which seems premised on the expectation that self-controlled order should remain the norm. Larivière (1989, II: 5–6) helpfully points out the underlying assumption that a final appeal lies to the king. But that does not mean that the ruler's verdict always overrules everything else.

Derrett (1968b: 148ff.) took the equivalent text of the *Kātyāyanasmṛti* as a basis for his own discussion of this hierarchy. He argued, firstly, that when both parties to a dispute act truthfully and the wrongdoer admits his misdeed, the decision or outcome is achieved through dharma (Derrett 1968b: 149), clearly a reference to self-controlled ordering (see also Jolly 1977: 7). This might imply informal extra-judicial dispute settlement, perhaps after admission of the objectionable act by the wrongdoer. Such settlement of a dispute 'before trial' would strongly confirm the continuing relevance of self-control mechanisms in real life. In this particular sense, dharma itself would then continue to be a source of dharma. It is rightly placed in the primary position, since the present hierarchy of four sources is given in a realistic chronological order, beginning with the least authoritative but most frequently applied source.

Continuing this dual image of sources of dharma and methods of dispute settlement, the second level in this hierarchy, *vyavahāra*, would imply a slightly more formal process of dispute settlement. The contested ascertaining of dharma makes sense here, particularly in view of the corrupted ideal of post-classical Hindu law. In the bad *kaliyuga*, self-control has largely broken down and other mechanisms for dispute settlement would need to be pursued. In this regard, Kātyāyana's view is that *vyavahāra* involves the settling of disputes by recourse to *smṛti* rules (Derrett 1968b: 149), while *Nāradasmṛti* 1.11 suggests that 'a judicial proceeding (rests) on the statements of the witnesses' (Jolly 1977: 7), which led the translator to comment that either party to a dispute may have lied and witnesses may have had to be called.

[97] Derrett (1968b: 148) indicates that this is a virtually unexplored issue. Lingat (1973) treated such verses as evidence of methods of dispute settlement or means of proof (see Derrett 1968b: 154–5).

[98] The translator notes on this duplication of terminology that this *vyavahāra* refers to the more general usage of the term as 'a dispute at law'.

All of this shows that formal methods of dispute settlement do not by necessity involve or demand recourse to shastric texts. Indeed, Derrett (1968b: 149) indicates that the authors of the ancient texts may here be conducting 'a self-conscious and tendentious debate' among themselves. Less concerned to explain how dharma is determined, they might rather wish to emphasize their own importance in view of the obvious social fact that textual authority remained a subsidiary source of dharma, needed to be adduced by experts and was probably not that popular, given the many textual statements from which one might choose. It is possible that the authors of *smṛti* texts might have argued for an increased role of these texts, hardly a surprise in a morally corrupt era such as the *kaliyuga*, in which self-interest is supposed to prevail. Another explanation might be that recourse to texts here means reliance on the new rules about evidence rather than older shastric sources. Both arguments lead to the same conclusion: The *vyavahāra* experts are seen to be effectively advertising themselves and their products. Here is a further potential growth point for legal business.

The third element in this scheme is *caritra*, a colourful term which can mean many different things, just as *ācāra* or *sadācāra* in the classical scheme of Hindu law. Derrett (1968b: 149) translates from Kātyāyana that 'whatever a person practises, whether it be in accord with *dharma* or not, is declared to be *caritra* because it is the invariable usage of the country'. At first sight, this means that appropriate behaviour in itself serves as a source of dharma, requiring no further intervention from anywhere, in which case it should be the same as the first category, self-controlled dharma, and one must wonder why it should be listed here separately. If we view *caritra* as a method of dispute settlement, however, it could refer to documentary evidence of what is right and proper (Jolly 1977: 7). Again, this does not need to imply recourse to *smṛti* texts but could be written or orally documented confirmation of particular local or caste practices, which would have evidentiary value. The precise meaning of this element needs to be investigated further. Surely it must be wrong, at this stage, to think of highly technical notarized affidavit procedures, but *caritra* probably involves more than just plain 'custom'; it is perhaps rather 'proof of custom'.

Lastly, and most important for the present debate, the ruler's verdict must also be seen in this dual fashion. As a source of dharma, it could be subsumed under the classical *sadācāra*, based on the personal and institutional authority of the leader figure. As a method of dispute settlement, it makes sense to envisage the ruler as an institution and a final arbiter, indeed a final court of appeal. But how would a ruler reach a decision? It could be the result of patriarchal despotism and brazen force, but this is not what the still somewhat idealistic texts appear to have in mind. While Jolly (1977: 8) thought of 'the pleasure of the king', Kātyāyana seems to indicate that recourse to texts would play an important role in ascertaining 'relative appropriateness' (Derrett 1968b: 150). This reference makes sense if we envisage that a conscientious ruler should consult experts in the shastric texts. This could again be read as evidence of cunning self-advertisement by experts, this time towards rulers, but it certainly does not mean that the ruler's verdict necessarily becomes the 'law of the land'. While the ruler appears to have the last word, he must consider a variety of factors within the dharmic context in order to fulfil his own dharma. Moreover, the end result is a resolved dispute, not a piece of legislation.

All of this shows clearly that late classical Hindu law, too, does not allow the ruler to make law as he pleases, but keeps him firmly within the framework of relativities. The fact that the ruler increasingly delegated his judicial functions to experts (Derrett 1968b: 183; Derrett et al. 1979: 65ff.), some of whom we may now call judges and/or jurists,[99] had some influence on the consideration of these relativities, but case law and statute would not appear to become a source of Hindu law until British intervention many centuries later. Speaking of these two sources within the realm of traditional Hindu law itself reflects infections of the writer's pen by legal positivist notions. Quite inconsistently,[100] Desai (1998: 35) concludes that '[t]here is no reference to any centralised judicial system and there seems to have been little interference by the king with the traditional local tribunals which functioned in matters of local importance including dispensation of justice'.

Late classical Hindu law, thus, represents an important conceptual shift in emphasis from internalized processes of ascertaining dharma to more visibly negotiated attempts at finding the right balance in conflicts or disputes. This happened probably through recourse to texts and various human agents who took their authority primarily from knowledge of those texts, and not in the first instance from secular political power. In real life, there can be no doubt that the majority of such conflict situations continued to be dealt with locally, and by more or less informal processes of dispute settlement, in which local customary laws remained in all likelihood the most important yardstick for ascertaining dharma. The increasingly detailed evidence of legal rules, especially in the later *smṛti* texts, and the concept of *vyavahāra* itself, should therefore not mislead anyone into imagining a highly formalized stage of late classical Hindu law and litigation. Most of Hindu law at this time remained informal, unrecorded and inaccessible to formal legal analysis and positivist control. Whatever the present leading Hindu law textbooks may say, in the light of the present analysis it appears that the traditional Hindu legal system as a whole remained firmly based on the primacy of self-controlled order and individual action, not on outside intervention through law-making authorities.

[99] On whether a legal profession existed in ancient India, the answer appears to be in the negative. See Kane (1968–77, III: 288ff.).

[100] I say this in view of the contrary statements by Desai (1998: 33–4) as cited above, and note his comment that by the time of the *Arthaśāstra* India was politically unified and there was consolidation of power in the hands of emperors 'whose writ ran in the whole country' (p. 36).

The Role of Custom in Classical Hindu Law

The late classical pre-eminence of localized, self-controlled order within the ambit of the *ṛta*/dharma complex is powerfully reinforced by considerable evidence that the shastric texts themselves continued to accord huge importance to customary laws.[101] For this reason, too, something is seriously wrong with the prominent perception, propounded by legal textbooks, that ancient Hindu rulers or shastric authors, as judges or simply as 'lawmakers', could in positivist fashion determine or lay down the law.[102] The supremacy of customary laws in daily social reality is further underlined by frequent statements to the effect that a valid custom need not be in accordance with *smṛti* rules. Diwan (1984: 4) seems to go further when he argues that 'the Punjab customary law throughout remained a secular law', a view which reflects that author's modernity, but not, I would argue, the perspective of the people concerned. Against this, the viewpoint of Roy (1911: 12–13) is to be preferred, indicating that under customary law, 'a person aggrieved complains not of an individual wrong but of the disturbance of the order of the entire little society'. While this could still be interpreted as a secular matter, the various degrees of awareness of Hindu interlinkedness would not exclude the realm of custom. While custom has secular elements, no doubt, its operation in the social context also clothes it with religious elements. Measuring such degrees may be beyond the capacity of lawyers, but an outright declaration that such customs were either secular or religious cannot be justified on any count.

The recognition that custom in derogation of *smṛti* rules can be perfectly valid in Hindu law and would be given effect in a dispute settlement process or even a formal court of law has many conceptual consequences. Such statements illustrate, more than anything else, the fact that 'Hindu law' is indeed only a label and governs many people who, on strict criteria, might not qualify as 'Hindu'. Undoubtedly with an eye towards some Indian Muslim communities who continue to apply Hindu customary laws, Mahmood (1981: xxxviii) complained:

> The expression 'Hindu law', which may once have been most appropriate, is now, surely, a term of convenience, if not a misnomer. At present the law described as 'Hindu law' is applicable, or may be applied, to a heterogeneous section of the Indian citizenry, many groups in which are certainly not 'Hindu' by religion. So, 'Hindu law' is not the 'law of the Hindus'. 'Hindus' are only one of those communities who are governed by this law.

[101] See, e.g. Jolly (1975: 3–4). On the general recognition that custom is older than law, see Roy (1911: 1). On its place as people's law see in detail Diwan (1984: ix), who is also trying to make the curious claim that the Punjab is the cradle of Indian customs.

[102] Diwan (1984: 11) correctly indicated that adherents of the analytical school of jurisprudence would have problems with the view that ancient custom was law.

While this statement describes the situation in today's India, the many people of ancient times who were more or less incompletely Hinduized, or who lived on the thick fringes of Hindu society, or indeed somewhere in its midst, would be governed by their own localized social norms and would not normally seek guidance from the lawmakers of ancient India which textbook writers seem to imagine. The ancient texts themselves make it quite apparent that local notions of appropriateness, and thus local customary laws, remained the inherently flexible major source of law in social reality.[103] A ruler who wanted to follow his own dharma would have to respect such customs and was enjoined to give them effect, thereby following his own *rājadharma*, as *Manusmṛti* 8.41–2 illustrates:

> A ruler who knows (his duties according to) dharma must inquire into the customary laws of castes, of districts, of guilds, and of families, and thus settle the law peculiar to each. For men who follow their respective occupations and who abide by their respective duties become dear to people, even though they may live at a distance.

Arthaśāstra 3.7.40 directs the ruler that '[w]hatever be the customary law of a region, a caste, a corporation or a village, in accordance with that alone shall he administer the law of inheritance'. Even when a new territory has been conquered, there should be no superimposition of the new ruler's law, as *Manusmṛti* 7.203 clearly indicates:

> Let him make authoritative the customary laws (of the inhabitants of that territory), just as they are stated to be, and let him honour (his representative) and his chief servants with precious gifts.

While such textual statements may not be taken as proof of their direct practical application, we find so many of them that even the positivism-focused Indian textbook writers have not been able to suppress such messages. Hence they have incorporated custom, thereby further contradicting their other legalistic claims, in particular the assertion that Hindu law is based on divine revelation and/or that it should ultimately be determined by the authoritative verdicts of rulers or the law codes of ancient law givers.

The leading text of Mayne's *Hindu Law* (Kuppuswami 1986: 14) starts off by accepting that custom is the third major source of Hindu law after the *smṛtis* or *dharmaśāstras* and the commentaries and digests. This is evidently a general view of the legal position which is coloured by Anglo-Hindu legal concepts.[104] Thereafter, this text does not pay any further attention to the role of custom in interaction with the numerous *smṛti* texts and concentrates on

[103] For details on the widespread toleration of custom at various levels see Derrett et al. (1979: 17–58).

[104] The same transpires from Mulla's tenth edition (Ramesam 1946: 9), which briefly cites some of the leading texts on which British Indian courts would rely to recognize custom.

legalistic concepts rather than the place of local custom. In contrast, Desai (1998: 2) is quite specific on the important role of custom:

> The ancient law promulgated in the Smritis was essentially traditional and the injunction was that time-honoured institutions and immemorial customs should be preserved intact. The law was not to be found merely in the texts of the Smritis but also in the practices and usage which had prevailed under it. The traditional law was itself grounded on immemorial custom and provided for inclusion of proved custom that is practices and usages that from time to time might come to be followed and accepted by the people. The importance attached to the law-creating efficacy of custom in Hindu jurisprudence was so great that the exponents of law were unanimous in accepting custom as a constituent part of law.

Taking the view that customary law was an important element of the sources of Hindu law in its own right, and had over time also become incorporated into the early texts,[105] Desai (1998: 13) also claims that the authors of the *dharmasūtras* took the law from earlier *smṛti* texts and customs which had grown up bit by bit, reducing them to some sort of order, a process that became more intricate still in the production of the *dharmaśāstras*. Desai (1998: 16) explains that the importance of these texts lies in the concepts of jurisprudence that they reflect and 'the reference that is traceable in them to previously unrecorded custom, and crystallisation in the form of precepts of usages and practices and the transformation of these into constituent law'. In this envisaged process of lawmaking through texts, the author sees a self-reinforcing pattern of reliance on various ancient customs. Desai (1998: 17) even appears to go as far as claiming that the ancient texts (rather than being expressions of private opinion) might represent the views of the ancient communities themselves:

> ... these Sutrakars primarily sought to express the *communis sententia* of the Indo-Aryans and were unanimous in their appeal to customary law. This adherence to the doctrine of accepted usage and the enjoined duty of the interpreter of law to see that customs, practices and family usages prevailed and were preserved is one of the outstanding features of Hindu jurisprudence.

Over time, thus, a process of harmonization of text and custom was envisaged by Desai (1998: 19) who emphasizes dynamic elements in the growth of the ancient texts, 'supplementing, altering and gradually moulding the ancient traditional law into [a] system. This evolution was going on for many centuries ...'. Desai (1998: 20) treats the *Manusmṛti* not only as a code, but as 'a landmark in the history of Hindu law' in which ancient customs have been recorded and

[105] Derrett et al. (1979) also discuss this in detail. Derrett (1963b: 2) portrayed the system of Hindu law as 'a rationalized and systematized body of customary law and observances, a collection of (for the most part) carefully justified "oughts" and "should nots"'.

legally sanctioned. Roy (1911: 13) stated that '[t]he Code of Manu was by far the earliest attempt at a compilation of the then prevalent customs and usages, though it contained but a very small body of such customs and usages'. Desai (1998: 20) claims further that '[t]he Code records many genuine observances of the ancient Hindu and gives a vivid idea of the customs of the society then extant. The ordinance of Manu is based on ancient usages'. A similar approach is taken (ibid.: 25) when discussing the *smṛti* assigned to Nārada, who is said to be 'categorical and emphatic in his statement that custom is powerful' and agrees that custom overrides any textual statement. Diwan and Diwan (1993: 24) similarly emphasize the unique position of custom in Hindu law and confirm that '[c]ustom not merely supplemented law but it prevailed over sacred law'. They also assert that '[t]o a great extent the *Dharmashastras* were themselves based on custom'. Mahmood (1981: xl) identifies different historical stages:

> Hindu jurisprudence has always had an extremely respectable place for custom and usage. No legal philosophy has perhaps given so much importance to custom as it received at the hands of the Hindu doctors of law. These doctors had, of course, begun with the concept of *sadachara*. It was after a long time that *sadachara* came to be regarded as a synonym of what is now known in English as custom or usage. The fact remains that custom and usage (whether they are the same as *sadachara* or not), which once were constituents of Hindu law, became its strong opponents in the course of time. Followers of Hindu law came to have a choice between the written law of their religion and the prevailing usage of the locality, class, caste or family; and the ancient jurists accepted it. This established juristic position got full recognition by the judiciary in British India ...

In socio-political reality, as in other early societies, various forms of social organization, from small family groupings and acephalous societies to centrally structured large kingdoms, would have maintained order at the local level. Due to the interaction of various spheres of the visible and the invisible worlds, customary rules will have been closely linked with culture-specific and local concepts of magic and chthonic religious elements, such as worship of the earth, trees, and rivers. To what extent such practices and accompanying rules were 'Hindu' in nature will be impossible to ascertain, but it seems safe to assume a gradual process of Hinduization, parallel to the transition from *ṛta* to dharma.[106] While dharmic perspectives became more prominent, customary diversity prevailed and is explicitly referred to in the dharma texts. The coexistence of local practice and textual model is regularly referred to in the context of marriage rituals (Derrett 1968b: 159), with the former clearly supreme. Thus, *Āśvalāyanagṛhyasūtra* 1.7.1–2 begins its treatment of marriage rituals with an important reservation about textual authority, indicating that such texts cannot be read as binding codes that laid down the law for all Hindus:

[106] This is also clearly reflected in the late Vedic models for marriage solemnisation, as detailed in RV 10.85 and AV 14 (Menski 1984).

> Very diverse, indeed, are the customary practices of different countries and villages; one should follow those in marriages. What, however, is common to all or most shall be declared here.[107]

Important questions must have arisen about the hierarchy of the various local and family customs and the *smṛti* rules, really about the relationship between customary flexibility and dharmic obligation, at a deeper level between individual discretion and divine order. But there is no contradiction here, since the dharmic system is not a uniform code of obligations but rather a situation-specific and context-sensitive method of expecting the best possible results in what may often have been quite inauspicious circumstances. This is why classical Hindu law cannot be essentialized. The *smṛti* texts do not provide much discussion of how individual obligations and cosmic expectations are to be matched in practice and were content to list a hierarchy of the sources of dharma. The practical application of such concepts was presumably familiar to those who produced or collated such texts. I suggest that this invisible but acknowledged element points us again to the *ṛta*/dharma complex, which may of course be defined as local normative orders with fairly little or even no concern for the cosmic dimension that the texts would stipulate as the norm. There is no jurisprudential debate over such questions in the old sources and *Manusmriti* 2.6 and 2.12, respectively, simply state the basic rule as follows:

> 2.6: The whole Veda is the first source of *dharma*, next *smriti* and the virtuous conduct of those who know (the scriptures well), also the example of good people, and finally the individual's conscience.
>
> 2.12: The Veda, *smriti*, the customs of good people, and one's own satisfaction they declare to be visibly the fourfold means of defining *dharma*.

Such statements establish an obvious and sensible hierarchy of sources of dharma, starting from the divinely inspired and reaching down to the Hindu individual's intuitive discretion, a very personal sense of what is right. However, this top-down hierarchy does not make sense in daily practice. Hindus would not ascertain their dharma by looking up rules in Vedic texts first, they would proceed in reverse order and would initially examine their individual conscience. It is essential to understand this before one can appreciate how much this genre of textual material was also distorted by positivist legal scholarship.

In practical terms, common Hindus would never have looked first to *śruti* and then to *smṛti* for ascertaining dharma, even though these are the highest sources. The texts indicate a hierarchy of authority, but do not purport to guide us on the practicalities of ascertaining that authority. Since these texts do not disclose how Hindus would gauge the dharmic needs of a particular situation, it is useful to turn to social reality. Common sense suggests that the textual

[107] My translation. Other texts indicate that old women, rather than learned men, are to be seen as an authority on customs (Derrett 1968b: 159). This is still true today and may be observed in contemporary rituals (Menski 1987: 197).

statements about the hierarchy of sources of dharma must be read in reverse order to retrace the methodology of finding the actual sources of dharma. The sequence of sources of dharma must therefore be examined in reverse, so that individual satisfaction about 'doing the right thing in the right way at the right time', individually experienced and socially sanctioned, is in fact chronologically the first source of dharma. This connotes with the statements in the immediately preceding section about the primacy of self-controlled order in processes of *vyavahāra* or dispute settlement. In other words, these texts are consistent with other statements of 'legal' hierarchy and make it quite clear that self-controlled ordering is the first and foremost method of 'finding' dharma, i.e. ascertaining the relevant Hindu law. This method, which results primarily in the invisible process of internal self-examination of one's conscience, may well settle nearly all disputes or situations of insecurity. It is a mental process, imperceptible to others, and thus of no interest and concern to lawyers. For this reason, and writing as a continental civil lawyer studying Hindu law, Lingat (1973: 6) did not find it proper to give a voice to the common Hindu in law-making, claiming that 'if "inner contentment"—we should prefer to say the approval of one's conscience—really is a source of dharma, it does not strike us as quite properly placed here, following upon sources which possess an authority exterior to man'.

To Lingat, 'law' is clearly something imposed on people from outside, and self-controlled ordering as a mental process does not qualify as a legal factor. This legalistic, negative scholarly reaction not only marginalizes the Hindu individual's rights to participate in the rule-ascertaining process, it excludes every Hindu from the most basic processes of law-finding to which he/she should in fact aspire according to the expectations of the *ṛta*/dharma complex. Typically, in view of positivist lawyers' denial of the role of society as a law-creating and rule-ascertaining agent, it appears that Lingat misunderstood what the textual sources attempt to say. Here again, it transpires that the positivist approach, brought by so many legal scholars to the study of Hindu law, is inadequate for the task in hand, namely to analyse a social situation in which the rules of the normative order are not found in legal codifications, but are internalized in the minds of those who live within that tradition and practise what they see as its norms.

The above conclusion, reinforcing the practical pre-eminence of *ātmanastuṣṭi*, the Hindu individual's self-satisfaction,[108] does not automatically mean that individual conscience is therefore the most authoritative source of dharma in Hindu social reality. No doubt it has a very important place as the first and most immediate and intimate instance of decision making, but how autonomous is the agent of that decision, the individual mind? While it is probably no coincidence that most of the shastric texts mentioned only three sources

108 Mahmood (1981: xli) overlooked the individual dimension and saw this concept as 'not much different from the modern concept of "equity, justice and good conscience"', thus offering another secularized, legalistic interpretation.

of dharma and left out the individual conscience altogether, the fact that it is mentioned, even in the *Manusmriti* which is constantly represented to the world as a code of law, should have given rise to deeper analysis.

Obviously, Lingat's interpretation of these verses reflects elitist thinking and feeds on the positivism of the civil law traditions with their binding norms as codified by the state. The conceptual mismatch becomes still more obvious if we consider briefly the meaning of *sadācāra*, 'model behaviour',[109] the third source of dharma as indicated in the above verses. Here again, the ancient Indian authors—as well as Western scholarship—have been more than happy to allocate authority to learned men (and thus indirectly to dharma texts) rather than to common people. This is caused by redefining *sadācāra* as *śiṣṭācāra*, referring to the behaviour of 'the great and the good', more specifically learned men, as many comments on the ancient verses signify. But *sadācāra*, in social reality, is first of all what an individual's peers consider right and proper. It could be what a young person's parents or grandparents might advocate as right or wrong, sage advice of the family elders or, from a different perspective, individual self-subjugation to the authority of the family. Whichever way one views this matter, *sadācāra* clearly does not depend on the advice or guidance of learned men, let alone on a 'holy man' of some description, nor need it rely on scriptural authority. The concept of *sadācāra* involves constructive recognition of local social realities and individual circumstances.[110] It does not mean that 'anything goes', since from the viewpoint of the *smṛti* texts, local normative orders have been put under pressure to conform to Hindu ideals of good behaviour. These are neither fully defined nor unchanging, as Datta (1979) showed through her fascinating examination of clashes over sexual morality. Also, the texts themselves contain different layers of provisions which reflect social change.

Overstating the roles of scriptural authority and its representatives in the form of learned men, the interpretations of Lingat and many others have once again overlooked social reality and have thus constructed another legal fiction. In the real life circumstances of a late classical Hindu, recourse to scriptural guidance was clearly a matter of secondary importance and a strategy of last resort. In other words, the ancient texts remained mostly a remote, residual source of law. To speak of the formal legal application of codes of Hindu law to every conflict situation does considerable injustice to the understanding of Hindu law as a whole. This significant element of distortion needs further debate, because in this way, too, the widespread schizophrenia of Hindu legal scholarship is amply illustrated. It cannot be conceptually harmonised that, on the one hand, we are asked to imagine ancient, divinely revealed codes of law, while on the other hand the very same authors who glorify such codes also

[109] On *ācāra* and its various forms and meanings see May (1985: 58–9).

[110] Conceptually, this comes close to the 'living law' perspective, which is such an integral part of the historical school of jurisprudence. See Ehrlich (1913) as analysed in Menski (2000a: 114–19).

suggest that custom remains the most critical source of Hindu law. After all, in indigenous terminology, custom is nothing else but *sadācāra*.

Modernists will say that here precisely is the proof that ancient Hindu law was bad for justice and human rights, and that adherence to the cultural *ṛta*/dharma complex disempowers individuals. But we found earlier that in the vast majority of cases, a split-second decision may be made by the individual himself or herself to ascertain what should be done, so the individual is not totally disempowered and actually retains enormous discretion.[111] When a Hindu individual cannot reach a decision without consultation with others, we find the element of *sadācāra* in operation. This again need not be a visible process, since one may simply observe others, or listen silently to guidance, not giving away (not even being aware, perhaps) that one is in fact ascertaining dharma. Of course, these are a matter of psychology, not law, but these processes are legally relevant. Lingat (1973: 6) protested rightly that from his perspective, such processes of ascertaining legal rules did not strike him as *sui generis* with law. But that is not the end of the matter.

Of course, the intangible processes of ascertaining dharma may be formalized, but unless they involve recourse to a source of guidance based on textual authority or knowledge, texts still do not appear as a source of legal authority, so that *smṛtis* and especially the more remote of the *śruti* texts could only ever be residual sources in this context. Given rural actualities, even to imagine shastric guidance in every formal dispute takes legal positivism too far. Derrett (1968b: 156–7) rightly considered *sadācāra* to be of prime importance, and reported this in many different ways, emphasizing the informal nature of the processes involved.[112]

While there is no disagreement that *sadācāra* refers in various ways to custom, it is perhaps better seen as 'good' custom, in view of the Hinduising efforts that needed to be undertaken all the time. As Derrett (1968b: 206) perceptively put it, customary law 'moved towards the *śāstra*' in various ways. *Manusmriti* 8.46 seems to recognize this explicitly when it advises the ruler to find an appropriate balance between the various local customary norms and the customs of high-caste Hindus:

> What may have been practised by the virtuous, by such twice-born people who are devoted to *dharma*, that he shall establish as the rule, unless it is opposed to the customs of countries, families and castes.

The inherent tensions between allowing every individual to decide for himself or herself and binding everyone into a more shastric network of obligations will have been felt in most situations of real life. The relationships of the various

[111] In her analysis of women's property rights, S. Basu (2001: 10) refers correctly to 'the pockets of equity that have seldom been utilized by Hindu women'. Such recognition of women's agency needs to be strengthened, for women as individuals *have* this power, but do not seem to use it often enough.

[112] See in detail Derrett et al. (1979).

customary laws and the *smṛti* texts show that customs, in principle even in derogation of textual rules, would be valid (Menski 1992b). Relying on other texts quoted above, Pathak (1986: 6) states that in this regard, 'Narada is categorical and emphatic in his statement that custom is powerful and overrides any text of sacred law', thus accepting the principal supremacy of custom as a source of dharma. This is summarised it seems, in texts such as *Manusmriti* 8.14–15, reiterating the supremacy of the *ṛta*/dharma complex itself, with no attempt to universalize any law for all Hindus. Significantly, Bühler's (1975: 255) old translation of the verses renders dharma as 'justice', thus creating the impression that the verse relates to dispute settlement alone, while in fact it contains a much broader, general message. This translation runs as follows:

> 8.14. Where justice is destroyed by injustice, or truth by falsehood, while the judges look on, there they shall also be destroyed.
> 8.15. Justice, being violated, destroys; justice, being preserved, preserves; therefore justice must not be violated, lest violated justice destroy us.

My own translation differs from the court-centred image of the above interpretation, using 'righteousness' for dharma instead of the law-centred 'justice', and emphasizes the general social nature of the common Sanskrit term *sabhāsad*, against a specialist legal meaning.[113] This wording clearly brings out the need for vigilance about righteousness throughout Hindu society, not just in courts of law and I would translate:

> 8.14. Where righteousness is destroyed by selfishness (*adharma*), or truth by untruth, while members of society look on, they too shall be destroyed.
> 8.15. Righteousness which is being violated, destroys (in turn); righteousness which is preserved, preserves (in turn); therefore righteousness should not be violated, since violated righteousness indeed destroys.[114]

In my interpretation, these two verses from the chapter on 'civil law' that lawyers have imagined in this part of the *Manusmriti*, make a general statement about the need to protect dharma at all times, thus alluding to the idealized self-controlled order system. In the late classical period, this is assumed to require the protective support of vigilant rulers. Whether we imagine only a restricted legal meaning for these two verses, or a wider connotation, the message is invariably to the effect that there exists something beyond the immediate

113 In the Sanskrit-English dictionary of Monier-Williams (1976: 1151), *sabhā* is clearly much more than just a courtroom, while *sabhāsad* is perhaps a little too narrowly interpreted as 'an assistant at a meeting or assessor in a court of justice'. May (1985:16) noted that the *sabhā* was one of the institutions that limited the ruler's power, rather than an instrument of his rule.

114 The general tone of the statement at the end is in my view reinforced by use of the little and innocuous Sanskrit word *naḥ*, which does not necessarily mean 'us' here, as it normally does. Thus I do not read at the end that 'violated righteousness destroys us', but suggest that the key message itself is being emphasized, to the effect that 'violated righteousness indeed leads to destruction'.

grasp of the human sphere that must be protected at all times. Whether we should really call this 'justice' is debatable, since the term in the Sanskrit text is dharma, and the holistic 'justice of a specific situation' is perhaps not quite the same as 'justice' in its supposedly modern sense of a rationally ascertainable legal outcome. Of course, we shall never get round the problem that dharma is polysemic (Nakano 1935) and poses a special challenge to the translator (Olivelle 2000: xvi).

Looking back at the official positivist non-recognition of the Hindu individual's role as the ultimate arbiter of dharma, and linking this to the present debate, I conclude that there is a deeper problem which requires further analysis. Apart from ideological opposition to the religious foundations of Hindu law, it seems, positivist thinking among lawyers and other scholarly commentators has systematically sought to deprive all Hindu individuals of their ultimate voice and agency in the never-ending process of ascertaining what is 'appropriate', i.e. in the law-making process itself. Scholarship and legal doctrine have formally divested Hindu society, and ultimately every individual, of their critical ancient role in ascertaining righteousness. Both anti-religious and anti-traditionalist modernism as well as the 'anti-people effects' of legal positivism have therefore conspired to pacify Hindus, on the one hand, by lip service to divine revelations of the Hindu legal foundations, while ripping apart those very foundations that empowered Hindus to define for themselves what is appropriate in any particular situation. I do not think that this complex conspiracy took place before the end of the late classical period. What we have seen above are manifestations of modernist, legalist distortions of what classical Hindu law was really about.

Thus, at the theoretical and conceptual level, it remains a fact that late classical Hindu law, as in the Vedic period, continues to be focused on maintenance of the pre-existing order, encompassing gods, men, and all creatures alike. However, there appears to be a shift of emphasis in the later periods, not only placing a duty on every individual to contribute to the maintenance of order, but now emphasizing the need for supervision of the all too flexible element of self-control and the added control mechanism of dispute settlement. This fluid diversity, together with strong evidence of the pre-eminence of customary laws and individual discretion, as recorded even in the supposedly leading *smṛti* text, continues to haunt and taunt the positivist images created by some Orientalists and most lawyers. If *ātmanastuṣṭi* and *sadācāra* are indeed so manifestly the major criteria for measuring what is 'right' and 'wrong', and for achieving justice in every situation, then there is no conceptual space for Manu's alleged code of universally binding Hindu law, for the law-making of absolutist traditional Hindu rulers or judges, or for the positivist distortions of classical Hindu law by legal writing many centuries later. We must ask, therefore, to what extent certain post-classical distortions may have prepared the ground for later massive colonial intervention in this arena.

4

The Post-classical Evolution of Hindu Law and its Colonial Distortions

In this chapter, an attempt is made to understand and depict how the critical transition from dharma to law occurred during the periods following late classical Hindu law. There can be no doubt that this transformation took place, albeit mainly at the official level, but it remains at issue whether this was a consequence of colonial intervention or of internal developments within Hindu law itself. It appears that a gradual process of legalisation and professionalization of Hindu law during this period led ultimately to the case-based Anglo-Hindu law, which was at first administered by a class of total outsiders who were largely ignorant of Hindu law.

How, then, did it happen that indigenous perceptions of Hindu law as a self-controlled order system, based ultimately on some form of revelation or immemorial traditions, could have shifted more or less totally towards positivist assumptions about the inherent superiority of state law over any form of religious or moral ordering? In Chapter 3, I showed that such assumptions and mental shifts are quite strongly manifested in the specialist secondary literature on classical Hindu law, but these were largely distortions imported into the analysis by a combination of Orientalist and legalistic scholarship. Even in late classical Hindu law, the pervasiveness of the *ṛta*/dharma complex remained a fact, virtually taken for granted and thus not discussed in so many words.[1]

This chapter demonstrates that in the post-classical period, leading towards medieval times, several further developments of Hindu literature and concepts occur, potentially throwing light on the official movement away from dharma and towards law. Short sections on the post-traditional and medieval legal developments of Hindu law are provided, focusing on the activities of commentators, digest writers, and philosophers. These new experts of Hindu legal tradition appear to have prepared the ground for the gradually increasing interaction with South Asian Muslim laws, the eventual reception of supposedly European concepts of law and the transition towards more explicitly English influences on Hindu law. But did these processes still operate within the conceptual framework of dharma, or to what extent had positivist temptations and ambitions taken over? The final section of this chapter contains a

[1] May (1985: 9) comments that dharma constitutes 'a by no means negligible factor of Hindu jurisprudence' and points out that it is 'still widely unknown outside its own tradition, in particular to Western jurists and legal philosophers'.

brief analysis of the impact of British legal administration on the conceptualizations of Hindu law. This stage of development definitely reflects positivist intervention and led to the emergence of a curious conceptual amalgam, Anglo-Hindu law. As a colonial construct, this represented a new official form of Hindu law for the convenience of British administrators, but what happened to the 'real' Hindu law?

Post-classical Commentaries and Digests

Given the 'house of cards' of the chronological situation (Larivière 1989, II: xx) and the multitude of 'floating traditions which are generally current among the learned' (Bühler 1975: xi), it remains impossible to give definite dates for the beginning or end of the post-classical period of Hindu law. While the borderline between this and the previous period remains fluid, dates of c. 200 AD to c. 1100 AD may be given for the later phases of the classical period, leading to the transition towards the medieval ages until c. 1700 and the subsequent British period.

A leading Indological expert, writing in 1928, described the later *smṛtis* as 'modern compilations of secondary importance' (Jolly 1975: 50) and provided a fairly detailed description and overview of all the texts known at the time.[2] He commented that '[n]one of these works deal with law proper (*vyavahāra*)' (ibid.: 51) and was not impressed with the late *smṛti* texts that had been created all over India. The growing mass of such texts in itself, as well as increasing evidence of contradictions between them, raised many questions. Diwan and Diwan (1993: 39) suggest that the commentaries and digests cover a period of roughly one thousand years from about AD 700 to 1700 and explain how the period may be divided:

> Till the 12th century, we find that the general tendency was to write commentaries (*tika*) on a particular *Smriti*, but from the 12th century onward the trend was to write Digests (*nibandha*) on several *Smritis*, and thereby to attempt to synthesise all the topics in the *Smritis*.

Pathak (1986: 7) provides a useful overview of why these new literary works were considered necessary, listing that '(a) The Smritis did not agree with each other; (b) The Smritis were often obscure; (c) The Smritis were silent on many points; (d) Most of the Smritis were in verse and not intelligible to the ordinary men.' Other legal textbook writers, working under the assumption that the *smṛtis* were codes of law, identified prominently the issue of gaps in the law—rather than contradictions within the increasingly crowded body of texts—as a

[2] Kuppuswami (1986: 23) refers briefly to the many fragments of *smṛti* texts which are only known from citations in later texts, a huge problem for Indological research in this field. Desai (1998: 42) emphasizes that a very large number of commentaries and digests were written during this period.

major factor responsible for the creation of new literary products.[3] Diwan and Diwan (1993: 39) offer a typical lawyers' explanation of why it was necessary to have yet more texts:

> In an ever-advancing society, a clear and systematic exposition of rules of law, legal concepts and principles was necessary. The rules of law enunciated in the *Smritis* were not always clear-cut and also they did not cover all situations. This was not all. One *Smriti* differed from another, and sometimes in the same *Smriti*, there were conflicting texts. Thus, the need arose for further analysis, systematisation and assimilation of law. This need was satisfied by the Commentators and Digest-writers.

Desai (1998: 37–8), similarly wedded to legalistic images of complete codification and extensive coverage of every gap, commented in 1958, at a time when codification was obviously prominent in lawyers' minds:

> However ponderous or exhaustive a code might be, it cannot provide for all varieties of matters or all situations that might crop up for consideration and this is particularly so of rules of procedure ... while the leading Smritikars gave elaborate rules on matters of substantive law, the rules of procedure which may be gathered from the extent work do not embrace all the heads of procedural law and are indeed wanting in fullness and scanty on some topics .... The provisions contained in these ancient treatises do not give any comprehensive code of procedure and there are a number of rules which must seem defective when judged by modern concepts.

Such comments confirm that the author did not focus deeply enough on why so many new texts were produced during the post-classical period, and what their purpose was. Diwan and Diwan (1993: 39) further describe the work of the digest writers, quoting also from other authors:

> However, even in the earlier period, the commentators, with a view to introducing order by synthesising the chaotic mess of *Smriti* [*sic*] rules and principles, adopted the style of digest writing. "The authors of the Commentaries and Digests assumed that the *Smritis* constitute a single body of law, one part of which supplants [*sic*] the other; every part of which, if properly understood, is capable of being reconciled with the other ... They modified and supplemented rules in the *Smritis*, in part by means of their own reasoning and in part in the light of usages that had grown up."[4] In the apt words of Mr. Justice Desai, "If the productive era of the *Dharmashastras* was the golden age of Hindu law, this was the period of critical inquiry, expansion and consolidation."[5]

[3] On details of these texts see Lingat (1973: 107ff.); Dasgupta (1973, Vol. I: 6). Kane (1968-77, I, Part 2); Kuppuswami (1986: 28-29).

[4] Here the authors cite from the eleventh edition of Mayne's *Hindu Law*, p. 40.

[5] This is a quote from the fourteenth edition of Mulla's *Principles of Hindu Law*, p. 41.

This long passage with its various quotations seeks to illustrate the intentions of the commentators, but merely throws some light on how their efforts were treated and evaluated by much later generations of lawyers trained in the English legal tradition. Pathak (1986: 7) indicates more cautiously that various conflicts between the *smṛtis* 'were inevitable as they had been written at different times. The Smritis had embodied the usages of their times and the difference in the usages led to a conflict between them'. Such a statement does not explicitly claim that law-making was necessary, but still emphasizes the perceived need for harmonization of textual rules.

Views among scholars over how such discrepancies and confusions were resolved, if at all, appear to be divided. Desai (1998:42) envisaged on the one hand a planned legal process 'which naturally helped the rational development of law', while emphasizing almost in the same breath a totally contradictory point, namely that '[t]he commentators did not at any time arrogate to themselves the position of lawmakers'. The duality of this purported law-making process and the internal contradiction within the statement is striking. Are these still efforts to circumscribe dharma, rather than just a fine-tuning of the law? Desai (1998: 42) offers merely a glimpse of this issue:

> Nevertheless their thought was to fashion the law into as perfect an instrument of justice as they could devise albeit within certain absolute formulae of the Smriti law and as far as possible by analogy to what was already settled and on lines parallel with usages and customs which were springing unconsciously from the habits and life of the people in their part of the country.

It is not clear what this reference to the 'absolute formulae of the Smriti law' is supposed to imply. Is this a subtle recognition of the fact that the authors of commentaries, in particular, were torturing themselves (and their eventual puzzled readers, centuries later, in East and West) in order to ascertain dharma in a variety of difficult situations? The modern writers of Hindu law textbooks, so much is evident, did not really think deeply about this issue. They have merely raced to the conclusion that sooner rather than later, the commentaries became authoritative sources of law in their own right, replacing the old *smṛti* texts.[6] But that legal position was only established by colonial rule, it did not naturally grow out of the old Hindu law.

What appears to have happened well before that, during the post-classical period of Hindu law, is that the confusions over textual authority and the diversity of opinions became more pronounced, and ultimately unbearable, for those who wanted to make use of the texts as a source of guidance. Through the constant addition of new *smṛti* texts, commentaries, and later the digests, the textual basis of post-classical Hindu law became so convoluted and outrightly messy that Hindu law turned literally into a morass of texts, from which

[6] The relevant section from Desai (1998: 43) is cited in a later section on medieval texts in this chapter.

virtually anything could be justified. This confused diversity, in addition to questions about the authority of the texts and conflicts between customs and texts, led to various attempts to decrease diversity and plurality. None of those strategies proved workable, nor would uniformity have been considered desirable.[7] Derrett (1968b: 221) recognized that there was an underlying pull towards some sense of unity and depicts this as a form of 'Hinduization': 'The system described was groping for unity. The *śāstra* was preaching cultural and jurisprudential harmony if not homogeneity. Gradually anomalous customs began to give way.'

This is quite a different issue from the above-cited purported attempts by law-obsessed experts to construct a uniform legal system. Desai (1998: 38) indicates that the *smṛti* authors themselves were especially conscious of conflicts between the various texts. In their efforts to achieve some kind of harmonization and unification—given that the underlying cultural aim of all this activity remained the constant search for criteria of appropriateness, for the *ātmanastusti* and *sadācāra* of classical Hindu law—the post-classical *smṛti* experts resorted to several techniques to iron out or explain away textual discrepancies. Pathak (1986: 7) lists three major rules for reconciliation of conflicting texts, as stipulated in the *Bṛhaspatismṛti*, *Nāradasmṛti* and *Yājñavalkyasmṛti* and helpfully reports that these three texts advocate quite different methods. While the *Bṛhaspatismṛti* stipulates that the rules given in the *Manusmṛti* possess superior authority,[8] the *Nāradasmṛti* is said to appeal to reason, while the *Yājñavalkyasmṛti* suggests that in cases of disagreement one should follow *nyāya*, translated here as 'equity ... guided by the people of old', which Pathak defines as 'natural equity and reason' (id.).

Desai (1998: 38) also reports that *Bṛhaspatismṛti* 27.3 was taken to insist that any text which contradicted the *Manusmṛti* should not be approved. However, rather than leading to uniformity and some form of streamlining, diversity was increased. Desai (id.) writes that in actual practice, this maxim was not strictly followed, and effect was at times given to later *smṛti* texts, on the ground that they were more in accordance with approved usage or by applying some principle of textual exegesis. Kuppuswami (1986: 24) confirms that '[o]ne rule, which has not always been observed, is that where the Code of Manu and other Smritis conflict, Manu's view prevails as against the other Smritis'. Thus, uniformizing attempts to establish practical guidelines on the relative authority of texts simply did not succeed in practice. It follows that the widespread assertion that the *Manusmṛti* is the universally binding code of law for all

[7] Derrett (1968b: 177 and 206) notes that the shastra turned a blind eye to the customs of non-Aryan peoples and showed 'marvellous unconcern' (p. 192) for some developments, concluding that 'this apparent unreality of the *śāstra* is no accident' (id.). Rather than seeking to subjugate all subalterns to high-caste Hindu norms, it appears that the dominant policy focused on compartmentalization.

[8] This is further evidence that the *Manusmṛti* was given superior authority in the post-classical system.

Hindus is clearly not maintainable on the evidence before us, despite many tall claims.[9]

Methodological Strategies to Harmonize Texts and Customs

The methodological intricacies pursued by the various authors of this period have been discussed under a number of further headings, some of which are briefly mentioned here.[10] Derrett (1968b: 86) writes that '[i]nterpretation alone could work marvels' and proceeds to discuss various tricks from the experts' repertoire. The fact that so many textual statements contradicted another *smṛti* should not have caused much concern given the holistic and outrightly pluralistic principle of *ekavākyatā*, according to which all the sages spoke really as one voice and thus were in harmony (Derrett 1986b: 86). According to this view, all the texts could only proclaim aspects of the same ultimate truth. However, manifest discrepancies gave rise to various techniques designed to make one statement superior to the other—or to explain away what one did not like. Kuppuswami (1986: 24) stated that the commentators, 'bound as they were to the orthodox rule to treat every text in the Smritis as equally valid, were obliged to adopt a different process of reconciliation by treating some as ARTHAVADA and others as relating to different subjects'. The distinction of *vidhi* (injunction) and *arthavāda* (explanatory material) and its practical use is also made by Diwan and Diwan (1993: 37):[11]

> Whatever text they considered to be inappropriate or inconvenient, they interpreted it in a manner as to appear to contain only explanatory material. This method of discussion ... was further fortified by another rule of interpretation, viz., if a rule was stated without reason in the *Smritis*, the rule was merely *arthvada* and if a rule was stated with accompanying reasons, it was *vidhi*.

[9] Many of these assertions about the pre-eminence of the *Manusmṛti* rely on Privy Council decisions, not on scholarship of classical Hindu law.

[10] Derrett (1968b: 75–96) is excellent on this topic and contains, at pp. 95–6, a section on 'distress *dharma*' (*āpaddharma*), a collection of rules about coping with exceptional circumstances. Derrett (1963c: 3) rightly emphasizes that being an expert in *dharmaśāstra* demanded knowledge of many different fields and asserts a little too confidently (from a lawyer's perspective that would not be shared by traditional Sanskrit grammarians, for example) that 'its majesty as the queen of all sciences was never disputed'.

[11] Treating this as an 'abstruse' method, Derrett (1968b: 8) remarks that '[o]ne is left with the conviction ... that each jurist approached the text from his own standpoint, and that those who were concerned with the practical application of the law did their utmost to expound the texts so that inconvenient or inappropriate rules should be seen as explanatory or subordinate matter'. On the role of this device, see also Baxi (1986b: 6–7).

This distinction between rules of greater and lesser authority, binding injunction, and descriptive account of how a problem may be solved, became a major device for harmonising texts and social reality (Derrett 1968b: 87–8). It allowed the authors and collectors of new *smṛti* material to develop rules in accordance with new preferences or their own taste, no doubt allowing an increasing amount of personal opinion to masquerade as authoritative rule. Given the complexities of Hindu law, all of these efforts indicate recognition of the many gaps between theory and practice. There are many attempts to make such gaps smaller (for examples see Derrett 1968b: 192 and 196). Statements in texts are now more closely related to actual problems, sometimes to legal cases in which appropriate solutions are sought by reference to texts (Derrett 1962: 17).

The interesting (and clever) device of declaring older and now unacceptable practices as *kalivarjya*, prohibited in the *kaliyuga*, the current immoral and bad era of human existence, was particularly used to circumnavigate textual statements that would seem obnoxious to later generations (Derrett 1968b: 88–9). For example, it was difficult to accept, later, that ancient sages apparently enjoyed eating beef, or that great women like Draupadī in the epic Mahābhārata could be married to five brothers at the same time.[12] Various devices to explain away such unpalatable evidence show concern to use the older texts as guiding models also in a new setting. As today, rewriting the ancient texts can never have been a realistic endeavour, but later generations of Hindu specialists certainly engaged in creative reinterpretation and much textual reconstruction. Of this we know far too little, because all these difficult texts are in Sanskrit and remain mostly untranslated. The late classical period is rich in a virtually unexplored literature of commentaries.

Diwan and Diwan (1993: 37) explain that the *kalivarjya* theory was developed to avoid conflict and to treat some texts as not binding. This theory holds the view that certain rules in the *smṛtis* later became obsolete and were to be avoided in the *kali* age.[13] Bhattacharjee (1994: 24) particularly highlights the fact that this technique challenged the 'theory of the divine origin of the scriptural laws'. Thus, this doctrine (ibid.: 25),

[12] See in detail Datta (1979). Current evidence in India that the Gurjjars of Rajasthan have begun to practise polyandry again, mainly because there is such a shortage of women in certain communities, but also for economic reasons, has led to mixed reactions. See *India Today*, 1 September 2001: 46–8 and the hostile email comments of readers in *India Today*, 17 September 2001: 4.

[13] Diwan and Diwan (1993: 37) also refer to the technique of holding certain texts as not binding on the ground that they are intolerable to the public (*loka viviṣṭa*). This links well with concepts of 'public interest', to which the traditional Hindu textbook writers evidently paid little attention, given that they were focused on positivist concepts of law and on the envisaged lawmakers rather than the wider public and its concerns. Derrett (1968b: 181) provides some early evidence that 'public opinion' was recognized and also makes reference to the consideration of 'public interest' by concerned political authorities (ibid.: 96).

> clearly goes to show that even the Hindu Jurists themselves did not regard the sacred laws of the scriptures to be divine and sacrosanct and could think of directing their avoidance to meet the changes of the society .... The so-called laws were not something imposed upon the society from outside by any divine will and revelation and recorded as such in the *Smritis.* But these laws were something which developed within the society on their own strength and changed with the changing needs of the society.

This turns into a useful discussion on the spontaneous growth of law itself, though most other legal authors did not go that far in their analysis. Derrett (1968b: 88) finds the *kalivarjya* technique 'a most interesting notion, which rid the law of a number of archaisms (ritual and legal alike)'. Derrett (1968b: 88–9) suggests:

> The commencement of this theory may have been a refusal to accept as binding legal precedents certain apparently immoral acts which the admired gods, heroes and legendary sages indulged in. In traditional language, their strength derived from spiritual merit was so much greater than ours that they could withstand the effects of such lawlessness. But a simpler point of view questioned the relevance of conduct that was good enough for those remote ages as our guide at present.

It is evident, however, that the enormous variety of customary laws was not reduced through the involvement of later commentators and their juristic speculations. Thus, as Baxi (1986b: 7) reports, Lingat (1973) warned against the assumption that custom was in any way canonized. Hence, it seems certain that in the purported search for legal development and certainty in post-classical Hindu law, no single text could achieve universally recognized code status. Neither the enormous textual diversity, nor the amazingly complex customary plurality, could in any way be centrally controlled and uniformed. The confusion, if it was even perceived as such, given the principle of *ekavākyatā*, only got worse.

Another important strategy to harmonize and uniformize the ancient textual sources, attempted with immense cerebral investment, is known under the collective term of *mīmāṃsā*. This was originally a term for the classical Hindu science of interpretation of Vedic ritual texts, comprising several ancient techniques and principles of textual exegesis, which were at first used to explore finer details of Vedic mantras or ritual pronouncements.[14] Developing originally from philosophical concern over precise ritual interpretations in the Vedic context, and thus ideologically linked to belief in the sanctity and supremacy of the Vedas, the scientific logic-based techniques of *mīmāṃsā* eventually came

[14] For some details see also Diwan and Diwan (1993: 38). Kuppuswami (1986: 25–7) is quite detailed on this subject and puts the date of some early specialist writers at about 600 BC.

to be seen as an important tool of 'legal' interpretation.[15] As to how that happened, Pathak (1986: 7) merely writes:

> Mimamsa is a science of interpretation, especially of scriptures. Assistance was derived in the task of interpretation of the texts from the rules of Mimamsa of which Jaimini was the greatest exponent. The Mimamsakas were not merely experts on interpretation but also logicians.

Diwan and Diwan (1993: 38) explain that, using logical methods, the main writers developed a variety of interpretative concepts, including one based on the 'literal construction' of texts, so that the eminent British scholar Colebrooke later found that '[t]he logic of Mimansa is the logic of the law' (id.).[16] Derrett et al. (1979: 33) suggest that the special qualifications of the *mīmāṃsā* experts gave rise to an intricate mental system that was eventually wide enough to include secular questions and legal issues. In fact, a legal branch of *mīmāṃsā* developed which had immense influence on the shastra and continues to influence current scholarship.[17] Lingat (1973: 143) argued that the mental labours of the commentators, and in particular the *mīmāṃsā* experts, were a key factor in the emergence of a 'true juridical science' in India, thus marking and facilitating the eventual segregation of law from dharma.[18] Baxi (1986b: 7) suggests that in this process, experts were originally more concerned with harmonizing textual rules and social reality than with achieving textual harmony or producing binding legal rules:

> ... the juristic concern with interpretation, overtly analytical and exegetical though it may appear, continually made *sastric* precepts responsive to social realities, within which they had to function as rules for conduct. Sometimes, such interpretation legitimized local custom ...

This observation is fully confirmed by Derrett et al. (1979: 33–4) with a number of examples, leading to the conclusion that the involvement of *mīmāṃsā* techniques brought about a detailed examination of the relationship between shastra and custom, and a wide-reaching revision of the latter. As a result, many local customs were treated as devoid of dharmic authority and were declared unauthoritative and even abominable.[19] The effect was similar to the application of the *kalivarjya* techniques. However, Derrett (1968b: 193) points out that the jurists did not go the whole way with the *mīmāṃsā* specialists. It seems

[15] Desai (1998: 40) writes that '[s]tudy of Mimamsa was regarded as an integral and essential part of the study of the Shastras'.

[16] On this see also Desai (1998: 40).

[17] Olivelle (2000: 15) distinguishes epistemological and theological definitions.

[18] Lingat (1973: 143–75) discussed the *mīmāṃsā* techniques in much detail.

[19] The technical term, given by Derrett et al. (1979: 35) is *durācāra*. Examples would include the drinking of alcohol by Brahmin women, or marriage with the daughter of a maternal uncle, which is incest according to some texts, but binding custom in some parts of south India.

that the ground was being prepared here for later declarations by judicial personnel, refusing to legally recognize certain customs.

The theoretical claim that the shastra alone, and thus textual experts, determined what was dharma and what was not, led to different approaches in the understanding of *ācāra* as a source of dharma. The discussion in Derrett et al. (1979: 37) explicitly recognizes that much local customary law remained outside the definitional grasp and immediate concern of the *mīmāṃsā* experts. In addition, there continued to be a well-recognized but perhaps not sufficiently documented basic rule that local custom, even in derogation of the *smṛti* texts, would prevail. This view of the matter suggests that *mīmāṃsā* scholarship as a theoretical edifice helped to highlight the basic division between an official shastric system of rules and multiple local normative orders, but achieved comparatively little in terms of harmonization.[20] It remained a theoretical construct of great sublimity, while social reality continued to be very diverse. Diwan and Diwan (1993: 38) report that the use of highly technical methods of logic and their application to 'law' has not been without controversy:

> The question whether they apply to the *vyavahara* portion has been a subject of debate among scholars. There is no doubt that they have been used by the Commentators and the Digest-writers in interpreting the *vyavahara* portion of the *Smritis* and in reconciling the conflicting *Smriti* texts.

Desai (1998: 39) confirms that the rules of exegesis 'were applied, though not with uniformity, in construction of texts also of Vyavahara or municipal law' and provides details of the various rules that were developed over time. As a complex body of rules arose, this was seen as a remarkable achievement in its own right. The analysis found in Desai (1998: 40–1) contains excellent pointers for the present discussion. It certainly does much more than simply glorify this period, as one might assume at first:

> In the history of Hindu law ... it was the post-Smriti period during which Hindu law and jurisprudence reached a remarkable stage of progress and assimilation .... This was the period of critical inquiry, expansion and consolidation. The ancient aphorisms of the Sutrakars and the earlier Smritis were compiled when the spiritual motive dominated life. The Smritis though accepted as 'revelations remembered' were themselves partially based on usages and practices ... as were approved by the conscience of the virtuous and followed by the people ... Usage when established outweighed the written text of law. The Smriti law had a rational synthesis ....

Desai's argumentation clearly recognizes the continuing importance of the *ṛta*/dharma complex during this period. Highlighting the internal contradiction between belief in the revealed ultimate sources of the *smṛti* on the one hand and customary norms on the other, he claims that the major contribution

[20] Kuppuswami (1986: 28) argues that the *mīmāṃsā* rules are now of doubtful utility.

of the post-*smṛti* period lies in harmonizing textual rules and customary norms, which is portrayed here as a secularising process and a 'rational synthesis'. But it is one thing to envisage more formal recognition for local customary norms and quite another to develop a formal legal system. The inherent flexibility and immense internal diversity of customary laws does not centrally concern Desai in his analysis but is mentioned in passing. That matter must have troubled most experts of *mīmāṃsā*, especially later generations, as they saw their exalted methodology gradually slip into a position of arcane expertise of little direct social relevance, reserved for a few specialists. Ultimately, nobody could survive simply as an expert of *mīmāṃsā*; other, apparently more secular issues gained greater importance. It also seems that some *mīmāṃsā* experts became commentators on shastric texts, so that their methodological tools were thus redeployed in a more practical manner.

Derrett's (1968b) views on the process of interaction between text and custom, filtered through a class of partly self-interested experts, were cited earlier. Desai (1998: 41) argues that the *mīmāṃsā* experts were eventually assisted by the commentators, 'who did not hesitate to interpret and mould the ancient texts so as to suit the needs of a progressive society'. By introducing new texts and a commentary literature, thus, another rule-building process began to evolve, which many later legal authors have seen as approaching proper law, away from dharmic domination. They could do this primarily by envisaging and arguing that the *smṛtis* were legal texts, focused on secular matters. Desai (1998: 41) portrays this well:

> A comprehensive and homologous view of the contents of the Smritis required synthesising of what was at times presented in an unsystematic form .... Some of the rules of Smriti law expressed general principles .... A number of rules were of the nature of maxims of the law, ... a species of legal shorthand requiring interpretation and exposition in the light of expert knowledge. Moreover, the fixed and authoritative formulae of which the Smriti texts were embodiments suffered from the same defects to which any *litera legis* is subject ... differences and even some conflicts of opinion on points of law were naturally to be expected.

All of this suggests that the process of legal development envisaged here simply concerns a formal system of legal rules. There is no explicit recognition of the dharmic dimension or of the difficulty, as May (1985: 12) saw it, of distinguishing between 'a perspective of reality and one of ideality'. Declaring the *smṛti* texts as *litera legis*, an undefined category of legal literature, looks like an elegant device to evade the crucial question: Were these commentators really engaged in making law, or were they still testing situations for compliance with dharma? Or did they perhaps aim for both at the same time? Desai (1998: 41) continues an explicitly law-centred approach and suggests that the *smṛti* authors themselves 'realised the various difficulties in the way of evolving one system of law out of numerous Smritis'. This image is continued in his description of the commentaries which, 'being dissertations on law had in the nature of things to take notice of all this' (id.) and, in Desai's view, really excelled in their various tasks. However, this was not a process without pitfalls, as Desai (1998: 42) confirms:

> There can be no doubt that the commentators at times stretched points, took precepts out of their context and on occasions gave strained interpretations to rules. As far as possible they tried to bring out the true import of the ancient texts but at times they made logic yield to convenience and clearness. Sometimes the reason given in support of an accepted construction would seem to be a sophism but their ingenuity was at times taxed to the utmost.

Without wishing to deny the partial ingenuity of this collective exercise and the many individual efforts, what were the perceived benefits of all this text torturing? Desai (1998: 42) clearly envisaged this process as contributing to 'the rational development of law', but his analysis is riddled with contradictions. Recognizing the absence of a system of authoritative or persuasive judicial precedents in classical Hindu law, and reporting correctly that the commentators did not see themselves as lawmakers, Desai (id.) finally pronounces on the intentions of the commentators:

> Nevertheless their thought was to fashion the law into as perfect an instrument of justice as they could devise albeit within certain absolute formulae of the Smriti law and as far as possible by analogy to what was already settled and on lines parallel with usages and customs which were springing unconsciously from the habits and life of the people in their part of the country. Although in form merely commentaries on the ancient Smritis and complementary [*sic*] to the same these treatises were independent works which embodied the law current at the time.

The results, as perceived by later practice-focused lawyers, were literary codifications of law, an image reinforced by further references to commentaries written under the patronage of kings, acquiring special importance in this way for legal administration. However, the picture might be quite different if one looks at the same material from the perspective of Indological rather than legal scholarship. For example, a perusal of the various commentaries on *Manusmṛti* 1.1ff. (Bühler 1975: 1–3) shows clearly that those later authors and commentators were not exclusively concerned with law, but operated as holistic philosophers with a much wider agenda. Jolly (1975: 66) wrote that the works of the *mīmāṃsā* school 'may in a certain sense be considered as explanatory works on the Smritis; the aim of this school was to explore the Dharma and to investigate the essence of Smriti and its relation to Śruti theoretically and practically'. This wording does not give the impression that *mīmāṃsā* scholarship is as legally focused as the later Anglo-centric legal experts imagined. Derrett (1968b: 199–200), too, retained a holistic perspective, writing that '[a]ll the available sources, of whatever quality and authenticity, attempt to restate Duty, including many legal details, in a more current form than that to be found in the sources they imitate or plagiarize'.

In an important study on the concept of duty in ancient Indian jurisprudence in O'Flaherty and Derrett (1978), Derrett clearly states at p. 55 that 'the wisdom of past generations was brought to bear by specialists whose conscious function was not that of legislation but pronouncement. They did not innovate—they were mouthpieces'.[21] There is a need to research such material in more depth, but this is precisely the kind of legal topic which academics, let alone practising lawyers with their focus on doctrinal law, have long since ignored.[22] In the discussion on the above topics, as produced by Desai (1998: 43), the logical next step is therefore to proceed to a heading 'Systematic building up of the law' and to steer the discussion to the late medieval and British periods with their creation of two principal schools of Hindu law, as discussed later. This amazing intellectual process, ultimately coagulating an immeasurably complex cosmic and chthonic legal perspective into two tangible texts of law, reflects the transition from classical Hindu law to its post-classical manifestation. But is this new book law still Hindu law, or is it merely a legal fiction created by the application of law-centred axioms, cultivated in the minds of legal writers who looked over all of this many centuries after the events?

While the standard legal textbooks offer no proper answer to such questions and remain fixed on law-centred assumptions, Baxi (1986b: 10) reports that even Professor Lingat (1973) had denied that classical Hindu law developed law in the sense of legislation and binding case law:

> Lingat does not feel that the royal recognition of custom constitutes any exercise of legislative power: such recognition is not an act of the legislator but rather one of the administrator "concerned to keep peace between the subjects". Lingat even suggests (here following Yajnavalkya) that even when thus royally recognized, an individual to whom custom applies may disobey it on the ground that it conflicts with the precepts of *dharma* (ibid., 228–29). Nor, finally, does the exercise of judicial power by the king result in any positive law: "even though his judgements are law-in-action they remain singular and unrelated, staccato, without any future" (ibid., 259).

From Lingat's perspective, whatever law-like manifestations there may have been in late classical India did not satisfy his criterion of proper 'law', which applies positivist standards. Lingat reaches his conclusions, which in my view are correct, given his narrow definition of law, through a combination of criteria, matching his application of external criteria for the definition of law with

[21] Derrett, in the same article in O'Flaherty and Derrett (1978: 55) goes on to emphasize that this remains relevant today: 'The prestige of such a method of ascertaining duty is evidenced even today by the popularity of *dharma* pronounced by traditional orthodox leaders, public recitals of scripture, and allusions to such criteria in nostalgic speeches and articles by public men. That they are not *articulate* in public life, however, is all too evident'.

[22] See, however, the detailed study by Derrett (1975a), in a field that abounds with untranslated Sanskrit texts and sources whose precise role remains largely unexplored.

recognition of internal methods of Hindu law. Thus, Lingat seems to have understood that even a royal declaration does not ultimately bind the Hindu individual, whose supervening loyalty should always be to the *ṛta*/dharma complex, while decisions of judges, too, would not acquire the power of precedent, but merely decided the case in hand, based on its particular facts and circumstances. Baxi (1986b: 10) thus concludes:

> Thus, by and large, we have here a denial that the classical Hindu law knew any 'positive' law, enacted by a 'sovereign' and, entitled to obedience on that very ground alone. The authority which sustained law was *dharma*, transcendent and immutable, an eternal moral law of interdependence which no one could conscientiously disobey.

In my view, this interpretation still expresses the binding nature of the *ṛta*/dharma complex a little too strictly. It overlooks the possibility (or rather, the fact) that many 'Hindus'—and at any rate many people at the fringes of Hinduism as a collection of sects and belief systems—might very well disregard what dharma suggested. Here we return to the ancient debate over who determines what is appropriate. As illustrated earlier in the section on the role of custom in Chapter 3, the ultimate test of what is right and wrong in the Hindu system depends more on individual conscience and *sadācāra* than on textual rules. Finding the appropriate answer relies on individualized assessments of situation-specific problems, not on application of fixed legal rules. This scenario works against attempts by the state to lay down rules and would legitimize total subversion of any form of purported 'official' law. Regrettably, Baxi (1986b: 10) did not pursue this issue, but insisted that Lingat's view of the absence of positive 'law' in ancient India should be questioned in view of the evidence provided by texts like the *Arthaśāstra*, which contained, in Baxi's view, at least the normative idea of the science of positive law. Was Professor Baxi a little too concerned not to underwrite a claim that the ancient Hindus did not have law?

Nobody denies, I think, that the ancient Hindus were capable of conceiving of law in a positivist manner. They constantly experienced rudimentary forms of positive law in the shape of local rule by heads of families and all kinds of strong men, more or less powerful little rulers. After all, they lived in a largely patriarchal environment, and like for their Greek cousins, abuses of power must have been part of the lived experience. Ancient Hindus must have been aware, as are Hindus today, that naked power could all too easily be abused. The transition from *ṛta* to dharma and the consequent involvement of all aspects of human life in the giant spider webs of macrocosmic order and microcosmic order, as discussed earlier in Chapter 3, also had the effect of subordinating all forms of human law-making to the higher pre-existing order. The logical consequence of the acceptance of cosmic interlinkedness, which was of course never total and complete even among people who are supposed to be 'Hindu',[23] was that any form of positive law-making could not be the final legal authority. Regrettably, Baxi's discussion (1986b: 10) is sidetracked by the issue of 'legality' and thus does not answer the questions that the current debate is concerned with. Suggesting that legislation existed in the late classical period and was made use of, Derrett (1968b: 96) wrote:

> ... the political authority has in fact supplemented and contradicted the *dharmaśāstra* where it seemed necessary in the public interest. The academic effort of bringing legislation into alignment with the *śāstra* was contemplated by Medhātithi amongst others. But the method chosen, as we shall see, was to argue that the *śāstra* contemplated only such legislation as its own silences rendered necessary, and there only provided that Vedic authority and valid custom knew nothing to the contrary. The capacity to legislate irrespective of śāstric authority undoubtedly existed, and was utilized in countless precedents before the coming of the British.

If we can take any indications from more recent Hindu practice, collective reference to 'the Vedas' as an authoritative corpus of texts has a long tradition as a standard strategy to back up the opinion of a learned individual (which, therefore, takes us back to *sadācāra*), already much before the British employed learned Hindu pandits to help them ascertain what they thought were the rules of Hindu law. The above analysis by Derrett does not challenge the elevated status of the Vedas as a matter of belief but he suggests, like other legal commentators, that the shastra had left gaps to fill, providing room for the growth of 'secular' law. But does his assertion that there was undoubtedly 'capacity to legislate irrespective of śāstric authority' therefore also assume that there were areas of life that the *ṛta*/dharma complex did not reach?

This secularized view of the ambit of Hindu law is reflected, as we have begun to see, throughout the specialist literature on Hindu law. It gained strength with reference to later periods of Hindu law and relies, as the sources appear to demonstrate, more on the secularized interpretation of key concepts like *artha*, *arthaśāstra*, *vyavahāra,* and *rājaśāsana* by outsiders and commentators many centuries later, rather than on the perceptions of socio-legal

[23] Recent debates in India about the wisdom (and political motivation in terms of alleged saffronization) of introducing astrology as an academic subject clearly demonstrate that there can be no agreement about the existence of cosmic interlinkedness itself. The editor-in-chief of *India Today* (17 September 2001: 1) calls it 'a regressive subject' and significantly refers to an environment of 'essentially modern ambiguity about the field'. At another level of debate, which the present study has also highlighted as critically contested, the same editorial discloses modern discomfort with individual freedom and uses the argument that 'astrology with its emphasis on individual interpretation can hardly constitute a science' (id.). This pointed attack on individual discretion indicates modernist, absolutist discomfort with the critical importance of the individual mind in understanding what can ultimately not be understood. It also displays ignorance of how human society, from a Hindu perspective, is presumed to function.

actors in late classical and medieval Hindu law. All of these later distortions have one crucial thing in common: they envisage growing scope for more or less purely secular law-making and have thus instigated a conceptual division of the internalized *ṛta*/dharma basis and externally imported scholarly superstructures. The next section demonstrates that the relevant medieval Hindu texts themselves, and their later commentators, operate on quite different conceptual levels. Thus, the process of intellectual debate and further distortion of Hindu law continued, in fact with special vigour, during the periods prior to Muslim and later British intervention.

Medieval Texts and their Purported Secularization

It is evident that during the post-classical 'dark ages' which extend throughout medieval times, Hindu law did not wither away but became somewhat fossilized and eventually, so the legal literature suggests, more specifically secular and 'legal' in its methods. But to what extent is this, again, a scholarly construct rather than a process that reflects the realities of Hindu law?

Earlier texts like the *Manusmṛti* were clearly anonymous products of accretion over time, despite impressive assertions of individual authorship. Later texts can be more or less firmly ascribed to individual authors, often high-ranking officials with expert status in the administration of justice (Lingat 1973: 110). This also goes for much of the commentary literature.[24] In all the leading legal textbooks on Hindu law, one finds the argument that the later texts, in due course, totally superseded the earlier ones.[25] However, this reasoning is based on statements by judges of the Privy Council, offering a glimpse of solid evidence for the massive distortion of Hindu law by lawyers, who also managed, through the same process, to deprive the entire range of classical shastric writing of direct relevance for legal studies. At a stroke, classical Sanskrit-based learning lost much of its earlier rank, since the later works would be available in English and their principles could eventually be gleaned from reported Anglo-Hindu case law. Nobody has written openly about this significant intellectual impact, but it is one of the major outcomes of such scholarly reasoning that Hindu legal tradition was virtually suffocated.

Several examples can be provided here to support my argument. The rather dramatic development that the old system of sources of dharma, viz. *śruti* and *smṛti*, was now replaced by a secularized understanding of the sources of law,

[24] On the commentary literature see in detail Kane (1968–7) and Jolly (1975: 66ff.). The commentaries on the *Manusmṛti* are briefly discussed by Diwan and Diwan (1993: 40–1) and Kuppuswami (1986: 29–30). The commentaries on the *Yājñavalkyasmṛti* are described by Diwan and Diwan (1993: 41–2) and by Kuppuswami (1986: 30–3). The various regional authorities are outlined by Diwan and Diwan (1993: 42–4), Kuppuswami (1986: 33–7) and Desai (1998: 49–55).

[25] Kuppuswami (1986: 28) points out that the commentary works and digests 'claim, and are admitted to possess, an independent authority'.

is indicated by Diwan and Diwan (1993: 39). These authors clearly took the view, already discussed in an earlier section, that the commentators perfected the body of shastric writing and thus concluded, based on later statements by the Privy Council (PC), that '[s]uch has been the masterly handling of the subject by the Commentators and Digest-writers that Digests and Commentaries in effect superseded both the *Shruti* and the *Smriti*' (id.). Discussing the practical importance of the commentators, Desai (1998: 59) asserted that 'when legislation in the modern sense was not originated and judicial precedents as now understood had no established authority, these juristheologians were virtually law-makers who systematised the personal law of the Hindus.

Desai (1998: 43) envisaged a systematic law-building process in which, almost by default, the commentators found themselves in the role of lawmaker, even if this was not their original intention.[26] This reformulation of textual statements and the production of new texts was also perceived as harmonization of customary laws, so that the authors were 'always having regard to rules of conduct and practices reflected in approved usage' (id.). Kuppuswami (1986: 28–9) explains this process and its consequences in more detail with reference to the various techniques discussed in the preceding section:

> The authors of the Commentaries and Digests assume that the Smritis constitute a single body of law, one part of which supplements the other, and every part of which, if properly understood, is capable of being reconciled with the other. They discarded what had become obsolete ... in the present Kali age .... They did their work so well that their Commentaries and Digests have in effect superseded the Smritis in very large measure.

While these rather general statements are made for a whole class of literature, the specialist authors on Hindu law have ultimately focused on two important texts, the *Dāyabhāga* of Jīmūtavāhana, an independent work of commentary on property law,[27] and Vijñāneśvara's *Mitākṣarā*.[28] The *Dāyabhāga* purports to be like a digest. It is 'a valuable dissertation on the law of inheritance and partition and is believed to be a part of a larger work known as Dharmaratna' (Desai 1998: 56). The author of this work is described as a 'progressive jurisconsult some of whose interpretations were in all probability tinged by established usages and must naturally have found favour with the Hindus of Bengal' (ibid.: 57).

[26] As pointed out earlier, Desai (1998: 42) claims that the commentators 'did not at any time arrogate to themselves the position of lawmakers'.

[27] On this see Desai (1998: 55–7) and Diwan and Diwan (1993: 43). Colebrooke (1984) provides a translation and publication dating originally from 1810, covering both texts. Much detail is contained in Sontheimer (1977) and Dammann (1993). An excellent new edition, analysis, and translation of the *Dāyabhāga* is now found in Rocher (2002).

[28] For details see Jolly (1975: 68–9), Kuppuswami (1986: 31) and especially Desai (1998: 45–7). Pawate (1975) is a specialist study of this text and its practical application.

Both texts appear to have been composed just after 1100, probably around 1120–25 (Rocher 2002: 24). It appears that they came to be used as a point of reference when the British took over the legal administration of India, and these texts acquired an interesting role under the Anglo-Indian system of legal administration.[29] It is evident that their superior status in the eyes of lawyers is due to the attention eventually lavished upon those two texts by Colebrooke and, in due course, the PC. Desai (1998: 43) hurries along blinkered paths, rushing to establish a connection between the envisaged processes of law-making and the eventual recognition of only two major schools of Hindu law as perceived by the British:

> So in course of time the law came to be ascertained and accepted in the main from the commentaries and digests of which the leading ones acquired almost *ex cathedra* character .... Facts of geography were massive and in different parts of the country different commentaries came to be referred to as the chief guides on law. The result was that the two principal schools of Hindu law, the Mitakshara and the Dayabhaga sprang into existence ....

This sudden 'springing into existence' seems to be an overstatement. A clue to relevant external factors is given by Desai (1998: 43), who explains how the PC eventually phrased the dominant, and henceforth official, legal position regarding the schools of Hindu law. It appears, therefore, that the resultant image of two major Hindu law schools is largely a British construct rather than an indigenous development.[30]

Diwan and Diwan (1993: 41) explain that Vijñāneśvara's *Mitākṣarā*, traditionally seen as the most important commentary on the *Yājñavalkyasmṛti*, was in reality more like an independent work with special emphasis on matters of property and succession. It was a South Indian work from Andhra Pradesh, composed according to P. V. Kane around 1100–1120.[31] Kuppuswami (1986: 31)

[29] Colebrooke (1984: i) emphasizes the practical importance of inheritance law and significantly expresses his disappointment over the limited usefulness of compilations commissioned from a learned pandit, Jagannatha, whose 'very ample compilation' (p. ii) had been translated into a *Digest of Hindu Law*. This was found to be of limited practical use since the learned pandits had cited so many different views on the same subject that it became extremely difficult to ascertain the law. Colebrooke (ibid.: iii) therefore argued that it was more useful to turn to 'the standard authorities of the Hindu law of inheritance in the schools of *Benares* and *Bengal* respectively' and thus appears to take these two works as codifications of the relevant law.

[30] Mahmood (1981: xli–xlii) suggests that '[f]rom the earliest years of the *Smriti* period of Hindu legal history, two distinct currents of legal thought had prevailed among the doctors of law', reflected in the eventual emergence of *Mitākṣarā* and *Dāyabhāga*. However, Rocher (2002: 21) clearly portrays Colebrooke's critical role in this process.

[31] Kuppuswami (1986: 31) reports that the latter part of the eleventh century is suggested by recent research and provides further details. Rocher (2002: 24) agrees with Derrett that the dates are about 1120–1125.

portrays the author as a great jurist and outlines how his treatise became a standard work and achieved, much later, an elevated legal standing throughout the subcontinent with the exception of Bengal and parts of Assam, where it was of some authority, too. While it would appear that this authoritative legal status is more the result of the involvement of Privy Council, and not a matter of popular agreement before the British arrived on the scene, Desai (1998: 46) blatantly inflates the importance of the *Mitākṣarā* which has for more than nine centuries occupied a place of ascendancy and authority unique and unrivalled in the annals of legal literature. To him, Vijñāneśvara was one of the greatest of the juristheologians who contributed to the making of Hindu law.

The author of the *Mitākṣarā* has also been praised as a real reformer of Hindu law. Kuppuswami (1986: 31) asserts that '[t]his far-seeing jurist and statesman, by practically freeing Hindu Law from its religious fetters and making it readily acceptable to all communities in all parts of India, established it on new foundations'.[32] This important issue is further explained by Kuppuswami (1986: 12–13) in a discussion of the limits of religious influence. He argues at p. 12 that '[t]he religious element in Hindu Law has been greatly exaggerated' and takes as an example that '[r]ules of inheritance were probably closely connected with the rules relating to the offering of funeral oblations in early times' (id.). Explaining, thus, that the traditional Hindu heir not only inherited property but also carried obligations towards the souls of the deceased, an intricate discussion is centred on the question whether inheritance of property is inevitably linked to religious obligations. Kuppuswami (1986: 12–13) argues:

> When the religious law and the civil law marched side by side, the doctrine of spiritual benefit was a living principle and the Dharmasastrin could coordinate the civil right and the religious obligations .... Vijnanesvara and those that followed him, by explaining that property is of secular origin and not the result of the Sastras and that right by birth is purely a matter of popular recognition, have helped to secularise Hindu Law enormously. Equally Vijnanesvara's revolutionary definition of sapinda relation as one connected with particles of body, irrespective of any connection with pinda offering, has powerfully helped in the same direction.

This intricate argument about the *Mitākṣarā*'s contribution to the secularization of Hindu law fails to explain quite how this transition between a religious and a secular system was made.[33] It is nevertheless quite clear as to how the

[32] See also Diwan and Diwan (1993: 41). Commentaries were, in turn, written on the *Mitākṣarā* during the medieval period. For some details see id., Kuppuswami (1986: 32) and Desai (1998: 46).

[33] Pawate (1975: ii) argues that the *Mitākṣarā* theory is older than the *Mitākṣarā* itself and even older than any work on *dharmaśāstra*. While that may be so, he also asserts that '[t]he great merit of Vijnaneshwara's work was that he insisted on the secular nature of the institution of property and indicated that the Smritis ... had had no hand in the making of the law of property'. This author also seeks to argue that the origins of such concepts are Dravidian rather than Aryan (p. v).

new legal regime operates. Thus, the phrase 'under present conditions' refers to the colonial state's rule of law model, which applies secular principles and thus becomes incapable of enforcing—and unwilling to implement—religious principles of Hindu law. But this segregation of law and religion merely proves that the new formal, official law took this particular perspective. It does not confirm with certainty that this was the original intention of the author of the *Mitākṣarā*. In other words, the present discussion does not resolve the question whether Hindu law experts themselves refuted and abandoned the *ṛta*/dharma complex, partly or as a whole. Whether or not they had argued that certain aspects of life could be seen from a secular angle—a perspective which is undoubtedly realistic, given the internal plurality of Hindu concepts—this particular element was later isolated and recycled by outsiders as a tool for the colonial administration of Hindu law. Here again, the construction of certain images by scholars or professional experts from outside seems to have occurred.[34] In fact, the process of declaring the *Mitākṣarā* so important and dominant looks remarkably similar to the earlier attempt of giving exalted status to the *Manusmṛti*, which is now being challenged.

The Indological scholar Julius Jolly (1975: 68) indicated that the great influence of the *Mitākṣarā* perhaps not only reflects that it became 'a standard work already at an early age in the Dekhan and also in Benares and a great part of North India', but also that 'even in the English period, it has exercised a great influence on modern judicature through Colebrooke's translation of that portion of it which deals with the law of inheritance' (id.).[35] Even more significantly, Jolly (1975: 69) argues that the fame for this work should be attributed more to the power and esteem of certain powerful south Indian princes and not to any intrinsic merit of the text itself, which contains a comprehensive system of dharma. This would appear to contradict the above-quoted assertions by Desai (1998) of the secular nature of the text and its message. Further research should be undertaken in this particular area. I am not convinced, at this stage, that the *Mitākṣarā* is the fountainhead of secularization of Hindu law.

Interestingly, Kuppuswami (1986: 31) observes, almost in an aside, that the long and anxious discussions in the *Mitākṣarā* about different types of succession indicate that its author 'found the law in a very unsettled condition'. While Kuppuswami uses this argument to emphasize the secularising and unifying impact of the text, the real effect was to highlight the existence of quite different patterns of inheritance and hierarchies of succession. The fact that one method was preferred over another does not mean that the customary diversity ceased to exist, it simply reflects the customary state of legal

[34] Kuppuswami (1986: 31) describes the *Mitākṣarā* as 'by far the most celebrated and authoritative of all the commentaries on the Yajnavalkya Smriti'.

[35] In a subsequent section on the impact of British legal administration, an examination of what Colebrooke said about the *Mitākṣarā* confirms that he preferred this fairly compact text to the unwieldy compilations produced by pandits in his time.

pluralism, given that various patrilineal and matrilineal patterns coexist in Hindu law even today. Vijñāneśvara's position as a southerner, working on the border between north and south, must have made him acutely aware of the totally contradictory patterns in this field of law. The conclusion that such a learned man's observations of differential customs should result in a secular perspective is not logically stringent. All he seems to have observed is that succession was a matter of popular recognition. As a Hindu, he must have been aware of the impact of *sadācāra* on this topic; his mind would not have rushed towards the secular principles that modernist outside observers have so prominently noted.

Much could be said about the developments in Hindu law during the middle ages, when many new compilations and digests (*nibandhas*) were produced.[36] Jolly (1975: 77) suggests that the fourteenth century was a period of invigorated growth of different scholarly traditions in places like Mithilā, 'highly important for the development of jurisprudence proper'. Diwan and Diwan (1993: 39) report that the last of the great commentaries on Hindu law is a work called *Vaijayantī*, a commentary on the *Viṣṇudharmasūtra*, composed by the learned Nandapandita in the seventeenth century. Such isolated statements here and there are mere snippets of information and prove nothing about the transition from dharma to law with which the present chapter is centrally concerned. It remains a fact, however, that this 'dark period' gave rise to masses of relevant textual material, most of which has neither been translated into European languages nor analysed in any detail.

While there can be no doubt that Hindu customary law continued to operate during this period as the main law in action, the development of Hindu texts did not come to a halt either. The various Hindu scholarly activities of text production and interpretation carried on throughout this period, and it does not appear that Hindu law declined in any significant way. It is simply our own deficient knowledge of this 'dark period' that makes it so difficult to come to any definite conclusions. The medieval centuries saw the collection of *smṛti* material into huge digests (or *nibandhas*) like the *Kṛtyakalpataru* of Bhaṭṭa Lakṣmīdhara, probably of the twelfth century, and many later ones, about which far too little is as yet known.[37] In such texts, subjectwise, often following the pattern of 'titles of law', the relevant statements from various earlier *smṛti* texts have been collected, frequently without any further comment. Such collections were never practically useful in ascertaining the law, but this was probably not their purpose, anyway, as such texts served as a databank (so to say) for the few remaining experts on the shastra. A well-trained pandit would be in a position to cite either all verses on particular sections, or only those that made a particular point useful to the case. Or indeed, he could simply articulate what suited his opinion on the matter.

[36] For much descriptive detail see Jolly (1975: 73–88). Desai (1998: 42–59) offers a few glimpses, as do Kuppuswami (1986: 38–9) and Diwan and Diwan (1993: 43–5).

[37] Kane (1968–77, Vol. I Part 2) produced some material on these texts.

The textual experts thus exercised a monopoly of knowledge and thereby achieved a position of tremendous power and discretion that could be abused and exploited, as the British were eventually to discover. It is evident that during the emerging process of cross-cultural communication between indigenous experts and British administrators, the transition from dharma to law had to be made. The new system would certainly not wish to underwrite Hindu concepts of order, but rather constructed a model of rule of law for its own time and place. However, to what extent would this transition already have been experienced and practised in those parts of the subcontinent where Muslim domination led to important legal changes?

Medieval Hindu Law under Muslim Rule

This section demonstrates that a particular conceptual segregation of 'secular' rule was indeed made by Muslim rulers when they rejected theocratic aspirations of learned Muslim scholars (Bose and Jalal 1998: 40). This would have occurred in the same way that earlier Hindu rulers, throughout history, opposed Brahminical domination and were always concerned to be visibly 'in charge', and not directly subject to superior guidance from pandits as representatives of Hinduism. But refusing claims to superior status of the religious spokespersons in a political scenario, whether Hindu or Muslim, is certainly not the same as discarding one's belief system and ruling in an outrightly 'secular' manner, as though the cosmic order of the *rta*/dharma complex or the Islamic concept of Allah's rule of the world no longer existed. Thus, the manifestations of secular rule that researchers have observed do not go far or deep enough to root out religion altogether.

It appears that the political fragmentation of medieval India made it fairly easy for any strong force to take over more and more parts of the subcontinent. At times, this had been achieved by Hindu and Buddhist rulers, but eventually the development of a politically unified central state in medieval India took the shape of Muslim rule.[38] The effects of this for Hindu law have not been as negative as is often claimed. Certainly, Hindu law did not cease to exist or be applied at various levels. In fact, medieval Hindu law seems to have flourished, especially within certain regional centres that remained under Hindu rule. However, the system as a whole was coming under increasing threat in some parts of the subcontinent, because of the influence of Islamic concepts and the strictness of some Muslim rulers, which might involve forcible conversions to Islam. Despite this situation, both during Muslim rule and later also under British domination, Hindu law continued to thrive and to develop conceptually, turning first into a personal law under Muslim sovereignty and in due course into the case-based official personal law which became known as Anglo-Hindu law, discussed in the next section.

[38] A good historical account of this is found in Bose and Jalal (1998: 23–56).

Apart from the conquering foreign elite and their offspring, the overwhelming majority of the Muslims of South Asia were former Hindus or their descendants.[39] As Sunni Muslims, following the Hanafi school, became the dominant grouping in the subcontinent, from *c.* AD 700 onwards Muslim rule was consolidated and the Muslim population continued to grow, so that Islamic law became the second most important personal law of the subcontinent. Even though there was eventually a Muslim ruler at the political centre, firmly established from 1206 in the Sultanate of Delhi, little may have changed for the average Hindu at the time. As before, any central ruler would have remained a remote and inaccessible power, and most Muslim rulers appear to have learnt very soon that it would be impossible to superimpose Islamic law on all their subjects, the vast majority of whom (a figure of 95 per cent is quoted) remained Hindu.[40] The expedient desire to sustain a viable central rule apparently (and quite sensibly) prevailed over ambitions to regulate the daily lives of all citizens. Thus the Islamic rulers upheld the authority of Islamic law for themselves, but vis-à-vis their non-Muslim subjects they developed a rather more secular approach, a subtle combination of sharia and political expediency which enabled them to stay in power without facing public rebellion.

For Hindus, this meant that their patterns of self-controlled ordering or 'assisted self-control' could in principle and practice be continued.[41] On the other hand, most Muslim rulers acted like their Hindu predecessors in leaving vast scope for local and even individual self-controlled order. As a result, the existing pattern of an 'essentially isolationist society' (Ingalls 1954: 37) remained almost totally undisturbed, and Hindu law continued to be applied at all levels of society. The effects of Muslim rule on the legal system remained largely restricted to the cities (Shrivastava 1981: 112–28) and the Muslim rulers were mainly concerned with the collection of taxes and the administration of criminal law (Banerjee 1962: 33–4). Allowing Hindu chiefs and rulers to remain in

[39] For details see Ojha (1978: 119ff.). While the Hindu roots of South Asian Muslim culture are often acknowledged only with some reluctance, Diwan (1984: 4) claims that in the Punjab, Muslims and Hindus paid much less attention to their respective religious authorities and followed local customary norms rather than, in the case of Hindus, the *dharmaśāstra*. Maybe that is not unique to the Punjab, but there it was officially recognized, if only for political reasons.

[40] Bose and Jalal (1998: 38) emphasize that most subjects were non-Muslims. For further details see Ojha (1978: 119–26) and Jain (1970). Muslims also tended to be city dwellers, with only very few among them engaged in agriculture (Ojha 1978: 126).

[41] Bose and Jalal (1998: 33) report on the exclusivist strategies of Brahmanical tradition at this time and refer to the advice of a certain Nrisinghacharya, in a *kumbha melā* gathering, 'to adopt ... the habit of a tortoise, in other words withdraw into a shell in order to be impervious to Islamic influences'. The authors add, interestingly, that '[i]ndeed, if one reads the *Dharmashastra* or Hindu law books of this period, to the exclusion of other sources, one would not even begin to suspect that there were Muslims in India' (id.).

place, provided they paid the appropriate tribute (Ojha 1978: 119), the central rulers did not interfere with the administration of justice in the local realm. It would appear, thus, that the duty of the common Hindu towards the central state was fulfilled merely by discharging the tax burden. The state offered little else in return than some degree of political stability, if that. Many Hindus would then, as now, have felt little impact of centralized rule.

Not only in this period, the preservation of Hindu customary laws must have been helped by the traditional reluctance to carry one's disputes beyond the immediate social group. There is evidence, however, that in the cities Hindu law cases did reach higher fora of dispute settlement. Such cases were normally interesting civil disputes, giving useful information about procedural details (Derrett et al. 1979: 76ff.). Some disputes involving Hindu law were also carried before Muslim rulers. The more open-minded among them applied Hindu law not only in disputes between Hindus, but also between Muslim and Hindu litigants. Derrett et al. (1979: 84) provide an instructive example of a dispute over the offerings made to the shrine of a holy man (*pīr*) who had converted from Islam to Hinduism. They note that even under Muslim rule, the assessors were Brahmins and the terminology was largely taken from the *dharmaśāstra*. The coexistence of technical terms like *mahazar* (a Persian term for the plaint) and *jayapatra* (Sanskrit for the document given to the victor) illustrates the emerging hybrid nature of dispute resolution in late medieval South Asia.

A further development, about which far too little is known, concerns the use of village Brahmins or 'neighbourhood pandits' as self-professed experts or advisers on dharma, indeed on a variety of *smṛti* matters.[42] Fitting the pattern of *sadācāra*, this process meant that shastric and more generally dharmic notions could continue to percolate to the villages and their inhabitants. The absence of Hindu central rule limited the economic prospects of Brahmins at the top level, while it probably brought better chances for their survival in villages and small towns than in urban centres. Thus, for a variety of reasons, the complex process of interaction between customary laws and Hindu scriptural authorities and their interpreters never ceased during this period, and the substance of Hindu law did not change simply due to Muslim domination.

By 1206, when Muslim central rule had been consolidated in the Delhi Sultanate, Sunni Islamic law became the official law of the land and Hindu law turned formally into a typical personal law, applying to a variety of people on the basis of religion. Since most Muslim rulers were content to restructure the tax systems and the criminal laws, this left the administration of most legal matters to local agents and to the people themselves, who were mostly Hindus. It was an inevitable result of political expediency that the Muslim state law, too, became a somewhat 'soft' and fragmented official legal system. It therefore followed the model set by earlier Hindu patterns of rule and

[42] Similarly, the ordinary Muslim might ask for a fatwa, a form of legal opinion, from the local maulvi.

concerned itself only with certain aspects of public law rather than comprehensive governance of the country by shariat. Moghul rule differed from time to time in the approach to non-Muslims, displaying a vacillation between leniency under more cosmopolitan rulers like Akbar, who even sought to fuse Hinduism and Islam, and parochial early forms of Islamic 'fundamentalism'. The latter sought to enforce a more strictly defined rule of shariat but had to acknowledge that the Hindus had their own ways of defining what was appropriate.[43]

Actually, rather little is known about the realities of legal administration prior to British rule in India.[44] Islamic law as applied by the Muslim rulers of India was not 'pure' sharia law, given the importance of local customary laws.[45] Local, pre-Islamic customary laws were recognized in many parts of India. The Khojas, Memons, and the south Indian Moplas or Mapillas are important communities that continued to apply various forms of local succession and property laws based on Hindu principles. With regard to criminal law—which was officially subject to Islamic law—Banerjee (1962: 62) has pointed out that '[i]n practice, what was the exact law on a particular crime or what was the punishment for it, would never be known before the pronouncement of sentence by the Quadi or Magistrate'. The traditional reluctance to go to official courts meant that Islamic law took time to develop into an official law. Many individuals formally subject to Muslim rule probably never had any direct contact with that formal legal system. As practically everywhere in Asia, it seems, avoidance of recourse to formal dispute settlement processes was seen as a virtue in itself.

Eventually, we find two officially recognized, authoritative juristic texts of Islamic law principles in South Asia, the *Hidaya* or *Hedaya* and the *Fatawa-i-Alamgiri*.[46] While details do not concern us here,[47] it is relevant to note that these texts, not unlike the Hindu *smṛtis*, were used as guidelines for certain situations, rather than strict and universally binding rules of law or textual precedents. Despite the Islamic concept of equality before God, it is no surprise

[43] Bose and Jalal (1998: 40) emphasize that during Akbar's reign 'the supremacy of temporal over religious authority was clearly maintained'.

[44] Banerjee (1962: 32-67) provides some useful material, while Pearl (1979) gives some attention to the British influence, but does not discuss the pre-British Islamic law of India.

[45] With particular reference to Punjabi customs, see Diwan (1984). Scholars of Islamic law, with few exceptions (e.g. Rosen 1989) tend to find the role of local custom a difficult subject. Pearl (1979: 21) and Mahmood (1986: 49–4) point to various factors which give an Indian flavour to the Islamic laws of the subcontinent. Hai (1977: 77) emphasizes consideration of local exigencies as a major source of rules.

[46] The Moghul Emperor Aurangzeb had commissioned a digest of mainly Hanafi statements to facilitate the administration of Islamic law. On the *Fatawa-i-Alamgiri* see Banerjee (1984: 55) and Mahmood (1982: 16). On the *Hedaya* see Hamilton (1891).

[47] Pearl (1979: 22) cast some doubts on the authority of such texts.

that South Asian patterns of differential statuses in society prevailed. What mattered most was the goal of achieving justice in view of the particular facts and circumstances of a case. Bose and Jalal (1998: 45) captured this well, but do not seem to realize that this is the old Hindu pattern, now in its Muslim manifestation, indeed a general model for how to operate a personal law system:

> Muslim law officers, such as qazis and muftis, enforced the Islamic sharia, less as a rigid legal code and more as a set of moral injunctions to be invoked in the light of circumstances. The goal was to assure the result of equity and justice rather than strictly apply the letter of the law. While brought under the purview of the Mughal system of criminal law in certain parts of India, non-Muslims had recourse to their own customary and religious law in matters to do with marriage and inheritance.

Mahmood (1981: xlii) confirms this, emphasising that in this period, 'the state did not disturb in any way the division of Hindu law into various schools and sub-schools'. Derrett (1968b: 229) is clearer on the practical implications:

> Where Muslims occupied the seats of power, disputes between Hindus which were brought before them were often remitted to Brahmin jurists for an opinion, upon which the parties were compelled to compose their differences. By far the greater part of litigation was never brought before Muslim officials, but was settled by recourse to traditional methods of resolving disputes, which differed according to the caste, the status in society, and the locality of the parties.

Thus, when Muslim political power in South Asia eventually began to collapse in the early nineteenth century, the legal system was bound to experience some change but not total reformation and reconstruction. Banerjee (1962: 133ff.) indicates that the weakening of central Muslim rule had the effect, at least in Bengal, that the local landholding elite, the zamindars, usurped more judicial authority and in fact virtually ruled their particular district or area, so that the involvement of an outside power, the emerging colonial rulers from Europe, could well appear as a blessing. That perspective does not tackle the key issue of concern here, namely to what extent British intervention in legal administration in the subcontinent changed perceptions of law itself.

The Impact of British Legal Administration

Despite a traditional tendency among historians to emphasize the role of important men, it must be noted here at the outset that basic facts 'on the ground' have had a crucial bearing on how South Asian laws developed under British influence.[48] Bose and Jalal (1998: 76) rightly observe that '[t]he old model of

[48] This is confirmed in many of the writings, even if it is not analysed any further. Mahmood (1981: xlii) states that '[a]fter the advent of the British, the courts which they had set up also applied in every case the law of that school to which the parties belonged'. Baxi (1986b: 40) notes that there are very few studies by lawyers on the use of law as an instrument of social reform.

studying the European impact and Indian response is gradually being replaced by approaches more attentive to Indian initiative and agency'. The assumption that fundamental legal changes were brought about by colonial rule seems to some extent exaggerated and skewed, reflecting the supposedly inherent superiority of the colonial system, as well as law-centred claims. These are clearly not maintainable, because much of Hindu and Muslim law remained outside the ambit of the formal law and worked through internal self-regulation in the social field.[49]

Looking at the personal law sphere, in particular, the formal and rather peripheral nature of the new legal influences becomes all too evident. Informal local methods of dispute settlement would not be of concern for the new rulers and would be left largely untouched. Colonial intervention therefore did not root out, replace, or displace Hindu law totally, but introduced important new methods, at a formal level, of dealing with the entire field of law and with legal proceedings in particular.[50] This had the impact not only of marginalizing Hindu law, but also of rendering it still more invisible and, in Chiba's (1986) sense, turned it to a larger extent into unofficial law.

Relying on Guha's work, Baxi (1986b: 22) emphasizes the centrality of property as a basic principle of colonial government. He also shows that law-making, following Bentham's utilitarian approach, was perceived as an instrument of planned social change. The extent to which there would be legal interference by the British depended on a variety of factors. Most of all, as Baxi (1986b: 42) has noted, the slow pace of legal intervention and legislative reform in the personal law sphere reflects 'the wariness of a colonial power to intrude in sensitive areas of group morality'.[51] Much depended on how the religious element in Hindu law was perceived by the foreign rulers. Derrett (1968b: 319–20) indicates that where the governing power 'is wedded to the notions (i) that the religions of the inhabitants must at all costs be respected and (ii) that the personal laws were "religious"', outside legal interference must necessarily be limited. Thus, on the one hand, early British involvement sought to preserve and respect this 'religious' element, however ill-defined. On the other hand, as Dhagamwar (1992: 71) has shown, colonial administrators like

[49] Derrett (1968b: 235) notes that '[n]o steps were taken to collect evidence of local or caste custom, and this is sometimes regarded as a mistake'.

[50] A detailed outline of the historical development of early British intervention in India and the emergence of Anglo-Indian laws is provided by Jain (1966), a study first published in 1952. See also Fawcett (1979) and Banerjee (1984). On the French role in Pondicherry, compare Bonnan (1999). Galanter's (1972) analysis of this issue is clearly based on wrong assumptions about the nature of law, which have not been revised (Galanter and Krishnan 2001).

[51] Banerjee (1984: 275) writes that between 1772 and 1859, the introduction of English law was a very slow process and lists in the subsequent discussion the reluctance of the British to interfere with religious sources, the difficulty of applying English law to Indian conditions, and the non-availability of judges and advocates well versed in English law.

Macaulay assumed that Hinduism was so absurd and backward that contact with Western concepts would sooner or later lead to its abandonment. Over time, the growing secularization of European legal concepts impacted on British India, where the pressures of administration demanded efficiency and financial prudence. Still later, the more legocentric elements of preference for precedent and legal certainty exerted a pull away from the fluid shastric sources, and towards a fairly rigid case-law system, which came to be known as Anglo-Hindu law. These processes must be seen as intimately linked to the physical and mental processes of colonialism. Nandy (1983: xi) explains that '[t]his colonialism colonizes minds in addition to bodies and it releases forces within the colonized societies to alter their cultural priorities once for all'. The self-distancing of Indians from Hindu law and other traditional personal laws would soon be manifest.

Crucially, given the historical circumstances, the first British traders in the subcontinent had no option but to fit themselves into existing local legal structures first—even if this was by ideological and religious rejection of such structures—rather than creating and influencing laws at the political centre from the outset.[52] The political centre was only penetrated in 1858 when British sovereignty was finally imposed.[53] However, as soon as they started trading under the Royal Charter for the East India Company of 1600, local British managers in India needed to develop systems of dispute settlement that would serve their purposes, which were practical rather than ideological. They needed to act fast because there were pressing economic concerns which required strategic responses. The resulting amalgam would eventually emerge as the complex hybrid of local laws and colonial input known as Anglo-Indian laws and Anglo-Hindu law.

The widespread assumption that Indian law today is merely a distorted form of English law, or that the British simply gave the Indians their law, as though there had been a legal void before, are strange myths that refuse to die and are being fed by inadequate education systems both in Europe and India. Legal textbook authors tend to perpetuate such myths. For example, Desai (1998: 64–5) writes:

> ... the spontaneous growth of Hindu law was retarded if not wholly stopped with the reduction of [*sic*] India under British rule. The difficulties of English

[52] The early administrators were also not trained lawyers, as Jain (1966) repeatedly emphasizes, stressing that early British legal administration in India was 'executive-ridden' (p. 2), which brought its own problems for achieving justice.

[53] The distinction of areas under direct British rule and the so-called Princely States remained important throughout. British India never became one solid legal entity but remained a fragmented patchwork, which had much impact on legal administration, preventing total legal reform. Bose and Jalal (1998: 69) describe the colonial construct of indirect rule as 'an ingenious device that complemented and did not contradict the efficacy of direct British colonial rule in other parts of the subcontinent'.

> judges, who did not know the language of the Dharmashastras, when called upon to administer a system of law which required understanding and appreciation of argumentative works, religious traditions, ancient usage and more modern habits of the Hindus with which they were unfamiliar, were indeed great.

As elsewhere in the Empire, the British who started trading in India had to provide legal mechanisms for the settlement of civil and criminal law matters which involved, first of all, their own staff. The application of local Muslim or Hindu laws to British personnel would have been resisted and was considered deeply inappropriate.[54] Action was very soon taken, loosely based on the principle of extraterritoriality,[55] to extend the application of English law to some parts of the subcontinent.[56] Inevitably, the crucial question then became to what extent the Indians living in those territories should also be governed by English law, and to what extent local laws should continue to operate at all. The British could have decided to abolish or ignore Hindu law (and Muslim law) during this early period, but they did not do so for a number of reasons. Derrett (1968b: 231) indicates that '[w]hen the East India Company stepped into the shoes of the Muslim emperor's deputies in Eastern India it found a flourishing, but not assertive or brilliant tradition of śāstric learning available both for intellectual exercise and for the direction of the Hindu public'. But by that time, earlier patterns had already been set in western India where the strategic decision to respect local religions became part of the survival strategies of insecure Company rule, heavily challenged by rival colonial powers. Early British administrators clearly realized that the application of English law to Indians would not be feasible and would lead to chaos (Derrett 1968b: 276). While the judicial system in the presidency towns became a replica of the English system, in the rural hinterlands of the so-called *mofussil* or *mufassil*,[57] 'the preponderant population was Indian, and the British administrators, Warren Hastings in particular, very well realised that it would not work if an alien system was foisted on them' (Jain 1966: 4).

[54] Abundant evidence of this is found in Jain (1966). At p. 2, and confirmed at p. 5, the 'Englishman's natural partiality for his own law' is emphasized. Jain (1966: 4) stresses that the judicial system 'was developed primarily to cater to the needs of the Englishmen residing there'. Reservations about Muslim law are said to be of a religious nature, since the English merchants 'did not ... cherish the idea of being governed by the Mohammedan Law which was religious in character' (ibid.: 14).

[55] Under this principle, a particular group of people in a given territory would not be governed by the local laws, but by the legal rules of a usurping power, often a trading company rather than a state, which claimed territorial jurisdiction without having political sovereignty.

[56] On the pioneering steps taken in Surat, before it was overtaken by Bombay, see Jain (1966: 12–16). On early criminal law and the role of English law until 1726, see Verma (2001: 125–8).

[57] This term, still often heard today, refers to 'the balance', in fact the greater part, of the early areas of influence.

After 1600, various royal charters had given the British East India Company the power to establish courts in their areas of influence. Such charters did not specify which law was to be applied, leading to considerable legal insecurity (Banerjee 1984: 1–27).[58] Under various new charters, granted from time to time, the East India Company was required to enact laws that would be reasonable, not repugnant or contrary to English law but as near and agreeable to it as possible, while also being acceptable to the natives (Derrett 1968b: 280). Since it was not expressly stated which law was to be applied, many choice of law questions arose, particularly in disputes between British and Indian litigants, and ignorance of local law and their principles posed huge problems for the emerging British administration of justice.

In litigation between Indians, the application of English law could bear rather strange results.[59] Banerjee (1984: 21) emphasizes that as the absurdity of enforcing substantive rules of English law on the Indians became more and more obvious early on, calls for restrictions on the applicability of English law were increasingly heard. Still, many authors argue that the Charter of 1726 implied the application of English law. English law was indeed introduced, but mainly for the colonial personnel and in the presidency towns.[60] However, it also proved attractive for litigants in Bengal who merely wanted to harass their enemies and saw new possibilities in this system (Derrett 1968b: 232), giving rise to allegations that Indians were litigious. Practical experience all over India soon showed, however, that English law and procedure would be quite unsuitable for the local population. As a result, custom and customary authorities were reluctantly recognized (Banerjee 1984: 9), leading to 'the beginnings of the co-existence of English law with Indian laws prevailing in the region concerned' (id.), an expedient arrangement that follows the historically tested South Asian pattern of the coexistence of a 'soft' general law with numerous concurrent personal laws.

There are various ways of viewing this scenario and its implications. Jain (1966: 5) observes that it is a peculiar feature of Indian legal development under the British that 'the chief endeavour of the government was to create a

[58] In Bombay, for example, English law was applied under a charter of 1661 (Pearl 1979: 22). Legal insecurity pervaded also when in a charter of 1726 mayor's courts were established in the presidency towns of Madras, Bombay, and Calcutta (Banerjee 1984: 11).

[59] Jain (1966: 60) refers to a dispute over some jewellery, which arose in 1730 after a Hindu woman in Bombay had converted to Christianity. The decision of the mayor's court led to vociferous protests of Hindus against interference in their religious matters.

[60] Banerjee (1984: 11) appears to support the 'general view' that the charter of 1726 introduced the laws of England, as they stood at that time, into these towns. Verma (2001: 125) captures this process more correctly, writing that the charter of 1726 enabled the East India Company staff to make independent laws (thus not just to apply English law), a process in which English practices and principles were the model, but not the only source of guidance.

system of courts without making any attempt to develop a body of law'. Jain (1966: 70) reflects some ambivalence about this, criticizes non-interference as a negative policy and alleges that this 'resulted in a whole-sale denial of justice to the people' (id.).

After the East India Company had obtained the *Diwani* rights over parts of Bengal, Bihar, and Orissa in 1765, they had to act like a local authority, still under Mughal sovereignty, and had to develop suitable methods of judicial administration. Again, it did not take long until practical decisions were made. In 1772, Warren Hastings, then Governor General of Bengal, issued his famous regulation which included provisions to the effect that,

> ... in all suits regarding inheritance, marriage, caste and other religious usages and institutions, the laws of the Koran with respect to the Mahomedans, and those of the Shasters with respect to the Gentoos, shall be invariably adhered to.[61]

This important declaration had several crucial consequences.[62] It effectively stopped the British from introducing English law as the 'law of the land', preserving the so-called 'listed subjects' of family law and religious matters—to which succession was added in 1781—as the exclusive domain of the personal laws. To this extent it clearly respected 'religion' in the shape of the personal laws. However, the declaration also gave notice that the British intended, at least to some extent, to exercise more direct control over the perceived 'secular' sphere, the realm of public law, with criminal law as a priority area. This pattern therefore appears to follow the historically tested South Asian method of legal development, marked by the coexistence of a general state law and various personal laws. But the perceived separation of the public law sphere from the influence of religion, whether Hindu, Muslim, or Christian, led eventually to the formal secularization of large areas of the law and of legal administration generally.[63] To most colonial administrators, there was nothing religious about procedure in a court of law, murder, or the making of contracts. Formally, this is the point at which a large-scale separation of 'law' and 'religion' was not only envisaged but was subsequently implemented. But this is not how the world was viewed from the perspective of the *ṛta*/dharma complex, leading to irreconcilable conceptual clashes, so that the attempts at

[61] The wording was amended in 1793 to read 'Mohammedan law', reflecting growing recognition of the complexity of Islamic sources of law and customary diversity within South Asian Islamic laws.

[62] For details see Banerjee (1984: 30), Derrett (1968b: 231ff.), and especially Jain (1990: 580ff.).

[63] After the enactment of the first Criminal Procedure Code of 1859 and the IPC of 1860, both promulgated from 1862, Islamic criminal law ceased to be applied. The Islamic law of evidence was superseded by the Indian Evidence Act, 1872. Derrett (1968b: 318) refers to 'numerous adjustments during the formative period'. Considerable detail is found in Banerjee (1962: 68–180) and the more recent work of Fisch (1983) and Malik (1994).

amalgamation of the two systems, Hindu and British, were doomed to failure (Derrett 1968b: 269).

Prior to 1793, when the so-called Cornwallis Code was introduced, there was no general code of laws and regulations in British India (Banerjee 1984:166). The new Code brought with it many innovations (Jain 1981: 137ff.). Influenced by British legal theorists of the time, in particular Bentham and Mill, codification began to be considered essential for good administration (Banerjee 1984: 167), which means that the pressure to respect indigenous religions had to be harmonized with a new reformist energy that began to assert itself more strongly. Soon, provisions were made for an Indian Law Commission, the first of which started work in 1835.[64] A major aim of this codification process was to achieve uniformity and certainty through the codification of existing laws (Banerjee 1984: 171). But since the usefulness of 'native laws' was not accepted by Macaulay and other important reformers at the time, the new codes took as their basis the law of England. The new legal provisions on criminal law were drafted to avoid superfluous technicalities and local peculiarities of the English law, introducing some modifications to suit the circumstances of British India (Banerjee 1984: 173, 177). While Macaulay also acknowledged some debt to the French Code and the Code of Louisiana, and thus to the civil law tradition—after all he was Scottish—on closer examination one finds many Indian elements, too (Banerjee 1962: 129ff.).

The result of Macaulay's labours was a systematically arranged, fairly precise, and intelligible code of criminal law. The draft code, having evoked considerable opposition among the British in India, was reworked several times and became official law only in 1862 as the IPC of 1860.[65] There appears to have been little opposition to this new Code from Indian subjects, but it has been questioned whether the Code was really widely known.[66] Silent non-acceptance seems a likely reaction of the general population. However, the fact that the Code offered new remedies, some quite cruel (Fisch 1983), made it popular with some of those who could afford to harass their enemies. The image of the litigious Indian was reinforced in this context, particularly in Bengal.

The British soon began to codify a large number of areas of the law, leading to charges of 'over-legislation' (Banerjee 1984: 180–90). During the

[64] For details see Jain (1981: 411ff.). The first task of the Law Commission was to prepare, under the leadership of Macaulay, a draft Penal Code, which was submitted in 1837, followed by a draft Code of Civil Procedure and a draft on the law of limitation.

[65] The IPC of 1860 is to this day hailed as a model of successful codification. It was introduced, with some modifications, into many other parts of the British empire, especially countries in east and west Africa. However, the Code did not govern all aspects of criminal law in all parts of India (Banerjee 1984: 179), so in practice the codification was less successful and comprehensive than appears at first sight.

[66] See Banerjee (1984: 179). Dhagamwar (1992: 9–10) presents evidence that, even today, the Code is not a matter of public knowledge.

particularly active period after 1860, the Third and Fourth Law Commissions operated under instructions to use the law of England as a basis, while making some concessions to local conditions, native habits, and modes of thought (Jain 1981: 430ff.; Banerjee 1984: 182). Banerjee's view (id.) that '[t]hus it was decided that India was to be governed under English law' is clearly overstated and wrong. The process of codification obviously meant the creation of a new legal system, in which English law had an important influence, but it was not the only law used. Acts like the Indian Companies Act, 1866 might resemble their English model, but at this stage English law per se could no longer become the law of India.

Codification was not restricted to the area of the 'unlisted subjects'. In derogation of Warren Hastings' declaration of 1772, from the earlier Sati Regulation of 1829 and the Caste Disabilities Removal Act of 1850 onwards, the British gradually began to interfere more and more in matters of Islamic and, more so, of Hindu law.[67] Despite much criticism over the speed and amount of Indian legislation (Banerjee 1984: 187), the general law was constantly expanded at the expense of the 'listed subjects', until quite vigorous Indian opposition to some amendments of the IPC at the end of the nineteenth century slowed down the British legislative zeal.[68] Thereafter, only a few selected reform measures were introduced,[69] often as a result of pressure from Western-educated Indian opinion makers. By this stage, it appears that the internal Hindu processes of ascertaining dharma had become irrelevant to the colonial administrators, who followed their own procedural models in a process of reconstruction of Hindu law.

The Emergence of Anglo-Hindu Law

Derrett (1968b: 225) observed that '[t]he administration of Hindu law by the British is a complex story with two distinct sides'. By this he meant firstly the changing role of shastric texts as a source of law under the British, and secondly the actual process of administering Hindu law through a subtle combination of English and Hindu principles, involving the use of precedents and the important formula of justice, equity and good conscience (Derrett 1978d; Pearl 1979: 27ff.).

The early British attempts to understand Hindu law from within included stimulation for native scholars to give their best in terms of cultural explanations and expert guidance (Derrett 1968b: 225). Once cross-cultural communication

[67] A list of several statutes is provided by Pathak (1986: 14).

[68] This arose in relation to the question of age of consent, i.e. minimum ages for marriage and its consummation. For details see Heimsath (1962), Anagol-McGinn (1992), and Ch. 9 of this book.

[69] The major Acts relevant here are the Child Marriage Restraint Act of 1929, the Hindu Women's Right to Property Act, 1937 and the Dissolution of Muslim Marriages Act, 1939.

became possible, the British asked specific questions from Hindus who were seen (or presented themselves) not only as 'legal' experts, but also as 'religious' authorities. The British appeared at first 'sincerely anxious to find out what native laws were' (Derrett 1968b: 274),[70] but proceeded on the false assumption that the Hindu law was found in books, particularly in the shastra, and that the textual experts were their key to the legal authority hidden in the texts. Despite the crucial role of custom, which was overlooked for a long time and ultimately disregarded to some extent, this was not totally wrong. Derrett (1968b: 229–30) argues:

> But it is certain that amongst Hindus the *dharmaśāstra* held very high prestige, served as the only indigenous system of jurisprudence, and supplied actual rules of law in a wide variety of contexts, especially (in Northern and Eastern India) in matters of inheritance. The native professors of the *śāstra* were therefore consulted on such matters as were indisputably within their province, and it was usual for the parties to obey the decision, provided that it was not open to doubt whether the report was biased in favour of one party.

Thus, despite the fact that the texts were essentially private works, they had evidently given rise to practical consequences in terms of dispute settlement. It is important to note that the texts *might* be used in such contexts, which is not the same as asserting that the texts *had* to be used because they contained 'the law' binding on all Hindus. In this context, the Indologist Julius Jolly (1975: 97) quite rightly emphasized that '[i]t should ... never be forgotten that the Smritis are purely private works and cannot be placed on the same footing with the law-books of other countries'. However, in practical reality, the system as a whole was being corrupted by scheming litigants and to some extent by the native experts who acted as court advisors. Derrett (1968b: 232) captures this well:

> As soon as it was evident that the power of the new rulers was at the disposal of a successful litigant, and that to be successful it was only necessary to make a case which the native assistants of the Judges certified to be good, the breakdown of the system was imminent. A flood of cases arose, and accusations of corruption and inefficiency against the native assistants multiplied.

Under the early British in India, probably because of Muslim political domination at the time, Hindu law was seen as an inferior system of law lacking official, i.e. political, authority. However, Hindu law was manifestly the personal law of the vast majority of people. The Warren Hastings Regulation of 1772 had put Hindu law on an equal footing with Islamic law, creating some

[70] Derrett (1968b: 283–84) claims that already by 1769 'the British had no intention of accepting more knowledge or interest in Hindu or Muslim customs or laws than was essential for performing the functions which had devolved on them'.

resentment among Muslim rulers at the time.[71] Many British administrators refused to pay much attention to Hindu law, but once the pattern had been set by the Regulation, the practical demands for settling disputes under Hindu law made themselves increasingly felt. Personal preferences might have had a bearing on individual discretion of an administrator, but the general pattern was set: Hindu law could not be totally ignored.[72]

The 1772 scheme also gave official recognition to the need for formal administration of the indigenous laws and involved the pandits in a critical role, which neither they nor their employers fully understood at first. The Administration of Justice Regulation of 11 April 1780 made the *śāstrīs* formally responsible for the law they reported and the cases decided on the basis of their evidence, but established the necessity of consulting those indigenous experts on the listed subjects only (Derrett 1968b: 232–233). Derrett (ibid.: 233) shows in detail that key figures like Warren Hastings understood the Hindu argument that certain areas of the law were subject to religious authority and that pandits should remain an authority on those topics.[73] Jain (1990: 580) discusses in some detail the underlying motivations for respecting Hindu law:

> In course of time, Hastings's policy of preserving the indigenous Indian laws came to be increasingly appreciated and eulogised. It came to be recognised that to ensure stability of the British Government in India, it was of fundamental importance that affections of the Indians should be conciliated, and that nothing could be more effective from this point of view than tolerance in matters of religion, and adoption of such indigenous institutions of the country as did not clash with the laws and interests of the conquerors.

At this stage, then, if not before, the vast holistic field of Hindu law was not only divided into 'listed' and 'unlisted' subjects in terms of the 1772 plan, but

[71] Starting from a position of relative strength as the dominant legal system when the British began to get involved in the administration of justice, the Islamic law of India had most to lose from the new arrangements. Bose and Jalal (1998) emphasize Muslim resentment over the loss of political domination. Derrett (1968b: 318) went too far in the claim that Islamic law died under the British, but it certainly suffered considerable loss of status and massive interference, which is vigorously criticized by Mahmood (1986: 49–94).

[72] I see parallels here with the predicament faced by earlier Muslim rulers who wanted to reduce or wipe out the influence of Hindu law. They could not do so effectively because the pattern of coexisting personal laws was already entrenched. The British later faced the same scenario and had no option but to live with the realities of Hindu law.

[73] More or less subtle resentment on the part of administrators shines through many comments. W. Sloan wrote in 1867, in the Preface to the third edition of Colebrooke's translation of the *Dāyabhāga* and *Mitākṣarā* (Colebrooke 1984: xv–xvi) that not enough was known through 'the replies of the Pundits whom the Courts were required formerly to consult when doubtful points of hindoo Law arose'.

was actually split into 'secular' and 'religious' laws. The pandits may not have seen it like that, but they were in effect asked only certain types of questions and were expected to give focused legal answers instead of lectures on dharma. Derrett's analysis indicates that there was a vast area of residual law, which included many topics of law not specifically covered by the 1772 Regulation. In these areas, too, the advice of the pandits might be sought, but was not taken as binding. Derrett (1968b: 234–35) shows how the British judges assumed that they were acting according to procedures familiar in England and treated the experts as religious rather than legal authorities:

> When the Anglo-Indian judges sent, as they subsequently constantly did, for 'opinions' (*vyavasthā*) on Hindu law from the pandits, and acted upon these certificates without bothering to see whether they agreed with others by the same persons in the like circumstances, they were imitating the practice of the King's Bench or the Common Pleas. This was a piece with the error perpetuated by Sir William Jones, that Brahmins were 'priests'. Very few Brahmins were priests, and there were priests who were not Brahmins: and similarly pandits were not Bishops' Officials, or anything of the kind. They were however jurisconsults, which had quite another implication.

The effects of the artificial segregation of listed/unlisted subjects demonstrate that the British appreciated the importance of religion as an element of Hindu law, but what sense did they make of the interaction between law and religion? Derrett (1968b: 225) noted that the early administrators were somehow sympathetic to the religious laws of 'heathens' and wondered whether they were all sentimental antiquarians like Sir William Jones. The wording of the 1772 Regulation indicates that the British had understood shastra as a collective term for the written sources of Hindu law, but were unaware of the complex nature of this literature and of the holistic concepts underpinning the Hindu legal system as a whole.[74] Derrett (1968b: 225) reported that the early British administrators 'stimulated the native scholars to give of their best and tell their own tale in a fashion intelligible to and useful for Europeans'. The British, in particular, thus 'played a sympathetic part in the revival of Hindu learning' (ibid.: 226), and they alone, of all colonial powers in the subcontinent, furthered the production of Hindu law treatises. The judges clearly needed guidance from indigenous experts, especially in the *mufassil* (Jain 1990: 581).

Despite such initial sympathies, however, the attempted cross-cultural communication over legal concepts during this crucial early period contains precisely the evidence of malfunction and distortion that we are looking for in the present analysis. The evidence takes us closer to understanding how dharma was (mis-) represented as either 'law' or 'religion', and how a

[74] Agnes (2000: 43–6) demonstrates the 'anglicization of scriptures' before turning to the subversion of women's rights under British rule.

secularized perspective of Hindu law was being created while assuming respect for the religious nature of Hindu law.[75] Obviously, it was too early for outsiders in the late eighteenth century to appreciate the finer points of the conceptual foundations of classical Hindu law, nor did the British obtain a complete picture of socio-legal reality. They observed, however, that experts on the shastra, the pandits, were often consulted by the general population in legal matters (Derrett 1968b: 235), though they also noticed that neither shastra nor pandits might be consulted in some cases (Derrett 1968b: 230). Consequently, the help of indigenous legal personnel (as the British saw it) was sought, and native experts on Hindu (and Islamic) law were appointed at all levels of the official court hierarchy until 1864, when it was believed that sufficient precedent had accumulated.[76]

The pandits and maulvis, in turn, treated their new employers almost like a Hindu or Muslim ruler (Derrett 1968b: 268) and it would appear that their methods in the use of textual authority were adjusted to the new expectations. The English-style court system demanded specific answers to often very complex issues. It appears that the questions asked by the judges sought to elicit responses about 'law', while the Hindu experts answered in terms of dharma—a classic case of failed cross-cultural communication. While the experts' responses were not intended to establish precedents, they were perceived by the British as universally binding rules and thus turned into 'law'. Hence, situation-specific solutions would be reconstructed as binding precedents, quite unlike traditional Hindu law, which had developed from case to case and remained context-sensitive. Initially, the traditional flexibility and a case-by-case approach prevailed, as Derrett (1968b: 235–36) explains:

> Thus at first Hastings and his colleagues were not concerned at discrepancies between the reports of pandits in different courts, or discrepancies between the reports of the same pandits on similar matters. After all, the *śāstra* being a complicated system, and the opinion of the great 'doctors' differing frequently, even within the major schools, there was ample room for honest disagreement and a change or growth of opinion. The pandits, having a sense of responsibility, would be likely to mould their answers to suit the needs of the situation, and they might take into account the effect which the decision would have. Tolerance of this somewhat fluid state of affairs was hindered by the existence of the Supreme Court at Calcutta, in which of course *stare decisis* would tend to be the rule and English practitioners functioned ...

[75] Derrett (1968b: 227–28) indicates that the British ability to administer justice (however defined) and to inflict punishment impressed some Indian observers, but does not go into detail. The attractions of litigation as a means of harassing enemies are highlighted (ibid.: 232).

[76] Derrett (1963c: 6) notes that at this point 'it was felt desirable to proceed as if the court had full judicial knowledge of the system'.

Thus, at the district level, the traditional English and Hindu patterns of looking for the justice of the situation, rather than fitting a case to existing laws, avoided immediate conflict. Matters became problematic only once the formal law and its insistence on precedent imposed themselves more firmly and made the law more rigid. While as Derrett (1968b: 236) shows, pandits were eventually appointed at all court levels, the fact that their reports were turned into decisions of an English court meant that the principle of *stare decisis* could not be totally ignored and eventually superimposed itself onto the system as a whole. This, as Derrett (1968b: 237) notes, 'gradually brought into the administration of Hindu law an entirely new feature, highly embarrassing to the pandits'. Hidden behind those cryptic words is the realization that the case-by-case approach of the pandits, who were still seeking for the dharma of the situation, was now being replaced by a formal legal approach that favoured certainty and fixed rules over flexibility and situation-specificity.

Derrett (1968b: 237–38) demonstrates how Warren Hastings planned education and training for the pandits, established Sanskrit Colleges for that purpose and prescribed a certain range of texts for study, with a clear bias towards sources from Bengal and Mithilā and no recognition of southern texts, which created its own problems. In essence, there was no easy way around the traditional diversity of texts and learned opinions. As the pressure grew to devise a more uniform system of rules, the British attempted to commission some kind of agreed text that might present the rules of Hindu law in virtually codified form. Derrett (1968b: 238–39) explains:

> The obvious course was to summon a 'synod' of the most learned and respected jurists, as if it were a kind of convocation, to induce them to compile a digest similar in form to the digests compiled in more or less recent times for emperors and kings in not altogether dissimilar circumstances, and to give to the results an authority which those pre-British compilations had never had.

Derrett's analysis reflects doubts over whether all pandits would fall in line with such a new compilation, but also highlights the considerable means at the disposal of the British to enforce compliance—other pandits would take the place of those who were unwilling to comply with the new methods. Another reason advanced for curtailing the discretion of the pandits was the allegation of corruption. Derrett (1968b: 239) writes:

> Moreover, it had been rumoured that certain pandits had been issuing *vyavasthā-s* which agreed with the wishes of the wealthier party to the dispute in question. If the law were digested by an authoritative and independent committee, it would not only be easier to learn and to refer to than the extensive and vague literature normally consulted, but would also render corruption difficult to hide.

Thus, it became an important advanced stage in the efforts to reconstruct Hindu law for colonial purposes that digests of Hindu law were commissioned by the

British.[77] Jolly (1975: 88–9) provided an early outline of the most important works:

> ... like the Vivādārṇavasetu written at the order of Warren Hastings ...—an elaborate treatise on law and judicial proceedings, written in 1773–75 by a commission [of] 11 Pandits from every part of Bengal and ... translated into English by Halhed in 1775 .... Similar works are the Vivādasārārṇava composed for Sir W. Jones in 1789 and the two works Dharmasāstra-saṁgraha and Siddhāntapiyūṣa written towards the end of the century at the order of Colebrooke. Most remarkable however is the Vivādabhaṇgārṇava written by Jagannātha of Calcutta at the instance of Sir W. Jones ... translated by Colebrooke .... This translation, completed in 1796 ... was the starting point of the study of Indian law in Europe.

Derrett (1968b: 239) explains that the titles of the early digests, signifying some kind of 'bridge across the ocean of litigation' implied thereby 'that the certainty now for the first time offered to litigants in the Company's territories would put some check upon the appalling flood of cases which inundated the courts'. The British attempt to gather the rules of Hindu law into a code-like basket promised certainty and some kind of codification, which would allow them to restrict the freedom of the indigenous experts as court advisors.[78]

These new texts are compilations of shastric rules, grouped under English legal headings, initially perceived by the British as a collection of authoritative statements on Hindu law. It was anticipated that these collections would eventually be followed by all court pandits (Derrett 1968b: 239) but, in Derrett's laconic words, this codification 'failed to deflect pandits from their normal sources of information, and merely added another to their many reference works' (p. 241). This confirms that the formal process of 'law reform' does not have the effect of superseding the older texts and their rules, as lawyers would like to believe. Colebrooke and others did not fully appreciate this, even though they worked in the interface of law, religion, and custom. It also dawned on the British only fairly late in the day that what was presented to them as shastra was rarely the oldest layers of such literature, such as the ancient *sūtras* and

[77] The first work so commissioned, the *Vivādārṇava-setu* or *Vivādārṇava-bhañjana*, has continued to fascinate researchers. See Derrett (1968b: 239), Jain (1990: 585) and Bhattacharyya-Panda (1995).

[78] Derrett (1968b: 240) notes that the pandits were not really trusted, and hence an English translation was commissioned to allow judicial supervision. Jain (1990: 582) explains the various doubts over the reliability of pandits. Macnaghten (1894: xviii) insisted that 'I am still of opinion, that to the Pundits is chiefly attributable the perplexity of the system which it is their province to expound' and provided several examples of how life was made difficult for the British administrators by the methods employed by pandits. Derrett (1968b: 258) records that in Madras, too, the judges did not treat the reports of their indigenous experts with total confidence.

shastras, or the *Manusmṛti* and similar texts,[79] but later commentaries and extracts from digests (Desai 1982: 48). This updated shastric material was heavily influenced by the personal opinions of pandits, which could, and did, create considerable mischief.[80]

The first digest was at best 'a somewhat qualified success' (Derrett 1968b: 242) as the huge basket of the shastra, even if reduced to a digest, continued to allow pandits to rummage in the textual bricolage until they found what to them seemed the most appropriate opinion. Derrett (1968b: 242) emphasizes that specialist pandits were needed even at the Supreme Court in Calcutta from 1777 onwards, which proves that the new code alone was not helpful enough to the lawyers and judges called upon to decide cases on Hindu law.

Other attempts at codification followed, and are linked to Sir William Jones, who arrived in Calcutta only to be appalled by the pandits and their methodology. Indeed, he was 'very soon impressed with their opportunities for corruption' (Derrett 1968b: 243) and began to search for better ways of dealing with Hindu law. The British administrators experienced much helplessness when faced with the intricacies of Sanskrit texts, and were keenly aware that the judicial process depended heavily on what the pandits were saying. Thus, 'the best way to avoid this dependence was to have some authoritative works in English on these legal systems' (Jain 1990: 584). The almost complete ignorance of the English judges about Hindu law, despite the earlier works, demanded remedies. As Derrett (1968b: 244) explains, the frequent court struggles involving large numbers of pandits 'led inevitably to a demand for further and better particulars about the Hindu law'.

It appears that Jones made serious efforts to understand Hindu law and worked closely with a number of pandits. His understanding of Hindu law, as Derrett (1968b: 244) shows, was more that of a lawyer than an Orientalist.[81] He was certainly not an adherent of the historical school of jurisprudence, as to him 'the law was not unwritten custom, but only the *śāstric* law' (id.). As the need for another code became clearer, Jones prevailed on the East India Company to obtain the necessary funds for a new compilation. The new venture was Jagannātha Tarkapañcānana's *Vivāda-bhaṅgārṇava* ('Ocean of resolutions of disputes'), which was even translated into English, was initially considered a success, and was quite often applied for some time (Banerjee 1984: 43f.; Derrett 1968b: 245ff.). In this code, as Derrett (1968b: 247) lays out in

[79] Most ancient texts were not known at this early stage and it is especially important to remember that the *Arthaśastra* was only discovered in the early years of the twentieth century.

[80] It is doubtful that this is really a new phenomenon, since the older shastric texts were also created by individuals who presented their own views, often in distinction to rival opinions.

[81] Cohn (1997: 73) notes that unlike Colebrooke, Jones's intellectual approach to Hindu law was marked by his training in English law and consequent knowledge of Roman law.

detail, there is considerable evidence that the learned Hindu author had been influenced by some English legal thinking. That apart, Colebrooke's translation of the text appears to be excellent, but Colebrooke himself was not as convinced as Jones that the whole venture would be practically useful. Derrett (1968b: 249) comments:

> Colebrooke knew better than Jones that no production, even that of a committee, could by any governmental authorization oust the textbooks and treatises which formed the existing *śāstric* learning. The pandits would be glad to cite Jagannātha, as they did more eagerly than he had expected or welcomed. But from such a work they would not find conclusive answers to all the questions put to them by the courts, nor be able to instruct the European Judges in the technique by which they were themselves bound. Jagannātha recorded the state the *śāstra* had reached, stimulated, as it were, by questions from some attorney or barrister. He aimed to do no more. This is where the misunderstanding lay ... Jagannātha would have rejected as comical the notion that he had preserved the *śāstra*, as it were, in cold storage.

Against this, as Derrett (1968b: 249) clearly shows, Jones had thought that it was possible to fix Hindu law 'at any given moment without doing it any harm' and that 'it seemed quite practical to cause a book to be written from which the lawyers of the new age could cite as they would cite the *Corpus Juris*'. Thus, as Derrett (1968b: 250) shows:

> It is obvious that Jones believed that the conscientious opinions of the *śāstrīs* could be made to assume a fixed form, from which neither they nor their successors would be able to deviate .... The need for certainty took precedence over the comfort of the science of jurisprudence. The *dharmaśāstra* as a living and responsible science in matters which might come before a court of law died when the courts assumed judicial knowledge of the system in 1864, but the death-sickness commenced with Jones's quaint act in 1786.

This reference to an act of 1786 relates to what Derrett called the 'extraordinary episode' of Jones forcing his pandit to admit in court that a particular legal position in the Sanskrit texts was 'the law'.[82] Was this an act of cultural imperialism, the blatant imposition of legal positivism, or mere despair at the size of the ocean of Hindu law? Bose and Jalal (1998: 77) portray this issue as a process of reinvention and reform of 'tradition', but discuss the subject only with specific reference to Muslim law, which was turned into Anglo-Muhammedan law:

> ... by injecting English procedural practices, such as precedence, into their rulings based on the sharia, the company's judicial officials transformed what Muslim law officers generally treated as a flexible set of moral injunctions into a strictly laid down legal code.

[82] See Derrett (1968b: 249). The episode is also recounted in Jain (1990: 582).

The above analysis applies to Hindu legal developments as well, where a parallel transformation took place.[83] In reality, as Derrett (1968b: 250) highlights, '[n]o translation of any *smriti*, even that of Manu, could enable the courts to administer to the Hindus the "law of the Shaster" or their "law and usages". In the same way no single text could do duty for an able pandit's learning if honestly applied'. However, such worrying thoughts, which seem to have occurred to Colebrooke,[84] were evidently overshadowed by the perceived practical needs of legal administration. Therefore, the next stage in this ongoing process of more or less deliberate distortion of Hindu law and its principles through the intervention of English legal practice produced the argument that it would be desirable to fine-tune the codified source that had been selected as the basis for textual authority. Thus, as Derrett (1968b: 250) shows, Colebrooke made preparations to supplement Jagannātha's work with clarifying comments and additions. He commissioned further work for this purpose from two more pandits but, sorely disappointed with the outcome of these efforts, Colebrooke himself considered writing a Hindu law digest. However, he was aware of the considerable scepticism for such a project since, '[a]s an English pandit his determinations of controversial matters might convince neither the native population nor the European judge' (Derrett 1968b: 251). Indeed, this particular project never matured, as Colebrooke turned his energy to other matters and thereby spearheaded a further process in developing methods of ascertaining and fixing Hindu law. Derrett (1968b: 252) briefly reports that '[h]e prepared an English translation of the *Mitākṣarā* (inheritance portion) and the *Dāyabhāga*, with a valuable introduction to both, in order that the judges might have the means of learning at first hand how the basic principles of the two schools of Hindu law were originally formulated'.

Derrett (1968b: 252) also mentions that, thirty years later, this particular translation was regularly used, which amounted to a change in climate that made Colebrooke drop his original plan to publish a supplementary digest to Jagannātha's work.[85] Indeed, conditions changed further and from about 1830 until 1860, "no further research was done into the textual bases of the *dharmaśāstra*" (id.).[86] It seems that the use of certain supposedly codified texts within the court system as administered by the British—original Sanskrit texts

[83] For details on the distinctions between moral and legal norms see Jain (1990: 597–8).

[84] This is subtly indicated by Derrett (1968b: 249–50).

[85] Further criticism of Jagannātha's work is found in Kuppuswami (1986: 39), calling it '[t]he best law-book for a counsel and the worst for a Judge'.

[86] Apparently, in the earlier period, between 1790 and 1830, learned men seeking appointment as pandits began to produce various types of treatises that focused on particular procedural questions or substantive points of detail. This, too, reflects a process of legalization in the perception and treatment of Hindu law, which helped smoothen the eventual transition to Anglo-Hindu law. Notably, this is not purely an internal Hindu process, but evidence of Nandy's (1983) colonialism of the mind.

that were now available in English translation—meant that especially the *Dāyabhāga* and the *Mitākṣarā*, i.e. a fairly recent layer of *shastric* texts, gained a prominence and level of authority which they would never have reached in the indigenous system.[87] This is evident from Colebrooke's (1984: ii–iii) complaint that the older digest of Jagannātha was not usable:

> ... indeed the author's method of discussing together the discordant opinions maintained by the lawyers of the several schools, without distinguishing in an intelligible manner which of them is the received doctrine of each school, but on the contrary leaving it uncertain whether any of the opinions stated by him do actually prevail, or which doctrine must now be considered to be in force and which obsolete, renders his work of little utility to persons conversant with the law, and of still less service to those who are not versed in *Indian* jurisprudence; especially to the *English* reader, for whose use, through the medium of translation, the work was particularly intended.

Colebrooke therefore argued that it was simpler to return to the original text; indeed he produced his own translations of the *Dāyabhāga* and *Mitākṣarā*. It is interesting to see how Colebrooke (1984: iii) presented those works as virtually codified entities:

> They are the standard authorities of the Hindu law of inheritance in the schools of *Benares* and *Bengal* respectively; and considerable advantage must be derived to the study of this branch of the law, from access to those authentic works, in which the entire doctrine of each school, with the reasons and arguments by which it is supported, may be seen at one view and in a connected shape.

It appears that such statements reflect a perception of the role of texts in Hindu law which now assumes that the Hindu texts are codes of law, with binding rules for certain legal issues. In their search for certainty, desperately trying to collect bricks for the altar of precedent, the British did not notice—and did not really want to know, as Rocher (2002: 39) confirms—that the traditional Hindu legal system operated on a rather different footing from English law. Despite all his knowledge of Sanskrit and the *shastric* literature, Colebrooke seems to have changed strategy, capitulating before the ocean of Hindu textual diversity. It appears from Derrett's analysis that the pandits did not really try to teach the British otherwise and kept a polite, perhaps even amused silence and distance. If they attempted to assert the flexibility of their textual sources, they were either accused of deviousness or even slapped down, as happened to a

[87] Derrett (1968b: 255) indicates, rightly I believe, that the importance given to these two texts meant that '[t]he pandit as a professor of a living science was rejected for the more or less fossilized treatises which would head the pandits' lists of references'. Rocher (2002: 21) notes that these two texts 'were elevated above all others as the main representatives of two distinct systems of inheritance', and that comparison of the two texts therefore became inevitable.

supposedly leading expert in Calcutta in 1786 at the hands of William Jones (see earlier note 82).

All of this prepared and founded the eventual view in the Privy Council that there were really only two schools of Hindu law.[88] This perception is clearly reflected today in the standard Hindu law textbooks and seems to have come from Colebrooke, as Kuppuswami (1986: 39) confirms, immediately adopting this perception as though it were an unchallengeable legal fact:

> The term 'schools of law' as applied to the different legal opinions prevalent in different parts of India, seems to have been first used by Mr. Colebrooke. There are in fact only two main schools, the Mitakshara and the Dayabhaga. Undoubtedly, there are fundamental differences of doctrine between the Mitakshara and the Dayabhaga schools ... the two works differ in very vital points ...

While the critical differences between the two texts and their principles do not concern us here,[89] it is interesting to follow up how Kuppuswami (1986: 41) perceives the role of pandits and texts in relation to the emergence of school traditions:

> At a time when the opinions of pandits who were only conversant with a few text-books in each province guided the decisions of Courts, it was natural to assume that the text-books they most frequently referred to were the special authorities in particular provinces. With the widening of knowledge and increased attention to Sanskrit law books, it is clear that the assumption then made is no longer correct. The commentaries that generally follow the Mitakshara are not the particular property of any one school. They have been and can be cited in all the schools .... The references in the Digests and the Commentaries to one another clearly show that all the treatises are the common property of all the schools.

However, the constructed image of separate school traditions was continued, and the differences were in fact soon enshrined in case law, confirming that British judges rather than native experts, at the end of the day, established 'the law'. Kuppuswami (1986: 42) writes that '[t]he differences between the Benares, Mithila and Dravida schools are only minor variations on very few points and are due chiefly to the courts in each province giving effect to their own earlier decisions on the principle of *stare decisis*, or to divergency in judicial opinion'.

The ridiculous cycle of reflections of chains of possible misconceptions is therefore neatly completed. At the end of the day, Hindu law is what the British judges declare it to be, a construct that is neither Hindu law proper, nor English law. Indeed it is a new amalgam, Anglo-Hindu law. By the time the system of

[88] Cohn (1997: 74) points to the mistaken analogy between Hindu law and Muslim law, which led Colebrooke to assume that Hindu law had schools, too.

[89] For details see Kuppuswami (1986: 40–2) and Rocher (2002: 25–8).

native officers was disbanded in 1864, the damage had been done: Anglo-Hindu law, a conglomerate of precedents built on shaky textual authority, developed its own momentum and became a new formal source of Hindu law in its own right. While recourse to earlier works became minimal, the whole process of restating Hindu law through textual exegesis came to be abandoned.[90] Derrett (1968b: 269) confirms that the experiment was probably not workable anyway, since the conceptual underpinnings of the two legal systems involved were so very different:

> ... what the British really required was hardly within the pandits' power to supply; had they been beyond suspicion they would have continued to be treated as experts, and it is just conceivable that under British pressure a working compromise between the two very different jurisprudential techniques might have arisen not too far from *stare decisis*. In the course of this it would have emerged that the Hindu religion was consistent with far more flexibility and far more novelty than the British observers of the period of Rāmmohun Roy and later could have believed. As it was, the British administrators insisted upon clarity, certainty and finality in terms foreign to Hindu tradition, and if the pandit was true to his *śāstra* he could not at the same time substitute the new attempts at legislation for his own old authorities. Perhaps the attempts were doomed to failure.

The British thus created Anglo-Hindu law, which Derrett and others have referred to as a bogus system (Derrett 1977: vii), a 'hybrid monstrosity' without parallel in the world (Derrett 1968b: 298), clearly because the Sanskritist did not understand the lawyer, and vice versa, and the concepts of law involved would not match. In the earlier section on medieval texts and their purported secularization, it was noted how Desai (1998: 43) portrayed the sudden emergence of the *Dāyabhāga* and the *Mitākṣarā* as major sources of law through the involvement of commentaries. Desai (1998: 44) uses the authority of the Privy Council to tell the history of Anglo-Hindu law and finds that '[t]hese schools born of diversity of doctrines mark a new stage in the evolution of Hindu law'. Desai (1998: 46–7), as shown in the section just referred to, engages in a deliberate construction of the superior role of the *Mitākṣarā* and, pushing for the central role of this text as a legal authority, claims at p. 47 that proper methodology would involve always checking this text first:

> Speaking broadly, therefore, the first thing is to inquire what the Mitakshara has laid down on the question under inquiry when it is not concluded by the judicial decision and then to turn to the other authorities. Error is almost sure to arise if this order of priority be changed. The first thing to be considered is what the Mitakshara states.

This significant methodological suggestion harks back to earlier techniques in Hindu legal history for referral back to the Vedas, or the mythologically embellished *Manusmṛti*, as the primary sources of law. Here is a contemporary Hindu

[90] See Derrett (1968b: 269), partly blaming the indigenous experts for this.

legal scholar at work, attempting to construct a fictitious raft of certainty for the ocean of Hindu legal texts. It should be evident that this approach precisely matches the view taken by Colebrooke, as shown above, to the effect that recourse to a mass of earlier texts would only lead to confusion and diversity, while reliance on one major current text would assist the process of formulating a rational system of Hindu law rules. In their search for certainty, lawyers are evidently prepared to go very far, and they may not even notice to what extent they distort particular legal traditions.

In British India, such problems in applying the textual sources inevitably led to the eventual departure of the pandits from the formal arena of Hindu law-making. To the extent that the *Dāyabhāga* and the *Mitākṣarā*, as two imagined Hindu codes, became the perceived basis of Hindu law, and were now available to lawyers in English,[91] it would be unnecessary to employ textual experts with wide-ranging knowledge of the *shastric* literature. Given the many criticisms of these indigenous experts and their methods, such obfuscations could now be avoided. It seemed that, after all, the Hindus had laws which could simply be ascertained from texts and applied in courts. Apart from that, nobody seemed to worry much about the growing gulf between the official personal law of the Hindus and the law as it existed in Hindu societies. The formal creation of 'Hindu law' was by then too advanced to allow many further questions.

Fragments of texts like the *Dāyabhāga* and the *Mitākṣarā* were then built into the system of precedents, on which the British-influenced system relied more and more, though not blindly, especially in later years when obvious mistakes were discovered (Derrett 1968b: 301). Case law as a new source of Hindu law, embodied in the principle of *stare decisis*, went fundamentally against the most elementary Hindu principles of justice, where (as we saw) consideration of the facts and circumstances of every case was paramount. However, the Anglo-Hindu case law became so persuasive that some authors now saw judicial precedent as the overriding source of Anglo-Hindu law, superseding the unwieldy digests (*nibandhas*) and commentaries (Sarkar 1940: 37).

This development had several important consequences. Firstly, as shown, British efforts to ascertain and re-state the traditional Hindu law were gradually abandoned. Instead, Hindu law was now administered on the lines of Western law, with precedent as the new major source of law.[92] Secondly, since

[91] Derrett (1968b: 255) also notes that the several early books on Hindu law by English authors, e.g. Macnaghten (1894)—the first edition of which appeared in 1828–29—'were of far more practical use than even the excellent printed copies of genuine Sanskrit *śāstric* works'.

[92] In addition, apart from the earlier attempt to outlaw *satī* through a regulation in 1829, from about 1850 onwards legislative interference in the 'listed topics' began. The effectiveness of such reforms remains doubtful. The quiet burial of the Hindu Widows' Remarriage Act, 1856 in India shows that it may never have been an

the commentaries were often more conservative than the early *shastric* texts (for example on child marriage),[93] this reinforced the impression that traditional Hindu law was in need of much reform, which could only strengthen the eventual move towards codification and further legal intervention by the state. Thirdly, ignorance of the *shastric* law persisted also after the indigenous experts had been relieved of their duties in 1864. Inevitably, the British judges were often faced with lacunae, and now they had to fill the gaps themselves. The problem was not new, however, and a potent solution had been found earlier when the Administration of Justice Regulation of 5 July 1781 introduced justice, equity and good conscience as a residual source of law. This turned into the most important device in the development of Anglo-Hindu law after 1864.[94] In this way, too, Anglo-Hindu law became heavily indebted not only to English law, but also to Roman law and other legal systems.

The haphazard introduction of fragments of imported law led to an even more hybrid system of court law, an official legal system known only to specialists, while the 'living law' of the Hindus was increasingly different. This very fact, however, partly explains the quite astonishing popularity of the Anglo-Hindu law with Indian litigants: it offered new remedies and alternative strategies to harass one's adversaries and, though the stakes were high, the gamble was often considered worthwhile.[95] As a result, a flood of litigation developed, and the litigiousness attributed to Indians by many authors appears to have been strengthened here (Derrett 1968b: 232, 279, and 286). Historians of south India, in particular, have shown that litigation with an army of lawyers replaced traditional warfare among ruling clans (Dirks 1987; Price 1979) and thus assisted the British cause, too.

Derrett (1968b: 261) mentions that a hardening of the case law had taken place since the 1830s and that precedent was gradually asserting its pull. Desai (1998: 63) speaks much more as a practising lawyer than as a scholar in justifying the need for Anglo-Hindu case law, following a legalistic chain of arguments that classical Hindu lawyers would have challenged as inevitably leading to injustice:

---

effective Act. It was simply taken off the shelf by the Hindu Widows' Remarriage (Repeal) Act, 1983 in India, but remains part of the Hindu law of Pakistan and Bangladesh.

[93] Olivelle (2000: 6) notes that the 'puritanism' of a text is not necessarily a sign of lateness, but what is puritanism?

[94] See Derrett (1968b: 289 and 311) and in detail Derrett (1978d). Though not originally meant as such, reference to justice, equity and good conscience often implied the application of rules of English law (or the judge's perception of them), because to many judicial officers English law appeared so very identical to the rules of universal law (Derrett 1968b: 311). Derrett (1963c: 9–10) emphasises the importance of this concept for understanding how Anglo-Hindu law was constructed.

[95] The use of litigation as a tool to harass the opposition is also reported from recent fieldwork on how women deal with claims to property (S. Basu 2001: 186).

> Since the reduction of India [*sic*] under British rule another element was added to the effective sources of Hindu law. The courts had to ascertain and administer the personal law of the Hindus in matters relating to succession, inheritance, marriage, adoption and religious usages and institutions except in so far as such law was altered by legislative enactment. The decisions of courts, founded on interpretation of the texts of the Smritis and principally on the views expressed by the commentators accepted as leading authorities in the different schools, although they immediately affected only the parties, necessarily operated as binding on the entire community. Judicial precedents became necessary and useful for in them the courts found reasons to guide them and the authority of those who made them had to be regarded. Unfortunately, however, the importance of custom was at times not fully appreciated ...

This discussion therefore turns towards the potential clashes between accepting what the community assumes to be its law and what the courts are saying. The increasing divergence between flexibility-conscious customary practice and precedent-focused official law now placed custom in conflict with case law and legislation, rather than with *shastric* texts. As those in charge of the official law preferred to follow the 'letter of the law' rather than vague, unwritten rules based on diverse socio-religious traditions, Anglo-Hindu law became still more of an elite phenomenon, focused on the written word. Thus, the gap between law and society became much wider than it could ever have been under traditional Hindu law. Earlier there was at least a harmony of principles governing the formal and the informal legal systems, the dominant and the subordinate. This conceptual unity is clearly lacking in the Anglo-Hindu law,[96] a key factor which contributed so much to the artificiality of the new construct, which was neither English nor *shastric* (Derrett 1968b: 274). In fact, the result was a gross caricature of the *shastra* (ibid.: 265).

One could say that the British administration of justice, unaware of the role of every Hindu individual in supporting dharma, and insufficiently informed about the Hindu ruler's function in maintaining dharma, acted within the conceptual framework of positive law,[97] while the Hindu system of law was built on very different foundations. The British, despite lip service to respect for Hindu law, were not really concerned about finding out what the common

[96] Stipulating an earlier conceptual unity here, I do not attempt to assert indirectly that there were uniformly shared values in ancient India. Peripheral and dissident groups, however, still share in the dominant paradigms, albeit by disagreement.

[97] Such positivist reflections appear everywhere, significantly also in Derrett (1963c: 1), who suggests that rules from the *Arthaśāstra* 'were still the ultimate authorities in and about 1750' and thus envisaged a formal rule system that could be formally administered and moulded into an official legal system. Later commentators were clearly wedded to the ideal of codification. Jain (1990: 590) sees the preparation of various Sanskrit texts under British patronage as 'the second best alternative to adopt in the absence of codification of these laws through the process of legislation which stage was to come only after a lapse of considerable time'.

Hindus considered to be their law, and ignored the many statements in the *shastric* literature requiring the ruler to implement the customary laws of his subjects. Public opinion, as Derrett (1968b: 316–17) put it, 'had no organ of expression' and it was unrealistic in the circumstances to expect the British to create a system based on local custom. Thus, by taking advice from some members of the elite only, and hearing only what they wanted to hear, the British developed a formal legal system of inadequate precedents, which were then strengthened by *stare decisis*, a formal smokescreen for what Guha (1997) has called dominance without hegemony.[98] Only very gradually and with obvious reluctance were maldevelopments admitted.[99]

Desai (1998: 63) simply argued that 'obviously the preferable course was to follow the doctrine of *stare decisis* and to uphold a decision already given', although it is recognized that this 'tended to impart a measure of rigidity to the law' (id.). Thus, predictably, the discussion ends in a classic, authoritative modernist restatement of the sources of Anglo-Hindu law (id.):

> With numerous superior courts administering law in different parts of the country, there grew up a mass of case-law and most of the important points of Hindu law are now to be found in the law reports and to this extent it may be said that the decisions of Hindu law, though not in theory yet in effect, have in part superseded the commentaries and limited and supplemented the rules of Hindu law. Modern jurisprudence endorses the importance of authoritative precedents and accepts them as legal sources of law being entitled to unquestioning obedience. The pronouncements of the Privy Council and now the Supreme Court are final and in practice recourse to them is of the utmost importance and necessity.

This is legal centralist ideology at its best, claiming that Hindu law is now found in cases and statutes, totally overlooking the continuing links between law and real life as perceived by Hindus in all their diversity. Statements like this explain to some extent why nobody seems interested in studying traditional Hindu law any more—it has been declared practically irrelevant by the most authoritative textbook writers on Hindu law themselves, who have literally set the torch to the funeral pyre of traditional Hindu legal scholarship.

[98] Guha (1997) demonstrates that it suited the British colonial agenda to assert certain positions at the cost of others, although this did not result in the total exclusion of subaltern positions. Asking why in India universalism failed to generate a hegemonic ruling culture, Guha (1997: 64) asserts that '[t]he answer is, simply, that colonialism could continue as a relation of power in the subcontinent only on the condition that the colonizing bourgeoisie should fail to live up to its own universalist project'.

[99] Nelson, in particular, had been an early warning voice in Madras. For details see Lingat (1973: 138) and Derrett (1961). Derrett (1968b: 310 and n. 3) provides further pointers about how some defects were later remedied. Albeit rarely now, the Supreme Court of India may still find itself asked to correct a position taken by the Anglo-Hindu law. For an example see Venkataramiah (1982).

Simultaneously, in an attempt to claim that the British also respected custom and thus bridged the gulf between formal law and local practice, Desai (1998: 65) argues that 'under the Hindu system of law, clear proof of usage will outweigh the written text of the law', a statement clipped from the important early Privy Council case of *Moottoo Ramalinga.*[100] However, as Desai (1998: 65–6) candidly explains, it was often impossible for litigants to satisfy the high standards of proof required to establish a custom. Rhetorically, the importance of customary law was recognized and even administratively regulated in some places (Lingat 1973: 137). *Moottoo Ramalinga* is often cited as having laid down that custom can override any text of *smṛti* law (Desai 1998: 60), but full-scale recognition of Hindu customs was evidently not considered a viable option. While Hindu customs were not totally abrogated, satisfaction of strict requirements of evidence was made extremely difficult.[101] The Anglo-Hindu case law laid down such stringent conditions for the proof of custom that very few managed to become judicially recognized (Desai 1982: 67f.). In effect, after *Moottoo Ramalinga*, any Hindu could try to prove that he or she was not governed by the Anglo-Hindu law in a particular matter, but by custom (Derrett 1957: 7). Custom, once proved, would totally displace the official Hindu law (ibid.: 27), but there was a strong presumption in favour of the official Hindu law (ibid.: 78).

Thus, at the end of the day, it seemed best to effect a change of method yet again—another new conceptual development in tune with new law-centred axioms—by attempting a fundamental reform of Hindu law through codification. Desai (1998: 66) argued that the creation of a judge-made law had led to unprecedented rigidity, so that '[t]he only remedy was comprehensive legislation in the form of a uniform code'. Thus, the story of the development of Hindu law under British rule ends with a further pronouncement on the impending death of this legal system, a sick patient lying on the operating table. In fact, some authors have gone further and have prematurely pronounced another death of Hindu law. Cohn (1997: 21) argues that the British converted Indian forms of knowledge into European objects to achieve their agenda of control. However, Cohn (1997: 75) concludes his analysis of this distortion process with an exaggerated and rather mixed message. He identifies correctly that the process of publishing authoritative decisions in English 'had completely transformed "Hindu law" into a form of English case law'. The important words here are 'form of', rather than simply assuming that English law as such was being recreated. The final sentence of this analysis, however, appears to pronounce the irrevocable death of Hindu law and clearly goes over the top in asserting colonial supremacy, for 'what had started with Warren Hastings and Sir William Jones as a search for the "ancient Indian constitution" ended up with what they had so much wanted to avoid—with English law as the law of India'.

[100] The full citation is *Collector of Madura v Moottoo Ramalinga* (1868) 12 MIA 397.

[101] This problem persists in Hindu law today and causes much confusion if the judges are not alert. For some details and examples of cases, see Menski (2001).

That statement clearly goes too far, but it reflects widely shared common perceptions of the nature of Indian laws as an inferior version of English law. Questioning whether the colonial development of Hindu law has been beneficial, one finds that most authors see the changes as positive, because 'the law became, for all its many anomalies, more certain and much more uniform' (Derrett 1968b: 316). But such views only take account of the official law, while 'the great chasm between custom and law remained', as highlighted by Derrett (1968b: 305). In other words, Anglo-Hindu law and the actual social reality of Hindu law remained quite separate and grew still further apart. Like an iceberg, most of Hindu law became submerged and virtually invisible to lawyers and modernist analysts.

In the context of difficulties to prove custom, Derrett (1957: 78) has written that 'the British period saw the elimination of a great many customs diverging from the Anglo-Hindu law'. But judicially unrecognized customs would of course not automatically cease to exist in social reality. Even if it had been acknowledged earlier that local customs were of major importance in Hindu law (as suggested by Lingat 1973: 137), it was too late to redirect the course of legal history. So Anglo-Hindu law developed vigorously as a formal court law (Derrett 1968b: 320), but as such covered only a slice of the total reality of Hindu law. It is evident that lawyers have only studied this particular narrow segment of the entire field, leaving the rest to anthropologists and others.[102] As a result, studies on Indian and Hindu law became even more of a specialist field of interest, while political correctness impeded initiatives, until fairly recently, to study the religious dimensions of Indian law, which ultimately achieved some impetus from interdisciplinary area studies.[103]

Thus, while genuine attempts were initially made by the early British administrators to understand Hindu law and to gather evidence of its rules,[104] the complex nature of Hindu law was either not understood by the early British or, if they had an inkling of the *ṛta*/dharma complex, they would not have wished to implement this as 'religious' law. Yet, at the end of the day, the British ended up respecting Hindu law on the ground that parts of it were perceived as religious law. It was only in the sphere of the 'religious' personal

[102] Baxi (1986b: 20) laments that almost all Indian books on legal history conceive of the subject too narrowly as a history of judicial and other legal institutions, devoid of social analysis. In typical positivist and myopic fashion, Galanter (1989: 15) claims that '[o]ne of the outstanding achievements of British rule in India was the formation of a unified nationwide modern legal system'. Guha (1997) clearly goes along with Derrett's analysis to the effect that the formal legal structures were not entirely dominant.

[103] See Baird (1993). He is also one of the contributors to the important collection of essays on religion and personal law edited by Larson (2001), reflecting renewed interest among scholars of American area studies in religion.

[104] Derrett (1968b: 257) provides evidence that in Madras, the East India Company 'had really attempted to know what the Hindu religion taught in law as in other spheres'.

law, as circumscribed in the 'listed subjects', that the British were prepared to make larger concessions to the ideational foundations of Hindu philosophy.

For the Anglo-Hindu lawyer, undoubtedly, the process of adapting Hindu textual statements into a case-based system of authoritative legal principles found in judgments represents hard evidence of the creeping secularization of Hindu law.[105] This formal legalization occurred, no doubt, but one must question how important this official development was in relation to the population as a whole.[106] Analysing this issue becomes inevitably a matter of perspective. The official legal view reflects manifestly only one particular perspective of how Hindu law developed during British times. What really occurred was that at least two types of Hindu law would now coexist, sharing the same social field, namely the 'old' Hindu law with its emphasis on *sadācāra* and the *ṛta/* dharma complex, and the 'new' Hindu law as created by the courts.[107] To that extent, then, Hindu law was neither displaced nor abolished during the present stage of its development, nor rendered extinct or disfigured beyond recognition.[108] It became part of the unofficial law but lives on in the lives of those hundreds of millions of common Hindus who would not have wanted direct contact with the state and its law-making apparatus, perhaps also because they did not see themselves as Hindus. No wonder that the definition of 'Hindu law' is so impossibly complex, there are clearly more forms of Hindu law than the textbooks on the subject wish to admit.

It appears that Derrett (1968b: 223) envisaged an inevitable clash between secular and spiritual jurisdictions and posited that the latter would have to give way. This resembles a modernist statement. At the level of the formal official law this may have been true, but for the purposes of the present analysis, 'law' remains much more than official law, and a simple dichotomy of law and religion does not enhance our understanding of how the British handled Hindu law. Notably, the way in which Derrett (1968b: 223) discusses the subject permits an interpretation to the effect that the full impact of secularization (in its

105 Galanter (1989: 15–36) discusses the displacement of traditional law in modern India and argues that a process of expropriation of law took place in several stages, making 'the power to find, declare and apply law a monopoly of government' (p. 17).

106 Baxi (1986b: 44) speaks of 'obstinate social realities' as a continuous challenge for modernizing law reforms.

107 Curiously, the latter came to be known as 'traditional' Hindu law in much of the more recent writing.

108 Yang (1989: 4) in his study of the 'limited raj' in a district of Bihar illustrates how going beyond the so-called 'steel frame' of the Indian Civil Service can be useful in 'uncovering the deep extensions of the colonial state into the countryside in order to delineate the contact points at which government impinged on the lives of the majority of the population'. The legal mechanisms operating at that level are portrayed as far removed from the official Anglo-Indian law, while massive evidence of the manipulation of the legal system leads Yang (1989: 164) to the conclusion that the courts were mainly used as arenas for speculation in control.

Western sense of division of power between state and Church) never materialized in India, and thus India was spared the 'severe shock to the conscience of Europe during the reformation, from which we never recovered' (id.). Derrett's highly strung analysis of this issue is complicated by reference to the modern Indian 'socialist pattern of society', which he did not seem to like, and which he assumed ancient Indians would have resisted.[109] However one interprets this, it is evident that fundamental communication problems—especially pertaining to the interaction of religion and law—persist. Indeed, the fundamentally religious nature of Hindu law, however fractional, has continued to trouble all those who wished to be involved in its reform during the period leading up to independence in 1947 and beyond.

Retracing the complex caricature of the *shastric* law under British influence in the present chapter, I found it remarkable how confused and insecure Indian writers, themselves mostly Hindus, seem to be about the concepts of Hindu law. It appears to be a fact, not only among the emerging Indian lawyers during the colonial period,[110] but also more recently, that legal positivism has implanted itself so firmly in Indian lawyers' minds that serious cases of legal myopia are not even perceived as such. Not only the basic understanding of 'law' itself as a concept, but in particular the relationship of law and religion have given rise to some strange comments.

For example, on the issue of dividing religion and law, Desai (1998: 65) asserts that '[n]o system of law makes the province of legal obligation co-extensive with that of religious or moral obligation'. One would have thought that this is exactly what traditional Hindu law—especially the classical self-controlled order ideal of dharma—was seeking to achieve, a harmony of life and law which made formal law superfluous.[111] Thus, the distinction of positive law and religious or moral obligation made by Desai and others is insignificant—even irrelevant—in relation to the *ṛta*/dharma complex.[112] It only

[109] The modernist concept of 'socialist pattern of society' which Derrett refers to, compared to its postmodern manifestation in the age of Indian public interest litigation, further confirms that Indian law has now moved beyond bipolar debates on tradition and modernity.

[110] Derrett (1968b: 304–05) noted that with a few outstanding exceptions, 'Hindu judges have been undistinguished for learning in *dharmaśāstra*' and rightly commented that *shastric* training and busy legal practice are fundamentally incompatible.

[111] African laws, among which there are innumerable indigenous variants, expound the same principle and would thus also rely on self-controlled order rather than state intervention. For details see Menski (2000a, Ch. 5).

[112] This is confirmed by Baird (1993: 3), who points out that the distinction between the religious and the secular did not always make sense, and 'indeed, for many Indian people it does not pertain even today'. Muslim authors will strongly support such views not only with regard to traditional beliefs but in postmodern debates. For example, Sayyid (1997: 4) argues that '[t]he Islamic resurgence marks the revenge of God; it signals the return of faith, the return of all that puts into question the idea of the progressive liberation of humanity'.

concerns lawyers who are oriented towards a positivist world view. The fact that such questions earlier occupied the Privy Council confirms that the British did not comprehend—and perhaps did not want to know—how the internal mechanisms of Hindu law worked. Kuppuswami (1986: 23) illustrates this when he argues that '[i]n interpreting and applying the rules contained in the Smritis and the Commentaries and treatises founded upon them, the principal [*sic*] question is whether a particular rule is a rule of positive law or only a religious or a moral precept'.

The subsequent discussion by the same author shows that British judicial discretion could indeed have the effect of mixing authoritative statement and moral precept, when it should have been clear that there is no positive law as such to be found in the *shastric* texts. And yet the Hindus had law, but their legal system is manifestly not built according to the axioms of Western model jurisprudence.[113] Raising this debate again at this critical juncture wakes many old corpses, tired of discussing whether the ancient Hindus had law at all, but it seems that reminders of ongoing misconceptions are necessary in the complex reassessment attempted in the present study.

Opening any of the leading Hindu law textbooks today, unwary readers are seriously befuddled as to the nature of Hindu law and its later manifestations. Since such confusing and irreconcilable statements are found in textbooks classed as leading practitioners' handbooks, selling thousands of copies and probably influencing what the next generation of Indian lawyers knows and reads, it is important to highlight those outdated and confused perceptions of Hindu law. For example, Kuppuswami (1986: 10) peddles positivist mind traps in stating that '[b]oth the Arthasastra and the Dharmasastras establish the fact that the king was the fountain of justice'. Evidently, this would be read by many unthinking lawyers as confirmation that ancient Hindus had law as we know it today, based on solid Austinian principles. All it says, really, is that the ruler constitutes the final resource for dispute settlement, and thus the final piece of driftwood that a litigant may clutch in the ocean of litigation, but surely not the source of all Hindu law. Unless modern editions of the leading textbooks on Hindu law are assiduously rewritten, future generations of Indian lawyers will continue to be forever confused.

Since Hindu law had, by the end of the British period, moved significantly along the path of becoming a formal legal system based on case law and some statutes, and formally resembled Western-style law rather than Indian or Hindu law, it becomes all the more important not to overlook those areas of the law that remained in the vernacular, in every sense of that word. Looking ahead to the post-independence period, there does not appear to be much hope that the non-elite elements of Hindu law would receive prominent attention. Falling

[113] Jolly (1975: 95–6) noted that 'the authors of the Smritis themselves fully recognised the necessity of the existence of other laws and regulations. It is a significant remark that the science of law (*vyavahāraśāstra*) like grammar ... is based on usage (*ācāra*)'.

under 'religion' and 'tradition', being unwritten and informal, they were bound to be further marginalized and to become even more invisible—which is certainly not the same as claiming that they ceased to exist. However, at the end of the period under review, as we shall see in the next chapter, the powerful impact of modernity allowed only the formal Anglo-Hindu law to be seriously discussed, albeit now from the perspective that this 'traditional' law was bad for many reasons, too, and was as unsuitable for an independent, modern India as the unreformed, old Hindu law. The agenda of modern Hindu law reform therefore further privileged modernization, codification, and unification as key elements of progressive development.

5

Origins of Modernity in Hindu Law: Emerging Discourses on Reforms and Codification

As the previous discussion showed, the ancient fluidity of Hindu law was transformed under British rule into a somewhat rigidified, positivist case-law system, which was neither just English law nor Hindu law, but a distorted variant of the latter, called Anglo-Hindu law. This chapter examines how this particular shift in the development of Hindu law lay the groundwork for the origins of the discourse on modernity in Hindu law. Following a discussion of the legal and ideological challenges posed by post-colonial law-making, in which the discourse on modernity has remained dominant, the chapter traces the origins of this discussion to the emergence of ideas about legal reforms and codification of Hindu law. It pinpoints the historical and conceptual origins of the processes of post-colonial law reform, in which the ascendency and resonance of modernity in Hindu law has taken shape. Analysing the discourses on reforms and codification during the colonial period and their conceptual underpinnings, the chapter traces the arguments for legislative reforms and codification of Hindu law back to the early colonial period and follows events and debates through to the end of the Raj. It is argued that the origins of the discourse on modernity in Hindu law can be largely seen as the product of colonial and Hindu elitist endeavours to reform and codify Anglo-Hindu law, rather than the traditional Hindu law.

Debating Modernity: Legal and Ideological Challenges of Reform

At midnight on 14–15 August 1947, India and Pakistan became two independent countries. While a historical watershed for South Asian history and politics, it also represents strong elements of continuity.[1] For postcolonial India,

[1] Bose and Jalal (1998: 201). Brown (1985: 308) emphasized that '[i]t can be argued powerfully that there was really far more continuity than change in the 1940 [sic]' and highlighted the role of Congress, which 'was itself responsible for this fundamental continuity in the institutions of government and consultation' (ibid.: 344). Baxi (1986b: 24) highlights that Dhagamwar's (1974) research on the IPC of 1860 'demonstrates some striking continuities between the British Indian legal system and Independent India's legal system' and notes such basic continuities also for agrarian conditions in Northern India (ibid.: 45).

one of the most prominent early challenges was posed by the hotly debated agenda of Hindu law reform, which was in full swing while Indians were struggling towards independence from British rule.[2] However, the colonial state had so seriously manipulated and distorted Hindu law that its remnants of personal law were barely—and to a large extent reluctantly—recognized as 'law' by the end of the Raj. All 'proper' legal subjects of the 'general law' had been formally manipulated, reformed through codification and Anglo-Indian case law, and had been successfully de-Hinduized, so it appeared. A crucial task before the new nation, therefore, was to decide the future role of the Hindu personal law.

The controversies in the present discussion of post-colonial reconstruction relate to two interlinked processes of law-making and ideology. After 15 August 1947, three major tasks awaited the new rulers of India in terms of law-making: (1) reconstructing and modernizing the various personal laws, with special emphasis on Hindu law; (2) modernizing the existing Anglo-Indian general laws; and, most urgently, (3) constructing a new constitutional framework for independent India. Deeply embedded within the efforts to tackle these law-making challenges, as well as academic analysis of them, has lain a persistent ideological problem of reconciling tradition and modernity. The dominant ideology during the early post-independence period was that in order to establish a democratic secular nation state, the new reformed laws would have to 'modernize' along Western, positivistic lines and be purged of all traditional religious elements. However, as this study seeks to illustrate, in all three fields of activity, albeit to varying degrees, Hindu law concepts, principles, and rules have continued to play a significant, but largely unacknowledged role in India's reconstruction of a new legal system. This was primarily because of the imperative for the Indian state and those who seek power in it to portray themselves as secular.[3] The generally unacknowledged role of

[2] Like India, Pakistan retained the whole gamut of personal laws, with Muslim law as the majority personal law. The continued presence of Hindu law as part of its legal system reminds everyone of the fact that Pakistan did not become just a country of Muslims. The Hindu personal law of Pakistan is being studiously ignored, while in Bangladesh Hindu law has a higher profile, demonstrated by frequent references to it in policy studies (Chaudhury and Ahmed 1981) and published research (White 1992; Ali 1992). Since Hindu law cases keep coming to court, there is a manifest need for expert knowledge, which has become rather limited and thin, leading to a process of 'mainstreaming' Hindu law (Menski and Rahman 1988). Chaudhury and Ahmed (1981: 33) confirm that '[n]either the Government of Pakistan nor the Government of Bangladesh have made attempts to amend the Hindu personal laws'.

[3] The term has been explained before. To avoid any doubt, it needs to be repeated here only that 'secularism' in its specific Indian connotation does not merely imply that no religious law should override state law, but that the state law should take equidistant account of all religions. In effect, this amounted to a constitutional guarantee that India would not become a Hindu republic, an axiom that needs to be respected and protected (Sathe 2002: 189), but also gave a place to religion as such,

traditional Hindu legal concepts in post-independence law-making is also in large part due to the ingrained ideological dispositions of legal scholars and commentators, favouring modernity, secularism, and formal unification of Indian laws.

However, it is gradually being realized today that Indian lawmakers, despite presenting outward secular appearances, have decidedly chosen not simply to follow the West, but have pursued their own culture-specific path of post-colonial reconstruction and even post-modernization. This development in India's approach to the challenge of law-making perturbs many scholarly egos, for whom third world still means 'third rate', and who suffer from superiority or inferiority complexes, as the case may be.[4] The rejection of Western models and their universalistic claims hurts not only Western protagonists, but also numerous Indian scholars who nailed their flag, as it were, to the mast of modernity and have more or less explicitly sought to distance themselves from their 'traditional' and supposedly backward environment.[5]

In the present and following chapters that analyse the 'modernizing phase' of Hindu law, it is necessary to counter persisting myths, not only about the supposed backwardness of ancient Hindu laws, their partly hidden genesis and messy development, but also about the nature of post-colonial Indian and Hindu laws. Such myths, perpetuated through semi-informed public opinion all over the world, are peddled by a large number of modernist scholars who have neither detailed knowledge nor experience of Hindu law, yet are keen to pronounce its irrelevance.[6] For example, the final paragraph of a well-known study on English law in India (Banerjee 1984: 288) is not only sycophantic, but culture-blind and sadly self-deprecating in denying any useful role for traditional Indian laws in the modern legal set-up and claming that '[e]xcept in the case of the personal laws of the Muslims the entire legal system of India today is based on English Law. Banerjee (id.) further asserted:

> Hindu Law has been cut off from its moorings by codification after Independence. The present laws of Hindu marriage and inheritance owe very little to ancient *Samhitas* and medieval digests .... Courts ... administer

which continues to perturb modernists. Nandy (1999: 412) emphasizes that 'modern India ... now fears religion'. The ongoing debates are captured well in Larson (2001).

[4] In various writings focused on psychology, Ashis Nandy has perceptively commented on this intricate phenomenon, which cannot be explored here in detail, but seems highly relevant for an understanding of post-colonial India.

[5] Nandy (1990: 69) criticizes deliberate abuse of the hegemonic language of secularism and the nation state, which 'has increasingly become a cover for the complicity of the modern intellectuals and the modernizing middle classses of South Asia in the new forms of religious violence'. The investment of modernists and secularists in secularism is also incisively discussed by Nandy (1999).

[6] It was shown in Ch. 4 earlier that Cohn (1997: 75) is wrong to assume and assert that the law of India is now English law.

> laws ... not infrequently in the light of the present laws in England. Finally, the Constitution ... is an imported product, and the English ingredients constitute its largest portion. The higher courts often appeal to English precedents in interpreting its provisions. The democratic values which we hold so dear cannot be traced even remotely to Hindu Law or Muslim Law.

While some of these assertions are simply factually wrong (see Chapter 8 on marriage), it may have been correct in the early 1980s to argue that Indian law was still in many cases relying on English models, but even this was never to the extent that Banerjee states.[7] By the mid-1980s, there was powerful evidence of a broad-based refusal by the Indian legal system to continue to rely on colonial crutches. Strongly worded judgments were reported, distancing Indian law from the English model.[8] Today, Banerjee's assertions simply do not reflect Indian legal reality. At the same time, the ideological problem of how to reconcile tradition and modernity has remained relevant to the core of Indian law-making and constitutes a challenge for interdisciplinary scholarship. Khilnani (1997: 5) observed in relation to modernity and the demands of the modern Indian state that there was a certain risk of losing cultural identity through the process of state-led modernization:

> ... the many civilizational strands on the Indian subcontinent have uncomfortably but inescapably been confronting modernity: a seductively wrapped and internally inconsistent mixture of instrumental rationality, utilitarianism, and respect for individual autonomy and choice. From this perspective one can focus on the question of whether a culture and its members can sustain their distinctive character once they entrust their destiny (as they must) to a modern state.

However, as far too few scholars have noticed, the post-1947 Indian state learnt fast that it was essential for its survival to become postmodern rather than simply modern or post-colonial.[9] While there is no space here to take up again the

[7] Such assertions continue to be used by more recent writers and underpin their modernist analyses. Agnes (2000: 209) not only imagines that 'all statutory matrimonial laws in India, except the Muslim law, are based on English laws of marriage' (which seems to come from Banerjee (1984) as cited above), she even suggests in blanket fashion that the HMA 'is based on archaic English principles', thus grounding her demands for modernist reforms.

[8] A powerful early refutation of the usefulness of British precedents, arguing that 'the validity of an Anglophilic bias in Bharat's justice, equity and good conscience is questionable today', is found in the famous, much-cited decision by Justice Krishna Iyer in *Rattan Lal v Vardesh Chander* (1976) 2 SCC 103, which concerned a landlord-tenant dispute.

[9] A political analysis might well find that the survival instincts of Indian politicians such as Indira Gandhi played a major role in this context. Mrs Gandhi had a variety of reasons to invoke an Emergency, as Dhar (2000) shows. In independent India, the power of the ballot box, at least to some extent, has restrained politicians from engaging in legal reform projects that ignore the interests of the wider public.

debate on post-colonialism and its distinction from postmodernity,[10] it must be stressed that the input of local, religious—and therefore largely Hindu—elements into the newly constructed secular edifice of post-colonial Indian laws has been far more extensive than lawmakers, and especially modernist scholars like Banerjee, have wanted to see.[11]

This huge divergence between observable reality and perceived positions lies in the insidious operation of modernist ideological blinkers, which urgently need to be removed through critical analysis of law and law-making in the religious pluralistic context of India. It is evident that expecting modern India to shed its Indianness through the process of law reform was asking rather too much and went too far in pushing law-centred axioms. Law-making is nowhere a culture-neutral process, as comparative analyses now clearly show.[12] To presume that hundreds of millions of people, who follow their own culture-specific forms of legal regulation, could be governed by a new law created for them by a modern state clearly does not make logical sense. Blind following of any particular ideology (and that includes *hindutva* ideology as well as secularism) does not recommend itself as a viable strategy for India.

Yet during the late colonial and early post-colonial periods, it became evident that the official secular agenda of Indian law-making precluded a revival of Hindu law as the official, national legal system. Hindu law would have to remain, if at all, a matter of personal law. India was not to become a Hindu state, but has of course a large Hindu majority, whose numbers were swelled by millions of refugees from East and West Pakistan. The critical question was therefore to what extent the Hindu personal law would continue to be operated and officially recognized by the post-colonial Indian state. If the earlier colonial regime had, after 1772, required the application of the *shastra* as a source of law,[13] the post-colonial lawmakers sought to pass statutes that would abolish recourse to that ancient law.

Similar observations are now being made about the moderating influence of coalition politics on the BJP (Ayres and Oldenburg 2002: 5 and 26–7).

[10] See Ch. 2. On distinctions of post-colonialism and postmodernity within their Marxist framework of reference, see in detail Spivak (1988) and Young (2001).

[11] The excellent Preface in Derrett (1970) provides a comprehensive overview. Young (2001: 339) refers negatively to 'Indira Gandhi's notorious political experiment', while in a classification of political actors, Nandy (1990: 76) highlights that she was a genuine non-believer in public, but a devout Hindu in private, which allows a glimpse of Hindu concepts as part of her politico-legal strategies.

[12] Recent studies in this field include above all Chiba (1986), Glenn (2000), and Menski (2000a).

[13] Derrett (1977: ix) wrote that '[t]his was as if a statute had been passed requiring lemon-juice to be produced from oranges', by which he clearly means that the rules of the old law were not of the same kind or genus as the new rules of the legal game. It is this strange process which earlier turned fluid principles of Hindu law and situation-specific statements into Anglo-Hindu legal precedents.

In this regard two specific theoretical understandings about the modernity of Hindu law and its future role in a modern secular state need to be examined. From a positivist perspective, it had until now been taken for granted among legal scholars, commentators, and lawmakers themselves that traditional Hindu law would be severely limited, and that the modern state would want and need to assert itself and its law-making powers to control and regulate an immensely diffuse and inherently conservative society. However, from a socio-legal perspective, following Sally Falk Moore (1978) and Masaji Chiba (1986), it would be equally arguable that no official state law would ever be able to assert itself totally over the myriad of unofficial laws operating in a huge jurisdiction such as India.

Even if the modern Indian state were to abolish Hindu law officially, this formally redundant law would live on in various forms and would make its pervasive 'invisible' presence felt in many ways. More than just a social phenomenon, it would remain a legal factor also after its formal abolition, in the sense of Chiba's 'unofficial law' and his concept of 'legal postulates', culture-specific value systems that interact with all aspects of any particular official and unofficial law. Taking a socio-legal perspective within the historical school tradition, one immediately recognizes that the formally abrogated law would still be more or less invisibly contributing to the 'real' law. This is precisely Eugen Ehrlich's (1913) 'living law', a situation-specific amalgam of the official law and people's law.

Post-colonial India, thus, had some tough decisions to make. Total abolition of traditional Hindu law and comprehensive adoption of Western-style modernity would not be feasible. Neither could be presented to the world, or indeed the hundreds of millions of Indian people, as a workable model for a huge, pluralistic fledgling state. The inevitable outcome would have to be a compromise between tradition and modernity, a middle way between outright abolition of Hindu law and its full-scale official recognition. Culture-blind positivist intervention would be counterproductive, most evidently in family law. The focus would be on the realm of personal law, but the place of Hindu law in that context would also have crucial implications on the basic structure of the Indian Constitution. The process of post-colonial Hindu law reform was therefore immensely comprehensive, and the spheres of private and public law could not be neatly segregated.

In independent India, two diametrically opposed perceptions of the future role of Hindu law were prominent, and can be regarded as approximate parallels of the theoretical positions examined above. At opposite sides of the ideological spectrum in terms of evaluating and using Hindu law as a factor in post-colonial India's future, Mahatma Gandhi (1869–1948) and Dr B.R. Ambedkar (1891–1956) stand out prominently within the conceptual structures of traditional historical analysis.[14] Ambedkar became a major protagonist

[14] On Ambedkar see in detail Chanchreek (1991) and Dhawan (1991). The major leader figure became Pandit Jawaharlal Nehru (1889–1964), independent India's

for the total abolition of Hindu law and went as far as burning the *Manusmṛti*, a desperate symbolic act being repeated in India today from time to time.[15]

In contrast, M.K. Gandhi, the Mahatma, envisaged a symbolic return to a Hindu golden age. Slogans of Indian self-rule (*Hind Swarāj*) were matched by the more explicitly Hindu but still ambivalent term *Rāmrājya* ('rule of Lord Rama').[16] This harks back to the ancient epic *Rāmāyaṇa* and thus the total idealism of classical Hindu law (see the section on Dharma and classical Hindu law in Chapter 3 earlier), while it also imports positivist notions about good governance by a morally upright, strong Hindu ruler. In other words, Gandhi combined dharma and *daṇḍa* in his ideas, clearly giving pre-eminence to the ideal of self-controlled order. Despite being a lawyer trained in England, unlike many of his contemporaries and those who were to follow, Gandhi did not believe in conventional government and thus rejected legal positivism and a 'strong state' in the Nehruvian sense in principle.[17] Mehta (1977: 214) pinpoints this well, citing K. Swaminathan:

> Gandhi felt that ninety per cent of our people didn't need to be governed. The only people who needed to be governed were the top five per cent, made up of the avaricious, the hoarders and the black marketeers, and the bottom five per cent, made up of the common thieves, the murderers, and

---

first prime minister, a keen modernist reformer who did not, however, entirely dismiss the Gandhian approach to law and politics. Khilnani (1997: 7) significantly reports that Nehru 'established a powerful and intriguing relationship with Gandhi'. Gandhi's influence, in the context of the present discussion, was probably mainly in terms of reminding zealous reformers like Nehru of the realities of village India, thus ruling out purely Austinian methods of law-making for postcolonial India. In theoretical legal parlance, the positivist inclinations of Nehru were tempered by the Gandhian legal approach, based on socio-legal theory.

[15] In 2000, this gave rise to Madhu Kishwar's (2000) pertinent comments on the irrelevance of Manu and her own potential role as a 'scriptural' authority on Hindu law through a *Madhusmṛti*.

[16] Brown (1985: 202–23) offers a detailed discussion on Gandhi and *swarāj*, which to him was more than freedom from colonial oppression, but an inner reform: 'It was a state of being which had to be created from the roots upwards, by the regeneration of individuals and their realization of their true spiritual being and goal .... His *swaraj* bore three hall-marks – unity among Indians of all religions, but particularly between Hindus and Muslims; the eradication of Untouchability; and the practice of *swadeshi*' (ibid.: 207).

[17] Brown (1985: 205) highlights that, in a sense, Gandhi 'can therefore properly be called an anarchist,' while she also notes Nehru's observation that 'Gandhi was "delightfully vague" about the actual form of government to be aimed for' (id.). The realisation that Gandhi wanted to use Hindu principles in the governance of modern postcolonial India made his suggestions totally impalatable to the modernists. Young (2001: 327) also notes that Gandhi's stance of anti-modernity 'was highly problematic for Indian feminism'.

> the gangsters. The rest were fit to manage their own affairs in the villages, because they were godly men and women, the custodians of ancient Indian wisdom, of India's morality and religion.

The multiple connotations of references to Hindu self-rule, a further manifestation of the ancient Hindu model of self-controlled order, and not merely a question of freeing India from the Raj at a particular time, requires careful analysis. It is evident that Gandhi's traditional 'soft state' model could not be acceptable for a Congress leadership that wanted a strong and secular post-colonial, modern state. Thus, ideological objections against reconstructing Hindu principles as tools of governance, as well as the pull towards positivist assertions of strong state power, precluded a formal revival of Hindu law in this period. With the early death of Gandhi, the engine that had driven official thinking in the direction of a soft Indian state fell silent.

But neither Gandhi's moralizing appeals nor Ambedkar's radical modernist agenda prevailed in the end, as India's legal development was set on the road to a carefully crafted compromise. The ancient culture-specific notions of governance and of the role of the state retained relevance for Indian governments of whatever political orientation and were not completely forgotten. These concepts also remain crucial today, but are not easy to detect, because they are in essence invisible 'legal postulates' in Chiba's (1986) terminology.[18] Even if those who governed did not themselves subscribe to such notions, they would be aware that large sections of the Indian electorate did not trust models of top-down government and would make their own sense of concepts like *swarāj* and 'self-controlled order'. Such divergencies of opinion and policy in India tend to be perceived by outsiders as messy lawlessness. However, there is a method to this pluralistic madness, an intricate formula of South Asian hybridity and legal pluralism that is built on compromises and subtle balancing acts.

Despite a huge literature on post-colonial development in India, such basic issues have remained insufficiently analysed, mainly because of certain political interferences and apprehensions. In the post-colonial parlance of Hindu activism, as well as Indian debates about good governance, obsessive focus on the ideal of Rama's rule on the one hand, and the perceived risks of rabid Hinduization on the other, have obfuscated the central issue of how to handle the pervasive presence of Hindu law and culture as a conceptual entity. There is clearly more to *hindutva* than majoritarianism or rabid fundamentalism. Whatever state there may be in India, it will not be able to simply govern in culturally neutral, plain top-down fashion. In practice, recognition of diversity will remain a crucial strategy. All over South Asia, the ideals of local self-controlled

[18] Drawing on Chiba's model, Menski (2001) analyses in detail how the Indian state, and especially the Indian judiciary, have constructed a new model of social welfare in explicit reliance on traditional 'legal postulates' to safeguard the survival of individuals.

order remain strong, and everyone concerned knows this.[19] Within the politicized struggles over *hindutva*, however, stereotypical Hindu ideals—or opposition to them—are being used for political purposes by participants on all sides in the fierce debates over how post-colonial Indian law should be structured and applied. The real issue is not an either/or binary pair of any kind, but an assessment of the actual extent of more or less invisible Hindu law input in any sphere of life. This has escaped notice, but more often than not, one must suspect, is actually being denied.

Thus the formal defeat of Hindu law as a tool of post-colonial governance for the Indian state as a whole was no victory for anyone; it did not bring the end of Hindu law, or its displacement. Clearly, this is what many enthusiastic modernist observers seem to have missed in their emphasis on progress and modernization. Galanter (1989: 15) explains legal modernism:

> The salient features of a modern legal system include uniform territorial rules, based on universalistic norms, which apportion rights and obligations as incidents of specific transactions, rather than of fixed statuses. These rules are administered by a hierarchy of courts, staffed by professionals, organized bureaucratically and employing rational procedures. The system contains regular and avowed methods for explicitly revising its rules and procedures. It is differentiated in task and personnel from other governmental functions; yet it enjoys a governmentally-enforced monopoly over disputes within its cognizance, permitting other tribunals to operate only in its interstices and subject to its supervision.

These are ambitious claims, particularly with regard to the claimed monopoly over dispute resolution processes. The observable and undeniable fact of a flourishing Hindu personal law jurisprudence *within and outside* the formal legal system in India should have given rise to detailed analyses many years ago. However, apart from some specialist studies,[20] the literature is oddly skewed by the positivist predilections of major legal textbook writers,[21] as noted earlier by Baxi (1986b), but not remedied.[22] Mainstream Indian legal writing has been dominated by a few men and their textbooks, which appear in slightly

[19] Significantly, but of course ideologically unrecognized and politically opposed, Muslim claims to local and individual self-control also assert themselves in India and have doubtlessly influenced the way in which the Indian legal system as a whole has reacted to the continued presence of personal laws.

[20] The leading studies are Derrett (1963c; 1968b; 1970; 1978a) and Galanter (1989). Derrett (1970: x) rightly emphasized that his *Critique of Modern Hindu Law* was the only effort of its kind and constituted a significant reversal from his earlier approach to writing about Hindu law (Derrett 1963c).

[21] Most prominent in this field are Mulla's *Hindu Law* (now Desai 1998) and Mayne's *Hindu Law and Usage* (now Kuppuswami 1986), but also the works of Diwan and Diwan (1993) and the more historically focused study of Jain (1990).

[22] Derrett (1970: 9) claims that '[b]ooks of authority are more of a nuisance than a help' and criticizes the approach of textbook writers in colourful terms (ibid.: 10):

updated versions every few years, but do not easily tolerate significant reassessments of an issue.[23] In contrast, but often equally unhelpful, much excellent and detailed writing on Hindu law issues comes from activists for the cause of women, who may be trained lawyers, but do not write primarily for practitioners.[24] Such non-mainstream writing has tended to veer to another extreme, turning into personalized crusades with anti-establishment venom (even if the authors are themselves establishment figures), anti-state rhetoric, and anti-law arguments that are often contradictory as they, in turn, expect law to solve perceived social problems. Dhavan (2001: 313) provides a trenchant assessment of the naive instrumentalism of law and development discourses and their 'crippling effect of forcing Indians to look down upon themselves'.

Remarkable gaps and significant inconsistencies persist in the academic coverage of modern Hindu law. Undoubtedly, a new comprehensive analysis of the modernization debates of Hindu law today is urgently needed.[25] However, if this fresh analysis, of necessity, involves recourse to the conceptual models of ancient Hindu law and their contemporary manifestations, many analysts are bound to feel that this is more than they can stomach. Since it will be necessary to revert to Sanskrit-based scholarship, as demonstrated in Chapters 3 and 4 earlier, such recourse to traditional Hindu concepts often stymies scholarly enthusiasm. Again, thus, ideology rather than purportedly objective and universal legal scholarship dominates the field. The powerful emergence and resonance of the discourse on modernity in Hindu law requires fresh critical analysis. The following section pinpoints the origins of British colonial rule and traces the evolution of this particular modernist discourse during that formative period.

'A mummified and quasisacrosanct subject, Hindu law cannot be seen by legal writers as a dynamic entity, but as some kind of mammoth, dug from the Siberian snows, its thousand-year-old flesh to be fed by bits and pieces to the judges whose chief aim is to evacuate the cases as quickly as possible. Piecemeal law-making provides the textbook writers with their public, and gives their productions a constant sale. Whether the law which the judges are handing down is good for the public no one knows, or cares—or so it would often seem'.

[23] A fine example of reluctant admission that the textbook writer had been wrong and the law had taken a different turn than the textbook said, is found in Diwan and Diwan (1991: 158–65).

[24] Notable recent exceptions are Lawyers Collective (2000) and Jaising (2001).

[25] The urge is clearly felt by many authors. See, e.g. Jois (1990a; 2000) and in detail Bhattacharjee (1994: 1–11). However, it seems that attempts by various Indian leading law schools to develop thinking and teaching on such issues run into familiar obstacles of resource allocation and, above all, lack of scholarly expertise. The old saying about 'lawyers without Sanskrit, and Sanskritists without law' applies today more than ever putting brakes on endeavours to make sense of the many links between Hindu traditions and today's legal systems. Dissatisfaction about the quality of scholarship is also being voiced in circles of Sanskrit scholars all over the world (Nanavati 1998; Michaels 2001b).

Early Colonial Debates on Codification and Hindu Law Reform

As demonstrated in the previous chapter, the colonial impact involved translating the classical concept of dharma as positivistic law. Yet this entailed more than mistranslation, ushering in a fundamentally different approach to, and understanding of, Hindu law. As demonstrated, dharmic self-controlled order was maintained primarily at the individual and local social level, by informal recourse to custom rather than formal litigation and textual authority (see Chapter 3). This is why *sadācāra*, officially 'the practice of good men, learned in the Veda' (Derrett 1957: 42), but ultimately local custom in its various manifestations, has remained such an important source of Hindu law.[26] By implication, this meant that justice was perceived as relative, law remained inherently flexible, and that there could never be one set of binding rules for all persons and situations in Hindu law. However, under British influence, which longed and groped for legal certainty, this flexible perception of law changed, providing legitimate space for rigidification and, ultimately, the perceived need to reform and codify Hindu law in modernizing Indian society.

The development of formal Anglo-Hindu legal structures led to a widening gulf between official law and unofficial laws and growing scholarly neglect for the sphere of Chiba's (1986) 'legal postulates', the specific value systems underpinning a system of official or unofficial legal rules. By the time of India's independence, the secularized views of Hindu law had gained prominence to such an extent that some legal positivists, led by Ambedkar, could argue for the total abolition of Hindu law as a manifestation of oppressive religion and irrational 'tradition' which had no place in a free, modern world. From this radical reformist perspective, there was also no room left for the legal recognition of Hindu customs (Derrett 1957: 78).

The seeds for such modernist arguments had been planted during colonial rule. The previous chapter showed in detail how the general trend towards modernization and unification of law, and later specifically of Hindu law, was first promoted by the British during the nineteenth century, in the interest of more efficient governance, not primarily as a strategy to uphold or reform the traditional Hindu law per se.[27] The movement towards formalization of legal rules gradually focused on remedying some perceived social evils among the Hindus (Jain 1990: 622) and was still later adopted by supposedly 'enlightened' sections of the Indian elite, who were instrumental in securing some general legislative reforms in the early twentieth century. Prime examples would

[26] This is interestingly confirmed for the Nepalese Hindu system by Michaels (2001a: 71), who sees the *pandit* in the *Muluki Ain* of Nepal as a guide on customary law rather than a textual authority.

[27] On British reluctance to interfere in Hindu and Muslim laws see Jain (1990: 496). The same study, at p. 509, argues that the Hindus themselves should have taken the initiative, but were unwilling to do so.

be the CMRA of 1929, which tried to do no more than its name indicates, and the Hindu Women's Right to Property Act of 1937, which gave Hindu widows a 'limited estate' in the share of their deceased husband to ensure their maintenance, but did not grant them absolute property rights.[28]

While independent India inherited the Anglo-Hindu law as it then stood, already before that date Hindu law had been formally applied only as a personal law, and its extent and operation had been limited by various procedural rules and civil court Acts.[29] Such formalistic statements confirm that scholars saw only the 'official law', when in fact there was much more to say about the wide socio-legal field of Hindu law. While it seems correct to find that the British reluctance to interfere in Hindu law 'stunted the growth of Hindu Law' (Jain 1990: 622), no legal study has clearly emphasized that common Hindus at that time were perhaps not really concerned about state-made Hindu laws and would studiously avoid any contact with the official law.[30] Other, more doctrinal writing has emphasized that in a colonial context, law reform imposed by the superior conquerors on a subject people is virtually an inevitable consequence. In retrospect, Banerjee (1984: 266) avidly legitimized such colonial law-making:

> The conquest of a country by an alien race is necessarily followed by the imposition of the legal system of the conquerors on the conquered people. The new rulers exercise power in accordance with laws, customs and administrative practices with which they are familiar in their own country, subject to local exigencies and political expediency. Moreover, they usually look upon their new subjects as peoples who are inferior to them and who would benefit by the replacement of their indigenous legal system by a system representing a higher stage of political development.

Such writing clearly reflects the perspective of legal positivism and inevitably leads to neglect for socio-cultural issues. Upendra Baxi (1986b) has convincingly argued that the poor state of sociology of law in India is a direct consequence of such traditional fixation on doctrinal legal studies and themes. Not surprisingly, the issue of law reform was prominently presented as a matter of

[28] This Act formally confirmed a right that Hindu widows had held within the traditional system, although not without challenge. On the various Hindu law Acts promulgated by the British colonial rulers, see Kuppuswami (1986: 54–61) and Desai (1998: 71–72). Diwan and Diwan (1993: 54) merely assert that 'the legislative modifications till August 15, 1947, are not insignificant' and list them, starting from the Caste Disabilities Removal Act of 1850 to the Hindu Marriages Validity Act of 1949.

[29] For details see Kuppuswami (1986: 13). Before the 1950 Constitution of India, the validity of statutes relating to Hindu law was determined under the Government of India Act, 1935 (ibid.: 81).

[30] While Baxi (1986b: 59) laments the lack of empirical literature on Indian law, he highlights some useful studies, particularly Chatterjee et al. (1971) and Dhagamwar (1974). Yang (1989) is relevant in this context. Guha (1997) recognizes the significant gaps between official policy and socio-legal reality.

codification, not of socio-legal amelioration and analysis. This was evident already during the late nineteenth century. Banerjee (1984: 280) cites a despatch of the Government of India to the Secretary of State, dated 10 March 1877, in which the utility of legal codification is emphasized and highly praised.[31] The historical analysis produced by Jain (1990) charts in abundant detail how the arguments for comprehensive codification of laws in India developed over time.[32] However, when Jain (1990: 463) highlights the chaos and great uncertainty of the law in British India, such comments relate first of all to the British-made Anglo-Indian law, not to Anglo-Hindu law:

> Codification envisages reduction of different branches of law to a clear, compact and scientific form. Only through codification it was possible to achieve certainty for uncertainty, a written and stable law instead of a wilderness of judicial precedents which were bewildering to the litigant and confusing to the court. It was only through codification that homogeneity of law in the country could be achieved, that the law could be systematised, simplified and made somewhat clear and precise.

Such arguments for codification imply criticism of the case law method, and appear to have been influenced significantly by Benthamite utilitarian thought,[33] on which Desai (1998: 66) offers a useful discussion:

> Codification is a well-worn subject. Its chief apostle was Bentham and its greatest antagonist was Savigny. It has been said that they were both giants, to each of whom half his prayers were granted, whilst the other half was scattered to the winds. According to Savigny, 'law should be gradually developed by the silent internal forces of national consciousness with the least possible interference by the legislature'. Modern jurisprudence ... accepts innovations on the substance of existing law and even extirpation and substitution of any part of that law ....

After the death of Bentham in 1832, the first Law Commission in India had enthusiastically advocated the introduction of a codified *lex loci* for British India.[34] This would have been based on English law and would have governed all persons who were not Hindu or Muslim. Relevant discussions can be traced to Lord Macaulay. In a famous statement of 1833, cited in Banerjee (1984: 276), he argued for codification and formalization of the law, saying that: 'Our principle is this—uniformity where you can have it—diversity where you must have it—but in all cases certainty'. This strongly expressed emphasis on legal certainty, more than anything else, reflects not only British despair about being

[31] Notably, even Banerjee (1984: 280) found this assessment of the virtues of codification over-optimistic.

[32] A useful discussion of the pros and cons of codification is found in Derrett (1957: 34–54).

[33] This is confirmed by Jain (1990: 464).

[34] This Law Commission acted under the authority of the Charter Act of 1833. For details see especially Jain (1990: 461–88).

dependent for expert guidance on *pandits* and *maulvis* at the time, but also a decidedly law-centred view of the world. Michaels (2001: 66) captures this well:

> ... the Company could not find what they were used to and what they also wanted to find in Hindu law: clarity, accuracy, certainty, uniformity and finality. Hindu law remained the law of different social groups, regions and schools. For the British it was too customary, too natural, too religious. After some time they were so desperate that they even compiled their own digest of Hindu law.

This search for certainty was and is presumed to be 'rational', as Baxi (1968b: 23) confirms with reference to Macaulay's law reform process generally. This leads inevitably to the claim that comprehensive codification would be desirable and feasible. Banerjee (1984: 277) emphasizes that '[t]he two chief features of the continuous import of English Law were centralization and codification'. These were important factors in unifying the country (ibid.: 279), although such assertions overlook that the whole subcontinent was not a contiguous colonial territory, but was interspersed with a variety of Princely States. In other words, even if the Hindu law in the territories under direct British rule had been unified through colonial legal intervention, there would still be numerous local legal systems in existence, and the perceived problems of plurality and uncertainty would only have been remedied marginally.[35] Hence, such wide-ranging proposals were simply too ambitious and could not be implemented, while the agenda of codification itself was not abandoned. Jain (1990: 487) highlights that the commission's Report clearly exposed the uncertainty of law in the country, directed attention to the complexity of the problems and warned of complications regarding codification.

In a departure from Benthamite optimism about the utility of comprehensive codification, the Second Law Commission, which was appointed on 29 November 1853 and reported on 13 December 1855, came to the conclusion that 'what India wants is a body of substantive Civil Law' (Jain 1990: 493), thus advocating a strategy of piecemeal codification of the 'general law', while the Commission 'was positively against the codification of the Hindu or Muslim law' (ibid.: 494) and gave detailed reasons for this (id.):

> The Hindu law and Mohammedan law derive their authority respectively from the Hindu and Mohammedan religions. It follows that, as a British legislature cannot make Mohammedan or Hindu religion, so neither can it make Mohammedan or Hindu law .... We think it clear that it is not advisable to make any enactment which would stand on such a footing.

[35] Guha (1997) could have taken more explicit notice of this issue, which fits his analysis of dominance without hegemony. Occasionally, a Princely State would go ahead and produce significant legal reforms. In Baroda, the *Hindu Nibandha* of 1937 created advanced, pro-women laws that generated much interest.

This is more than mere respect for Hindu or Muslim religion in line with the Warren Hastings Regulation of 1772, or a reflection of a policy of non-intervention for fear of native uprisings, but a glimpse of recognition that positivist legal intervention has definite limits and that law-making itself cannot solve all the problems of humanity. While the language of the quote above focuses on religion as a basis for legal rules,[36] the central element of traditional social norms remains unacknowledged, but was silently present at all times, confirmed by explicit recognition elsewhere of the views of Savigny, in particular, as the protagonist of the historical school of jurisprudence. As a result of such officially unacknowledged realizations, the Hindu personal law was left alone and '[t]he Commission's significant recommendation against codifying the personal laws of the Hindus and Muslims was observed rather scrupulously in later years' (Jain 1990: 496).

The British thus left all matters of Hindu personal law to self-regulation, unless there were certain atrocious violations of civilized norms of decency and justice. While the Indian colonial regime never developed a formal 'repugnancy clause', as introduced in African law, colonial intervention in Hindu law subjects did eventually focus on perceived social ills in Indian society. The inherent tension between the civilizing mission and the desire for smooth colonial rule and undisturbed exploitation of resources is brought out well by Banerjee (1984: 282), who appears to criticize the conservative attitude of those Orientalists, like Warren Hastings and Burke, who were ready to accept what the Hindus did and argued against legal interference. Banerjee (id.) shows that until 1813, the British 'followed a policy of non-interference in the religious, social and cultural life of their Indian subjects'. Derrett (1957: 55) reports that the project of the codification of Hindu and Muslim law 'was dropped as impracticable in 1855'. Yet this was not the end of the agenda to codify and reform Hindu law during the colonial period.

Following the assumption of British sovereignty in 1858, legislative activity concentrated on the field of general laws. Only then did the so-called conservative attitude gradually abate as it 'gave way to radical criticism of Indian society and culture, and a powerful section of public opinion in England demanded reforms which would transform and reform the allegedly decadent society' (Derrett 1957: 55). Discussing specifically the codification of Hindu law, Jain (1990: 632–34) traces the earlier motives for non-interference and charts the growth of Anglo-Hindu case law as laying foundations for further British intervention in Hindu law. Jain (1990: 634) observes:

> The growth of Hindu law was very fast as would be evident if one were to look through the various editions of Mayne's Hindu law. During the period 1878 to 1938, there were ten editions of this treatise, and between one

[36] Then as now, the favourite but utterly simplistic Muslim argument that Islamic law cannot and must not be subjected to state control resurfaces here, demonstrating that the complexity of interaction between state, religion, and society continues to befuddle analysts.

> edition and another, so many important decisions were rendered by the courts, and so many new points settled, that each subsequent edition needed a lot of rewriting. Case law multiplied very fast and important decisions on several branches of Hindu law came in quick succession.

As a result of such rapid changes in Anglo-Hindu case law, which began to cause much confusion, a programme of comprehensive codification was energetically put through, especially during 1861–1879 (Jain 1990: 499–514). The Fourth Law Commission, which made only one report in its brief life, submitted on 18 November 1879, focused on the process of codification itself, distinguishing two stages: first the orderly and systematic arrangement of the rules relating to particular subjects into specific Acts, and secondly compilation of all these Acts into a general code (Jain 1990: 505). This line of reasoning demonstrates that the concept of a uniform civil code as a project of complete codification of all laws, the ultimate pinnacle of legal positivist ambitions, has been hovering around India for a long time.[37] At that historical stage, there was certainly much belief in the need to have codified laws. Jain (1990: 506) indicates that '[e]very settled community desires to have fixed laws. India had a special need for legislation in view of the introduction of English law there which gave rise to anomalies, inconsistencies and difficulties'. But it should not be overlooked that again, the perceived deficiencies in the law are explicitly related here to the Anglo-Indian law, not to Hindu law. An assessment of the general law in India is provided by Jain (1990: 510) in a passage that imports a typically law-centred image of legal voids and gaps,[38] needing to be filled and plugged through Codes:

> The period of codification was ushered into the country in 1833 with the Macaulay Law Commission .... The state of the law before the Codes was extremely chaotic. India then was singularly devoid of law on many branches .... No rules existed on a number of subjects. Whatever laws existed were uncertain, conflicting, contradictory and vague. The courts, found it very difficult to administer law in a sound manner. When cases came before them for decision ... they began to make law in ....

It is quite remarkable in this quote, as well as from further comments in the same source, that judicial law-making was so strongly seen as a negative phenomenon at that time. The definite preference for codification is evident, and Jain (1990: 510) argues that codification has on the whole been 'very beneficial to the people in the country', emphasizing again the increase of certainty and

[37] A reference to Art. 44 of the Indian Constitution and the ultimate goal of total codification is found in Jain (1990: 513), observing that, 'even today, the formulation of a uniform code yet remains a distant and far-fetched goal'.

[38] In my view, such wording hides the fact that those who felt empowered to apply the law simply did not know enough about the traditional rules of Hindu law on various subjects. To argue simply that there was no law is not only myopic, but also devious, unless we exonerate such views by reference to positivist conceptualizations of law.

uniformity. Further, relying on the earlier study of Rankin and the observation that English law had been transferred to India by codification rather than direct reception, Jain (1990: 513–14) considers the difficult question about the extent to which the codified English law could be said to have become indigenous:

> But looking at the development from the Indian point of view, one entertains a doubt whether it was right to throw overboard lock, stock and barrel all that was indigenous in favour of importing English law wholesale. Doubts remain whether the foreign system of law has remained confined to the elite or has permeated the Indian soil and come to be accepted by the common man. A question remains whether or not it would have been more prudent for the law givers to ascertain the principles of indigenous law, to test which of them had vitality and viability in the contemporary social conditions and then seek to codify them.

Jain (1990: 514) argues that 'there may be some value in giving to the people the law which is a part of their culture, traditions, heritage and outlook', thus partly explaining the British reluctance to get involved in the codification of Hindu personal law. At this stage, it may well have been realized that the Hindus had their own laws on virtually every aspect of life, but did the colonial regime really want to implement and develop such laws? If so, the preferred method would still be through codification. The need for eventual legislative reform of Hindu law was not really doubted, while the practical difficulties at the time were recognized. Jain (1990: 509) reports that as early as 1882, Sir Courtenay Ilbert, a Law Member, had written in a minute that there was much litigation concerning Hindu family law and that there was a need to consider the potential for reforms. But it was felt that the initiative should come from the Hindus themselves. When Ilbert tried to ascertain privately whether leading members of the Hindu community would consider any reform project of family law, he found much general reluctance and formed the view that 'no part of their law was ripe for codification and that it had better be left for the present to the more gradual and less direct action of judicial decision' (id.).

There was, thus, a growing perception that Hindu law was becoming 'ripe' for legal reform.[39] Such statements seek to legitimize legal intervention, but deny the capacity of Hindu society for creating internal rule systems that could be seen as 'fair and equitable', particularly for low-caste Hindus and women. Rather than maintaining a concern for society, the energies of legal scholars focused on the magic remedy of codification in Benthamite mode, blurring the lines between general law reform and legislative intervention in the Hindu personal law. Desai (1998: 67) reflects this rationale:

> Bentham wrote that the great utility of a code of laws is to cause the debates of lawyers and the debates of former times to be forgotten and that its style

[39] Desai (1998: 66) explicitly argues in favour of Hindu law codification, since 'the social, economic and political transformation in the country had rendered imperative substantial and radical changes in that law'.

> should be characterised by force and harmony. The code of his dreams, one that would not require schools for its explanation or casuists to unravel its subtleties and be a complete self-sufficing enactment, was indubitably an ideal to be pursued but he pushed his theory too far when in his aim at finality he minimised all practical difficulties in the way of such legislation.

The powerful arguments in favour of codification were certainly not unchallenged. Desai (1998: 67) explains that '[c]odification has all along been opposed by those who deprecated legislation in any shape or form in Hindu law on religious grounds', as well as by those who argued that it would be impossible to give legislative form to the complicated structure of Hindu law. While it was alleged that '[m]uch of the opposition was grounded in sentiment and not in reason' (id.), it was not realized by some traditionalists that the *shastric* authors had been progressive and had tried to keep the law in harmony with their changing environments. Rather than addressing the substantive reservations against the transition from a situation-specific system of law to a uniform code, Desai (1998: 67) alleges mere sentimentality for 'tradition', insinuating that Hindu arguments could not be based on reason, while modernity is equated with rationality. Other legal writers have rushed to pronounce that Hindu law was in danger of death anyway and needed to be revived by modernist reforms. Diwan and Diwan (1993: 54) declare that 'Hindu law became static and did not conform to the changed context of Hindu society. The progressive section of Hindu society always clamoured for reforms'.

The patronizing approach taken to legal regulation by the British, whose 'rule of law' is supposed to have been very different from what the Hindus knew, and was perceived as far superior to traditional despotism (Cohn 1997: 62–5) or the alternative model of the theocratic state (ibid.: 65-72), is strongly reflected in modernist writing. Banerjee (1984: 269) emphasises that '[t]he idea that rights and privileges must be derived from legally constituted authority was a peculiar inheritance of the English people', while on the other hand, '[t]he English rulers knew that the history of India did not provide even a crude precedent for constitutional government' (id.). Banerjee (1984: 275) argues that the precious legacy of the rule of law was given to India, and an entirely new concept of justice took firm roots.[40] Banerjee (1984: 281) further launches into a discussion of why it was essential for English law to be brought to the fore:

> On the whole, codification, despite its imperfections, was a progressive force; for, through the importation of English legal principles, it contributed to the modernization of India's legal and administrative structure .... The

[40] That this is not quite so simple is evident from the detailed discussion in Cohn (1997: 62–75). As shown in Ch. 4 earlier, Cohn discussed the same process, but not explicitly from a legal angle, emphasizing the process of construction of colonial knowledge. Cohn (1997: 57) begins to discuss the invention of a colonial state system in India, but is quite wrong to assume that in all colonial situations '[t]he laws of these colonies were the laws of Great Britain'.

> uniformity of laws led not only to uniformity in the administration of justice but to uniformity of social conduct as also of general outlook on life. A society brought into contact with Western civilization and passing through diverse socio-economic changes could not have been re-built upon the foundations laid by the *Dharmasastras* or the four Schools of Muslim Law.

This still conflates the codification of the general law and the Hindu personal law, as the debate appears to be primarily about the former. Banerjee's classic modernist statements deny the relevance of tradition and see the future of 'civilized' Indian laws secured by copying models from English law. A related assumption appears to be that legal change in the general law would somehow engender positive developments in the personal laws, presumably through some form of legal osmosis. In this context, Banerjee (1984: 281–7) discusses the modernising impact of British legislation 'for the removal of certain social abuses which formed a part of our medieval inheritance' (ibid.: 281–2), focusing on specific legal problems such as sati abolition. One wonders, though, whether presenting the problems of law reform from this angle was perhaps a device to disguise the colonialists' realization that deeper and systematic interference in Hindu (and Muslim) personal laws would be counterproductive for governance, and would also simply be ineffective because of the strength of social norms. There are certainly numerous indications that the British hesitated to interfere in Hindu law. Banerjee (1984: 282) tellingly emphasizes that '[t]he best policy was to let the sleeping dogs lie as undisturbed as possible'. Towards the end of the colonial period, however, there were certainly enough educated Indians to push the British more or less gently towards allowing them to experiment with legal reforms in Hindu law.

Late Colonial Reform Debates: The Role of the Hindu Elite

As we began to see above, the debates on Hindu law reforms in the run-up towards August 1947 have an impressive pedigree. Jain (1990: 634) reports that resolutions in favour of Hindu law reform were sought as early as 1921 and resurfaced from time to time until the early 1940s. By 1938, a large number of bills on Hindu law were pending, giving rise to concerns about fresh confusions rather than increased clarity and legal certainty. The last statute in this series, the Hindu Married Women's Right to Separate Residence and Maintenance Act of 1946, enabled a married Hindu woman to claim separate residence and maintenance from her husband in certain circumstances, for example if he took a second wife or a concubine, became an apostate, was guilty of cruelty or desertion, or suffered from a loathsome disease (Jain 1990: 623). This kind of legal reform went well outside traditional Hindu norms of conjugal life, and reflected the growing reformist zeal of an Indian elite of foreign-trained lawyers. Similarly, when the Hindu Women's Right to Property Act of 1937 was promulgated, this immediately presented a number of intricate problems of interpretation, since the entire traditional *Mitākṣarā* system had of course not been abolished.[41]

As a result, renewed calls for Hindu law codification continued to emphasize certainty and simplicity, arguing that comprehensive codification would be better than piecemeal effort. However, the indigenous proposal for a comprehensive Hindu code was initially rejected by the British as 'too contentious and costly' (Jain 1990: 634), while leading Hindu writers on Hindu law, such as Dr Ganganath Jha, an early leading authority on Hindu law (Derrett 1957: 55), began to argue more and more vociferously for legislative involvement, reflecting a change of view within the Hindu elite about the 'ripeness' of Hindu law for legislative intervention.

Being eventually convinved of the strength of indigenous support for law reforms, the government appointed a Hindu Law Committee on 25 January 1941 under the chairmanship of B. N. Rau (hence known as the Rau Committee),[42] with the specific initial task to suggest amendments to the Hindu Women's Right to Property Act of 1937, but also a wider brief to examine various reform proposals for Hindu law. The Committee reported on 19 June 1941, pointed out several defects in the 1937 Act, and argued that such defects were an inevitable consequence of the piecemeal process of legislation. Their advice was that since it was not safe to make small piecemeal changes, it would be best to codify the entire field or, if that was not possible, to tackle at least those branches of the law that were said to be in need of reform. In effect, thus, the Rau Committee Report of 1941 'merely urged the Government to go ahead with comprehensive legislation' (Derrett 1957: 57) and suggested that this would be a fairly easy task.[43] As Jain (1990: 635) reports, the view was that internal differences might be ironed out without too much difficulty and that it would really be a great achievement if Hindu law could be unified and a code produced which might apply uniformly to all Hindus throughout the country. 'On points of difference amongst the Schools and Sub-Schools, that view which appeared to be the most liberal .... could be adopted'. Thus, the reformers would simply pick and choose from the rich sources of Hindu law and the code 'generally speaking shall be a blend of the finest elements in the various schools of Hindu law' (Derrett 1957: 58). In addition to unification arguments,

[41] Derrett (1957: 57) wrote that '[t]he Act gave rise to several real difficulties of interpretation, some of which may not be capable of satisfactory solution'.

[42] The Committee was composed of three more members, a former Calcutta High Court judge, D.N. Mitter, a law college principal, J.R. Gharpure, and a lawyer from Baroda, V.V. Joshi, whose Princely State had first-hand experience in passing comprehensive modern legislation on Hindu law matters.

[43] Derrett (1957: 58) cites the words of the Report, but is scathing about the scope for executing the process of law reform as envisaged by the Committee, saying that 'this prospectus, with somewhat visionary direction, could hardly have been expected to come to fruition as planned; the successive drafts of the "Hindu Code Bill" have been alike in failing to reach any such standard'.

the need for harmonization of the often outdated legal norms with more progressive and flexible social norms was highlighted. Jain (1990: 635) summarizes this significant new perception well:

> The Hindu society was undergoing vast socio-economic changes .... In the absence of the law keeping pace with the change, a gap, a dichotomy, had arisen between law and society. Hence the need to modify the law so that it might satisfy the legitimate wants, aspirations and needs of the people. In modern times, this can only be done through legislation'.

Interestingly, this recognizes that Hindu society had moved ahead of the law. The reference to 'the people' here is most certainly taking account only of the Hindu elite. Their members had already begun to experience the impact of some legal reforms. The reaction had not been entirely positive, since piecemeal codification had manifestly created its own unforeseen difficulties. Inevitably, this led to further arguments in favour of comprehensive codification, advanced by the Hindu intelligentsia and reported by Jain (1990: 636), who claims that '[t]he only way out, therefore, is to take the law in one piece and introduce reform in all those places where reform is desired all at once so that an integrated and co-ordinated body of law could emerge. This can be done only through the process of codification of Hindu law'.

It is interesting to see how, in its focus on the desirability of codification, the Committee linked perceived past and present methods of law reform. It imagined ancient Hindu lawmakers at work, whose efforts now needed to be undone, if necessary, in radical fashion.[44] Jain (1990: 636) quotes from the Committee Report, which again makes reference to ancient Hindu lawgivers as though the classical Hindu law had been a positivist edifice:

> In the view of the Committee, the time had arrived to codify Hindu law. In the old days, the task of codifying the law from time to time was performed by successive law-givers and commentators "who by a judicious process of selection and exposition of the ancient texts moulded the law to the needs of the time. But there are no *Smritikars* and commentators now; we have the Legislature and the Courts, but the Courts are bound by the law as interpreted by the commentators. This means that the growth of Hindu law has been arrested at the point at which it was left by *Vijnaneswara, Jimutavahana*, and other recognised commentators." "It follows, therefore, that the main agency for altering the law according to the changing needs of the community must in future be the Legislature." But the Legislature must deal with the subject as a whole. "The aim must be to produce a logical and coherent code of Hindu law".

[44] Derrett (1957: 70) reports that Dr Ambedkar, who chaired the Select Committee which received the Rau Committee Report, saw himself as a second Manu, but with the additional title, 'breaker of the pride of the twice-born classes'. It is no surprise, therefore, that his ideas for Hindu law reform were not carried, and he ultimately resigned in disgust.

The Committee also argued in a familiar phrase that '[c]odification does not necessarily mean the abolition of the Schools: the aim should be uniformity where possible and divergence where inevitable' (Jain 1990: 636). The Committee floated the idea that a judicious selection of the best elements of traditions of various schools might be made, and finally recommended that Hindu law should be codified in gradual stages, beginning with the law of intestate succession and marriage.[45] Significantly, Derrett (1957: 59) argued that '[t]his must frankly be dismissed as an amateurish approach, since every part of Manu and every part of all the *shastras* is effective and valid only in its traditional context, and the meaning can by no means be made out by the first Sanskrit-knowing person to read them'.[46]

The Committee was then asked to draft two bills, one dealing with intestate succession and the other with marriage. The former received particular attention because of its implications on property law. It was referred to a Select Committee, 'which expressed an opinion in its report that action be taken to codify the whole of the Hindu law as far as possible' (Jain 1990: 637). It appears that this encouraging response motivated the colonial Government of India to throw its earlier caution about involvement in Hindu law reform to the wind. The Rau Committee was revived on 24 January 1944, with the explicit brief to formulate a Code of Hindu Law, which should be as complete as possible, dealing with succession, maintenance, marriage and divorce, minority and guardianship, and adoption. Jain (1990: 637) reports how several steps were taken to draft the Code in stages and to elicit opinions from selected lawyers, bar associations, and interested individuals. However, this project of a comprehensive Hindu code soon ran into serious opposition and Jain recounts that 'orthodox opinion was aroused by certain proposed provisions of the code, particularly, the provision for divorce and the provision for daughter's share in her father's property' (id.).

Convinced that the proposal to codify Hindu law was a sound project, the Committee argued that it would benefit Hindu society, and the reforms would make this complex law available to all literate persons in the country. Further, it was seen as necessary to create a Hindu Code in which the principle of equality before the law was entrenched and in which distinctions of caste and gender would cease to be recognized. Interestingly, the argument that only the legislature could actively modify the law was again repeated in this context. Jain (1990: 637–8) reports that 'as the courts would not recognise the validity of any new custom, there was no scope for any fresh customs to grow. Nor could the courts themselves effect any large improvements and changes in the law ... bound as they were by the theory of *stare decisis*'.

[45] Desai (1998: 67). The same information is briefly given by Diwan and Diwan (1993: 54).

[46] Derrett, in O'Flaherty and Derrett (1978: 55), cited in Ch. 4 earlier, rightly emphasized the role of the shastric experts as social mouthpieces rather than law-makers.

The revised Code was published in the Gazette of India on 19 April 1947 and the original plan was that it should become law on 1 January 1948 (Derrett 1957: 60). Opposition to the projected Code was met by the astounding assertion, as reported by Jain (1990: 638), that 'the aim of the ancient law-givers, the writers or compilers of the *Smritis*, was always to produce a Code of law which would be applicable to all Hindus in the land'. Such positivist fantasizing was hardly a proper response in view of the shattered myths of ancient Hindu law-making. The claim that Hindu law had been uniformly applicable earlier certainly does not reflect reality; yet in the heat of the argument, such assertions passed uncriticized. More immediate concerns were the threatened abolition of the joint Hindu family and increased property rights for women.

We are not told by Jain (1990: 638) if the distortions about the role of ancient lawmakers led to opposition to modern legislative intervention. Diwan and Diwan (1993: 54) identified much opposition to the bill, concluding that, by and large, this opposition was from the uninformed and orthodox sections of Hindu society. This juxtaposition of Hindu irrationality and modern rationality seems to imply that Hindu opposition could be ignored: the lawmakers somehow knew better.[47] Jain (1990: 638) emphasizes that the so-called Hindu orthodoxy questioned the legitimacy of the government to introduce Hindu law reforms on religious grounds, since '[t]he conservative and orthodox element in the Hindu Society had raised the argument that the State had no power to alter Hindu Law which was religious in nature and was laid down by the Hindu sages'.

Here again, it is evident that conservative Hindus themselves claimed—for whatever reason—that the ancient *smṛtikars* were virtual legislators. If indeed it was assumed that ancient Hindu law had been laid down for all Hindus, any arguments against state intervention could hardly be successful now. So they were predictably dismissed out of hand by the Committee, which staunchly defended the legal competence of the Indian government to legislate on Hindu law. However, while the Committee was clearly in favour of comprehensive codification, the emerging opposition to this strategy led to the suggestion that piecemeal reforms might, after all, be more palatable to the people of India than a comprehensive code of Hindu law.

The grave atrocities accompanying the independence of two new states in mid-August 1947 temporarily halted the project of Hindu law reform. It was shelved for some time while other urgent business was seen to. Various factors in connection with the process of making the Constitution and resettlement of millions of refugees took priority. However, debates about modernizing Hindu law through codification soon regained prominence when the agenda of modernizing Indian society along socialist, democratic lines were redrafted.

[47] Derrett (1968b: 329) notes in this regard that 'the villager is accustomed to paternalistic government, and ... used to being told that he is ignorant and does not know what is best for him'.

6

Contesting Modernity: Post-colonial Evolution of Hindu Law

The previous discussion pinpointed the origins of the discourse on modernizing Hindu law and purging it of undesirable traditional elements as lying in colonial and Hindu elite endeavours to reform and codify Hindu law. This chapter develops that analysis to examine the discourse of modernity during the post-colonial period and the agenda and processes of Hindu law reform that accompanied and shaped it. It is demonstrated that the self-imposed task of transforming the traditional Anglo-Hindu law into the modern Hindu personal law involved a large amount of codification and reforms between the 1950s and 1970s. The process followed secularizing Austinian models of law-making rather than Hindu law principles.

Ultimately, as we saw, the modernist ambition of codification and reform went as far as formal de-Hinduization through a projected uniform civil code.[1] As this chapter shows, however, despite the onward march of such 'progressive', modernist agenda, formal attempts to reform and codify Hindu law were constantly contested and undermined. These forms of resistance were perceptible from the beginning of the early independence period, and more so over the following decades, as the discourse and practice of modernizing Hindu law increasingly lost momentum in the face of the stark realities of legal pluralism and social diversity in the Indian polity and society.

The Modernizing Process of Hindu Law

The formal future of Hindu law as the majority system of personal laws in India was safeguarded in 1950, despite a Constitution that appears to speak the language of modern Western constitutionalism and guarantees equality before the law for all citizens. Not just Hindu personal law, therefore, but the entire legal system of post-colonial India was subjected to an intricate compromise

[1] On the politics of this code see Menski (2001: 345–402). Derrett (1970: 1) still favoured such a code, but clearly saw that an Indian uniform civil code would be 'based firmly in the then state of the Hindu law, the personal law of the majority'. He proceeded to analyse 'the needs of Hindus in the delicate stage immediately prior to the drafting and eventual enactment of a civil code which will replace the personal laws' (ibid.: 8).

from the 1950s onwards, which would constantly need to be fine-tuned. The most significant fact for the present analysis remains that Hindu law was neither abolished altogether and declared irrelevant, nor formally imposed, in what would be an act of majoritarian violence, on the new nation as a whole. Instead, Hindu law continued to apply to Hindus in India, whoever may be included in that vast category. As the dominant personal law, it was given space to undergo an interactive process of synthesis, reconstruction, and reinvigoration, allowing us to view Hindu law today as a phenomenon that has moved well beyond the parameters of adversarial discourses about tradition and modernity. Here, then, is another classic example of overlapping consensus: we see that Hindu law was banned from openly infusing the Constitution, and yet it has been recognized in the shape of the Hindu personal law and, in carefully chosen secular language, even in numerous constitutional provisions. In addition, rather than being on the wane as a legal influence, indigenous conceptual ideas about relative justice have made a huge comeback throughout Indian law during the late 1980s and 1990s and are now manifesting themselves more openly as sociocultural influences that shape postmodern Indian legal realities (Menski 1996b; 2001).

The present analysis needs to bring out and examine to what extent the post-colonial leadership of modern India has considered use of the traditional Hindu framework of reference in reshaping and rebuilding modern Indian laws and the Hindu personal law system. In this context, the guiding state policy of Indian secularism evidently meant that India could not, and should not, formally become a Hindu state, only a state with an overwhelming Hindu majority.[2] Thus, after the rapid vanishing act of Mountbatten in 1947 (Bose and Jalal 1998: 198), the general Indian law would remain based on secular principles, while the personal law system would be retained, despite criticism about this concession to religion.[3] India was initially too busy with massive refugee problems, national reconstruction, and the wider political and legal restructuring process to give much attention specifically to Hindu law reforms. However, there had already been substantive debates on Hindu law reform during the Raj and especially in the 1940s. Perhaps for this reason, too, India moved fairly fast during the 1950s to bring about a major restructuring of Hindu law.[4]

[2] That issue has continued to be contested, too. On representations of secularism, see in detail Madan (1987; 1998), Sheth and Nandy (1996), and Nandy (1999). M.K. Gandhi was murdered in 1948 by people who wanted total Hindu rule and did not appreciate the pluralistic Indian strategy of secularism.

[3] Many commentators continue to see personal laws simply as a matter of religion. In fact only the criteria for determining jurisdiction are based on religion, while the rules by which people live largely come from local and family customs.

[4] Pakistan, in contrast, not only took much longer to tackle reforms in Muslim personal law but also hoped that the Hindu personal law might just become irrelevant. While there has been no attention at all given to Pakistani Hindu law, it continues to exist as a largely Anglo-Hindu system of official law which in social reality is operated as a customary legal system.

Like the British before them, therefore, the post-colonial Indian lawmakers continued the ancient Hindu system of personal law regulation and again made few changes to the legal system as a whole. As before, the top of the political pyramid was once more removed as a new ruling elite gained the mandate to remould the legal system along purportedly new, yet familiar, formal lines. It was a historic opportunity to make a fresh start,[5] but to what extent would this be feasible when it came to legal reform, given that lawyers (and post-colonial politicians) have tended to be protective of the status quo?

Legal conservatism exerted its pervasive influence also with regard to the general legal framework, which was at first simply inherited from the colonial system and only later subjected to minor modifications,[6] and some cleaning-up operations to throw out old laws.[7] The approach to Hindu personal law appeared to be quite different, however, as the modernizing post-colonial state developed an appetite and ambition for personal law reform. The ambition itself had been nurtured during the final decades of British rule, partly as a result of the British forms of 'civilizing mission' and its perceived fruits in the form of Indian social reform movements.[8] Almost by definition, the modernization of Hindu law in India was perceived as a historical opportunity for removing 'tradition', a chance to wipe out the remaining vestiges of traditional norms in the Hindu personal law as they had developed and sheltered under Anglo-Hindu law. It was a revolution, but it remained by its very nature incomplete. In reality, despite all the hype, the reformed law was no more than a half-way house in the ongoing legal process of harmonizing law and society.[9] Even in the new field of constitutional law-making, which is carefully phrased in secular language, Hindu law concepts are not totally absent.[10]

[5] Brown (1985: 307) refers in this context to Nehru's famous midnight speech at the end of an era, on 14–15 August 1947, which 'was passionately hopeful, claiming the end had come of "a period of ill fortune" and that India was about to rediscover her true self'.

[6] Several authors have noted that Indian lawyers were only too happy to use the newly instituted laws, because it was in essence the system that they knew as a tool of trade.

[7] On this process, which extended into the 1960s and is by no means complete, see Jain (1990: 568).

[8] Young (2001: 22) indicates that for the British, this method of cultural imperialism was really a later product of imperialism in its nineteenth century form. His analysis highlights the various forms of *mission civilisatrice* and the ambivalence of colonial powers towards local cultures.

[9] Derrett (1957: 49) remained unimpressed, observing that 'in any event the result would be patchwork, difficult to expound and use, a happier hunting-ground for the expert practitioner than even the existing jungle of authorities'.

[10] Sometimes, even the most careful secular drafting cannot avoid giving away that we are dealing with a legal system in which Hindu concepts remain an all-pervasive element. Art. 48 of the Constitution of 1950 provides, regarding 'Organisation of agriculture and animal husbandry', that '[t]he State shall endeavour

As we saw, the legalistic positivization of Hindu law was one of the major results of British legal intervention. When the originally context-sensitive rules of Hindu law were turned into precedents, something important was overlooked and lost that had always intimately connected Hindu law and society, namely the situation-specific concern for an appropriate solution to any particular problem. Brushing this aside, for the sake of legal certainty, marginalized the implied recognition in Hindu law that all individual legal actions had not just a 'seen' purpose but also reflected invisible linkages in the Hindu mind. The post-colonial Indian leaders had a unique historical chance to make fundamental changes to the Indian legal system and to mould and reform Hindu law as they saw fit. While Hindu traditions were seen as inherently defective and corrupted, overlooking the impact of such culture-specific elements of the legal system was bound not to inspire confidence in the wider public. A compromise, therefore, had to evolve over time to balance modernist ambitions with public opinion.

Setting the Debate for Reforms: The 1950s

On independence in 1947, India had inherited the complex colonial legal system, characterized by extreme plurality of laws and built around a large existing nucleus of secular, general Anglo-Indian laws created under colonial rule. As false myths about India's legal heritage are constantly repeated, by a misinformed general public as well as so-called comparativists and even historians,[11] it is necessary to reiterate here that this was not English law as such, but rather a hybrid legal system based on principles and rules of English and Scottish laws, which was tailor-made for British India.[12] It had many characteristics of common law and had retained this flavour through the importance given to judicial involvement, but Anglo-Indian law was also to a very large extent codified and thus in form and substance recognizable as a civil law system.[13] This manifestly hybrid body of laws included earlier elements of constitutional law, particularly the Government of India Act of 1935,[14] which came to signify the

to organise agriculture and animal husbandry on modern and scientific lines and shall, in particular, take steps for preserving and improving the breeds, and prohibiting the slaughter, of cows and calves and other milch and draught cattle'.

[11] Guha (1997:1) vigorously attacks the 'elitist bias in British Indian historiography', but does not go far enough in his critique of law-centred assumptions.

[12] On the curious love-hate relationship between India and Britain, which 'must be taken seriously, since it completely transcends individual attitudes or personal psychologies', see Derrett (1970: xv).

[13] Jain (1990) emphasizes the importance of English law in India, but also provides evidence that many of the early laws were either gradually rendered defunct or abolished. Today, the notion that India is a common law jurisdiction therefore primarily implies a political statement about the historical impact of British colonial rule, rather than an accurate description of the present legal system.

[14] On this see Jain (1990: 553–4).

legal order of the oppressive colonial rulers, but was largely retained to promote administrative stability. Thus, entirely typical of post-colonial transitions, this partially tainted colonial law became the structural basis for post-colonial governance,[15] and most provisions of the 1935 Act were incorporated into the Indian Constitution. There was thus, at all levels of law-making, a significant opinion and trend in favour of legal continuity. While one wonders to what extent any rhetoric of fundamental post-colonial reform could have matched reality, the outcome, whether in constitutional law or in the Hindu personal law reform project, had to be a tricky compromise.[16]

One of the central themes in the development of modern Indian law as a whole has remained the constant tension between uniformity and diversity: between official legal regulation emanating from the federal centre and various regional centres of power; between formal central rule and the lively spontaneity of India's many communities; between certainty and fluidity, as embodied in official law and unofficial law, state law and 'people's law' (Baxi 1986a). Although the state law is, in the world's largest democracy, supposed to represent the people's law, in reality the two did not match well at the time of independence. While this could be explained by the constellation of colonialism,[17] would self-government improve this gap of communication and overcome the lack of fit between the rulers and the ruled? Asking such questions presumes that legislative reform could actually achieve a significant transition from fluidity to certainty. This raises profound questions about the relationship of law and society, to which the present analysis must frequently return.[18]

[15] However, it goes too far to assume, as Brown (1985: 343) and Bose and Jalal (1999: 204) mistakenly do, that India simply copied the Westminster model. Such assumptions of British influence draw from patronizing myths about India as a common law country to which the British gave their laws and hence, their civilisation. The Westminster model is defunct now, even in the UK itself, and its repetitive citation merely serves to reflect British superiority complexes. The Indian Constitution of 1950 clearly sees the people of India as the sovereign, and not any elected representative or body of representatives. It is highly significant that this crucial element of difference between the Indian and British polities should have escaped the notice of so many commentators for so long and is perpetuated even in the most recent writing (Larson 2001).

[16] This compromise nature of post-colonial laws and the post-colonial Indian system as a whole has been commented on by many recent writers. Some were cited in Chapters 1 and 2 earlier.

[17] In particular, one would not expect the Government of India Act of 1935 to be consciously democratic, while the Indian Constitution grabbed the bull by the horns and, quite radically, made the people of India sovereign. This, as we know today, gave rise to significant constitutional developments such as public interest litigation (Menski et al. 2000, Ch. 4), which is deeply inspired by Hindu notions of good governance.

[18] Baxi (1986b: 59) bemoans the lack of empirical legal literature on legal reforms. Derrett (1968b: 347) notes that, when the Indian Constitution was framed, no pains were spared to make comparative studies, while the same did not occur during the process of Hindu law reform in the 1950s.

Post-colonial India has been trying to find methods of legal regulation that would privilege above all, as lawyers keep emphasising, certainty, simplicity, and uniformity. It is evident from the debates that these were considered central values for lawyers following positivist models of legal analysis and evaluation (Jain 1990: 635). Going down this route, under the guidance of British-trained lawyers like Ambedkar and Nehru, modern India sought to abandon the difficult but historically familiar compromise between formally enforced uniformity and virtually rudderless diversity. This helps to explain why Article 44 of the Constitution, requiring the state 'to endeavour to secure' a uniform civil code for the whole of India, was eventually inserted into the Constitution as a Directive Principle of State Policy, but has remained a pious declaration, despite continuous rhetoric about the supposed advantages of legal uniformity.[19]

In its 1947 Report, the Rau Committee recommended reforms of Hindu law on various important points, signifying that the major policy aim was an improvement of the legal status of women.[20] This concern, while not new, now gained prominence, as did the argument that from a wider perspective of international law, newly independent India had become a role model for other post-colonial states and should introduce modern laws. Jain (1990: 639) reports the views of the Committee in this respect:

> The eyes of the world are upon her now and it would be more than a misfortune if at this juncture she were to fail to enact within her own borders a Hindu Code in which there was equality before the law and in which disabilities based on caste or sex were no longer recognised.

Jain (id.) lists seven major controversial areas of reform in Hindu family law. Some of these were already being addressed in separate legislation during the sitting of the Rau Committee. The Hindu Marriages Validity Act of 1949 accepted all inter-caste marriages, so that caste differences could no longer be relevant in marriage law. This removed the legal insecurity caused after a number of High Courts had declared such marriages void (Jain 1990: 625). The Rau Committee was concerned to evolve a uniform code of Hindu law, which would apply to all Hindus by blending the most progressive elements of the various schools of Hindu law from different parts of the country (Desai 1998: 67).

While this draft Code was meant to be an integrated whole, in the process of passage through the ministry of law, a Select Committee chaired by Dr Ambedkar, and finally the Constituent Assembly, numerous alterations were

[19] Allott (1980: 214) observed a virtual standstill of policy with regard to bringing legal uniformity in India more than twenty years ago. On the current perception of stagnation, see Sathe (2002: 193).

[20] This point is also emphasized by the important Report of the Committee on the Status of Women in India, *Towards Equality* (1974: xii and 102–3). Agnes (2000) critically examines to what extent this was mere modernist rhetoric, designed to increase state powers rather than to emancipate women.

made, especially by the Ambedkar Committee, mainly in relation to the abolition of all customs. The most revolutionary step of all planned legal changes was the abolition of the birthright, 'the technical fountain-head of the Mitakshara joint-family law' (Derrett 1957: 62). Derrett (1957: 68) reports that when the Ambedkar Committee Report was published on 12 August 1948, 'public indignation, which had been aroused by certain of the proposals in the First Draft, broke out with renewed vigour'. Worse was to come, as the third draft of the 'Hindu Code Bill', as it was called then, provoked widespread antagonism. Derrett (1957: 69) elaborates:

> The abolition of the Mitakshara joint family, equal shares for daughters, the abolition of the widow's limited estate, and the harsh heavy-handed treatment meted out to customs summoned from all quarters opposition to the Code as a whole. Every argument that could be mustered against the project was garnered, including many that cancelled each other out.

Derrett (1957: 70–1) charts the unhappy story of the battles, particularly in the Constituent Assembly, which ultimately led to the lapse of the Bill and the resignation of Dr Ambedkar in 1951. It had become clear that there was no unanimous support for the Bill in its fully codified form. Even the president of India at the time, Rajendra Prasad, was against the project of codifying Hindu law in this way.[21] Derrett (1957: 71–2) identified an important lesson for the reformist lawmakers of modern India:

> From that gruelling experience one very useful lesson was learnt, namely that compromise might achieve what rigid adherence to principle and common-sense might fail to attain. Practical utility and theoretical perfection had to come to terms, and the battle revealed that the practical approach might be in everyone's interests. The necessity for compromise had made itself felt at the last stages of the bill's unhappy fight for survival.

This clearly shows that the path of the modernist bulldozer of comprehensive Hindu law reform had been blocked. As Derrett (1968b: 327) put it, '[a] storm of objections, and a temporary failure of political nerve, wrecked the original Hindu Code Bill', which was now strategically divided into various separate bills to facilitate their passage through Parliament. Jain (1990: 640) reports that 'instead of enacting the whole Code in one piece, and attempting to enact one comprehensive Code at one stretch, it was broken up into separate parts dealing with separate matters, and separate Acts were thus enacted'. Desai (1998: 67) criticized the delay in law-making and the decision to split the Bill into four parts:

> ... one disadvantage was that it meant legislation by instalments. Such codification, however carefully done, cannot derive the full benefit of a

[21] Austin (1999b: 22) writes of the Bill as 'an omnibus measure' designed to speed up the process of secularization, and uses it as an illustration of early confrontations over presidential powers in Indian constitutional law.

> pre-conceived plan of the whole system to be wrought upon. Instalments of a law intended to be uniform and to operate as an organic whole have come into operation at intervals during 1955 and 1956 and this must raise some problems and create some anomalous situations ... apart from the fact that the enactments ... leave an undetermined residue.

Remarkably, the argument proceeds as if legislated, codified law could ever cover everything without loopholes. In reality it must have been evident that the modernist ambition of comprehensive codification could simply not be fulfilled. Especially from the reference to the 'undetermined residue' above, it is clear that a total break from the past was not made. Rather, the ongoing project of law reform was part of a historical continuum, during which important shifts of emphasis would take place. Indeed, as stated later by the Fifth Indian Law Commission in its 59th report in 1974, the four new Acts spearheaded the message that the Hindu personal law 'is a social and secular matter and not a part of religion properly so called. These four Acts thus constitute the first decisive step in implementing the important Directive Principle enshrined in Art. 44 of the Constitution' (Jain 1990: 640).

This comment seems to indicate that the reformers were now said to have tackled the problem of bringing socio-legal uniformity, rather than the formal abolition of the supposedly 'religious' Hindu law. This amounts to an official admission that the modern post-colonial Hindu law is officially presumed to be secular. This not so subtle reconstruction of the nature of Hindu law must at once have raised questions over its legitimacy in the eyes of Hindus. Professor Derrett identified the resulting crisis of duty-discovery in modern India (in O'Flaherty and Derrett, 1978: 55):

> The law enacted by Parliament and the State legislatures has little or no claim to correspond with *dharma*, or with the *shariat* of the Muslim population. Indeed much of it (e.g. birth control programmes) is flatly opposed to *dharma*. But the forces pressing upon the individual still create a 'duty' which transcends individual-centred prudence. The society is still 'duty-orientated' rather than 'right-orientated'. Why, otherwise, do men still enter into arranged marriages in the face of constant romantic encouragement from all media of entertainment? The crisis of duty-discovery in modern India arises from the absence of prestige-figures whose own claim to authority can be based *both* upon a self-validating scripture *and* upon state patronage.

The lawmakers at the time were not, it appears, deeply concerned about such questions and pressed ahead with as many reforms as they could. Derrett (1957: 73–4) shows in detail how first the civil marriage law was passed, in the form of the SMA of 1954, an optional law that caused comparatively little controversy. Derrett's coverage at the time ended with a brief report of the then recent and successful passage of the Hindu Marriage and Divorce Bill, which became the HMA on 18 May 1955. The HSA became law on 17 June 1956, the HMGA on 25 August 1956, and the HAMA was enacted on 21 December 1956. Diwan and

Diwan (1993: 54) confirm that through these four enactments of codified Hindu law, 'some fundamental changes have been introduced, though a total break from the past has not been made'. Derrett (1968b: 328) noted that 'considerable uncertainty remains' and found it most remarkable that the Acts were passed at all (ibid.: 329), given the many inconsistencies of style and substance. Desai (1998: 68) summarizes the new development in a positive light:

> The objects achieved by the new legislation are substantial unification of Hindu law by blending much that was progressive in the various schools of law which prevailed in different parts of the country and removal of many anomalies and incongruous injunctions. One aim of this legislation was to act, it is submitted rightly, on the principle that where the reason of the rule had ceased to exist there was little justification for insistence upon its perseverance .... Renascent India of the post-independence era appreciated the value of the fresh and broadened outlook in matters affecting the rights social, economic and political of the citizen regardless of sex. Adult suffrage and political parity were fore-runners to the recognition of all that was implicit in the constitutional directives and fundamental guarantees of equality of status and equality before law enounced in the Constitution. The underscoring of the rights of women to be in *equali jura* finds concrete shape in the new legislation.

The concept of 'blending' desirable rules from a variety of sources is traced back by Derrett (1978a: 8) to the pattern of 'patching' (*talfiq*) known from Muslim jurisprudence, which allowed such borrowing in view of the principle of mutual orthodoxy of all major schools. The emphasis on women's rights, a most difficult subject, has been commented on by many writers,[22] but there was and is no discernible agreement as to how far the specific legal concerns of women should and can be protected by modernist legislation.[23] It is significant that calls for further reforms in this regard are still being made now,[24] while more analytical writing observes 'a mixed legacy of hesitations, of questions opened up in one domain only to be shut out elsewhere' (John and Nair 2000: 26).

While regulating many aspects of family law, the four separate Acts on Hindu law were certainly not a comprehensive code. Leaving so many gaps gave rise to much criticism.[25] The major, though still only piecemeal, reforms

[22] Derrett (1968b: 333–8) produced a detailed discussion of many aspects of women's legal emancipation, arguing that the abolition of Hindu polygamy constituted the most dramatic step towards gender equality. For much relevant detail, see *Towards Equality* (1974) and Agnes (2000).

[23] Rajan (1999: 4) highlights the role of gender 'as a point of *crisis* in the cultural, social, and political space of nation'.

[24] For details of the modernist arguments, supported by an international legal perspective, see Lawyers Collective (2000) and Anand (2002).

[25] Derrett (1970: 11) found that '[n]ot a word of praise emerges. No case is defended, except from attacks by some foreign observer. And the more celebrated

of Hindu law do not imply a total break with the past, nor a total embracing of modernity. Hence Derrett (1978a: x) mockingly noted: '"Hindu law is dead". Or is it? One can argue that there *are* fields in which Hindu rules must be applied still'. Significantly, Derrett (1957: 80) envisaged as a major benefit some unifying effects of the new Hindu law:

> The result ... will undoubtedly be a very substantial bid for unity among Hindus and those not belonging to the minority religious groups. It is hoped that within a reasonable period the exceptions can be reduced in number, as community after community voluntarily abandons the irregular customs which are at present to be preserved. Precedents for this gradual conversion are not far to seek, and the plan is both practical and realistic.

It seems correct to say that the main sources of the official modern Hindu law have now become the new legislation and precedent, and only to a very limited extent custom and the traditional texts. To that extent, Derrett's initial assessment in his 1957 study was correct. However, the trustful approach to the ameliorative effects of codification, unification, and modernization leaves out the vast field of unofficial law and the conceptual realm of Hindu consciousness, which were by no means superseded by the new state law.[26] For any postmodern study of the subject today, this means that an analysis of Hindu law statutes and cases remains rather ephemeral unless one takes into account the vast sphere of the unofficial law and considers relevant aspects of indigenous jurisprudence and 'legal postulates'. Again, to simply view this as evidence of dysfunction or of 'crisis' in the modern legal system indicates ignorance of comparative jurisprudence and of Indian as well as global legal history. The continuing operation of officially 'extra-legal' forces may be perceived as an element of irritation, but from an indigenous legal perspective all of this is 'law', as much as the modern state law.

The legal writing on reform in this period itself is curiously fixated by the idea that comprehensive codification, the ultimate ideal of the reformers, had been made impossible by the vocal opposition of 'traditionalists' to the Hindu Code Bill. This opposition, it is alleged, ruined the modernizing project of law reform by allowing only piecemeal intervention instead of comprehensive renewal and a total abolition of tradition. At the same time, it is evident that the post-colonial Indian state asserted itself in this field, insisting on its legitimate claim to reform the Hindu personal law. The state sought to superimpose legal positivism onto the Hindu model of law-making (where, as we saw, the state used to be a somewhat remote guardian of law and order), and would get involved in procedural aspects and punishment of severe crimes, but not simple matters of everyday life. Clearly, the prevalent assumption among legal

---

departures made from the Anglo-Hindu law by Parliament in 1955-56 are subjected to criticism and complaint incessantly'.

[26] Derrett (1970) explained this in detail, continuing his critical analysis in later studies (Derrett 1978a).

scholars at the time was that the Hindu law reforms were effective steps to achieve the desired aims, but that more would be needed. The ultimate aim remained comprehensive codification, as Jain (1966: 724) confirms in typically doctrinal fashion:

> In the area where legislation has been enacted, the Hindu law has become certain and uniform; reforms have been introduced so as to bring it in conformity with the facts of modern life, as for example, in the area of marriage, monogamy and divorce .... In those areas, however, which have not yet been codified, the old difficulties still abound. It may be hoped that sooner than later the whole of Hindu law would be codified into one single code.

Taking a socio-legal approach, one could not share such unquestioning optimism about how modernizing law reforms simply create new legal facts. Did anyone other than a tiny elite of Indians know anything about these reforms? Was polygamy really abolished and divorce made available to all Hindus? What would happen in those cases where ignorance of the law was manifestly a fact? Derrett (1968b: 323) demonstrates that the reformers believed to be acting in the interest of the nation:

> Those who strenuously advocated reform of Hindu law did not, in our submission, have any interest in Hindu law as such: they had other, simple and obvious interests, and once these were successfully served the question of further law reform could be shelved indefinitely. The two things everyone cares about seriously are marriage and inheritance and these two topics received a thorough overhaul ... in a direction subserving the personal interests of a class of Hindus, in fact a class which had given to Hinduism a relatively new flavour, pioneers in the modification of a culture.
>
> This is not to suggest that they imagined that they were foisting upon the remainder of the public something for which they alone had any use: they believed that sooner or later the remainder, the submerged six-sevenths of the iceberg, would share their outlook and their needs. They were leaders and were giving to others as well as to themselves benefits which, in their view, had been withheld from them by the foreign government. And in this there was a grain of truth ...

However, it must be noted here that the impact of the modern reformed Hindu law did not extend as far as in a Western legal system. From a modernist, positivist perspective, it is all too easy to overlook this. Understanding the limited practical impact of the Indian compromise solutions found for official Hindu law regulation in 1955–56 is crucial for a postmodern evaluation of India's current legal realities.

Taking only the simple, central example of marriage (Chapter 8 later), the modern state law provided for compulsory registration of marriages by the state bureaucracy, but only for marriages registered under the secular SMA of 1954, and not for Hindu marriages. It is a fact that hardly any Indians register their marriages under this Act, so that formal state-controlled registration of such a couple's marriage has remained a virtually optional minority phenomenon in modern Indian law.[27] A Hindu marriage, on the other hand, need not be registered by the state to achieve legal validity. Under Section 7(1) of the HMA 1955, it is simply provided that '[a] Hindu marriage may be solemnized in accordance with the customary rites and ceremonies of either party thereto'. This critically important matter of contracting Hindu marriages is therefore left entirely to custom and to the social realm. Clearly, the modern Indian state's ambition did not extend to bureaucratic control and validation of all Hindu marriages through formal registration.[28] Indeed, Derrett (1978a: 24) recorded that this is the case for 99 per cent of all Hindu marriages in India, and that figure will not be much different now.[29]

This one example must suffice here to indicate that the intricate compromise achieved through the Hindu law reforms of the 1950s did not eradicate the traditional Hindu law, but merely formally restructured the law, so that it now appears in statute form, while many rules must still be ascertained from the old sources, even in some cases from Sanskrit texts.[30] Derrett (1957: 37) produced a quite negative assessment of this:

> Undoubtedly reforms and restatements of the law ought to flow from first principles, but the story of the "Hindu Code Bill" is a story of baulked ambitions and frustrated theories in this connection—for the Hindu Marriage Act and the Hindu Succession Bill are alike in leaving it to the text-bookwriters, if any such can be found, to rationalise and justify, to expound and portray, the living principles behind a mass of regulations, which do not appear to have any underlying thread within them at all. No doubt, this is not the way in which a Code ought to be framed.

[27] Unpublished research on the extent of marriage registration in India, conducted by some of my students during the late 1980s, found that couples would register their marriage officially if they anticipated the need for official documentation. In those parts of India from which substantial populations have moved abroad (e.g. the Punjab and Gujarat), leading to much transnational movement of secondary migrants, the figures for marriage registration were clearly much higher than elsewhere.

[28] Agnes (2000) shows in detail that this basic fact has been disregarded in all recent reform proposals regarding compulsory registration of Hindu marriages. It is evident that this is a big hidden issue in many jurisdictions in the world (Bainham 1998). Conflicts may also arise where Hindus move abroad and marry there in accordance with Hindu law.

[29] Agnes (2000: 244) reproduces statistics for 1968–72 and 1986–96 which confirm the low uptake of marriage registration even in Mumbai.

[30] Derrett (1957: 273) speaks of 'mere fraud' with regard to what he calls the 'pathetic mention of *saptapadi*', an ancient Hindu ritual of solemnizing a contract, in which bride and groom at the end of the main marriage ceremony take seven steps together. This is found, in rather distorted form, in Section 7(2) of the HMA 1955. Predictably, this gave rise to confused judicial decisions, which have implications for women's rights even today (see Menski 1995b; 2001 and Ch. 8 later).

Thus, the formal assertion of the modern state's authority through the process of codification begins to look somewhat hollow. The reformist ambitions were clearly limited by various considerations of realism and practicality. For example, how would the Indian state police a comprehensive system of marriage registration, if it had been decided that legal validity should depend on formal registration? The truth is that such comprehensive reforms would have been totally unrealistic, leading ultimately to social chaos. Hence, the modern Indian state has never ventured as far as claiming the sole right to determine the validity of marriages, and manifestly delegated this task to society. The reformist rhetoric of modernism could not be practically imposed by the reformers during the 1950s, and the situation has not changed now. This is a clear-cut case of recognized limits of law.

Another central conceptual issue in the present context must be whether a legal reform can abolish or even significantly influence social norms, even if it does not seek to strengthen legal regulation. Most Indian legal scholars have simply not been interested in analysing such questions and have remained focused on doctrinal legal approaches.[31]

Derrett depicted the nature of the Hindu law reforms as a significantly watered-down compromise. In particular, Derrett (1957: 78) noted that '[a]ll customs were to have been abolished, but the present position is that they will to a great extent be saved'. In his concluding chapter, Derrett (1957: 267–8) explained that traditional law had by no means become irrelevant:

> At once we shall see that the Hindu law will continue to draw its inspiration from divergent sources. The fundamental source of the Hindu law will not be the Code alone, though that will, of course, be the source most frequently resorted to. The reason for this is the fact that the Code deliberately (and no doubt rightly) leaves room for customs in certain regards, particularly Marriage, Adoption and Succession, while in numerous instances the law set out in the Code cannot be administered entirely without reference to the law existing at the moment of codification. Thus the mixed background and muddled origins of the present Anglo-Hindu law will not be entirely dispensed with, though they will obtrude themselves for practical purposes to a distinctly subordinate degree.

Derrett (1957: 272) argued that the Hindu Code, therefore, 'will be a direct descendant of the *shastra* only in the sense that no one can understand it without reference to the history of Hindu law'. While in Derrett's view it would be misleading to say that the Code is based upon the shastra, he also emphasized that '[f]rom *shastric* texts, and from general *shastric* sources, much material may be culled which will explain features in the Code' (id.). Therefore it seemed that 'the content of the Code itself will be a unique mixture of the

[31] It is noteworthy in all the leading Hindu law textbooks that their coverage, after 1955, switches away from historical analysis and focuses more or less exclusively on the new statutes and their interpretations, thereby reinforcing a doctrinal, black-letter approach in legal study.

traditional and the modern' (Derrett 1957: 268). But it was also anticipated that the legislated reforms would bring about a significant movement of Hindu law along the developmental paradigm of legal progress. In this regard, at least, Derrett (1957: 269) seemed to share the ambitions of the modernist reformers. He felt that the result would inevitably be the gradual elimination of 'that esoteric and complicated technique of administering Hindu law which is hardly adequately describable in terms of anything other than a *mystery*. Hindu law will come down out of the clouds and will take on the guise of a statutory law similar to the law of Contract or Evidence'. He felt that this would be beneficial in the long run and saw the Hindu law reforms of the 1950s as one further planned stage in the journey towards the projected Indian Civil Code. Derrett (1957: 275) went even further, predicting significant legal change:

> So far as may be conjectured at the time of writing, the Code will hasten, or at least facilitate, the eventual disappearance of the *legal* Hindu joint family ...
>
> ... Hindus will begin to wonder why they have a special family law and will urge non-Hindus to join them in a Civil Code. They will forget that there was an historical justification for the oddities that will be found in the Hindu Code, and will readily accept further adjustments of a rationalistic type, such as at present are too much for most Hindus to swallow. The total abolition of personal laws will become a reality, which may not be achieved within the lifetime of anyone now living, but which cannot be long delayed thereafter.

This prediction of rational, modern 'unlimited progress' (Derrett 1957: 277) reflects, therefore, that even the leading Western expert on Hindu law at that early time assumed that Hindu law was firmly set on a road to reform and on a path towards modernity in which women, in particular, would have a much better life.[32] At the same time, Derrett (1957: 270) was also quite critical of the Hindu Code and somewhat hedged his bets:

> It is not an intellectual whole, it is not founded upon clear principles or rational doctrines. It is hardly a typical Anglo-Indian Code: rather it is more like an English codification than some of the more splendid Indian Codes such as the Penal Code. Practice and experience will soon demonstrate whether it is a mighty banyan tree sending down its roots into a variety of soils, or whether it is a lifeless creature unable to progress because it is equipped with every means of propulsion, operating simultaneously in different directions and without stearing-gear.

Interestingly, Derrett (1957: 270) also commented on the question of the public image of India to the outside world, 'one which, though most often unspoken, is generally seldom far from the minds of reformers in India to-day'. For

[32] Derrett (1957: 275–76) concludes with a long paragraph arguing, in essence, that greater legal freedom for Hindu women will lead to enormous changes that most people could not even imagine.

'[i]f advanced countries admire, the Indian inventor is doubly pleased' (id.), and foreign encouragement for reforms seemed to be welcome at that stage. Thus, the case for reforms, and for further legislative intervention, had been made out in so many words. Derrett (1968b: 96) suggested that legislative intervention was nothing new to the Hindu system of law, since '[t]he capacity to legislate irrespective of śāstric authority undoubtedly existed, and was utilized in countless precedents before the coming of the British'. Derrett therefore seemed to share the modernist assumption that codification was the ideal tool for law reform. He vigorously rejected the argument that, as a religious law, Hindu law should not be subjected to reform by the state. Indeed, Derrett (1963c: 1) emphasizes his awareness of the internal dynamics of Hindu legal development and justifies further legal intervention: 'The partial abolition of what we call the Anglo-Hindu law during the codification of 1955-6 was yet a further stage in the process whereby the system was adapted to suit current needs, and it will not be the last.'

At the same time, the realization that the reforms had not been made for the explicit benefit of the Indian masses was also expressed. Derrett (1957: 271) found that 'it is evident that Parliament has not legislated so far with the interests of the poor and illiterate citizens (i.e. the majority) in mind'. We saw earlier that Derrett (1968b: 323) was a little more kind to the reformers, assuming that they had acted not only in their own narrow interests, although that was undoubtedly served first. Derrett (1968b: 350) offered a typically British class-based analysis:

> Thus the real reasons which propelled Hindus into the 'Hindu Code age' were not in any sense religious any more than they were anti-religious. They had to do with the formation of a new nameless caste, the caste of the 'haves', who naturally have the instincts of all previous castes. And a thoroughly reasonable programme it was. The aid of the lawyers was taken at the right moment.

In addition, as Derrett (1968b: 341) indicates, the legal profession, rather than the general public, benefited from the legal reforms. He argues that '[t]he Code puts much business into the hands of the Bar, instead of diminishing litigation: it tends to diminish uncertainty, but the certainty which has been achieved will bring with it the strife and perplexity which the law itself, perhaps by developing the Family Arrangement, must strive to mitigate'. He predicted that, for some time, the common Hindu would find the new system less familiar, more hazardous, and more expensive. Derrett's initial assessments thus remained ambivalent, albeit cautiously optimistic. The new law was undoubtedly and officially 'the law'. Only time would tell how it would work out. Derrett (1968b: 341–2) concluded:

> In India theory got the upper hand of the Hindu law, but it was theory almost uncontrolled by experience. That the Code is in operation no one can deny, and the spread of popular 'guides' throughout the country must have acquainted many with its broad outlines. But in order to see whether it is a success ... we shall have to enquire into its faults of matter and manner.

In the light of the above discussion, it may safely be assumed that many such faults were bound to make themselves felt, not only in law. The project of the Hindu law reforms of the 1950s, however fragmentary and incomplete, had been pushed through by the law-centred leadership of independent India as an experiment with modernity. The new rules now faced multiple tests, as Sunil Khilnani (1997: 5) notes from a political economy angle, describing modernity as 'a seductively wrapped and internally inconsistent mixture of instrumental rationality, utilitarianism, and respect for individual autonomy and choice'. Assessing the uneven economic picture of India which, for most Indians, has been a failure, Khilnani (1997: 10–11) concludes:

> Competing ambitions collided to create this lopsided pattern of economic modernity followed after 1947: the interests of big industrialists, the hopes of Gandhian miniaturists, the ambitions of Nehru's intellectuals, and the power of those who controlled the land and its produce. No single vision triumphed.

As in economics and politics, in the legal sphere there was bound to be much scope for finding a new path that would suit the new nation. The direction that this modernist train on its journey into the future would take could evidently not be fully predicted by anyone, but it seems that, at this early time, modernist hopes were high.

The Onset of Realism: The 1960s

At first, it seemed that the Hindu law reforms of the 1950s had brought about a virtual legal revolution, as reflected in the writings of Jain (1966: 724) cited above. Jain (1990: 641) discusses what he sees as the drastic impact of the four new Acts on Hindu personal law, which in his view brought about fundamental changes. The argument is still that a large part of Hindu law has been secularized and detached from its religious base. It also appears that these reforms were indeed not introduced for the benefit of the Hindus, but for the convenience of lawyers. Jain (id.) indicates this, summarizing the modernizing mission of the Acts of 1955-56:

> Henceforth a lawyer does not have to look beyond the statutes, and the court cases under these statutes, for decisions of any dispute falling within the scope of these four Acts. To a large extent, thus, Hindu Law has been modernized by these Acts. These Acts have also made law certain and uniform and have also reformed the law so as to bring it in conformity with the facts and realities of modern life. These statutes eliminate the caste-factor from the law. These statutes seek to confer equality of the two sexes.

However, these are merely modernist slogans, reflecting post-colonial positivist optimism among lawyers. Would more detached scholars take the same view? In his early leading study on modern Hindu law, Derrett (1963c: 2) observed that the movement from the classical law to Anglo-Hindu law had been more gradual than the transition to modern Hindu law, which had been achieved rather rapidly, in fact within two years, although the debates about these reforms took much longer. Derrett (id.) discussed the recent legislative changes to Hindu law, which he portrayed as a code, and he envisaged an eventual uniform civil code for the whole of India. Interestingly, a few years later, Derrett (1970: vii) looks back at his 1963 study and admits that, 'in that book I took a conservative and technical stand, as I think a law teacher of the old school should be expected to do'. While he had earlier tried to explain the law as it was, in the new study he attempted to produce 'substantial and evaluative comment' (id.), to provide a constructive criticism of the modern Hindu law, the personal law system as administered after the reforms of the 1950s.

Emphasis had shifted during the late 1950s from Parliament to the arena of the courts, and thus to the practical application of the law. Derrett (1968b: 274) had earlier referred to the status of legal decisions as the makers of ideals, particularly in the context of the curious amalgam of Anglo-Hindu law, which 'is not English, and it is not the attitude of the *śāstrī-s*' (id.). This ambivalence about modernism and its influence now continued and can also be traced in judicial decisions.[33] Derrett (1968b: 353) emphasizes that by the mid-1960s, the Supreme Court of India 'has yet to pronounce on many of the intricate legal problems involved, and its policy ... is still in a formative stage'. But one wonders whether there ever was a discernible policy. In view of the distance between Parliament and the public, Derrett (id.) noted that '[r]ustic spouses can pose puzzles for Judges having English decisions as their guides'. He was scathing about some of the quaint early decisions that came out of the courts, reflecting what he called 'the dreadful incongruity of the new law with the mentality of many of the people' (Derrett 1968b: 355).

Within this project of national education about new socio-legal values, an early case like *Kusum Lata v Kampta Prasad* AIR 1965 All 280 illustrates how a High Court judge, a Muslim in this case, criticized the lower courts for lacking in understanding for the complaints of a Hindu wife about the husband's persistent cruelty. It was evident to the learned judge that, '[r]ightly or wrongly, the Legislature in this country has adopted the modern view of cruelty of one spouse to another in the eye of law' (p. 284). Referring to Halsbury's *Laws of England* and the legal position then obtaining in English law, but also under the Indian Divorce Act of 1869 and the Dissolution of Muslim Marriages Act of 1939, it was held that the approach of the lower appellate court towards the subject of conjugal relations 'is completely out of tune with the times and in conflict with the ideas underlying the concept of cruelty' (ibid.: 285) as found at the time in Section 10(1)(b) of HMA 1955 as a ground for judicial separation. Hence, 'selfish brutality or disregard for the health, needs, desires and feelings of the other by either spouse even in a matter such as sexual relations between the two' (id.) qualified as cruelty. The lower courts were therefore criticized for having 'completely disregarded the views on matrimonial matters embodied

[33] Derrett (1977, 1978b) contain useful guidance on many points of detail that go too far here.

in all recent legislation and case law on the subject in this country' (ibid.: 286) and for showing undue bias in favour of the husband.

Judicial statements of this kind were bound to become more frequent, as the essentially Victorian attitudes of Indian judges to women and matters of matrimonial law began to change. However, the opposite trend was also discernible from the very start, and 'occasional rare glimpses of the "Old" India at work' (Derrett 1968b: 355) gave rise to the telling comment that 'we must not make the mistake of supposing that India stands still here or elsewhere, and the follies of the 1950's may not necessarily endure into the 1970's' (id.). This still reflects reformist optimism at this early stage, in which it is also significant that the case law on divorce was not yet considered interesting, because it merely relied on English precedents (ibid.: 365).

It was increasingly recognized, however, that in the Hindu world view, with all its contested internal diversities, there always remains something above the realm of human law-making that a state legal system cannot overrule and remove. Derrett's above reference to the old India, and other similar phrases indicate this, but his own position at the time remained firmly tied to that of the reformers, although he doubted whether the new law would bring about unqualified humanitarian progress. Derrett (1968b: 397) concluded that law should be used as a means of social change, but he soon began to warn that the urge to copy Western models can indirectly work against that agenda in a fashion not contemplated by the reformers. The emerging question may well have been whether the judges of the Supreme Court of India would be happy to decide cases involving Hindu spouses (who would more often than not be members of extended families) as though they were an English family. Discussing the case of *Lachman v Meena* AIR 1964 SC 40 in which such a clash of values between Old and New India was apparent, and the modern view prevailed in a majority judgment, Derrett (1968b: 398–9) concluded his analysis in typically ambivalent style:

> Time will tell which approach will gain favour. In the meanwhile the question remains whether the habits of Indian families will alter to take account of the new matrimonial reliefs and matrimonial practice. One may be forgiven for doubting whether there is strong ground for expecting that they will, at any rate in the near future.

While Anglo-Hindu law had been turned into an official legal system based mainly on case law, post-colonial Hindu law was initially characterized by increasing use of legislation as a source of law. Thus, modern Hindu law, as a hybrid legal system, has taken characteristics of both the civil law systems and the common law and now looks, from the outside, like a Western secularized legal system. But post-colonial Hindu law also retained its conceptual roots, its Hindu elements, which continue to infuse the Indian legal system as a whole rather than just the Hindu personal law. To reiterate, these are the 'legal postulates' that Chiba's (1986) instructive model treats as powerful interlocutors with the official law and unofficial laws.

The main points of conflict that arise now, therefore, are between customary laws on the one hand and statutes and case law on the other, rather than between custom and cultural texts, as was the case earlier during the colonial period in particular. But the underlying tensions are really about different kinds of legal postulates rather than any formal legal rules. To that extent, indeed, the classical Hindu law system lives on in the shape of concepts like dharma, constantly interacting and potentially conflicting with the claims and aspirations of the modern legal concepts. In the never-ending search for justice,[34] dharma has not become irrelevant in post-colonial India. To that extent, therefore, the modern codified Hindu law also remained a 'religious' system, in the same way that Islamic law recognizes the supremacy of a divine force beyond and above mankind, but is also forced to take account of the need for human lawmaking (Menski 2002). At the same time, Hindu law's secular dimensions also emerge, specifically in matrimonial litigation. Hence, post-colonial Hindu law remained religious *and* secular, as it had always been. The reformers of the post-independence phase were aware of such complexities and for that reason, we must assume, had not blindly followed Ambedkar's path of pure rationalism, which had simply denied any place and role to Hindu religion and tradition.

The resulting ambiguities began to be challenged in the academic analysis of Hindu law during the 1960s. In his major reassessment of modern Hindu law in 1970, Derrett's position shifted and he now emphasized much more than ever before the need to go 'back to the spirit of the old system as it existed in pre-British times' (Derrett 1970: ix). While the modern Hindu law was merely 'a sorry remnant of the *dharmashastra*' (id.), it had always been clear that 'the real law which would ultimately rule Indians must be customary and rooted in ancient and traditional *mores*" (ibid.: xi). Derrett (1970: xiii) noted that 'the coming of the New India has not changed all that" and declared that '[i]nherited rules can well be worked, but the spirit in which they are worked need not issue, like a bad smell, from a grave' (ibid.: xv). This line of argument culminated in a defence of the indigenous characteristics of Indian laws and the need to develop legal solutions appropriate to the country and her people. Derrett (1970: xvi) argued:

> In our present context there will be a need to fight off an urge to copy an English precedent here and there. India's attitude is the reverse of China's.

[34] There seems to be no disagreement in principle that justice is the ultimate aim of all legal activity, but writers disagree over *how* to secure it. Archana Parashar, in Dhanda and Parashar (1999: 1) argues forcefully that 'a feminist understanding of law is essential for anyone interested in achieving social justice through the law' and expresses her belief that 'no one can absolve themselves of the responsibility to pursue social justice for all members of society' (id.). Rajan (1998: 11), relying on Hayek, argues that individual liberty and social justice are incompatible. She also asserts (ibid.: 46) that 'most cultures—in particular the Hindu culture—are not democratically structured and demand obedience, not dialogue'.

> China is not now open to juridical influence from abroad. India is, and is glad to be. Yet she is irremovably Indian: attempts at reform which do not spring from within are defied, and rightly. I do not think, by the way, that foreign approbation has, or should have, any part at all to play in the development of Indian law. It is up to India to map out her own path: she does not need crutches from an indifferent, and perhaps slightly contemptuous, foreign legal world. English, American, or Australian authorities are not to be spurned as irrelevant, but they should not be leant upon as if they absolved India from working out her own solutions.[35]

These solutions would have to be worked out by Indian judges. Derrett (1970: xvi–xvii) argued that 'a surprising scope of Hindu law is still case-law, and some of the more fascinating of the open conflicts of opinion to be observed, at the time when I write, relate to what is virtually judge-made law, and will remain judge-made law for a long time to come'. In the introduction to the same study, Derrett (1970: 2–3) constructed an elaborate argument about the intrinsic nature of Hindu law as a constant search for the appropriate way to live, as a living and growing system, with its own internal norms:

> I come to my point: competition in this environment is not sterile and sheer self-seeking. Its ambitions and jealousies have as their background some presuppositions about life, death and eternity, and these must be taken seriously even by people whose chief claim to prestige for the time being is their cosmopolitanism. Righteousness in its Indian form subsumes, and requires, competition and conflict for the attainment, by the maximum number, of the practical application of the ideals which that co-existence demands.

Observing that some aspects of the Sanskrit texts were still considered relevant by the judges, Derrett (1970: 4) argued that it only appeared as though 'the ideas to be found in the *shastra* are abandoned on the surface, but the attitude of mind and the conception of life remains the same' (ibid.: 5). Thus, he argued in detail at p. 6:

> The texts have no more authority than the people give them, but they make a perennial claim on the Hindu mind such as few foreign productions, however prestige-worthy, can ever do, because they express what the people from time to time believe in. Whatever may go on upon the surface, and however people may direct their lives, the old laws of duty in their essence, the old tensions between the desire to be righteous and the temptation to be unrighteous, the pull upwards of the commandment to act *without* desire and to know and seek absorption in the Self, these remain; and the more India's miseries and frustrations become the stronger these will grow and the more pervasive will be their call .... The Sanskrit texts

[35] Derrett (1977: xx) commented that '[t]he awkward relation between the Indian courts and their opposite numbers in England, in which the former only seem to imitate the latter, is no longer taken for granted'.

> which I shall use have no authority which people do not give them, but I shall submit that they express perennial truths active in Hindu society in India (if not always out of India), and that they are to be neglected at the public's peril. It is here that the continuity of Hindu law lies.

Professor Derrett was not constructing some *hindutva* model of Hindu law here, but was reflecting on his long observations of Indian social reality, a reality that has in some respects not significantly changed even as the twentieth century came to an end. He saw what he called 'an alternative intellectual system, not as vocal, not as well armed, not as well documented as the legal system which is represented in English print, but pervasive and effective for all that' (ibid.: 12).

Derrett was well aware that his new approach would upset some readers, who might not like his conclusions. However, his concerns were not with scholarly politics but 'the higher interests of the public' (Derrett 1970: 8) in India, a place to which he evidently had a very close link.[36] Without using the now fashionable phrase of 'public interest', he made it quite clear that his overriding concern was to find principles 'in keeping with India's needs' (Derrett 1970: xiii). He thus emphasised the need 'to concentrate entirely on the factual, empirical situation' (ibid.: xiv) and to realize that law exists for the solution of actual problems. To Derrett by the early 1970s, it was a fact that 'the Hindu point of view' was an internally pluralistic phenomenon which needed to be treated with caution, but which would continue to play a vital role in Indian law-making. His conclusion, to the effect that Indian law had its own culture-specific contribution to make to the world's legal systems,[37] and would not simply disappear, led to a critical analysis of modern Hindu law as a system whose usefulness needed to be tested in all respects. Derrett (1970: 8) therefore saw the reforms of the 1950s in a new light, and no longer just as an embodiment of positivist law-making:

> Parliament hardly knew what it was doing, and it did it with great energy and enthusiasm. Its main task was to abolish the Anglo-Hindu law and to substitute it for something more modern but no less 'Hindu'. On the whole it succeeded, but nowhere perfectly, and nowhere to everyone's satisfaction.

This, interestingly, confirms the view that the modernist reforms did not tackle traditional Hindu law as such, but rather the partly unsatisfactory Anglo-Hindu

[36] Derrett (1970: xvii) pleaded: 'I see no reason why I should be disqualified from attempting to pay the debts I owe to that system and to the people who are subject to it. Perhaps, writing at the distance fate has set for me, I see that system in its complexity with more objectivity than those hundreds of millions who at present knowingly or unknowingly groan under its inconsistencies, insufficiencies, impracticalities and even absurdities.'

[37] The full quote from Derrett (1970: 13–14) is found as part of the earlier discussion in Ch. 2. Nanda and Sinha (1996: xi–xii) reiterate that the cosmology of Hindu law is unique and 'produces a general and all-pervasive way of life as an organizational principle of existence' (ibid.: xii).

law. It is also worth reiterating here that the law itself is still seen as a form of Hindu law, and not just a type of English law.[38] While the law had to some extent become more certain, there was also new litigation emerging in the matrimonial field, in particular, which almost of necessity brought local and social concerns back into the formal, national legal system. Derrett (1970: 9) observes that 'the advantages which the so-called "Hindu Code" has brought with one hand it may be accused of diminishing with the other, since it tends to make the public depend more upon the aid of lawyers than it did previously'. In terms of practical analysis, Derrett (1970: 18) emphasizes that 'a satisfactory symbiosis between custom and the Hindu law has yet to be achieved'. As far as the analysis of sources of law was concerned, in particular the prominent use of foreign precedents, this gave rise to a discussion of the role of judges in this context. Derrett (1970: 20) observed with characteristic sharpness:

> But though this using of foreign authorities is psychologically explicable, and traditionally understandable if not actually correct, Indian judges desperately want to be Indian in all they do. The few instances where true Indian authorities are cited by Indian judges in contexts where they were not obliged to do so are excellent evidence that the judiciary wants the best of both worlds: they want to have the "best" law cited to them, and they want that law to coincide with Indian values and Indian traditional principles. This is where the *shastra* comes in.

Derrett (1970: 21) argued that Indian judges would be correct to use more indigenous authorities and less foreign ones, but at the same time he was well aware that the reforms of the 1950s had suggested recourse to 'modern' models. But what was modern, and what was appropriate? Derrett (1970: 21–2) argued forcefully that there was never a legislative intention to turn Hindus into English people:

> Indian judges say from time to time that it is wrong to rely blindly on English cases. How right they are! English authorities subsuming a totally different state of society, and conditions of life known only to the "top" (or would-be "top") half per cent of the Hindu population, can hardly be a reliable guide. It is true that when statutes were passed in New Delhi in 1955/56 introducing what were virtually new rules based historically on English models the legislature virtually directed the judiciary (as they have noticed) to consult English decisions construing comparable provisions in England. In Company Law, and revenue law, for example, this is the usual practice and there is little harm in it. But in the realm of family law it can hardly have been the intention of Parliament that the judiciary should assume for purposes of argument that the population were constructive Englishmen! The numerous variations from the English pattern which we find in the Hindu Marriage Act, for example, alert us to the intention of Parliament to create something new, new both to India and to the West. Even if we assume

[38] But see Cohn (1997: 75) as cited in Chapters 4 and 5, and Galanter's (1972) perspective that Hindu law had been displaced by a modern reformist edifice.

> for a moment that Parliament wanted English decisions to be consulted, we are not obliged to suppose that the judiciary must blindly apply English law to so complex and unknown a mass of un-English people, the Hindus, without regard for the welfare of the public. Granted that ... law, like *dharma*, has an effect similar to "suction"—it is an educative force—, it does not follow that we can impute to Parliament the intention that Hindus should be educated to be English people.

Derrett (1970: 22) therefore skilfully detected a judicial preference for applying indigenous principles, if only they could be found:

> Thus two additional facts to be borne in mind are (1) that English and other foreign authorities may be consulted eclectically, tolerantly, intelligently; and (2) that the frequent warnings that such authorities are to be used only with the greatest caution are good evidence that the judiciary would like to apply Hindu principles if they knew what these were, and would like not to apply foreign principles where these are inconsistent with indigenous continuous tradition.

Derrett (1970: 22–3) predicted that over time, a general tendency would emerge, continuously evidenced in the Supreme Court: 'A definite drift was seen there in the context of property rights within the Indian Constitution. A definite drift is yet to be seen in Hindu law. Let us hope that it will not be too long in coming'. In the fundamental principles which Derrett (1970: 24–44) established as a touchstone for developing appropriate guidance in Hindu law, he emphasized especially the careful consideration of custom and the social facts and circumstances of cases. Three major principles emerged from this analysis, namely, 'law must treat the parties as Indians; it must be apt to educate the public; and it must be in keeping with the principles of the Constitution' (ibid.: 32). These suggestions demand some interactive linkages between these three potentially competing considerations. Derrett (1970: 32–3) critically examined the concept of uniformity, and put it in relation to the fluidity of moral values among Hindus:

> It is a principle of Indian thought and Indian law that no one standard or method is ideal in its details for all. No one has the right to lay down a single pattern for the lives or the thoughts of Indians. Hindus believe that several ways of life will be, in a transcendental sense, equally meritorious. Preferences can be made on moral grounds which no one has the right to enforce *except in relation to the relevant group or social unit.*

Since the moral values of Hindus are insufficiently well known, despite the numerous teachings, and their application in relation to the individual Hindu's merit cannot fully be anticipated, there is no way in which law could pin down fixed obligations for every Hindu. Thus, not in reliance on Hindu 'religion' as such, but within the broad confines of the *ṛta/*dharma complex, which this study has identified as the central Hindu conceptual phenomenon, every Hindu individual should ideally be enabled by the law to fulfil his or her chosen path.

This is not a purely religious argument any more, since it is as much moral and social as religious. As Derrett (1970: 37) phrased it:

> ... the Hindu believes that the individual has a right to follow his chosen path to salvation, and that salvation is the natural right of the individual. His brief appearance in this phenomenal world should be regulated by the State in such a way as to enable him to reach that goal, consistently with the rights of his contemporaries to do the same by their own chosen paths. This belief is a fact, not a fancy. To ignore this belief is to fail to implement a moral value operative amongst Hindus.

The final principles highlighted by Derrett (1970: 43) therefore emphasize that 'no requirement exists that all Hindus should be governed by the identical rule in all circumstances, but rather that different regimes should be contemplated for persons treading different paths of social life; and ... that the moral values of Hinduism should be observed and fostered'. This is finally linked by Derrett (1970: 432) to the limited role of the 'soft' Hindu state:

> For it is a traditional principle that the King does not make law, he makes regulations. These can be changed at any time and are of no more value than their suitability to meet the circumstances of their origin. But *dharma* does go on for ever, and the arm of *dharma* reaches through generations. The King cannot create it, nor can he destroy it; the most he can aspire to do is to find out what it is and apply it. And if he does this and protects the people, he need do nothing else.

These Hindu principles, as restated by Derrett, form part of Hindu consciousness in society and operate at all levels. It is no surprise, therefore, to find evidence that reformist energies were sagging after the big effort of the mid-1950s. Having achieved their aim of legislating for modernity, India's lawmakers and policy planners realized that law reform was only a formal aspect of social engineering which had to compete with other forces in the field. Hence, it soon became obvious that the enthusiasm for law reform seemed to have exhausted itself by 1956. Derrett (1968b: 322) observed that 'few now seem really interested in that class of law reform'. But Derrett (1970: 401) also noted that 'Parliament is far too busy to amend personal laws from year to year'. The post-colonial Indian state had not totally given up on reformist agenda, but the piecemeal nature of the process manifested itself in many ways. The modernist claims about comprehensive law reforms and abolition of tradition were shown to be ambitions that could only be partly fulfilled.

Political scientists and historians, having almost completely stayed away from detailed legal analysis, have made some relevant observations about the difficult role of the state, which can be related to the present discussion. Khilnani (1997:2) noted:

> For nationalists, 1947 marked a keypoint on a still building crescendo, a thrilling movement to a brighter future, where a settled and defined modern Indian nation, mature in its 'emotional integration', would come to preside over its own destiny.

> But over the past generation the presumption that a single shared sense of India—a unifying idea and concept—can at once define the facts that need recounting and provide the collective subject for the Indian story has lost all credibility.

Khilnani (1997: 4) also argued that the responsibilities of the modern Indian state to act for the welfare of the citizens 'have raised expectations often very distant from the state's practical capacities'. While this comment was primarily related to economics, in the light of Derrett's aforementioned legal analysis from the late 1960s, it appears evident that the early post-colonial Indian state made a critical mistake if it assumed that it could rewrite Indian law, reform Hindu law out of existence, and eventually create a uniform national legal system, claiming to promote social welfare. In the light of what we know about ancient subcontinental forms of governance in terms of artha and dharma, it does not surprise that the modernist ambitions have led to frustrations, or more realistic recognition of the limits of law, as Allott (1980) was to demonstrate in detail later. Khilnani (1997: 207) comes to the conclusion that, ultimately, the viability of India's democracy 'will rest on its capacity to sustain internal diversity, on its ability to avoid giving reason to groups within the citizen body to harbour dreams of having their own exclusive nation states'. While this argument veers off into the much-debated issues of communalism and separatism, the general lesson for the modern Indian state was rather similar to the experience of enforcing ambitious legal reforms in the field of Hindu law.

Other legal scholars have come up with similarly realistic assessments of the need for modern Indian law to cater for plurality and culture-specific diversity. An excellent article by John Mansfield (1993) analyses whether a uniform civil code for India would be preferable to the personal law system. Mansfield (ibid.: 175) highlights what he calls the 'identity value', in other words various aspects of ethnicity, and notes, at p. 176, that despite certain compromises and limitations, 'the state administration of the system of personal laws does give substantial support to the identity value, so that the system should not be abandoned simply on the ground that it fails to achieve what it sets out to do'. Mansfield (1993: 176–7) goes further in his concluding discussion:

> But even within the familiar list of personal law topics, it may be sensible to make distinctions. For instance, from the point of view of the identity value, the rules relating to marriage may be more important than the rules relating to succession .... Such a particularizing approach, of course, has something in common with what has been going on since 1772. But the weight to be ascribed to the identity value ... may be significantly different than in the past ... an open-minded approach seems called for, one unconstrained either by the hesitancy of a foreign ruler to interfere in the laws and customs of subject peoples, or by a purely theoretical notion that a nation-state cannot exist without a uniform substantive law on all subjects. The nation-state that India needs is one that is adapted to its special circumstances.

It would be expecting too much to ask for a national consensus on this complex question. While perceptive scholars like Derrett (1970) and some Indian writers pursued a socio-legal approach to further Hindu law reforms in India, there continued to be substantial support for further legislative intervention in the direction of modernity, secularization, and an eventual uniform code of family law. As we saw earlier, despite all his reservations, Professor Derrett also still believed that a uniform family law for the whole of India would be the eventual outcome.

Legislative Counter-move: Reforms of the 1970s

During the 1960s, it became increasingly evident to academic observers that the modernist ambitions of the new Indian state to reform and codify Hindu law were not likely to be effective in creating a more just and equitable social order. Nevertheless, modernizing reformist efforts were continuing during the 1970s, while voices of caution were marginalized and brushed aside. The modernist legislative efforts continued to pursue a reformist agenda and partly reflected dissatisfaction with what had been achieved earlier. In the view of many, the reforms of the 1950s had not gone far enough. However, since most of the Hindu personal law had been codified, the reformers now gave less attention to the methodology of codification, an earlier concern that was deemed more important, if mainly for the benefit of lawyers. Now, several problematic practical issues were addressed, so that the emphasis shifted more towards substance rather than form, and specifically aimed at a number of social reforms designed to improve the position of women and minorities. The list of Reports of the Law Commissions of India between 1956 and 1988, provided by Jain (1990: 575–9), indicates that several subjects of personal law reform came up for consideration. However, little of this was ultimately translated into legislation.

The only noteworthy modernist legislative reform to Hindu law during the 1960s had been the introduction of two extra grounds for divorce by the Hindu Marriage (Amendment) Act of 1964.[39] Basically, divorce now became available to Hindus on the ground that there had been no conjugal relations over an extended period, clearly a reformist move towards adoption of the breakdown principle in divorce law, following debates and developments in English law at that time. The effect of the 1964 amendments was, in a nutshell, that following a decree for judicial separation or restitution of conjugal rights, if the spouses did not resume cohabitation within two years,[40] this became in

[39] Act 44 of 1964 is very short and amends Section 13 of the HMA 1955. For details see Derrett (1978a: 28–33). Derrett argued, at p. 30, that this amendment 'caused immediate differences of judicial opinion, and no little heat' about the critical question of how to relate sections 13 and 23 of the HMA of 1955 to each other.

[40] This was reduced to one year under the Marriage Laws (Amendment) Act of 1976.

itself a ground for divorce. Derrett (1978a: 31) found that 'this was repugnant to the sentiments of many, and not only orthodox or traditionally-minded people'. Inevitably, this led to the 'own wrong problem', since it became rather easy for a husband to engineer a situation in which the wife could not possibly return home,[41] would be pushed out of the marriage against her will, and possibly without any fault of her own. As atrocious cases of this type began to be reported,[42] not only Derrett protested that Hindu women needed to be protected against such male machinations.[43] But not everyone agreed, and many judges took a much more 'modern' view than Derrett thought good for Hindu women and Indian society.

Reformist pressures continued to build up during the 1970s, in particular on the question of women's rights. An important report, *Towards Equality* (1974), one of India's major contributions to the International Women's Year 1975, was the outcome of the task set to the Committee on the Status of Women in India, to review the achievements of the reforms of the 1950s and to suggest further measures for reform. This report, which was not specifically focused on Hindu law reform and had a much wider brief, stated, at p. 4:

> The period after Independence witnessed the enactment of a number of laws that sought to apply the principles underlying the Constitutional guarantees to the sphere of social life. The reforms in personal law governing marriage and inheritance, the labour laws ... tried to remove the disabilities that contributed to the low status of women in our society.

The report highlighted positive and negative factors influencing women's progress and made reference to 'the centres of resistance to the desired change in women's status and roles and the disabilities that still hamper many groups of women at different levels of existence' (p. 5).[44] In Chapter IV on 'Women

[41] She might be beaten with leather slippers (chappals) every time she tried, so that the act of beating her was compounded by the ritual impurity of contact with the leather footwear—a double act of ritual humiliation, not only for the woman of course, but her parents, too. On the importance of footwear as a cultural status symbol, see Cohn (1997: 43) for the colonial period.

[42] *Laxmibai v Laxmichand* AIR 1968 Bom 332 is a good case, in which an alert judge spotted that the husband was taking advantage of his own wrong. Bad examples of judicial focus on modernity rather than justice are *Madhukar Bhaskar v Saral* (1972) 74 *BomLR* 496 and *Bimla Devi v Singh Raj* AIR 1977 Punj 167 FB. In the former case, at p. 498, it was held that the enactment in 1964 is 'a legislative recognition of the principle that in the interest of society if there has been a breakdown of the marriage, there is no purpose in keeping the parties tied down to each other'. Eventually, the leading case became *Dharmendra Kumar v Usha Kumar* AIR 1977 SC 2218 but 'own wrong' problems continue to arise.

[43] Derrett (1981) vigorously criticized the undesirable social effects of the 1964 Amendment and the scope for the husband in taking advantage of his 'own wrong'.

[44] One of the perceived centres of resistance was Professor Derrett, whose views on the need to protect Hindu women from modernizing reforms were not widely accepted at that time.

and the law' (pp. 102–47), detailed evidence is found of how the Committee viewed legal reforms and their role in the process of modern development. Modernity is here portrayed as 'heavy reliance on law to bring about social change' (p. 102) and the report continues (id.):

> Inequalities and exploitation, generated or intensified by colonial regimes, cannot certainly be eliminated by freedom from foreign rule only. The tasks of social reconstruction, development and nation-building all call for major changes in the social order, to achieve which legislation is one of the main instruments. It can act directly, as a norm-setter, or indirectly, providing institutions which accelerate social change by making it more acceptable ...
>
> Like other colonial countries, independent India has also relied heavily on legislation in its effort to usher in a society where there will be no discrimination or inequality ... By clearly emphasising the principle of equality and removing all legal discrimination *inter-alia* between sexes, our leaders have shown their acceptance of the view that to achieve liberty there must be complete liberty for women and "all legislative traces of the inequality of women without exception must be removed".

This high-sounding statement, ending with a quote from Lenin, therefore argues for 'total equality' and in particular 'complete liberty for women', as though these were universally valid ideals that can simply be implemented through legal reform.[45] The 1974 report blamed the British for adopting the personal law system and argued in essence that both Muslim and Hindu law were thus segregated and made to stagnate.[46] Some kind words were reserved for Mahatma Gandhi because of his untiring efforts in demanding major changes to free women from social and legal disabilities, noting that '[u]nder Gandhiji's leadership the demand for improvement and modernisation of the law grew and ultimately the Government was compelled to move' (*Towards Equality* 1974: 103). However, as the report complained (id.), these reforms were long in the making, and predictably they were not the result that the reformers wanted:

> Only after independence, under the leadership of Pandit Nehru could this matter be taken up. Even so, the law had to be passed piecemeal owing to

[45] Similarly, Rajan (1998: 204) insists that '[n]o serious social scientist today, even on the extreme left of the ideological spectrum, can afford to ignore the value of individual liberty, given the international political climate of the last decade or so'.

[46] This is another persistent stereotype and legal myth, so popular with scholars that they forget to check basic facts and even contradict themselves. As shown earlier, the British never invented or created the personal law system; it predated colonial intervention, as the evidence relating to Parsis and Christians clearly demonstrates. This should have struck Agnes (2000: 128–9), who neatly outlines how the Parsi personal law appeared in India in the seventh century under local Hindu protection, but still repeats the mantra that the 'edifice of personal laws was erected' by colonial rule (ibid.: 58).

> the resistance from those who believed in the status quo. It is significant that the same body which, sitting as the Constituent Assembly, adopted the equal rights clauses in the Constitution without any debate, while functioning in its capacity as the Central Legislature, blocked the Hindu Code Bill which attempted to provide only partial equality to women.

Such comments reflect dissatisfaction with the extent of Hindu law reforms during the 1950s and insist that the intricate compromise between constitutional guarantees of equality and continued existence of personal laws is wrong and inadequate to achieve the desired aim of 'total equality'. The argument of this Committee therefore became that a Constitution that had promised equality should not now tolerate the continuation of personal laws. Long since, though, the courts had decided that the personal laws were in fact protected by the Constitution.[47] The report of 1974 was unhappy with such developments, asked for more reforms and, equally important, better implementation of existing laws. In that respect, *Towards Equality* (1974: 103–4) makes some useful comments, echoing Nehru's views:

> But legislation cannot by itself change society. To translate these rights into reality is the task of other agencies. Public opinion has to be moulded to accept these rights. The judiciary and the executive have a major role to play in this. This effort has not always been forthcoming. Sometimes the judiciary has interpreted new legislation strictly and failed to give effect to the principle underlying the legislation, as for example in dealing with cases of bigamy or the right of women to work. The executive branch of the government has seldom made an effort to set up the machinery to educate the people about the socio-economic changes. The mass media used for publicity for certain measures taken by government has been conspicuously silent about social legislation .... It is therefore necessary not only to legislate but to see that it is implemented.

The suggestion that implementation is the critical element is certainly sensible, but the way in which the report tackles the question of implementation of polygamy, child marriage, dowry, divorce, and other topics shows not only an unhealthy focus on Muslim law and the alleged unwillingness of Indian Muslims to fall in line with all other Indians, but an avid insistence on 'full equality of sexes' as a starting point for any debate.[48] Thus it is concluded on polygamy that public opinion in the Muslim community against abolition or control of polygamy 'cannot be reconciled with the declaration of equality and social

[47] *State of Bombay v Narasu Appa Mali* AIR 1952 Bom 84. The most recent case on this issue, *Ahmedabad Women Action Group (AWAG) v Union of India*, AIR 1997 SC 3614 provides a detailed overview of the relevant case law, but refuses to give in to reformist pressure.

[48] This is evident from the very first sentence on polygamy at p. 104: 'Full equality of sexes can hardly be possible in a legal system which permits polygamy and a social system which tolerates it'.

justice. We are, therefore, of the opinion that ignoring the interests of Muslim women is a denial of social justice' (ibid.: 107).

The Committee reserved particularly harsh comments for Professor Derrett's suggestion,[49] to the effect that in certain cases there might be 'carefully regulated polygamy' (id.) on economic grounds. The Committee refused to accept such evidence in a plainly politicized tone, showing its unwillingness to address the critical issue that Derrett raised, namely concern for any women caught up in polygamy. It was simply stated at p. 108:

> We are not aware of a sympathy for bigamous unions or an opinion in favour of them in the absence of a systematic survey. A survey made some years ago showed 85% of the men and 96% of the women to be in favour of compulsory monogamy.

Thus Derrett's claim was haughtily dismissed as anecdotal evidence, although the response of the Committee itself points to existing evidence of the partial acceptance of polygamy in Indian society. This method of responding to a reform suggestion discloses the high level of ideological politicization among modernists and a marked unwillingness to discuss the real legal issue, namely how to assist those women who, despite the prohibition on polygamy, got caught up in it and should not be made to suffer further. We shall see in Chapter 10 later how the Indian courts have, especially during the 1990s, followed Derrett's broad guidance to take account of polygamy rather than to outlaw and deny its existence. Indeed, the courts have begun to use economic measures (as Derrett anticipated and the Committee failed to recognize in proper perspective) to protect those women who are a party to polygamous marriages, especially if this happened against their wishes or even without their knowledge (Menski 2001: 189–230). At the height of modernist hubris, the report of 1974 was not even willing to engage in any discussion about such compromises and asserted firmly, at p. 108, that 'there can be no compromise on the basic policy of monogamy being the rule for all communities in India. Any compromise in this regard will only perpetuate the existing inequalities in the Status of women'.

However, this only seemed to address the policy issues raised by alleged continued Muslim opposition to a basic rule of monogamy. What about implementation of strict monogamy for Hindus? The report admits that despite legislative reforms, namely straightforward abolition, 'bigamous marriages are still prevalent among Hindus .... The Government had failed to enforce the law' (*Towards Equality* 1974: 110). A number of formal suggestions were thus made to improve the implementation of anti-polygamy law, but this unsatisfactory discussion remains marked by dogged insistence on certain basic principles, rather than consideration of the socio-economic predicaments for polygamously married women. This discussion also does not address the critical question

[49] This suggestion was made in Derrett (1970: 309) and quoted verbatim by the report at pp. 107–8.

whether a modern state law can indeed change the Hartian 'primary rules' (Hart 1994) operative among people simply by the stroke of a pen.

This ideologically loaded approach to polygamy appears even more politicized when we compare it to the Committee's attitude to the question of child marriage (see Chapter 9 later). Here the central observation is that despite having been 'restrained' and made subject to certain penalties, such marriages remain legally valid. In this case, the Committee shows its capacity for social realism, arguing against holding such marriages void, since 'in the present social and economic conditions such a rigorous measure may create more problems than it seeks to solve. We suggest, therefore, that it should be envisaged as a future goal' (*Towards Equality* 1974: 113). While such social realism can become the guiding spirit on this point of detail, it appears to remain outside the ambit of reform debates on the modernization of Hindu law. Indeed, it was decidedly less realistic on the part of the Committee to argue that registration of all marriages should be made compulsory in Indian law (p. 115). On the dowry problem, the Committee was clearly overwhelmed by massive evidence that the modern law, the Dowry Prohibition Act of 1961, 'has signally failed to achieve its purpose' (p. 115). On the huge topic of divorce, the Committee's presumption was evidently that the introduction of a number of divorce grounds in the 1950s was a step in the right direction. Indeed, it was found, at p. 118, that '[f]rom the cases reported, it appears that many women have benefited from this provision'.

However, the 1974 report focuses on Muslim divorce law. It recommends the abolition of the Muslim husband's unilateral right to divorce (p. 121) and adherence to the general principle that parity of rights regarding grounds of divorce for both husband and wife should be observed (p. 124), although not even three quarters of the respondents of a survey conducted by the Committee agreed with that strategy. This means that a very substantial minority either thought that the husband should have enhanced rights to divorce or, one suspects, had maintained that wives should have specific grounds on which to divorce. Here again, the Committee produced survey evidence to the effect that strictly uniform legal provisions were not totally socially realistic, agreeable nor desirable, but pushed for uniformizing reforms nevertheless, relying on the principle of democratic majority.

The fixation on legal uniformity for all Indians comes through most clearly in the Committee's comments on the uniform civil code. Reporting on the debates during the 1950s and the contradictory views then taken, culminating in the modernist argument that maintaining the old diversity 'violated the principle of Fundamental Rights that there should be no discrimination between citizens' (p. 142), it was stated:

> These arguments remain as valid today as when they were placed before the Constituent Assembly. The absence of a uniform civil code in the last quarter of the 20th century, 27 years after independence, is an incongruity that cannot be justified with all the emphasis that is placed on secularism,

> science and modernisation. The continuance of various personal laws which accept discrimination between men and women violate the fundamental rights, and the Preamble of the Constitution which promises to secure to all citizens 'equality of status', and is against the spirit of national integration and secularism.
>
> ... We, therefore, recommend expeditious implementation of this constitutional directive by the adoption of a Uniform Civil Code.

While the Committee was otherwise unanimous to a surprising extent (Derrett 1978a: 1–2), a note of dissent from two major Indian women scholars, Lotika Sarkar and Vina Mazumdar,[50] emphasizes their views about the nature of special representation for women. They evidently felt strongly about that particular subject. We read, in *Towards Equality* (1974: 356):

> A political system cannot be based on ideology alone but must keep in touch with the actualities of the social situation and so adjust its operation as to achieve the desired goals of the society. The mechanics of a system, if they do not grapple with the needs of a society, can defeat the ultimate objective in the long run. It is for this reason that we are compelled to dissent ...
>
> Our reasons for dissenting on this matter are consistent with the findings that run throughout the Report, that despite progressive legal changes, the actual condition of life of the mass of Indian women has not changed much.

This came very close to the realization that the social reality of Indian women—rather than just modernist ideology—should inform legal reform policy, as well as the reformers' ambitions. This is of course what Professor Derrett (1970) had been arguing in so many words, but without being taken seriously. Somehow the point was acceptable for the political representation of women, but not for the legal sphere, in which everyone was blinded by the glittering goals of modernity and eventual total legal uniformity.

In parallel with the considerations of the Committee on the Status of Women, the Indian Law Commission (typically comprising only men) became involved in specific thinking about further reforms in Hindu divorce law because of the controversies caused by the implications of the Hindu Marriage (Amendment) Act of 1964. The Law Commission produced its major Report No. 59 of 1974, on the consolidated reforms to the HMA 1955 and the SMA 1954 in record time.[51] These recommendations were put before a gathering of law teachers in 1975 and there was 'a consensus that further reform of some kind was not only inevitable but also desirable' (Derrett 1978a: 34). In fact, as Derrett (1978a: 34–5) reports:

[50] This is found in *Towards Equality* (1974: 355–7).

[51] It was asked to consider both statutes and to make recommendations about law reforms on 17 January 1974 and produced a well-researched report on 6 March 1974. Derrett (1978a: 33) saw this as 'an impressive piece of comparative law'.

> No one took the view that the Rishis' principles commanded acceptance, let alone adherence. The cry 'religion in danger', so loud in 1941 and 1947–51 was not heard at all. The thin end of the wedge had been driven home by the practice of the courts during the two decades that had intervened. A few lonely voices urged caution and pointed out, what we shall repeat, namely that divorce is not by any means a panacea for women's ills, and that quick divorce may be much less valuable than tardy divorce ... There was no general excitement.

Derrett (1978a: 35–9) provides a detailed summary of the main reforms that were ultimately introduced in the Marriage Laws (Amendment) Act, 1976. In essence, these were individualising, 'liberating' provisions.[52] Above all they made divorce available on a number of new grounds, such as cruelty, desertion, and adultery. Nullity for fraud was to be more easily granted,[53] and divorce by mutual consent was introduced.[54] However, the breakdown principle—which many reformers (and some judges) had desperately wanted to see introduced—was not formally and fully made a part of the new Act, although the principle lurks in many of its provisions and was bound to be invoked in protracted divorce cases. The new law gave some attention to the difficult issue of reconciliation, but was otherwise totally pro-divorce and thus, as Derrett (1978a: 39) solemnly pronounced, 'the Hindu marriage system is dead'. Derrett (1978b: ix) commented that 'the really astounding development of 1976' was the passage into law of the 1976 Act, which 'puts an end *at the statutory level* to the traditional Hindu marriage' (id.).

Since 1976, the field of Hindu personal law has hardly experienced any further legislative activities and has instead been subject to much judicial involvement and intervention.[55] Derrett (1978b: xi) found that '[i]n the summer

[52] In particular in relation to express consent to a marriage, which was not yet introduced, but appeared on the horizon.

[53] This very soon had disastrous results for women, as discussed in Menski (2001: 106–110).

[54] Derrett (1978a: 38) found it 'clear that divorce by consent is dangerous in a country where freedom of will and action is rare'. Indian divorce law therefore has a useful rule in Section 23(1)(b) of the amended HMA of 1955 to the effect that the court must satisfy itself that the consent to divorce has not been obtained by force, fraud, or undue influence on the respondent. In fact, such a provision would be useful in English law today, where a South Asian spouse may, under the so-called 'quickie divorce' of the 'Special Procedure', be forced to sign the relevant affidavits (and thus sign away all sorts of potential rights as well) without this pressure ever coming to the knowledge of a judge.

[55] This happened immediately, as indicated by Derrett (1978b: ix) in *Bimla Devi v Singh Raj* AIR 1977 Punj 167 FB. It confirms that Indian judges were and are quite comfortable to be seen making law, albeit not in a strictly positivist sense. It might be more appropriate to say that they are shaping legal policies. Some legal scholars in India have been prepared to accept this. For example, Diwan and Diwan (1993: 53) state that, 'in the process of interpretation, [the] judiciary does make law'.

of 1978 the prospects for further law reform seemed dim'. It appears that activism in the field of women's rights, for example, was directed into areas other than law-making.[56]

The only exception, which must be briefly mentioned here because it is highly significant for a postmodern analysis, is the failed Marriage Laws (Amendment) Bill of 1981. This Bill, which aimed to introduce the breakdown principle as the sole ground for divorce, as in English law, came to grief because, significantly, it was opposed by women's groups. Women who claimed to act in the best interests of all Indian women realized that this kind of individualizing, modernizing reform would do more harm to defenceless Indian women than any other measure before it.

But modernist, feminist pressure has not abated and still comes to a significant extent from the National Commission on Women, which has been busy drafting new pro-women legislation,[57] only to see their efforts frustrated by government unwillingness to be bullied into legislative measures that cost the state (or men, for that matter) extra money. There has since been a failed Marriage Bill of 1994, which clearly confirms the Indian state's ongoing reluctance to promulgate further modernizing reforms in the field of family law.[58] However, that Bill also seems to have failed because it linked reforms in family law to financial issues, a problematic area analysed further in Part II of this study.

Thus, overshadowed today by the general Indian law, but of central relevance to the present study, the old structure of concurrent personal laws remains in place and was not significantly changed by the new legal regime and its various reformative interventions. Rudolph and Rudolph (2001: 56) observe that everywhere in the world, the modernist hope that religion and difference would fade away has receded in the last two decades. In India, the opposition between legal pluralism and legal uniformity is not likely to yield a smooth progressive historical narrative in which society moves from plurality to uniformity: 'Whether regarded as benign or malign, identity formation, in the form of religiously based personal law, seems to be alive and well' (id.).

Apart from the modern successors to the Anglo-Hindu and Anglo-Mohammedan laws, also the Christian, Parsi, and Jewish personal laws have remained integral elements of modern Indian law. With the exception of Muslim and Jewish law, all other Indian personal laws are now codified to a very large extent. Since much of this codification, especially that of the Christian and Parsi law, took place in the nineteenth century, these earlier statutory laws have now become somewhat arcane and socially outdated and were increasingly subject to criticism after independence. Significantly, the abolition of such

[56] Omvedt (1993) provides a detailed overview of new movements during the 1970s and 1980s.

[57] For details and the text of some of the draft legislation, see Agnes (2000).

[58] *India Today* (15 October 1996) reported that this concerned the proposed abolition of child marriages and the compulsory registration of all marriages. The measure is further discussed in Ch. 10 later.

minority personal laws could only be achieved by their merger into a uniform civil code.[59] Since that has turned out to be 'no more than a distant mirage', as Allott (1980: 216) rightly predicted, minority personal laws have continued to exist and actually prosper in India today. The Parsis of India, evidently again mainly for reasons of ethnic self-preservation,[60] managed to persuade Parliament to legislate on marriage and divorce reforms for themselves in the Parsi Marriage and Divorce (Amendment) Act, 1988, which closely follows the Marriage Laws (Amendment) Act of 1976 in all material respects. It is therefore possible to effect modernist reforms in Indian family laws, but it seems to matter who is asking for what, and how the lobbying is done.

In contrast, the old Indian Christian law, long under vigorous attack for being discriminatory against women, has not been modernized by statute. The opposition of the Catholic Church to divorce is well known and has left some impact in Indian law. The central government's reluctance to legislate on Christian law reforms, and opposition from the Bishops to modernizing divorce reforms, have led activist judges of the Kerala High Court to rewrite the outmoded Indian Divorce Act of 1869, thus to indulge in judicial legislation, making divorce available also to Indian Christian spouses on the basis of cruelty.[61] But it has become necessary to prevent the emergence of 'shark rule' in this field, too, so that the most recent cases again look 'traditional' in their attempted control of male exploitation and discretion, since it was immediately found that Christian men were fastest in using the new law for seeking a quick divorce.[62] As these examples show, legal modernity remains an ambiguous goal difficult to implement in practice.

[59] It is evident that the Parsis, in particular, know this very well and have therefore since the nineteenth century made sure that the central law-making authority would give them their own personal laws in a form that the community finds acceptable. Jain (1990: 525) refers to the fact that as early as 1836, the Parsis asked for their own laws to be codified.

[60] Details of recent legal developments are found in an unpublished study by Ms Laila Caruso (London: SOAS 2001), which is based on fieldwork in India to ascertain the current position. Agnes (2000: 136–8) confirms that the Parsis use their personal law to maintain a separate community identity. The same strategy of quiet lobbying was even applied successfully in Pakistan, where the surprisingly modern Parsi Marriage and Divorce (Amendment) Act of 1998 governs just a handful of families.

[61] For details see Champappilly (1988) and the remarkable developments in Christian law triggered off by *Mary Sonia Zachariah v Union of India* 1995(1) KLT 644 FB. This case has since been followed not only in Kerala, but is gradually being adopted by other Indian High Courts, despite continuing resistance from the Churches.

[62] In *Philip v Susan Jacob* 2001(1) KLT 890, it was held that a divorce on the ground of cruelty and desertion is not available to the husband, thus opposing the application of the breakdown principle also for Christian spouses.

7

Transcending Modernity: The Postmodern Reconstruction of Hindu Law

The previous two chapters demonstrated that during the colonial and post-colonial periods Hindu law was subjected to a plethora of elitist strategies to reform and codify it in an endeavour to achieve modernity. The present discussion examines how post-colonial law escaped from this programmed modernization and metamorphosed into a postmodern legal system designed for achieving situation-specific justice within a culture-specific context, mainly through creative judicial interpretations. If these assumptions are correct, Nehru's post-colonial regime was right to extol diversity, while being fearful of too much of it (Dhavan 2001: 314), and it looks like misguided scholarship to assume that modernist laws in India 'had too many design faults to be wholly effective' (id.). Hindu law, whatever shape it would eventually take, assumes first of all that there is something of higher validity than any human construct of law.

However, it seems to be suggested by the projected uniform civil code in Article 44 of the Constitution that Hindu law could be discarded altogether, and modernist analysis is largely based on the eventual disappearance of Hindu law. On the other hand, Indian lawmakers—and in particular the higher judiciary—began to recognize that what had been legislated was not a fixed body of rules, but an idiosyncratic combination of modern secular rules and old indigenous concepts. This realization ushered in a process during the late 1970s and early 1980s whereby Hindu law was increasingly reconstructed by an activist judiciary to revert to a more outrightly pluralist shape, emphasizing situation-specific justice over certainty of legal rules, and thereby giving new respect to Hindu law's customary plurality and internal diversity. Within Derrett's modernist analytical framework of the 1970s, this can be characterized as the gradual reassertion of practice over theory. The present analysis goes further, however, arguing that this development reflects a postmodern transition in Hindu law-making from formerly dominant, positivist methods of law reform to socio-legal perspectives and pluralist theories. It is demonstrated here that this reconstruction process of Hindu law occurred in such a way that it involved neither complete recourse to tradition, nor total abandonment of the modernist agenda. As a result, Hindu law has transcended the axioms of tradition and modernity to the extent that it can now be more accurately conceptualized as a postmodern legal system.

The Re-indigenization of Hindu Law: Statutory Precursors

Even while further modernizing, uniformizing reforms were being promulgated during the 1960s and 1970s, it was beginning to be accepted in some scholarly debates that post-colonial Hindu law had remained a form of Hindu law rather than turning into some culture-neutral offshoot of English law. The logistical, practical, and indeed political feasibility of implementing a uniform civil code as the ultimate aim of modernist efforts was also increasingly being questioned in the context of India's legal pluralism and diversity.[1] As noted early on by Derrett (1957: 55), 'expediency and foresight, practice and realism have modified what theory alone originally projected as the ideal scheme'. Derrett's later writing (especially Derrett 1970: vii–xvii) reflected the gradual rethinking of the Hindu law reform process in India. Today, it is virtually unthinkable for India to implement the constitutional programme of a uniform civil code for all Indian citizens, and yet enormous progress has been made in creating uniform legal rules for the various personal laws of India (Menski 2001).

This process of uniformizing the personal laws through the 'back door', as it were, has largely occurred through judicial interpretations. As legal scholars and even lawyers themselves often seem to be ignorant of recent developments in case law, this process has largely passed unnoticed. However, before proceeding to examine the role of those judicial reconstructions which laid the foundations for the emergence of postmodern Hindu law, it is important to note that a pluralizing trend became discernible in the legislative field, too, as manifested in the Hindu Marriage (Madras Amendment) Act of 1967 and a number of other state enactments.

The 1967 Act constitutes evidence that the national system of Indian law is quite able to take account of local norms, even of new customs.[2] In Tamil Nadu (then Madras), blatant injustice and social confusion had been created by a pre-1955 Hindu law case, which had refused to recognize as legally valid a local, informal method of Hindu marriage solemnization.[3] The people involved called themselves 'self-respecters', refused to follow ancient Sanskritic modes of elaborate shastric rituals, did not employ Brahmins, and were happy for the spouses to simply garland each other, or to put a ring on each other's

[1] This is now confirmed by several articles in Larson (2001). On secularism and the need for more explicit toleration of differences, see Bharucha (1998).

[2] At a higher level of organization, the Indian Constitution makes a distinction between laws that may be passed by the federal government, by a state government, or in concurrent jurisdiction. Mansfield (1993: 159) observes that '[i]f territorial legal pluralism is desirable—and no one doubts that it is to some extent—why not non-territorial ethnic and religious legal pluralism?', and would thus appear to support such local legal amendments.

[3] *Deivaini Achi v Chitambaram Chettiar* AIR 1954 Mad 657.

finger, in the presence of some relatives and friends.[4] It took a long time for the legislative machinery of the then state of Madras to remedy this blatant injustice, but ultimately it was officially recognized that new local customs had developed and required full legal effect to avoid creating havoc in society.

For the present analysis, the importance of this otherwise only locally relevant Act lies in the victory of diversity over uniformity, of local norm over nationally legislated rule, and of concern for local social justice over adherence to a general principle that is presumed to bind all citizens of the state in an equal manner. It could be argued that the modern law of Hindu marriage solemnization is not a subject area in which uniformity may even be attempted, since Section 7(1) of the HMA of 1955 left the field entirely to custom (see in detail Chapter 8). The more significant element in this context is, however, the explicit recognition of situation-specific justice for 'little' local people, whose lives should not be disrupted by the state law, and who should be able to derive some assistance, rather than experiencing grief, from the official law.

This particular Act is symptomatic, therefore, of a largely hidden or 'unofficial' parallel process of gradual indigenization and pluralization of modern Hindu law, at least since the late 1960s. Careful study would demonstrate that there are many small state amendments in India's family laws which take care of local sensibilities, though not always to the benefit of women. Details of the full story of such laws will have to be told in a separate study, since it involves myriads of cases, only some of which the labours of Derrett and a few others have managed to bring to our notice. Derrett (1970) prepared the ground for such an analysis with a detailed critique of Hindu case law from the 1960s, but much has of course happened since.[5] An overview must suffice here to take us to the present postmodern state.

ORIGINS OF POSTMODERNITY: JUDICIAL RECONSTRUCTIONS

My argument here is that at a formal level, too much attention has been focused on the official processes of law reform and modernizing uniformity. At the same time, and largely unnoticed, Hindu law on the ground, as it were, retained its plural and situation-specific characteristics, which were constantly

[4] John and Nair (2000a: 33) explain that this type of marriage also had rational and gender-equal implications, as 'a social contract animated by a vision of chosen reciprocity, based on mutual desire, and, especially, on reason'. This actually looks close to the ancient *gandharva* type of 'love marriage'. On the Tamil self-respecter movement and its leader figures, see Subramanian (1999).

[5] A useful analysis of cases on marriage law is found in Derrett (1978a) and is widely spread in Derrett's four volumes of *Essays in Classical and Modern Hindu Law.* Menski (2001) was not designed to be a comprehensive analysis of family law, but focuses on how the Indian courts have developed a coherent jurisprudence that is, at the same time, justice-conscious and efficient in terms of guaranteeing social welfare without burdening the state's coffers.

imported via litigation. Thus, while the statutory provisions may not have changed, Hindu law as played out in socio-legal reality in the courts has indeed experienced a shift through judicial interpretations. Evidently, Derrett's later writings constitute the most valuable source of evidence, apart from the cases themselves, for an analysis of postmodern developments of Hindu law especially during the 1970s. In a detailed Preface to the third volume of his *Essays in Classical and Modern Hindu Law* (Derrett 1977: x), we find the comment that legal decisions by Indian judges are so difficult to analyse and apply because '[t]he Indian judgment is written to a pattern and with the object of avoiding, so far as may be, being itself reversed on appeal'. This technical approach to the process of determining disputes clearly links to the public image of law itself, as Derrett (1977: x–xi) explains with reference to the traditional Anglo-Hindu system:

> This is because law is something handed down to the public by the legislature and the judiciary, much as medicines are handed out by apothecaries. One cannot complain that one does not like the taste of medicine. One goes to law, and one must take the consequences. The teacher must therefore teach and write as if the matter which is handed down as law *is* law, for it is so by statute.

However, was this a satisfactory and sensible position to take? In Derrett's view, the state of Anglo-Hindu law was dreadful, and he argued that 'no worse chaos has (so far as I know) ever plagued the common-law milieu' (ibid.: xvi). However, Derrett (1977: xx) detected that the earlier common complacency about the use of foreign precedents and the formalistic handling of litigation no longer prevailed and he found that '[a] notable indigenous movement for rethinking the Anglo-Indian legal heritage is in the air' (id.). Strong evidence of this revision was provided through a remarkable judgment by the prominent SC judge, V.R. Krishna Iyer, arguing in a protracted landlord-tenant dispute for the Indianization of Indian laws.[6] In view of Indian circumstances of life, the learned judge, as cited by Derrett (1977: xxi), held:

> We have to part company with the precedents of the British-Indian period tying our non-statutory areas of law to vintage English law, christening it "justice, equity and good conscience". After all, conscience is the finer texture of norms woven from the ethos and life-style of a community, and since British and Indian ways of life vary so much the validity of an Anglophilic bias in Bharat's justice, equity and good conscience is questionable today. The great values that bind law to life spell out the text of justice, equity and good conscience and Cardozo has crystallized the concept thus: "Life casts the mould of conduct which will some day become fixed as law". Free India has to find its conscience in our rugged realities—and no more in alien legal thought. In a larger sense, the *insignia* of creativity in law, as in life, is freedom from subtle alien bondage, not a silent spring nor a hothouse flower.

[6] *Rattan Lal v Vardesh Chander* (1976) 2 SCC 103.

Much stronger judicial statements have been made in the past few years, while whole new areas of law (such as public interest litigation, consumer protection law, and environmental law) have been developed, outwardly built on secular rhetoric and human rights principles, but actually founded on indigenous concepts of justice and sustainable balances (Menski 1996b). In much of this new Indian jurisprudence, inspired by Hindu principles, the focus on common people's concerns and a new form of social justice is clearly discernible—provided the analyst knows enough about indigenous and specifically Hindu legal traditions to perceive that such subtexts exist. It is not the case that such statements are only made in formal speeches or articles by former judges in *Bhavan's Journal*,[7] they have become part of Indian law-making, especially during the 1980s and 1990s.

Derrett (1977: xxi) began to observe that the traditional reliance on English cases 'is no longer quite taken for granted'. Thus, it is certainly no longer true today that the Indian courts 'often appeal to English precedents' (Banerjee 1984: 288) when interpreting constitutional and other legal provisions.[8] English constitutional law has always been of limited relevance to modern Indian law, which now seems miles ahead in its explicit concern for situation-specific justice and the supremacy of judicial review, rather than the parliamentary sovereignty of the Westminster model.[9] Not surprisingly, given such elementary differences in legitimizing supreme legal authority, the Indian courts have actually thrown out many English precedents with increasing vigour, and strongly refute slavish dependence on foreign jurisprudence.[10] Thus, the modern Indian legal system has become acutely alert to the need for substantive, relative justice rather than formal uniformity, operating a complex ordering process of disparate units, rather than a simplistic and uniformly egalitarian approach as preferred—at least rhetorically—by Western legal systems. In this context, English law is certainly not ignored, but it does not have any more persuasive value than other legal systems and models that might be looked at.

Focusing on marriage law, Derrett (1978a), in his last major study on Hindu law, provides a trenchant critique of the reformist legal interventions of the 1976 Marriage Laws (Amendment) Act, proclaiming that 'for practical purposes, Hindu law died on the 27 May 1976' (p. vii), when the president of India gave his assent to the 1976 Act. He clearly felt that these reforms went too far in

[7] For a recent example of judicial pontifications in the *All India Reporter*, see Yadav (2001).

[8] Significantly, Jain (1990: 460) points out in his discussion of 'Justice, Equity and Good Conscience' that the scope for application of this maxim is now much reduced, citing *Rattan Lal v Vardesh Chander* AIR 1976 SC 588.

[9] Yet, as we saw earlier, authors continue to assert, for example, that the Indian elite 'fixed their choice on the Westminster model of government' (Baxter et al. 1993: 37).

[10] See *M. C. Mehta and another* (1987) 1 SCC 395. Many other examples could be given, e.g. *Forasol v Oil and Natural Gas Commission* AIR 1984 SC 241, at 259f.

copying Western models. Critical of the modernizing elite, Derrett (1978a: vii) likened it to a benign Orwellian liberator:

> One of its characteristics is to be only partially aware of its own nature, and assuming without question hegemony of the remainder of the population .... The élite now insist on being treated as a cosmopolitan whole, and scout the continued existence of personal laws. These, in spite of Art. 44 of the Constitution, which promises to eliminate them, are a standing monument to India's failure as yet to unify the legal structure of the most ordinary aspects of life.

But was this a failure, or was there a purpose in continuing legal plurality? Rather than focusing on the uniform civil code issue, an ideal which Derrett (1978a: 189) seems to defend to the very last, his trenchant analysis homes in on the evident and now glaring contradiction between elitist modernist ambition and real life. Linked to his earlier *Critique of Modern Hindu Law* (1970), Derrett (1978a: viii) reiterates the central confusion, observing that until recently, India used to be proud of her indigenous legal system and even now, '[t]here is not the smallest doubt that the élite value Hindu culture as such. There is no such thing as a conscious rejection of traditional Hindu values'. Based on the fieldwork-based study of Rama Mehta (1975), Derrett (1978a: ix) highlights the critical contradiction that has emerged in post-reformist Hindu law as a clash of expectations:

> Thus, a deplorable, but inescapable, contradiction is, at present, woven into the marriage-picture of the modern middle-class Hindu family. We must take account—and the judiciary must notice—a fact to which Rama Mehta draws repeated attention, based on her interviews with actual participants in this drama. The fact is that, for the Hindu woman, an unsatisfactory marriage ... is far better than no marriage at all.

Remaining optimistic about the potential for social change, Derrett (1978a: x) argued that in due course the elaborate, ultra-modern new Hindu law might fit the social facts. To that extent he remained a modernist, too. However, in the meantime, it was his express concern that women should not be made to suffer because the modern Hindu law, stipulating and assuming gender equality, further privileged men and therefore seriously disadvantaged women. While on the surface Hindu law was as good as abrogated (id.), and only 'an aroma of Hinduness' (ibid.: xi) remained,[11] its underlying principles were clearly still valid and relevant for the majority of Indians. Thus, any presumed gender equality was not a reality, and Derrett (1978a: xxi) warned that the amended HMA carried torpedoes, posing a huge danger to Hindu society, and ultimately to India as a nation. While the latter concern has clearly become prominent during the 1990s in the context of expectations of the welfare state (Menski 2001),

[11] Derrett (1978a: xix) also noted, with a sense of resignation, that '[m]y first stay in India coincided with the first dramatic progress in reforming the ancient system and my lifetime coincides with its destruction'.

Derrett's major focus was on the predicaments caused to Hindu women's status and the resulting problems in society.

Derrett (1978a: xxi) even claimed that in the *Critique* of 1970, 'I tried to show that traditional Hindu ideas, shorn of the outmoded and obsolete elements, still had a vital role in the administration of justice in the regular courts'. This might even lead to some form of integration of the formal court systems and the myriads of local informal dispute settlement practices. But it should be noted that this is not the same as reintroducing ancient Hindu law by the back door. Derrett (1978a: xxvi) took it as virtually irrevocable given that the modern Hindu law had been imposed on the nation 'in one of its many bursts of optimism', since '[t]he Act of 1976 is a fait accompli; and a return to a traditional, disciplined régime of Hindu marriage is impracticable, and virtually impossible' (p. 2).[12] At the same time, Derrett (1978a: 38) was quite certain that the introduction of divorce by consent, in particular, was dangerous in a country and society where individuals acted as members of families and were, more often than not, not free to decide critical issues for themselves. Thus the law presumed individuality and envisaged Hindu men and women as autonomous actors, but that was not social reality. Derrett (1978a: 43–4) predicted that India would find her own way out of this labyrinth, significantly through the involvement of judges:

> There are quite a number of misconceptions, and it will take us some more patient thought before we make our way through the labyrinth. When (if I may anticipate my conclusion?) we come out at the Exit we shall discover something rather unexpected: marriage in India is worth what it was before, and the Judges will see to it that that is what it remains. Modern styles, modern manners, modern aspirations will all have had their way: but a synthesis of the old and the new will leave the essence of the old in the ascendant. In this department of life ... it does not matter what use India makes of western 'precedents'; she will go on her own way in her own time, and woe betide any that get under her feet!

Such wise, culture-sensitive predictions are matched with a clear explanation of the dilemma of the modern lawmakers wishing to undo Hindu traditions. Derrett (1978a: 60) not only stated that the ancient rishis 'can by no means be abolished by a few men and women sitting in New Delhi' but produced a conceptual explanation that matches the central arguments of the present study, as discussed particularly in Chapter 3 and 4 earlier. Derrett (1978a: 67), having cited the typical words of a learned Hindu judge who had sermonized about ancient religious preceptors as lawgivers, states:

> Now practically all these manifestations are mistaken. Manu, Brihaspati, Narada, etc. could be called 'codes', but they never had the force of law,

[12] Derrett (1978a: 42) argues that this was a fait accompli in two stages, which did not make the reform process any less difficult at the end of the day. Another image used is the cuckoo in the nest (ibid.: 43).

> which indeed, would have left no one the option whether to apply them or not; and before the advent of digests no one knew how to reconcile the divergencies and contradictions between them. The idea that they ever even resembled statutes is misleading; for there was no promulgating authority. But that incorrect notion is of value for *us*, since it explains how the reformers seriously understood that the *dharmashastra* could be *repealed*, and that all that was necessary for legal and social change was legislative enactment. This last idea we now see was careless or naive.

Derrett missed a chance at this point to highlight and reiterate that, therefore, the positivist assumption that laws can just be changed by a legislature at will, has serious flaws when it comes to regulating social norms.[13] Instead, he refers readers to the excellent study of Lingat (1973) for a 'correct' picture of the nature of the *dharmaśāstra*.[14] I would go further and challenge here again the indeed naïve idea that legislation can simply undo types of traditional law based on social and religious norms. These are not of the same genus, and a state-made enactment does not just overrule something like the shastric rule system. Law cannot abrogate religion or sociocultural tradition by a stroke of the pen. The traditionalist distortion of presenting the shastra as codified law created an impression of legislative viability that had sooner or later to be defeated by social reality.

Derrett's major concern since 1970 was not with the preservation of religion or tradition, but with the growing evidence of social distress caused in Hindu society by the new Hindu laws. Reading cases all the time, which are prime evidence of sickness in society, he clearly had more than his fair share of insight into the problems caused by the new law, which had especially negative consequences for women. Based on the studies by Rama Mehta (1975), who had interviewed many divorced middle-class Hindu women, Derrett found that Hindu men were evidently lagging behind women in adjusting to 'modern' conditions. Derrett (1978a: x) therefore argued that Hindu women had to bear the brunt of the legal reforms of 1976, which were offering tempting remedies like faster divorce and nullity, 'used both *against* the woman, and *for* the woman: in either case to her detriment!' In a section on the traditional Hindu family and the costs of modernization, Derrett (1978a: 107–8) concluded:

> The cost to the *sastrically* perfect family when it works well and is undisturbed is the low cooperation between spouses and the excessive power-rating of the husband: but that did not matter, as in the integrated whole neither party felt much loss thereby. The cost to the modern family

[13] As we saw, Derrett (1970: x–xi) was more forthright about the usefulness of the historical school of law as an interpretative model.

[14] It is necessary to be critical of Lingat's position, which appears still too much influenced by the civil tradition from which he came, and too much wedded to the power of learned old men as lawmakers. For details of such criticism, see Menski (2000a: 154–6). Olivelle (2000) now translates dharma as 'law' throughout, purportedly to make life easier for the reader, but in my view this is not appropriate.

> cut off from the village and from tradition, doubly deprived, was much higher. Unless they are élite or nearly élite people, brought up to élite ambitions and élite standards, they are not adapted at all to modernisation and their religious and social traditions fit them only for distress and mutual distrust.

One can anticipate the modernist response that, therefore, Hindus would do well to modernize more completely, getting rid of all vestiges of their religious and social traditions. But what should they adopt instead? What does it mean to advise Hindus to modernize?[15] While in the 1970s it may still have been admired by many Indians, 'Western' or even specifically 'English' society is arguably not a role model for India of the twenty-first century any more.[16] Too much has happened in modern Western societies that suggests to states like India that following Western trends of unmarried cohabitation, easy divorce, and especially abandonment of wives and children to the care of the welfare state, would be detrimental for the nation, extremely damaging for many families, and even more difficult for many individuals, especially women and children. In view of this, Derrett (1978a: 96–7) significantly revised his views about the desirability of modernist Hindu family law reforms in Indian conditions, observing that, during the 1950s,

> ... every legislator's mind was full of the eventual need for a Uniform Civil Code, and was sure that B. N. Rau was right, that piecemeal reform horizontally applied was undesirable, and that comprehensive reform vertically was inevitable—the only problem seemed to be what form the 'Hindu Code' should take. There was general agreement that castes that had customary divorce should not be deprived of it; no one considered that the gift of divorce in a cosmopolitan form to the large number of respectable castes was a Trojan Horse, a poisoned gift. It certainly did not occur to me then. Like, I am sorry to say, others very much more *au fait* than myself, I was preoccupied with the correct choice between *sastric* rules and Anglo-Hindu rules, the selection to be made between Indian and foreign expedients, for, as I supposed and as many must have thought, everyone's advantage. Baroda, Mysore and the B. N. Rau Committee, both in 1941 and in 1947 were clear that what was wanted was a renewed *sastra* and therefore something universally and compulsorily applicable to all Hindus saving insignificant exceptions. It hardly occurred to anyone that that aim was itself out of date.

On the other hand, for the majority of Hindus, dharma has remained a reality, as Derrett (1978a: 157–8) clearly saw:

[15] Derrett (1978a: 111) asks the key question: 'Is it necessary to "westernise" in order to "modernise"?'.

[16] Bharucha (1998: 171) criticizes the media for presenting 'imaginary utopias that are at once unaffordable and decontextualised from the realities of people's lives'.

> The 90 per cent of Hindus for whom I am showing concern, whose laws have been tampered with at the behest of those who have better access to the legislature, still equate law as an ideal standard with *dharma*, and are (i) most reluctant to dissociate the two, and (ii) reluctant to take statute law seriously (except when it offers them cash benefits or the equivalent) or to think of it or manipulation of it as morally binding.

Derrett (1978a: 16 and 141) wisely predicted that property matters would become more important in the context of Hindu matrimonial litigation, rather than the grounds for divorce.[17] But the developments of Hindu marriage law would also affect the nation as a whole, not just relations between spouses or families. Derrett (1978a: 164) realized that the Indian state had a deep interest in the stability of marriages and thus predicted that the judges might well intervene and rescue Hindu women from being thrown out of their marriages on the slightest pretext. However, commenting on the well-meaning but probably ineffective attempts to strengthen reconciliation procedures, Derrett (1978a: 197) saw the risk of continuing to follow 'modern' developments in England and warned of the likelihood 'that India, like England, will develop a divorce-production-line', since 'parties who actually get as far as the court are unlikely to treat attempts at reconciliation seriously' (id.). Ultimately, Derrett (1978a: 182) saw the future of Hindu marriage law dependent on the balance of power between modernist individualism and local resistance to it. He identified the speed at which individualism in the form of 'contract' society instead of 'status' society is adopted all over the world including India, and, secondly, saw the resistance to it which will be created by Indian, particularly Hindu ethno-characterology.

This is actually not that different from the 'identity value' brought into the discussion by John Mansfield (1993: 175), which is also about recognition of sociocultural difference, and thus ethnicity as well. Derrett's sharp analysis took account of many factors, including the inevitable impact of modernization, to a point where Hindu consciousness perhaps evaporated altogether in diasporic situations.[18] But in this regard, Derrett (1978a: 183) observed that even the most elitist Hindus could ultimately not reach the position of the West:[19]

[17] The same point is now made by Agnes (2000: 215).

[18] Derrett was not centrally concerned about this, but specialist research, such as Ballard (1994), shows that the children and grandchildren of South Asian immigrants abroad may become hybrid 'skilled cultural navigators' rather than somewhat inferior 'brown' British citizens with poor English skills.

[19] Despite the end of colonialism, which treated the colonized as a child (Nandy 1983: 11–12), colonialism of the mind has continued to exert its influence. Madan (1996: 244) shows more generally that 'notwithstanding the bow to the oneness of humankind ... anthropology had contributed ... to the gradation of cultures, with Western civilization providing the *criteria of excellence*', thus dividing humanity. Hence, Madan (1996: 246–47) argues that the logical fault lies 'in implying that, ultimately, the alleged benefits of Western industrial civilization will, *and should*, become available to all humankind'.

> The *ecology* of our élite has changed, for they have moved from the joint family in the village or township to the nuclear family in the city: some of them oscillate between cities and even between countries. But their psychology has not. Note their double stance: on the one hand a prestige-rating group vis-à-vis the bulk of the population, and on the other hand an apprentice-group vis-à-vis the West, with which they intimately wish to be associated. This is essentially a hangover from the caste-society, and the fact that they have been busy building a super-caste makes no profound difference.

While the elite would, therefore, forever struggle to be accepted on account of its own modernity,[20] the pulls of 'tradition' and the basic presumption in Hindu society in favour of preserving marriages would remain strong. Derrett (1978a: 183) rightly pinpointed the fact that '[m]en have changed much less than women. Women's situation has changed, and is changing alarmingly', so much so that over time the maturity of women would mean that control over chastity would be in their hands. The most serious criticism of the new Hindu law of marriage and divorce, advanced by Derrett (1978a: 185–6), relates to the fact that this modern law promised Hindu women freedom, but actually damaged many of them:

> Surveys of actual cases go far to confirm this disturbing picture. Therefore a marriage law which was professedly intended for the relief of suffering wives may quite as easily be used to browbeat, oppress, deprive and corrupt women! 'Philanderers' charter' or not, the new marriage-law available to all the majority community is a means whereby vast numbers of women, whose fault is merely that they were married off into unsympathetic and unscrupulous families, will be put on the street with a few rupees a month and with a psychic trauma which no amount of 'freedom' will assuage. For however low their expectations might have been when they married, consummation of that marriage has anchored them psychically in that family, and cannot be simply washed out by litigation.

Derrett (1978a: 186–8) also reconsidered the crucial role of the judges in this dilemma. Derrett (1970: 29) had earlier criticized that the courts' work is seen

[20] Outright assimilation is now largely seen as impossible because of racial and cultural factors, which play a much larger role than official bodies are ready to admit. While he was right to emphasize the impossibility of becoming English, Derrett (1970: xv) was less correct when he declared that the presence of South Asians in the UK was ephemeral and not really relevant to his analysis. By now, we can see that most Hindus in the UK are clearly not abandoning their cultural norms in favour of total assimilation or outright modernization. Indeed, they have been reconstructing their lives as they saw fit—as British Hindus with a hyphenated identity, constructing a British dharma, which may be referred to as *angrezi* dharma and appears in various manifestations (Menski 1987; 1993a). Ballard (1994: 8) comments in this regard that 'nothing can alter the fact that the new minorities have become a part of the British social order, and they have done so *on their own terms*'.

as 'a kind of mystery or *hocus pocus*, to which the public resort not only to obtain their rights but also to bring pressure to bear upon opponents' and had doubted the aptness of the courts to cope with family quarrels. Derrett (1978a: 186) still identifies the same problem, in that '[t]he search for the aroma of *undue influence* has become particularly important', making it an obligation on the judges to throw out false and contrived cases. But where the evidence before the court points to the breakdown of a marriage beyond repair, '[o]nce that is clear, and only then, *expeditious* termination of the dispute is enjoined upon the courts' (p. 187). Otherwise, as Derrett (id.) argued:

> Parliament knows that the judges' *values* will colour the application of the Act. Parliament's values and the judges' values are the same: the basic presumption in favour of marriage. The unwritten clause of the Act runs, 'No one shall dissolve a marriage unless no other course is conceivable, taking into account the welfare of (i) the spouses (*not* their families!) and (ii) the children of the marriage'. There is no question ... of the judiciary being neutral as might well be the case in England, many jurisdictions in the United States, or Japan. Very important implications emerge from this.

Derrett (1978a: 195) thus painted a fairly optimistic picture, and he trusted the Indian judges, many of whom he knew well, to come to the assistance of Hindu women.[21] But in one of his last published essays, he can be found criticizing Indian judges for being still insufficiently alert to the limits of modern law, or for being too insensitive to the predicament of the woman in a case. Thus, Derrett (1981), in a brief article on the 'own wrong problem', voices dissatisfaction with a leading SC case, *Dharmendra Kumar v Usha Kumar* AIR 1977 SC 2218. This case is seen by Derrett (1981: 14) as 'another slap in the face, not of the present writer (who does not matter), but of the Hindu women of India, which is quite another question. Why did they do it? ... it is ridiculous to treat matrimonial litigation as irretrievable breakdown of marriage—understanding 'marriage' as a matter between two spouses'. While Parliament gave the right to a divorce, there must be effective mechanisms to prevent unscrupulous husbands from engineering an easy divorce for themselves. While he was particularly critical of northern Indian courts for tending to take patriarchal perspectives, Derrett (1981: 15) lauded a decision from the Madras HC, refusing a divorce:[22]

> Here is a situation which has, in many parts of India, attracted the Courts' sympathy towards the husband! Justice Sathiadev openly points out what everyone knows, and this present writer has been vainly urging for years, namely that unless such divorce petitions are rejected by discerning judges every Hindu marriage exists at the whim of the husband: and in a land

[21] Some judgments have had an unfair and outrightly discriminatory effect against women. A bad case for widowed Hindu women is *Surjit Kaur v Garja Singh* AIR 1994 SC 135.

[22] This was *Soundarammal v Sundara Mahalinga Nadar* AIR 1980 Mad 294.

> where arranged marriages are proper, child marriages are common, dowries are endemic, and female virtue is prized above all virtues, such a situation is absolutely intolerable.

During the 1980s and 1990s, many decisions on Hindu law appeared which would still have made Professor Derrett despair over whether his expert advice would ever be listened to. However, from about 1988 onwards, as my own recent detailed analysis has shown (Menski 2001), the Indian courts have more clearly taken account of the potential and actual social problems caused by the modernization of Hindu law. In other words, we have strong evidence from the case law itself that the process of postmodern reconstruction of Hindu law is not some random aberration in some odd cases, but a thickly represented development that requires urgent critical analysis.

Earlier, the extremely long case report of *N.G. Dastane v S. Dastane* AIR 1975 SC 1534 had been a major social document of modernist judicial views on the breakdown of marriage and matrimonial cruelty in India. The new guiding authority in the postmodern phase became the case of *V. Bhagat v D. Bhagat* AIR 1994 SC 710. In this case, two learned judges, Kuldip Singh and B. P. Jeevan Reddy JJ, ultimately granted the warring spouses (who were themselves highly placed professionals, the husband being a senior lawyer) the divorce they needed to escape from a living hell. But this divorce was not granted without serious warnings about the unsuitability of the breakdown principle for the average Indian couple. Thus, this case was not to be treated as a precedent for the coveted modernist symbol of 'irretrievable breakdown' of marriage. *Bhagat* was to remain an exceptional case, and the SC was extremely careful to stress that its decision to grant divorce in this case was made 'to clear up an insoluble mess' (p. 721) and should not become a precedent for the acceptability of 'irretrievable breakdown' in Hindu law.

The learned judges in *V. Bhagat v D. Bhagat* (the judgment is given by B.P. Jeevan Reddy J) do not claim to construct postmodern Hindu law, but that is exactly what they did. Rather than pursuing the strategy of the formal legal system, which had been held to ransom by this warring Hindu couple for eight years, the judges looked at the tangled facts before them and decided that the mess needed to end forthwith, to save further embarrassment as well as precious judicial time. The judges did take notice of the fact that the Hindu wife in this case was tenaciously claiming that she was still ready to live with her husband, but found, as a matter of fact, that her own conduct was such as to make this option totally impossible.[23] They therefore granted divorce on a ground that technically does not exist in modern Hindu law, achieving a socially and economically 'good' result, which was as much motivated by disgust over the protracted process of washing dirty linen in court as concern to save judicial

[23] She probably wanted extra maintenance from the husband, even though she had independent means, but this is not discussed.

time and 'face'.[24] Not a word about Hindu traditions, *saṃskāra* or the like, but a decision, nevertheless, that remains cautiously aware that such exceptional cases must not be used as a model for all Hindus.

The positive assessment of this particular case is not shared by some modernist women advocates in India. Ms Indira Jaising, in an email communication, claimed that *Bhagat* was a bad case, because it still carried the risk of chaining a Hindu wife to an unsatisfactory marriage and of leaving her without adequate maintenance. It did not appear to me that Mrs Bhagat was genuinely interested in her marriage, nor that she should actually require maintenance. Here was a woman who harassed her husband (not that he was lily-white himself) through years of litigation. Is this a proper and socially desirable benefit resulting from the modernization of Hindu law?

This debate shows, above all, that the modernist proponents of the 'breakdown principle' have not given up arguing that their principle constitutes a better policy than the perceived restrictiveness of the judges about granting divorces to Hindu couples. Yet this argument is too simplistic. It overlooks precisely the postmodern dimension of Hindu law development, namely the fact that the current judicial sensitivity about the facts and circumstances of individual cases would not preclude a Hindu wife from seeking divorce, but she would be expected to provide reasoned grounds—and the husband would need to provide her (and of course any children of the couple) adequate maintenance. *Bhagat* shows that the modern statutory system of Hindu law permits individual spouses to torture each other through exploitative use of legal procedures. Where such legal processes lead to improper results, the postmodern law has a duty to intervene, and it does so quite effectively, as shown in *Bhagat*.

While modernity, as we saw, is often propounded on the basis of a single linear 'progressive' line of development, such as abolition of polygamy, introduction of divorce for every Hindu couple, or the abolition of all personal laws, the complex socio-legal reality of modern India demanded a more sophisticated, indeed a postmodern approach. Under that paradigm, it is no longer necessary to waste time debating whether tradition or modernity are a good thing, because postmodern reality is manifestly hybrid and there is anyway no right answer that fits all situations. It is significant that in postmodern Hindu law regulation, more mental energy is now being spent on solving the real problems of real Hindus, in line with recognition of their means and practical needs, instead of pursuing ideological goals and pushing certain agenda which might damage the many millions of 'little Hindus' for whom the modernist lawmakers have had so little time and patience.

[24] Kusum (2000: 250) asserts that in this case, '[t]he apex court with its sensitive and pragmatic approach to the problem of broken marriages has thus imperceptibly inducted the breakdown theory', but also warns that this ground 'should be applied with utmost discretion' (id.).

An Evolving Postmodern Condition: Constitutional Reawakening

While there had been protests and opposition to the reforms of the 1950s from the very start, once litigation under the new Hindu law appeared, it gave rise to vigorous criticism on all sides (Derrett 1978a: 125). Traditionalists deplored many of the new decisions, while the reformers remained unhappy about the piecemeal nature of change and the continuing complexity of using lengthy court proceedings to settle matrimonial disputes. This criticism is abundantly documented in the widely dispersed writings of Professor Derrett.[25]

Derrett had been clear from the beginning that India's judges would play a key role in this venture of modernizing Hindu law and/or reworking it. They were the critical agents when it came to harmonizing the new legal rules and the expectations and needs of Hindus as individuals and members of families. Much was in fact explicitly left to judicial law-making, for example the definition of 'cruelty' as a ground for judicial separation and (after 1976) of divorce, or of 'fraud' for the purposes of nullity petitions. In the 1970s, most judges still pursued strictly modernist arguments and strategies, but there has been a most remarkable reorientation of judicial law-making in India since about 1975, the time of Indira Gandhi's Emergency. This crisis point in post-colonial Indian history not only led to significant changes in Indian constitutional law, but also affected the entire area of family law, although that took some time to become evident.

A few words on constitutional developments must suffice here to provide the wider context for the genesis of postmodern Hindu law in India. Influenced by post-Emergency developments in the arena of constitutional law, the realization of an 'unfinished revolution' (Gandhi 1992: 21) led to amendment processes which basically reintroduced Hindu concepts into the Indian Constitution, secular in language but Hindu in spirit. This constitutional reconstruction soon contributed to an enormously fertile interpretation of such basic guarantees as the right to life in Article 21, which now comprises many aspects that the original lawmakers would not have dreamt of connecting to the formal legal understanding of the right to life (Sathe 2002). Not just Western models were used here for the fundamental reassessment of rights and duties in postmodern Indian law. Hindu concepts, too, have made their impact in the new case law of the 1990s. These cases have not yet been analysed in depth, because most legal analysts remain fixated on the established categories of legal analysis and have not found it easy to adjust their framework of reference to the new realities. Much of the supposedly leading modernist writing is simply not up to date.[26]

[25] A full bibliography of almost all of Professor Derrett's writing on Indian laws is found in Sontheimer and Aithal (1982: 411–58).

[26] For example, Austin (1999b: 10) explains that his analysis stops in 1985. The fourth edition of Seervai (1991), the leading constitutional law text, extends only into the early 1990s.

The present, extremely brief excursion into constitutional law demonstrates that it is now impossible to analyse developments in the Hindu personal law in isolation from other legal areas. Justice does not respect the subject borders of legal specialisms. Since the 1980s, in particular, the Indian higher judiciary has become instrumental in creating a postmodern Hindu law that tries to be economically sustainable and remarkably justice-focused, but not ideologically bound to Western-style prescriptions of formal equality and Western interpretations of human rights (Menski 2001).[27] It appears that the issue of diversity (and its usefulness, hardly a new issue) hit those who govern India through the realization that the wonderful promises of the Constitution about equality and basic human rights had remained meaningless for increasing millions of Indian citizens as time went on. It was gradually recognized that the guarantees on fundamental rights in the Constitution meant nothing for many millions of deprived and impoverished Indians. Just as the post-colonial, modernist system of governance began to settle, it became increasingly evident (some would say, painfully obvious to politicians around election time) that the great promises of the state could not and would not be fulfilled. In particular, the twenty-point programme of Indira Gandhi and her slogans about beating off poverty (*garībī hatāo*) during the 1970s reflect a desperate realization that those aims were becoming increasingly unrealistic. The result appears to have been a fundamental reorientation of the modern Indian state, which far too few observers have been able to understand because it involves interdisciplinary insight and a good dose of knowledge of the principles of classical Hindu law.

To promote a better quality of justice, thereby recognizing that justice was not guaranteed by the Constitution merely on paper, postmodern Indian law reintroduced ancient special techniques for achieving easier access to justice, such as public interest litigation with its relaxations about locus standi, to provide at least justice within reach of the citizen (Singh 1996). Significantly, helpful provisions like Article 32 of the Indian Constitution were already in place, but now received a new interpretation, focusing on the needs of those citizens who had no means to engage lawyers and follow fully formalized procedures. The revolutionary reinterpretation of the simple little phrase 'by appropriate proceedings' in *S.P. Gupta v President of India* AIR 1982 SC 149, at first sight a matter of judicial politics, had eventually enormous implications for the entire Indian system of adjudication, weighting the scales of justice in favour of the disadvantaged and the dispossessed or, from the perspective of opponents of

[27] Modernist analysis, however, continues to insist that 'the state is an irreversible feature of modernity' (Rajan 1998: 108) and that 'it would be naive to underestimate its staying power' (ibid.: 111). Parekh (1996: 49) analyses the nature of the modern state, arguing in view of many criticisms that '[t]he state cannot give up its enabling, coordinating, and socially creative role' and needs to develop 'an institutionalized partnership with major social institutions' (id.). While this seems to suggest that the modernist and positivist ambitions of the state have been frustrated, Parekh (1996: 49) rightly concludes that 'it is too early to write the obituary of the modern state'.

'public interest litigation', giving undue favours to certain litigants rather than the elite repeat players of the early post-colonial era. In this way, plurality was explicitly recognized as legally relevant, and the fake modernist claim of equal status was thus exposed. Of course, the legal fraternity and the elite were not happy.

Similarly, by explicitly recognizing the social fact that Hindu men and women are different, having learnt that assuming formal equality may actually hurt women and children,[28] India's higher judiciary developed an advanced approach to gender sensitivity for which the judges have been given little credit. While the leaders of scholarship remain wedded to Western-dominated models of legal modernity,[29] Indian socio-legal reality has therefore moved on. It was demonstrated earlier that some of the most recent feminist legal scholarship is now beginning to recognize this (Dhanda and Parashar 1999), but the present state of analysis seems still set in confrontations between haplessly loaded binaries of 'tradition' and 'modernity', 'East' and 'West', 'developed' and 'undeveloped', and above all, 'religion' and 'law'.

Nowhere is this more obvious than in the assessment of the recent powerful movement of Indian public interest litigation, which seeks to ensure social justice and, prominently, better access to justice for the many millions of Indian citizens to whom the official legal system has remained a remote institution without meaning, and to whom justice is an empty shell without the means to survive the next day. Recent research shows that Indian public interest litigation can be best conceptualized as an intricate blend of modern human rights concerns *and* traditional Indian concepts of relative justice and balance in society. It is a hybrid phenomenon and clearly goes beyond the idioms of modernity.[30] Thus, it was never correct to assume that only a few maverick judges of the Supreme Court of India promoted this movement, or that the judiciary became activist to enhance its own image or power. Rather, public interest litigation is a broad-based phenomenon carried by public opinion, to the effect that the state legal system is not in all instances sufficiently concerned to achieve the standards of justice and efficiency that the Constitution so vigorously preaches. Cruel injustices have come to light in petitions under public interest litigation,[31] remedies are not always readily available, and the courts are recognizing such limits. Through this movement, much progress has been made in alerting the Indian public to the need for greater accountability of those in positions of power, which is also a form of self-controlled ordering.

[28] Recognition of this is already found in the basic constitutional foundation of Article 15(3), which provides that '[n]othing in this article shall prevent the State from making any special provision for women and children'.

[29] See in this respect my critique of Paras Diwan's tenacity in trying to tell the judges to follow modern models (Menski 2001: 133). Rajan's (1998: 204) insistence on the central value of individual liberty has already been noted.

[30] See e.g. Hurra (1993) and Bakshi (1999) for India and for South Asia as a whole Hossain, Malik and Musa (1997) and Menski et al. (2000).

[31] On the early prominent cases in many areas of law, see comprehensively Ahuja (1997).

Today, India appears to lead the way in the world in terms of judicial activism and concern for public accountability.[32]

To an observer familiar with traditional Indian law, all this looks like a reincarnation of concepts of *rājadharma*, which emphasize that those in positions of power have duties towards their fellow citizens, rather than just political and legal authority and rights. The rise of awareness about public accountability in India, by no means on a steady curve of progress, is a sure indicator that concern for justice, which is neither Hindu, nor Muslim, nor secular, but constitutes a universal target, can be linked to ancient concepts about ordered spheres, in which state law is but one small aspect. It seems that we have come back, full circle, to the fluid parameters of the old Hindu systems of *ṛta* and dharma, culture-specific forms of natural law, which are remarkably similar to their ancient Greek counterparts. The latter are certainly not as universal as has been made out in Western scholarship.[33]

However, this does not mean that there has been no change on this circuitous route. The more recent developments in Indian laws, from Anglo-Indian law to the latest statutory reforms, have distracted us from the fact that the old system was never fully superseded and totally displaced, as placatively assumed by Galanter (1989: 15). It was simply added to all the time, and the accretions—provided they were part of the official law—received much publicity, thus making the traditional basic and largely conceptual forces ever more invisible. In particular the informal and invisible parts of Hindu law did not succumb to simple displacement.

It appears now that the politicians and lawmakers of modern India, having satisfied most of their reformist ambitions by codifying modern Hindu law in the 1950s and up to the mid-1970s, began to realize the need for greater introspection and moral integrity. This has been built into the most recent Indian law-making processes at levels that escape notice, unless the observer is familiar with ancient Hindu concepts. It also appears in speeches by leading Indian politicians, such as the significant statement by A.B. Vajpayee, quoted at p. 59 earlier, that 'a modern India must also be a moral India'. In other words, a combination of modernity and morality must be aimed for.[34] This is not so

32 See Menski (1996b) on India and Menski et al. (2000) for South Asia as a whole. Sathe (2002) provides a more ambivalent assessment. Abraham (1999) briefly analyses the relevance of ancient conceptual models in modern Indian environmental law. Jois (1990b; 2000) concentrates on public law. Bhattacharjee (1994) makes a useful contribution to the debate, but does not go far enough in combining tradition and modernity.

33 For details see Menski (2000a: 76–85).

34 Modernists would of course ridicule this and deny the strength of morality. Quite explicitly, Rajan (1998: 98) seeks to demonstrate that 'tolerance alone is too weak a concept to achieve communal harmony and gender justice in India'. Advocating what they call a 'substantive approach', Kapur and Cossman (1995: 110) in fact allow for elitist determination of what is, and what is not, conducive to justice, sidestepping deeper analysis of the question whose perspectives should prevail.

much a rejection of hedonist modernity,[35] as a sign of the open-minded adoption of postmodern thought. This does not mean that individuals will resist temptations to be corrupt or unjust, or that foreign global companies will renounce ambitions to snatch control over key resources from little local people.[36] By itself, a postmodern approach achieves and solves nothing in terms of promotion of justice, just as 'tradition' by itself is neither inherently good nor bad. Thus, insinuations that a postmodern analysis of Hindu law will be undermining women's rights, and their gains so far, must be rejected. They are just as unreasonable as the claim that following modernist axioms brings about instant salvation.[37]

While at least one major political party in India is trying to make capital out of the current reassessment of the order foundations of Indian law, judges and policy makers alike have been extremely careful not to portray their strategies in terms of Hindu law or of dharma. This is so because the secular nature of the modern Indian polity demands a secular discourse and would declare anything else unconstitutional (Sathe 2002: 189). Since express reference to the *ṛta*/dharma complex has virtually been banned in modern secular India, while reference to foreign precedents used to be seen as unproblematic, one cannot expect judges to speak explicitly about the cultural reasons that underpin their reconstruction of postmodern Indian laws. The discourse, if there is any at all, will therefore be conducted in terms of natural law models, and within the general idioms of 'rule of law' and justice.[38] In the Indian case, this will be relative justice, not absolute standards guaranteed to all citizens, given the

[35] In his critique of modernity, Bhikhu Parekh (1997: 63) characterises this phenomenon of modern industrial civilization 'by such features as rationalism, secularization, industrialization, the scientific culture, individualism, technological mastery of nature, the drive towards globalization, and liberal democracy'.

[36] For a particularly audacious and outrightly cheeky attempt at subversion, vigilantly spotted by the Supreme Court of India, see *Monsanto Company v Coramandal Indag Products* AIR 1986 SC 712.

[37] Tamanaha (2001: 98), relying on Raz (1979), notes that 'the idea of the rule of law is the dominant legitimating slogan of law at the close of the twentieth century', but 'the crucial point is that the rule of law, as formulated, is substantively empty'. It says nothing about justice, leading Tamanaha (2001: 99) to the conclusion that 'the rule of law is compatible with, and may be instituted by, a system that contains the most immoral of laws'.

[38] The writings of V.R. Krishna Iyer, a prominent former Supreme Court judge who retired in 1980, offer extremely rich inspiration in this context. For example, Iyer (1979: 113), in an essay on 'Legal reforms in the Indian perspective', emphasizes that '[l]aw or *dharma* is not a self-validating *veda* but is legitimated by its ability to serve society in the vital area of delivery of justice .... Law, to endure and command, must be sustained by justice; people-conscious law must be the vehicle of people's justice ...'. See also Iyer (1985) on judicial justice, and Iyer (1990) on human rights from an Indian perspective. Chander (1992) analyses his thoughts and writing.

manifest impossibility—now more or less fully recognised—of such endeavour. Thus, as Krishna Iyer (1979: 114) put it in an early programmatic address:

> ... the law's linkage with society, especially the numerous weak, should loom large in the legal engineering process. And if the glory of the law be protection of the weak our jurisprudential undertaking must constantly remember that (a) the great rights that make man should be unbreakably written in favour of the little man and (b) the censorial power is not in government over the people but in the people over the government. Lastly, no country can attain material and spiritual affluence without planned development and law must be at the intelligent service of developmental processes .... The rhythm of a vibrant legality must be set to the national wavelength. And our *dharma* or code of conduct is not *ad hoc* pragmatism but rooted in morality and founded on the divinity individuated in every entity.

Such thinking along a secular, progressive route, tailor-made for India and nurtured by indigenous traditions, is not phrased with specific reference to Hindu law. It concerns the entirety of Indian laws, and it did not remain without impact in the courtroom. Detailed research would confirm that the general law of India, too, has been moving along the road to further indigenization and towards a particular form of postmodernization, in two ways. First, increased awareness of the persistence of traditional legal concepts has stimulated fresh thinking about the potential relevance of Hindu concepts, despite many ideological reservations. It helps in this context that concepts of Hindu law are never just a matter of 'religion', but have social and secular dimensions that can hardly be ignored by a justice-focused legal analysis. Bhattacharjee (1994: 8) argues that India has recently realized at great cost 'that too much pampering of the Individual Rights erodes the welfare of the community', showing how the abuse of individual rights by the elite led to frustration of major constitutional programmes.[39]

Second, reliance on foreign models has been put under the spotlight, and is currently being tested with specific regard to international legal norms such as those found in the Convention on Elimination of Discrimination Against Women (CEDAW), which has generated much excitement among women activists.[40] This process, far from subjugating Indian law to international legal norms, has brought about an even stronger realization that the application of

[39] Shourie (2001) argues that India's superior judges have not been vigilant enough in controlling the efforts by various elites in subaltern societies to secure benefits for themselves at the cost of the nation.

[40] See in particular Lawyers Collective (2000) on the issue of domestic violence. CEDAW principles were referred to in *Vishaka v State of Rajasthan* (1997) 6 SCC 241 and AIR 1997 SC 3011.

Western legal concepts masquerading as global legal norms does not necessarily suit Indian conditions and needs.[41]

In Hindu family law cases, such issues are being reflected in decisions like *Saroj Rani v Sudarshan Kumar Chadha* AIR 1984 SC 1562, which held that a decree for restitution of conjugal rights is not violative of Articles 14 and 21 of the Constitution. Here, the SC upheld the detailed reasoning of a learned single judge in the Delhi HC, Avadh Behari Rohatgi J, in *Harvinder Kaur v Harmander Singh Choudhry* AIR 1984 Del 66.[42] It had been held in that case, at p. 75:

> Introduction of Constitutional Law in the home is most inappropriate. It is like introducing a bull in a china shop. It will prove to be a ruthless destroyer of the marriage institution and all that it stands for. In the privacy of the home and the married life, neither Art. 21 nor Art. 14 have any place. In a sensitive sphere which is at once most intimate and delicate the introduction of the cold principles of Constitutional Law will have the effect of weakening the marriage bond. That the restitution remedy was abolished in England in 1970 by Sec. 20 of the Matrimonial Proceedings and Properties Act, 1970 on the recommendation of the Law Commission headed by Justice Scarman is no ground to hold that it is unconstitutional in the Indian set-up.

The partly confused, detailed discussion of this issue in Jain (1990: 642–51) focuses on the uniform civil code rather than restitution of conjugal rights (on which see in detail Chandra 1998). This discussion indicates that modernist arguments remain very strong today, but may not be shared by the judges. Jain (1990: 645) argues that 'the Founding Fathers were convinced that it was not necessary to have legal pluralism for a pluralistic society and that, as a multireligious country, India's salvation lay only in having a secular uniform civil code'. Jain (1990: 645–6) avidly underwrites this with reference to the recommendations in *Towards Equality* (1974): 'The absence of a uniform civil code so far is an incongruity that cannot be justified with the emphasis that is placed on secularism, science and modernisation'.

In this kind of discussion, the Indian judges are virtually blamed for not listening to the modernists. Jain (1990: 646) argues that '[t]he courts have either avoided or bypassed evaluating the family laws on the touchstone of Art. 14 or rejected these challenges'. As confirmed by a more recent analysis of postmodern Hindu divorce law (Menski 2001: 130–3), this demonstrates that Professor Derrett was entirely correct when he predicted that only the judges would be able to protect Hindu law from the individualizing reformative

[41] Recent writing now increasingly recognizes that globalization does not feed people and that the incursions of globalization may actually lead to an erosion of human rights (Bharucha 1998: 168).

[42] The case is also cited by Jain (1990: 646) as an example of the alleged prominent strategy of the courts to either avoid or bypass the key issue. Modernists are of course critical, as Chandra (1998: 207–9) confirms.

pressures of the modernizing elite.[43] This reorientation away from blindly modernist reformism and a strengthening of judicial policies towards constructing postmodern Hindu law began in earnest by the early 1980s.

The Blossoming of Postmodernity

As the dominant personal law in modern India, Hindu law has undoubtedly been secularized by statute, but as we saw, the spirit of Hindu law and its continuing concern for the relativities of justice are not controllable by state law. Thus, the gradual re-emergence of Hindu principles in the operation of modern Indian law generally and especially the traditionalist restructuring of the personal law sphere by judicial decisions should not surprise.[44] This was not done to reinstate Hindu traditions, but to serve an alternative sophisticated modernist agenda, focused on developing a culture-specific form of family law that suits today's common Hindus and their circumstances of life, rather than to strive towards a system of modern legal rules that resembles the laws of England, or modern 'filmstar law'.[45] There is plenty of evidence in recent developments in Hindu law to demonstrate that postmodern Hindu law has arrived, and is here to stay. It makes sense socially as well as economically (Menski 2001).

Rather than evidence of some kind of ethnic revival, or even the dreaded *hindutva*, this is proof that South Asian legal systems have retained their flexibility and capacity for justice-conscious adjustment. This potential flexibility needs to be understood also in the wider context of comparative law and socio-legal studies, because it is bound to be dismissed as messy, cumbersome legal pluralism. Postmodern Hindu law is unashamedly plural, not so much Hindu in name and credo as testing appropriateness for Hindus as they live today. As a pluralist system, it is designed to maximize social welfare and justice. The foregoing postmodern analysis yields the conclusion that there is in fact no room for absolute equality in law, because equality does not exist in social

[43] Baxi (1980) provides a detailed analysis of the people-oriented activism of the post-Emergency Supreme Court of India. He reports that 'the judiciary and especially the Supreme Court, is increasingly seen as the only surviving assurance of fair play and justice' (p. xi), and has become a last resort for the oppressed. The post-Emergency SC 'appeared determined to bury its emergency past by an astonishing range of judicial activism' (ibid.: 123).

[44] Agnes (2000: 208) protests about the Hinduization of the SMA in 1976, which 'went unnoticed by scholars and the media except for a few stray protests'.

[45] Typical in that category is the famous south Indian actress Sareetha, who successfully fought to get rid of her rustic husband once she had become a star, relying on Constitutional law arguments and the abolition of restitution of conjugal rights in English law. However, the modernist decision in *T. Sareetha v Venkata Subbaiah* AIR 1983 AP 356 was later overruled in *Saroj Rani v Sudarshan Kumar Chadha* AIR 1984 SC 1562. This, again, is a postmodern decision, preserving the stability of marriages as far as possible, and for the sake of general social stability.

reality. So what is the point of doggedly pursuing uniformizing agenda? Indeed, the uniform civil code now 'largely remains a frozen ambition' (Iyer 1979: 47).

While it is a fact that modern Hindu law in India has been codified and reformed almost beyond recognition, we must recognize today that the spirit of the old system, the 'legal postulates' of Hindu law, could never have been legislated away. These are not rules that can be superseded by a statute or a case, they are cultural norms and values, which retain their vitality despite formal legal regulation, and which therefore only *appear* to have been abolished and reformed. Since we are dealing with different categories of law here, some of which are not subject to statutory amendment in the same way as a pre-existing statute would be, the field is much more complex than the standard legal textbooks care to suggest.

Indeed, it is fair to state that Indian legal textbooks generally disappoint and seem not to grasp the central socio-legal issues in Indian legal development today. Even within the field of legal scholarship, there is insufficient interaction between those who study family law matters and those who focus on constitutional law, commercial law, and other lucrative areas of practice. The purposeful myopia of legal centralists, for whom only state-sanctioned law counts as valid law, is clearly overrepresented in the doctrinal writings of Indian legal scholars. Officially, we are indoctrinated to believe that Hindu law was almost reformed out of existence and is close to extermination by the projected uniform civil code. In reality, the informal sphere of legal regulation among Hindus persists in full strength, including the primary consideration of dharma, and recourse to all kinds of informal dispute settlement mechanisms, not just traditional panchayats, but *lok adalats*, legal aid camps, and similar initiatives, if not simply family arrangements.[46] The presence of dharma in India's legal field is often not mentioned, because it is an all-pervasive known element and thus gives rise to meaningful silence, while postmodernity makes meaningful recourse to it and treats it as an informally dominant legal force.

Postmodern Hindu law remains at present characterized by the uneasy coexistence of official formal sources of state law and continued adherence to informal value systems which are extremely diverse, are anchored in religion, culture, and social reality, and may be instantly called upon in situations where conflicts arise. In fact, before any matter goes to court, it may be resolved in the informal sphere. Formal recourse to law is neither the only, nor necessarily the most appropriate method of solving Hindu law disputes.

The self-control syndrome is most evident in the Hindu personal law, but clearly affects the operation of the entire Indian legal system.[47] It is also shared

[46] Derrett (1978c) emphasizes that family arrangements are favoured by equity, and refers to a number of cases from the Supreme Court of India on this subject.

[47] Writers have been hesitant to acknowledge this, even if the evidence was there before them. Abraham (1999), originally a thesis written under my supervision, reluctantly argues that dharma plays a critical role in the development of Indian environmental jurisprudence.

by other Asian jurisdictions.[48] If, as before, most Hindus in India operate by recourse to individual conscience within their respective socio-economic environment, rather than citing the Constitution to each other, the modern law's impact would at best be to contribute to a new 'living law' of India. The emergence of that new 'living law', and within it of a new Hindu law as a classic postmodern phenomenon, will be charted and discussed in more detail in the substantive chapters of Part II of this study. The new success story of internal postmodern legal reconstruction is rarely told because it challenges the axioms of legal positivism and legal centralism. In the Indian case, it involves modernist concerns that India should to a large extent have fallen back on elements of indigenous tradition, rather than Western models and modernizing influences. In addition, India's judges, the activist carriers of such innovative energy, have been forced into partial silence by the constitutionally dictated secular requirement to be detached and neutral about religion.

It is thus necessary to examine in more detail the conceptual consequences of the barriers for Indian judges to explain fully what they think while making decisions that appear to reintroduce tradition into modern laws. Why have they developed a decidedly postmodern Hindu law, rather than advocating—as many judges did earlier—its abolition and merger into a general law? While most judges are not in the habit of talking about their motives anyway, and tend to restrict themselves to technical explanations, a detailed analysis of the links between reported legal decisions and known social facts from the case concerned often helps to explain why a particular legal development in Hindu law took place. In India, as elsewhere, justice is not blind, but continuously struggling out of a blindfold. Within the postmodern Hindu framework of reference, concern for basic justice has had to remain situation-specific and context-sensitive, an approach which appears to be able to serve the avowed purpose of safeguarding justice better than a purportedly universalist, clinically sterile modernist approach to law-making.

In this context it is instructive to refer to an otherwise fairly insignificant SC case, *M. Govindaraju v K. Munisami Gounder* AIR 1997 SC 10, which appears to be about evidence law. The case concerns the legitimacy of a child, now a grown man, in a succession dispute. Rather than producing a detailed dissertation on 'caste', 'equality', or issues of legal uniformity, the learned judges, M.M. Punchi and Mrs Sujata V. Manohar, JJ swiftly addressed the nitty-gritty detail of Shudra custom and found, without difficulty, that the claimant must be recognized as a legitimate child. This judgment fills little more than one page, but is

[48] Such reluctance to deal with culture-specific issues is not unique to Indian law and can be shown for South east Asian laws. My colleague Andrew Harding at SOAS earlier challenged researchers from the region to provide evidence of 'Asian values', but received only polite silence in response. Harding (2001: 220) now accepts that future South east Asian legal developments, given the complexity of legal transplants from all over the world, cannot be expected to be a mirror image of Western law.

an embodiment of the new, efficient postmodern spirit among the superior Indian judiciary. There was no doubt for the Supreme Court that a situation-specific decision would have to be found, and that ignoring 'caste' in such a case, and low-caste status, could not be conducive to justice. Throwing out all legal technicalities, the decision addresses instead the factual matrix in a refreshing spirit of common sense.

This case embodies postmodern Hindu law, premised on the explicit recognition of the variable sociocultural, ethnic, and economic conditions of the litigants. Those who argued for formal stratification, codification, and unification of Hindu law and continue to fight for its eventual abolition, have evidently, and probably purposely, forgotten to remember the very first lesson which Professor Derrett (1970: 1) attempted to teach more than thirty years ago:

> In tackling Hindu law the first thing to remember is the tension between the past and the present, the desire to be traditional and the desire to be up-to-date. It is usually said that the old are traditionally-minded and the young are progressive, that the towns are progressive and the villages backward: and perhaps there is some truth in this. But it is too readily forgotten that the tensions to which we allude were present centuries ago, though not always in the same form, and the conflict between 'foreign' manners and ancient ways is endemic in India and has been going on since the Vedic age. Far too few critics of the present order realise that their ancestors were engaged in corresponding if not actually similar complaints centuries ago.

Derrett's sage guidance was of course not accepted everywhere. It appears that the state of Kerala in south India, under Communist rule at the time, went furthest in reforming the Hindu family law by attempting to abolish the Hindu joint family altogether. However, even though the Kerala Joint Hindu Family System (Abolition) Act, 1975 (Act 30 of 1976) is now the official law, at least in Kerala, in the many villages of that state various forms of traditional joint Hindu family law continue to operate (Menski 1986a; 1986b), and I am told that this is not only a rural phenomenon. Even such radical law-making confirms, therefore, that Hindu law is not a legal system that can simply be legislated out of existence overnight. Its principles and concepts have been showing a remarkable resilience, which is entirely in line with the postmodern jurisprudential axiom that all legal systems are culture-specific.

However, studies on Hindu legal developments tend to omit this important point, a tendency that draws largely from the inability to appreciate the conceptual idiosyncrasies of non-Western legal systems and the misplaced adherence to dominant modernist conceptions of what 'law' means. Indeed, on the subject of the conceptual core of Hindu law, the first chapter ('Hindu law: Age-old yet Age-less') in Bhattacharjee (1994: 1–11) is quite instructive, but something is still missing in this debate. It appears too much like a glorification of the law of *dharmaśāstra* and does not appear to question what the learned author was told as a law student in the early 1950s. Thus, Bhattacharjee (1994: 9) argues for duty orientation, claiming that '[t]he Dharmashastras convinced us that welfare of the Society benefits and enriches not only the Society or the State, but all its Individual members also'.

In retrospect, however, the modernist agenda for Hindu law reforms in India contained some hidden explosives that caused considerable damage in society, particularly to women and poor people.[49] Many judges realized that such maldevelopments occurred and sought to provide certain remedies. Looking at all the Indian personal laws together, we see now that the Indian state values all of them and has become more interested in substantive reforms across the board rather than rhetoric and formal allegiance to uniformity.

While many lawyers have been too distracted by the political football of the uniform civil code to notice the massive problems over justice that were beginning to build up in modern India, political scientists have tended to focus on the dilemmas for the nation state. Bose and Jalal (1999: 242) reflect modernist ambitions when they emphasize that '[t]hose who set their sights on the acquisition of power at the helm of a unitary nation-state displayed increasing impatience with articulations of cultural difference and diversity'. But maybe such modernist agenda and ambitions of simply following 'the West' were misguided. What if the modern state promised too much, and is now made to admit this? Bose and Jalal (1999: 243) observe that '[t]he failure of post-colonial states to assure equal citizenship rights and to deliver on the promise of redistributive justice has brought these entities into some disrepute', but they do not pursue the legal consequences, as we have done here, nor explore the problems of redefining what justice might mean. As political scientists, they emphasize instead that '[a]s the general concept of the modern, centralized nation-state has been drawn deeper into a crisis of legitimacy, a raging battle has begun between state-sponsored and anti-state nationalisms' (id.).

That issue itself is by no means irrelevant to the postmodern development of Hindu law and of Indian laws, since the modernist Indian state would constantly need to legitimize its role vis-à-vis the citizens.[50] A state run by a small elite for its own private interest would not be a viable nation, a message that Indira Gandhi understood very well when she imposed the Emergency in 1975. Looking back, we see that the ambitious modern Indian plans of the 1950s for unification and secularization of Hindu law looked ideal on paper, but were

[49] Derrett (1970: 436) expresses his disgust about the 'craze for matrimonial litigation' among modern Indians and argues that the HMA 'has opened a new door, through which filth and lies pour in an unending stream. The fears of *some* women that divorce laws would do more harm than good were justified. Much more harm than good has been done'.

[50] Rudolph and Rudolph (1987: 9), emphasizing that the Indian state must be concerned to find an appropriate balance between being a 'strong' or a 'weak' state, argue that '[f]inding the proper balance of responsiveness and firmness ... will be critical to the meaning of secularism ...'.

destined to fail on conceptual as well as substantive socio-legal grounds. In essence, such ambitious plans for social engineering through law were inherently dehumanizing, disempowering the key role of the individual in deciding what is good and bad and replacing it with compliance of state laws. This positivist method of law-making inevitably clashed with the internal mechanisms of traditional Hindu law, even if this was not immediately obvious.

To that extent modern Hindu law tried to prevent Hindus, unsuccessfully as it turned out, from using their individual conscience and the views of the community (*sadācāra*) as the final arbiter for justice. It is Hindu society, assisted by the judges, that has preserved for itself the agency to develop a justice-centred approach which is today increasingly hidden from the official law. This has in turn given rise, as we saw, to complaints about lawlessness and village anarchy. Criticism of the positivistic model of law reform is also evident from the discussion in Jain (1990: 556–7), which emphasizes the need for law and society to remain in harmony, without engaging in a debate about the relevance of Hindu concepts. Even if the legislators forgot such basic messages at times, the legendary capacity of the holistic Hindu traditional system to manifest itself in yet another avatar is shown in the recently emerged postmodern manifestation of Hindu law.

It is likely, therefore, that India will never have a purely modern and uniform legal system and will instead strive towards maintaining an equitable balance between competing equalities, not only in family law, but also throughout the legal system.[51] As we know today, the diverse Hindu foundations of modern Indian law, as well as the considerable conceptual input from Muslim law and other personal law systems, preclude a strategy of legal development that merely copies and imposes what are, after all, predominantly Western models. The Parsis show the way in this regard, insisting on legal reforms that actually mirror postmodern Hindu law. Overall, Indian law today has become a culture-specific postmodern Asian legal system in its own right, rather than an imperfect copy of some Western model. Within that wider framework, Hindu law in India has long since crossed the boundaries of tradition and modernity. It is to be found today in a postmodern condition, whose precise bearing and character in the various areas of Hindu law requires more detailed critical analysis. We now turn, therefore, to Part II of this study, where the substantive evidence for this postmodern metamorphosis of Hindu law is examined.

[51] In some areas of the law, it has long been accepted that competing equalities form the central challenge for law and policy. Specifically on protective discrimination policies, see Galanter (1984).

Part II

Substantive Hindu Law Beyond Tradition and Modernity

8

Hindu Marriage Law

While marriage law has been quite prominent in Indian family law cases, litigation has almost always involved other legal problems concerning the status of the female spouse, her financial entitlements, or inheritance rights. The legal recognition of customary Hindu marriage arrangements also often relates closely to bigamy, maintenance law, succession, or joint family property. As a result, there is much fuzziness over what is actually meant by 'marriage law'.[1] To clarify this term, it is necessary to distinguish the process of marriage itself, i.e. marriage solemnization and registration, from the social consequences of marriage. Many of the latter are not of central concern to the present chapter, but have given rise to comments about Hindu marriage traditions and their legal relevance.

The solemnization of Hindu marriages is first of all a matter of social conventions and ritual elaboration, involving the dramatization of social norms and all kinds of related beliefs.[2] In the traditional Hindu system of marriage, there was no role for the state, as marriage remained a private affair within the social realm. In the traditional system, the solemn performance of a long sequence of traditional Hindu marriage rituals was assumed to evoke mental awareness of being married, both for the spouses concerned and for those who celebrated the marriage with them and witnessed it (Derrett 1963a). Hindu society, and not the state, legitimized and publicly 'registered' all proper Hindu marriages. Once the British became involved in the administration of Hindu law and sought fixed rules, it became an issue of central importance for lawyers how such Hindu marriages are solemnized and legally validated.

The present chapter shows that neither the Anglo-Hindu interventions, nor the modernist reforms of the 1950s in independent India, have brought

[1] Following the sagacious advice of Professor Derrett, I wrote my Ph.D thesis on Hindu marriage concepts and the solemnization of Hindu marriages (Menski 1984).

[2] Derrett himself had long been interested in what types of marital expectations the Hindu wedding rituals dramatized, and he set me on a rich seam of material that still requires exhaustive research. Derrett (1978a: 197–8) contrasted the presuppositions of Western spouses and the trend towards easy remarriage with the observation that Indian spouses 'have only the most basic and crude expectations. Those who marry with low expectations are seldom disappointed with each other' (ibid.: 198).

about any substantive change in Hindu marriage law. Even today, a Hindu marriage in India does not normally require the involvement of the state. Thus, behind a modernist smokescreen of formal legal reform and codification, the traditional Hindu law remains more or less fully in place.[3] Agnes (2000: 210) correctly states that 'under the present statute, a Hindu need never approach a state functionary or a religious institution either for solemnization of his/her marriage or for its dissolution'.

Here, then, is our first substantive case of postmodern Hindu law in post-colonial India. Analysing this postmodern condition of Hindu marriage law within a historical context, we need to ask whether the virtually complete blanket approval of ancient Hindu practices (which now of course appear in their current, contemporary avatar) constitutes a hidden surrender to Hindu traditions. Does it signify postmodern realism, namely that marriage is such an intimately social affair that its formal regulation is best left to the respective societies? Or should we apply the 'limits of law' argument as an explanatory model for why the modern state law admits so comprehensively that it is unable to regulate the relevant normative traditions?

It appears that there could not be a more clear-cut case for the preservation of the ethnic characteristics of Hindu communities, or the identity value of different social groups (Mansfield 1993), as discussed in Part I of this study. The modern state recognizes that it seems best to leave the solemnization and even registration of Hindu marriages to the jurisdiction of society, while offering judicial fora for dispute settlement and judicial supervision as a safeguard. This clearly reflects an acknowledgement that within the Hindu sociocultural framework—and not primarily therefore on account of Hindu religion—legal mechanisms exist which remain able to exercise meaningful social control at the lowest level, also today. In this field of analysis, there was evidently little room for positivist intervention in the first place. But since the reformers did not hesitate to interfere in other areas of the law, why did they not intervene in Hindu marriage law too? The reason lies in the postmodern condition of Hindu marriage law, where to date there remains an uneasy coexistence of reformist rhetoric and sociocultural realism.

The Traditional Hindu Law of Marriage

The existing literature on Hindu marriage has developed into a complex combination of oddly mismatched evidence and comments. The painstaking study of ancient Sanskritic marriage rituals is not a mainstream job for lawyers, but a matter for Sanskritists, historians, anthropologists, and researchers of religious

[3] Like everyone else, Hindus have the option to register their marriage under the SMA 1954. In some cases of marriage between spouses of different religious and/or cultural backgrounds it is not only advisable but also required by the legal system to register the marriage formally with the state authorities.

studies. There are many serious attempts by Sanskritists to make sense of the phenomenon of traditional Hindu marriage and its consequences in a traditional context.[4] However, these studies tend to become embroiled in ritual detail and thus discourage the legal reader who looks for certain, quick answers. Writers working within a modernist conceptual framework of reference, and generally without addressing details of Hindu marriage law and practice, have produced a barrage of criticisms of the institution of Hindu marriage.[5] Somewhere in between are those writers who describe the patterns of traditional marriage but cannot resist glorifying Hindu tradition, fantasizing about certain aspects, or simply getting sidetracked into other related issues.[6]

As a result, there exists a segregation of specialist literatures. The remarkably detailed literature on Hindu marriage includes hardly any writing by legal scholars, while a researcher on Hindu marriage will draw a blank in legal textbooks, returning to literature produced by scholars who are not lawyers. Nevertheless, at least non-legal researchers have been able to elucidate the conceptual framework of Hindu marriage and its central social functions for all levels of society. Within a Hindu framework of reference, it is agreed that every single Hindu marriage solemnization is a more or less conscious attempt to link the spouses to the cosmic dimension of Hinduism through the performance of certain rituals.[7] These may be minimal, in certain circumstances,[8] as Hindu marriages need not be elaborate, costly celebrations that last for several days.[9]

[4] The leading studies in this field have been produced by Sanskritists. See in particular Pandey (1969); Chatterjee (1972–4); Chatterjee (1972); Apte (1978); Chatterjee (1978).

[5] Most recently, Basu (2001) is an example of such writing, while Thomas (2000: 14) takes a dim view of marriage itself, treating it as 'an institution of sex-slavery'. Here is a modern author who apparently has ideological problems with marriage itself and fumes about all aspects of patriarchy. Such writing does not enlighten readers to understand basic key concepts.

[6] A critique of such works would be long and tedious. One of the most recent examples of such writing is Dogra and Dogra (2000). I have used only some elements from such studies, as indicated in the references later.

[7] Stein (1998: 52–3) points to the role of Agni as chief priest in Hindu marriage rituals. In the present context, it would be useful to perceive this 'fire god' as the *ṛtic* link for a Hindu marriage, making the role of the state redundant.

[8] In the extreme, it is possible to identify a potential 'zero-ritual' as the accepted customary pattern, for example, for the remarriage of a Hindu widow (Menski 2001: 20–4).

[9] Bumiller (1991: 25) emphasizes the costs of weddings: 'In India, a wedding is a chaotic pageant that can last until six in the morning, and more and more has become a public validation of a family's status and wealth. If a family is rich, it is not unusual to have a thousand guests. Even a working-class family will put on a feast for two hundred, ensuring crippling debt for the next decade'.

Conceptual Core: Unity in Diversity

A full discussion of traditional Hindu marriage law must be placed within the appropriate conceptual framework and should therefore begin from the central premises of the *ṛta*/dharma complex (see ch. 3). Right from the earliest Hindu literary sources onwards, in *Ṛgveda* (RV) 10.85 and in *Atharvaveda* (AV) 14,[10] we find two detailed sequences of Hindu marriage rituals. Beginning from such Vedic foundations, we have massive evidence of ancient Hindu marriage rituals, which elaborate and ritually dramatize the centrality of marriage as a cultural, social, and religious institution among Hindus. The detailed contextual interpretation of such ancient sources has remained problematic. My Ph.D thesis (Menski 1984) cracked some of the sophisticated codes of language and presentation that distinguish the Vedic texts as extremely intelligent and complex representations of human marriage vis-à-vis the Hindu universe. From this Vedic perspective, a Hindu marriage is seen as the microcosmic equivalent of the macrocosmic togetherness of the universe, as symbolized in the daily cycles of sun and moon.

Contrary to assertions by many modern Hindus, the Vedic patterns of marriage solemnization did not constitute a fixed, uniformly binding model for every couple. Furthermore, my research confirms that the ritual element of the *saptapadī*, which appears to have been given such prominence later, and even appears in Section 7(2) of the HMA 1955, cannot satisfactorily be traced back to the Vedic stage of marriage solemnization.[11] Instead, it appears in full-fledged form only in the domestic ritual sections of the important classical *sūtra* literature. It thus belongs to the realm of classical Hindu law with its emphasis on dharma rather than *ṛta*. It also fits there conceptually, rather than in the Vedic model, as it focuses primarily on the two spouses that are being joined in matrimony, rather than the cosmic links recreated through their marriage. The full-fledged *saptapadī* is a ritual of friendship (Menski 1991b), a solemn promise of 'going through thick and thin together'. It thus emphasizes the microcosmic sphere of dharma more than anything else, ritualizing the emerging close bond between the spouses within that conceptual mould.

The multiple transitions within Hindu traditional practices are well reflected in the specialist literature. Pandey (1969: 153) wrote that '[w]hen religious consciousness developed, marriage was not only a social necessity but became a religious duty encumbent upon every individual'.[12] Nair (1978: 2) confirms

[10] This is a slightly younger text, still belonging to the pre-classical Vedic period, and thus dateable to around 1000 BC or possibly later.

[11] This is in essence, as the name says, a ritual involving seven steps, but there are so many variations of it, and such amazing distortions of theory and practice, that a whole book could be written just on that topic. Some relevant details are discussed later.

[12] Chatterjee et al. (1971: 58) also observe that marriage is a universal phenomenon in South Asia.

that an orthodox Hindu must marry, 'whether he be an idiot, impotent or imbecile, for the proper discharge of his socio-cultural and religious duties'.[13] During the classical period and its elaboration of dharmic duties for every Hindu individual, the central importance of marriage was further reinforced. Now it supposedly became the only *saṃskāra* for women.[14] Within the framework of the ashrama theory and its sequence of stages of life, it became a major expectation that everyone, male or female, should be married.[15] Detailed fieldwork confirms that such norms are also strongly reflected in contemporary Indian society.[16]

The topic of traditional Hindu marriage solemnization was in itself an ocean of diverse beliefs, rituals, and practices. These made sense, if at all, only to those who practised such complex ritual dramatizations of the transition of a couple from one stage of life to the next within the *varṇāśramadharma* model of Hindu stages of life. As the ancient texts tell us in clear terms, there was virtually unlimited scope for local, caste, and family customs to be combined with these 'traditional' Hindu ritual elements. *Āśvalāyanagṛhyasūtra* 1.7.1–2 (tr. Sharma 1976) significantly begins the marriage section of the text with a comment that emphasizes plurality and the overriding importance of customs:

> Now, manifold indeed are the customs of different areas and villages, those one should observe at the marriage. Only what is common (to all), that we shall state here.

It has evidently been impossible, from the start, to bring any order into this complex pattern of unending diversity, despite the unifying conceptual core.

[13] Nair (1978: 2) argues that the universality of marriage among the lowest strata of Hindu society is also exemplified by the marriage of prostitutes to mock husbands before initiation into their profession.

[14] Where this leaves the Shudras is an important question that is not properly addressed in the literature, which has an obvious Sanskritic bias. I am less than impressed with the traditional model of the 'eight forms of marriage', in which the worst methods of getting married (by rape and pillage, it seems) are simply allocated to Shudras, as though they knew nothing else. The prevalence of local and caste customs of marriage in such communities was confirmed by the Supreme Court of India in *M. Govindaraju v K. Munisami Gounder* AIR 1997 SC 10. Another recent case stressing the value of oral evidence about a Hindu marriage is *Rajan Baboo v UP Public Service Commission* (1998) 8 SCC 580.

[15] Feminist interpretations often forget the pressure on Hindu men in this respect and behave as though only women were under such compulsions. The ancient literary evidence on this is clear and strong, because the 'fashion' among men of bypassing the stages of life and becoming a renouncer on an accelerated 'route to salvation' (*mokṣa*) was perceived to threaten the future of society as a whole. The work of Patrick Olivelle (1993) is most relevant in this regard, as is Sprockhoff (1976) on the wider phenomenon and its philosophical representations.

[16] Weinberger-Thomas (1999: 128) emphasizes the central role of Hindu marriage (and of women) in Rajasthani society today, showing how this links to concepts of the 'ideal wife'.

This is exactly where a postmodern analysis of Hindu marriage law needs to begin, in the early Vedic times. Hindus, as we know, have not been worried about the possible fissiparous tendencies of such diversity and plurality, since virtually from the start, Hinduism as a religious tradition accepted a variety of coexisting interpretations of this religion, its origins, motivating forces, concepts, and purposes. Not much seems to have changed in this scenario of overlapping consensus since the earliest Vedic times. Throughout the traditional Hindu law periods, as we saw, this recognition of diversity is manifest in the texts themselves. Significantly, attempts to introduce uniforming models have been made from time to time,[17] and the label of 'Vedic marriage' is being used for all kinds of purposes.[18]

The Socio-legal Status of Marriage as a Sacrament

Within the traditional framework of reference, there is no doubt that the most important transitional point in a Hindu's life is marriage. The leading studies confirm marriage (*vivāha*) as the most important of all the Hindu *saṃskāras* or life-cycle rituals.[19] Shastri (1990: 25) notes that it is difficult to say when marriage as an institution came into existence but it appears that Vedic marriage was already a fully developed social institution. Shastri (1990: 26) argues that marriage was regarded as a sacred religious union brought about by divine dispensation, but not a contract. The marriage sacrament united the parties in an indissoluble union. Husband and wife were on equal footing and prayed that their love and friendship should be lasting, genuine, and indissoluble. This sounds like glorifying Hindu ideology, but is a paraphrase of certain verses that might be used ritually in connection with the *saptapadī* (see Menski 1991b). Nair (1978: 1) describes Hindu marriage in contrast with the contractual tribal marriage system:

> The orthodox Hindu marriage is a *sanskara* or sacrament, the last of ten enjoined by the sacred scriptures of Hindus .... The legality of a marriage depended upon ceremonies. The consent of third persons was as essential to the validity of a Hindu marriage as were the religious ceremonies.

Marriage is undoubtedly of vital interest to society, since it is seen as the foundation of the family. Fruzzetti (1990: 108) emphasizes the nature of Hindu marriage as a sacred union and as the most auspicious *saṃskāra*, saying that the sacred conception of marriage in India can be traced back to the age of the

[17] For some misguided positivist efforts to 'lay down the law', see further later.

[18] In our time, the aim may be to prevent the abuse of tradition and to increase public awareness of the significance of the Hindu marriage rituals. An interesting recent example comes from South Africa, under the title of 'Vedic wedding ceremony' (*Vaidik vivāha vidhi*), compiled by Rambilass (2001). Dogra and Dogra (2000) aim to provide a general guidebook for modern readers, but are often too prescriptive on ritual details, while also making some efforts to emphasize plurality.

[19] See Pandey (1969: 153); Shastri (1990: 31).

Vedas. She also asserts that 'Manu regards marriage as an individual and social necessity' (id.). On Hindu legal tradition generally, Agnes (2000: 11) takes a typical feminist starting point that, seems to damage Hindu women forever:

> It is generally believed that the 'pristine' Hindu law was particularly harsh towards women and denied them sexual and economic freedom. These two freedoms, in fact, are coordinate. The Hindu joint family structure based on male coparcenary, was the institution through which sexual control was effected by denying women the right to own property. In this realm of patriarchal domination, women were treated as chattels and upon marriage domination over them was transferred from the father to the husband within the confines of perpetual tutelage. In support of this premise, it is emphasized that Manu, the arch law giver of the Hindu religion stipulated: 'A woman must be dependent upon her father in childhood, upon her husband in youth and upon her sons in old age. She should never be free.' The strict sexual control was also effected through ordeals. Sita's ordeal by fire is set out as an example. It is also believed that the modernity ushered in during the colonial rule and post-independence period helped to loosen out this strict sexual control by granting women the right of divorce and property ownership.

Agnes (2000: 11) asks whether 'within these strict dictates, the Hindu law permitted any space for negotiating women's rights'. But she also notes that '[p]lurality of laws and customs and non-state legal structure were the essential characteristics of the ancient Indian communities' (ibid.: 12). How then can one maintain that there were or are strict norms that are binding on everyone? It appears that such writing only perpetuates modernist stereotypes about Hindu 'tradition' and its anti-women effects. At the same time, some writers are now beginning to recognize that the traditional methods of Hindu marriage solemnization continue to perform a useful function today. While this is not phrased as a postmodern analysis, some modernist authors realize now that insistence on formal registration of all marriages with the state 'would adversely affect the rights of women and children' (Agnes 2000: 170).

Legal textbooks have no difficulty reiterating the central concept of sacramental Hindu marriage or *saṃskāra*,[20] but do not offer much insight into Hindu marriage solemnization. From a Sanskritist's perspective, Pandey (1969: 153–233) discussed in elaborate detail how the traditional Hindu understanding of rituals and sacraments developed. Pandey (1969: 153) emphasized that marriage is the most important of all the Hindu sacraments and confirmed the assumption that every Hindu male is expected to marry, run a home, and create a family. Pandey (1969: 155) places Hindu marriage within a sociocultural framework of reference:

> Marriage was a family affair rather than a personal one; indeed the generation of offspring was the supreme motive of every union to the end that a man's

[20] See e.g. Derrett (1963c: 137–8); Variar (1985: 19). On Hindu marriage ceremonies, see Desai (1998: 663–4).

> house or family might not die out. Then religious motives were equally operative in assigning such a great regard to marriage. Worship of ancestors and gods was dependent on progeny, which could be obtained only through marriage. In later development of Hinduism, the last idea became more prominent than the social and economic ones.

Modernist writing also emphasizes the joint family context of traditional Hindu marriages, but clearly sees it in a less positive light. M. Basu (2001: 3) goes a little too far when she claims that '[t]he western concept of the nuclear family consisting of only a husband, wife and children had not emerged then'. Surely that concept was known, if only because premature deaths and disasters of all kinds constantly broke up joint families, which were not the only known form of social organization. Basu portrays marriage as a social alliance between two families and argues that '[i]t was believed that the woman's sole aim in life ought to be to ensure the happiness and well-being of her husband's family—her own happiness was of least importance' (id.). The chief objects of marriage 'were *dharma* or religious duty, *praja*, procreation and *rati*, sexual pleasure' (M. Basu 2001: 4).

The leading sociologist Kapadia (1972: 167) placed Hindu marriage explicitly within the wider context of dharma, and found it obvious that 'the Hindu thinkers regarded *dharma* as the first and the highest aim of marriage and procreation as the second best'. Kapadia (1972: 168) also reflected on the performance of Hindu marriage rituals, but seems rather too strongly influenced by the lawyers' dogmatic insistence on certain central ritual elements of Hindu marriage:

> There are certain rites which must be performed for marriage to be complete. The main rites are: *homa*, or offering in the sacred fire, *pānigrahaṇa*, or taking the hand of the bride, and *saptapadī*, the bride and the bridegroom going seven steps together. All these rites are performed by a Brahmin in the presence of the sacred fire and are accompanied by the Vedic *mantras*. They are necessary for marriage to be complete, because when they or any of them are not properly performed, the marriage may be legally questioned. Hindu marriage is a sacrament. It is considered sacred because it is said to be complete only on the performance of the sacred rites accompanied by the sacred formulae.[21]

Sharma (1993) discusses the multidimensional importance of marriage in ancient India in great detail, emphasizing the need for a man to progress in the stages of life (*varṇāśramadharma*). Sampath (1969: 29) argues that marriage leads to a different status in that it brings not only physical intimacy between the two individuals, but also effects important changes in the legal and social status of

[21] In modern India, Bumiller (1991: 36) observed what looks like a proper traditional *saptapadī* ritual: 'The couple took seven steps, each one representing a blessing: food, strength, wealth, happiness, progeny, cattle and devotion. After the seventh step, the marriage was irrevocable. The priest sprinkled holy water on the couple'.

the parties. Sharma (1993: 3–4) indicates that marriage was the centre and root of life and its basis was sexual power, i.e. the procreation of the next generation.[22] More specifically, Sharma (1993: 9) states that, '[f]rom the biological point of view the institution of marriage was necessary for self-preservation and procreation of children'. Kapadia (1972: 168) emphasized the role of marriage as a rite of passage to one of the major stages of a Hindu's life, and placed it firmly within a social context:

> Marriage was a social duty toward the family and the community, and there was little idea of individual interest. The social background provided by the authoritarian joint-family, and caste with its domination in all spheres of life, afforded no scope for the recognition of any personal factor, individual interests or aspirations, in the relations between husband and wife (ibid.: 169).

Again, the language used here suggests fixed patterns within a patriarchal setting, whereas in social reality all these arrangements would have remained negotiable. Similarly, Nair (1978: 16) makes the overstated claim that patrilocal residence is 'absolutely necessary among Hindus after marriage'.[23] Qureshi (1978: 39) repeats the usual ideological humbug over Hindu husbands as gods and also takes a typically uncritical view of sages as lawmakers. This passage is only cited here to illustrate scholarly lack of care:

> The Hindu sages in clear terms hold that the husband is 'the lord and master of his wife'; he must be adored and obeyed, even if devoid of all virtues. He must be obeyed as long as he lives and the wife should remain faithful to his memory even after his death. He should be worshipped like God, even though he is a man of bad character.

There are many repetitive comments in the literature about whether Hindu marriages are contractual or sacramental. The Hindu concept of marriage as a sacramental union implies several things. Above all, the marriage is declared to be 'divine' in nature and not a mere human contractual union. One would imagine that it has elements of both, but authors have been emphasizing one concept or the other to suit their other agenda.[24] Sastri (1988: 176) describes Hindu concepts of marriage emphasizing the wider dimensions:

[22] In the context of dowry, Bumiller (1991: 112) states that an unmarried woman in rural India would have been shunned for the rest of her life, hence there is huge pressure on the parents to arrange for her marriage.

[23] For some details on the fascinating case law about this question in post-independence India, see Agnes (2000: 84–5), who notes a change in favour of women's perspectives from about 1975 onwards. Arguments that women have no rights in this field overlook various traditional patterns of post-marital residence in which the husband, often for sound economic reasons, agrees to move to the wife's family and works with (and often for) them.

[24] Derrett (1968b: 558) rightly warned that '[t]he differences between Hinduism and Christianity and Islam as known in India have been exaggerated'.

> They view marriage as a sacrament, as a holy act whose real meaning and purpose are beyond the ken of material and moral science. They regard it as a subject of injunction, of spiritual law or Dharma strictly so called, which should be learnt from the Shastra, from the Veda itself which deals with super-physical and purely spiritual matters.

Qureshi (1978: 39) argues that marriage under ancient Hindu law was not a civil contract. In the patriarchal society of Ṛgvedic Hindus, it was considered a sacramental union, binding not only in this life, but even in the life hereafter.[25] However, it has also been argued that Hindu marriage is a contract. Qureshi (1978: 40–1) states:

> A marriage under the Hindu law is a sacred covenant. In a Hindu marriage, the bridegroom has to promise that he will look after his wife. On the other side, the bride also promises that she will be faithful to her husband. In the approved form of marriage the essence is the transfer of the gift (*kanyadan*) by the guardian.

Does this amount to a contract between two men, then, as representatives of two joint families? The irksome conceptualization of the bride herself as a mere gift has led to protests about how callously Hindu tradition allows women to be treated as a piece of property, to be given and received in marriage. While M. Basu (2001: 2) blames Muslims and other raiders for the bad position of Hindu women, other writers become defensive. Sastri (1988: 208) emphasizes the Aryan ideal:[26]

> Marriage, with us as with several other peoples more or less civilised, is a sacrament, an institution having a deep spiritual significance, and whose value cannot be judged from its uses and purposes which our external senses alone can give us to understand. The breeding of progeny and mere satisfaction of the natural craving for sexual companionship are not the only aims of married life cherished by cultured peoples all over the world. Among the advanced and cultured races of people, married life is intended to serve other and nobler purposes than these, however essential and valuable these are in themselves.

Many authors address specific aspects of marriage arrangements. Mishra (1994: 25–35) discusses the qualifications of the bride and groom, while Karve (1994: 60) distinguishes marriage and widow remarriage, since '[a]ll over India the words for "marriage" are always different from the words for "widow-marriage". The second marriage of a woman needed no ritual and vows. It is merely considered a living together of a man and woman after letting a few friends and relatives know about it'. Agnes (2000: 20) also shows that differences in terms of social strata and the status of the spouses were highly significant:

[25] According to Derrett (1968b: 89), Manu developed the one-flesh doctrine of marriage.

[26] The language of this author reflects to some extent that this was originally written in 1918.

> Marriages among the various lower castes were less sacramental and more contractual. The ritual of *saptapadi* (seven steps round the sacrificial fire, which is essentially a Brahminical ritual) or kanyadan did not prevail among these communities. Child marriages were not the norm. The contractual marriages were based on consent of adult women and the rituals and ceremonies reflected this element of consent and contract. The rituals of remarriage of widows and divorcees varied from those of virgin brides.

The eight forms of traditional Hindu marriage are covered in great detail by many authors.[27] Pandey (1969: 170–1) specifically discusses the role of rituals in Hindu marriages, arguing that religious ceremonies are essential to make a Hindu marriage valid (p. 170) and that they are performed for legalising the marriage, legitimising the children, and avoiding public scandal (p. 171). In his view, '[t]he nuptials were supposed to impart sanctity to the marital relation. Hence it was thought necessary that they should be performed in every case' (id.). Shastri (1990: 40) claims further that the presence of the wife is absolutely necessary for these rituals. According to Pandey (1969: 199), these Hindu marriage rituals have developed from inelaborate beginnings:

> In the beginning they must have been very simple. A woman was given to a man by the constituted authority by which they became wife and husband. But as marriage was a very important occasion in the community, many rites, practices and customs arose, which were regulated by the community itself. In course of time the society became complex and many local and chronological differences came into existence.

A variety of cultural festivities surrounded a Hindu marriage as well. Pandey (1969: 200) briefly discusses the major Vedic ceremonies. Fruzzetti (1990: 121) writes that 'Hindu marriage as a sacrament requires sacred rituals of two types, Brahmanic rituals handed down from Vedic times, and local rituals performed by women, without the involvement of a priest and without Sanskrit *mantras*'. She shows that '[b]oth types of ritual are concerned with the same theme: male and female union through the complementary roles of the sexes in securing the immortality of the male line'. This again shows the critical context of the joint family. Fruzzetti (1990: 123) also emphasizes life-cycle rituals:

> Marriage is seen as a journey to a new locality, status, role, position, way of conduct—a new set of relationships. Bride and groom are reborn as husband and wife .... The rites highlight the severance of a married woman from her father's house and the tying of a wife (*strī*) to a new environment in her in-laws' house.

While this focuses on the cultural construction of the category of 'wife', Pandey (1969: 233) commented on the expected social transformation of the couple:

[27] See in particular Pandey (1969: 158–170). Also useful are Nair (1978: 16); Mitra (1965: 30–43); Sharma (1993: 21–32) and Desai (1998: 651–53). Derrett (1963c: 147) writes that it used to be important to know in what form a woman was married, but does not go into detail on this point.

> The nuptials in their utterances, promises, hopes and fears symbolize a great social transition in the life of the bride and the bridegroom. They are no longer irresponsible youths depending for their bread and views on their parents. The seriousness of life dawns upon them .... This involves a great compromise and mutual sacrifice .... Marriage acquires its true meaning and reaches perfection only when the conjugal relationship is based on the realization that marriage is a willing sacrifice for the good of the partner, the family, the society and the world.

In their discussion of Hindu marriage concepts, Bedwa and Ullah (1992: 67) note that observance of shastric ceremonies or of customary rites of the particular community brings about a valid marriage. They, too, comment on the diversity of customs, so that 'it is not possible to state with certainty what formalities are required to be observed .... It is indeed a question of fact to be ascertained from the social context of the particular community' (id.). These legal authors then elaborate on the rituals, highlighting that the *dharmaśāstras* 'have prescribed elaborate and complex ceremonies' (id.). Through a gradual process of elaboration, Hindu society has developed a plethora of ceremonies. However, as Bedwa and Ullah (1992: 67) assert:

> ... there is a wide agreement among the leading works with regard to the performance of certain necessary ceremonies such as *Kanyadan, Panigrahana, Saptapadi* and *Lajhoma*. It is very difficult to say with any degree of certainty which of these ceremonies occasions the creation of matrimonial status. From the legal stand point it is the ceremony of *Saptapadi* which brings into existence the matrimonial status, for it along [*sic*] puts the stamp of finality on the transaction. Could it be then said that a marriage is valid even if *Kanyadan* and *Panigrahana* have not taken place since *Saptapadi* is the decisive factor regarding the validity of a marriage? Such a situation is most unlikely to arise for Saptapadi is the culminating ceremony, the Kanyadan and Panigrahana being the preliminary ceremonies. This position is still continuing even after the passing of the Hindu Marriage Act, 1955.

Here we are entering the realm of current legal debates on Hindu marriage in the light of Hindu traditions. The above quote demonstrates how easily modern legal authors conflate and confuse the Vedic and shastric ingredients of the traditional ritual plurality. In the end, the reader is left confused, as no clear guidance is given.

Deconstructing Modernist Misconceptions

Many of the existing writings do not address the ritual or legal detail surrounding Hindu marriage solemnization and simply challeng the institution as a whole. We saw earlier that Thomas (2000: 14) takes a totally negative view of marriage, describing it as a form of sexual slavery:

> It is an institution by means of which the ownership of a woman is transferred from her father or guardian to her husband. While the rights of a parent

> over his daughter is [*sic*] restricted at least by the taboos of incest, those of a husband over his wife were complete and absolute. An abject slave to her owner, a married woman could not plead lack of virtue in her husband as an excuse for disloyalty, any more than a bond-slave could with regard to his owner .... The sanctity of matrimony is the sanctity of subtle tyranny. Perhaps the ancients had good grounds for sanctifying tyranny ....

Thomas (2000: 15) continues this argument by saying that in modern conditions, there ought to be significant changes. While sanctifying tyranny may have been suited to ancient society, today we know better forms of government than those founded on tyranny and 'it ill-behoves us to retain the sanctity of an institution which has its roots in iniquity'. While this looks like a case of throwing out the baby with the bath water, Thomas (2000: 26–7) goes on to blame marriage ceremonies, in particular, as giving men totally disproportionate powers and allowing them to do with women what they want. At p. 27 she argues:

> All these undesirable aspects of marital morality are but offshoots of its essential vice, which is the absolute power the marriage ceremony gives a man over a woman. In certain respects this power is more despotic than that enjoyed by political tyrants. Marriage gives a man power to condemn an innocent woman to confinement in a cell he calls his home. It gives him power to disrobe a woman whenever he wants to and even against her will. It gives him power to demand work from her without remuneration.

While this amounts to a call for abandoning Hindu marriage rituals altogether, it is not explored what would or should replace them. To what extent is legal recognition by the state, through a secular ceremony or no ceremony whatsoever, going to circumvent the androcentricity of society? Instead, Thomas (2000: 28–9) gets carried away into comparing a 'good' Hindu wife to a dog who anticipates the master's will: 'And a woman knows, much better than a dog, that her daily bread, her happiness, and her honour depends upon the caprice of her husband and she takes infinite pain to see that she gives him no cause for complaint'. This author therefore concludes that '[o]ur marriage morality can best be described as a vicious circle in which husband and wife chase each other into disastrous ruin' (p. 36). This is hardly constructive scholarship on marriage law.

Such negative conceptions of marriage appear to originate in deeper modernist (mis)constructions of traditional Hindu marriage. To a large extent these have developed as a result of the hegemony of modernist, positivistic assumptions about 'law', which distort our understanding of the legal status and role of marriage in Hindu society. Nair (1978: 11) shows how the knowledge of Indian scholars about Hindu marriage ceremonies has been influenced by the modern law, rather than traditional Sanskritic scholarship:

> The orthodox Hindu wedding is a ceremonial marriage and it is solemnised in accordance with customary rites and ceremonies of the parties. Its

> essential validity depends upon (1) invocation before the sacred fire and (2) *Saptapadi*, whenever these two formed the essential rites. Marriage is completed only when the seventh step is taken if *Saptapadi* is observed; till then it is imperfect and revocable. Consummation is not necessary to make a marriage complete and binding.

This is almost a paraphrase of Section 7 of the HMA 1955, carefully phrased to avoid pitfalls. A similar passage, but full of mistakes, is found in M. Basu (2001: 22), to the effect that generally speaking, 'a Hindu marriage is solemnized with the customary rites and ceremonies practised by both the families involved'.[28] Basu then continues to emphasize the key role of the *saptapadī*, but makes another critical mistake when she writes, at p. 22, that '[o]ne of the most important Hindu marriage rituals is *saptapadi*, i.e. seven steps taken together by the bride and the bridegroom around the sacred fire. It is only after the seventh step of *saptapadi* is taken, that the marriage ceremony is considered complete'.

While this also attempts to be a paraphrase of Section 7(2) of the HMA, the Act itself does not say or explicitly assume that the seven steps have to be taken *around* the sacred fire, but actually uses the words 'before the sacred fire'. Since Basu's book is one of the most recent pieces of writing on Hindu marriage law, some warning about the current state of scholarship in this field must be given, for even the plain legal information is not accurately presented.

Unfortunately, the situation is also unsatisfactory when it comes to legal textbooks. Derrett (1970: xiv) had argued that the law of marriage was central to legal regulation and needed to be carefully studied in its own right. He warned that despite the focus on property, the highly sensitive topic of matrimonial status must be treated with a certain degree of discrimination, isolated partly from other topics. Derrett himself (1970: 287–301) discussed various aspects of Hindu marriage in detail. However, when we turn to Indian authors on this subject, we locate more cases of deliberate blindness, or at least a good deal of obfuscation. A leading author on Hindu law, Paras Diwan (1979: 78) wrote at the beginning of a chapter on ceremonies of marriage that '[p]erformance of certain *shastric* ceremonies is still necessary for a valid Hindu marriage. The ceremonies have been laid down in minute details in the *Grihya Sutras*'. Then follows a rather long, haphazard summary of some Hindu wedding rituals and other details, until Diwan (1979: 79) comes to the *saptapadī*:

> Then comes the fourth and the most important and indispensable ceremony: the *saptpadi*. Near the *vivaha-mandap* the bridegroom leads the bride for seven steps in the north-eastern direction while reciting certain hymns. This is followed by an address by the bridegroom to the bride. Water is then poured on the hands of the couple and certain prayers are recited. Upon the completion of the prayer, the bridegroom joins hands with the

[28] However, this is not correct, since Section 7(1) specifies 'either party', not both.

> bride and says to her, "Give thy heart to my religious duties, may thy mind follow mine. Be thou consentient to my speech. May Brihaspati unite thee unto me". On the completion of the seventh step the marriage becomes final and irrevocable.

This idiosyncratic description and summary of the law conveys what a *saptapadī* ritual might consist of, but remains confusing. Evidently, the author combined his own knowledge and observation of (Punjabi) Hindu marriage rituals with elements taken from relevant specialist literature. But having declared the *saptapadī* indispensable, this particular discussion then concludes by stating that most of what has been described would not be performed in a Hindu wedding today. In fact '[t]he performance of all the above ceremonies is also not necessary for the validity of the marriage' (Diwan 1979: 80). What then is necessary? A few paragraphs later, the author reiterates, having had a brief look at Section 7 of the HMA:

> Thus, the *shastric* ceremonies and rites are still necessary. These can be dispensed with only if one of the parties to the marriage can establish a customary ceremony in substitution of the *shastric* ceremony .... *Saptpadi* is absolutely necessary for all Hindus. Whether the other ceremonies are also necessary for the validity of marriage is not clear (id.).

This confusing discussion continues for another few pages. Although this particular textbook has been re-published many times,[29] the relevant passages are still not adequately modified and the readers, mainly legal practitioners, are not given clear and unambiguous guidance. A cynic might think of the professional habit of lawyers to avoid clarity to protect their own interests. It is doubtful that Professor Diwan sought to uphold Hindu tradition as such, since he argued vigorously elsewhere for its abolition and for modernizing, secularizing reforms.[30]

Few legal textbooks avoid such mischief, which could be seen as deliberate abuse of Hindu marriage traditions (Menski 2001, Chapter 1). However, the application of a presumption of validity of marriage in accordance with the Hindu concept of *saṃskāra* has been found useful to uphold the legal validity of Hindu marriages and the financial claims of married women. For example, Desai (1993: 100–1) states:

> There is of course a strong presumption in favour of the validity of a marriage if from the time of such marriage the parties are recognised by the people concerned as man and wife and such presumption applies also to determine

[29] At least nine editions of this book have appeared. See Diwan and Diwan (1993) and their later works under different titles.

[30] In Ch. 8.3 later, we return to the question of essential ceremonies under the modern Hindu law. It will become apparent there that Diwan's obfuscating stance actually protected Hindu polygamists from criminal prosecutions (see Ch. 10), which may be taken as evidence of collusion among male lawyers.

> the question whether the formal requisites of a valid marriage ceremony were satisfied.

In conclusion, it must be admitted that our knowledge of the complex field of traditional Hindu marriage law has remained patchy and rather inadequate. It is evident that this has worked to the potential detriment of women and children in a male-dominated legal environment, as stereotypes rule the roost, and the diversities within social reality are inadequately captured by the literature. In view of the male bias of the entire Hindu sociocultural system, it is tempting to suggest that reformist efforts might be directed at the regulation of Hindu marriages by the state. However, it is evident that for traditional Hindu rulers, there would be no perceived need for legal intervention, since the area of marriage falls squarely under the idealistic self-controlled order model of *sadācāra*. Within the realm of traditional Hindu law, therefore, and also under Muslim rule in medieval India, this particular area of the law remained remote from state intervention. We need to discuss next to what extent that situation may have changed under colonial rule and under the modern Indian legal system.

Hindu Marriage Law under British Rule

Derrett (1978a: 10) reports that *dharmaśāstrīs* had threatened people with hell if they interfered with the sacred institution of marriage. Perhaps the British were gradually becoming aware of this, but they had their own reasons for not getting involved too deeply in Hindu marriage law. We saw in Chapter 4 that the general reluctance of the colonial rulers to interfere in the personal law sphere became a prominent pattern. Some writing on this period suggests that legal intervention by the colonial powers could bring no good anyway. Chandra (1998: 4) argues that the institutional sexism underlying the androcentric patterns of Victorian England was transposed, through the colonial claim to universality, onto the colonial framework of British India. However, as Chandra (1998: 73) emphasizes, there were many limits to the process of colonial intervention:

> Reflecting the paradoxical structure of the larger imperialist exercise, a contradiction was inherent in the British Indian judicial practice. Driven by an expansionist urge for unquestioned jurisdiction over the affairs of the ruled, it was, simultaneously, obliged by the force of indigenous laws and usages into a self-limiting minimalist conception of its mediation.

Chandra claims that after 1857, a slight shift occurred, but eventually 'the experience of 1857 had introduced a new stress in the structural ambivalence of the colonial dispensation' (id.). Pujari and Kaushik (1994, III: 283) blame the British for maintenance of the personal law system, leading to the argument that the colonial rulers could not involve themselves in the customs and religions of their subjects, which then resulted in further stagnation. Taking the famous case of Rukhmabai as a mirror of such tensions,[31] Chandra (1998: 100) argues that after the 1860s, the gradual experience of codification of the general law emboldened the British to go further:

> ... massive codification of indigenous laws and usages had meanwhile induced a sense of knowledge about the subject people, and an attendant sense of power that could dispense with the earlier hesitancy and uncertainty. The British would now be the sole arbiters in India, even settling cases relating to the subjects' private lives. They would assume the powers of the king and the functions of the caste .... They would not only exercise jurisdiction over conjugal rights as determined by Hindu laws, they would enforce those rights according to their own modes of procedure.

The process of judicial intervention, thus, allowed the British to become more closely involved with questions of Hindu marriage or, to be more precise, its social consequences. Did a child wife who had been married to an unsuitable, sick man have to agree to consummation of her marriage? In Rukhmabąi's case, it appeared that the colonial system asserted itself and intervened in favour of the husband's traditional rights. However, since the negative judgment against Rukhmabai was not enforced, the law was deliberately left without implementation. Chandra (1998: 186) observes that the colonial officials, enjoying a monopoly of power, also claimed a monopoly of wisdom. As before, '[t]hey rationalized any position that helped to ensure their power and safety. They had developed cold feet on the question of altering the existing law for fear of popular discontent'. Thus, there was no scope for large-scale intervention in Hindu marriage law, and the British merely dealt with a few peripheral matters, such as removing the legal obstacles to widow remarriage.[32]

Agnes (2000: 46–52) examines in detail the subversion of women's rights under the British through the indirect introduction of English concepts and principles. Despite the initial policy of non-interference in personal law matters, she observes a gradual process of tampering with established local customs through various means, prominently by law. Agnes (2000: 46) confirms what we found in Chapter 4 earlier:

> At this stage, the process of evolving laws at the local level through commentaries, which incorporated within them the local customs, was arrested. The British interpretations of the ancient texts became binding and made the law certain, rigid and uniform. This clear marker of modernity was welcomed by the newly evolving English-educated middle class of Bengal and provided the British a moral justification for ruling India as

[31] In this case, Rukhmabai (who had been married at the age of eleven) opposed the legal claim of her husband to restitution of conjugal rights eleven years after the marriage. The British Indian courts ultimately held that the Hindu husband was entitled to the company of his wife, but did not enforce the decision.

[32] These efforts were socially not effective, as Weinberger-Thomas (1999: 146) demonstrates with reference to a case in the 1920s from Rajasthan.

> harbingers of enlightenment. Through their interventions the Hindu society could rid itself of its 'barbarism' and enter an era of 'civilization'. An image of the cruel and superstitious natives who needed Christian salvation was deliberately constructed by the Evangelists. The entry of Hindu social reformers into the campaign against Sati at the advent of [the] nineteenth century strengthened the process of interventions not only by judicial decisions but also by legislative reforms.

Agnes (2000: 46–7) lists four legal areas in which significant reforms were spearheaded, the Sati Regulation Act of 1829,[33] the Hindu Widows' Remarriage Act of 1856, the Age of Consent Act, 1860 and the Prohibition of Female Infanticide Act of 1872. None of these legislative interventions concerns Hindu marriage solemnization directly, but all are linked to marriage-related arrangements among Hindus and sought to remedy perceived abuses in society. Agnes (2000: 47) comments that these laws, focusing on 'barbaric' native customs, create the impression that interference in the realm of 'personal' laws was for the benefit of Indian women: 'There is a presumption that by incorporating the concepts of modernity into the native jurisprudence, the status of women in India was alleviated. But recent scholarship has questioned this premise'. Agnes (2000: 52) goes further in her criticism of British legal intervention, identifying the effects of bias in favour of high-caste Hindu norms and male-centred assumptions:

> The period between 1850 and 1930 witnessed the elimination of a wide range of customs which diverged from the Anglo-Hindu law as the standard of proof required was very high. Unless it could be proved that the custom was ancient, certain, obligatory, reasonable and not against public policy, it had a very slim chance of survival. Derrett comments that in this manner, the Anglo-Hindu law with its Dharmashastra background was spread more widely than it had ever been before. The only customs which were saved from the crushing effects of the British courts were the customs of the agricultural classes in the Punjab and matrilineal practices of the Malabar region. The tendency of both the British courts and of the urban Hindu middle class was to ignore the diversities and to impose a legal Hinduism upon these communities. Contrary to popular belief, many of the customs which were crushed were those in favour of women.

However, while various Acts were passed under British rule around the 1920s, with some regulating the consequences of marriage in terms of property relations, no direct intervention in Hindu marriage as such took place. Few further reforms then occurred in this field until after the Second World War, during which, as Derrett (1978a: 7) observes, social activism began to flourish:

> Ladies of good family, and high educational attainments, pressed hard for a wholesale reform of the law of marriage since the 1920s at the latest. As

[33] There were earlier Sati Regulations from 1813 onwards, as Weinberger-Thomas (1999) stresses.

> happened in both World Wars in England, national emergencies placed women's claims to equality in a new light. The leaders of the movement had personal access to Indian jurists and public men; which meant that before Independence, indeed as early as 1941, they were able to inspire numerous Bills before the Legislative Council.

Kapur and Cossman (1996: 45) show that social reformers in colonial India used the women's question for a variety of purposes. Some legal changes were sought from the colonial administration to improve the status of women, tackling specific social problems like sati and widow remarriage, as well as child marriage. Reforms of Hindu personal law were first looked at during the 1920s as an aspect of achieving women's uplift (Kapur and Cossman 1996: 55). By 1928 the focus was broadened to encompass female inheritance rights. Agnes (2000: 204) notes that rights for Hindu women in the traditional periods were based on traditional notions of equity, while during the colonial era, the British influence had been negative. Agnes (2000: 205) explains that,

> ... the English common law contained several stringent anti-women biases. These biases crept into India through the Anglo-Saxon jurisprudence and subverted the traditional legal systems which provided women with a certain measure of economic security. The traditional systems were remoulded into linear, formal and stringent structures, which exercised greater patriarchal control over women and their right to property.

Agnes (2000: 206) argues that '[c]oncepts of justice, equity and good conscience became the direct channels of introducing English laws, principles and puritanical notions of morality into India'. Agnes (2000: 205–6) also clearly recognizes that the ancient texts were distorted in this process of colonial superimposition:

> The colonial interventions also facilitated the construction of distinct and mutually hostile religious communities of Hindus and Muslims, to be governed by their respective personal laws along the model of the canon law. The basis of the legal system were the ancient scriptures translated with a western mind set. These scriptures were never meant to be used as rigid legal principles of an adversarial legal system. The translated texts drastically changed the nature and character of the customary and scriptural Hindu law and the Hindu woman's right to property suffered a severe set back. In the process of streamlining the pluralistic society several customary rights of women were crushed as they could not meet the legal requirement set by the British courts to prove a custom. Ironically, in this process the character of the communities was fixed and the mutually exclusive communities of Hindus and Muslims were constructed through litigation over property disputes.

The colonial intervention could not, and did not, interfere in traditional patterns of Hindu marriage solemnization, which remained as complex and custom-dominated as ever.[34] Anglo-Indian case law upheld the Hindu concepts of *saṃskāra. Venkatacharyulu v Rangacharyulu* (1891) ILR 14 Mad 316, is a case on the validity of a child marriage, which also concerns Hindu concepts of marriage. The parents of a young bride were restrained from giving her in marriage to someone else and it was held at p. 318:

> There can be no doubt that a Hindu marriage is a religious ceremony. According to all the texts, it is a samskaram or sacrament, the only one prescribed for a woman and one of the principal religious rites prescribed for purification of the soul. It is binding for life because the marriage rite completed by saptapadi or the walking of seven steps before the consecrated fire creates a religious tie, and a religious tie when once created, cannot be untied. It is not a mere contract in which a consenting mind is indispensable. The person married may be a minor or even of unsound mind, and yet, if the marriage rite is duly solemnized, there is a valid marriage.

An impression has thus been created that, in this area of the law, traditional Hindu practices, even Sanskritic scriptural traditions, have been strictly maintained and preserved. Exaggerated assumptions about the fixed nature of 'tradition' in this context abound. Bedwa and Ullah (1992: 68) engage in myth making when they claim that, even though we do not know much about Manu and other sages,

> ... even a few decades back, the Hindus were mainly and scrupulously following the injunctions prescribed by them. There were unbroken traditions continued from the earliest time upto the present period. This continuity of the tradition speaks a volume about the efficacy and the usefulness of the said injunctions which could not otherwise command so great a reverence and so faithful an observance by the entire Hindu society. As a matter of fact, until the passing of the Hindu Marriage Act, 1955, there was hardly any momentous change in the law of Hindu marriage.

The authors here conflate customary traditions, textual norms and legal rules, overstating the continuity and uniformity of traditions. On the other hand, most writing pays little attention to 'tradition', comments straight on the need for modernist legal reforms, or discusses the effects of the legal interventions brought about by the HMA of 1955, to which we must now turn.

Modernist Reforms to Hindu Marriage Law

As we saw, it has been a standard technique in post-colonial South Asian countries to reform the majority personal law first and to ignore the minority laws.[35]

[34] However, pre-1955 case law confirms that recognition of customary patterns remained a grave problem, as shown in *Deivaini Achi v Chitambaram Chettiar* AIR 1954 Mad 657.

[35] Minority laws, everywhere, are seen to be under siege. While Indian Muslim law is often portrayed as being threatened by modernist reforms (Mahmood 1986),

The aim, it appears, was modernization as well as unification, in total conceptual opposition to traditional legal systems with their emphasis on context-specificity rather than legal uniformity. In India, the debates about Hindu marriage law and its reforms have therefore been tied up with uniform civil code debates and the politics surrounding the perceived intransigence of the Muslim personal law.

In modern Indian law, Hindus, Buddhists, Jainas, and Sikhs were eventually to be governed by one uniform Hindu law, ostensibly for the sake of reducing diversities within the Hindu personal law, and to promote nation building.[36] In this way, an artificial unity of Hindu law has been created to foster a national spirit.[37] Desai (1998: 68) claims that '[t]he conditions and requirements of a ceremonial Hindu marriage are considerably simplified and any two Hindus, which expression includes not merely Hindus by religion but Buddhists, Jains and Sikhs as well, can solemnize the ceremonial marriage recognised by the Act'.[38] Whether this has been successful—in a purportedly secular democracy which claims to value equidistance from all religions—must be doubted. Some Sikhs, in particular, have violently objected to this legal intervention, demanding among other things greater recognition of their own personal law.[39] Even today, local and tribal customary laws continue to play a much larger role in the Indian legal system than most lawyers readily admit. Custom remains evidently relevant and is a topic discussed in all major textbooks.[40]

---

in Pakistan and Bangladesh the Hindu law remains an unwanted and unreformed colonial relic (see Menski and Rahman 1988 for Bangladesh).

36 Mahmood (1981: 4) writes that '[t]oday, Hindus, Buddhists, Sikhs and Jains—all four compendiously known by the legal term "Hindu"—are the proud possessor of the most progressive marriage law of India .... There has thus been a real upheaval .... The Hindu marriage law ... has travelled a long way from where it stood in 1856'. The Anand Marriage Act of 1909 had earlier legalized Sikh marriage rites known as *anand karaj*.

37 On similar policy aims of nation building for Tanzania and their limited social impact, see Moore (1986). Jain (1990: 601–2) shows that a different strategy than bringing these groups under Hindu law would have made them subject to the secular general law.

38 See also Desai (1998: 650), which creates a total legal fiction and is quite misleading in view of the wording of Section 7 of the HMA, cited later.

39 In *Partap Singh v Union of India* AIR 1985 SC 1695, a Sikh Don Quixote managed to come all the way to the Supreme Court of India, challenging the claims to a share in the family property by his father's two widows, to be told that he definitely could not lawfully assert his patriarchal claims to the exclusion of the women. On Jaina law, see Menski (1993b).

40 On various aspects of legal debates relating to social norms and the extent of their legal recognition, see Kuppuswami (1986: 43–54); Diwan and Diwan (1993: 20–25 and 45–50); Desai (1998: 85–8).

Modernist Agenda and their Problems

Legal intervention in marriage law by the post-colonial Indian state has been justified in classic eurocentric modernist statements. Qureshi (1978: 81) claims that '[t]he role of social engineering is complete in the west and it should be applied to India, if necessary, in remodelled or rectified form'. Qureshi (1978: 251–2) explicitly justifies such intervention in marriage law through the idealized concept of the welfare state:

> In ancient days the ceremony of marriage was necessary because the state was not expected to see every aspect of human life. At that time the main task of the state was to maintain law and order. The reason of prescribing marriage ceremonies was to impose a moral binding on the husband to give shelter to his wife and children. Today, the state is a welfare state. It has to make laws for every aspect of human life. Therefore, if a marriage has been registered with the Registrar of Marriages, there should be no need of a marriage ceremony.

By stipulating that a 'religious' marriage ceremony may not be necessary, this author apparently suggests a secularizing agenda, a rather radical step for a Muslim writer.[41] While the precise extent of state involvement remains debated, marriage as a major building block of society is now perceived to be of relevance also to the state. Earlier, Altekar (1978: 368) had clearly pleaded for reforms:

> ... even orthodox Smriti writers like Manu have recognised that a time might come when their rules would become obsolete, and have therefore declared that if any rules framed by them are found to be not conducive to the welfare of society, or against the spirit of the age, they should be unhesitatingly abrogated or modified. As a matter of fact they themselves have done so in many cases.

Modernist legal authors such as Ranbir Singh (1991) claim that the state should exert ever more control over marriage law and must make greater efforts to control the social aspects of marriage. Singh (1991: 39) argues in particular that compulsory registration of marriage 'is certainly [the] need of the hour to prove the validity of a Hindu marriage' and claims that 'compulsory registration holds a key to the eradication of social maladies which are [a] by-product of defective marriage laws' (ibid.: 40). Asserting that all kinds of benefits will accrue to women, Singh evidently relies on arguments by Professor Cretney from England, to the effect that registration is essential to ascertain a person's status. But is this equally relevant in India? Singh (1991: 40) claims that 'dogmatic insistence on the observance of essential ceremonies for the solemnisation of a Hindu marriage has provided a fertile ground for the nurture of many social evils'. As discussed further in Chapter 10 later, one of the modernist key

[41] In a subsequent section dealing with postmodern evolution of Hindu marriage law, another passage from the conclusions by the same writer will be cited to show that he eventually reconsidered his suggestions.

arguments, as in Singh's essay, is that formal registration of marriages would reduce polygamy.[42] However, such claims remain highly doubtful. Qureshi (1978: 251) insists on the importance of marriage registration, while recognizing that customary forms of marriage cannot just be legislated away:

> ... it is clear that in all the religions, some ceremony has been prescribed for the validity of a marriage. The performance of the ceremony is a religious matter and it should not be abandoned. I feel that it should be provided in the Uniform Civil Code that no ceremony is essential for performing the marriage. Every member of the society should be allowed to perform the marriage in accordance with his conscience. But the registration of that marriage within 30 days after the performance of the ceremony, should be made mandatory. If a marriage has not been registered, it should not be treated as valid. However, the courts should be given the discretion to accept any reasonable explanation for failing to get the marriage registered.

Qureshi (1978: 251) also argues that the intention of the parties to a marriage is the most important point for matrimonial relations. If the spouses are willing to live as husband and wife, the state should give full protection to them.[43] More important for this author, though, appears to be the uniform civil code issue, leading to a surrogate debate which is not really concerned about marriage solemnization. Qureshi (1978: 290) writes:

> There was a time in the history of human civilization when the duty of the State was only maintenance of law and order, protection of life, liberty and the property of the subjects. This concept of state has completely changed. Today we are living in a welfare state which has to guarantee prosperity and well being of all the people. The Indian Constitution, therefore, contains the chapters of Fundamental Rights as well as Directive Principles of State Policy. The chapter of Directive Principles of State Policy imposes on the state a duty to take positive actions in certain directions in order to promote the welfare of the people and achieve economic independence. One way of achieving economic independence is by having uniform matrimonial laws.

While one must question the logic of such arguments, Qureshi (1978: 292) is even more explicit that the uniform civil code is 'intended to give equal facility of law to all sections of our people', stipulating that all Indian citizens should be governed by the same set of laws, since '[t]here cannot ordinarily be any justification for having one set of laws for one section of the society and a different one for the other' (id.). The simplistic argument promoted here, which

[42] Tiwari (1991: 44) also argues avidly for registration of marriage. See also Shams (1991).

[43] This is an old issue in debates about Hindu marriage solemnization; see Jain (1961) and Mathur (1962). Derrett (1963c: 137) noted that 'the formation of *intention* is somewhat handicapped in the majority of Hindu communities' because marriages tend to be arranged.

totally ignores the cultural input into legal norms, is to the effect that a uniform matrimonial law for all Indians would constitute one step towards social justice (ibid.: 293). Thus, as Qureshi (1978: 342) argues further, uniform marriage laws should give equal status to both spouses irrespective of caste, creed, and religion, since '[i]t is the duty of a good Government to introduce a good system of laws, which is certain, simple, lucid and uniform without giving rise to disputes or fostering disharmony among the people that are governed by it' (id.). Qureshi (1978: 343) suggests finally that Parliament should introduce laws keeping in view the recent trends in private international law to establish uniformity in marriage laws all over the world.[44] This chain of arguments clearly arises from modernist thinking and wishes for a globally standardized legal system, divorced from the sociocultural needs of local people outside the Anglo-American realm.

Discussing the practical mechanics of marriage registration, Singh (1991: 51) rightly suggests that this should be located at the village level: 'It is not a naïve suggestion because when births and deaths can be registered and a proper record can be kept for that, why should marriages not be compulsorily registered, too?' However, contrary to Singh's claims, a full-scale system of registration for all births and deaths simply does not exist in India (Sarkar 1993: 1875). Any system of registration would therefore create its own problems of unreliability.

Pujari and Kaushik (1994, III: 304) uncritically repeat the assertion that registration of marriages would serve as an effective check on all kinds of social problems related to marriage.[45] Singh (1989: 65) notes that Section 8 of the HMA 1955 enables the state governments to provide for compulsory registration of marriages but that failure to register a marriage will not affect its validity. Singh (1989: 65–6) notes that registration is compulsory among Parsis and Christians and for all marriages performed under the SMA 1954, although that Act has had very little social impact, as Singh (1989: 66) confirms, arguing that: 'The ultimate object is to recognise registration as the sole and conclusive proof of marriage, irrespective of the religious rites under which it was solemnised'. This author also asks that India should sign or ratify the UN Convention on Consent to Marriage, Minimum Age for Marriage, and Registration of Marriage and proclaims that it is necessary to introduce a system of compulsory registration for all marriages (id.). Pujari and Kaushik (1994, III: 282–3) note that independent India relied heavily on legislation in its effort to promote total gender equality.

[44] The country reports in Bainham (1998) confirm that there is no such international agreement or system, and in legal practice many problems occur.

[45] This argument relies on *Towards Equality* (1974), which appears to have inspired a lot of reformist writing. Similarly, Singh (1989: 65–6) claims that compulsory registration serves as an effective check on child marriage and polygamy and offers reliable proof of marriage.

Stress on the removal of discrimination and special protective legislation for women was necessary in post-colonial India, because the British policy in the field of family law had such a crippling effect on women (Chandra 1998). Calls for modernist reforms suggest capacity on the part of the modern state to control the sphere of marriage solemnization. However, it has remained a central characteristic of Hindu law that the route of entry into marriage for Hindus, with very few exceptions, goes through adherence to 'traditional' customs and rituals. In practice, the social process of getting married has vigorously resisted central state control.[46]

Limits of State Law and the Modernist Discourse

Indeed, careful scrutiny of the state's law-making devices to reform Hindu marriage law would suggest that modern Indian law in this field simply underwrites Hindu tradition. This is contrasted by prevailing modernist assertions in the legal literature which continue to claim otherwise. Even today the legal criterion for validity of a Hindu marriage in India is not whether it was registered in some form by the state, but whether it was performed in accordance with traditional rituals and ceremonies. Thus, one must indeed wonder if any reforms have been achieved in this field at all. The relevant law in this field is found in Section 7 of the HMA of 1955, which reads as follows:

> S.7 - *Ceremonies for a Hindu marriage.*
> (1) A Hindu marriage may be solemnized in accordance with the customary rites and ceremonies of either party thereto.
> (2) Where such rites and ceremonies include the *saptapadi* (that is, the taking of seven steps by the bridegroom and the bride jointly before the sacred fire), the marriage becomes complete and binding when the seventh step is taken.

This means that subsection (1) has entirely preserved the old customary position under Hindu law, whereby solemnization of a marriage is a matter for the respective families concerned and is to be governed by family, community, and caste custom. As we saw, these vary by locality, caste and family, and from case to case, so that custom needs to be interpreted flexibly and undue rigidity is to be avoided.

When the legal validity of a Hindu marriage is at issue before a court, questions need to be raised about what is customary in a particular kind of marriage. Given the flexible framework of Section 7(1) of the HMA as cited above, several important questions may arise about when an action falls under

[46] Weinberger-Thomas (1999: 188) reports from her fieldwork in Rajasthan that 'many villagers do not know their exact date of birth; and not so many years ago, the registration of births and deaths was regarded as a British eccentricity'. In a footnote to this point she adds: 'It is still common today not to register births and deaths, a fact that 1991 census procedures acknowledge. As for marriages and divorces, these are never registered' (ibid.: 264 n. 31).

'custom'. On the definition of customs, Section 3 of the HMA 1955 is the guiding provision:

> S.3 - Definitions.
> In this Act, unless the context otherwise requires -
> (a) the expressions "custom" and "usage" signify any rule which, having been continuously and uniformly observed for a long time, has obtained the force of law among Hindus in any local area, tribe, community, group or family;
> Provided that the rule is certain and not unreasonable or opposed to public policy; and
> Provided further that in the case of a rule applicable only to a family it has not been discontinued by the family;

Our traditional understanding of custom in relation to the nature of a Hindu marriage suggests that large numbers of people would follow exactly the same patterns of solemnization, and a group of people would have done so as long as they could remember. However, as indicated in an earlier section on the traditional Hindu law of marriage, there is simply no such thing as a uniform traditional Hindu marriage ceremony that could be held up to all Hindus as *the* binding model. Anybody who doubts this should turn to Pandey (1969: 199), who clearly emphasized the complexity of local and different scriptural traditions. More specifically, while discussing the Vedic marriage rituals, Pandey (1969: 200) admitted that 'we cannot be certain as to in what order they occurred'.[47]

Thus, a Hindu marriage is customary in the sense that it constitutes a specially constructed sequence of ritual steps that have elements of customary traditions in them. In essence such Hindu marriage rituals are ad hoc situation-specific reconstructions of cultural bricks that are being recycled as the rituals of marriage solemnization proceed.[48] Viewed in this manner, every single Hindu marriage becomes an entity in its own right, operative within the conceptual framework of 'custom', yet not rigidly defined in every minute point of ritual detail. Taking this pluralistic and flexible view clashes with the formal, more restrictive understandings of the legal concept of 'custom', which are too rigid and inflexible.

After 1955, further reforms to the HMA were made in the Hindu Marriage (Amendment) Act, 1956 (Act 3 of 1956), the Hindu Marriage (Amendment) Act, 1964 (Act 44 of 1964), and the Marriage Laws (Amendment) Act, 1976 (Act 68 of 1976). None of these brought any significant changes to the law on

[47] Pandey (1969: 200) himself states that he followed the fuller model of the *Atharvaveda* sequence, but from what he tells us about the *gṛhyasūtras*, it is evident that there is no *one* customary or textual pattern.

[48] In the context of sati rituals, Weinberger-Thomas (1999: 141) finds a similar picture, arguing (much more elegantly than lawyers) that '[t]radition reinvents itself by drawing on the bric-a-brac of cultural artifacts at hand'.

solemnization of Hindu marriages. Therefore, much of the legal literature conveys a misleading picture when it suggests that the modern Hindu law on the subject of marriage has been drastically changed. This was neither the case under the HMA 1955 itself, nor under its subsequent amendments. Reddy (1999: 13) claims there were radical changes in the marriage laws of Hindus, but does not actually mention marriage solemnization when he writes that '[s]ection 5 has the effect of abolishing the prohibition on widow remarriage, child marriage and polygamy in one stroke. The woman stands on the same footing as the man in all these matters'.[49] Variar (1985: 21) summarizes the present position in typical dogmatic lawyers' fashion:

> ... finally in 1955, the Parliament has enacted a law codifying and amending the law of marriage among the Hindus. Therefore at present the entire law is embodied in the Hindu Marriage Act of 1955, which supersedes the previous law contained in the Dharmaśastra works, commentaries and digests, customs, statutes, and decisions of courts, subject to the exceptions relating to certain aspects expressly recognised in the Act.

This very general position, carefully worded, prevails at a formal level, which assumes the supersession of Hindu tradition. But this general statement is clearly wrong as far as Section 7 of the HMA is concerned. Desai (1998: 650–70) claims that substantial changes were introduced in 1955, but totally overstates this in positivist fashion:

> The Act abrogates all the rules of the law of marriage previously applicable to Hindus, whether by virtue of any text or rule of Hindu law or any custom or usage having the force of law, in respect of all matters dealt with in the Act. It also supersedes any other law, contained in any Central or State legislation in force immediately before it came into operation in so far as such legislation is inconsistent with the provisions contained in it.

Jain (1983: xxii) notes correctly that the HMA does not prescribe any particular form of marriage, but nevertheless claims that the Act introduced radical changes, brought about uniformity in the Hindu law of marriage, and abrogated custom. Other authors appear to agree. For example Reddy (1999: 12) summarizes the position after the HMA:

> The Hindu Marriage Act, 1955 was the first of the codified Hindu laws. The Act does not specifically provide for any form of marriage. It made the marriage more consensual and secular than religious. It no more considers the marriage as a 'Samskara' as considered by Dharma Sastras. The marriage is solemnized as per the customary ceremonies prevalent in the community to which the bride and bride groom belong.

[49] Singh (1989: 59) also indicates that the major concerns relating to marriage have been polygamy and its effective abolition, age of marriage, compulsory registration of marriages, and dowry.

In fact, as is obvious from Section 7 of the HMA as cited above, the post-colonial Hindu law on marriage has simply restated and confirmed the dominance of customary law, but this rule now appears in codified form. Bedwa and Ullah (1992: 68) also seem to make exaggerated claims about the effects of modernist legal intervention:

> The immediate effect of the Hindu Marriage Act, 1955, according to conservative view, has been an abrupt severance from the ancient tradition and acceptance of certain principles and nations [*sic*] hitherto generally quite alien to the genius of the people. But at the same time the Act removed uncertainties in the matter of certain aspects of marriage which were formerly under the traditional law ... in doubtful state.

But what has been this abrupt severance when it comes to the law of marriage? Again, the examples discussed concern formal abolition of polygamy and a number of other issues, but not solemnization of marriage. Bedwa and Ullah (1992: 80) write:

> Section 7(1) of the Act provides that a Hindu marriage is to be solemnised by the customary rites and ceremonies of the parties. No preference is given to any party whose ceremonies are to be performed. It has been left to the option of the parties. As the rites and ceremonies to be observed are customary, they must possess the qualities which are necessary for the validity of a custom as defined u/s 3(a) which requires that for maturing into custom a rule should have been observed for a long time, continuously and uniformly.

Diwan (1978: 60) also suggested that the concept of Hindu marriage has undergone a tremendous change under the Act, asserting that '[t]he *dharmic* institution of marriage, in which marriage was meant to be an indissoluble religious union of man and woman, is sought to be transformed into a union of convenience'. Diwan (1978: 75) claimed that by repudiating the inviolable and sacramental character of the Hindu marriage, the HMA 'treats marriage as a conditional socio-legal agreement between adult and equal parties with their free consent to establish a home as husband and wife'. Qureshi (1978: 41) also argues that the HMA introduced a contractual element into Hindu marriage, which is now a union of one man and one woman to the exclusion of others. M. Basu (2001: 36) observes that '[t]he traditional concept of marriage is now greatly changed and Hindu marriage today has assumed more or less the nature of a contract for the mutual benefit of the parties concerned, duly aided by different legal provisions and reforms', although she recognizes that there are limits to what law can achieve. Singh (1993: 371) even claims that 'the sacramental character of Hindu marriage has evaporated as a result of induction of the remedy of divorce by the statutory law of Hindu marriage'.

Thus, despite their inflated assertions of the effective uniforming reforms of state law-making, such modernist authors are conceding their dissatisfaction with the extent of reforms to Hindu marriage law, which was clearly not totally abolished or reformed. Diwan (1978: 62) complained that the HMA was merely 'paper legislation in several respects' and criticized that it 'still allows customary marriages and marriages replete with religious ceremonies'. Diwan (1978: 63) argued that all these loopholes needed to be plugged, while trying to pronounce on the ideal of modern marriage:

> The question that occurs to every one is, what is the ideal form of marriage that suits the modern conditions? Marriage ceremony in the present society must be a simple one, secular or civil, without any pomp and show, and it should combine all the sanctity and solemnity of the *shastric* marriage and the secular content and modernity of marriage by choice, in which the parties to the marriage actively participate without undue interference from elders, who may be, at the most, consulted before marriage.

Diwan (1978: 68) was therefore critical of retaining traditional Hindu marriages under the law, claiming that 'the retention and recognition of *shastric* marriages under the present law of marriage is a retrograde step'. Arguing that the development of a secular outlook should be cherished by the modern Hindu law of marriage, Diwan (1978: 68) suggested that the law 'should be either amended suitably so as to break the religious shell of the marriage or be removed completely from the statute book'.

Such comments and suggestions reflect the hegemony of modernist discourse on modern Hindu marriage law, continuing to inflate and extol the power and virtues of state law-making. Yet despite their language of uniformity, secularism, and value-free modernity, these are actually culture-specific modernist phrases inspired by legal developments in England, where during the 1970s important divorce law reforms were being debated in such terms. Clearly, a more realistic perspective is needed to critique such suggestions. For example, how would India remove marriage law from the statute book? The HMA 1955 was indeed an odd compromise of the old and the new, which initially left some litigants and judges confused. Interestingly, Bedwa and Ullah (1992: 80–1) observe:

> It is submitted that even after the codification, the courts are not still certain as to which are the essential ceremonies of marriage, except saying that "Saptapadi" is an obligatory ceremony. It is denying the fact that among the Hindus there is no clarity about the essential "sastraic ceremonies". Different classes and castes of Hindus and Hindus in different parts of the country perform different ceremonies and even the priest who officiates at Hindu marriage is unable to identify what are the essential ceremonies, as distinct from the non-essential. The result is that whatever the ceremonies right or wrong the priest performs, are essential ceremonies for that marriage.

It is therefore argued, at p. 81 that 'it is very doubtful whether non-performance of essential ceremonies would now have a fatal effect on marriage'. These authors also recognize that long cohabitation as husband and wife would raise a presumption of valid marriage. Bedwa and Ullah (1992: 81) therefore almost stumble across the finding that 'the law relating to a Hindu marriage is the same after the passage of the Hindu Marriage Act as it was before its passage'. This is indeed the correct position, provided that the courts are ready to apply a presumption of marriage as liberally as they should. Yet this has continued to be constantly contested in the context of creating a modern legal order in the Indian courts.

Contesting Modernity in the Courts

Closer critical scrutiny of Section 3 of the HMA would appear to suggest that it actually supports such a flexible stance. The section does not speak of 'ancient' customs transmitted and followed 'since time immemorial', but explicitly mentions observance 'for a long time'. Problems have arisen when communities have more or less radically changed their customs and have introduced new elements that seem to clash with the provisions of Section 3 of the HMA. In such cases, critical questions arose about how long is 'a long time'.[50] The legal requirement is manifestly not that such customs have to be 'ancient'. Nevertheless, Indian courts have in many cases used precisely that word, or have even demanded evidence of customs 'since time immemorial', a phrase coming from Anglo-Hindu law. This remarkable imprecision in statutory interpretation should not have gone unnoticed, but the Hindu law on this subject remains confused today.

One famous early case exemplifying the imposition of such modernist, positivistic conceptions in Hindu marriage law concerns the pre-1955 case of the Tamil self-respecters, who refused to involve Brahmins and complex Brahmanical rituals in their marriage ceremonies and devised instead new, simpler, and cheaper customary forms of marriage solemnization, which were followed by a large number of people. In *Deivaini Achi v Chitambaram Chettiar* AIR 1954 Mad 657, it was held by the Madras HC, in conflict with local social norms, that a simple marriage solemnization without full rituals did not lead to a legally valid Hindu marriage. In other words, a full-fledged shastric marriage ceremony was held to be essential for legal validity. Denying the scope for the development of new customs and operating in favour of high-caste shastric norms, this decision created a grave social problem, for it legally invalidated thousands of Hindu marriages and confused people about their property rights and standing in society. Remarkably, it took the legislature of Tamil Nadu a good thirteen years to come round to resolving this conflict. Nevertheless, the resulting legislative amendment constitutes a significant victory for customary law.[51]

[50] The important case of *Baby v Jayant Mahadeo Jagtap* AIR 1981 Bom 283 reduced this period to some twenty years, given that a large community of people, in this case neo-Buddhists, had followed those 'new customs'.

[51] The eventual result was the Hindu Marriage (Madras Amendment) Act of 1967, which modifies Section 7 of the HMA for the state of Tamil Nadu (then Madras) only, inserting a new Section 7-A after Section 7 in the main Act. For details of the original text see Menski (2001: 14–15).

Later cases on Section 7 of the HMA, starting from the well-known precedent of *Bhaurao Shankar* AIR 1965 SC 1564, have tended to use the concept of 'ancient' custom and demand *shastric* rituals, especially the *saptapadī*. The insistence on custom having to be traced 'from time immemorial' is definitely a relic of British legal education, since in traditional Hindu law there was no such requirement. *Rabindra Nath Dutta v The State* AIR 1969 Cal 55 takes rather too strict a view of customs in Hindu marriages, virtually ruling out that any changes may be introduced. In this case, Hindu marriage is treated as a sacrament and it was held, at p. 58:

> The Hindu Marriage Act does not lay down any special or particular kind or form of ceremonies to be compulsorily observed in all Hindu marriages. In fact, the form of marriage, prescribed by the Sastras, is subject to modifications by custom or usage. But the expression 'Customary Ceremonies' cannot be taken to mean that 'Sastric Ceremonies' have been totally ignored. The expression 'Customary Rites and Ceremonies' naturally means such sastric ceremonies, which the caste or community to which the party belongs is customarily following. Customary rites and ceremonies to be accepted must be shown that such custom as an essence of marriage ceremony had been followed definitely from ancient times and that the members of the Caste, Community or Sub-Caste had recognised such ceremonies as obligatory. Once it is proved by evidence what ceremonies had been followed as customary rites, it is no longer left to the will of the Caste, Community or Sub-Caste to alter them as the essence of custom is that on account of its definiteness it had been recognised and adopted by the caste or community with certainty and without any variation.

This is clearly a strict legalistic approach that is not going to be feasible in practice. Given that the inherent customary flexibility of Hindu marriage rituals caused legal problems in some cases, some writers began to criticize the strictures of modernist, positivistic models. Anand (1992: 184), for example, while not consciously couching his analysis in this theoretical framework, observes that the official strictness of proof of marriage should be relaxed in view of social changes and new patterns of rituals:

> Meanwhile ceremonies to a marriage be simplified so as to include the intention of the parties manifested by exchange of garlands or rings or the likes in the presence of relatives and friends. Such simple forms be recognised as valid marriage statutorily. After all, many rituals and ceremonies in connection with marriage are already not in vogue any more. Panditji is generally bribed to skip *mantras* at the *Saptapadi* and to hurry the whole show. Should not law keep pace with society? Should the law not recognise those ceremonies which society has evolved to grant approval to a marriage?

This interesting suggestion means in effect that the law should recognize what society does, rather than seeking to dictate to people from above. Is this a conscious switch away from the colonial mode of the social reformers, or even an early glimpse of the emergence of a postmodern condition? Other debates that reflect upon the contestation of modernist conceptions within the courts relate to the issue of prohibited relationships for Hindu spouses in Section 5 of the HMA. Here the legal need was to protect certain local customs, especially from south India. In view of the size of India, and the variety of customs about prohibited degrees, a uniform legal regulation could simply not be achieved. Similarly, clauses (iv) and (v) of Section 5 of the HMA make an exception in favour of a custom or usage governing each of the parties to the marriage when it comes to prohibited degrees. Some reported cases from the South are very instructive on this subject. In *Balusami v Balakrishna* AIR 1957 Mad 97, a marriage between a grandfather and his daughter's daughter came up for consideration. The Court held this marriage to be void. In *Meenakshisundaram Pillai v P. Nammalwar* AIR 1970 Mad 402, a man had married his sister's daughter after his first marriage remained without offspring. It was held, at p. 405:

> The said marriage having taken place, after such marriages have been prohibited by law, it would be invalid and the position of his wife who is also his niece is no better than that of a concubine. But he took his sister's daughter in marriage as his second wife, as he had no issues by his first wife. Such a marriage was not prohibited by Sastras, or Hindu Law, as administered prior to the prohibition of such marriages by statutes.

This was a case about the Hindu law of charitable endowment, and the marriage issue was only a minor point. It is significant that nobody asked whether maybe, in this community, marrying a niece was within the scope of customary laws. It is certainly not the universally accepted position, as Bedwa and Ullah (1992: 72) seem to suggest, that all such marriages are necessarily void. In fact these authors themselves provide further case references (ibid.: 72–3) to the effect that a woman's marriage with her maternal uncle may be considered desirable in some communities, but not in others.[52] Bedwa and Ullah (1992: 73) add a touch of legal realism when they suggest that not much harm is done if people go on solemnizing such marriages since, 'if the families are well educated and financially sound, it would make no difference to them if they marry by breaking the provisions of the statutory laws. Their action would not bring any social stigma in the society to them and their children'.

Predictably, an important aspect of writing on Hindu marriage concerns the position of women. Singh (1989: 157) argues that the reformative efforts of the 1950s ended up being reduced to 'a tenuous and emaciated body fragmented into many laws' and thus throughout the 1950s, male hegemony continued to rule. Many authors complain that modernist legislation was not radical enough and has not improved the lot of women. Singh (1980: 85) makes

[52] Such cases also come up in the UK nowadays. While it is difficult to defend the position of custom in this field, some English judges are willing to recognize that Hindu law may have different methods of dealing with marriage solemnization compared to English law.

reference to Chinese family law reforms, arguing that the result has not been a copying of modern Western love marriage, but a 'situation where young couples agree to marriage on the basis of both traditional and modern Chinese values, keeping in mind their parents' preferences and advice'. For India, Singh (1989: 161) even asks for a degenderized society and, in a style reminiscent of Martin Luther King, Indu Prakash Singh (1990: xiv) imagines her own ideal society of the future:

> I envisage the end of all oppression of women and exploitation in a *depatriarchised socialist democratic society.* Let us join hands in building such an egalitarian society where we would not be having women and men (gendertypes) but humans.

More realistic and academically cogent, Agnes (2000: 77) speaks of stilted efforts at gender justice in the post-independence period, finding that:

> ... the underlying motive of the reform was consolidating the powers of the state and building an integrated nation. This crucial objective could be achieved only by diluting women's rights to arrive at a level of minimum consensus so that the agenda of reform could be effected without much opposition. Several customary rights were sacrificed to arrive at uniformity. The statutes that were finally enacted were merely ornamental instead of being markers of genuine and concrete efforts at rectifying the gender discrimination written into the Hindu law.

The fact that using the official mechanisms of the state law may even be counterproductive is evident from *Sanjay Mishra v Eveline Jobe* AIR 1993 MP 54. This case concerns a Hindu man and an Indian Christian woman who allegedly married, but the 'husband' refused to acknowledge that a lawful marriage had taken place. The woman had distributed copies of a marriage registration document under the SMA 1954 to her friends, while the man admitted to having signed certain marriage registration documents in a Registrar's office, but claimed that this had happened under duress. The woman alleged further that they were married in 1985 in a famous Hindu temple in Calcutta, in accordance with Hindu customs and rites, and had thereafter lived as husband and wife. The judge found that under the provisions of the HMA, a Hindu man and a Christian woman could not validly marry, thus the 'wife's' claim to have followed Hindu customary rituals of marriage could not be maintained. The lower court was criticized for overlooking the details regarding the personal law of the parties:

> The trial court has merely gone by the registration certificate; but such registration is valid only when it is found that there is a valid marriage. Where the factum itself is disputed, essential ceremony constituting the marriage in the instant case in accordance with Hindu rites must be pleaded and proved and the performance of such rites must be brought on records (p. 58).

While it was quite inappropriate to presume in the present case that a *saptapadī* ritual would be an essential element of this Hindu marriage,[53] the decision reached by the court seems correct. The registration document by itself is not sufficient conclusive proof in law that there was a properly solemnized marriage between the parties. The husband's appeal was therefore allowed, and he managed to extricate himself from his unwanted lover. This case would appear to confirm that if women want to secure their legal position as a Hindu 'wife', they would have to ensure that they follow the customary Hindu law on marriage solemnization.[54] Formal recourse to the secular state law on its own, as this case shows, is insufficient.

Thus, despite the prevalence of modernist, positivistic conceptions, modern Indian state law has not asserted itself through abrogation of the traditional Hindu law on marriage solemnization. Derrett (1963c: 137–8) summarized the legal position succinctly, saying that '[t]he *sastric* concept of marriage as a *samskara* ('sacrament'), a union of two persons for all purposes, spiritual and secular, indissoluble even by death, has been trimmed but not destroyed by legislation'. This points to the fact that the modernist reforms of the 1950s were not just an awkward, haphazard compromise. As a method of legal regulation, the legislative non-intervention in Hindu marriage solemnization reflects a recognition that law cannot just be imposed by the state. In this sense, the post-colonial modernist lawmakers already implanted the seeds of a postmodern condition into the regulatory system which they created during the 1950s.

Postmodern Evolution of Hindu Marriage Law

The implantation of these postmodern seeds, combined with a growing realization that modernist legal reforms in post-colonial India were not quite what they claimed to be, laid the foundations for the postmodern evolution of Hindu marriage law during the past few decades. Going beyond a mere critique of modernity and its elements, postmodernist approaches—both in scholarship and in the legal domain of cases and legislation—have searched more critically for appropriate solutions, while recognizing that no perfect simple remedy may be found to govern complex situations.

With specific reference to Hindu marriage law, the realization that Hindu marriage, as a central element of society, cannot be subjected to legislative intervention, forms a major element of Hindu law's current postmodern condition. This realization has led to legislative inaction, a form of nihilistic refusal by the state law to get involved in regulation of Hindu marriages. It seems to have been realized more recently that the reformist ambitions were too grand and the modernist task is just too enormous. One indication of this is that

[53] The relevant details are found under paragraph 23 at p.58 of the judgment.

[54] A useful authority for this position is *Sumitra Devi v Bhikhan Choudhary* AIR 1985 SC 765.

successive Parliaments have been unwilling to turn a number of statutory proposals by women's groups, in particular, into formal legislation.

The same scenario motivates the Indian judiciary to devote explicit recognition to traditional Hindu values related to marriage (which may be expressed in secular language about the need for a stable society), a process which has implications beyond the narrow realm of Hindu marriage law. The practical end result is that the rules and concepts of traditional Hindu law have been granted a new lease of life.[55] They now appear within the formal framework of 'modern' Hindu law, undermining this modernity, as it were, by exerting traditional sociocultural and legal influence through the formal mechanisms of modern Indian law. The traditional Hindu law of marriage solemnization has steadfastly resisted modernist attempts at its abrogation.

Derrett predicted, throughout his later writings,[56] that despite some evidence of modernization, the dominant view in Hindu society for the foreseeable future would remain that marriage is a form of social obligation. Mitter (1992: 20) notes that, 'nothing, apparently, can be worse for a woman than to remain unattached, a social pariah. In all the separate and unequal social worlds cohabiting in an Indian city, there is consensus on one point: a woman needs to have married status. At the least, she needs to have had a husband, once'. However, Nair (1978: v) observes significant social change, noting that '[m]arriage is perhaps the only institution which has undergone a rapid change' and even suggests that 'present-day marriage practices lead one to believe that the institution is becoming an unwelcome affair'. Yet this does not amount to suggesting that the abolition of marriage is viable in Indian society; it reflects at best the possibility of an individual, private choice, which was, after all, familiar to ancient Hindu tradition, too.[57]

Towards a Postmodern Discourse

In this regard it is instructive to refer to the Dowry Prohibition Act of 1961, which is widely seen as an example of the futile attempts by the state law to abolish socio-legal practices in Indian society.[58] Jain (1990: 625–6) argues that

[55] One must be conscious of the fact that the language could also be criticized as being too positivist. Is it really the case that the modern law has granted tradition a new lease of life, or does the law just have to admit defeat? This will always remain a contested issue.

[56] As we saw, Derrett (1957: 276–7) earlier envisaged virtually unlimited progress for Hindu society in the direction of modernization, but later reconsidered his modernist enthusiasm.

[57] On details regarding renouncers and ascetics, see Sprockhoff (1976); Olivelle (1993).

[58] The Dowry Prohibition Act of 1961, too, with a series of important amendments during the 1980s, illustrates that the threat of state-imposed legal sanctions alone does not induce desired behaviour in society. It has been estimated that more than 25,000 women die or are seriously maimed in India every year as a result of

'[i]t remains very doubtful whether some of the bad social practices which are ingrained deeply in the social psyche can be abolished merely by legislation'. Disgusted with the horrible stalemate over thousands of dowry deaths every year, some women activists began to call for a moral reappraisal (Kishwar 1990). Yet, does this mean that the wheel of history should in fact be turned back to Aśoka's idealism? Postmodernist analysis recognizes (albeit with some reluctance) that the old Hindu concepts of 'examining one's conscience' (*ātmanastuṣṭi*) and 'model behaviour' (*sadācāra*) retain their relevance today. While some modernist commentators have tremendous difficulties with this kind of approach, it cannot be just dismissed out of hand. While it clearly remains politically incorrect and ambivalent to highlight the operation of traditional Hindu concepts in modern India, global comparative jurisprudential theory suggests that all legal systems continuously feed on their particular, culture-specific 'legal postulates' (Chiba 1986; Menski 2000a). So, what is wrong with India relying on Hindu concepts to reconstruct its legal system?

Modernist analysis simply presumed that any elements or traces of Hindu law belong to medieval times.[59] Warnings from Professor Derrett and a few others that modernizing legal reforms could go too far and would end up producing injustice in the name of the law, were not taken seriously for a long time. While such arguments are more directly relevant for Hindu divorce law, problems have arisen not only at the substantive level of legal rules, but also clearly in the sphere of legal theory. Is state law really able to dictate to society and alleviate social problems in the process?[60]

However, some recognition of the limits of modernity is now provided by modernist writers such as Agnes (2000: 90), who argues that the new rights given to women in the 1950s 'are more conceptual than actual. While attempting to resolve some issues, the codification has foregrounded others which have yet to find a satisfactory solution'. Agnes (2000: 211) notes further that the family law debates are only conveniently brought into the public arena 'in support of other hidden political objectives'. While earlier the uniform civil

---

dowry-related domestic violence, while it is evident that attempts to control the so-called dowry problem through the state's legal framework have remained largely ineffective. On this problem and its various dimensions, see Menski (1998b).

[59] Banerjee (1984: 281–2) speaks of 'our medieval inheritance' and roundly criticizes 'conservatives' like Warren Hastings and others after him who had suggested that Indian civilization was different from European civilization, though not necessarily inferior. His final concluding paragraph at p. 288 roundly and pompously dismisses the notion that Hindu traditions contain anything useful for constructing modern democratic values and systems. Such views are strongly reflected in modernist feminist literature (e.g. Sarkar and Butalia 1995; Rajan 1998).

[60] Seeking to improve on H.L.A. Hart's theoretical model of law, Tamanaha (2001) challenges the 'mirror thesis' of law and society, and begins to write about 'order' as a coordination of behaviour in society, which comes rather close to the concept of *sadācāra* in traditional Hindu law (last section of Chapter 3).

code and increased property rights for women were focal points for debate, Agnes (2000: 177) confirms that women's groups and feminist activism are now concentrating on legal issues around violence against women. The literature reflects a growing realization that, just as the colonial intervention actually disadvantaged women further, as it imported androcentric Western notions which damaged South Asian women (Chandra 1998), post-colonial modernist reforms were not able to get rid of the patriarchal framework of reference either. In her concluding discussion, Agnes (2000: 203) observes:

> While examining the evolution of family laws situated within a patriarchal social structure, discrimination against women is a foregone conclusion. Caste, class and clan purities are maintained through a strict sexual control. Punitive deterrent measures and denial of economic rights are the means through which this control is exercised.

Agnes (id.) also argues that the history of women's rights is not linear, with religious and customary laws at one extreme end of the scale, and statutory reforms slowly progressing towards the other end, as is popularly believed: 'The history is complex with various interactive forces constantly at play ... it has been a case of "gain some, lose some"' (id.). Taking a different approach, but thinking along similar lines, Parashar (1992: 113) asserts that the Indian law reformers were not actually aiming to fundamentally redefine the roles of women. She observes that, in the 1950s, there was no radical break with Hindu traditional law. The Marriage and Divorce Bill prepared by the first Hindu Law Committee was ostensibly designed to incorporate the 'best parts of the code of Manu rather than those which fall short of the best' (id.). In other words, there was no real modernist legal revolution, but rather a slight tinkering of Hindu law at the edges, which is certainly the case in Hindu marriage law.

Feminists have often highlighted that some institutions which are considered necessary are not in fact tested as such (Singh 1989: 23). They thus engage in talk of counter-institutions and the obliteration of patriarchal institutions like family, marriage, and the legal system, aiming for an overthrow of the patriarchized society in toto. Yet dissenting voices, such as Singh (1989: 31), argue that revolution alone is not enough, as shown in the socialist countries: 'What more is needed is a conscientizing revolution—a phenomenological reality—which would not only emancipate women but also men'. Derrett (1978a) emphasized that point a long time ago. The challenge is huge and largely beyond the ambit of the state law.

From the angle of constitutional law, it has been evident for some time that the project of modern law reforms in India could not meaningfully guarantee and offer to the citizens the ideals that the law promised. Minattur (1980: 165) highlighted that under Article 15(3) of the Constitution, nothing shall prevent the state from making any special provision for women and children. So there was an explicit provision permitting the state to discriminate in favour of women, if such discrimination was found necessary. Minattur (1980: 166) noted that 'a number of laws were adopted with a view to ensuring equality of status and opportunity for women', while in practice, equality continues to elude women. Minattur (1980: 178) concluded:

> ... it is clear that something more than legislation is required. Perhaps the first thing to be attempted is to make women aware of their rights, however this is done. It is also necessary to change the attitudes of both men and women, of society in general, to social objectives sought to be achieved by legislation. A radical change in the attitudes of women induced by an awareness of their rights which are constitutionally guaranteed and legally protected will be the first step in the complex process of transforming the social structure so that women may enjoy full equality with men in every sphere of life.

Agnes (2000: 206) also observes that the Constitution with its mandate of equality brought in visions of gender justice:

> Restructuring of the feudal family laws to suit the needs of women within a modern democracy was the challenge before the newly independent state. But the much-trumpeted Hindu law reforms of the post-independence period were concerned more with homogenizing the culturally diverse Hindu community through a uniform set of state regulated enactments than widening the scope of women's rights. Hence crucial women's rights located within customary laws were compromised. The enactments turned out to be a curious mixture of the English law and the shastric law with the worst biases of both written into them.

In view of such shortcomings of the modernist law reform project, many modernists have developed cold feet. We saw in the previous section in this chapter how Qureshi (1978) argued vigorously in favour of significant state intervention in marriage law. In his conclusions, Qureshi (1978: 371–2) takes up the issue of marriage registration again, but this articulate Muslim author is now back-pedalling on his earlier reformist zeal, advancing religious arguments:

> As regards the essential ceremonies, there is a similarity between all the laws. It is submitted that this is purely a religious matter and the state cannot interfere .... Complete de-emotionalisation in marriage is not a healthy practice and is most unsuitable to Indians who are vibrant with emotion temperamentally. Merely signing the marriage agreement will not satisfy the psychology of Indians. Therefore, all citizens should be allowed to marry according to their own ceremonies. However, these marriages should be got registered. The method of registration should be 30 days from the date of marriage.

Evidence of the actual extent of marriage registration in India contradicts loud modernist assertions that state control would be a viable method of regulating Hindu marriage law. Pujari and Kaushik (1994, III: 305) report statistics of marriage registration under the SMA 1954 for the period 1968–72.[61] In Bombay,

[61] Earlier, Derrett (1963c: 139) had argued that this secular law was still virtually irrelevant in practice.

601 marriages in 1968 and 816 in 1972 were registered in this manner, no more than thirteen per year in Rajasthan, and not even 250 in Delhi. The figures for registration of marriages solemnized under other laws but registered under the SMA are much lower, with no more than forty-three marriages in 1970 for Bombay as the maximum.[62]

While reformers and modernist academic commentators still push for compulsory registration of marriages, it is quite evident that Indians are not ready to accept such a formal, bureaucratic regime.[63] A postmodern analysis would suggest that, in actual fact, no legal system in the world achieves absolute certainty of marital status.[64] Basu (2001: 36), whose arguments for modern reforms were cited above, also admits that there are limits to what law can achieve:

> Attempts to bring about changes in the status of woman either through legislation or judicial activism can achieve little success without a simultaneous movement to transform the social and economic structures and the culture (values, ideologies and attitudes) of society.

Iyer (1993: 1) similarly emphasizes that social justice in India means also gender justice, but notes that no quantum leaps have been made and that this is not just an Indian problem, since the USA has 'failed to ratify into its constitution equality of the sexes' (ibid.: 2). Much depends on private and individual initiative, but there is also a role for the state in promoting gender justice. Iyer (1993: 16) advises in this respect that Indian women must demand more economic and social dignity in practical terms. He also suggests that the private sector, like the public sector, shall be bound to respect equality of sexes 'on pain of the state withdrawing all licences, loans and other facilities. The State shall, through all its processes, compel the private sector to comply with the demands of gender justice'. These are again much wider agenda that have lost sight of marriage law as a key issue.

In an early mixture of modernist and postmodern analysis, Derrett (1978a: 159) noted that the Indian judges eventually underwrote Hindu marriage as a sacrament but were initially unsure:

> Judges, confused by the initial error of commentators who neglected the great shift in allegiance which occurred in the élite during those vital years,

[62] Agnes (2000: 244) reproduces the same figures as Pujari and Kaushik for 1968–72 and adds statistics for registration under the SMA in Mumbai between 1986 and 1996. The yearly totals never go beyond 2000 registrations.

[63] Evidence from fieldwork among Hindus in Britain confirms, in addition, that even in a legal system that officially insists on registration of all marriages, Hindus (and other 'ethnic minorities') tend to give more importance to the socio-religious solemnization of the marriage than to the formal registration with the state (for details see Menski 1987; 1991a; 1993a).

[64] Significant evidence of non-registration of marriages in England is discussed by Allott (1980: 259–86).

> and oblivious of the quaintness of a single marriage law being applied to all Hindus indiscriminately, have come out, almost intuitively, with the suggestion or rather apprehension that marriage is still a *samskara*, as for the vast majority it is.

Derrett (id.) also observes that 'this is understandably less evident in recent years', which one may take as a reference to the growing strength of modernist notions. However, the idea that marriage must be upheld, not for the sake of Hindu tradition, but for the good of society and the protection of women themselves, also comes through, at p. 163. While the English courts were not interested in reconciliation, Derrett (1978a: 197) stresses that Indian Hindu law did retain the judicial duty to check whether a marriage could still be rescued. This subject belongs more properly into a discussion on divorce, but the links between marriage and divorce law do not permit watertight segregation. How a state legal system will handle one of these areas of the law will inevitably influence the other.

Another example of links between different areas of law has been identified by Agnes (2000: 180), who challenges the modernist assumption that compulsory registration of Hindu marriages will automatically be beneficial, pointing to a crucial confusion:

> If the rights of cohabitees are on par with the rights of spouses then registration serves no purpose at all and there would be no compulsion to register a marriage in a society where marriages are viewed more as social functions than as legal contracts. Also if marriages and informal cohabitations are granted similar weightage and are deemed as offences then the whole premise upon which conviction for bigamy is based collapses. Here the existing law makes a clear distinction between solemn marriages and illegitimate and informal alliances where the ceremony of solemnization and permanency of the relationship is of greatest relevance. The widening of the scope would render adultery an offence rather than bigamy. But in the same stroke, it is recommended that adultery ought not to be deemed as an offence. So there is an ambiguity about whether the focus of the reform is curbing sexual immorality by a penal provision or protecting women's economic rights through widening the scope of maintenance to include women in informal alliances.

Agnes (2000: 183) observes that many countries in South Asia stipulate compulsory registration, but no country has extended this so far as to invalidate an existing marriage, with adverse implications for women and children.[65] She

[65] Agnes (2000: 195–6) wrongly assumes that Pakistan has reformed its traditional Muslim law through modernist legislative interventions by the Muslim Family Laws Ordinance in 1961. In reality, these are merely reformative 'paper' statements that have little practical impact. Pakistan neither requires compulsory marriage registration nor has it controlled polygamy or abolished the 'triple *talaq*', as Agnes (2000: 196) claims. Such mistakes confirm that there is an urgent need for Indian legal scholarship on Pakistan to be updated.

notes that, '[i]n fact, the modern trend is towards granting rights and benefits to people in informal relationships' (id.), while in India the official trend is still tilting towards greater regimentation in family relationships. However, she fails to identify that something must therefore be wrong with modernist Indian scholarship on family law reforms.

In fact, in moving towards a postmodern discourse, Agnes (2000: 176ff.) has diligently prepared the ground for a critical analysis of Indian family law by producing a detailed modernist discussion of a number of Marriage Bills formulated by legal scholars, women's organizations, and other bodies.[66] Her stated aim is to test these various reform suggestions for their modernity. In turn, she concludes that the existing suggestions do not go far enough and, above all, do not consider sufficiently well the economic needs and entitlements of women.

Agnes thus finds that in the highly politicized climate of modernist law reform debate, rhetoric dominates over a clear understanding of policy and a sense of realism. The dominant agenda of the uniform civil code have given disproportionate attention to Muslim law, communalizing and thereby blocking any progressive debates. Agnes (2000: 209) is highly critical of the legal reform proposals of various bodies. In her view, suggestions for reform in family laws which set out to redefine gender relations within marriage and the family, would have to take into consideration various social, political, legal, and economic realities. But, as she rightly claims (id.), 'the drafts for the enactment of a Uniform Civil Code framed by the legal academia, do not seem to have contextualized women's rights within these diverse complexities. The model for reform is the *Hindu Marriage Act* which in turn is based on archaic English principles'.[67]

The author therefore seems to have much reason to find fault with everything she sees in modernist debates. For example, Agnes (2000: 182) notes that the Marriage Bill, 1994 as formulated by the National Commission for Women 'makes sweeping and unrealistic recommendations, throwing all caution to the winds'. Agnes (2000: 182–3) notes:

> The primary concern of the Bill seems to be abolition of polygamy by ensuring compulsory registration of marriages. But instead of a facilitating measure (of providing proof in case of dispute), registration becomes an end in itself.

[66] In two appendices, Agnes (2000: 216–21) reprints and discusses the Domestic Violence to Women (Prevention) Bill, 1994, and the Married Women (Protection of Rights) Bill, 1994. None of these became official law, they were clearly too radical, especially in terms of financial implications for married men.

[67] Agnes (2000: 209) again overstates the English influence when she claims that 'all statutory matrimonial laws in India, except the Muslim law, are based on English laws of marriage'. Such assumptions seem to be uncritically copied from Banerjee (1984).

> The Bill stipulates that a declaration of marriage must be sent to the Registrar of marriages within three days of its performance. A fine of Rs 100 per day is levied for default for a period of one month and thereafter the marriage is deemed void.

Agnes is vocally critical of such proposals and comments in various contexts on the pernicious effects that such formalistic legal regulation would have for women and children, in particular. Apart from warning about an increase in state control over people's lives (ibid.: 187), an important element of her analysis, Agnes (2000: 183) also notes the resource implications of such reform proposals:

> While prescribing such stringent measures of compulsory registration, the fact that the government has not been able to provide bare necessities like clean drinking water, primary education and basic health facilities to a large section of its people has been overlooked. The Bill does not spell out the measures through which the government will make it possible for people to register their marriages within three days of its performance.

In a consolidated discussion of the main points, Agnes (2000: 186–7) examines the major elements of the various modernist reform proposals. Her first point is focused on the uniform civil code agenda. Agnes (2000: 186) finds that 'a consensus seems to be steadily, albeit gradually, emerging that the process of family law reform has to be cautious. Enforcing a compulsory uniform civil code from above may not be the best solution'. Significantly, Agnes (2000: 187) opposes the use of the term 'spouse' and demands explicit recognition of the specific needs of women.[68] Arguing that any recommendations have to be based on the substantive model of equality, she asks for greater clarity regarding the theoretical framework, particularly for academics. Agnes (2000: 188) does not appear to see much hope for significant legal reforms in the near future and therefore issues a rallying call:

> Women's rights seem to be lost in the larger controversy around Uniform Civil Code which today, has become a political question. Only through a step by step approach to bring in small and specific reform through concentrated campaigns can the rights of women be salvaged from the political entangle within which they are currently enmeshed.

Agnes (2000: 211) concludes that 'women's rights is [*sic*] not a primary concern of the dominant forces' and argues finally that 'there is a need to locate property at the centre of matrimonial law reform' (ibid.: 215). There is much in this rich analysis which can be salvaged for a postmodern analysis of Hindu and Indian family law. With specific reference to marriage law, it is highly significant that Agnes (2000: 210) also notes that the modern state may in fact be as good as irrelevant when it comes to Hindu marriage and divorce:

[68] In this context, she is extremely critical of the fact that Hindu men are able to claim maintenance from their wives under certain provisions of the HMA 1955.

> The fact that the *Hindu Marriage Act* has validated diverse customs of marriage and divorce, seems to have been overlooked by the zealous reformers. Although the *Hindu Marriage Act* set out to 'reform' Hindu law and bring it under the state control and regulations, sufficient scope was provided for Hindu customs and practices. Hence under the present statute, a Hindu need never approach a state functionary or a religious institution either for solemnization of his/her marriage or for its dissolution.

On the ground, it will always remain tempting for some litigants (and their legal advisers) to misuse the state-sanctioned customary flexibility of Hindu marriage traditions for obvious pecuniary benefit, thereby damaging the interests of women, especially widows and remarried women. The case law confirms that problems for the female claimant may be multiplied if she was previously married to someone else.[69]

Many reported cases under Section 7 of the HMA constitute bona fide petitions by Hindu women seeking to assert their rights arising from their marriage to a Hindu male. Still, the argument that any woman who claims to be married to a Hindu male must automatically be believed, does not recommend itself. It would encourage false claims of formal marriage, when in fact there was perhaps only an informal liaison. Actually, this kind of scenario points to unresolved legal problems over the boundaries between polygamy and unmarried cohabitation. The existing academic and legal discussions, while moving towards a postmodern discourse in studying and understanding Hindu marriage law, have hardly begun to realize that any strictly formal regulation of Hindu marriage would have potentially negative consequences for those many women who are party to a quasi-marital relationship that may not have full social sanction (see Agnes 2000: 180, cited earlier). It is more than clear from the existing case law that such women often need special protection through flexible and situation-specific application of the criteria for Hindu marriage. Thus, while scholarly debates have begun to realize the limits of modernist discourse, this recognition has developed in ignorance of the reality of the postmodern condition that has been evolving and blossoming through the application of Hindu marriage law in the Indian courts.

An Emerging Postmodern Condition: Case Law Evidence

Detailed research on case law shows many reported and unreported disputes in which the strict official legal position on 'proper ceremonies' was exploited by ruthless husbands during the 1970s and 1980s to the detriment of women.

[69] *Bibbe v Ram Kali* AIR 1982 All 248. In *Surjit Kaur v Garja Singh* AIR 1994 SC 135, discussed further later, the SC deprived a twice-widowed Sikh woman of her due share on the ground that she was not validly married under Hindu law, even though she also produced a marriage certificate. For details and a critique, see Menski (1995b and 2001: 33–5).

Looking more closely at the cases, however, I found that the case law under Section 7 of the HMA actually falls into two types, namely appeals by Hindu husbands seeking to avoid a prosecution for polygamy, and cases by Hindu women claiming their entitlements from the marriage. Where Hindu husbands were accused and convicted of bigamy, and went on appeal, the courts tried to assist the man, developing in the process a strictly formal case law that seems to grant only completely ritualized Hindu marriages full legal recognition. This strictness, however, is only partly explained by the evidentiary requirements of the criminal law;[70] it is also based on a pro-men interpretation, simply to avoid that the polygamous husband should be punished or even sent to jail.

By the mid-1980s, the consequences of taking this biased angle in the case law became very bad for women and children and judges realized that there was a second type of case concerning Hindu marriage solemnization. Here the key issue was the entitlements of the wife as a result of the marriage. Some Supreme Court judges began to realize how dangerously easy it had become for Hindu men to divest their wives of rightful claims. Where could they go for help if the courts did not intervene in a balanced manner? This realization apparently went hand in hand with growing judicial activism and awareness about the maintenance rights of divorced wives.[71] However, rather than making a big issue out of this, for example by publicly demasking the old pro-men precedent of *Bhaurao Shankar* AIR 1965 SC 1564, the Supreme Court chose a more subtle strategy, applying a presumption of marriage instead of demanding strict proof. Because of the subtlety employed here, most legal writers did not notice the second type of Hindu case law on marriage solemnization, while many practising lawyers were only too happy to overlook the emergent postmodern legal position in the case law on Hindu marriage solemnization.

It appears that the subtle transition of the Hindu marriage law into a postmodern condition, under the second type of case law, can be located in *Sumitra Devi v Bhikhan Choudhary* AIR 1985 SC 765. This was an appeal by a Hindu wife from Bihar against the refusal of her claim to maintenance, resisted by the husband on various grounds, including the allegation that she was not properly married to him. This brief case report contains an important restatement of the law by the SC, which hardly anybody seems to have picked up at the time.[72] Ranganath Misra J, criticizing the technical approach taken by the lower court and the HC, held at p. 766:

[70] The relevant legal principle here is that an accused should be presumed innocent until proven guilty, since in a criminal prosecution, proof 'beyond reasonable doubt' has to be adduced.

[71] An influential early case on Hindu women's maintenance is *Soundarammal v Sundara Mahalinga Nadar* AIR 1980 Mad 294. After 1985, the discussions about the Shah Bano case obviously had an impact, too.

[72] For example, the normally quite comprehensive *Annual Survey of Indian Law* for 1986 does not mention this case, and it was also overlooked or purposely ignored by other commentators. Diwan and Diwan (1990: 100–1) discuss this case in the context of maintenance.

> There is no doubt that in order that there may be a valid marriage according to Hindu law, certain religious rites have to be performed. Invoking the fire and performing Saptapadi around the sacred fire have been considered by this Court to be two of the basic requirements for a traditional marriage. It is equally true that there can be a marriage acceptable in law according to customs which do not insist on performance of such rites as referred to above and marriages of this type give rise to legal relationships which law accepts.

We hear not a word about modernism or postmodernism, but the learned judge is in effect decreeing postmodern pluralism, laying down that explicit recognition of the facts and circumstances of individual cases is more important than following the Supreme Court's own precedents in the other line of cases on marriage solemnization. Justice, in other words, is more valuable than the formality of the law. This decision clearly refutes the modernist, uniforming, formally rigid legal position that had built up in the line of cases involving polygamous husbands. The judge avoids further discussion by swiftly remitting the case to the lower court for disposal. In *Sumitra Devi*, the tangible issue was the entitlement of the Hindu wife to recognition of her married status and her financial claims. Here we see postmodern Indian social welfare law in action. But only if we understand the inherent principles of Hindu law are we able to recognize that the SC relied in this otherwise insignificant case not on a state-based modern form of legal regulation, but on the flexible traditional Hindu concepts of self-controlled ordering—if necessary with a little push from the courts. The reason for doing so was again to avoid injustice to women, not glorification of Hindu norms or principles of Hindu law. And yet, in effect, this case strongly upholds the customary diversity of traditional Hindu methods of marriage solemnization. It is, however, not a backward-looking decision that ties Hindu men to religious obligations, but a forward-looking social welfare approach designed to protect the interests of weaker sections in society.

As indicated, this was primarily a maintenance case, so hardly anybody noticed the link with the law of marriage solemnization.[73] The predicaments of Hindu women in this regard have been complicated when the marriage rituals in question were truncated or in some way modified from earlier customary patterns. As seen in the earlier section on modernist reforms to Hindu marriage law, this was already the case in *Deivaini Achi* AIR 1954 Mad 657, on account of social changes in that particular community of 'self-respecters'.[74] Problems have arisen for remarried women, especially widows marrying a widower, who would customarily perform only minimal rituals. The women in such cases should be protected under the wide umbrella of Section 7 of the

[73] The headnote of the case only mentions maintenance, so time-pressed lawyers would not easily find this case if they were looking for material on marriage solemnization.

[74] On this particular community and the agenda of its leaders, see Subramanian (1999).

HMA, but the twisted case law on Hindu polygamy has posed considerable risks to many Hindu women.

More detailed research on such cases would show various customary forms of truncated or even totally absent marriage rituals, and the consequent application of a presumption of marriage.[75] Apart from Sikh marriage customs which have long allowed for remarriage in the *karewa* form, there are cases involving Hindus from Maharashtra,[76] Kerala,[77] and other parts of India, all accepting the legal validity of unusual marriage ceremonies, with some of them concerning widow remarriages.

In contrast, the dreadful case of *Surjit Kaur v Garja Singh* AIR 1994 SC 135 concerned a Sikh widow's claim to a share in the deceased husband's property, which was fiercely resisted by the husband's family. Alleging that the widow was not a decent woman, evident character assassination was employed through the allegation that 'Surjit Kaur was in the habit of changing husbands frequently' (p. 136). Both the Chandigarh HC and the Supreme Court appear to have been impressed by such anti-women rhetoric and sexual innuendo, thereby overlooking the overall justice involved and its watchdog function. This case provides strong evidence of lack of judicial sensitivity about gender and Hindu marriage solemnization, and is simply a bad case (Menski 1995b; 2001: 33–5). It is of course not unique to Indian law or Hindu law that there should be conflicting legal positions. But in this case something else went seriously wrong: This woman's claim to property entitlement was treated, in terms of evidence law, like a man's defence against polygamy. As a result, the strict criteria for customary rituals were applied, instead of considering a presumption of marriage, as was done in other cases at the same time, in the same year, and even by the same court.[78]

An easy suitable solution to this kind of legal problem cannot be found, as modernist reformers are always tempted to argue, by removing Hindu marriage traditions and bringing in modern secular state law. Marriage remains a human social institution resistant to totalitarian modernist regimentation. Moreover, the Indian legal system is clearly not in a position, for financial as well as organizational reasons, to introduce a compulsory marriage registration system

[75] On presumption of marriage see Desai (1990: 639), a leading practitioners' handbook.

[76] *Ningu Vithu Bamane v Sadashiv Ningu Bamane* AIR 1987 Bom 27 recognizes a *pat* marriage as an approved, customary form of marriage among Hindus in Maharashtra and followed an earlier case to that effect.

[77] *Narayanan Namboodiri v Bhargavi Amma* 1989(1) KLT 547 explicitly relies on *Sumitra Devi* AIR 1985 SC 765 holding that the customary local form of marriage known in Kerala as *sambandam* was fully recognized by the law.

[78] The case of *S.P.S. Balasubramanyam v Sutturayan* AIR 1994 SC 133 arose from Madras, but that itself should not have made a significant difference. In this case, remarkably, a presumption of marriage was applied by the same judges who refused its operation in *Surjit Kaur*.

as a basis for determining the legal validity of all marriages, a prerogative that English law and most Western jurisdictions have claimed, but are evidently failing to maintain.[79]

Therefore, here is another element of postmodern analysis relevant to the present case: Unlike prosperous and fairly small Western countries, a huge nation like India will evidently never be in a position to attach welfare right entitlements to married status. At any rate, the number of potential claimants would be unmanageable. The legal system therefore must continue, of necessity, to rely on the traditional customary patterns of marriage solemnization. Public recognition of marital status through social processes must remain the main criterion. If the aim is to protect women, their position and bargaining power in society has to be strengthened. We do not need new laws for that, but activist engagement for protection of individual rights.

At the same time, there are deeper sociocultural reasons for why Hindu marriage solemnization without duly elaborated ritualization (however diffusely perceived in any particular situation), or simple registration of marriage, will remain widely unacceptable.[80] Firstly, within the *ṛta*/dharma context, an unsolemnized marriage between Hindus is simply not a Hindu marriage, because the invisible links between macrocosmic world and microcosmic sphere have not been created. It is arguable that for this basic cultural reason alone, and not just out of a fear of 'illicit sex', most Hindus find a system of unmarried 'cohabitation' deeply unsatisfactory and even offensive. It follows that they would therefore not be satisfied with state-controlled formal registration procedures by themselves. They would treat themselves as married only after the Hindu rituals of solemnization have been completed.[81]

All of this puts paid to modernist hopes from a 'law and development' or 'social engineering through law' angle. By the early 1990s, it was becoming increasingly clear all around that Indian law no longer even tries to follow

[79] In modern English law, 'cohabitation' has become increasingly equated with formal marriage, at least as far as property and succession law, and the rights of any children are concerned (Allott 1980: 259–86). More recent evidence from England shows that the state will eventually have to grant formal legal recognition to all kinds of marriages (including Hindu marriages) which did not, at their inception, follow the prescribed legal pattern. See *Gereis v Yagoub* [1997] 1 FLR 854 and particularly *Chief Adjudication Officer v Bath* 2000 [1] FLR 8 (CA), a Sikh case in which the couple had married only in a gurudwara in London thirty-five years ago, but the English Court of Appeal had to recognize the widow's pension claims.

[80] Most modernists would now not venture to suggest that Muslims should abandon their contract of marriage before God, the *nikah*, while members of other religions are somehow still expected to shed their sociocultural and religious traditions more easily.

[81] Indeed, Asians in Britain do not, with few exceptions, follow a pattern of cohabitation. In effect they end up 'marrying twice' (Menski 1987; 1991a; 1993a). For similar evidence regarding Muslims in Britain, see Pearl and Menski (1998: 73–7).

such Western models (Menski 1996b; 2001). Then, what would be the point of an elaborate system of marriage registration if the information produced would anyway be of no real use to the state and could not be fully and reliably collected in the first place? The new system would inevitably create more problems than it might ever hope to solve.

Indeed, as seen from the discussion by Agnes (2000) as outlined above, it is more widely recognized today that the formal introduction of compulsory registration of all marriages in India would only create many new socio-legal problems and is not a sensible item of reform programmes for the state.[82] Most crucially, it would not be an effective remedy for women who are in danger of being denied marital status. This does not simply mean that India has failed to modernize, therefore, but that this important country and its legal system have consciously chosen not to follow the route of Western modernizing models and are relying instead on indigenous methods of self-controlled ordering. Derrett (1978a: 121) anticipated this long ago, pointing to the fact that the overwhelming majority of Hindus lived in villages and to them, 'a civil marriage implies a negation of everything that they live by'.[83]

A combined reading of Sections 7 and 8 of the HMA 1955 confirms that the dominant criterion for legal validity of Hindu marriages in India remains observance of customary marriage rituals, and not—as in most Western countries—compliance with the state's law on marriage registration. Given that customary norms and conventions are decided by people and at the local level, this constitutes a comprehensive abdication of the Indian state's claim to regulate marriage law. This is a critical and significant finding which, somehow, modernist scholarship has been reluctant to recognize.

The court system, therefore, remains the only formal element of supervening state control in this field. From a Hindu law perspective, this is little more than a supervisory mechanism, a kind of safety net to prevent blatant injustice, a role that is familiarly known in Hindu legal tradition. It is thus not an institution whose involvement must be sought in every case. In fact, like the ancient Hindu ruler's court, and in tandem with the principles of *vyavahāra*, formal recourse to dispute settlement mechanisms should not be made unless attempts at self-controlled ordering have failed. This confirms the finding by several authors that Hindus in India today do not need the state to marry and

[82] Corbridge and Harriss (2000: 167) rightly point to the violence of cutting primary education in India to the bone. So where and how would money for marriage registration systems be found?

[83] Similarly, Kishwar and Vanita (1991: 15) criticize the misguided modernist assumption that urban models have become dominant for the rural masses of India, arguing that 'in reality it is the family structure of the dominant peasant castes and their forms of property organization that act as the norm in India .... Most urban centres in India are like islands intimately influenced by the vast ocean of the countryside'.

to divorce. Rather than being seen as some deficient aberration, this actually reflects the postmodern condition of Hindu marriage law.

The present analysis, thus, points to a polite refusal on the part of the Indian state to carry any real responsibility for the maintenance of any formal law on marriage solemnization. The Indian postmodern state, in a more or less silent process of surrender, recognizes the internal power and strength of Hindu concepts and customary norms, and thus relies on society to self-regulate, without explicitly using ancient terms like *sadācāra*. In effect, the state has handed ultimate authority not to some saffron men, but to the people of India, who are after all—at least in constitutional rhetoric—the sovereign authority of the nation. Even from a constitutional angle, thus, this subtle regrouping of legal authorities is beyond reproach. It is about time that anthropological and legal scholarship recognizes this scenario as a postmodern condition and embarks on new critical research that moves beyond modernist paradigms and indoctrination to analyse the resulting legal questions which this postmodern condition poses.

9

Child Marriage

Strictly speaking, the topic of child marriage is not a matter of Hindu personal law, but falls under the general law of India, which applies to all citizens irrespective of religion and background. This theoretically uniform application of the law against child marriages gives rise to questions about how far any form of general, state law (rather than personal law regulation) can effectively influence different people's behaviour. The discourse about child marriages and their legal control in India is also relevant here since it has been taking place within the same sociocultural environment as Hindu marriage law and other subjects which this book covers.

Historically, debates and case law about child marriages have mainly concerned Hindu practices, with some apprehensions about early marriages among Muslims.[1] The discourse about child marriages in Hindu law has been focused on the marriage age of girls, rather than boys, though early marriages of boys are by no means unknown. Discussions about child marriage are often closely linked to debates about Hindu marriage (Chapter 8), in particular registration of marriages. They are often lumped together with other social problems such as child widows, taboos against widow remarriage, and sati. Verma (1993: 18) argues that '[a]ge at marriage is a very strong demographic indicator of the status of women in a society' and posits that the lower the age at marriage, the higher the potential for exploitation of women.[2]

While historians of colonialism, focussing on social and legal reform efforts during the late nineteenth and early twentieth century, play a prominent role in the literature on child marriage,[3] lawyers have not been

[1] Muslim law is not, in principle, opposed to child marriages, since it treats a young person who has reached puberty as an adult (Pearl and Menski 1998: 141). There is, however, some concern about pre-puberty marriages among Muslims, since a Muslim marriage contracted before God is unlikely to be nullified on the ground that one or both spouses were below some stipulated minimum age.

[2] Such arguments overlook that in the West today, marriage ages for an increasing number of people are also very low, with the result that the law is under pressure to recognize and deal with the consequences of sexual activity among young people.

[3] See in particular Heimsath (1962; 1964), Engels (1983), Anagol-McGinn (1992), Sarkar (1993), and Chandra (1998).

interested in this topic.[4] Child marriage has been relegated to the rank of a subsidiary issue.[5] Child brides lack the panache of the daring sati, on whom disproportionate publicity and attention has been lavished by sensation-hungry foreigners, media-conscious activists and vote-seeking protagonists of *hindutva*. Child marriage also lacks the constructed sense of drama surrounding 'forced marriages', which recently have become a prominent issue in the UK, serving a variety of agenda.[6]

The perpetual suffering of many Indian women today has little to do with sati or child marriage. It is located elsewhere in the vast site of patriarchal domination, although it appears correct to argue generally that the constant outward subordination of women in a male-dominated social hierarchy remains at the core of suppression techniques against virtually all Indian women. But child marriage concerns primarily children, not women. The absence of a vibrant literature on child marriage reflects not only frustration with the lack of effective legal control, but also a serious deficiency of concern among academic and policy-making circles for the rights of the child in India, which have tended to remain a peripheral consideration of the Indian state.

Concentrating on early marriages as a socio-legal problem, the present chapter first investigates the extent of child marriage practices in Vedic and classical Hindu traditions. We find again that 'Hindu tradition' has been by no means uniform and static and that there have been significant changes in perceptions and social practices over time. In particular, it is quite clear that Vedic Hindus did not support and practise child marriages, while classical Hindus and their later descendants modified their views on the matter. As a negative spiral began to lead to shifting perceptions among Hindus about ideal ages of marriage for women, this began to be reflected in ever lower ages at marriage within society. Where this was accompanied by insistence on early consummation of such marriages, it was inevitable that various serious medical problems would arise.

Later sections of the present chapter discuss significant evidence about how the problem may have escalated during medieval times and even under British rule. Early consummation of marriages, leading to early pregnancies,

[4] The most useful contributions come from Chatterjee et al. (1971) and Sagade (1981).

[5] However, articles complaining about Indian practices of child marriage and reinforcing impressions of Indian backwardness, continue to appear in the popular press at regular intervals. An article in the *Japan Times* of 19 May 2002 ('Ending the outrage of child marriages') by an Indian correspondent, B. Gautam, simply repeats all the stereotypes and behaves as though registration of marriages would be a magic remedy.

[6] The Home Office in London published a Report of a Working Group on Forced Marriage, entitled *A Choice by Right* in 2000. A critical review of this was produced in an interim report by the Southall Black Sisters Trust in 2001—*Forced Marriage: An Abuse of Human Rights One Year After 'A Choice by Right'*.

coupled with allegations of the systematic, legitimized rape of child brides by older men, would give rise to prominent and stinging social criticism of Hindu practices by outsiders (Mayo 1927). While there was never one view on this matter, it appears that Hindu opinion gradually moved towards recognizing the problematic nature of premature marriage and its negative repercussions. However, there was also a strong view that outsiders' interference in such intimate matters should not be tolerated and British involvement was vocally resented on political grounds.

Indeed, as we saw in the previous chapter, there was no significant British interference in Hindu marriage law. For child marriages, too, legal intervention has remained limited to remedying grave social abuses rather than seeking comprehensive socio-legal reform. After prohibiting sexual intercourse with a girl below ten years in the IPC of 1860, the Anglo-Indian law proceeded with a mixture of timidity and caution. The British did not interfere again until 1891, when a projected increase of the minimum age to 12 years sparked off a major public outcry. The result was that reform efforts were left to the indigenous elite, the 'enlightened sections' of which eventually managed to persuade the British to pass the CMRA of 1929.[7] However, under that Act any child marriage, once solemnized, remains a legally valid marriage. Even though illegal, it is merely punishable, but is not a void marriage. Significantly, since the 1929 Act is conspicuously silent on this issue, it was left to the courts to clarify the legal position. Unsurprisingly, everywhere in South Asia, child marriages remain valid today.[8]

Independent India has thus merely tinkered with the minimum ages for marriage, raising them to such a high level in 1978 that any discussion of 'child marriage' becomes almost meaningless.[9] It has been quite frustrating for modernists that the courts, as even the latest cases show,[10] continue to uphold the legal validity of child marriages.[11] While the courts are only confirming the legislative position, the gradual changes in sociocultural practices, earlier

[7] As its name indicates, the 1929 Act did not intend to outlaw or nullify child marriages, its purpose was mainly educative. On the earlier history of this legislation see Baxi (1986b: 41–2) and the studies by Heimsath (1962; 1964).

[8] For the position in Pakistani and Bangladeshi law see Pearl and Menski (1998).

[9] In India, the *Child Marriage Restraint (Amendment) Act* of 1978 raised the legal minimum ages to eighteen years for the bride and twenty-one years for the groom. For demographic reasons, Bangladesh copied this law and adopted the same high minimum ages.

[10] Following a long period of silence, one of the latest reported cases to this effect is *Gajara Naran Bhura v Kanbi Kunverbai Parbat* AIR 1997 Guj 185, discussed in a subsequent section later.

[11] The only prominent case that attempted to invalidate child marriages, *Panchireddi Appala Suramma v Gadela Ganapatlu* AIR 1975 AP 193, was swiftly overruled by a Full Bench of the Andhra Pradesh HC to avoid social problems in that state. See *Pinninti Venkataramana v State* AIR 1977 AP 43 FB.

reflected in Sanskrit literature, point to continuous structural shifts in the politico-economic, cultural, and social make-up of Indian perspectives on child marriage. It is these structural shifts in thinking, within the prolonged interaction of law and society, that indicate how Indian child marriage law has now moved beyond the axioms of tradition and modernity into a postmodern condition.

This chapter shows that since the practice of child marriage has declined in its extent today, it could be said that child marriages no longer constitute a grave problem. Indeed, social developments have taken care of the issue, but it does not follow that individual young people and women, in particular, remain completely free of this practice.[12] What irks and confuses modernists, however, is not only that society has shown its capacity for internal self-reform,[13] but that modernist reform ambitions in the legal control of child marriages appear to have been more or less completely defeated. The state law recognizes that the illegal solemnization of a child marriage still leads to a legally valid Hindu marriage. Again, modernists are confronted with the dilemma, created by their own inflated claims, that law cannot just abolish traditional practices.

In the postmodern condition of the current Indian scenario, we see the culmination of a temporal process of interweaving traditional and modern perspectives on child marriage. The judges, with an acute consciousness of social welfare and social justice, are first and foremost seeking to protect Hindu women and children from devious men who seek to shirk their social and legal responsibilities. The courts, confronted with male efforts to pull the wool over their eyes, have become alert to the abuse of modernist arguments by traditional androcentric forces. The judges have clearly been influenced by traditional *and* modern approaches, and have found a way of moving beyond both. They reject the traditional position of condoning child marriage, stating that it is bad and that social reform is necessary. However, vigilant as ever, the judges also reject the modernist position, arguing that to simply try and abolish a social practice in the eyes of the law is unhelpful for the creation of a cohesive and stable society.

[12] S. Basu (2001: 29–30) reports that in one of her sample areas in Delhi, most girls were married by their late teens and had several children a few years later. In a study of 400 rural and 200 urban households in two districts in Karnataka, Varma (2000: 73) found that in total nearly 67 per cent of her sample married between sixteen and eighteen years of age. While 11 per cent of her total sample of women had their first child below the age of fifteen, 35 per cent of the women had their first child between fifteen and eighteen years, and 27 per cent between twenty-one and twenty-five years (ibid.: 75).

[13] Weinberger-Thomas (1999: 194) confirms for Rajasthan that '[c]hild marriages have decreased almost to the point of vanishing: infrequent in the rural areas, they have disappeared entirely from the cities, although traces of this practice were still present in the 1961 Census'.

As shown in Chapter 8, it is highly significant that the state has declined to take any responsibility for the regulation of Hindu marriage itself, so that India has not—and I dare say will never have—a compulsory system of marriage registration. While the logistics for such a bureaucracy are well beyond the capacity of the state, the facile modernist argument that a system of marriage registration would be able to effectively prevent further child marriages is itself a modernist illusion. In the field of child marriage, too, the Indian state law has stepped back to allow local Hindu societies to regulate their own affairs, notwithstanding some educational efforts. Yet this does not mean that the state has abdicated its role as a protector of justice—or the protection of 'order' in the conceptual context of the *rta*/dharma complex and the constitutional framework. The pervasive influence of Hindu concepts as well as constitutional directives have provided important building blocks for the postmodern manifestations of Indian child marriage law today.

Child Marriage in Traditional Hindu Law

Legal writers tend to be much less circumspect than other social scientists in making distinctions between different types of 'tradition' within Hindu literature. Sampath (1972b: 386 n. 3) claims that '[t]he traditional Hindu texts exhorted the parents to celebrate the marriage of a girl before she attained puberty', which seems to allow little room for variation within Hindu tradition. Mishra (1994: 16–25) provides a detailed summary of the Vedic and classical Hindu position regarding qualifications of the spouses and sees marriageable age as one of the most interesting questions. Early marriages were no doubt in vogue in ancient days, as socio-political and religious circumstances compelled a father to have his daughter married as early as possible (Mishra 1994: 16).

However, if one wants to blame tradition for the evil of child marriage, it is clearly not the most ancient Hindu tradition that is responsible for the marriage of babies. There is significant evidence that during Vedic times there was no preference for early marriages of girls and it appears that the majority of brides were adults.[14] The old ritual models of marriage solemnization assume that the bride is fully matured and that the marriage rituals culminate in sexual intercourse.[15] Pandey (1969: 182–3) indicates that it is evident from the Vedic marriage hymns that 'the parties to marriage were grown up persons competent to woo and be wooed, qualified to give consent and make choice' and that '[t]he Vedic rituals presuppose that the married pair were grown up enough

[14] Mishra (1994: 17). This is confirmed by Augustine (1991: 23) who adduces various indicators to suggest that child brides were unknown and widows were permitted to remarry in the Vedic as well as epic period. M. R. Sharma (1993: 58–61) provides a useful, detailed discussion. Thomas (2000: 62) states that child marriages were unknown in Vedic India; only grown girls were eligible for marriage.

[15] See in detail Menski (1984). This was also noted earlier by Jolly (1892:421) and Bhandarkar (1893:148).

to be lovers, man and wife, and parents of children' (ibid.: 183).[16] All this is clearly confirmed by the earliest evidence of Hindu marriage rituals from RV 10.85 and AV 14, as well as later evidence that a Hindu marriage was to be consummated fairly soon after the ritual solemnization of the marriage.[17]

If, as Bhandarkar (1893) argued more than a century ago, the *smṛti* texts collectively reflect a change of the ideal model towards earlier marriages, this does not mean that this ideal model ever became mainstream practice. The gradual acceptance of child marriage may be one of the best-documented examples of how the interaction of custom and *smṛti* texts may have worked in practice. Descriptions of early travellers in India and other observations prove nothing. As today, sensationalism and emphasis on the quaint rather than the normal tend to distort our perceptions of social reality. If, therefore, one cites today certain *shastric* texts in favour of child marriage, one commits a critical mistake in assuming, firstly, that such texts ever represented 'the law' and, secondly, that they fully reflected social reality at any given time. All we know from the texts themselves is that they gradually advocated an earlier age of marriage. Starting off from the position that a bride should be physically mature and able to bear plenty of strong offspring, the earliest textual statements reflect the marriage of mature girls. This changes to arguments for marriage soon after puberty (puberty plus three years), then puberty plus three months, then marriage on puberty, and finally pre-puberty marriage (Menski 1984: 751ff.). The main consideration at this later stage appears to have been that as few fertile periods as possible should be lost and illicit sexual relations should be kept to a minimum. Later customary traditions focused particularly on the latter concern, to the effect that even very young children were married.

This chain of arguments, however, does not amount to a law in favour of child marriages. Rather, it represents a string of Hindu cultural comments on the desirability of protecting female chastity and seeks to ensure compliance with this newfound primary purpose of Hindu matrimonial law, which dates back to well over a thousand years. Early marriage, in this context, safeguards what is nowadays, at least in north India, subsumed under *izzat,* the honour of the family, which often manifests itself prominently in guarding the chastity of the females in a family. Early marriage, then, is primarily a device for avoiding pre-marital sexual irregularities, maybe not only for women but both genders.

Thus, while there are some indications that child marriage might have been practised in Vedic times (Mishra 1994: 17), the preponderance of evidence points in the other direction. The main explanation for this may well be that in Vedic times there was a marked emphasis on progeny and on procreation of strong children, especially sons. In such a scenario, a child bride would obviously not be suitable as an ideal mother, and marriages would have been

16 On the ideal expectations of a Vedic couple see in detail Shastri (1988: 6–9).

17 On this see also Sharma (1994: 15) and Shastri (1988: 11–16).

deferred to a point where the girl was physically mature and able to bear healthy children. Significantly, in some *smṛti* texts, a girl of marriageable age is compared to a ripe cucumber, full of seeds, to be plucked off from the stem (her natal family) and given to the husband's family for the explicit purpose of procreation.[18]

Jolly (1975: 119–20) also highlights that the ancient marriage hymns assume the presence of a physically mature bride and more or less instant consummation of the marriage after the completion of the rituals. According to Pandey (1969: 184–5) this would still be correct for the older domestic *sūtra* texts as well. Shastri (1988: 18) sums up the Vedic ideal of marriage to the effect that marriage should be entered into by a man and a woman at a mature age, 'when they may be fully alive to the responsibilities of the householder's life, both of them having been duly educated for a proper discharge of their duties. Such is the conclusion one will arrive at by an independent study of the Vedic texts'.

Pandey (1969: 186) indicates that by about 500 BC there was a tendency towards lower marriage ages. Shastri (1988: 19) finds that the Vedic ideal of marriage was only partly upheld and notes that it now was 'enjoined as a duty of the parents to get their daughter married as soon in life as possible before her attaining the age of puberty'. Later marriage texts, therefore, had to undergo considerable adjustment to reflect the fact that the marriage might now only be consummated years after the performance of the rituals.[19] Altekar (1978: 56) states that from about AD 200, 'pre-puberty marriages became the order of the day' and that 'Smriti writers of the period AD 500–1000 began to encourage marriages *much before* the time of puberty' (ibid.: 57). As Mishra (1994: 18) confirms, it was in the later *gṛhyasūtra* literature that a lower ideal age of the bride becomes reflected in the term *nagnikā*, which basically means a small girl who has not started menstruating and is still walking around more or less naked.[20] Mishra (id.) therefore assumes that 'the traditional post-puberty marriage was gradually disappearing ... and a tendency of pre-puberty

[18] Bhandari (1989: 67) reports that among tribals, physical maturity is virtually a precondition for marriageability, for both men and women. He asserts that the Bhils have recently taken to child marriage in an attempt to imitate Hindus, although his own discussion indicates that objective financial concerns are more often than not the most influential causative factors. See also Nair (1978: 5) who states that tribals do not practise pre-puberty marriages, while Pujari and Kaushik (1994, I: 300) report that only a few tribes indulge in child marriages, and most groups see puberty as the critical boundary. African traditions also tend to assume that early marriage is bad for health and is declared a sin (Moore 1986: 107).

[19] Menski (1984) discusses these issues at length. The topic is too specialized for the present analysis.

[20] See also Jolly (1975: 120) on the possible meanings of *nagnikā*, who does not have to be a naked baby girl. Similarly see Mani Ram Sharma (1993: 60–1). Madhu Shastri (1990: 48) confirms that the term itself has given rise to many debates.

marriage was slowly emerging' and claims that 'all the s*mrtis* from *Manu* downwards [*sic*] stress the necessity of marrying girls before puberty' (id.).

In fact, even according to the traditional texts, this was no absolute rule,[21] and there are plenty of verses to the effect that a girl should be married when the time is right and the best possible bridegroom has been found, rather than at any pre-determined early time. Social practices were thus likely in flux, and there was no one method or agreed rule about the ideal age of marriage for all Hindus. Mishra (1994: 18) refers to two texts which clearly state that a girl may be kept unmarried for three years after puberty if there are difficulties in obtaining a suitable partner. However, the trend towards earlier marriages is clearly reflected in the *shastric* texts. Mishra (1994: 19) refers to *Manusmṛti* 9.94 which Bühler (1975: 344) translated as follows:

> A man, aged thirty years, shall marry a maiden of twelve who pleases him, or a man of twenty-four a girl eight years of age; if (the performance of) his duties would (otherwise) be impeded, (he must marry) sooner.

This seems to say that Hindu men, after having completed their Vedic education (and being as old as indicated in the above verse) should marry girls many years younger. The general rule is clearly that the groom should be older than the bride (Mishra 1994: 22). Doniger (1991: 208) calculates that he should be about three times the age of the girl. Other authors view the significant age gap between the spouses in the context of patriarchal arrangements that seek to keep women under male control. Sagade (1981: 28) asserts that, '[t]he idea of marriage was the transference of the father's dominion over her in favour of her husband and this transference should take place before she reached the age when she might question it'.

A few additional points on the marriageable age of men must suffice here. In the traditional system, the ideal was that a young Hindu male, before entering the stage of householder, should have studied the Vedic literature. This could take many years, even decades, so there was really no need to be concerned about the ages of men at marriage.[22] Later, however, as Vedic studies declined and fewer men needed to defer marriage for that reason, the marriage ages of men appear to have decreased as well. It goes too far, however, to claim that the blame for the early marriage ages of men should fall on the illiterate *Sudras*, since they were not allowed to study.[23] Sampath (1969: 30) suggested a marked reversal of Sanskritization, which remains doubtful:

[21] Notably, Shastri (1988: 20–1) takes the strict view of the *mīmāṃsā* experts that only the Vedas are authoritative, whereas 'the Smritis are only record of rules based on empirical generalisations, and of conventional practices ... current at the time of their composition, and are therefore not of equal authority with the Vedas'.

[22] Sampath (1969: 30) reports that for Hindu men, 'there has been a unanimous presupposition of adulthood'.

[23] Mishra (1994: 22) refers to an earlier study by R. S. Sharma in this respect. Bedwa and Ullah (1992: 65) rely on Sampath (1969: 30) as cited here.

> Since such a prescription was inapplicable to the Sudras ... probably they adopted the practice of marrying away their boys of nonage, a practice that was neither forbidden in the Sastras nor discouraged by the three higher castes. It is likely that this practice emerging from the Sudras influenced in bringing down the age limit of the boys belonging to the three higher castes also.

This does not square with the evidence that tribals tend to defer marriage until after puberty. It is amazing, further, how many authors treat the ancient shastric writers as lawmakers without any second thoughts. However, the 'laws' assumedly made by sages like Manu were by no means the only type of textual authority and other guidance that Hindus might choose from, and in that sense, too, they were not even 'law'. Mani Ram Sharma (1993: 57) rightly states that there is no fixed age prescribed anywhere in the texts regarding the marriage age of Hindu males. A few samples of texts demonstrate the plurality of Hindu perceptions of this subject. *Manusmṛti* 9.88–91 (tr. Bühler 1975: 343) suggest:

> 88. To a distinguished, handsome suitor (of) equal (caste) should (a father) give his daughter in accordance with the prescribed rule, though she have not attained (the proper age).
> 89. (But) the maiden, though marriageable, should rather stop in (the father's) house until death, than he should ever give her to a man destitute of good qualities.
> 90. Three years let a damsel wait, though she be marriageable; but after that time, let her choose for herself a bridegroom (of) equal (caste and rank).
> 91. If, being not given in marriage, she herself seeks a husband, she incurs no guilt, nor (does) he whom she weds.

Such statements, found in a text that is constantly cited as a prototype of obnoxious anti-women positions taken by traditional Hindus, call for a rather drastic reconceptualization of scholarly assumptions about ancient Hindu thinking and practice as regards marriage and sexual relations. Far from suggesting a law of compulsory early marriage, these *Manusmṛti* verses make it quite clear that early marriage may be preferable, but finding a suitable groom for one's daughter is a more important consideration than the age of the bride herself.

But the *smṛtis* also take a pessimistic view of chastity and female virtue and treat early marriage arrangements as prudent on that count (Jolly 1975: 119). In addition, Hindus were threatened with negative consequences, and even 'hell',[24] if they did not facilitate the early marriage of their daughter, since every lost fertile period of a woman was said to count as equivalent to the murder of

[24] Teja (1993: 16) asserts that '[t]he father of a girl married after puberty goes straight to hell. The father therefore passed sleepless nights when his daughter approached marriageable age', and also links this to spending on the marriage in order to attract a desirable match.

an embryo.[25] This argument comes out in many different ways. For example, Mishra (1994: 19) refers to *Manusmṛti* 9.93, which seems to indicate that a father who fails to arrange his daughter's marriage before she menstruates loses all authority over her.[26] Jolly (1975: 122–3) reports, correctly, that later texts favour child marriages and that 'the later the work the earlier is the age'.[27] Altekar (1978: 57), who appears to agree, shows that the age of ten years, even eight years, became a kind of social norm and links this to new ways of looking at Hindu marriage rituals, which now reflected the presence of child brides.

The observable decline of women's status in the late classical period of Hindu civilization has been linked to a number of issues; these do not concern us here in detail.[28] It is evident, though, that the average marriage age of girls declined in this kind of cultural climate. Pandey (1969: 189) even reports that '[t]he hold of child-marriage became so strong that the commentators, who flourished in the mediaeval and the Muslim periods of Indian history, tried to explain away ancient passages in favour of adult marriages'.

Mishra (1994: 21) reports that according to P. V. Kane, the leading authority on Hindu law in the early twentieth century, as a rule, Brahmin girls were to be married between 8–10 years during the sixth and seventh centuries. M.R. Sharma (1993: 61) suggests that after the sixth century, the marriage age of girls continued to decline and links this to the loss of women's status as a result of declaring women unsuitable for Vedic studies. Further, he claims that the early invasions of Greeks and others in north India made the local populations change their marriage customs in order to safeguard chastity (ibid.: 62), a claim which seems tenuous, but is often made.[29] M. Basu (2001: 2) asserts that under Muslim occupation, Hindu customs of child marriage were strengthened, since

[25] Mishra (1994: 20); Mitra (1965: 22). Similarly, Jolly (1975: 119) adduces material to state that a father who fails to get his daughter married in good time commits a great sin. See also ibid.: 121 on the issue of 'killing of an embryo'. Meyer (1952: 216–7) emphasizes the risks of extra-marital liaisons if marriages are arranged too late. Weinberger-Thomas (1999: 147) confirms the strength of such notions in traditional Rajasthani society today.

[26] This reflects the position, known from other Asian and African legal systems, too, that on puberty a child becomes an adult.

[27] This is also evident from the *Dāyabhāga* (Colebrooke 1984: 186).

[28] Sharma (1994: 20–1) refers to Altekar's argument that the presence of non-Aryan wives led to the general deterioration of women's status in ancient India. Nair (1978: 4) claims that '[t]he orthodox Hindus adopted child-marriage as a counter-measure to the sexual freedom that prevailed among the indigenous people of India'. Shastri (1988: 22) identifies neglect of female education as a major reason for the loss of Hindu women's status and lower marriage ages and calls for a revival of ancient education (ibid.: 25–7).

[29] What is most suspect in those kinds of arguments is that a marauding raider should make a distinction over whether a young woman he desires to carry away is already married or not. Shastri (1988: 53) argues interestingly that under British rule there was no longer any necessity to adhere to early marriage practices.

'[w]hen raids and warfare became a common occurrence, the fear of insecurity which affected unmarried young women was, perhaps, largely responsible for the emergence of the system of early marriage'.[30]

The important shift in Hindus' concerns from the earlier emphasis on progeny and procreation to chastity and control of women at a later stage is clearly reflected in the literature (see in detail Datta 1979). Now it was seen as more important to control the sexuality of women than to consider the quality of offspring. Interestingly, the ancient Hindu medical literature of the Ayurveda had advised that in order to produce strong children, a man should not be below twenty-five years, and a woman not below sixteen years.[31] Pandey (1969: 190) elaborates on this, asserting that despite conservative textual guidance, there could not have been one uniform pattern:

> Although these sacred regulations received ever wider acceptance and finally became essential for an orthodox marriage, marriages at an advanced age must have been common for centuries till about the middle ages. Local differences also must have been there, as they are at present. Otherwise it will be difficult to explain the disregard of this custom in the Sanskrit dramas, epics and the mediaeval Rajput custom of grown-up marriages.

Kapadia (1972: 140), who originally wrote in the 1950s, clearly linked the lowering of marriage ages to growing concerns over chastity:

> Once virginity was regarded as a batch of respectability, it came to be encouraged as a sign of the *êlite* and an index to high caste. Consequently marriage would be desired before any scope for suspicion regarding the virginity of a girl presented itself. This explains why girls who have attained puberty are objects of great anxiety and care in the eyes of their parents even today. This extolling of virginity is a conducive factor in the contemporary Brahmanic trend towards pre-puberty marriage, and insistence on it as a requisite qualification of an *êlite* marriage has accelerated pre-puberty marriages among the Hindus.

Despite much evidence of diversity, a picture of almost universal early marriage appears to have been created in the literature.[32] Mishra (1994: 21) sums up his discussion by claiming that 'the custom of child marriage evidently was

[30] Similarly, M. Basu (2001: 33–4) also claims that such apprehensions 'established polygamy and child-marriage firmly in Hindu society and, as a natural consequence, society was faced with numerous problems from the practice of child-marriage—child-mothers, a high mortality rate among child-wives and the children born to them, and the most distressed, the child-widows'. Kapadia (1972: 143) is less convinced that such foreign influences should be responsible and blames instead some tantric cults for fears about moral corruption.

[31] For details see Mitra (1965: 23) and Pandey (1969: 190).

[32] Derrett (1978a: 62) also reflects this, stating that 'the rule about pre-puberty marriage was adhered to strictly for all the twice-born castes, but was regarded as optional for Sudras'.

as universal in ancient times, as it is now in some interior parts of India'. The Arab traveller Albiruni in the eleventh century reported that Brahmins were forbidden to marry girls above the age of twelve (Mishra 1994: 21) and was astonished about the early marriage ages among Hindus (Jolly 1975: 127). By the time we reach nineteenth century Bengal, the strictness of the rules about early marriage is quite distinct, and Katherine Mayo could point to the interpretation by Rabindranath Tagore of early marriage as a means to control women and their sexuality.[33] M. Basu (2001: 4) argues that child marriage, 'known as *gouridan*, was a bane of Hindu society. Girls were often given in marriage at the age of ten or even below'. Thus, as Mayo (1927: 51) concluded in total disapproval, '[i]n other words, a woman must be married before she knows she is one'. Altekar (1978: 60–1) indicates a variety of social reasons for early marriages among Hindus, prominently the protection of female chastity and the desire to socialize the young bride into the new environment. Meyer (1952: 216) emphasized economic factors rather than traditional religious grounds for arranging early marriages. Because of heavy competition in the marriage market, the father must find his daughter a good husband, and he should do so in time.

Mishra (1994: 22–5) attempts to produce ten plausible reasons for why Hindu girls would be married at a very early age. There is a lot of sexual fantasizing in this account, but some of the reasons given make logical sense, in particular the argument that 'early marriage keeps girls out of mischief' (ibid.: 23) and the observation that the desire to acquire a most suitable groom might have led to competition and thus earlier marriages for girls. The fifth ground, that 'by marriage at pre-puberty age the girl goes to her husband's family, where her unframed mind and character [are] bent to adjust very nicely into her in-laws' house' (id.), makes sense not only from an anthropological point of view. The sixth ground is the potential economic usefulness of the child bride, especially among poor people. Ritual reasons are also advanced in abundance. Finally, the argument that Brahmin practices were copied by other sections of society through the process of Sanskritization has been raised (Mishra 1994: 24–5; Qureshi 1978: 56). As we saw, other authors have claimed that low-caste practices led to a decrease in marriage ages.[34]

Weinberger-Thomas (1999: 147) notes that child marriage used to be common in Rajasthan until the end of the nineteenth century and often led to early widowhood. She also explains that the traditional advice regarding the 'religious' duty to arrange a daughter's marriage before puberty led to the marriage of girls in their infancy. In her leading early study on the Hindu family and marriage, Aileen Ross (1961: 245–50) showed that the arrangements for early marriage among traditional Hindus depended on many factors, not just

33 Fruzetti (1990: 96) observes that 'a girl's menstruation is a sure sign of her readiness for marriage' and analyses the consequences for the young girl in her family context and in relation to early marriage in Bengal.

34 See on this Altekar (1978: 59–60); Sampath (1969: 30).

religion. Thus, '[e]ven when the age is supposedly set by custom, it varies according to convenience of the families concerned' (ibid.: 245), and it might be influenced by natural disasters and economic factors. Ross (1961: 246) argued further:

> But the main consideration which determined the girl's age of marriage until recently was that she was supposed to marry before she attained puberty. This custom was due to the high regard for the chastity of women ...
>
> Another reason for early marriages ... was that marriage meant that the bride shifted from the domination of her father to that of her husband. And it was easier if this transfer occurred before the girl arrived at the age at which she could question his authority. Pre-puberty marriage for girls began in the higher castes and was gradually taken over by the whole society. In this way the custom began with high prestige and continued until the latter half of the nineteenth century when changing circumstances altered attitudes to it.

Jolly (1975: 127) reported from the end of the nineteenth century that 'child marriage is the standing custom particularly in all the castes attached to Brahmanism', confirmed the existence of a variety of marriage rituals at different stages of the process of implementing a marriage, and also confirmed, at p. 128, that even the marriage of boys at a tender age was quite common by that time. He concluded (id.) that '[t]he rule of the Smṛtis, that a mature girl who remains unmarried in her father's house is a cause of shame to the whole family, still rules the modern ideas in a potent form, so that even the lowest castes are more and more running into child marriage'.

It is no surprise that reforms should have been advocated, since the evidence produced by Mayo (1927) in particular, does not point to a healthy society in which women are given their rightful place. Whether Hindus like to admit this or not, by the time of the colonial period, something had gone seriously wrong in their traditional idealistic systems of marriage arrangements. The stark and growing evidence of sex-related atrocities against very young Hindu girls in the name of tradition points to systematic abuse of vulnerable young women by men in a society and culture that should know better.

Colonial Efforts to Curtail Child Marriages

In a general climate of reluctance on the part of the colonial administrators to become involved in the reform of intimately social practices, the British were unlikely to seize on child marriage and its consequences as a chance to intervene in the lives of their subjects. Early marriages were common in England, too, and there was little explicit concern over the victimization of Hindu girls through early marriage, early consummation, and premature childbirth. It appears that the energy needed to push for legal intervention in this area was generated from within the Hindu elite rather than by colonial administrators. Since reforms in the field of child marriage were not driven by the state, but by vocal sections of the Indian population, they developed an explicitly reformist, semi-modernist flavour. Instead of seeking to abolish practices that were felt to be obnoxious and unacceptable, the focus fell on curtailing the worst excesses to alleviate the suffering of Indian women. The resulting legal regulations took the shape of 'restraint' rather than 'prohibition'.

The Emergence of Social Activism

Sharma (1994: 32) notes that by the eighteenth century, the position of Hindu women had deteriorated to a very low level and disquiet about this eventually sparked off social reform movements. Altekar (1978: 61) claims that through the introduction of Western ideas and civilization, the educated sections of society began to see the need for social change. Sharma (1994: 34) portrays child marriage as 'the root cause of physical and moral degradation of Hindu society'.[35] Pujari and Kaushik argue (1994, III: 282) that the prevalence of child marriage, often leading to early widowhood, was one of the major concerns of the early social reformers. This resulted in the enactment of the Hindu Widows' Remarriage Act, 1856.

M. Basu (2001: 39) asserts that the movement against child marriage started in Bengal around the mid-nineteenth century. Women's groups managed to raise the issue and get the press to accept that child marriages were not only bad for girls, but also for boys, because it would disrupt their education and spoil their future. Other writings are less Bengal-focused and it appears that a crucial pioneer in the field was actually a Parsi from Bombay, Behramji Malabari, who in 1884 published two famous notes that set off a national debate.[36]

The emergence of social activism is also indicated by the increasing preponderance of cases coming to court, which raised awareness of the extent and abuses of child marriage and propelled Hindu elite demands for ameliorative action by the colonial state. Kusum (1993b: 132–3) reports on *Queen Empress v Huree Mohun Mythee* (1891) 18 Cal 49, an early case under the IPC, which gave much fuel to reformist fervour and offered a suitable pretext for the colonial government to take further action (Engels 1983: 108). An adult Hindu male had caused the death of his very young wife due to internal injuries after the consummation of the marriage.[37] The husband sought to rely on the law, claiming that his wife was more than ten years old, but this was not accepted. It appears that he was convicted under the IPC to one year in prison, but was later exonerated by the court (Kapur and Cossman 1996: 49–50). Based on this case, in particular, modernist writers have argued that the existing law was inadequate in dealing with child marriages (ibid.: 50).

[35] Altekar (1978: 61) claims that '8 or 9 was the usual marriageable age of girls at the advent of the British rule'.

[36] Heimsath (1962: 492). See also Chandra (1998: 26–7).

[37] M. Basu (2001: 48) also reports this case and claims (incorrectly) that the girl was only nine years old. See also Sarkar (1993: 1873).

Similar other cases from Bengal came to light (M. Basu 2001: 50) and it became apparent that early consummation of marriage was a widespread practice especially in that part of India.[38] Kusum (1993b: 133) argues that an '[a]wareness was beginning to grow on the evil consequences of early marriage and early consummation'. M. Basu (2001: 39) reports that as the movement grew in strength between 1860 and 1880, and spread to other parts of India,[39] more reformist voices were heard. State intervention was seen as essential (Anagol-McGinn 1992: 107), but the measure was also perceived as evidence of a culture clash and as anti-Bengali, rather than just colonial intervention (Engels 1983: 124).

Colonial Intervention in Early Marriages

While articulate women wanted an end to child marriages (Augustine 1991: 169) and voices were heard from almost all parts of India, nothing much happened until 1891. Sarkar (1993: 1872) observes that '[t]hrough much of the 1880s we find a studied silence' and a 'rather defensive discourse' (id.). From a legal perspective, Kusum (1993b: 132) states that prior to the IPC of 1860, there was no legal regulation by the state of marital cohabitation at all, irrespective of the age of the spouses.[40] The IPC had fixed the legal minimum age for cohabitation at ten years and treated contravention of this provision as rape, with strict penalties up to transportation for life (Qureshi 1978: 56). The relevant sections read:

> 375. Rape
> A man is said to commit "rape" who, except in the case hereinafter excepted, has sexual intercourse with a woman under circumstances falling under any of the five following descriptions: -
> *First.* - Against her will.
> *Secondly.* - Without her consent.
> *Thirdly.* - With her consent, when her consent has been obtained by putting her in fear of death, or of hurt.
> *Fourthly.* - With her consent, when the man knows that he is not her husband, and that her consent is given because she believes that he is another man to whom she is or believes herself to be lawfully married.
> *Fifthly.* - With or without her consent, when she is under ten years of age.

[38] Mayo (1927) still makes shocking reading on this topic. On the ritual aspects of early consummation at puberty, and resulting religious arguments, see Engels (1983: 116).

[39] Augustine (1991: 118–28) reports on reform movements in Andhra Pradesh and Maharashtra. Anagol-McGinn (1992) concentrates specifically on the perspective of Maharashtrian women.

[40] Heimsath (1962: 497) suggests that this had been passed without much opposition in 1860. Sagade (1981: 29) argues that such legislation was hardly expected to be successful.

> *Explanation*. - Penetration is sufficient to constitute the sexual intercourse necessary to the offence of rape.
> *Exception*. - Sexual intercourse by a man with his own wife, the wife not being under ten years of age, is not rape.
>
> 376. Punishment for rape
> Whoever commits rape shall be punished with transportation for life, or with imprisonment of either description for a term which may extend to ten years, and shall also be liable to fine, unless the woman raped is his own wife, and is not under ten years of age, in which case he shall be punished with imprisonment of either description for a term which may extend to two years, or with fine, or with both.

Evidently, this was not a law that regulates the age of marriage, but it concentrates on the unacceptability of early sexual intercourse with a young, immature girl. The stipulated limit of ten years is quite low, reflecting the fact that there must have been real social problems in this area which required focused legal intervention, as well as British caution in tackling this issue.[41] Pujari and Kaushik (1994, III: 300) recount that the first relevant legislation controlling marriage age was what they call the 'Civil Marriage Act', in fact the Special Marriage Act of 1872, which laid down a minimum age of fourteen years.[42] However, because this Act was hardly used by anyone, the problem of child marriage was not affected by this legislation. Since the existing law was not seen as satisfactory, a view developed that young women needed to be better protected. This is precisely where the Parsi social reformer Behramji M. Malabari (1853–1912) became most active and spearheaded the discourse about further reforms.[43]

After much debate, a Bill was finally introduced in 1891 to raise the minimum age for marital cohabitation from ten to twelve years. This became the so-called Age of Consent Act, 1891 (Act X of 1891), which Banerjee (1984: 285) saw as 'a poor substitute for prohibition of early marriage of girls' and Sarkar (1993: 1875) depicts as 'an unbelievably messy and impractical measure'. Derrett (1978a: 81) merely comments that '[a]fter an incredible amount of foot-dragging, the Indian Criminal Law Amendment Act, 10 of 1891, was passed whereby, amending Section 375 of the Penal Code, 45 of 1860, it became rape to have intercourse with all girls under 12 years of age'.[44]

[41] The age limit was subtly raised further in various amendments discussed later.

[42] See also *Towards Equality* (1974: 111) from which this is evidently copied.

[43] Chandra (1998: 26–7) provides a brief summary of his life and work. Anagol-McGinn (1992) provides a good literature survey. The earlier studies of Engels (1983) and Heimsath (1962) are useful sources for the extent of the debates which, as Engels (1983: 114) highlights, was really 'the result of an encounter between two types of male domination and female suppression'.

[44] Rather than the more widely used label of Age of Consent Act, the title used by Derrett is the correct, official name of the Act. The text of the Act itself, as far as it

Bose and Jalal (1999: 109) note a 'markedly more conservative atmosphere' during the controversy over the Age of Consent Act, 1891. There was undoubtedly an element of local opposition to the new law, and resentment at British interference in Hindu social practices. In addition, as Banerjee (1984: 286) indicates, a good deal of emerging nationalist pride was mixed with an implied claim that self-controlled order could make a contribution to social reform:

> When Tilak took the lead in opposing the Age of Consent Bill he did not object to its provisions, but he repudiated the right of a foreign Government to interfere in the social affairs of the Hindus. Generally speaking, the Hindu society desired that reform should come from within instead of being imposed from without through laws. But the internal forces working for reform were very weak, and they accomplished little in practice even when their efforts were supported by legislation.

Kapur and Cossman (1996: 48) produce a good analysis of the controversy over the age of consent question between Malabari and Tilak, which they see as a conflict between social reformers and political revivalists-cum-nationalists. Malabari had dedicated himself to the regeneration of his society (Chandra 1998: 26) and embraced a social reform agenda based on personal sacrifice as an instrument of social action (id.). He pushed hard to initiate a public discussion about early marriages that might facilitate governmental intervention.

Balgangadhar Tilak saw state law as an ineffective means of changing behaviour and practices within the family. Although he agreed that marriages should not be consummated below the age of puberty, he did not believe that legislation was an appropriate or effective method of eliminating child marriages. He argued that 'reform which was imposed upon people through law could not be effective because it could neither ease family pressures upon the young couple, nor help the young couple to control its emotions; only education and knowledge could bring about this change' (cited in Kapur and Cossman 1996: 48). More significantly, within the colonial context, he saw law mainly as an instrument for legitimizing British rule. Since Tilak and other nationalist leaders of this period rejected the legitimacy of the colonial regime, they refused to engage in projects of law reform.

It becomes quite clear that the British lost their appetite for further family law reforms during the struggles over the 1891 Act. Kapur and Cossman (1996: 49) indicate that the debates of the Legislative Council over the 1891 Bill 'suggest that even the most avid supporters of the Bill recognized that the law was

---

is relevant here, simply provides that: 'In section 375 of the Indian Penal Code, in the clause marked *Fifthly* and in the *Exception*, the word 'twelve' shall be substituted for the word 'ten'.' The Indian Penal Code (Amendment) Act of 1925 (Act 29 of 1925) increased the relevant age to thirteen years. The Code of Criminal Procedure (Amendment) Act of 1949 (Act 42 of 1949) raised the relevant age of consent to intercourse in Section 375 IPC under 'Fifthly' to sixteen years, while the Exception in Section 375 now provided for fifteen years.

unlikely to bring about an end to the practice. Since the law was non-cognizable with respect to husbands and wives, there was some question as to whether it could ever be enforced'. While the potentially educative effect of this law was seen as a beneficial outcome, the colonial regime was simply not sufficiently interested to pursue further reformative measures for some time. Thus it was the case that, rather than the colonial government, the princely states of India, led by Mysore and Baroda, pioneered legislation against child marriage in India.[45] Mysore passed the Infant Marriages Prevention Regulation of 1894 to stop marriages of girls under the age of eight years and especially to prevent marriages of young girls with older men (M. Basu 2001: 51). The princely state of Baroda, despite some opposition, passed the (Baroda) Early Marriage Prevention Act of 1904, which outlawed all marriages of girls below nine years of age and demanded consent by a local tribunal for the marriage of a girl below twelve or a boy below sixteen years. In 1918, as reported by Kapadia (1972: 152), the princely State of Indore prescribed fourteen years for boys and twelve years for girls as minimum ages for marriage.

Under the Baroda Act, consent for an early marriage might be given if the family circumstances or emergency pleaded were deemed appropriate and sufficient grounds. Kapadia (1972: 152) reports that 695 applications were presented within the first year of operation of the Act, and 68 per cent of the applications were granted. Punishments were recorded, and were rather low. Of 718 offenders punished with a fine, 78 per cent were made to pay less than five rupees, and only 4 per cent paid more than ten rupees. The evident leniency in the implementation of this law is explained by Kapadia (1972: 153) in that 'the officers in charge could not enforce the law strictly, as they themselves did not always regard it as necessary and desirable. Customs die hard, and initial breaks with custom are always moderate and slow'.[46]

The Inefficient Restraint of Child Marriages

The Census of 1921 had shown that 104,850 girls below the age of five were married, while the total number of wives below the age of fifteen years was given as 8,451,744 (M. Basu 2001: 52). This led some social reformers to ask the British for further reforms, but the characteristic response was that suggestions

[45] For a fairly detailed discussion of this period see Kapadia (1972: 151–3). Shastri (1988), originally written in 1905, offers a detailed reflection of thinking in Mysore learned circles at the time. Sagade (1981: 29) refers to a few other small states which followed the reformative efforts of Baroda, namely Kota and Rajkot in 1927, and Mandi in 1928.

[46] Kapadia (1972: 155) reports that Baroda amended its Act in 1929 and introduced punishments for marriages below the minimum ages of sixteen and twelve years, respectively, for boys and girls, while making any marriage below the age of eight years void. In 1932, the minimum ages were raised to 18 and 14, respectively, i.e. the law was brought in line with that of British India at the time. Indore did the same in 1933.

for reform should come from private individuals rather than the government, thus reflecting continuing British reluctance to become involved in matters of Hindu family law. Various initiatives were promoted, but came to nothing until Dr Hari Singh Gour introduced a Bill in 1924 to further amend Section 375 of the IPC to increase the minimum age for cohabitation to fourteen years. Not surprisingly, this Bill also failed because of enormous public opposition, but the age of consent was raised to thirteen years in 1925.[47]

After much further debate, an Age of Consent Committee was set up in 1927, and Rai Sahib Haribilas Sarda introduced the Child Marriage Restraint Bill to restrain the solemnization of child marriages among Hindus, declaring such marriages as invalid if the girl was below twelve or the boy below fifteen years. It was proposed to penalize men over eighteen marrying girls below fourteen years (Kusum 1993b: 134), as well as parents, priests and guardians. Kusum (id.) reports that it was realised at this time that it would be beneficial to prevent early marriages altogether, rather than focusing solely on the age of consummation after marriage, as had been done earlier. During the debates it was decided that the only effective method to stop early marriages would be to prohibit them, and to impose a penalty in cases of contravention of prescribed age limits. Kapadia (1972: 156) further elucidates that it came to be seen as desirable that 'instead of raising the age of consent, age at marriage should be legally fixed. The Child Marriage Restraint Act was therefore a step in the right direction'.

There was fierce opposition, however, on the ground that legal intervention by a foreign power in the social and religious affairs of Hindus was unacceptable. Nevertheless, the Committee insisted on reforms, applying civilizational arguments, and in particular its concern about early motherhood, a widespread problem with enormously negative consequences for the social and physical well-being of women. The upshot of the reformist arguments was that 'early marriage was a great evil which resulted in many women becoming widows and even hindered women's education' (M. Basu 2001: 57). As Kusum (1993b: 135) claims, the main focus was on preventing early maternity, while Sagade (1981: 28) states that child widows were perceived as the main problem. It appears that the views of Katherine Mayo (1927) exerted some influence in this context. She had asserted that all of India's woes 'could be blamed on the effects of widespread child marriage' (cited in Bumiller 1991: 21). Indeed, Mayo (1927: 39) was fiercely critical of the reluctance of the government to do more to eradicate child marriages, but also saw the difficulties of implementing social legislation:

> A study of the attitude of the Government of India as to the subject of child-marriage shows that, while steadily exercising persuasive pressure towards progress and change, it has been dominated, always, by two general

[47] See note 44 above. *Towards Equality* (1974: 111) indicates that this became the forerunner of the CMRA of 1929.

> principles—the first, to avoid as far as possible interference in matters concerning the religion of the governed; the second, never to sanction a law that cannot be enforced. To run counter to the Indian's tenets as to religious duties, religious prohibitions and god-given rights has ever meant the eclipse of Indian reason in madness, riot and blood. And to enforce a law whose keeping or breaking must be a matter of domestic secrecy is, in such a country as India at least, impossible.
>
> Indian and English authorities unite in the conviction that no law raising the marriage age of girls would be to-day effectively accepted by the Hindu peoples. The utmost to be hoped, in the present state of public mentality, is, so these experienced men hold, a raising of the age of consent within the marriage bonds.

Altekar (1978: 62) interestingly suggested that the minimum ages laid down by the 1929 Act already 'followed the actual practice of the advanced middle classes of society' at the time and that the economic impact of the Second World War soon led to further rises in marriage ages.[48] M. Basu (2001: 53–9) provides a detailed account of the debates,[49] highlighting that the Bill was eventually amended to cover all communities in India and not just Hindus, and also indicates that the original plan of the reformers was to outlaw child marriages completely. However, that had to be changed and provision was merely made for penalizing the offence, avoiding and bypassing the question of validity.[50] The CMRA 1929 was thus introduced, but is completely silent on the question of legal validity of marriages that violate the Act. Derrett (1978a: 81) reports:

> In spite of great pusillanimity the British did find it possible, further, to pass the so-called Sarda Act (1929), whereby after prolonged agitation, marked

[48] Altekar (1978: 63) made the interesting remark that '[i]n accepting and following the theory of post-puberty marriages Hindu society is merely returning to the old custom of the Vedic and Epic times. It need not therefore be regarded as anti-religious at all'.

[49] Basu (2001: 59) emphasizes that this initiative against early marriage was entirely Indian in origin. Indeed, Britain was put under pressure to introduce corresponding reforms in English law, also in 1929, when the minimum age of sixteen years for both parties was promulgated in England. Poulter (1986: 18) claimed that the British reform efforts were designed to assist the Indians in raising the age of marriage.

[50] Confusingly, M. Basu (2001: 59) criticizes as the most glaring defect of the 1929 Act that it did not make child marriage a cognizable offence, when in fact it did, but only during the first year after the marriage, as Diwan (1983: 58, cited later) correctly stated. The one-year rule clearly takes account of the principle of *factum valet*, according to which something that is not supposed to be done may nevertheless be legally valid (see in detail Derrett 1958). Subba Rao (1994: 115) emphasizes that the post-1978 regulation of child marriages is 'a special case where the doctrine of *factum valet* is recognised and the validity of the marriage is left unaffected' and refers to the leading case of *Pinninti Venkataramana v State* AIR 1977 AP 43 FB, which firmly held child marriages to be valid.

> by emotional evocation of cases of girls killed or maimed by premature forced intercourse with their husbands, the age at which a woman could lawfully be *married* was raised to 14. This certainly flew in the face of Manu, whose recommendation of marriage at 8 was, and in some places is, observed by vast numbers of people, particularly in poorer strata. Alas, it is far from certain how far the better-off public at large has taken this reform to itself.

The Act itself clearly says that it is designed 'to restrain the solemnisation of child marriages'. It defines 'child' in Section 2 as a male under eighteen years of age and a female under fourteen. The only other major provisions of the Act provide punishments. These make a distinction between a groom not older than twenty-one years and all other persons, who might be punished for being party to or involved in a child marriage. It is specifically provided in Section 3 of the CMRA that '[w]hoever, being a male above eighteen years of age and below twenty-one, contracts a child marriage shall be punishable with fine which may extend to one thousand rupees'. This recognizes that a young male may not have been in control of the timing of his marriage and the choice of an under-age spouse. However, for older males, the penalties are stiffer, as laid down in Section 4. They are punishable 'with simple imprisonment which may extend to one month, or with fine which may extend to one thousand rupees, or with both'.

In Sections 5 and 6 of the Act, persons who solemnized a child marriage and the parents and guardians of child spouses are made punishable 'with simple imprisonment which may extend to one month, or with fine which may extend to one thousand rupees, or with both'. In every case, it is provided in Section 6 that 'no woman shall be punishable with imprisonment'. The remaining sections of the CMRA in its original form are of a procedural nature and concern mostly the hotly debated question of cognizance of the offence, on which the literature is full of contradictory, confusing, and sometimes factually incorrect statements. The offence itself appears to have been always cognizable in some form, but this was limited in practice. For example, Section 9 of the Act provided that '[n]o Court shall take cognizance of any offence under this Act after the expiry of one year from the date on which the offence is alleged to have been committed'. This provision, coupled with the total silence of the Act over the question of legal validity of a child marriage, suggests that the legislative intent was to let society decide about legal validity of marriages and, after the passage of one year, to accept the fait accompli of a child marriage.

Much attention has also been given by lawyers and commentators to the question of injunctions under the Act. The original CMRA made no provision for this, but the Child Marriage Restraint (Second Amendment) Act of 1938 introduced a new Section 12:

> 12. Power to issue injunction prohibiting marriage in contravention of this Act. –

(1) Notwithstanding anything to the contrary contained in this Act, the Court may, if satisfied from information laid before it through a complaint or otherwise that a child marriage in contravention of this Act has been arranged or is about to be solemnised, issue an injunction against any of the persons mentioned in sections 3, 4, 5 and 6 of this Act prohibiting such marriage.
(2) No injunction under sub-section (1) shall be issued against any person unless the Court has previously given notice to such person, and has afforded him an opportunity to show cause against the issue of the injunction.
(3) The Court may either on its own motion or on the application of any person aggrieved rescind or alter any order made under sub-section (1).
(4) Where such an application is received, the Court shall afford the applicant an early opportunity of appearing before it either in person or by pleader; and if the Court rejects the application wholly or in part, it shall record in writing its reasons for so doing.
(5) Whoever knowing that an injunction has been issued against him under sub-section (1) of this section disobeys such injunction shall be punished with imprisonment of either description for a term which may extend to three months, or with fine which may extend to one thousand rupees, or with both:

Provided that no woman shall be punishable with imprisonment.

This provision clearly shows that civil courts have, in the interest of the child, the authority to issue an injunction to prohibit a child marriage from being performed. Such an injunction may be issued if the court is satisfied, from information laid before it, through a complaint or otherwise, that a child marriage has been arranged or is about to be solemnized. The difficulty in practice appears to have been not so much that the offence was not fully cognizable, but that hardly anyone would want to complain about a child marriage or take action against it. Complaints about the alleged non-cognizance of the offence cannot be quite correct, therefore.[51] The underlying reason for the ineffectiveness of the Act is clearly that those who wish to solemnize child marriages will simply continue to do so, and no court may ever become involved because society, and not state law, continues to determine the rules in this field.

Not surprisingly, scholarly opinion on this Act has not been positive, but many commentators tend to confuse details in their eagerness to be critical. For example, Qureshi (1978: 57) is completely wrong on the punishment for the child spouses and M. Basu (2001: 59) misleadingly states that once a child marriage was performed, 'it was validated after the payment of a nominal fine', complaining that 'the Act lacked teeth and failed to serve its purpose' (id.). But what was its purpose? It is totally wrong to suggest that only payment of a fine would validate a child marriage, for such a marriage was normally valid the

[51] Pujari and Kaushik (1994, III: 301), relying on *Towards Equality* (1974: 113) claim that as a non-cognizable offence, it is not very effective legal regulation and copy the recommendations about making the offence cognizable and appointing special officers.

moment it was completed under the respective personal law, which continues to provide the guiding principles.

Diwan (1983: 57) explains correctly that the Act 'is a penal legislation and provides for punishment for the violation of the provisions of the Act'. Diwan (1983: 58) rightly points out that the offences under the Act are cognizable, also for the purposes of investigation. However, no cognizance of the offence can be taken after the expiry of one year from the date on which the marriage was solemnized, as shown above. Sharma (1994: 34) simply claims that the Act proved ineffective and the government lacked adequate means to enforce it. Tiwari (1991: 49–50) goes into a little more detail in his critique of the CMRA, arguing that merely passing an Act and then watching it being violated simply perpetuates the existing situation. Thus, '[t]he continuance of child marriages specially in rural areas on mass scale with pomp and show, without any fear of being punished under law, is nothing but a teasing illusion, a mockery of [the] present legal system' (ibid.: 50). Pujari and Kaushik (1994, III: 300), again copying from *Towards Equality* (1974: 112), show a slightly better understanding of the tenuous link between law and practice:

> Perhaps the realisation that legislation, while one of the major instruments of social change, is not sufficient by itself to fight against deep rooted prejudices and traditional practice made the legislators compromise by leaving the validity of child marriage untouched but making such practice a penal offence.

The reformers had obviously managed to alert the Indian public to the legal reform in 1929, since many thousands of child marriages were solemnized in the period between the passing of the Act and its coming into force to beat the perceived ban.[52] But beyond this, there was clearly little direct social impact. M. Basu (2001: 59) complains, in view of the 1931 Census, that the 1929 Act had made virtually no difference, as though such an Act would be expected to have instantaneous effects, anyway. Indeed, the statistics provided by Basu (2001: 60) confirm that the problems of child marriages and child widows at first got worse rather than better. Whether this was a result of the legislation or due to other factors, it became an accepted fact that the issue itself was put on the backburner during the 1930s and 1940s. Altekar (1978: 62) reported that child marriages continued to be practised in the lower sections of the community. He also provided a glimpse of census figures to the effect that about 39 per cent of girls were married before the age of ten in 1921, while this figure went down to 17 per cent of girls below the age of fourteen years in the 1941 Census and to 14 per cent of the same group in the 1951 Census. This is a very significant reduction indeed, more than expected by the reformers, but it would not be possible to claim that this massive social change occurred simply because of the CMRA.

[52] Altekar (1978: 62) confirms that the initial reaction among some orthodox Hindus was to break the law consciously and openly.

Thomas (2000: 26) characterizes child marriage as '[p]erhaps the most obnoxious feature of our marriage code' and refers to the cruel atrocities that may be committed on child brides by mature men who should know better. Thomas (2000: 27) laments that this Act 'has not brought about any appreciable change in the morality of the people in British India'. Mishra (1994: 25) reports that P.V. Kane had observed that the age of marriage in India was rising rapidly due to economic changes, increased literacy, and the impact of the CMRA of 1929. Thus, around the end of the colonial period, despite signs of improvement in this socio-legal field, neither had the problems been brought under control in society itself, nor had the colonial state been as strict as might be in abolishing, rather than merely restraining, practices of child marriage. Whatever modernist intervention there had been so far, it clearly did not go far enough, failing to protect women effectively.

Child Marriage in Independent India

We saw in previous chapters that the post-independence Indian leadership had more pressing matters to deal with than child marriages. Reformist pressure was maintained to some extent during the early independence period and eventually brought some results. Derrett (1978a: 19) noted that the battle against child marriage was by no means won by 1947 and that the problem persisted. Kapadia (1972: 164–6), writing in the 1950s, observed changing social practices and attitudes and argued forcefully in favour of raising the minimum age for women at least to sixteen, if not eighteen years. Derrett (1970: 305) claims that India cannot yet dispense with child marriages, which are nominally prohibited by law, but in practice prosecutions seldom follow as participants escape punishment by an over-strict interpretation of the CMRA. Derrett (id.) felt that 'so many personalities involved were themselves participants in child marriages (or are the fruit [*sic*] of them) that in many areas of India the statute is virtually a dead letter'. Derrett (1970: 305–6) also highlights that the relevant law was somewhat dishonest:

> The HMA makes it appear that there is a minimum age for marriage (as there most certainly is under the Special Marriage Act), but this is hypocrisy: a child marriage, in which one or both spouses are below the age prescribed ... is perfectly valid and cannot be annulled (for want of consent) during the years before the bride reaches majority. Since consummation, actually or supposedly, takes place before majority a change in the law allowing *girls* to renounce their marriage at majority or even at puberty would be of little value, since it would place a premium on a girl's refusing to consummate marriage with her husband, which is at present regarded in some quarters as a sign of insanity. The present dynastic nature of marriage makes it impossible now to render such marriages void or voidable, but the hypothetical Code of Family Law could quite properly refuse registration of marriages without proof of the spouses having attained the statutory age, and could refuse all matrimonial relief to parties to unregistered marriages.

This quote confirms that Derrett, too, assumed that modernist reforms could eventually curtail child marriages. It was thus inevitable that further debate should ensue. Bedwa and Ullah (1992: 76) voice a widely shared view when they complain about the fact that child marriages remain legally valid and see this as 'a sad commentary on the state of social legislation in India'.

New Statutory Reforms

M. Basu (2001: 61) indicates that the passing of the CMRA in 1929 had not satisfied the movement against early marriages. Following independence, new proposals were made, essentially seeking to raise the minimum ages further and to tighten up the law. Three bills were moved in April 1949, designed to amend the 1929 Act by raising the marriageable age of boys to twenty-one years and that of girls to fifteen. A second reform measure sought to prevent girls below the age of eigthteen years being married to men over the age of 45, and the third amendment related to cognizability. Interestingly, M. Basu (2001: 62) argues against making the offences under the Act cognizable as this would permit police officers to exploit people.[53]

The Child Marriage Restraint (Amendment) Act, 1949 was introduced on 15 July 1949. It is a very short, but important Act, which basically raises the minimum female marriage age from fourteen to fifteen years. This Act also adds a prison sentence of up to fifteen days to the monetary fine of up to Rs 1,000 for a male below twenty-one years who marries a child bride. Significantly, through deleting Section 7 of the original 1929 Act, this amending Act took away a clause that might have avoided the imprisonment of impoverished young men who could not pay such fines, indicating a will on the part of the legislator to toughen up the legal regime, even for young men. Further, this Act increased the maximum prison term for males over twenty-one years marrying a child bride, those who solemnized the child marriage, or the parents or guardians, from one month to three months. In addition, the amendment removed the ceiling of Rs 1,000 on the monetary fine and allowed the courts discretion to impose any fine they deemed fit—potentially a further toughening measure. Finally, it was made easier for the courts to receive complaints about child marriages and to take cognizance.

These amendments signify the intention of the lawmakers to deal more strictly with those who violate the 1929 Act, but this was clearly still a weak compromise solution (M. Basu 2001: 62), which one could not see as a tough criminal law approach. Kusum (1993b: 136) notes that when the minimum age under the CMRA was raised to fifteen years in 1949, Section 375 of the IPC was

[53] Indeed, a student of mine who conducted fieldwork in Baroda in 1985, Ms Priti Patel, reported precisely this—but only for certain scheduled castes, who had clearly experienced harassment at the hands of the police, and as a result knew much more than any other community about the relevant law against early marriages and the legal minimum ages.

also amended to fifteen years. Thus, a man may be legally married to a woman below the age of eighteen years, but it is only an offence for him to cohabit with her if she is under fifteen. This, again, shows legislative recognition of the limits of state law. Kusum (1993b: 136), concerned about legal protection of women against rape in various forms, found that this law 'acquiesces in non-age marriages in several ways'. Sampath (1969: 29) noted that child marriage is 'the price Indian society has to pay for the preservation of premarital chastity'.

When the major Hindu law reforms were being debated during the 1950s, there was no longer any discernible drive to completely abolish child marriages through legal prohibition. It seems to have been understood by the reformers that Hindu society would continue to operate its own rules in addition to those of the new official Hindu law, if not in opposition to it. The scheme of the HMA of 1955 in relation to child marriages is therefore deceptively simple and can easily mislead Western observers into assuming that child marriages were totally abolished. The opposite is true, as can be ascertained from Section 5 HMA, which specifies the conditions for a Hindu marriage and provides:

> 5. Conditions for a Hindu marriage. -
> A marriage may be solemnized between any two Hindus, if the following conditions are fulfilled, namely: -
> ...
> (iii) the bridegroom has completed the age of eighteen years and the bride the age of fifteen years at the time of the marriage;

Further, under Section 18 of the HMA, punishments are provided for violation of this minimum age requirement:

> 18. Punishment for contravention of other conditions for a Hindu marriage.-
> Every person who procures a marriage of himself or herself to be solemnized under this Act in contravention of the conditions specified in clauses (iii), (iv), (v) and (vi) of section 5 shall be punishable –
> (a) in the case of a contravention of the condition specified in clause (iii) of section 5, with simple imprisonment which may extend to fifteen days, or with fine which may extend to one thousand rupees, or with both;

Notably, the HMA is otherwise silent about the question of legal validity, while it is evident from a perusal of Section 11 HMA concerning void marriages that a child marriage is not listed, and thus is not explicitly declared void. This is mildly criticized in *Towards Equality* (1974: 112), as this Act was passed in the post-independence era, and yet did not say anything about the validity of child marriages, with the manifest result that they have been held to be valid. Kusum (2000: 233) observes in this context that 'Parliament seems to have deliberately excluded non-age marriages from the purview of void marriages'. Diwan (1979: 99) critically comments on the lack of enforcement of the prohibition on child marriages:

> It seems ... Parliament has attempted to prevent child-marriages, though not to prohibit them. Under the Special Marriage Act, 1954 such marriages

> are void. The reason is that [the] Special Marriage Act is meant for literate, educated and advanced people who alone, ordinarily, contract civil marriages ... the Hindu Marriage Act affects great masses of illiterate, backward and tradition-ridden people .... An attempt to prohibit such marriages would have failed and we could have been faced with 80 to 90% void marriages in the countryside. With the advance in education the child marriages are already receding. In cities and towns such marriages are rare.

Diwan (1979: 99) also notes that, apart from education, the child marriage restraint law aims to prevent a child marriage from being solemnized by obtaining an injunction from the court.[54]

However, even if such an injunction was issued, the child marriage would still be valid. This leads inevitably to the conclusion that the state law itself has quietly given in to social practice and virtually condones violations of its provisions. It is therefore more than a little misleading when Diwan (1983: 56) claims that 'in India no male can marry below the age of 21 years and no female below the age of eighteen years. Marriage below the specified ages lead [*sic*] to penal consequences'. But the author also recognizes that 'under the personal law in no Indian community is a child marriage void' (ibid.: 57), for 'the Act does not affect the validity of child marriages, which is governed by the personal law of the parties to marriage' (id.). Diwan (1983: 215) also confirms that despite the CMRA, child marriages continue to be performed among Hindus as well as Muslims and such marriages are neither void nor voidable under Hindu law.

Saxena (1994: 142) argues that the penalties for non-observance of the CMRA are too mild,[55] while Sagade (1981: 35) wrote earlier that she did not believe that punishments under this Act are effective. Gujarat tried to improve on the existing legislation by passing the Child Marriage (Gujarat Amendment) Act of 1963, which was widely seen as a pioneering piece of legislation. It sought to overcome the tricky hurdle of cognizance by appointing a special group of social workers as child marriage prevention officers. The Gujarat Amendment of 1963 inserted a new Section 7 into the 1929 Act and made the offences under the CMRA explicitly cognizable. It then added a new Section 13 to the CMRA, providing for the appointment of child marriage prevention officers. Singh (1989: 65) lauds these efforts; similar comments are found in *Towards Equality* (1974: 113), noting large-scale violations of the CMRA and asking for the offence to be made cognizable nationwide, as well as special officers to be appointed to deal with such cases.

[54] The same comment is found in Diwan (1982, reprint of fifth ed.), (1988, seventh ed.) and in the ninth edition of 1993.

[55] Saxena (1994: 144–5) points to several interesting cases in which the costs for the performance of a child marriage were held not to come under expenses for legal necessity in a joint family.

On paper, the Gujarat reforms looked good, but in social reality, as I know from first-hand sources,[56] the picture was less bright.[57] The lack of effective implementation, as well as the strength of local social norms, were outlined and confirmed in a position paper prepared for me in 1985 by Mr N.V. Dave, a former child marriage prevention officer from Baroda. He stated that the CMRA used to be implemented by the police department, which 'considers this act of child marriage as a minor offence and did not take much cognizance of it'. Mr Dave also complained that the police completely neglected the educational and reformatory aspects of the Act, hence the Gujarat government appointed child marriage prevention officers like him in each district from 1956 onwards. However, as noted by Mr Dave, 'the procedure of preventing child marriage is very clumsy'. Since the child marriage prevention officer or police officer are not empowered to prevent child marriages, they can only act as a deterrent. Punishments were low, around Rs 50 per person, and the whole Act was a failure:

> Though provision for punishment has been made in the Act, the Court usually fines nominally, say Rs. 25/- to Rs. 50/- each. Hence, that comes to Rs. 125/- to Rs. 250/- as total fine. Both the parties, though poorest people, spend Rs. 2000/- to Rs. 5000/- after performance of [the] marriage. They don't mind paying this little fine, and consider it to be additional expenses of the marriage. Hence filing a case in the court does not result in awakening the community.

While this kind of evidence does not claim that payment of a fine validates the marriage, Dave and his colleagues were quite clear about the fact that a Hindu marriage, once solemnized, could not be undone by officials of the state or the law itself. Since they observed even their educative efforts being undermined, they did not find much reason to be optimistic about the role of the law. Still, by the time I interviewed these officers, social patterns had significantly changed.

[56] My father-in-law also worked as a child marriage prevention officer in Gujarat during the 1960s, and I met some of his former colleagues (including Mr Dave) during the mid-1980s, when they were retired old men. They did not have happy memories, since when they tried to do their job properly, they would often be threatened or even beaten up by villagers. A motorbike became not just a convenient conveyance in the rural hinterland, but a life-saving device if one had to beat a hasty retreat. The readiness of villagers to defend their decisions about child marriages is confirmed by Rai and Badhwar (1986: 38), who write that '[s]trangers and people who look like bureaucrats who might file a report are spotted easily by villagers and often menacingly herded out'.

[57] Further practical problems are indicated by the Child Marriage Restraint (Gujarat Amendment) Act, 1973 (Gujarat Act No. 4 of 1973), which introduces two further subsections after Section 13 of the 1929 Act as applicable in Gujarat. Section 13A provides that a child marriage prevention officer appointed under Section 13 of the Act shall be deemed to be a public servant within the meaning of Section 21 of the IPC, which defines 'public servant'. Notably, the new section 13B protects child marriage prevention officers against legal proceedings.

Ms Priti Patel, who conducted fieldwork in Baroda at the same time, found not a single case of child marriage among the middle classes of that city during the period 1980–85, while there was evidence of some early marriages in urban slum pockets and rural areas.

Mr Dave also produced figures concerning the disposal of child marriage cases from Baroda District for the years 1982–83, 1983–84 and 1984–85. These indicate yearly case file totals of ninety-one, 153 and ninety-seven respectively. While twenty-three, fifty-one and fifty-eight inquiries respectively were conducted in those three years by a child marriage prevention officer, seventy-six, 102 and thirty-nine inquiries respectively were conducted by the concerned police authorities. Under disposal, Mr Dave listed thirteen, eight and five cases of prevention of child marriage respectively for those three years. A total of twelve, seventeen and nine cases were admitted in courts and were subject to sentence and fine. There were no cases in which either only a fine or only a sentence was given, and eighty-five cases during 1983–84 resulted in acquittal. In addition, twenty-seven cases in 1982–83 and twenty-five cases in 1984–85 resulted in a finding that there was no evidence of child marriage and the parties were above the minimum age. In eighteen cases in 1982–83 and twenty-one cases in 1984–85, the allegations about child marriage were found to be untrue, and twenty-nine cases were disposed of in other ways during 1982–83. In 1985, forty-three cases were pending from the 1983–84 case files, and fifty-four cases from the 1984–85 files.

This brief glimpse of the actual operation of the child marriage restraint law 'on the ground', even where dedicated and experienced social work officers were handling such cases, confirms that the state law and its personnel lacked the will and the resources to implement a total ban on child marriages. In social reality, some child marriages continued to be solemnized, and only more or less tokenistic actions were taken by the enforcement agencies.

Perceptions of Social Change

At the same time, as indicated, there is much evidence that the average marriage ages have slowly been going up. A somewhat dated specialist study (Agarwala 1962: 4–5) noted that '[t]he prevalent impression in India these days is that the age at marriage is rising, but a reliable quantitative measure of the suspected trend in published form is lacking because of the non-existence of a system of marriage registration in India'. M. Basu (2001: 62–3) observes that child marriage have gradually begun to go out of fashion:

> In fact, it began to disappear quickly during the forties and fifties, and the age of marriage of girls rose far beyond the expectations of legislators and reformers. The credit for the reforms, however, was not due to social or educational progress, but mainly due to the fact that society at that time was adversely affected by political and socio-economic changes .... Economically hard hit middle classes were forced to defer the marriages of their daughters because of their inability to meet the heavy expenses of weddings.

Mitter (1992: 19) discerns new trends that reflect significant shifts in market values, with teenage marriage on the wane. She claims that 'prospective brides are twenty-three, twenty-five, even thirty. Top-value girls are graduates, not totally unfledged nestlings. But more, along with looks and domestic virtues, the proferred or desired girl holds a job. She is a teacher'. There are numerous indications that today the earning capacity of a marriageable woman has become a major consideration in marriage negotiations (e.g. S. Basu 2001: 102).

Based on her extended fieldwork in Rajasthan, Weinberger-Thomas (1999: 147) reports that child marriage remains 'a custom which has not entirely disappeared'. This is confirmed by other authors with fieldwork experience and detailed local knowledge. Bumiller (1991: 263) notes the limits of legislation, saying that '[a]lthough the legal marriage age for girls in India is eighteen, in rural areas this was almost completely ignored, and the government estimated that three million out of the four million marriages in the country each year involved an underage bride'. While such estimates appear on the high side, there can be no doubt that the practice itself has not disappeared. Minattur (1980: 167) observed that '[c]ertain conservative sections of the community regard child marriage as a good, if not a proper, thing and would prefer to pay a fine rather than keep their infant sons and daughters unmarried'.[58]

Altekar (1978: 63) reported that the main reason for higher marriage ages was female education. Sinha (1993: 74) also identifies significant recent changes in the marriage patterns as prominently related to education. Parental aspirations for their offspring have risen so high during the past two or three decades that most parents do not now marry their sons and daughters at an early age. Several village studies have shown that rural Indians also prefer higher marriage ages.[59] The average Indian is not as backward as some writers from their urban desk perspective would suggest and is aware that early marriage is bad for the woman's health.[60] Sinha (1993: 76) finds that since boys would now often marry around thirty and above, the ages of girls have also gone up to about twenty-five and even up to thirty. This is obviously a middle-class picture, as confirmed by Priti Patel in her unpublished field research in Baroda city in 1985, when she did not find a single recent case of child marriage among the middle classes. Verma (1993: 18) reports that the 1981 Census for the first time showed an average higher age at marriage than the legal minimum of eighteen years, it was 18.3 years as opposed to 17.2 years in 1971.

Sinha (1993: 76–7) notes from his own fieldwork that the age of marriage for girls has again been coming down slightly during the past few years, claiming

[58] Minattur's experience relates mainly to Kerala. The case of *Gangadharan v Rajendran* 1986 KLT 543 involved a bureaucrat from Kerala, whose socially unacceptable marriage arrangements were brought to the notice of the courts by political opponents.

[59] Chekki (1968) is excellent on this. For rural Bihar see Chatterjee et al. (1971: 68–9).

[60] For some evidence see ibid.: 67–8.

that one of the main reasons for this lies in the growing emphasis on emotional stability of the girl. Since it is commonly believed that emotional adjustment is possible before the girl attains maturity, and that adjustments before twenty-five are easier, parents try to marry their daughter before she crosses that age. But that is then no longer an issue of child marriage, but a subject within the fierce current debates about domestic violence. The key issue is not any more the gruesome death of little girls as a result of premature 'marital' intercourse that might virtually rip them apart, but the equally pernicious evidence of tens of thousands of women being killed or maimed in India every year in circumstances often linked to the 'dowry' problem (Menski 1998b).

Ross (1961: 246) still noted that despite the CMRA, many child marriages took place all over India, but also confirmed a general upward trend (ibid.: 248). Analysing the problem of early marriage within the context of the Hindu family, Ross (1961: 246) highlighted some of the continuing arguments working in favour of arranging early marriages for girls:

> Child marriage meant that the bride learned to fit into the ways of the new household and carry on its traditions to a much greater extent than girls who marry at a later age, for the child bride changed her environment before she had become too strongly attached to her parents and family, and before she was too deeply immersed in family customs to be able to change to those of the new home. As she was in a subordinate position to her husband and in-laws she had to fit into the new pattern with no chance of asserting her own individuality.

Conversely, as Ross (1961: 151) noted, there is change in the mother-daughter relationship as daughters stay at home longer than they used to:

> The mother-daughter relationship has probably changed more markedly than any other family relationship since child marriage has been abandoned. The daughter no longer leaves home when a child, but remains close to her mother until a young woman, and in this longer interval they develop common interests and comradeship. This is bound to strengthen the relationship between them.

Derrett (1968b: 366–7) commented on the process of taking in a child bride to the effect that '"[r]espectable" classes are often unfeeling towards young brides, once the formal present-giving is over. They can afford to be. They take them in marriage, as young as possible, in order to break them in to the family's ways'. While there was no longer any strongly voiced concern over the early consummation of Hindu child marriages during the 1950s, such psychological reasoning would make sense to families that depend on the new daughter-in-law's cooperation for their own welfare. Experience must have shown that marriages of mature girls might cause problems of adjustment, with which the men, in particular, did not cope well.[61]

[61] Derrett (1978a: 183–4) sharply depicts the childishness of supposedly modern Hindu men and their frequent inability to cope with their more advanced wives.

Derrett (1968b: 342) noted that '[i]t is hardly satisfactory that Section 5 of the HMA should have left it uncertain whether or not marriage between children is voidable'. But already during the 1970s, as Derrett (1978a: 25) highlights, the Hindu nature of the scheme of the HMA was once again becoming more evident, in that child marriage would still be perfectly legal,[62] and actual consent of a Hindu spouse was not required for the validity of the marriage. Derrett (1978a: 81–2) therefore writes that the various amendments to the CMRA:

> have progressively raised the minimum legal age for marriage to 15 for a girl and 18 for a boy, but there is only too much evidence that child marriages are contracted—though not necessarily forcibly consummated—to this day all over India. In spite of a well-meant but unsuccessful attempt at judicial reform of the law, child marriages are common, and are legally valid at present.

Many Indian observers have continued to call for further reforms. Augustine (1991: 169) complains that the practice of child marriage continued, even half a century after the promulgation of the CMRA. Singh (1989: 64) notes that while penalizing child marriages is necessary, 'the benefit of such legislation is greatly offset by the fact that the marriage itself is held valid' and argues that therefore it should be 'a long-term objective to amend this aspect of the law and to declare child marriages as legally void' (id.). Shastri (1990: 335) expresses her dismay over the fact that even the modern Hindu law as found in Section 5 of the HMA had not rendered a child marriage void. She claims that the CMRA and the HMA 'are without teeth and therefore have no practical effect to curb this social evil of child marriage' (id.). There is some recognition of socio-legal reality when Shastri (1990: 336) claims that the prime need is to implement the prohibition of child marriages, but also recognizes that declaring child marriages void would create chaos in society. Still, she argues for stricter implementation and calls for drastic steps, in particular the punishment of parents and compulsory registration of marriages.

Qureshi (1978: 373) observed in his conclusions that the consequences of the CMRA have never been realized in those rural areas where child marriage is still considered appropriate and common, while in urban areas the practice has virtually died out. He therefore suggested, in true reformist fashion, that making a minimum age of eighteen and twenty-one respectively for boys and girls compulsory 'will be a mere formality'. While he seemed to admit that '[t]he legislature did well in leaving the issue slightly vague while enacting the Hindu Marriage Act, 1955' (id.), he also argued that '[i]t will be better if the legislature completely abolishes child marriage and prescribes severe penalties in case of contravention. A national policy in this regard is essential. If we are able to stop child marriage, we shall be able to control the growth of population as well' (id.). Shiv Sahai Singh (1993: 10) even propounds the argument that if the CMRA 1929 could override and unify all personal laws in India

[62] The case referred to here is *Gindan v Barelal* AIR 1976 MP 83.

regarding age of marriage, 'there is no reason why all the personal laws cannot be made to agree on the issue of the minimum age for a valid marriage'. Such formalistic arguments quite clearly overlook the social dimension of the problem and are too fixated on legal uniformity and certainty.

Reforms of the 1970s

A number of further legislative reforms were indeed introduced during the 1970s, but child marriages have continued to be valid in Indian law. The Committee on the Status of Women deliberated further changes to family laws during the early 1970s, as recorded in *Towards Equality* (1974: 112). It felt that the lesser minimum age of marriage for women is perhaps not appropriate, but most importantly, it was felt desirable to increase the minimum age of marriage for women to eighteen years. Notably, one reason given is that 'child marriage is one of the significant factors, leading to the high incidence of suicide among young married women in India' (id.). It is also highly significant that the Committee raised the issue of making child marriages void, but decided against this strategy. *Towards Equality* (1974: 113) argues:

> 4.66 Another effective approach to this problem is to render such marriages void. But in the present social and economic conditions such a rigorous measure may create more problems than it seeks to solve. We suggest, therefore, that it should be envisaged as a future goal.

This softening of the reformist zeal was matched by other measures to assist Hindu women in asserting their rights as individuals. The Committee suggested above all the introduction of an 'option of puberty' into Hindu law, in analogy from Muslim law,[63] and its final recommendation relates to denial of any form of relief through courts for parties to child marriages. *Towards Equality* (1974: 114) suggests:

> 4.69 We recommend legislation prohibiting courts from granting any relief in respect of a marriage solemnized in violation of the age requirements prescribed by law unless both the parties have completed the age of 18 years.

The Committee (id.) also suggested that registration of all marriages should be made compulsory, but noted that India had neither signed nor ratified the United Nations Convention on Consent to Marriage, Minimum Age for Marriage, and Registration of Marriage. Nevertheless, *Towards Equality* (1974: 115) urged:

> 4.73 We regret that for over a decade no attempt has been made to introduce legislation to implement the objects of the UN Convention. This attitude

[63] This would permit a child wife to seek virtual annulment of her marriage on the ground that she was married without her own consent earlier and, on reaching a specified age, had decided not to implement the marriage. The critical questions

> indicates a casualness and lack of concern on matters affecting the status of women. *We recommend that registration should be made compulsory for all marriages.* We have a clear precedent for a uniform measure in the Registration of Births and Deaths Act.

Relying on this source, Pujari and Kaushik (1994, III: 304) also recommend compulsory registration of marriages as an effective check on child marriages and reiterate this strongly (ibid.: 328):

> Registration of marriages should be made mandatory and the parties to the marriage should produce evidence of their date of birth at the time of marriage. In order to better implement the law restraining child marriages a mandatory minimum term of imprisonment and fine should be imposed on the parents of the couple and if the parents of one or both are dead then on the legal guardians. Facilities for registration should be made in addition to the ones in the cities, to be made in the villages and talukas.

Pujari and Kaushik (1994, III: 304) mention the Egyptian Civil Code under which, during the 1920s, a marriage in contravention of the minimum age rules was not made invalid, but would not be registered. Under Article 99 of the Code, such a marriage would also not be recognized for the purpose of giving any relief, except relating to legitimacy of children. The authors fail to point out that these well-meaning reforms in Egypt were in fact one of the most famous examples of legislative failure. They also overlook the fact, established in Chapter 8, that most Hindu marriages do not involve the state in any form. Such writing merely shows that reformist activism in this field was by no means exhausted by the 1970s.

Derrett (1978a: 36) reports that the fifty-ninth Law Commission Report of 1974 did not discuss whether a further attack on child marriages should be made, and such marriages be outlawed completely, because it 'was probably supposed that the existing penal law was strong enough', although this had been contradicted by many experts. It was, however, felt that further reforms should be made, but these did not materialize until 1978. In the meantime, the Marriage Laws (Amendment) Act of 1976, which significantly amended some provisions of the HMA 1955 in relation to divorce, left the minimum age requirements of fifteen and eighteen years undisturbed and did not tamper with the question of legal validity of child marriages.

However, the 1976 Act introduced a new ground of divorce for Hindu wives, which led to some excited discussions, as it involved the transplantation of a concept from Muslim law, the traditional 'option of puberty', into Hindu law. In the climate of the time, this could be interpreted as a confidence-building gesture towards Indian Muslims, demonstrating that elements of Muslim law have a potentially useful role to play in the anticipated uniform

---

concerning consummation of early marriage—and the wife's consent to it—cannot be explored here in detail. On the Muslim law principles, see Pearl and Menski (1998: 143).

code of family law.[64] The relevant amendment was inserted into Section 13 of the HMA and became Section 13(2)(iv), to the effect that:

> (2) A wife may also present a petition for the dissolution of her marriage by a decree of divorce on the ground -
>
> ...
>
> (iv) that her marriage (whether consummated or not) was solemnized before she attained the age of fifteen years and she has repudiated the marriage after attaining that age but before attaining the age of eighteen years.

Mahmood (1978: 24) argues that the introduction of this 'option of puberty' had put an end to any doubts over the validity of a child marriage, because it confirmed impliedly that such a marriage was not void ab initio. Derrett (1978a: 36) saw this option of puberty in Hindu law as 'an attempt to mitigate the evil of child marriage, and incidentally to come nearer to the Muslim law'. Bhattacharjee (1994: 148–9) notes that under Section 13(2)(iv) a young Hindu wife has virtually been given what in Islamic law is known as the 'option of puberty'. Tahir Mahmood, while pleased about this borrowing from Muslim law, opposed the restriction of the 'option of puberty' to the wife and asked that it should be extended to the husband. He also criticized that a wife should be allowed to wilfully consummate her marriage and then be permitted to ask for divorce nevertheless, which 'amounts to permitting her to have her cake and eat it too' (Mahmood 1986: 127).[65] Bhattacharjee (1994: 149) argues that it is more reasonable not to make the option depending on non-consummation of the marriage, and suggests that the option should be made available to Hindu males also.

However, in the Child Marriage Restraint (Amendment) Act of 1978 (Act 2 of 1978), the only significant change in the law is that the minimum marriage ages were raised to eighteen years for the wife and twenty-one years for the husband. Thus the option of puberty issue died a sudden death, though it is not irrelevant and is still part of the HMA. The CMRAA of 1978 also provided a new Section 7 about cognizability,[66] and made consequent amendments in the Indian Christian Marriage Act of 1872 and the HMA of 1955. For the Indian

[64] In this context, Mahmood (1976: xiii) argues that while the future civil code will certainly differ significantly from traditional religious concepts of the Hindus, 'the corresponding Islamic concepts, devoid of their time-worn traditional interpretation, can be a potential component of the emerging Indian civil code'. An excited foreword by V.R. Krishna Iyer speaks of the envisaged common code as 'a new dharma—a progressive, just, common family code' (ibid.: ix). Qureshi (1978: 373–4) argued for the introduction of an 'option of puberty' for Hindu girls similar to the one that exists for Muslims.

[65] Ten years after the 1978 Act, Singh (1989: 64) still pleads for the introduction of the option of puberty similar to Muslim law, irrespective of whether the marriage was consummated or not.

[66] Sagade (1981: 29–30) states that with few exceptions, all offences under the Act are made cognizable. Jain (1983: 504) explains that offences under the Act may now be investigated by a police officer under the CrPC 1973 as if they are cognizable

Christian marriage law, the simple effect was to raise the minimum ages to eighteen and twenty-one years respectively, as was also done for Section 5(iii) of the HMA.

For Hindu law, however, a further consequence was that the entire legal regime on marriage guardianship, as earlier found in Section 6 HMA, had now technically become superfluous and was omitted from the HMA.[67] This is of course a legal fiction, since the law on marriage guardianship must remain relevant in practice as long as under-age marriages continue to be solemnized.[68] While the critical importance of consent is emphasized by Chandra (1998),[69] the sacramental elements in Hindu marriages were perceived to militate against individual expressions of opinion, especially from young girls and the view has prevailed that express consent is unnecessary in Hindu marriages. But because Section 6 was taken out of the statute, the discussion on this topic has died a quiet death.

Mahmood (1986: 114–5) argued that raising the minimum ages to eighteen and twenty-one resulted in a number of anomalies and created confusions about when a person is a 'minor' or a 'child'. His suggestion, therefore, was to reduce the age of marriage for men to eighteen years under all laws concerned, thus achieving harmony between different provisions on majority, but also gender equality in terms of marriage ages. Dhagamwar (1987: 15), reporting on the results of field surveys to ascertain the legal knowledge of respondents about marriage laws, notes that at the time when the CMRAA was introduced, there had been significant press and media coverage, so that more young people in her sample knew about the official higher marriage ages. Still, as we saw, observers have continued to find that child marriages are solemnized in various parts of India.[70]

---

offences, but such officer shall not have the power to arrest a person without an order of a magistrate. Again we note here some reservations about trusting the police to handle such matters.

67 Thus, for example, Diwan (1979: 78) and Diwan and Diwan (1993: 86) merely say that the question of guardianship in marriage has now become irrelevant. Mahmood (1986: 113–5) contains a thought-provoking discussion of this issue.

68 A few smaller amendments were made to Sections 12 and 18 of the HMA of 1955.

69 The basic principle would be that '[a] marriage—even a Hindu marriage—ought not to be binding on a spouse who had not consented to it' (Chandra 1998: 23).

70 For example, there was a fairly detailed report in *India Today* (15 April 1985: 62–4) about one particular community of Reddis in Andhra Pradesh and their economic arguments in favour of early child marriages. The excellent study of Chekki (1968) among Lingayats shows a neat picture of an age gap of eight years between husband and wife and, most interestingly, a difference of two years on average between perceived ideal ages of marriage and the actual age at marriage. Chatterjee et al. (1971: 62) found in their field research among rural people that about two thirds of all marriages violated the law. Sagade (1981: 33) observes a slight social change, but does not accept that this may be due to legislation.

Among the reformist agenda child marriage was closely associated with population control, which is hardly a novel connection. In 1884 Behramji Malabari had highlighted this issue, and a significant number of recent writers touch on the population dimension.[71] Legal authors, too, make much of this: Sampath (1969: 28) begins his discussion with this concern and Sagade (1981: 33) argues forcefully that child marriage definitely leads to population problems. A search in the literature on population control locates the perceived linkages. Sehgal (1989: 112) confirms that the CMRAA of 1978 was promulgated due to the acute population problem, but does not explain this further. At p. 117, he writes that a higher marriage age for women obviously cuts down the reproductive span and notes that 'girls marrying at a later age favour and adopt family planning more readily', thus leading to a clear correlation. Seen from this angle, the need to combat early marriages in India remains manifestly a socially and economically desirable goal.

Case Law on Child Marriages: Towards Postmodernity

While the relevant statutes are conspicuously silent on the question of legal validity of child marriages, advise leniency, and in fact whisper condonation of social practices, what do we know about the case law? The analysis produced below shows that cases on the issue of child marriage have been arising in all kinds of circumstances and concern many other issues than age at marriage or legal validity of an under-age marriage. Significantly, from the very first case in 1933 onwards,[72] the courts have upheld child marriages as valid, with only one major exception, discussed here. Sampath (1969: 31) complained vigorously that the ineffectiveness of the CMRA is evidenced by the fact that in over forty years just over 100 cases had been reported at High Court level. Thus, at best a few hundred prosecutions had resulted from millions of child marriages. Sampath (id.) also notes that 'where the parties have been prosecuted, the motivations have come from family feuds and factional fights rather than from the diligent enforcement of the provisions of the Act'.

A frequently cited early case is *Munshiram v Emperor* AIR 1936 All 11. The bride was over fourteen years, but the groom had been below eighteen years. The two fathers had been dragged to court and sought to avoid punishment

[71] Verma (1993: 18) emphasizes the link of marriage ages with fertility. Sharan (1992: 127) indicates the negative impact of early marriages on the extent of India's population explosion claiming that only intelligent people are using birth control methods. Brown (1990: 371–2) blames population growth for the failure of development plans to obliterate poverty and to lead to self-sustaining growth, portrays the age of marriage as an extremely sensitive religious topic among Hindus, and complains that the law was too loosely enforced, so that child marriage has continued to exist in practice.

[72] Sehgal (1989: 113) refers to *Jalsi Kaur v Emperor* AIR 1933 Patna 471, as the first case that upheld child marriages and provides further case references.

by claiming that the marriage was not valid, advancing all kinds of reasons. Ganga Nath J was clearly not impressed and took the stance, at p. 12, that '[t]he question of validity or invalidity of the marriage is beyond the scope of the Child Marriage Restraint Act. Marriage is solemnised by the performance of certain ceremonies, which depend on the race and religion of the parties, who enter into marriage'. Reasoning that the father of a Hindu bride would always be taking part in the marriage, even though his daughter was not below the minimum age, the judge upheld the convictions of both fathers under Section 5 of the CMRA, but acquitted them otherwise. The case does not disclose the severity of the penalty, but the principle is clearly established.

Birupakshya Das v Kunja Behari AIR 1961 Or 104 also confirms that the CMRA does not deal with the validity of a Hindu marriage. This is an early case in which an alienation of joint Hindu family property for necessity is at issue, the necessity being the expenses of the illegal marriage. It was held at p. 105:

> It is indisputable that the marriage is a valid marriage. The Child Marriage Restraint Act does not affect the validity of the marriage even though it may be in contravention of the provisions of the Act. In spite of the marriage being valid, it is transparent from the provisions of the Act that the marriage in contravention of the provisions of the Act is a criminal act punishable under law .... To incur expenses for performing a ceremony which is a criminal act, in my opinion cannot be taken to be legal necessity for which a karta of the family is empowered under the Hindu law to effect an alienation.

In *Premi v Daya Ram* AIR 1965 HP 15, a husband's case for restitution of conjugal rights, the wife denied her marriage on the ground of age. However, she did not succeed, for it was held, at p. 16:

> A marriage which contravenes the condition, specified in clause (iii), or clause (vi), of Section 5 of the Act is not declared to be void by Section 11 or any other section of the Act. The omission to declare such a marriage to be void by the Legislature does not appear to be merely accidental. The Legislature has provided punishment in Section 18 of the Act, for the breach of the aforesaid conditions. It is not for the Court to speculate upon the reasons for the aforesaid intentional omission. But, it may be that the Legislature did not intend to declare child marriages ... as void, as, though such marriages are discouraged by society and law, yet the evil is deep-rooted and child marriages are not rare in the country and declaring such marriages as void must have resulted in unfortunate consequences and unnecessary hardship to the parties.
>
> The Legislature, therefore, stopped short of declaring such marriages as void, and contended itself by making such marriages merely punishable.

In *Naumi v Narotam* AIR 1963 HP 15, the question was whether under the relevant provisions of the HMA the marriage of a Hindu girl below the age of fifteen years to a man of about sixty years was legally valid. The girl, aged about 13–14 years, complained of having been forcibly married to this man, who already had a wife or a mistress, and treated her with cruelty. The desperate young woman tried to argue that there was an inadvertent lacuna in Sections 11 and 12 of the HMA, but the judge held firm and found that 'the irresistible conclusion is that the Legislature did not intend that a marriage solemnized in contravention of clause (iii) of Section 5 could be avoided' (p. 16).[73]

During the 1970s, a remarkable episode is provided by the case of *Panchireddi Appala Suramma v Gadela Ganapatlu* AIR 1975 AP 193. This case explicitly dissented from *Naumi v Narotam* AIR 1963 HP 15, and sought to break the mould of condonation of child marriages by declaring them void. The wife had been about six years old at the time of the marriage in 1957, and the husband eleven. Disputes broke out between the families involved, and eventually the wife pleaded that her marriage was void, on the simple ground that under Section 5(iii) of the HMA alone, it fell foul of the law. The husband's lawyer argued against this that the combined reading of Sections 5(iii), 11, and 18 of the HMA meant that the marriage had always been valid. Having taken a detailed look at the statute and the contrary pleadings, Obul Reddi CJ then held, at p. 195 that the object of the HMA is:

> ... to prevent and eradicate the evil of child marriages. This is why the marriageable ages of the bridegroom and bride are prescribed. A marriage between the bridegroom and the bride, if their ages do not satisfy the requirements of clause (iii) of Sec. 5, cannot be solemnized as it is prohibited under clause (iii) of Section 5. It is not necessary that, in the event of contravention of clause (iii) of Section 5 either party to the marriage should rush to the court for declaring that marriage as null and void. Such a marriage is void ab initio .... Where the bride and bridegroom are minors, as in this case, there is no question of presenting any petition. Such a marriage is no marriage in the eye of law and it cannot be solemnized in the event of the bride and bridegroom being below the ages prescribed in clause (iii) of Section 5. It is for that reason that there is no reference to clause (iii) of Section 5 either in Section 11 or Section 12.

The learned judge therefore allowed the wife's petition, refused to agree with *Naumi* and relied instead on an earlier case in his own court, *Rayudu Pallamsetti v Dommetti Sriramulu* AIR 1968 AP 375. This is a case under the Contract Act of 1872 for recovery of presents and money given in connection with a contract of marriage involving minors. The suit was over Rs 3,000 worth of gold ornaments, given by the father of the groom to the family of the girl. However, the relations between the families then broke down, evidently over dowry demands, the marriage was never solemnized, and the girl's family refused to return the presents, pleading that they were part of an illegal transaction. Obul Reddi J found, at p. 377:

[73] The judge referred also to the case of *Kalawati v Devi Ram* AIR 1961 HP 1, in which an under-age Hindu girl had been given in marriage by her minor brother prior to the HMA, but was held not entitled to a decree for nullity.

> All that has happened in the instant case is a contract was entered into to perform a marriage which is prohibited by law and is opposed to public policy. The mere intention to celebrate such a marriage, if celebrated will be ab initio void, is not sufficient to disentitle the plaintiff from recovering what he gave as present to the prospective bride.

Since the marriage had not been performed, the parties had reverted to their original position. The mere fact that the contract was one prohibited by law would not disentitle the boy's father from recovering the money. It was held, at p. 378:

> Although in this case, presents and moneys were given for an illegal purpose, namely, to celebrate the marriage of two minors, who had not attained the requisite age, as prescribed by the Hindu Marriage Act, the purpose itself was not carried out and the contract was repudiated, and in cases of this nature money is recoverable as the parties revert back to their original or previous positions as there could be no question of any part-performance of marriage.

The girl's parents, thus, lost their claim, but the judge's comments about the illegal nature of an under-age marriage lingered on and were applied, as we saw, in *Panchireddi Appala Suramma* in 1975, when Obul Reddi had become Chief Justice. Child marriages in AP were therefore void marriages from at least 1975 onwards. The reactions to this case have been extremely mixed. Mahmood (1978: 24) states that this decision 'raised many difficult problems'. The decision was enthusiastically welcomed as representing a healthy trend by Tiwari (1991: 50):

> Though this decision is not going to operate as a uniform law for all Hindus and obviously for other communities, the legislature should amend the law suitably and try to curb child marriages with all vigour and reasonable force, in the interest of a healthy society and nation. As the things stand at present legislation alone cannot bring about social change and abolish centuries old practices, overnight. It is strong and concentrated public opinion also that can put an end to such harmful practices. It is submitted here that the compulsory registration of marriages will help greatly in putting an end to such marriages as at the time of marriage parties to the marriage should be asked to enter respective age of the person marrying. It may be provided that any marriage solemnised in contravention of the age clause shall not be [a] valid one.

Such recommendations are concluded with the suggestion that the adult persons responsible for child marriages should be punished more vigorously (ibid.: 50–1) and that the process of marriage registration should start right from the village level. Tiwari (1991: 51) argues that when births and deaths can be registered, why not marriages, but fails to admit that the system of registering deaths and births in India is not at all foolproof. This approach, thus, idolizes the usefulness of a state-controlled system of public records and does not consider the fiscal implications of such a system and, more crucially, its limited use by peripheral local populations.

Other academic commentators, notably a local law lecturer, expressed their concern about the apparent conflict between the High Court declaring child marriages void, while millions of people carried on solemnizing them. Rao (1975: 1) argued that the decision 'gives rise to serious social problems, and heavily tells upon those that are married at an early stage either by way of custom or usage'. Noting that the decision would have serious repercussions especially for rural women, it was also emphasized that '[t]he decision is very much against the current judicial practice, in which various other High Courts have declared minor's marriages as valid'. (id.). Thus, as noted by Rao (1975: 2):

> However progressive and reformative this decision may be, it calls for comment in view of its serious consequences upon all couples of early marriages, particularly in the rural areas where 80 to 90 per cent of the people must have been married in violation of the rule regarding the age.

Rao (1975: 5) thus found that the weight of scholarly opinion as well as the trend of judicial practice went against the opinion held by the AP High Court and submitted that this decision 'is unrealistic and unacceptable in view of the present conditions in the society'. However, at the same time, the author also recognized that it marked a step forward towards eradicating the evil practice of early marriages, and goes much ahead of Hindu society.

Meanwhile, in other parts of India, High Courts continued to treat child marriages as legally valid marriages. In *Gindan v Barelal* AIR 1976 MP 83, a wife unsuccessfully resisted the husband's petition for restitution of conjugal rights on the ground that she had only been ten years old at the time of her marriage and that her marriage was void. It was held, at p. 85, that contravention of the minimum age requirements is only punishable under Section 18 of the HMA and that it is difficult to hold, in view of the statutory provisions, that such a marriage should be void. The judge was well aware of the AP High Court's decision of 1975, but firmly disagreed with it. It was held, at p. 85:

> If the Legislature intended otherwise, the Act certainly would have made a specific provision in that regard in the like manner as it has been done in the case of contravention of clauses (i), (ii), (iv) and (v) of Section 5 and Section 11 of the Act. Thus, the marriage would remain valid in law and enforceable and recognizable in the Court of law.

There is actually another decision from the High Court of AP at this time which holds that a child marriage is valid. In *Panchada Chitti Venkanna v Panchada Mahalakshmi* 1976 (2) *AnWR* 45, a child marriage had remained unconsummated and the husband had abandoned the wife. It was held that the marriage was not a nullity, and that the wife was entitled to maintenance, on the ground that the marriage had been performed prior to the promulgation of the HMA. It is therefore evident that in AP itself, there was a strong view that child marriages could not simply be declared null and void. The judges recognized this, and at the next possible opportunity, which presented itself in *Pinninti Venkataramana v State* AIR 1977 AP 43 FB, a Full Bench was set up by the HC to rectify the situation. This case overruled the 1975 decision in *Panchireddi Appala Suramma*, AIR 1975 AP 193, holding that a child marriage was neither void nor voidable, but was merely punishable. This carefully researched and well-reasoned judgment by a new Chief Justice, B.J. Divan, shows that he was evidently aware that the progressive decision of his predecessor had created a huge social dilemma and was also not quite in line with the provisions of the HMA itself. Examining the HMA, it was held at p. 45:

> It is well settled law that the old Hindu Law, as it prevailed prior to the enactment of the Hindu Marriage Act, is to continue in force except to the extent to which that law was altered by the provisions of the Hindu Marriage Act, 1955. It is in the light of this well settled principle that we have to approach the question that arises for our consideration.

Considering the wording of the HMA, it was found that 'neither in Section 11 nor in Section 12 is there any provision for what is to happen if a marriage is solemnized in violation of the provisions of clause (iii) of Section 5' (p. 46). Thus, as held at p. 47:

> This analysis of the different provisions of the Hindu Marriage Act clearly brings out the fact that the Legislature itself has made a distinction between contravention of one or the other clauses of Section 5 and such contravention is to be visited with different consequences.

After referring to some earlier cases which had treated child marriages as valid,[74] the Court then turned to *Panchireddi Appala Suramma*, which had held that a child marriage was illegal.[75] At p. 48, the Chief Justice expressed his reasons for disagreeing with this earlier decision of his own HC:

> We find that the consequences of accepting the view of the Division Bench would be very serious. It is well settled principle in the law relating to marriages that the Court should lean against the interpretation of any provision of law which is liable to render innocent children of the marriage bastards. It seems that this aspect of bastardized children, who were

[74] In *Sivanandy v Bhagavathyamma* AIR 1962 Mad 400, it was held that a child marriage was valid under the CMRA 1929, based on the doctrine of *factum valet.* See also *Kalawati v Devi Ram* AIR 1961 HP 1; *Premi v Daya Ram* AIR 1965 HP 15 held that the marriage of a minor wife is neither void nor voidable; *Mohinder Kaur v Major Singh* AIR 1972 P&H 184 confirmed that a child marriage constitutes no defence against a decree for restitution of conjugal rights.

[75] The only other decision said to be holding child marriages void is *Krishni Devi v Tulsan Devi* AIR 1972 P&H 305. Here, after the death of a polygamously married husband, one of the co-widows filed a petition for nullity of the other widow's marriage and won her appeal. However, this is a case of polygamy, and not of child marriage.

> otherwise innocent and who would be treated as illegitimate children of the couple was not present to the minds of the learned Judges.

While the consideration of the best interests of children weighed strongly, it was also evident that statutory interpretation worked against a finding that child marriages were void. It was thus held, at p. 49:

> If each of the clauses in Section 5 is to be treated as a condition precedent, the violation of which would render the marriage void ab initio, the Legislature itself would not have given out its mind by providing for contravention of the different clauses of Section 5 differently.

It was also noted, at pp. 50–1, that the introduction of an 'option of puberty' in 1976 had confirmed that the legislature never treated an under-age marriage as void ab initio. It was thus held, at p. 51, that the decision in *Panchireddi Appalasuramma* 'does not lay down the correct law and it must be held that any marriage solemnized in contravention of clause (iii) of Section 5 is neither void nor voidable'. That settled the law for AP and restored harmony between official law and local practice, as well as resolving the brewing conflict between different High Courts.

The only Supreme Court case dealing with this matter provides only an obiter dictum, since it is a case about the hitherto unexplored question of legal validity of a Hindu marriage solemnized in contravention of Section 15 HMA and not Section 5.[76] In *Lila Gupta v Laxmi Narain* AIR 1978 SC 1351, a bench of three judges took a close look at the various relevant provisions of the HMA and came to the conclusion, at p. 1353, that '[a] comprehensive review of the relevant provisions of the Act unmistakably manifests the legislative thrust that every marriage solemnised in contravention of one or other condition prescribed for valid marriage is not void'. This was the case under Section 5(iii) of the HMA and also under the CMRA, as held at p. 1358:

> Similarly, a reference to [the] Child Marriage Restraint Act would also show that the Child Marriage Restraint Act was enacted to carry forward the reformist movement of prohibiting child marriages and while it made marriage in contravention of the provisions of the Child Marriage Restraint Act punishable, simultaneously it did not render the marriage void. It would

[76] Section 15 of the HMA is to the effect that '[w]hen a marriage has been dissolved by a decree of divorce and either there is no right of appeal against the decree or, if there is such a right of appeal, the time for appealing has expired without an appeal having been presented, or an appeal has been presented but has been dismissed, it shall be lawful for either party to the marriage to marry again'. This was followed by a Proviso, which was taken out of the section by the *Marriage Laws Amendment Act* of 1976, and which ran as follows: 'Provided that it shall not be lawful for the respective parties to marry again unless at the date of such marriage at least one year has elapsed from the date of the decree in the Court of the first instance'. Interestingly, the court in *Lila Gupta* refers to this change of law at p. 1355 and does not find any critical words.

thus appear that voidness of marriage unless statutorily provided for is not to be readily inferred.

The position that contravention of the minimum age requirements will lead to punishment by fine and/or imprisonment, but that the marriage is still legally valid, has been upheld by the Indian courts ever since. In *Sukram v Mishri Bai* AIR 1979 MP 144, a husband was granted a decree for restitution of conjugal rights on the ground that even though his wife was only about ten or eleven years old at the time of their marriage, it was a valid marriage. *Ratnamma v Ammalu Amma* 1982 KLT 980 was a case under a local Kerala Hindu law enactment, in which the question arose whether a spouse below the minimum age for marriage could enter a valid marriage. In this case, the relevant statute lays down sixteen years as a minimum, but the bride had only been fifteen years old. It was held at p. 982, relying on *Lila Gupta* AIR 1978 SC 1351, that this contravention 'does not render the marriage void but merely invalid'.

In *Shankerappa v Sushilabai* AIR 1984 Kant 112, a wife was claiming maintenance from a husband who totally denied the validity of the marriage on a number of grounds, including the wife's age at marriage. The Court, at pp. 118–9, enters into a detailed discussion of the issue but relies on *Lila Gupta* AIR 1978 SC 1351 which is said to have concluded the matter. In *Rabindra Prasad v Sita Devi* AIR 1986 Pat 128, a husband's divorce suit was refused. He claimed divorce on all kinds of grounds, alleging that his wife had no right breast but plenty of paramours, and claiming that since he was less than eighteen years old at the time of his marriage, the marriage was void anyway. The Court was swift to hold that a Hindu marriage in violation of Section 5(iii) of the HMA remains unaffected, being neither void nor voidable.

It then appeared that for about ten years, there were no cases, but in 1997, as shown below, some important new decisions were reported. These new cases reflect acute awareness of the social problems posed by law reform in this area. They speak much more elaborately than a lot of reformist campaigning, which has moved into other, more fashionable topics. As observed elsewhere (Menski 2001), the Indian judges have their finger closer to the pulse of Hindu ideals than anyone else, and reading judgments remains the most instructive method of understanding the current state of judicial thinking. It is the judges who have clarified the law, and certainly not legal scholarship, most of which is either confused or blind to social realities because of the powerful lense of modernist agenda.

The Postmodern Condition of Child Marriage Law

India's postmodern legal condition with regard to child marriages and their validity is not marked by sentimental philosophizing about Hindu values and a distant past, but is centrally concerned with immediate and tangible risks to the social welfare of Indian women and children. This should not surprise, given that child marriage law is not a matter of Hindu law but falls under the general law. This confirms that it makes, at the end of the day, no real difference whether personal law regulation or general law provision are operative. In either case, the social realism of the judges appears to have ensured that social and legal development stay in some kind of harmony.

The courts have therefore found a way of moving beyond traditional and modern views of child marriage, not wholly rejecting either idea, but modifying each and incorporating them both together in the search for solutions to socio-legal problems while adhering to principles of dharmic justice. This is evidenced by the fact that the judges have been instrumental in upholding the legal validity of child marriages for solid reasons of social welfare. This appears to underwrite 'tradition', but not to do so would have further disadvantaged Indian women and children, which would be out of line with the expectations of India's Constitution as well. Hence, postmodern Indian law finds itself, to some extent reluctantly, underwriting an aspect of local and/or Hindu tradition to construct a justice-focused family law system. The extent of this reluctance and the underlying reasoning are worth some further analysis. Derrett (1978a: 159) notes that post-reformist Hindu law has retained many traditional features that make it unsuitable for easy amalgamation with a general marriage law:

> Hindu law has thus taken to itself a matrimonial régime which is distinguishable from the 'special marriage' only in that *samskaras* are perforce comprehended within it. A Hindu marriage can still come into existence without the spouses' consent, and at ages below 15 and 18. If Parliament had felt strong enough to abolish that (it would only have been eyewash if they had), the Hindu law of marriage could have been merged in the Special Marriage Act and thus become lost, so far as the law-books are concerned, without trace.

This implies that, precisely because child marriage is at the same time a matter of Hindu personal law and of the general law, the legislature would not move to avoid impairing the status of Hindu law. While that makes sense as a theoretical argument, in practice there are more obvious arguments for why the Indian state systematically refuses further legal intervention. Significantly, in the legislative field, there is some recent evidence that the state is not willing to be pushed by radical modernist agenda when it comes to dealing with child marriages. *India Today* (15 October 1996: 15) reported:

> Stating that it was apprehensive of interfering with "personal laws of minority communities", the Government has rejected a draft bill to curb child marriages. The provisions of 'The Marriage Bill, 1994', drafted by the National Commission for Women, makes it mandatory for all marriages to be registered. The marriages of minors would not be registered. Had the draft bill become law, the Hindu Marriage Act, 1955, the Muslim Personal Law (Shariat) Application Act, 1937, the Parsi Marriage and Divorce Act, 1936, The Indian Christian Marriage Act, 1872 and the Special Marriage Act, 1954, would have had to be repealed.

This muddled statement is certainly factually wrong as far as the need to repeal the various personal laws is concerned. What the National Commission for Women wanted, however, was a legal regulation of marriage that focuses on compulsory registration of marriages and thereby on supervening legal control of entry into marriage by the state. One stipulated side effect is that this new law would abolish child marriages once and for all.

It is unsurprising that the Indian lawmakers declined the offer to intervene in this heavy-handed way. The evolving postmodern approach to legal regulation has clearly taught them that to do otherwise would be pointless, which the Women's Commission in its modernist fervour has not yet been willing to accept. As we saw in Chapter 8, Agnes (2000) discussed the various recent proposals for reforms of marriage law, including that by the National Commission for Women, and clearly saw them as unrealistic. Agnes (2000: 183) reports that '[t]he Bill stipulates that a declaration of marriage must be sent to the Registrar of marriages within three days of its performance. A fine of Rs 100 per day is levied for default for a period of one month and thereafter the marriage is deemed void'.

It is evident that such a law is not practicable at all, given Indian conditions of life for hundreds of millions of people. More dangerously, such strictly formal legal regulation would leave women totally vulnerable to exploitation and would create legal insecurity over married status at their expense. By refusing to act, the Indian legislature not only leaves the field to the judges, but also indicates that the existing law is considered appropriate and conducive to social welfare. Evidently, many modernist authors disagree. As indicated, the law on child marriages is actually quite clear, but the commentators are confused, caught up between tradition and modernity, and unable to analyse the current position from a holistic perspective.

Social Awareness in the Most Recent Case Law

The above analysis of the earlier case law on child marriages clearly showed that the judges had taken up the challenge of developing the legislative foundations into a socially meaningful system of regulation. Their major concern was not really over punishment of offenders or prevention of direct physical violence against child brides through deterrent sentences. Rather, the courts have been busy to prevent certain individuals, who tend to be men, from taking duplicitous advantage of the argument that child marriages are against public policy and thus should be void. Thus, the courts have again found themselves upholding the legal validity of marriages, also in cases where women wished to nullify their marriage. Even if the judges, as modern highly educated individuals, would not for themselves accept that there is any social good to be had from arranging such early marriages, they have upheld child marriages for ideological as well as practical reasons. Unlike many social reformers and textbook writers, some judges realize the extent of their social responsibility. We are fortunate that at least some of them have begun to tell us about their thinking.

I focus here particularly on two recent cases that indicate with surprising clarity the position of child marriage law in India today.

In *Gajara Naran Bhura v Kanbi Kunverbai Parbat* AIR 1997 Guj 185, a Hindu wife had asked for maintenance in 1974, while the husband claimed that the marriage was void on account of the wife's age being less than fifteen years at the time of the marriage in 1967. The court first examined the CMRA and argued that there would have been no need for injunctions under Section 12 of the Act if a child marriage had been considered void. Looking at the HMA, it was again found that an under-age marriage could not be void under that Act. Thus, it was held at p. 189 that:

> ... marriage solemnised between two Hindus who are of the age which makes one of them punishable under the Child Marriage Restraint Act does not render the marriage itself invalid or void. Therefore, rights and obligations arising from such valid marriage cannot be avoided by not recognising the marriage at all.

This decision clearly protects the financial interests of the married woman but is too short to enlighten us on current judicial thinking about marriages. A similar case, argued much more elaborately, is *V. Mallikarjunaiah v H.C. Gowramma* AIR 1997 Kant 77. Here an opportunistic husband sought a declaration that his marriage, solemnized in 1990, was void because he had been under twenty-one years at the time of the marriage. Having lost in the lower court, the husband appealed to the HC of Karnataka, which evidently had not seen such a case for some time and found it 'a very unusual aspect of the law relating to Hindu marriages' (p. 78). This was certainly not a bona fide case, evidenced for example by the fact that *Panchireddi Appalasuramma* AIR 1975 AP 193, decided more than two decades earlier, was relied on by the husband's lawyer, who kept ominously quiet over the fact that this case had been overruled by the HC of Andhra Pradesh in 1977. The learned single judge, M.F. Saldanha J, took great effort with this case and clearly looked through the husband's scheming. On the legal and social position, it was held at p. 81:

> ... one needs to take cognizance of the fact that matrimonial laws do make various special provisions principally because of certain irreversible consequences that the parties find themselves faced with. One of them is the situation in which if certain infirmities are disclosed in a marriage, and if there are children born out of that marriage, that the law through a process of legal fiction, incorporates the provision of deemed legality. The whole purpose of this is in order to prevent the social consequences and the serious harm and damage that could occur to the parties as a result of infirmities in a marriage .... It is for a very valid reason that the Legislature excluded sub-clause (iii) of Section 5 from the grounds specified in Ss. 11 and 12 as also from the grounds that are set out in section 13 ... where misguided parents or relations may bind a young couple through a ... marriage, if at a subsequent point of time, merely on the basis of under-age, the marriage is to be declared as void, the consequences particularly to the girl or the young

> woman are absolutely irreversible. In situations such as the present one, they would have lived together as husband and wife for some time. There could also be situations in which children are born out of that wedlock and ... it would not only be harsh, but absolutely brutal if a Court were to technically void the marriage merely because the parties were under-age. Obviously, in such a situation, the grave consequences of such a Court order could be visited upon the parties virtually for no fault of theirs.
>
> To my mind, therefore, there is considerable substance in the argument that decrees voiding marriages can only be passed on the grounds or in the situations set out in Sections 11 and 12 of the Hindu Marriage Act. It is not permissible to accept the argument canvassed by the petitioner's learned advocate that the provisions of sub-section (iii) of section 5 must also be added on to the aforesaid.

This demonstrates very clear awareness of the social welfare dimensions of the present scenario and constitutes a frank assessment of the responsibilities of the courts in that context. The use of the word 'brutal' in the above context is remarkable. The learned judge, at p. 82, highlights in yet more detail his concerns about social justice for women, in particular:

> ... it is very clear that though the Legislature desired to discourage marriage between under-aged persons, that it did not go to the extent of providing that such marriages would be void or voidable or that this can be a ground for divorce principally because, it was concerned with the consequences of such a situation. Having regard to the strata in which such marriages were likely to take place, the Legislature was contuious [*sic*] of the fact that such a provision should not have the result of rendering a large number of girls or young women virtually unmarried and destitute for life. The only security that a girl or a woman in such a situation is entitled to is within the framework of the marriage and if that marriage can be loosely undone or if it is not recognised by the law, it would result in disastrous social consequences which is the only reason why this section was specifically excluded from Sections 11 and 12 of the Act .... Perhaps, in the light of ... the fact that cases of this type are still relatively common, it would have been advisable for the Legislature to have to provide for harsher penalties particularly as far as the parents, guardians and relatives who are responsible for the commission of these offences are concerned. In order to cure social evils and particularly having regard to the current thinking, it is highly desirable that the penalties provided in Section 18 should be considerably stepped up.

There is much in these two long quotes that tells us how securely entrenched postmodern legal thinking has become in the minds of many of India's best judges. It is quite clear that the judges are not upholding Hindu traditions or some other imagined ancient law, but are concerned to protect women and children against 'shark rule' by unscrupulous men.

In effect, deeper analysis uncovers another layer of postmodern legal construction that has escaped notice so far because we are used to dealing with legal topics under separate rubrics like 'marriage law', 'child marriage', or 'restitution of conjugal rights' and as a result do not see the wood for the trees. In cases like *V. Mallikarjunaiah v H.C. Gowramma* AIR 1997 Kant 77, the unspoken application of a presumption of marriage, clearly without saying this in so many words, is centrally concerned with protecting the social welfare of women and children. However, there are several important side effects of this protective judicial stance. The first is that marriage (and thus mainly Hindu marriage) as an institution also is protected, and more specifically even the Hindu joint family, as Chandra (1998: 208) has quite correctly pointed out in his modernist analysis.

The judges, thus, have been acting and reacting in a way that is remarkably similar to their decisions on Hindu marriages, but without talking about the obvious parallels. A typical case of this kind is *Gindan v Barelal* AIR 1976 MP 83, which involved a child wife's unsuccessful resistance to a decree for restitution of conjugal rights. It appears that historical research, feminist scholarship, and even legal comment on such cases have tended to see only the restrictions on the freedom and human rights of the wife, not the wider social environment within which this kind of dispute between spouses takes place. Holistic analysis of this field is somewhat lacking.

Chandra (1998) analyses in detail the issue of restitution of conjugal rights, taking the child bride case of Rukhmabai as his major evidence. Opposing a law that forces unwilling women to subjugate themselves to men because of a marriage in which they had no say, or which they no longer want to be party to, Chandra cites three leading cases from India on restitution of conjugal rights to support the main argument of his study, namely that 'the restitution of conjugal rights has brought no relief to women' (Chandra 1998: 209). We have no space in the present study and at this point for a detailed analysis of the case law on restitution of conjugal rights.[77] But it is highly significant that Chandra (1998: 207–9) refers to these cases with apparent distaste for the eventual outcome of the debates in the Supreme Court, where it was held that the remedy of restitution of conjugal rights acted as a check against the easy break-up of marriage and served a constructive social purpose. In that field of law too, the Indian judiciary took a postmodern stance which modernist analysts have failed to recognize and appreciate.

Postmodern Reflections

So, is the problem of child marriage no longer existent in the legal field and has it become a matter of gender politics? While it is difficult to argue that there is no socio-legal problem, we should be aware that the discourse on child marriages, like much of the writing on sati, is periodically used to depict India as a weird country teeming with backward people and customs, reinforcing the

[77] The relevant cases are *T. Sareetha v Venkata Subbaiah* AIR 1983 AP 356, *Harvinder Kaur v Harmander Singh Choudhry* AIR 1984 Del 66, and *Saroj Rani v Sudarshan Kumar Chadha* AIR 1984 SC 1562.

image that Mother India and her children are as strange today as ever.[78] The underlying suggestions, that there is no real social progress and change in India, no concern for human rights and children's rights, serve to highlight that modern India refuses to comply with Western standards.

Concern over child marriages is still not irrelevant, since child marriages continue to be a reality. One must ask, however, whether there is any problem if a young man of twenty marries a girl of seventeen, which is technically a child marriage under Indian law, but would be perfectly legal in English law, for example. Curiously, the raising of the minimum ages for marriage to eighteen and twenty-one years for girls and boys, respectively, by the CMRAA in 1978 significantly increased the statistical numbers of Indian child marriages. The critical question of how to define 'child marriage' has actually received hardly any attention in the literature. It is evidently crucial for statistical purposes in particular where one draws the lines of definition.[79] If we look at the marriage of very young children alone, it must be doubted whether child marriages were ever the dominant norm in Indian society, as some writers have suggested.[80] At best, they were a prominent minority feature.[81]

Basically, two major objections have been raised against early marriages in the West. First, that it creates considerable doubts as to whether free and informed consent has been given by the child. Second, that the chances of a successful and lasting union may be reduced where the spouses are immature and their personalities have been given insufficient time to develop.[82] Both these arguments are closely related to concern over the stability of marriages and are substantiated by statistical evidence of a disproportionately high marital breakdown among young couples in some Western countries, especially the UK. However, as Derrett (1978a: 198–9) highlights, the social environment for marriage and marital breakdown in India is very different from that in Europe.

With regard to Indian law, modernist reformers are now somewhat unsure whether further measures are actually useful. Qureshi (1978: 58) refers to the argument by a Parsi author (Master 1968) that child marriages ought to be declared void, though she had recognized that this is a position for which India is hardly ready. However, it is also argued that once consummation has taken place, the marriage should be valid. Many commentators, but

[78] Press reports of child marriages, even mass weddings of little children, appear from time to time in *India Today* (e.g. Rai and Badhwar 1986).

[79] Sampath (1972b: 386–7) points out how crucial it is to be clear about the boundaries of 'minor' and 'adult', giving the example of Australian statistics, according to which child marriage now hardly exists.

[80] See for example Sagade (1981: 28) and Sampath (1972b: 388 and n.15).

[81] A feature which does not constitute more than half of the incidents that feature.

[82] Summarized by Poulter (1986: 17), who discusses child marriages at pp. 16–22.

significantly not all, continue to believe in the usefulness of registration of marriages as a means to control or prevent child marriages. While Singh (1989: 65) claims that '[c]ompulsory registration of marriage operates as an effective check on child and bigamous marriages and also offers reliable proof of marriage',[83] Pujari and Kaushik (1994, I: 299) argue that '[c]ompulsory registration of marriage would never help to curb the evil of child marriages'. These authors claim that since early marriages and lack of education constitute a vicious circle, determined educational efforts should be made and observe that 'education of girls is both a cause and an effect of raising the age of marriage' (ibid.: 300). The need for education and publicity for the law is also stressed by Sampath (1969: 34) and Sagade (1981: 34). Tarachand (1991: 5) raises quite different concerns, claiming that child marriage leads to further evils in Indian society:

> Many such couples on coming of age cannot adjust themselves, which results in desertion or divorce. Such women are forced to enter into the profession of prostitution and gratify their sex urge. Child marriage has also brought about the problem of child widows ... the young widows are forced to go without sex gratification or satisfy it through immoral means. Those who resort to the latter means gradually drift towards prostitution.

Here again, ancient concerns over female chastity are mixed with contemporary efforts to protect young women. We saw that the legal regulation of child marriage was motivated originally by concern over child widows, virtual child rape, and early pregnancies being imposed on child brides. While such concerns are still not irrelevant today, it appears that these specific problems have now become subsumed under wider issues of violence against women and do not inspire much analysis and activism in their own right. Kusum (1993b: 139) confirms this wider concern when she writes that '[i]n India, child marriages are still rampant despite laws against it. However, not only child brides but all wives need protection. The dignity and freedom of a woman over her body must be honoured'. Such comments by a leading legal researcher indicate that modernist reformers have lost interest in the specifics of child marriage during the 1990s, if not before. The focus is now on more topical issues such as domestic violence.

Rather than dismissing Indian child marriage law as ineffective and tradition-bound, one might perhaps return to the question what the law in its purportedly modernizing ambitions was actually seeking to achieve in the first place. Here we clearly see subtle ameliorative and educative efforts at the centre of legislative involvement. The state law has never gone into this arena

[83] Such blue-eyed visions clearly overlook reality. In practice, once a system of marriage registration appears to exist in an overseas country, official agencies, especially immigration authorities abroad, will demand to see those documents, which may be lost, purposely not given to the woman, or otherwise not available because the law does not actually demand compulsory registration. In such cases, a presumption of marriage will still have to be applied, but this may not be granted unless expert evidence of the 'foreign' law is provided.

heavy-handed, aiming for total abolition of particular practices, but has responded to evidence of social illness and stress with mildly deterrent threats and punitive measures designed to educate the public.

As elsewhere, thus, the onus remains on society to regulate itself and its affairs. This means that the aim of colonial and post-colonial legal intervention has in effect been remarkably similar to the agenda of the ancient Hindu system of self-controlled ordering. The absence of explicit statutory rules for completely outlawing child marriages, both in the CMRA and in the HMA, reflects not so much incomplete or inefficient legal regulation, as modernist scholarship asserts, but provides evidence of the early genesis of postmodernity in this particular field. The realization of the colonial rulers that outright prohibition of child marriages could not be effectively policed and implemented, quite apart from the disastrous negative social consequences, contributed to a purposely 'ineffective' and incomplete legislative scheme. Rather than bringing in the heavy guns of the law, India's child marriage legislation falls in effect back on *sadācāra*, working through education and persuasion. This reliance on making people accept that later marriage is perhaps more beneficial to them in the long run than rushing little children into marital liaisons which they might later seek to undo, causing multiple problems in society, reflects traditional Hindu values, without saying this in so many words.[84] Apart from such evident conceptual links with Hindu tradition, the single most important practical issue in the discourse on child marriage today, also for legal practitioners outside India, remains that all Indian child marriages, if they are otherwise good in law, are legally valid. A superficial positivist reading would not spot this postmodern legal condition.

[84] As we shall see in Ch. 11, modern Hindu and Indian family laws provide various escape routes for individuals who are unhappy about their marriage arrangements.

10

Polygamy

The previous two chapters demonstrated the continuing centrality of marital status and its social consequences as a major consideration in Hindu law. The discussion of Hindu polygamy and its legal regulation in India presents a slightly different, yet related scenario from marriage law and child marriage. At first sight, there appears to have been a violent clash of tradition and modernity over polygamy and it would appear that modernity has decisively won the contest. Post-colonial Hindu law abolished polygamy by statute in 1955 and appears to follow modern principles and legal models. However, triumphant modernist declarations of legal and moral victory in this field cannot ignore the fact that in social reality polygamous arrangements of various kinds remain operative among Hindus and are legally condoned in a variety of ways. The present chapter analyses why and to what extent the formal legal abolition of polygamy in Indian Hindu law does not fully represent social reality in India today and examines the consequences for the postmodern analysis of Hindu law.

The clash of tradition and modernity over polygamy is a classic case of bipolar ideological contestation. Agnes (2000: 194) expresses this well when she writes that 'the doctrine of monogamy (which is the basic tenet of Christianity) also draws the unquestioning support of liberals moulded in the western ethos. Here bigamy is reflective of pre-modern barbarism and monogamy symbolizes civilisation, enlightenment, modernity and progress'.[1] Hindu tradition represents cultural evidence of permission for Hindu men to engage in numerically unlimited polygamy,[2] while Hindu women appear to have no such right.[3] It was deemed essential, in the view of modernists, that Hindu polygamy should be completely outlawed. It was certainly easier to prohibit polygamy (more technically correct: polygyny) for men than to allow polyandry for

[1] Mahmood (1986: 115–6) claims that '[t]he West regards monogamy as an absolute ideal in itself and would never pardon the East for any of its laws that may permit the slightest deviation from this western ideal even in the most abnormal circumstances of an individual couple'.

[2] Indeed this is what the *kulin* Brahmins of Bengal were doing at some point (see p. 385 later).

[3] However, this is contested by some mythical and real exceptions to the general rule of Hindu law.

women, and human rights arguments were used to justify the formal abolition of Hindu polygamy.

However, modernity also stands for free choice and individual discretion. Since both men and women all over the world are known to engage in various forms of sexual relations outside the formal framework of marriage, despite numerous taboos and more or less strict prohibitions, what approaches should modernist laws take to such phenomena? It is one thing to outlaw formal polygamy, but then quite a different matter to control all forms of sexual relations. As we shall see, the fuzziness of controlling polygamous relations of various descriptions calls for some critical rethinking about the consequences of strictly legal non-recognition of polygamous liaisons. Is it really desirable that the state should aim to exercise full control over this field?

The colonial law of India, certainly as far as the general law and Christian and Parsi personal law are concerned, responded to Christian and modernist challenges by asking the government for the legal abolition and criminalization of polygamy for their communities.[4] A similar process can be observed under the Hindu law reforms during 1955-56.[5] The only pocket of resistance in Indian law today concerns continued official condonation for Muslim polygamy, as an alleged traditional 'religious right' of Muslim men to have up to four wives at the same time continues to be respected by the post-colonial Indian legislature. While we are not concerned with the legal control of Muslim polygamy here, the presence of about 130 million Muslims in India has had important implications on debates over the legal abolition and control of Hindu polygamy. In particular, it is not surprising that Hindu polygamists should have complained about the 'favourable treatment' granted to Muslim men under Indian law.[6] They have challenged the legislative interference with Hindu polygamy as discriminatory on religious grounds, but have been unsuccessful. Due to the intensely politicized nature of the debates around polygamy, it will be necessary from time to time to return to issues concerning Muslim polygamy.

Beginning with the traditional position in Hindu law, this chapter demonstrates that polygamy was originally tolerated among Hindus, but not to the extent that it gave blanket permission for men to take as many wives as they

[4] Already during the nineteenth century, the Indian Christians and the Parsis had successfully asked for legislation that made their marriages monogamous, as shown in the Parsi Marriage and Divorce Act, 1865 and the Indian Christian Marriage Act, 1872. On the pioneer function of these two communities, see *Towards Equality* (1975: 104).

[5] The Hindu law of Pakistan and Bangladesh maintains its Anglo-Hindu condition and permits unlimited polygamy. In Bangladesh this has led to critical debates about reforms of the antiquated Hindu personal law through a uniform family code, which would inevitably amount to Islamization.

[6] Curiously, the dominant assumption among Indian legal scholars appears to be that in Pakistan, the Muslim Family Laws Ordinance of 1961 has regulated polygamy for Muslims (Agnes 2000: 196). This is a convenient modernist fiction which needs to be deconstructed in the present analysis.

wanted, though that was possible. The Hindu cultural ideal was and clearly still is monogamous marriage in the sacramental form of the *saṃskāra*. Polygamous arrangements were apparently seen as a deviation from this ideal, exceptional measures to support and uphold the *ṛta*/dharma complex, especially when the first wife turned out to be infertile, had only stillborn offspring, gave birth to daughters only, or was otherwise seriously deficient. It was an option that a man could exercise, and not some sort of divine right, rather in the nature of a pious obligation if it was for the explicit purpose of procuring offspring. It has been impossible to ascertain how widespread polygamy actually was in various Hindu societies in the past, but there is much evidence to indicate that it was always practised by a minority and treated as an exception from the general rule of monogamy.

Under colonial rule, this position remained largely undisturbed since the British had more important things to do than worry about the marital arrangements (or infidelities) of their Hindu subjects. Towards the end of the colonial period, however, indigenous reform movements, influenced by Christian views on polygamy filtered through English law, pressed for the abolition and criminalization of polygamy among Hindus. While various local Acts were promulgated during the 1940s, polygamy was finally banned for Hindus by the HMA of 1955 and was made a criminal offence under the existing relevant provisions of the IPC of 1860.

While the modern Indian reformers formally achieved their aim of abolishing Hindu polygamy, there remains much dissatisfaction in India today over the fact that Muslim men continue to be allowed to have up to four wives. The debates about polygamy in modern India therefore focus on this assumed Muslim privilege and have mainly turned into a debate on equality before the law and the perceived need for the uniform civil code.[7] While the central argument of the modernists is persistently voiced, to the effect that the abolition of Hindu polygamy must be followed by reform to the Muslim law in this respect, many Indian Muslims continue to oppose state interference in their personal law. In this context it is often pointed out that Hindus continue to practise polygamy, too.

In this stalemate on the statutory regulation of polygamy, the Indian courts have intervened, bridging the formal gulf between Hindu and Muslim legal regulation of polygamy. They have done so by avoiding the implementation of a strict prohibition on Hindu polygamy and by punishing polygamous Muslim husbands financially. Thus, the simplistic modernist construct of inequality in Indian law, namely that Hindus have to remain monogamous while Muslims may have up to four wives, is deeply misleading. Yet this 'thin reality' of modernist accusations can not only be uncovered from careful scrutiny of statutory provisions. In the light of case law evidence, we now find that men of either community may make polygamous arrangements, but are then expected to bear the financial consequences (Menski 2001, Chapter 3).

[7] For details see Derrett (1975b); Khodie (1975); Mahmood (1976; 1986).

The outcome of cautious judicial intervention, which appears to have been purposefully hidden from view owing to the politicization of the debates over polygamy,[8] as well as simply drowned by blind shouts for further legal intervention, is another manifestation of the postmodern condition of Hindu law today. It appears to protect the polygamous inclinations of Hindu men, and thus admits that state law cannot fully control sexual relations, while hitting all polygamous Indian men where it hurts—in the pocket. Hindu husbands in India today may continue to violate the law by arranging polygamous unions, but later pay the price when they seek to exercise that privilege as they wish. It could not be in the interest of the state to concentrate purely on punitive enforcement of the abolition of polygamy, given the negative social and financial consequences for women and children. As a result, here too, judge-led legal realism seeks to balance gender equality with social welfare concerns. The Hindu law on polygamy has thus moved beyond condoning 'tradition' as well as blind adherence to modernist axioms of formal abolition. It now lies in a condition of postmodernity, drawing from, and yet ultimately discarding, both positions to maintain justice in a heavily contested field.

Traditional Hindu Law on Polygamy

Notwithstanding the Hindu ideal of monogamous marriage as a *saṃskāra*, a one-to-one union for life, traditional Hindu law clearly permitted polygamy to men in certain situations and on certain grounds.[9] In this, Hindu law is similar to Islamic law in approach,[10] as well as to Chinese law and African laws,[11] all of which tolerate polygamy to some extent. Meyer (1952: 108) wrote that

[8] This politicization is impressively evident from much anguished writing about *Sarla Mudgal v Union of India* AIR 1995 SC 1531, which concerned the tactical conversion of a Hindu husband to Islam.

[9] This, evidently, has given rise to much bickering about gender discrimination in the context of modernist debates on full equality before the law. See *Towards Equality* (1974: 108). Such purely rhetorical positioning is unproductive in terms of finding solutions for those women who may become victimized as a result of polygamous arrangements. At the same time, there are well-known ancient examples of polyandry, particularly the polyandrous marriage of Draupadī to the five Pāṇḍava brothers in the epic *Mahābhārata*. M. Basu (2001: 28) emphasizes that 'polyandry was not the customary practice in the Vedic age'. Altekar (1978: 112) comments that polyandry as a custom 'was practically unknown to Hindu society' but refers, at p. 114, to the existence of polyandrous arrangements among a few non-Aryan tribes of Kashmir and Tibet. Berreman (1994: 257–72) wrote a detailed chapter on Himalayan polyandry.

[10] Islamic law claims to limit polygamy to four wives, but this means four women *at any one time* and can therefore easily be exploited.

[11] Derrett (1978a: 54) claims that '[p]olygamy as practised in Africa today can give us some idea of the motives behind and consequences of such a life in ancient India'.

polygamy in India is 'as old as the hills and does not form the slightest offence in the Brahmanic system', although since Vedic times monogamy is seen as the ideal. This is confirmed by Mitra (1965: 49) with quotes from earlier sources, to the effect that 'the fundamental conception of marriage was monogamous and not polygamous'. M. Basu (2001: 28) summarizes the traditional position:

> Vedic literature generally endorsed monogamy and [it] was considered the best practice of the highest virtue. However, polygamy was also in practice, especially among the nobles. A number of such instances of polygamy are available not only in later Vedic literature, but also in the *Rig Veda*.

From this, it is not clear how Vedic Hindu law would justify polygamy. Sharma (1993: 108) observes that both monogamy and polygamy were practised and also indicates that the latter was found mainly in royal families and among the nobility. Confirming this, Sharma (1994: 17) claims that '[p]olygamy was never recommended openly though it was generally tolerated'.[12] Mitra (1965: 50) suggests that '[i]nsistance on the interest of the family led to a compromise of the monogamous ideal', which means that in certain specified conditions polygamy would be allowed. Tiwari (1991: 22) merely states that because of Vedic woman's high status, polygamy was rare and confined to the ruling classes. Altekar (1978: 104) also indicates that monogamy was the rule, while polygamy existed for a number of reasons:

> It is true that monogamy normally prevailed in Hindu society. The word *dampatī* 'two joint owners of the household' excludes a third person from the conjugal life. The ritual too does not provide for the association of more than one wife in the normal sacrifice. The Vedic gods also are monogamous. In practice, however, polygamy often prevailed in the rich and ruling sections of society. It was fairly common among kings and nobles, who often found it a useful instrument in strengthening their political power by contracting numerous but judicious matrimonial alliances. The rich probably regarded plurality of wives as a proof of their wealth, reputation and social position. References to polygamy are fairly numerous in the Vedic literature.

Sinha and Basu (1992: 81) claim that in Vedic India both polyandry and polygamy 'were almost the prevailing custom, but the succeeding Epic Age leaves them far behind and weds itself to a monogamic ideal'. This seems to suggest that over time, polygamy was reduced, while other authors try to claim exactly the opposite. It goes too far, however, to assume that polygamy ever became the norm among Hindus and that this should have been the law. However, this is what Mishra (1994: 158) misleadingly asserts:

> In ancient Hindu law polygamy is the rule rather than the exception, the norm rather than the ideal and it has an unquestioned place ... there was no

[12] Sharma (1994: 85–128) contains an excellent, detailed discussion of polygamy from ancient times and its inefficacious legal regulation in modern India.

> limit to the number of wives a man might have; he could have as many as he might afford to procure by the different modes of marriage.

This kind of statement helps to construct an image that traditional Hindu law stands for the obnoxious tradition of polygamy, thus building up a target for modernist ire. Mishra (1994: 158–9) is not concerned with such agenda, however, and merely attempts to justify his stance by reference to the need for men to fight and protect their realm. This seems to indicate that allowing for polygamy would mean a higher birthrate, which was at that time seen as desirable.[13] Altekar (1978: 105) argues that polygamy probably reflects a certain social and economic standing in society:

> There are some observations in the late Vedic literature to show that polygamy was well-established in certain sections of society. In later times also society thought it to be nothing unusual that men should have several wives; .... Polygamy, of course, was a luxury beyond the means of the poor.

Apart from economic and status considerations, however, there was a more explicitly Hindu rationale for allowing polygamous marriages, namely the desire to have male children, which is vigorously portrayed in the Vedic literature (Sharma 1993: 108; Apte 1978: 61). Specifically, 'failure to get children or the sterility of the wife was quite a strong reason for the prevalence of polygamy' (Sharma 1993: 108–9). As Altekar (1978: 105–6) explains in detail, the occasional occurrence of polygamy even among ordinary Hindus reflects concern for the preservation and continuance of the family:

> For offering the prescribed oblations to ancestors so as to secure their continuance in heaven, a son was absolutely necessary, and so society permitted the husband to take a second wife, if the first one was barren. Nay, we find some writers laying down that it was the duty of the wife to urge her husband to contract a second marriage, if she had failed to present a son to him.

While this is undoubtedly a prominent argument, we should not forget that in normal family circumstances lack of fertility would not pose a problem, so that there was no need for polygamy on that account. At any rate, the traditional discretion to marry polygamously was to be exercised cautiously and without haste, since 'polygamy never led to domestic peace and happiness' (Sharma 1993: 109). Key verses from the ancient texts are quite clear on this. For example, *Manusmṛti* 9. 81 (Bühler 1975: 342) states that '[a] barren wife may be superseded in the eighth year, she whose children (all) die in the tenth, she who bears only daughters in the eleventh, but she who is quarrelsome without delay'.

Other texts, for example *Arthaśāstra* 3.2.38–9, are to similar effect, stipulating a waiting period of up to twelve years, but emphasizing the necessity of

[13] This argument resurfaces, as we shall see later, in current debates about Muslim polygamy.

having a son.[14] As Altekar (1978: 106) demonstrates in some detail, making allowances for polygamy in order to obtain a son and thus to strengthen the joint family pattern would by implication endanger the sanctity of the *saṃskāra* ideal of Hindu marriage as a monogamous union. Indeed, Altekar's discussion confirms that there was considerable theoretical and practical opposition to any permission for polygamy in ancient India, since it infringed the Hindu ideal of *saṃskāra*.[15] The oldest of the four *dharmasūtras*, the *Āpastambadharmasūtra*, dated by Olivelle (2000: 10) to the beginning of the third century BC, encourages monogamy and clearly advises against taking a second wife if the existing wife is able to partake in ritual activities and to bear children (ibid.: 17–18).[16] Rather than leaving Hindu women out in the cold, important safeguards were stipulated for the protection of first wives in Hindu marriages.[17]

Over time, however, it appears that the carefully controlled discretion to enter a polygamous Hindu marriage turned virtually into a perceived right or privilege of Hindu men. This, as Sharma (1993: 109–11) brings out, needs to be seen in relation to the lowering of the status of Hindu women generally during the late classical period, which marginalized women, reduced the sanctity of the marriage ceremony, and probably also led to an increase in polygamy. Tiwari (1991: 23) claims that in the shastric period, Hindu women lost their earlier respected status in society and polygamy became one of the indicators of the decline in female status. Sharma (1993: 114) goes as far as stating that '[a]s a matter of fact the history of the evolution and prevalence of polygamy was the history of the social, economic and religious decadence of women in ancient India'.

In this context, as Altekar (1978: 106) excellently pinpoints, the problem was that Hindu men might simply supersede their wife for another and might then be tempted to wriggle out of traditional obligations to such a wife.[18] If we assume that supersession is virtually a divorce, this would no longer be polygamy, therefore, but serial monogamy.[19] In addition, if the traditional law

[14] Shastri (1990: 54) refers to a number of texts that stipulate such conditions.

[15] The obvious remedy for a sonless couple might be adoption, but that involves a legal fiction to which there are also many objections. Hindus therefore prefer adoption of close relatives, most ideally a brother's son. On adoption law, see Dhagamwar (1989); Venkataramiah (1982); Manooja (1993).

[16] For the relevant Sanskrit text and its translation see Olivelle (2000: 90–1).

[17] This leads Olivelle (2000: 17-18) to argue that Āpastamba's views with regard to sexual morality and women were progressive because he opposes polygamy. An alternative interpretation could be that the preservation of the *saṃskāra* ideal as a superior consideration makes this text look more conservative. However, Olivelle is quite correct to emphasize that protection of the interests of the dutifully married Hindu wife is evidenced from this early text (see also Olivelle 2000: 67).

[18] This subject, equally relevant to Ch. 12, is also discussed by Sharma (1994: 24–5).

[19] This particular issue becomes a matter of grave concern in the context of debates about prohibitions against divorce among Hindus and is discussed later in Ch. 11.

had been too strict about formal recognition of polygamy, Hindu men might simply arrange various forms of concubinage, which would probably have undesirable socio-economic consequences for Hindu society, especially for women, in the long run. The fluid borderlines between a formal polygamous marriage and more or less informal concubinage are discussed further below. Classical Hindu law as reflected in the dharma literature provides much evidence of the various situations in which a man might marry polygamously. M. Basu (2001: 28) explains, albeit in typically misguided positivist fashion, the role of ancient Hindu lawgivers:

> In fact, polygamy was sanctioned by the ancient law givers under certain specific circumstances, for example, Manu and Yajnavalkya approved of second marriages under special circumstances such as the wife's barrenness or lack of religious-mindedness, that is, if she was unfit to participate in the performance of the religious rites of her husband. The husband had the right to remarry if the wife failed to deliver a male child, so that he could beget a son.

While some texts thus specify in what conditions a Hindu male might take another wife, many other texts did not underwrite polygamous marriages and sought to preserve the sanctity of the shastric marriage. Derrett (1978a: 54) claims that the intervention of shastric experts provided a clearer picture:

> The Rishis became, on the whole clear, that the first marriage in the approved form was a dharmic marriage, a marriage for *dharma*. Other marriages and unions could not claim this quality. In course of time all legal distinction between them vanished, but in the earlier days a polygamous marriage was regarded as somehow lacking in the dharmic quality unless the first wife were deficient in *dharma* and/or offspring.

These arguments reflect distinctions between a 'proper' marriage and some kind of concubinage, but this issue remains vague. Other authors have emphasized that the growing practice of inter-caste marriage led to an increase in polygamy (Sharma 1993: 113), and that caste was a central factor in this context (Mishra 1994: 161). The shastric statements that appear to be treated as relevant in this context are the ones that permit a Brahmin husband to marry a wife from all four castes, while a Kshatriya male could marry only from three castes, a Vaisya male only from two, and a Sudra male should only ever marry a woman from his rank. But such simplistic formal interpretations relate first of all to the general *anuloma* rule that the ideal Hindu husband should be of equal or higher status than the wife. The argument that such texts, therefore, justified polygamy for higher castes, but not for members of the lower castes is plainly too simple. It overlooks social reality and is blinded by the unlimited classification mania of many late classical shastric texts. If anything, economics and the particular circumstances of the family would have determined why, or why not, a particular man would enter a polygamous arrangement. It is also difficult to give much credence to arguments, advanced by some writers, that polygamy was necessary to satisfy the sexual urges of hot-blooded men.[20]

While Sinha (1993: 63) claims that "[e]xcept for certain kings and rulers who were given a special licence in the historical times, polygamy was never favoured by the Hindu social organisation', Derrett (1978a: 4) summarizes the traditional position of Hindu law on polygamy by saying that there was little difficulty in accepting it:

> A wealthy husband could take a second or even third wife from social groups which would not lose in status and hopes by their daughters being disposed of in such a manner. The first wife was protected because she remained the husband's *dharmapatni* or wife for the sake of righteousness, subsequent wives being considered a matter of self-indulgence on their joint husband's part. Speaking practically, this facility took care of husbands for whom the first wife had lost all charm, and who could not divorce with a view to remarriage.

To what extent this was actual practice will obviously never be known. Shastri (1990: 53) rightly indicates that 'what percentage of Hindu males followed the practice of having more than one wife is difficult to say'. The leading Indologist Julius Jolly (1975: 140–7), writing originally in German in 1896, contributed a detailed discussion on polygamy. He showed, at p. 141, that '[g]enerally a man should at first marry a woman of his own caste and only afterwards proceed to take wives from the lower classes in the order of the Varnas, so that only the Sudra is restricted to a single wife of his own caste'. Here again, too much focus on caste boundaries precludes fuller analysis of the phenomenon of polygamy itself and the various reasons for it.

Curiously, many authors are tempted to blame the Muslim presence in India for the existence of Hindu polygamy.[21] Historically, this is a flawed claim, since Hindu polygamy is, first of all, much older than Muslim polygamy.[22] A fairly typical example of such writing, which links all kinds of issues together to furnish an ideological argument, is found in M. Basu's (2001: 33) statement that '[t]he position of women deteriorated further with the advent of the Muslim invaders and, consequently, customs and practices like purdah, polygamy, and infant marriages slowly took deep roots in Hindu society'. Since the Hindus

[20] But see Mishra (1994: 164–5) who produces a number of questionable arguments for the causes of Hindu polygamy. This echoes similar Muslim arguments, reproduced and discussed in Menski (2001: 148–60). Qureshi (1978: 350) is useful on this issue, too.

[21] A typical example of this reasoning is found in Thomas (2000: 98–100), who also suggests, at p. 171, that whereas Christian law enforces strict monogamy, '[i]n all Asiatic countries, the law favours polygyny'. This amounts evidently to the argument that Christianity is civilized and 'Asian values' are inherently inferior and deficient.

[22] Muslim authors claim against this that the Islamic regulation of polygamy (its restriction to four wives instead of an unlimited number) represents an important progressive civilizational step in terms of protecting the rights of women.

felt that their religion and social practices were under threat, they protected caste boundaries more avidly than before, which in turn led to shortages of grooms. As Basu (id.) sees it, '[d]esperate parents, therefore, began giving their young daughters away even to old infirm men who already had a number of wives. This established polygamy and child-marriage firmly in Hindu society'. Such placative assertions are of dubious empirical validity, as we saw earlier with regard to child marriage (Chapter 9).

Whatever the real reasons for Hindu polygamy, there is no doubt that it remained permitted throughout as part of the traditional Hindu system of family law but was not as prominent as writers such as M. Basu (2001) would suggest. While traditional Hindu society was clearly not concerned about modernist discourses on gender equality, it could not be said that the socio-economic interests of polygamously married women and their offspring were not a concern of traditional Hindu law. However, such concerns come out in other areas of law than polygamy, namely maintenance law (see Chapter 12), or succession and joint family law. In other words, the legal consequences of traditional Hindu polygamy made themselves felt in other legal areas. Polygamy itself was hardly a 'big issue' within the traditional system.

Hindu Polygamy under British Rule

M. Basu (2001: 34) notes that by the time the British arrived in India, Hindu women suffered from a number of social problems, but does not even specifically mention polygamy. Indeed, the British did not, as we saw, wish to interfere more than necessary in the social and family affairs of Hindus. Not much activism is identifiable in terms of restricting or prohibiting polygamy for Hindus, let alone Muslims, during British rule.[23] The issue simply kept a low profile.

The basic framework of British legal policy (see section on impact of British administration in Chapter 4), as laid down in 1772 by the Warren Hastings Regulation, effectively guaranteed Hindus and Muslims non-interference by the British in matters of family laws. Polygamy was treated as a matter of marriage law and fell within the ambit of 'religion' and local social regulation under the personal law.[24] Hindu polygamy was protected under this system of legal administration, while attention was given to other perceived social problems, such as the abolition of sati, or permitting widow remarriage, despite traditional Hindu reservations, through the Hindu Widows' Remarriage Act, 1865.

[23] At the same time, Indian Christians joined modern civilisation by accepting the legal prohibition of polygamy under the Indian Christian Marriage Act, 1872. Similarly, the Parsis accepted monogamy as a rule under the Parsi Marriage and Divorce Act, 1865 and later the 1936 Act of the same name.

[24] In theory, Hindu polygamy could have been declared a crime and would then have fallen under the provisions of the IPC for punishment.

As far as developments under the Anglo-Hindu case law were concerned, Hindu wives would not, in such a climate, be successful in opposing polygamy through a court case. Mishra (1994: 162) reports that it was held in 1863, in the Madras High Court,[25] that Hindu law permits polygamy, but does not approve of the practice. In another case during the 1870s, the discretion of a Hindu husband to marry polygamously, despite an earlier undertaking not to do so, was upheld, because an agreement restricting the husband's discretion would be opposed to traditional Hindu law (id.). Qureshi (1978: 182) refers to two other cases from the 1870s, *Jeebodhan v Sindhoo* (1872) 17 WR 522 and *Sitanath v Haimbutty* (1875) 24 WR 377. In both cases the husband had married a second time, but this was not treated by the courts as cruelty against the first wife. In *Dular Koer v Dwarka* (1907) 34 Cal 971, a Hindu husband had introduced a low-caste mistress as a concubine into the matrimonial home, to live as a member of the family. The wife was then driven out of the home, which the Calcutta HC treated as cruelty. It is evident that what constituted cruelty in the eyes of the court was not the husband's polygamy, but the manner in which the lawful wife had been mistreated and expelled. Such behaviour violated not only norms of decency, but also the recommendations of traditional Hindu authorities about fair treatment to wives in a polygamous marriage.

It is instructive to look for a moment beyond the realm of Hindu law to test whether Hindus were given undue liberties. It appears that this is not the case. In *Joseph v Joseph* AIR 1934 Pat 475, decided under the Indian Divorce Act of 1869, it was held that a Christian husband's action in introducing another woman into the matrimonial home, coupled with threats against the legally married wife, amounted to cruelty. As far as Muslim law is concerned, there appear to be no early cases on polygamy. Indeed, there were vigorous protests when, well after independence, a famous Indian decision began to tackle Muslim polygamy.[26] Jolly (1975: 146) links this emerging stance on polygamy to reservations about divorce in India during the late nineteenth century:

> Even at the present day polygamy is as common as it is permissible, and separation proper, at least among the higher castes, is rare. The number of castes in Bombay, among which ... polygamy is permitted and practised is very large and includes many Brahmanical and aristocratic communities. There are similar data about other provinces too. Nevertheless, the percentage of people actually practising polygamy is nowhere very high. Thus in Madras where polygamy is most popular, only 4 per cent of the men have two wives and in the Punjab the number of men wedded to

[25] The case is *Viraswami v Appasami* (1863) 1 MCHR 275, also referred to by Derrett (1978b: 110) as an example of an old Hindu law rule being abandoned by the Anglo-Indian courts.

[26] In *Itwari v Asghari* AIR 1960 All 684, a new meaning was given to 'cruelty' in the light of changed social circumstances. It was held, for the first time, that the action of the Muslim husband in taking a second wife involved cruelty to the first wife. For details see Pearl and Menski (1998: 249–50).

> more than one wife does not even amount to [more] than 1 per cent. Sterility of the first wife is usually said to be the cause of polygamy and it is fully in conformity with the principles of the *Smṛtis.*

There is some evidence of early campaigns among women's groups to abolish polygamy through legislation. Augustine (1991: 118) reports that on 6 August 1866, the Governor General advised the Bengal government to postpone such legislation, reflecting colonial timidity about legal intervention in Hindu personal laws. A specialized committee report on the problem of polygamy in Bengal was then submitted on 3 February 1867. This report exposed the shocking conditions of the particular local practice of *kulin* Brahmins marrying huge numbers of women and making a lot of money out of it.[27] Nevertheless, no legislative action was taken by the colonial government.

As independence became imminent, some parts of India went ahead and restricted or abolished polygamy among Hindus. The Princely State of Baroda, forerunner in reforms, took such a position. However, the Baroda Hindu Nibandha of 1937 did not outlaw polygamy as such, but rather made it a ground for divorce if the respondent had married a second time during the lifetime of the petitioner, who would normally be a woman (Derrett 1978a: 6), or permitted a woman separate residence on the same ground (ibid.: 12).[28] Derrett (1978a: 13) reports that the Hindu Law Committee of Baroda had been advised by very learned pandits who, in view of evidence that polygamy was very rare in the state, agreed to the 'abolition' of polygamy and thus 'swallowed this drastic reform'.

Despite these piecemeal attempts at abolishing polygamy, no further reforms were promulgated in India until after the Second World War, though inspiration for their realization developed with the growth of various women's movements, which were actively supported by Mahatma Gandhi. Derrett (1978a: 9–10) argues that the women's movement 'kept up a vocal and literate campaign to such good effect as to instill into Hindu professional men a sense of guilt'. These women managed to convey the message that Hindu women had been treated badly for centuries, and that reforms were now overdue. Derrett (1978a: 10) writes that he found it 'difficult to imagine that any Hindu males conceived any of the impending changes as other than 'concessions' to their womenfolk, however merited'. Still, he also observed that there was a process of 'leaning over backwards', an early form of affirmative action, to be fair to women, which developed during this time. The major focus of the reformist efforts appears to have been concentrated on divorce and succession rights, not on the abolition of polygamy. Derrett (1978a: 11) reports that women's opposition to polygamous arrangements against their will needed to be strengthened:

[27] For some details on this particular problem, see also M. Basu (2001: 9–11).

[28] Sharma (1994: 89) points out that the Madras Marumakkathayam Act of 1932 made certain marriages in that part of India strictly monogamous.

> One of the complaints which the women's movement had ventilated was a certain indignity married women could be forced to endure if they ran away from unbearable or polygamous husbands: they could do so (if escape was indeed practicable) only at the cost of their maintenance.

Here again, ideological objections to polygamy are mixed with concerns about the financial implications for women who oppose polygamous arrangements. This particular problem was taken care of, as far as law can take care of such social problems, by the Hindu Married Women's Right to Separate Residence and Maintenance Act of 1946, which became law on 23 April 1946.[29] Under this Act, one of the grounds for a Hindu wife to ask for separate residence and maintenance from her husband was if the husband had married again, or kept a concubine in the house or habitually resided with a concubine. Tiwari (1991: 25) mentions briefly that within the wider context of a number of reformist activities, the Bombay Prevention of Hindu Bigamous Marriages Act, 1946 and the Madras Hindu (Bigamy Prevention and Divorce) Act, 1949 'provided improvements in the marital life of Hindu women', but gives no further details.[30] Sharma (1994: 34) adds to this list the Saurashtra Prevention of Bigamy Act, 1950 and reports that according to the Bombay Act, which was the model for the other Acts,

> it was illegal to have a second wife during the lifetime of the first wife. If a man wanted to remarry, he had to dissolve his first marriage. It further provided that a bigamous marriage was void not only if it is contracted in Bombay but even outside, if one or both the parties to the marriage were domiciled in Bombay State.[31]

In addition, the Bombay Hindu Divorce Act of 1947 permitted a Hindu wife to petition for divorce on a number of grounds, including the fact that the husband had married a second wife (Sharma 1994: 34–5). The reformative measures to abolish and control Hindu polygamy thus necessitated further activism in providing grounds for divorce on the basis of the husband's polygamy or his liaison with a concubine.[32]

[29] The relevant rules were later brought into the HAMA, 1956.

[30] For some details and the wider context of this Act, see Derrett (1978a: 15). The discussion in Sharma (1994: 89–90) is also useful.

[31] Derrett (1978a: 13) indicates that such extraterritorial provisions could easily be circumvented by simply moving to another territory.

[32] There is substantial evidence that inter-religious marriages, and especially marriages where a spouse converted from one religion to another, might lead to bigamy prosecutions. Such specific, often highly politicised issues do not concern us here. The most recent high-profile case on this was *Sarla Mudgal v Union of India* AIR 1995 SC 1531. Deshpande (1993: 22) vigorously criticizes the continuing discrimination between personal laws in this field. For details, see also Kusum (2000: 250–4).

The Modernist Abolition of Hindu Polygamy

Studying the modern Hindu law on polygamy, one sees at once how complex this once relatively insignificant issue has become. Reformers of Hindu law have been proud of the abolition of polygamy for Hindus, but many critical voices demand improvements to this law, as it appears far from perfect in its modern shape. In the discussions about the Hindu Code Bill during the post-independence period, the abolition of Hindu polygamy was not actually considered a controversial issue. Modernism demanded the abolition of polygamy, and presented a strong case as far as Hindus were concerned. Mishra (1994: 166) claims that today 'the West regards monogamy as an absolute ideal in itself and would never pardon the East for any of its laws that may permit the slightest deviation from this western ideal even in the most abnormal circumstances of a particular couple'.[33]

As Derrett (1978a: 20) shows, during the debates on Hindu law reforms, 'Ambedkar made it clear that the goal was one civil law for all Indians. Therefore if polygamy was to be abolished for Hindus in, say, Uttar Pradesh and Bengal, it ought to be abolished for Muslims also'. However, Ambedkar's uniforming vision did not prevail: polygamy was eventually abolished for Hindus, but continues—officially—to be permitted for Indian Muslims.[34] This now constitutes the main grievance of modernist observers, as is clearly documented in *Towards Equality* (1975: 104–8) and writing that relies on this report. The following sections examine the origins of this curious state of affairs by analysing the historical development of modernist failings, from the earliest reformist agenda to the gradual realization by the Indian judiciary that outright abolition of polygamy would mainly be detrimental to the social welfare of women and children.

Reformist Agenda

Derrett (1978a: 19) contextualizes the modernist attempts to abolish polygamy within the wider political dimension of reform debates, stating that '[p]rior to 1938 the aspersion that Hindus were polygamous, married without their personal consent and for money and did not allow divorce was used to demonstrate how unfit they were for the modern world and so for independence'. Sharma (1994: 89) reports that by the early 19th century, modernist condemnation of

[33] These are almost the same words as used by Mahmood (1986: 115–6), cited in n.1 earlier. This kind of modernist approach is also adopted by Poulter (1995: 85) who singled out polygamy as one of three intractable issues in terms of demanding adherence by immigrants to British 'core values'.

[34] This has given rise to many critical comments about Muslim conservatism and the resulting block on the implementation of the uniform civil code. For details see Sharma (1994: 87). Singh (1989: 60–1) vigorously criticizes the non-implementation of gender equality. Qureshi (1978: 382–91) discusses the position of Muslim law and concludes that the time has come to restrict Muslim polygamy, too.

polygamy had become stronger. Especially in the west, legislation was increasingly used to outlaw polygamous unions.

It appears, however, that the 'Western' modernizing agenda were not the only ones in the field. Sharma (1994: 89) notes that because among traditional Hindus, monogamy was the exception rather than the rule, '[d]uring this period Hindu social-reformers wanted that monogamy should be translated into a rule of law'. It seems therefore that Hindus themselves argued for restrictions on polygamy, since the ancient texts (as we saw earlier) had not given unqualified permission to Hindu men.[35] Parashar (1992: 94–5) refers to the debates during the 1940s about the modern state's power to legislate on Hindu law, showing that there were no doubts about the competence of the Indian legislature to codify Hindu law, since that law had always been subject to change and debate, rather than being an immutable rule system. Precisely such arguments were then used to justify legal intervention, as Parashar (1992: 96) explains:

> Monogamy for all Hindus was recommended on the grounds that under the *dharmashastra* the Hindu husband did not always have an unfettered, unqualified right to polygamy .... This line of reasoning suggests that ... the State was upholding the superiority of the true principles embodied in the *shastras* .... No consistent pattern was, however, followed. There is no evidence that the State made any serious effort to find out how its proposals could conform to *sastric* ideals.

Parashar (1992: 97) therefore concludes this discussion by stating that 'even while modifying the rules of Hindu law, the State was at pains to portray its efforts as not being contrary to the religious texts' and reports that the state even went so far as to claim that the purpose of the legal reforms was to save Hindu society and culture. Most commentators, however, assume that the main direction of reformative effort was provided by the reformers' desire to promote modernity and to implement the constitutional principle of gender equality.[36] Sharma (1994: 86) states that Hindu marriage was made monogamous to 'give concrete expression to the principle of equality enshrined in the Constitution'. Arguing that monogamy is beneficial to society, since it ensures conjugal happiness, promotes domestic peace and maintains the equilibrium of both sexes for the purpose of marriage, she states that, '[f]or monogamy, both the husband and wife are placed on equal footing in the matrimonial home' (id.).

Mishra (1994: 163–4) considers three reasons for and against polygamy, including cases in which the physical inability of the wife to either bear children or to produce a male heir is at issue. First, as seen earlier, this scenario was traditionally used to justify polygamy on the ground that a Hindu should

[35] Some evidence of this is also provided by M. Basu (2001: 106–7).

[36] Parashar (1992: 98) confirms that '[f]rom now on the State claimed the authority to reform Hindu law on the ground that the Constitution demanded that all laws be in conformity with its principles'.

ideally not die without a son, lest the chain of ancestors in the joint family context would be broken.[37] Second, polygamy was traditionally justified as bringing a man prestige and status, but this does not make it acceptable in modern conditions. Third, there could be economic reasons for polygamy, which might make sense to people in their particular local circumstances. However, most writers indicate in one form or another that polygamy is simply an outdated form of marital arrangement. Tiwari (1991: 44) claims that the system "has outlived its value in the modern world", but recognises later on in the discussion that "[b]igamy seems to persist because social norms have not been able to keep pace with legal reforms" (ibid.: 46).

Statutory Regulation of Hindu Polygamy

Despite the polemical character of modernist agenda, the introduction of Hindu monogamy by modernist legislation was a straightforward process. The HMA came into force on 18 May 1955 and simply abolished and criminalized Hindu polygamy, introducing monogamy as the only rule for Hindu law. This looks like a classic case of no-nonsense legislative intervention. The Act retained the distinction between void and voidable marriages and leaves no doubt that a Hindu spouse cannot enter a second legally valid marriage in the lifetime of an existing spouse (Derrett 1978a: 25). The main relevant provisions under the HMA of 1955 are found in Section 5(i), 11, and 17. Section 5 deals with conditions for a Hindu marriage and provides that:

> A marriage may be solemnized between any two Hindus, if the following conditions are fulfilled, namely: -
> (i) neither party has a spouse living at the time of the marriage;

Thus the HMA recognizes only monogamous marriages among Hindus as legally valid marriages. As we saw in Chapter 8 earlier, the legal validity of a Hindu marriage depends above all on the performance of customary rituals. We saw from the reported case law that a major loophole has developed in this regard because of pleadings by polygamous Hindu husbands that they were not validly married to a second or subsequent wife (or perhaps even the first wife) in accordance with the provisions of Section 7 HMA. This issue is further

[37] However, in the early Indian case law, this reliance on Hindu freedom of religion has not been accepted as an argument to justify Hindu polygamy. For details see *State of Bombay v Narasu Appa Mali* AIR 1952 Bom 84. In *Shrinivasa Aiyar v Saraswathi Ammal*, AIR 1952 Mad 193, the husband had claimed that it was necessary for Hindus to have a son so that spiritual debts could be redeemed and appropriate religious ceremonies performed. The Court rejected this argument, relying inter alia on American law. The case, which has various aspects, is briefly summarized by Parashar (1992: 206). *Ram Prasad v State of UP* AIR 1957 All 411, also unsuccessfully challenged those provisions of the HMA which restrict polygamy as unconstitutional, and as an infringement of the fundamental right of Hindus to freedom of religion.

analysed below. The second relevant provision under the HMA for the abolition of Hindu polygamy is Section 11, which concerns nullity and is unambiguously worded to the effect that a polygamous Hindu marriage is void in law:

> 11. Void marriage. -
> Any marriage solemnized after the commencement of this Act shall be null and void and may, on a petition presented by either party thereto, [against the other party][38] be so declared by a decree of nullity if it contravenes any one of the conditions specified in clauses (i), (iv) and (v) of section 5.

The third provision in the HMA regulating polygamy concerns its punishment and is found in Section 17 of the Act:

> 17. Punishment of bigamy. -
> Any marriage between two Hindus solemnized after the commencement of this Act is void if at the date of such marriage either party had a husband or wife living; and the provisions of section 494 and 495 of the Indian Penal Code (XLV of 1860) shall apply accordingly.

According to Section 494 of the IPC of 1860, a Hindu polygamist becomes liable to a prison sentence and a fine, since the provisions of this Code were extended to Hindus in 1955:

> 494. Marrying again during lifetime of husband or wife. -
> Whoever, having a husband or wife living, marries in any case in which such marriage is void by reason of its taking place during the life of such husband or wife, shall be punished with imprisonment of either description for a term which may extend to seven years, and shall also be liable to fine.

Section 495 of the 1860 Code provides for the more serious offence of not only committing polygamy, but concealing it from a spouse, more particularly the second wife:

> 495. Same offence with concealment of former marriage from person with whom subsequent marriage is contracted. -
> Whoever commits the offence defined in the last preceding section having concealed from the person with whom the subsequent marriage is contracted, the fact of the former marriage, shall be punished with imprisonment of either description for a term which may extend to ten years, and shall also be liable to fine.

These statutory reforms, in typical positivist fashion, would appear to have completely outlawed and criminalized Hindu polygamy. Desai (1998: 68) asserts that '[t]he outstanding feature of the new Hindu Marriage Act is that monogamy is now enforced as a rule of law and bigamy is rendered punishable as a crime'. It seems that the legislature has done its work and has brought

[38] The words in the bracket were added to the section by the Marriage Laws (Amendment) Act, 1976.

about a significant, modernizing legal reform.[39] Pant (2000: 23) notes that the prohibition of polygamy by the HMA brought one of the biggest changes in Hindu law in 1955/56. Mahmood (1981: 17) claims that Hindu polygamy was abolished, 'following the modern world-wide trend in this regard',[40] though Hindu religious law allows it.

However, virtually every commentator admits, in one form or another, that this reform measure has not been effective in practice. Reformist rhetoric obfuscates analysis at two levels. Gloating about the success of legal reform, as evidenced through the formal abolition of Hindu polygamy, is matched with vigorous criticism about the fact that Muslim polygamy was not abolished and Hindus continue to flout the law. Singh (1989: 61) notes that '[w]hile bigamy has been made an offence for the Hindus and the second marriage is void in law, such marriages are still prevalent'.[41] Tiwari (1991: 26) claims on the one hand that the enactments of the 1950s 'bring about a sea change in the status and position of Hindu woman', but also notes that bigamy 'seems to persist because social norms have not been able to keep pace with legal reforms' (ibid.: 46).

Barriers faced by women in accessing the legal machinery are seen as a major factor for inhibiting enforcement of anti-polygamy laws. Singh (1989: 61) claims that '[q]uite often an economically dependent woman who is also uneducated has neither the knowledge nor the means to go to the court'. It is well known from a variety of sources that women may be reluctant to approach courts, because it means giving publicity to an intensely private affair.[42] There may be various methods to assist women in reaching the courts, prominently through social workers (Singh 1989: 62) or specific NGOs, but the question remains whether that is actually in the best interests of women. Qureshi (1978: 51) argues that the abolition of polygamy occurred only in theory. While bigamy had declined during the past twenty years, the practice had not been eliminated mainly because of the reluctance of the aggrieved wife to go to court:

[39] In addition, as part of the introduction of a new divorce regime, based on a number of fault grounds, living in adultery (S. 13(1)(i) of the HMA) and the husband's polygamous marriage, under S. 13(2)(i) of the HMA, became grounds for divorce. For details see Virdi (1972: 236–9) who shows, at p. 237, that in 1955, 'the legislature left it to the choice of the wife of a polygamous husband either to remain with him or to seek divorce on that ground'. This is because bigamous marriages contracted before 1955 'do not become *ipso facto* void, but continue to be valid' (p. 238).

[40] One wonders, of course, why the same reasoning is not advanced for Muslim law.

[41] This is measurable, for example, from the census reports for 1961 on the incidence of polygamous marriages.

[42] Tiwari (1991: 46) writes that '[a]n Indian woman devoid of economic security or social awareness accepts her husband's lapse meekly as her fate and she is afraid of even going to courts of law'.

> She is between the devil and the deep sea; if she takes recourse to the law, her husband may be sent to jail (which she does not want) and if she does not, she has to share her husband with another woman.

Thus, as Qureshi (1978: 351) reiterates on the basis of a field survey, the HMA 'could not help much in abolishing polygamy'. In his conclusions he states, in view of evidence that both Muslims and Hindus in India continue to practise polygamy, that merely making a provision about abolition of polygamy in a uniform civil code will not work, since '[t]his practice cannot be stopped by an Act of Parliament or State legislatures' (ibid.: 390) and public education is needed instead to bring about social change.[43]

The Deficient Penalization of Hindu Polygamy

The legal commentaries on the extent of punishment for polygamy among Hindus are often disappointingly simplistic and tend to be purely doctrinal. The official legal view became that once the modern state had decreed the abolition of polygamy among Hindus, the legal task of modernizing reforms had been completed: Hindu polygamy has been outlawed in the HMA; the job is done. State law here claims, in typical fashion, to have created facts that are deemed to be social reality.

While the statutory regime for the formal abolition of Hindu polygamy is firmly in place, a critical analysis finds more or less clandestine legal tolerance for Hindu polygamy in India at various levels. The general social science literature continues to politicize the issue of polygamy in wider terms of gender equality and persists in advocating (with very few but significant exceptions) strict abolition and criminalization of polygamy in all situations, including Muslim marriages. The courts as ultimate dispensers of justice (Kusum 2000: 231) are dealing with real people and their specific socio-economic struggles and predicaments. It is notable that the judges have focused their energies more on devising techniques to regulate Hindu polygamy instead of outlawing it completely and punishing it to the fullest possible extent. This may fly in the face of legal doctrine, as found in positivist theory,[44] but is a fact.

Since in this area of the law, there appears to be some evidence of male collusion in undercutting the legal prohibition of Hindu polygamy, the picture is complex. To some extent, the condonation of polygamy feeds on traditional patriarchal predilections, allowing men discretion over how to arrange matters

[43] Agnes (2000: 245) reproduces figures for the community-wise incidences of polygamous marriages from *Towards Equality* (1974). Tribals are shown to have 17.98 per cent (1951-60) and 15.25 per cent in later years, while the figures for Hindus are 5.0 per cent for 1951-60 and 6.83 thereafter, and for Muslims 4.31 per cent and 5.7 per cent respectively. This seems to indicate that polygamous marriages are more common among Hindus than among Muslims, and that the numbers have increased rather than declined, except among tribals.

[44] This doctrinal view is evident, for example, when Desai (1990: 635) asserts that a bigamous Hindu marriage is simply non-existent.

in the home sphere and expecting women to put up with this. From that angle, the focus of the law has been on getting Hindu polygamists 'off the hook', once they got caught. If this was the only approach, it would clearly be bad, because it unfairly favours men and allows them to get away with much devious behaviour.[45] However, this is manifestly not the whole story, since the widespread non-prosecution of polygamous Hindu males also appears to be socially and economically motivated to protect, in particular, the financial interests of women and children. In a nutshell, the critical question has been whether a social purpose is being served by putting men behind bars if their wives and children end up suffering.[46] While all textbooks reproduce the system of penalties, few authors go beyond this to examine the extent of punishment in cases of violation of the law. Mahmood (1981: 117) compares the legal position of a Hindu wife married polygamously prior to the promulgation of the HMA (i.e. 18 May 1955) and of a wife who finds herself party to a polygamous marriage solemnized after that date:

> The relief is strictly available to wives married before the commencement of the Act .... Having a rather naive expectation that all Hindus would abide by the anti-bigamy provisions of the Act, the relief is not made available to a wife whose husband marries again after 18 May, 1955. Of course, in this case the second marriage would be void. But, since the first wife cannot seek its annulment by a decree of nullity, in order to save her from the curse of a co-wife's company she could have been given at least a right to seek a divorce on that ground. The law as it stands, however, does not grant her such a relief.

It would appear, however, that a Hindu wife could seek divorce on the ground of the husband's adultery under Section 13(1)(i) of the HMA and thus has such a remedy, at least under the Marriage Laws (Amendment) Act of 1976. Mahmood (1981: 139) correctly points out that the HMA has no retrospective effect, so where both marriages of a Hindu husband were solemnised prior to 18 May 1955, either wife might petition for divorce, but the husband would not be liable to the penalties stipulated under Section 17 of the HMA.

Despite the legislative prohibition of Hindu polygamy, virtually all writers concur that the law has not been effective.[47] Mahmood (1986: 115–6)

[45] Kusum (2000: 232) finds it 'distressing' that the Supreme Court should insist on strict compliance with essential ceremonies 'even in case of bigamous marriages' and thus seems to miss the point that this really only happens in bigamy prosecutions, and for a specific reason.

[46] Instructive cases involving children are *Laxmibai v Limbabai* AIR 1983 Bom 222 (see also *ASIL* 1983: 308), *Yamuna Bai Anantrao Adalia v Anantrao Shivram Adalia* AIR 1988 SC 644, which held that a polygamous marriage is void as far as the general law is concerned (see *ASIL* 1988: 301), and *Perumal Gounder v Pachayappan* AIR 1990 Mad 110, which gives limited rights of inheritance to the children of void bigamous marriages.

[47] A useful chapter on polygamy is found in Nijjar (1994: 20–64).

emphasizes that criminal prosecution of a bigamist would not really help the first wife, since her husband can easily wriggle out of the prosecution. While many polygamous marriages among Hindus never come to the attention of the legal authorities because nobody complains, the reported case law is highly instructive about the limited extent to which Hindu polygamy is being controlled. Many commentators have been negative and quite hostile about this. Desai (1993: 39) briefly discusses the strict penalties for bigamy under the SMA of 1954 and then turns to polygamy under the HMA at pp. 100–1, providing many indications that punishment for polygamy under Section 17 of the HMA is not in fact a simple, straightforward matter at all:

> Before a person can be found punishable under this section it is necessary to determine the fact whether there had been a subsequent marriage of a spouse during the lifetime of the other spouse. From that point it has to be determined whether the prior marriage was duly solemnized. In case where either of the two marriages is found to be not duly solemnized the position is that in the eye of the law there is only one legal and valid marriage making the charge of bigamy unsustainable.

Mishra (1994: 165) points to the notorious fact that many bigamy prosecutions fail because there is no proof of proper solemnization of the second marriage.[48] Courts have held in many cases that bigamy is committed only if the required ceremonies of marriage have been performed in both marriages. This has led some commentators to describe Section 7 of the HMA as a kind of bigamist's charter of freedom. Professor Derrett (1970: 307) was highly critical:

> The criminal courts are sympathetic to bigamists, holding that in order to commit the crime the ceremony must have been such a ceremony that, according to the custom of the parties, a valid marriage would have been contracted but for the first marriage. This is unfair...
> ... The whole law on bigamy by Hindus is unsatisfactory, since Parliament's intention has been turned into oppression.

Even in the rare cases resulting in convictions for polygamy, the punishments given appear to remain rather lenient. Despite tough rhetoric in *Gopal Lal v State of Rajasthan* AIR 1979 SC 713, the courts have not focused on heavy criminalization of Hindu polygamy, with a maximum penalty of seven years' rigorous imprisonment. In *Gopal Lal*, it was held, at pp. 715–6, dismissing the husband's appeal but treating him in effect leniently:

> Bigamy is a serious offence and the maximum punishment under Section 494 is seven years. Therefore, where the offence of bigamy is proved the court cannot take a very lenient view. In the instant case the appellant was sentenced to two years and a fine of Rs. 2,000/-. It appears that the appellant has already paid a fine of Rs. 2,000/-. In these circumstances therefore, we feel that the ends of justice will be met by reducing the sentence of

[48] See also Kusum (2000: 232–3). This issue is discussed in detail at pp. 395–404 later.

> imprisonment from two years to one year but maintaining the sentence of fine. With this modification the appeal is dismissed. The appellant will now surrender and serve out the remaining portion of the sentence.

Such a soft approach by the Supreme Court of India towards Hindu polygamists does not indicate explicit toleration of polygamy, but comes quite close to official condonation. A number of cases show that socially recognizing the factum of a legally void polygamous marriage, and taking legal notice of it does make sense to Indians. Above all, it allows the courts to grant the women in such cases substantial financial relief.[49] There is manifest judicial concern about social justice for women, which is not automatically achieved by formal abolition and criminalization of polygamy. Judicial protection of the economic interests of women and children has therefore become an overriding concern that prevails over the moral and ideological objections to polygamy and the desire to punish male offenders.

Case law has firmly established that certain Hindu values are not protected by the modern legal regime after 1955. Even before that, in *State of Bombay v Narasu Appa Mali* AIR 1952 Bom 84, a polygamous Hindu husband had appealed against his prosecution under the Bombay Prevention of Hindu Bigamous Marriages Act of 1946. Chagla J rejected the husband's argument that having a son is a religious requirement for all Hindus and an integral part of Hindu religion which must be protected under the Constitution. It was held that a Hindu male whose first wife has not produced a son, may not simply contract a second marriage on that ground. Chagla J observed in this context that if certain religious practices run counter to public order, morality or health, or a policy of social welfare upon which the state has embarked, such religious practices must give way for the sake of the greater good of the nation. In this case, the court tried to justify the ban on Hindu polygamy by saying that religious faith is different from religious/social practices, but at the same time it also tried to justify Muslim polygamy by saying that polygamy does not discriminate against women on ground of sex. The court seemed to be in an acute dilemma.[50]

Following such early court battles, the case law on Hindu polygamy in relation to Section 7 of the HMA developed some serious deficiencies. The leading case of *Bhaurao Shankar Lokhande v State of Maharashtra* AIR 1965 SC 1564, still treated by virtually all textbooks as a precedent in this field, appears to be firmly biased in favour of polygamous men, but is in my view no

[49] A case in point is *C. Obula Konda Reddy v C. Pedda Venkata Lakshamma* AIR 1976 AP 43, where a woman who was party to a polygamous and therefore legally void marriage was nevertheless granted maintenance from the 'husband' because she was a 'Hindu wife' under the terms of Section 18 of the HAMA 1956.

[50] Other cases challenging the constitutionality of the ban on Hindu polygamy were unsuccessful. See *Haisnam Baruniton Singh v T.N.H.O.B. Devi* AIR 1959 Manipur 20 and *Ram Prasad v State of U.P.* AIR 1957 All 411, discussed by Parashar (1992: 219).

longer good law. A neo-Buddhist husband appealed against his conviction for bigamy after he had been found guilty by all lower courts under Section 494 of the IPC. He had married one woman in about 1956 and another in 1962, during the lifetime of the first wife. On appeal to the Supreme Court, it was argued on behalf of the polygamist that the essential ceremonies for a valid Hindu marriage were not performed when he underwent the second marriage ceremony in 1962. Thus, the impugned marriage was not a legally valid marriage under Hindu law, and thus could not give rise to a prosecution for bigamy. Considering the wording of Section 17 of the HMA, the Supreme Court concentrated on the word 'solemnized' and held, at pp. 1565–6, that it is 'essential for the purpose of Section 17 of the Act, that the marriage...should have been celebrated with proper ceremonies and in due form. Merely going through certain ceremonies with the intention that the parties be taken to be married, will not make the ceremonies prescribed by law or approved by any established custom'. The SC had consulted the twelfth edition of Mulla's *Hindu Law*, which states, at p. 615, as cited in the judgment at p. 1566:

> '(1) There are two ceremonies essential to the validity of a marriage, whether the marriage be in the Brahma form or the Asura form, namely -
> (1) invocation before the sacred fire, and
> (2) saptapadi, that is, the taking of seven steps by the bridegroom and the bride jointly before the sacred fire.
> (2) A marriage may be completed by the performance of ceremonies other than those referred to in sub-section (1), where it is allowed by the custom of the caste to which the parties belong.

Bhaurao Shankar appeared to be a clear-cut case of Hindu polygamy; nevertheless the man escaped conviction. By assuming that a fully valid Hindu marriage must include ritual elements involving the holy fire as a witness and a rite of *saptapadī,* the SC virtually held that these two rituals are essential to all legally valid Hindu marriages. The Supreme Court found that the two essential ceremonies stipulated by Mulla's textbook had not been performed. Since the form of Hindu marriage chosen was the *gandharva* form, a kind of 'love marriage' rather than a full-fledged Sanskritic ritual had occurred. Mulla's *Hindu Law* in its twelfth edition claimed that a *gandharva* marriage also required full Hindu rituals, and the performance of the essential marriage ceremonies, unless there were customs to the contrary. Since there was no evidence before the Court that the marriage customs of this community had been modified or abrogated, the Supreme Court stuck to a rigid technical definition of custom. Oblivious of the fact that a second Hindu marriage may customarily not be performed with full rituals anyway,[51] the Court held, at p. 1567, that the marriage in question 'was certainly not performed in accordance with the essential

[51] On this see Menski (1983; 1995b). Singh (1989: 62–3) notes correctly that the burden of proof in many cases 'cannot be discharged owing to the fact that second marriages during the subsistence of a prior marriage, are seldom performed with usual pomp and show'.

requirements for a valid marriage under Hindu law'. Thus the appeals against conviction were allowed.

This case seems technically correct until one examines the factual backdrop in more detail. There was evidence of a simple marriage ceremony involving mutual garlanding and certain other rituals, in particular the touching of the foreheads of bride and groom, which was said to constitute the final rite.[52] The community concerned were former low-caste Hindus following Dr Ambedkar's lead in converting to Buddhism in the 1950s. As a result, they had modified their marriage customs, but this is not clearly brought out. The Court was evidently unwilling to accept evidence of new or changed customs during the past five or seven years, emphasizing at p. 1567 that 'the departure from the essentials cannot be said to have become a custom, as contemplated by the Hindu Marriage Act'.

In my view, the Supreme Court committed a critical mistake here in handling Hindu customs and produced a misguided statutory interpretation: Section 7(2) of the HMA makes it quite clear that there can be Hindu marriages without *homa* and *saptapadī*, and even Mulla's textbook, as cited above, indicates this. We also saw, in Chapter 8 earlier, that Section 3 of the HMA does not insist that customs have to be 'ancient', so that the modern Hindu law on this matter is purposely quite different from the traditional Anglo-Hindu law. The inadequate decision in *Bhaurao Shankar* represents an obvious example of judicial conservatism and blindness to social realities, ignoring not only the law and its social purpose, but also disregarding the legitimate expectations of women caught up in polygamous marriages. Decided wrongly in the first place, however, this case has been misused ever since.[53] It became a much-used precedent, which has evidently helped many Hindu polygamists to escape conviction.[54] Hindu husbands faced with a prosecution for bigamy would now simply try to argue that the marriage rituals they had performed did not result in a legally valid Hindu marriage. In fact, some ritual element might purposely be left out to avoid a prosecution for polygamy.[55]

[52] This appears to be a modified, simple form of the *saptapadī* ritual, which is widely considered to be the crucial marriage ritual for high-caste Hindu marriages. Touching of the heads of the spouses is a symbol of friendship (Menski 1991b).

[53] Singh (1989: 62) highlights that '[w]hether the interpretation put by the Court will subserve the policy and purpose of the Act or the social objectives of the legislation was never in their contemplation', noting at p. 63 that '[t]his judicial interpretation facilitates widespread evasion of law'.

[54] This position is also reflected in more recent editions of Mulla's *Hindu Law*, see now Desai (1990: 638–9), which is still misleading and has given rise to more wrong decisions. Tiwari (1991: 45) criticizes that judicial insistence on such high standards of evidence 'deprives the drive against bigamy of its spirit'.

[55] Kusum (2000: 232–3) claims that '[i]t is common knowledge that such marriages are performed surreptitiously so as to evade the law' and cites a number of cases to substantiate this point.

In *Kanwal Ram v Himachal Pradesh Administration* AIR 1966 SC 614, it was reiterated by the Supreme Court, relying on *Bhaurao Shankar*, that a conviction for bigamy could not be sustained unless the essential ceremonies for a valid Hindu marriage had been performed. Here, almost unbelievably, even the husband's own admission that he had taken the second woman as his wife was not accepted as evidence. In this case, the first marriage had taken place in 1940 or 1941, and the second marriage after the promulgation of the HMA. It was stated, at p. 614, that '[t]he parties belong to a village in Himachal Pradesh among whom a customary form of marriage called Praina, is recognised. Both the marriages were performed according to that form'. The Court went into some detail about this customary ritual but insisted, in reliance on Mulla's *Hindu Law* and *Bhaurao Shankar*, that certain Sanskritic ceremonies were essential. Taking a strictly technical approach on matters of proof, it was held at p. 615 that, 'it is clear that in law such admission is not evidence of the fact of the second marriage having taken place. In a bigamy case, the second marriage as a fact, that is to say, the ceremonies constituting it, must be proved'. Thus, even where the husband had admitted the second marriage, and there were plenty of indications that local custom allowed for such simple marriage rituals, there was no valid marriage, and hence no bigamy. This is pure formal legal reasoning, totally blind to social reality and devoid of any responsibility towards women.[56]

Given the presence of two strong precedents in this field, subsequent cases have come under the shadow of *Bhaurao Shankar*, but the judges have gradually become more alert and have convicted Hindu polygamists in a number of cases.[57] In *Rabindra Nath Dutta v The State* AIR 1969 Cal 55, a first wife complained that her husband had married a second woman and should be punished. The husband claimed that he had never validly married the first wife, but had been sentenced to rigorous imprisonment for three months by the lower court, hence his appeal. Since the second marriage had been registered under the SMA, it was clearly taken as proved. The new legal policy was highlighted by the court's statement, at p. 57, that monogamy has become the law of the land for Hindus. So, a second marriage would be punishable. However, the mere fact that a man had lived with a woman with whom some ceremonies

[56] *Towards Equality* (1974: 108) argues that while judicial decisions have rendered the enforcement of the penal provision against bigamy in Section 17 of the HMA difficult, 'it would only be fair to say that this stemmed not from a sentiment in favour of bigamy, but from a deep seated judicial attitude that penal provisions should be construed strictly'.

[57] Useful discussions of the case law on Hindu polygamy are found in an early article by Derrett (1967) and in Derrett (1970: 307–10). Derrett (1963c: 152–3) merely presents the formal legal position, while Gupta (1979: 155–76), Verma (1993) and especially Nijjar (1994: 20–64) and Sharma (1994: 85–128) discuss the case law well. Derrett (1977: 141, 485) considers Hindu law and polygamy in Goa. Derrett (1978b: 54) points to conversion to Christianity and related problems of polygamy under the Native Converts' Marriage Dissolution Act, 1866.

of marriage had been performed would not automatically satisfy Section 494 of the IPC for the punishment of polygamy. It was held, at p. 57:

> There is, of course, a strong presumption in favour of the validity of a marriage if from the time of such marriage the parties are recognized by the people concerned as man and wife and such presumption applies also as to the question whether the formal requisites of a valid marriage ceremony were satisfied.

In criminal prosecutions, however, the courts have applied a rigorous standard of proof beyond reasonable doubt and it was held, at p. 58:

> In this criminal case the prosecution must prove their case beyond reasonable doubt and for that the onus is heavy upon the prosecution to prove first of all that Sovarani was a legally married wife of the petitioner and secondly that during the subsistence of the marriage tie the petitioner had entered into another marriage duly solemnised in accordance with law. The presumption of innocence always stands in favour of the accused. There cannot be presumption in favour of a valid legal marriage as between the petitioner and Sovarani just merely on the basis of evidence that some ceremonies of marriage had been performed.

However, it was found in the present case that the parties had performed the major ceremonies of a Hindu marriage, including *homa* and *saptapadī*. Thus the husband was found guilty of polygamy.[58] In *re Dolgonti Raghava Reddy* AIR 1968 AP 117, it was correctly held that in the Reddy community of Telangana, a polygamous marriage performed without *homa* and *saptapadī* would be valid, and would give rise to a prosecution under Section 494 of the IPC. In this case, the polygamous husband had been sentenced to three months rigorous imprisonment and sought acquittal. The court, through a detailed examination of marriage customs among the Reddy community, found that neither *homa* nor *saptapadī* were customary, but that the customary rituals of this community had been performed. Thus, the marriage in question had been validly solemnized and the conviction stood.

In *Trailokya Mohan Nath v State* AIR 1968 A&N 22, a Hindu male had been sentenced to three months rigorous imprisonment and a fine of Rs 100. His lawyer tried to rely on *Bhaurao Shankar* and *Kanwal Ram* to argue that there was no valid marriage, but the husband had admitted in court that he had married polygamously and there was further evidence of a valid marriage. Applying a presumption of marriage, it was held, at p. 24:

> When there is celebration or solemnisation of a marriage which has been intended by the parties to be binding on each other and the form of it has not been wholly opposed or against the customs of the community or the caste to which the parties belong, the presumption that the ceremonies were complete and the marriage is legal arises ...

[58] Tiwari (1991: 53 n.19) refers to a number of other cases in which convictions were achieved during the 1960s and 1970s.

But cases could easily go the other way. In *Ram Singh v R. Susila Bai* AIR 1970 Mys 201, the first wife had complained that the husband had married another woman, and he had been sentenced to six months rigorous imprisonment. Since there was no proof that a *saptapadī* ritual had been performed, and in fact there were considerable discrepancies in the evidence, the husband was given the benefit of doubt. In *Subbarayudu v Venkatiah* AIR 1968 AP 107, it was held at p. 108 that '[m]ere tying of "Tali" is not enough to establish that the marriage has been solemnised'. The court found that since there had been no invocation before the sacred fire, and no *saptapadī*, there was no valid marriage.

In *Priya Bala Ghosh v. Suresh Chandra Ghosh* AIR 1971 SC 1153, a Hindu wife was trying to have her bigamous husband put behind bars, appealing against his acquittal by the HC of Calcutta, but she did not succeed. Thus, even where a woman vigorously objected to the husband's polygamy, the courts would not necessarily act in her support. This couple had been married in 1948, the wife had allegedly been driven out of the house, and by 1962 the husband had married again. In defence, the husband claimed that he was not married to the first wife, but admitted the fact of the second marriage. The magistrate's court had found the husband guilty of bigamy, sentencing him to rigorous imprisonment for one year and a fine of Rs 500, half of which was to be paid to the complainant wife. On appeal before the sessions judge, the husband had been acquitted, holding that both his marriages were legally invalid. The HC had upheld the validity of the first marriage, but confirmed the husband's acquittal, hence the furious pursuit by the wife and her infructuous appeal to the Supreme Court. This is an overly technical, and quite unsatisfactory decision, which merely relies on *Bhaurao Shankar* and *Kanwal Ram*, refusing to consider details of the social circumstances. It was held, at p. 1158:

> ... both the learned Sessions Judge and the High Court have categorically found that the Homa and Saptapadi are the essential rites for a marriage according to the law governing the parties and that there is no evidence that these two essential ceremonies have been performed ... No reliance can be placed on the admissions ...

In *Lingari Obulamma v L. Venkata Reddy* AIR 1979 SC 848, the polygamous husband had earlier been sentenced to six months rigorous imprisonment and a fine of Rs 100, but had been acquitted by the HC. The first wife appealed to the Supreme Court to have her erring husband punished. This is again a case on Reddy customs. It was basically held that since 'there was no evidence to show that there was any custom among the Reddys which outweighed the written text of law' (p. 849), there could be no conviction. Such acquittals of men who had allegedly or actually married polygamously were interpreted by some commentators as a result of judicial caution about evidence. For example, the Committee on the Status of Women in India (*Towards Equality* 1974: 108) noted:

> While judicial decisions have rendered the enforcement of the penal provision against bigamy in section 17 of the Hindu Marriage Act, 1955

> difficult, it would only be fair to say that this stemmed not from a sentiment in favour of bigamy, but from a deep seated judicial attitude that penal provisions should be construed strictly.

In contrast, academic comment has often been scathing and generally negative. Sharma (1994: 85–128) provides a useful discussion of India's law on polygamy, criticizing the technical constructions placed by the courts on Section 17 of the HMA.[59] At p. 95, she argues that '[f]or decades, the Judges have treated the issue with remarkable nonchalance and leniency, thus, lending a helping hand to their fellow men by discharging the clever bigamist'. There has been no agreement among scholars over this issue, however. Diwan (1985: 100) clearly took the male perspective, reiterating the standard position with reference to *Laxmi Sahuani v Maheswar Sahu* AIR 1985 Ori 11 and arguing that it is an established proposition of Hindu law that the offence of bigamy is committed only if it is conclusively established that the required ceremonies of Hindu marriage were performed. The second marriage cannot be proved merely by admission of the parties and the petitioner must prove that the essential ceremonies and rites were performed. Ten years later, Diwan and Diwan (1995: 104–5) still justified the actions of men in the same manner and saw no reason to review their position:

> A prosecution for bigamy will fail if what is established is that some sort of ceremonies (not the essential ceremonies as prescribed by law or custom) were performed with the avowed purpose that the parties were to be taken as married .... The mere intention of parties, however serious, will not make them husband and wife and the accused will escape prosecution even if he deliberately performed defective ceremonies.

Remarkably, the above reasoning entirely omits reference to the important concept of presumption of validity of a Hindu marriage and virtually refutes the idea that such a concept may come into play.[60] Turning to Desai (1990: 639), we find a very different perspective:

> There is an extremely strong presumption in favour of the validity of a marriage and the legitimacy of its offspring if from the time of the alleged marriage the parties are recognised by all persons concerned as man and wife and are so described in important documents and on important

[59] I would say Section 7 of the HMA as well as Section 17 was misinterpreted. Many authors mention only the latter.

[60] On the other hand, Professor Diwan was of course aware of presumptions of marriage. See e.g. Diwan (1987: 292) with reference to *Ningu Vithu Bamane v Sadashiv Ningu Bamane* AIR 1987 Bom 27. However, Diwan (1989: 213) maintains that 'it is essential that such ceremonies and rites must be proved to be ancient, continuous and definite and that these should have been recognised either in the community of the bride or bridegroom'. The reference to the requirement of 'ancient' custom is certainly not appropriate in view of the wording of Section 3(a) of the HMA which speaks of 'for a long time'.

> occasions. The like presumption applies to the question whether the formal requisites of a valid marriage ceremony were satisfied. Similarly the fact that a woman was living under the protection of a man who generally lived with her and acknowledged her children raises a strong presumption that she is the wife of that man. But this presumption may be rebutted by proof of facts showing that no marriage could have taken place.[61]

Therefore, it is clearly not uncontroversial that the Supreme Court of India should inevitably have to acquit Hindu polygamists because of the nature of Hindu law, as Diwan and Diwan (1995: 105) suggest. On presumption of marriage, *Sumitra Devi v Bhikan Choudhary* AIR 1985 SC 765 has escaped the notice of most commentators because it is a very brief case and has been listed under a different statute, namely the CrPC of 1973. However, this case is also about polygamy, involving a complaint by the second wife seeking maintenance for herself and a child. The Supreme Court held in this case that various customary forms of marriage are just as acceptable as the high-caste, ritualized Sanskritic forms of Hindu marriage and thus impliedly challenged *Bhaurao Shankar* AIR 1965 SC 1564. It was held in *Sumitra Devi*, at p. 766:

> There is no doubt that in order that there may be a valid marriage according to Hindu law, certain religious rites have to be performed. Invoking the fire and performing Saptapadi around the sacred fire have been considered by this Court to be two of the basic requirements for a traditional marriage. It is equally true that there can be a marriage acceptable in law according to customs which do not insist on performance of such rites as referred to above and marriages of this type give rise to [a] legal relationship which law accepts.

Other important polygamy cases which clearly took account of social facts and resulted in conviction of the polygamist have also been ignored, perhaps because they arose only at HC level. *Baby v Jayant Mahadeo Jagtap* AIR 1981 Bom 283 is a case of polygamy among neo-Buddhists. As an HC case, it could of course not overrule the Supreme Court precedents, but it skilfully bypassed them. The Bombay HC accepted that customary forms of marriage among persons governed by the HMA could be modified over time. Hence, the new marriage customs among the neo-Buddhists of Maharashtra obviously qualified for full legal recognition. The court could take judicial notice of the fact that during the last twenty-five years a different form of marriage had been devised, adopted, and socially recognized by these Buddhists. Thousands of marriages had been solemnized in this new form, and these rites and ceremonies had been the only ones adopted and followed uniformly amongst the members of this community for more than two decades. Hence it could successfully be argued that the test under Section 3 of the HMA, to the effect that a custom has

[61] See also, to the same effect, Desai (1982: 748). This presumption was applied in many recent cases, e.g. *S.P.S. Balasubrahmanyam v Suruttayan* AIR 1994 SC 133.

to be followed 'for a long time', was satisfied. *Baby* therefore challenges the position that only 'ancient' and fully ritualized customs of Hindu marriage solemnization could qualify for official legal recognition. However, as a High Court case, it could do nothing to get rid of the unsatisfactory precedent of *Bhaurao Shankar*, to which, for good reasons, no direct reference is made.[62]

The court was, however, quite clear about the undesirable social effects of refusing to accept social reality. It was held at p. 294 that '[t]he refusal to recognise the solemnization of such ceremonies of marriage as a valid and legal marriage will visit these people with untold miseries of grave social consequences'. The husband in *Baby v Jayant* was therefore sentenced to two years rigorous imprisonment and a fine of Rs 1,000. The court also directed that steps should be taken to disseminate this judgment to all law officials in Maharashtra. The HC was clearly concerned to stress that the offence of bigamy was a serious matter when it held, at p. 299:

> Once the offence of bigamy is proved, the court cannot take a lenient view regarding the sentence. In this country specially in this part of the country, it is not infrequent that the husband marries [a] second time and leaves the first wife to her fate to lead a life of untold miseries for the rest of her life. No sympathy can be shown to such persons...
> ... The attitude of such persons who marry the second time is not only a cavalier one but a wanton one. Such types of persons allow themselves to be under the impression that the long arm of the law cannot touch them inasmuch as there can be no proof of the solemnization of the second marriage.

The husband was therefore convicted, and a clear signal set that his particular excuse would not work in future cases. However, *Santi Deb Berma v Kanchan Prava Devi* AIR 1991 SC 816 is still an unsatisfactory Supreme Court case. A bigamous husband appealed against his conviction by the HC of Assam, which had applied a presumption of performance of all the required ceremonies, in view of evidence that the husband and his second wife had lived like a married couple. However, it was held by the Supreme Court at p. 817, falling back to the doctrine of the necessity of a *saptapadī*, that 'the High Court is not at all justified in drawing such an inference in the absence of any reliable and acceptable evidence, in regard to the performance of Saptapadi'. The second marriage was therefore declared invalid, and the husband swiftly acquitted. The insistence on performance of *saptapadī* by the Supreme Court in this case seems entirely misguided.

More recent case law has shown two fairly clear trends, which have not been noticed by legal academics and activists (but see Menski 2001), while practitioners seem to know the law but want to keep their options open. In the first type of case scenario, where polygamists are subject to criminal trial, the

[62] *Sumitra Devi* was applied, for example, in *Narayanan Namboodiri v Bhargavi Amma* 1989(1) KLT 547, which concerns a particular local customary form of marriage in Kerala called *sambandam*.

courts will still often support the male's case and will acquit the bigamist, hiding behind evidence law and the Sanskritic position as stated in *Bhaurao Shankar.* In the second type of case,[63] the factual situation is quite different, in that a woman or those claiming through her will seek financial entitlements from a polygamous marriage or liaison. Polygamous husbands in both case scenarios routinely attempt to deny the marriage, because they want to avoid punishment and evade their financial or social responsibilities.

We saw what happened in the first type of cases—polygamists tend to be acquitted. In the second type, which appears to be much more frequent, the higher Indian courts have clearly taken a different approach to the question of validity of Hindu marriages, liberally applying presumptions of marriage, trying to protect women and thus to give them a basis for claims of maintenance or other relief.[64] In addition, the courts are now particularly vigilant when it comes to the position of children and protection of their legal status, despite the fact that the marriage of their parents may be void.[65] But *Bhaurao Shankar* is still widely presumed to be the leading case on the subject, as reflected in legal textbooks, so that legal advice to any potential complainant would probably still be given on that basis.[66]

The above case analysis therefore confirms that despite the legislative prohibition of Hindu polygamy, the courts have continued to take a rather lenient approach towards polygamous Hindu men when it comes to protecting them against criminal convictions. But the courts are not lenient when financial claims of women and children are at stake. Thapalyal (1986: 11) comments that the law is confused and its evasion all too easy, so that 'prosecution does not often lead to conviction'. If the courts were to become more aware of the manifest abuse of the law on marriage solemnization in relation to cases of polygamy, Hindu wives would be better protected against the polygynous inclinations of

[63] *Ningu Vithu Bamane v Sadashiv Ningu Bamane* AIR 1987 Bom 27 concerned a widow remarriage and also applies a presumption of validity to protect the property entitlements of the claimants.

[64] This was the situation in *Sumitra Devi* AIR 1985 SC 765, already discussed. An instructive more recent case is *Vimala v Veeraswamy* (1991) 2 SCC 375, where a husband was seeking to defeat his second wife's claim for maintenance on the ground that her marriage was void, but did not succeed. *Nirmala v Rukminibai* AIR 1994 Kant 247 is a dispute over joint family property and the entitlement of certain individuals. This case achieves an equitable result by applying a presumption of validity of marriage and of the required rituals.

[65] In *Laxmibai Nagappa Maliwadar v Limbabai Nagappa Maliwadar* AIR 1983 Bom 222, it was held under Section 16 HMA that the children born of a void marriage are not disentitled to inherit from their parents. *Perumal Gounder v Pachayappan* AIR 1990 Mad 110 clarifies the legal position of illegitimate children in a joint Hindu family, denying them a status as coparceners, but holding that they are entitled to inheritance on the death of the parents.

[66] As indicated, however, *Sumitra Devi* AIR 1985 SC 765 has been followed by several courts.

Hindu men. As we saw also in Chapter 8, the Indian courts are demonstrating that they can handle the complex law of marriage solemnization with compassion and with an eye to the needs of women and children, but some judges continue to take a soft approach for Hindu polygamists faced with a jail sentence. The statute law by itself has not created a situation where Hindu polygamy has been wiped off the legal map.

The differential legal treatment of men and women in this field of law is rather starkly illustrated by the deeply unsatisfactory case of *Surjit Kaur v Garja Singh* AIR 1994 SC 135, where a remarried Sikh widow was dismissed by the Supreme Court in disgrace and was deprived of her rightful share in the deceased husband's property. [67] This decision turned on sexual innuendos of polyandry, and was apparently viewed by the judges like a female polygamy case, given the public insinuations that this widow was 'in the habit of changing husbands frequently'. This decision is seriously out of line with the rest of the case law, given that this widow asked for property entitlements, not punishment of the husband for polygamy. This case has thankfully remained an exceptional aberration, though it continues to represent a risk for remarried women (Menski 1995b). Notably, this marriage was refused legal recognition despite formal proof of registration and even though the core issue was not prosecution of a man, but protection of a woman.

Another difficult issue connected to polygamy is the question how Indian courts should react to arguments by a Hindu wife that her husband should be allowed to be polygamous. In *Santosh Kumari v Surjit Singh* AIR 1990 HP 77, a Hindu woman from Himachal Pradesh went to court asking for her husband to be granted the right to marry polygamously. A district magistrate had permitted the husband to contract a second marriage on this basis because his existing wife was weak and ailing. The judge had ruled that the existing wife should remain the legally wedded wife, and she and her daughter should be entitled to appropriate maintenance for life and, in the case of the daughter, until her marriage. At the HC, the learned Chief Justice himself, N.M. Kasliwal, held at p. 78 that '[t]he above order is absolutely wrong and illegal and against the clear provisions of the Hindu Marriage Act, 1955'. The lower court judge was severely reprimanded for his lack of knowledge of the relevant law and the order was set aside, at pp. 78–9:

> The Sub Judge has clearly ignored the provisions of the Hindu Marriage Act as well as the Indian Penal Code in this regard. The Sub Judge is expected to know such elementary principle of law and it is a gross mistake on his part to have ignored such principle of law and to have given a decree contrary to the provisions of [the] Hindu Marriage Act and perpetuate a criminal offence of bigamy punishable under the Indian Penal Code.

[67] Diwan (1991: 83–4) commented on this case after it had been decided by the HC in Chandigarh. I totally disagree with his interpretation and reasoning, as well as with further comments on the same case in Diwan (1994: 295–6).

It was of course an entirely proper course of action on the part of the HC to make this decision, and to publish it in those terms.[68] However, this does not solve the social dilemmas of any couple in India who seem to have agreed privately that a polygamous arrangement may suit them best. To be sent away from the official courts in such a situation creates an obvious blockage of communication between the formal law and local societies and does not allow for an open debate about the best possible solution to a particular family's dilemmas of law, dharma, and justice. The absolute legal prohibition of polygamy prevents the courts from playing a supportive role in consensual arrangements—while they do of course have a crucial function when any arrangements are contested. Many socio-legal researchers are aware of the fact that only certain disputes, or certain segments of disputes are brought to the official courts.[69] The key lesson from *Santosh Kumari* is therefore that a couple who agree to arrange some form of polygamy within the family should not approach an official court to have this family arrangement formally sanctified, because it clearly violates basic principles of current Indian public policy. If, however, the modern Indian system of family law regulation relies, as it clearly does, ever more on self-help and extra-judicial arrangements, this does not control and preclude bigamous family arrangements.

The Postmodern Scenario

The analysis of Hindu law on polygamy locates many confused modernist attempts to assess a scenario that is much more complex than lawyers and activists realize. While modernists tend to boast that the abolition of Hindu polygamy was successfully pushed through, many commentators now complain that because polygamy has not been effectively curtailed in Hindu law, and is not implemented for Indian law as a whole because of Muslim resistance, more needs to be done. The postmodern scenario of Hindu polygamy is therefore buried under a barrage of reformist assertions that are, at the end of the day, contradictory in themselves. Calls for further reforms and restrictions on polygamy, examined in the next section, are closely linked to demands for uniform regulation of all Indian family laws and the consequent assumption that Muslim polygamy will be put under state control in this way. This entirely unrealistic reform programme is examined further in the subsequent section.

However, the justice-centred approach of the Indian higher judiciary seems to have finally borne some fruit, since some activist researchers are now beginning to see that strictly formal prohibition of polygamy will drive the practice underground and would deprive the courts as agents of the state of the chance to intervene in situations of crisis and to secure justice for women and children. Within postmodern paradigms, but still phrased in modernist terms,

[68] See also the comments of Diwan (1990a: 125) on this case.

[69] See in detail Dhagamwar (1992) and Agrawala and Ramanamma (1994).

it has begun to be realized that the abolition of Hindu polygamy per se is not a panacea for women to effect liberation from the shackles of a patriarchal society and legal system. The purposeful silence around many issues of sexuality (John and Nair 2000b) also links into the current debates, as formal polygamy needs to be understood as only one variety of plural arrangements made by Hindu males. The wider context of sexual relations throws up fresh doubts about the effectiveness of law in this field too. Self-controlled ordering, with judicial supervision as a safety net, comes through as a viable postmodern model, but it will irk modernists no end that this self-regulation might involve the formal recognition of polygamy in certain situations.

Continuing Modernist Demands for Reform

Based on the earlier findings from a detailed field study (Chatterjee et al. 1971), Baxi (1986: 62–3) complained that current knowledge of the law against bigamy or polygamy is 'very meagre'. It is evident that in the various communities of India, polygamy still appears in all kinds of forms.[70] The reported cases most certainly only scratch the surface of a deep barrel of hidden practices. For example, in a number of recent cases we find evidence of husbands remarrying while an appeal relating to their divorce is still pending. While this is not a new phenomenon, it has achieved some notoriety. Diwan (1992: 206) found strong words to criticize this practice, but most courts seem to be too busy to take explicit notice of such obvious contempt of court.[71] This may lead to strange results, such as court-induced polygamy, which arises when a divorce decree is refused, but the husband has already married another wife.[72]

While there can be no doubt that most Indian women do not like polygamy and would presumably oppose such family arrangements, there are many indications that Hindu society as a whole is not ready to underwrite a complete official ban on polygamy. Shiv Sahai Singh (1993: 122) states that [i]nspite of this statutory prohibition the practice of polygamy continues in Hindu society and refers to statistics from a study conducted in 1972, which produced evidence that in a survey of 500 Indian villages, 5.1 per cent of Hindus had polygamous marriages, whereas 4.8 per cent of Muslim marriages were polygamous. These statistics have often been quoted to claim either that legislative abolition of Hindu polygamy has remained ineffective, or that Muslims should not be subjected to such reform, since they do not even indulge in

70 Dhagamwar (1992: 205) links the practice of *dhareecha*, the virtual sale of women, and bigamy.

71 See for example *Katari Subba Rao v Katari Seetha Mahalakshmi* AIR 1994 AP 364.

72 Protests about this can be found in the *ASIL*. For example, in the volume for 1992, at p. 206, it is stated that remarriages during the pendency of an appeal for divorce 'should be viewed with utmost gravity as they show scant respect for appellate courts and open contraction of bigamous unions'.

polygamy to the same extent as Hindus. Sharma (1994: 357–8) confirms in her final recommendations that modernist legal reforms remain only partially effective, arguing that '[t]he statutory ban on bigamy as laid down in the Hindu Marriage Act, 1955 is still resented and flouted in some cases', referring primarily to the legal loophole of the need for essential customary ceremonies.[73]

Desai (1998: 68) and Sharma (1994: 358) confirm that the abolition of polygamy was demanded as a matter of social change and was seen as the most outstanding feature of the reforms during the 1950s. Derrett (1968b: 333–8) produced a detailed discussion of many aspects of women's legal emancipation, arguing at p. 337 that, 'the most dramatic step towards equalizing the status of men and women was the abolition of plural marriages'. Jain (1990: 641–2) also mentions the abolition of polygamy as a major achievement of the reforms in 1955-56, seeing it in exaggerated terms as part of a larger process of copying Western laws into Hindu law:[74]

> ... in the area of marriage, monogamy and divorce have been introduced. Both these concepts constitute fundamental departures from the traditional Hindu Law .... A number of other Western concepts, such as, restitution of conjugal rights, judicial separation, desertion, cruelty, nullity of marriage, have been introduced into the marriage law by the Hindu Marriage Act.[75]

It appears that it became a matter of modernist credibility that Hindu polygamy should be outlawed. As *Towards Equality* (1974: 104) claims, full equality of sexes can hardly be possible in a legal system which permits polygamy and a social system which tolerates it. This particular statement frequently reappears in the writing on polygamy of the 1980s and 1990s. Much academic energy has been spent on arguing for the compulsory registration of all Hindu marriages and even the abolition of Hindu customary marriages in favour of simple, secular procedures which would provide a check on polygamy as well. Diwan and Diwan (1995: 105) conclude with reference to the issues of uniforming and bureaucratization of modern Indian laws that '[t]he solution lies in prescribing one ceremony for all Hindu marriages, and by providing for registration of marriages. So long as we recognize all sorts of ceremonies, such things are bound to happen; dupes may take advantage and innocent persons may become their victims'.

[73] Sharma (1994: 102) also notes that 'most second marriages are celebrated without pomp and publicity', and thus recognizes the social reality of plurality and diversity in this field.

[74] Such assumptions are now found elsewhere, too. Mansfield (2001: 93) asserts rather placatively that the HMA and SMA 'embody modern Western ideas' and would thus be a likely model for a uniform civil code.

[75] Whether these are really 'Western' concepts needs to be carefully investigated rather than just asserted in blanket fashion. I do not accept without further study that traditional Hindu law did not know such concepts.

This statement shows that these modernist authors envisaged wider agenda, namely to argue for the abolition of Hindu marriage ceremonies as the sole indicator of legal validity, and to push for the introduction of official marriage registration, as in Western legal systems. Tiwari (1991: 46) argues similarly that '[t]he solution lies in prescribing one ceremony for all Hindu marriages and by providing for registration of marriages'. Vijay Sharma (1994: 108) writes about the need to have independent and infallible proof of a marriage. Singh (1994: 357–61), identifying the lack of official documentation of marriage as a problem, also writes at p. 358 that '[t]here exists, therefore, a need for an independent and infallible proof of marriage. Compulsory registration of marriage provides a proof of marriage and it would help those women whose husbands disown them for lack of proof of marriage'. In a detailed article arguing in favour of compulsory registration of all Hindu marriages, Ranbir Singh (1991: 44–7) also argues for prescribing one ceremony for all Hindu marriages and compulsory registration. In his view, recognizing all sorts of ceremonies, shastric as well as customary, allows devious individuals to take advantage of legal insecurity, victimizing innocent persons. It is also submitted that Section 7 of the HMA should be amended to emphasize the intention of the parties to enter into matrimony.[76]

However persuasive they may sound, these are totally unrealistic, simplistic proposals in view of the size of India's population and the complexity of the issue. It is not practically feasible for the Indian state to introduce a complex bureaucracy of compulsory marriage solemnization, which anyway would not be foolproof and would be undermined in many different ways.[77] The resultant fundamental changes of law would create enormous social problems, placing a huge, new administrative burden on the Indian state which is simply unrealistic. Modernist authors all fall into the same trap of demanding more state intervention, which is supposed to lead to legal certainty and uniformity, when it should be self-evident to Indian observers, at any rate, that the socially complex Hindu law of marriage solemnization could not possibly be unified by any Act of Parliament.

It is of course correct, as Singh (1994: 359) reiterates, that many Indian judges have helped polygamists by insisting on unrealistically formal standards of proof of solemnization. However, to discard the ritual elements of marriage solemnization altogether and to argue for compulsory registration of all Hindu marriages by the state would be a classic case of throwing out the baby with the bath water. I can only reiterate here my earlier observation that the Indian

[76] It should be noted that these arguments are almost verbatim copied from Paras Diwan's writings, discussed above. The suggestion about intention is an old theme from the 1960s, raised in Ch. 8 earlier. The criterion of intention was criticized by Derrett (1963c: 137) as "somewhat handicapped in the majority of Hindu communities".

[77] Allott (1980: 259–86) critiques English law in this respect, based on his 'limits of law' thesis.

state has more important and urgent things to do than trying to establish a marriage registration system in order to control polygamy. In addition, there are deeper layers of analysis, debated further in Chapter 13, which relate to the extent of positivist claims about the powers of the modern state in juxtaposition to traditional social methods of self-controlled ordering. In view of the case law on Hindu marriage solemnization and its close links with polygamy, it is evident that the judges have bridged this conceptual gap in an almost ingenious way. Having found that the most cost-effective method of protecting Hindu wives against allegations that their marriage was not valid is the liberal use of presumptions of marriage, already a well-known and well-used concept, the judges have constructed a postmodern system of legal regulation of Hindu polygamy rather than remaining mired in modernist ideology. It is evident that most scholars have not understood this as yet. Sharma (1994: 95) discusses the legal loophole for bigamists in strongly critical terms, blaming the courts as well as the legislature:

> This law has become harmless to [the] bigamist because of some procedural as well as substantive lacunae in it ... the decisions rendered by the Supreme Court are no less responsible than legislative somnolence. For decades, the judges have treated the issue with remarkable nonchalance and leniency, thus, lending a helping hand to their fellow men by discharging the clever bigamist. Even after 35 years of the enactment of the Hindu Marriage Act, the bigamists are having their ways and mandatory provisions relating to monogamy are broken by males with impunity.

Lack of clarity over whom to blame is also evident in the comments by Agrawala and Ramanamma on bigamy (1994: 257), to the effect that '[t]he law of bigamy, and the judicial interpretation under the Hindu Marriage Act, 1955, are no deterrent to the Hindu husband. This attitude of law evidently discourages the Indian woman from expecting relief under the formal amended law'. These authors suspect that '[u]nderlying this is probably a compromise of the Indian legislator and the judge to help the woman while yet not being too hard on the man. This ambivalence of the legislator and the judge is, however, at the cost of the woman's interests ... it amply establishes lack of conviction of the lawgivers in the offence of bigamy' (id.).

Is it really justifiable, though, to group legislators and judges together in this way? Other commentators have brought law enforcement agencies into the picture and focus on the inefficiency of the legal machinery. Thus, Sharma (1994: 112) criticizes that the legal provisions against Hindu polygamy suffer from being non-cognizable, to the effect that courts can only act if an aggrieved person makes a complaint:

> Therefore, the police and the law enforcing authority should be empowered to act on their own since the status of marriage is one in which the whole of society has an interest and not just parties to the marriage. Thus, the evil practice of bigamy can be effectively put down if the offence is made cognizable.

It must be highlighted here that such arguments demand involvement of the modern state and its agencies with the daily life of the citizens. That is a deeply problematic positivist, modernist assumption which runs diametrically counter to traditional Hindu legal concepts like *vyavahāra* as a last resort, rather than a routine procedure. Huge conceptual issues aside, even in purely practical terms, direct involvement of the state and its agents does not appear to be a satisfactory solution because of the way in which law enforcement agencies such as the police work in India. Instead of arresting a bigamous husband, officers would probably try to extract some money from him, most likely after having 'charged' the complainant some token amount. The track record of such authorities in promoting justice is not at all impressive and gives rise to many concerns about the role of the state.[78]

Profound modernist dissatisfaction with the extent of legal reforms is apparent when Archana Parashar (1992: 136) claims that, at the end of the day, '[t]he State sought to give women better rights so as to bring about a limited social transformation but it did not intend to alter fundamentally the family structure or the balance of power within that structure'. While that seems a fair comment, Parashar (1992: 136) continues:

> The wives of polygamous unions were given no safeguards, and at the same time polygamy was not made unattractive for men. Polygamy was made a non-cognizable offence, so that only the parties to the marriages could prosecute the polygamous male and more often than not women do not have the power to initiate such prosecution.

Such comments, which seem primarily designed to improve the practical operation of a purposefully imperfect law, lead to the argument that the entire reform package was not serious, hence remained ineffective for the protection of women, constituting little else than eyewash.[79] Latent modernist complaints have here swollen to a deep feeling of betrayal, to the effect that the state has let women down and has abandoned the modernist cause. There is no concentrated attempt anywhere to understand the limited but constructive compromise that the judges have been engaged in. Instead, confused analysts blame the judges, the legislature, and as a surrogate scapegoat, the Muslims of India, whose role in this scenario cannot be overlooked.

Surrogate Debates on Muslims and Legal Uniformity

While Muslim law permits polygamy to men, it is not a practice that many Muslims indulge in, nor do most Muslim women appreciate it (Khanam 1960). Still, because of its Quranic foundations, there continues to be definite opposition

[78] On cases about police powers see in detail Ahuja (1997, I: 90–146). On the ineffectiveness of the police in relation to dowry-related violence see Chowdhary (1998).

[79] Singh (1989: 63) complains vigorously that the status of women has not really improved.

to the formal abolition of Muslim polygamy by any modernist state. Such resistance to modernist and state-sponsored legal intervention comes out with particular force in Indian law because of the minority status of Muslim law. The continued presence of Muslim polygamy everywhere in South Asia constitutes an uncomfortable reminder for modernists of their partial defeat in this field. In the Indian scenario, much of the debate about Muslim polygamy aims really at testing positions concerning the relative strength of uniform, secular state law and personal laws.

While Hindus as the majority community were formally subjected to state supervision, the Muslim minority appears to have managed to evade that net of control. Reformists have argued that Indian Muslim women, too, desire the legal abolition of polygamy so as to be put on par with co-citizens from other religious groups. Alka Singh (1992: 82–5) provides a report on fieldwork among Muslim women in Lucknow and Delhi, confirming that only a tiny minority of women found polygamy acceptable:

> The data show that in Lucknow 95.33 per cent women spoke against it. However, 4.66 per cent thought it to be acceptable under certain specific conditions such as barrenness of the first wife or in the case where the first wife is not keeping in good health.
>
> Similarly, in Delhi, 3.33 per cent spoke in favour of polygamy whereas 96.6 per cent firmly believed that the present-day circumstances including social and economic factors do not leave any scope for men to marry more than one time.

It was also found that in most cases, the first wife did not know of the existence of the second marriage, and often vice versa. Singh (1992: 84) issues a call for 'some legislation putting a ban on this practice' and cites, at p. 85, a Muslim author from the 1970s to the effect that '[t]he state can validly enact measures of social welfare and reforms in respect of the matter governed by the Muslim Law'.[80] Such comments, typically made with reference to Muslim law, display considerable confusion about the potential role of agents in lawmaking. Do the various authors ask for legislation, or do they recognize that judges can also make law? Judges certainly can and do make law in the Indian legal system, despite pious lip service to some colonial concepts of judicial restraint.[81]

Given the continued official toleration of Muslim polygamy, much energy has been spent on simply demanding the abolition of Muslim polygamy in Indian law. Academic writing here quite openly becomes an alternative form

[80] See Ghouse (1973). The excellent research report by Khanam (1960) on Pakistan is also relevant here, stressing the difficulties caused to Muslim wives by traditional allowances for polygamy.

[81] Kusum (2000: 231) argues that '[t]he Blackstonian fiction that judges merely declare and apply the law no longer holds good'. This is now widely recognized and not peculiar to India. On Australia, see Chen (1999: 54) to the effect that '[i]t is now well recognised that judges do make law'.

of public demonstration for certain causes. Vyas (1993: 194–6) argues vigorously that if any religious practice runs counter to a policy of social reform and social welfare, the modern state should repeal such religious practices. A similarly positivist perspective is espoused when Singh (1993: 11) argues that the social reform measure of abolishing Muslim polygamy would be justified under Article 25(2)(b) of the Constitution, notwithstanding alleged interference with the right of a citizen freely to profess, practice, and propagate religion. Singh (1993: 11) asserts:

> A Muslim who wants to have more than one wife is engaged neither in professing and practising nor in promoting or propagating his religion. In India the Muslim law acquired binding force not because of its divine origin but from the Constitution of India. The state, therefore, can validly enact measures of social welfare and reform with respect to the matters governed by the Muslim law.

These are huge positivist claims, which are debatable, and probably entirely wrong. For, like Hindu law, Muslim law in India pre-existed the modern legal regime, continues to coexist with the modern state's law and cannot simply be abolished by positivist state intervention. Leading legal luminaries have, however, continued to voice inflated positivist claims. Sorabjee (1991: 262–3) complains that leniency towards Muslim polygamy has focused too much on arguments about the sanctity of personal laws. In his view, permission for Muslim polygamy constitutes a clear case of discrimination against women on the grounds of gender and religion. Noting that the real reason for the state's leniency of Muslim polygamy was the anxiety not to ruffle the sensibilities of the Muslim community, the learned author introduces a comparison with the United States' Supreme Court, which 'readily upheld a federal law making polygamy a crime at a time when the Mormon Church regarded it as a religious duty'. Such comparisons seem unhelpful, and could easily be matched by new evidence of how Muslims in Euro-American jurisdictions today undercut uniform national legal systems and their prohibitions on polygamy.

Mahmood (1978: 23) proposed a different line of argument, to the effect that 'bigamy is neither enjoined nor encouraged in Islam; it is only permitted, subject to certain difficult conditions'. In Mahmood's view, the SMA of 1954 therefore, in not allowing bigamy, 'does not violate any fundamental principle or obligatory tenet of the religion of the Muslims'. However, the SMA is of course only an optional law and has no regulatory impact on Indian Muslims unless a couple chose to marry under that Act. This specific line of reasoning avoids and sidesteps the real issue.

A more general argument about limited traditional permission for Muslim polygamy has been cultivated over many years by Tahir Mahmood, one of India's leading academic writers on Muslim law. Mahmood (1976: 15) points out that in *Itwari v Asghari* AIR 1960 All 684, Dhawan J had emphasized the moralistic guidance of the Koran that it was better for Muslims not to enter polygamous marriages. While this was 'in effect, a judicial effort to prepare the

Muslims psychologically to accept the ideal of monogamy' (id.), Mahmood (1976: 77–8) argues that 'certain aspects of the Muslim personal law presently prevailing in India have outlived their utility and do need a reconsideration', including the man's uncontrolled freedom to contract a bigamous marriage. This clearly plays lip service to modernity and endeared Mahmood to many proponents of positivist state intervention.

In broad agreement with this line of reasoning, Iyer (1987: 4–5) discusses Muslim polygamy and the question of religious sanction, continuing this debate at pp. 66–9. Iyer (1987: 68) harshly criticizes Derrett, who had earlier suggested that polygamy should not be totally outlawed but might be carefully controlled by the judges, offering 'an involved solution—a long route to reach monogamy—which makes a new tort and inhibits indirectly a second marriage'. As an avid modernist, Iyer (id.) is scathing about Derrett's argument:

> His error is in reading the Prophet as conferring a polygamous franchise, coupled with mawkish solicitude for Indian Muslim "religiosity". Many Indian Muslims need to be saved from their friends .... Living law has to be interpreted in a living way.

The underlying assumption here is that the Prophet of Islam was a social revolutionary, and that the practice of polygamy did not agree with the spirit of gender equity as promoted by Islam.[82] The continuing spirit of social reform in Muslim law justifies modernist social reforms, if necessary through state intervention. Mahmood (1986: 68-71) further elaborated on this discussion, asserting that he was not apologetic for Koranic law on polygamy, since personally he did not regard monogamy as an ideal in itself. But in his view,[83] the formal abolition of polygamy for Hindus, Buddhists, Jains, and Sikhs had neither given any meaningful relief to wives, nor had it really abolished polygamy. Prosecution of a bigamist in a criminal court did not really help the first wife. The modernized Hindu law had clearly not succeeded in eradicating bigamous marriages, which continue to take place as freely as before 1955. Qureshi (1978: 389–90), another Muslim author, similarly argues that the legal reforms have not been effective enough and suggests a combination of better implementation and relaxation of the legislative prohibition, which has engaged many authors, as we shall see:

> Complete abolition of polygamy is neither possible nor desirable. The best way is to control polygamy. There may be circumstances in the life of a man when he may be in need of a second wife, i.e. perpetual sickness of

[82] Such arguments have been used in Turkey, Tunisia, and lately by one prominent judge in Bangladesh to justify legal prohibition of polygamy among Muslims (for details see Pearl and Menski 1998). This of course gives rise to the argument that if in Muslim countries polygamy can be outlawed by the state, why does the same not happen for Indian Muslims?

[83] An extensive discussion is found in Mahmood (1986: 115–7), which is paraphrased here.

> the wife etc. Under such circumstances a man may be allowed to marry a second time.
>
> Merely making a provision in the Uniform Civil Code about the abolition of polygamy is not sufficient .... To have a complete check on this institution, it is necessary that the common man should be told the demerits of this institution ... through cinema houses, newspapers and posters.

Mahmood (1986: 117) made a significant contribution to the debates on polygamy by not only criticizing the blind following of Western models, but suggesting additional supervisory roles for the judges:[84]

> Much more effective than legislative abolition of bigamy would, in fact, be its judicial control .... Under such a law, in a case of exceptional hardship the court can even give permission for a second marriage, instantly dissolving the first marriage at the same time, should the other spouse insist on it. Similar provisions may be introduced, *mutatis mutandis*, into the Special Marriage Act, 1954.

In view of the decision in *Sarla Mudgal v Union of India* AIR 1995 SC 1531, it appears that some of Mahmood's argument, have actually been followed by the case law. However, the Indian courts, as shown in *Santosh Kumari v Surjit Singh* AIR 1990 HP 77, would not be prepared to underwrite polygamous arrangements made by Hindu spouses, even if the existing wife expressly agreed to this. Mahmood (1986: 117) rightly sensed that his proposals would not be agreeable to Indian lawmakers, because it would mean a partial abandonment of the ideological commitment to modernity. He argued that '[f]or appreciating and accepting these suggestions we shall, of course, have to give up our blind imitation of the West in regarding monogamy as an ideal in itself and not as one of the means to attain the real ideal—*viz.*, mutual welfare of the couple' (id.).

What Mahmood really argues here, hidden behind much rhetoric, follows an attractive line of argument that characterizes much of his work. In essence, the suggestion is that Islamic law offers useful models for the whole of Indian law and could form the basis of the projected uniform civil code. This is quite an ingenious argument—each personal law including the SMA becomes harmonized with Muslim law as far as bigamy is concerned. Thus, Mahmood seems to argue that there is no need to reform Muslim law, but one needs to weed out unworkable Western ideas from all non-Muslim personal laws and to make these laws compatible with Muslim law, leading to a truly common Indian civil law. This elaborate chain of arguments, tolerating that Muslim law allows polygamy, but making it subject to some kind of overriding judicial supervision and scrutiny, seems attractive, but who will actually control or restrain the discretion of the Muslim husband who simply contracts a polygamous

[84] Similarly Ganai (1990: 423) observes that over time, the development of Indian Muslim law has been shaped not only by sharia, but in particular by judicial power.

marriage?[85] Nobody seems to have noticed that this is precisely the postmodern scenario that Hindu law has meanwhile developed in this field. Silence about this betrays Mahmood's hidden agenda of preserving the influence of Muslim law against state intervention.

Since polygamy is now prohibited by all personal laws of India except Muslim law, this has led to politicized arguments by non-Muslims that the Muslim minority in India is getting favours from the government, as though it is necessarily a privilege to be allowed to have several wives. Many of the contributors to these debates raise related questions about the loyalty of Muslims to the state, and their obedience to state law. But if the postmodern Indian state is a soft state, there is not much justification for such arguments. The dominant feeling that comes across is merely some kind of majority psychosis, as identified by Agnes (2000: 193):[86]

> The root of the communal propaganda is centered around the growth in the Muslim population. As per this premise, non-implementation of Art. 44 of the Constitution has resulted in a growth of the Muslim population and this constitutes a danger to the majority community. The image of a polygamous Muslim has been constructed to serve this propaganda. It is in this context that monogamy imposed by a compulsory code becomes the need of the hour. The gains to the gender concerns by the imposition of monogamy seems [*sic*] to be only incidental.

From a Muslim perspective, Mahmood (1986: 70) raised sexual agenda in a different way, noting that while until 1947 both Hindu and Islamic law permitted polygamy, '[t]he West ridiculed and rebuked both. Overawed, the modern Hindu code legislated for a western-type absolute monogamy, little realising that the West has stuck to that ideal at the cost of first ignoring mass-scale adultery and finally legalising it and also various forms of sexual perversion'. This turns into a discussion on sexual morality, which from a Muslim perspective, because of the supreme concern over avoiding *zina* (any form of illicit extra-marital sex), makes good sense. From that perspective, polygamy becomes actually a convenient and effective remedy to avoid *zina*—the man will simply marry a woman he desires as a sexual partner.[87] But how is this licence for men to make polygamous arrangements that suit their specific agenda any different, at the end of the day, from the alleged 'serial monogamy' and licentious sexual relations of the decadent West? Here we enter the shadow

[85] This, precisely, has been the predicament in Pakistani and Bangladeshi case law. For details see Pearl and Menski (1998: 256–73).

[86] Austin (2001: 20) notes that '[t]he most absurd claim by Hindu agitators is that Muslims are outbreeding Hindus and that Hinduism is bound for extinction'.

[87] Some forms of Islamic jurisprudence went as far as accepting the concept of temporary marriage, known as '*muta* marriage' among the Shias, while the Sunni schools refuse it recognition. The fierceness of the debates over this subject among Muslims reflects not only deep concern over sexual morality but also criss-crosses the boundaries of marriage and concubinage.

boxing arena of Orientalist myth making and its Occidental responses. In this mutual smear campaign, there is not much evidence of attempts to consider how justice for women and children can be improved.

Another prominent diversion from the key issues of polygamy, and thus an additional confusing element in these debates, has been the persistent assertion that many Hindu men would convert to Islam merely to be able to enjoy polygamy. This argument builds on and reinforces the assumption, recently shown to be quite misguided (Menski 2001), that there is a huge difference between Hindu and Muslim law on the subject of polygamy. Conversion is an old politicised debate, frequently commented on by Professor Derrett several decades ago.[88] More recently, this matter came before the Supreme Court in *Sarla Mudgal v Union of India* AIR 1995 SC 1531, leading to modernist calls by Kuldip Singh J for the introduction of a uniform civil code.

Given that modern Hindu law does not actually seem to implement its fairly strict anti-polygamy statutory rules, there should be little need for such conversions by Hindu men, and it does not seem to be a big issue in practice. Rather, it appears that this matter has also been blown out of proportion for political and 'communal' reasons. The issue is constantly aired in the popular media, confirming that the polygamy debates are being used in India, in a variety of ways, as a surrogate for inter-communal rivalries and politics. What is centrally at stake, however, in a way that the shallow modernist debates on Hindu polygamy do not bring out, is the extent of state involvement and supervision of polygamy. By standing out as opposed to modernist, state-sponsored legal control of polygamy, Muslims remind everyone that maybe the extent of positivist, modernist claims regarding state supervision of polygamy does need to be questioned further.

Limits of Modernist Intervention

Postmodern realism has struck modernist commentators to varying degrees and in various modestly enlightening ways when it comes to discussions about Hindu polygamy. Shiv Sahai Singh (1993: 124) favourably contrasts the Hindu law regime of monogamy, combined with ample grounds for divorce, with the 'archaic concept of absolute discretion of the husband to have four wives without any restriction on his divorce power against his wives'. This author does not seem to realize that both elements of his progressive modernist equation may have disastrous effects for some women and their children. More recently, Parashar (1992: 114) rehearses the modernist arguments:

> Polygamy was thus described as necessary for the protection of Hindu society. Among other things a warning was sounded that monogamy

[88] See for example Derrett (1967), which is an important early article on bigamy. More recently, Parashar (1994) focused on legal conflicts in situations of conversion to another religion.

> imposed by law may compel Hindu men to convert to Islam in order to be able to marry polygamously or it would result in an increasing number of men keeping concubines. Some persons made it clear that their objection to monogamy was only because it was being imposed on Hindus alone .... Others however supported the institution on economic grounds, namely that in the villages more than one wife is necessary to carry out the work.

Parashar (id.) further explains that monogamy was to be made the absolute rule of law without any exceptions, because the *smṛtis* permitted a second wife only in very limited circumstances. There was no need to keep those somewhat archaic rules alive and to tolerate any form of polygamy. If a wife was childless, the husband could still adopt a son. Parashar (1992: 115) also notes that strictly enforced monogamy may encourage men to enter into concubinage with women to whom marriage, even if polygamous, is unlikely to be offered.

Does this mean, then, that the legal reforms were mainly concerned with the protection of certain elite women, rather than all Indian wives? Nobody except for Flavia Agnes (2000, cited later) seems to address that issue, but it may be suspected that the outlawing of male polygamy was to some extent a symbolic act of feminist revenge from the perspective of those Indian women leaders who could prevail on a male-dominated legislature to abolish male polygamy. Given that polyandry was supposedly considered impermissible in an androcentric set-up, prevailing on the state apparatus to outlaw polygyny was clearly designed to achieve formal gender equality.

But within the social context, androcentricity continues to prevail. Sen (2000: 96) rightly emphasizes that from a male perspective, and especially among the lower and many intermediary castes, peasant and labouring groups, 'marriage was a means of extracting women's labour'. While, as Sen shows for Bengal, the relative fluidity of marriage practices, the availability of divorce and the possibility of remarriage meant that 'women frequently took recourse to flight' (id.), it is evident that for some women, putting up with polygamy may still bring definite advantages. Karve (1994: 59–60), a leading researcher on social issues, claims that there continue to be solid social reasons in favour of polygamy:

> The most powerful motive for polygamy besides the display of social status and wealth is the desire for male progeny. Not only does a man marry again if the first wife proves barren but the author has known cases in which the first wife insisted on a second marriage of her husband in order that children should be born in the house. When asked why she would not adopt a child, she replied, 'An adopted child is a complete stranger. A co-wife's child is at least the child of my husband and I could love it as such. I would hate to bring up strangers as my children.' Far more usual is the attitude where, in a polygynous household, a woman hates her rival's children who are a constant living reminder of her defeat and a symbol of her humiliation.

One may wonder to what extent lack of legal literacy is a relevant factor in this context. Vijay Sharma (1994: 330) reports on fieldwork to ascertain women's knowledge of the law, which shows that about 70 per cent of the female respondents knew the law, observing that a husband cannot contract a second marriage; if he does, the marriage would be null and void. 20 per cent were of the opinion that the husband can contract a second marriage if the first wife consents. 10 per cent were not aware of the law and thought that a husband can keep more than one wife if he likes. Five respondents thought that barrenness and the happiness of husband and family should make the first wife agree to the husband's second marriage. Two respondents had left the matrimonial home because of the husband's second marriage. About 30 per cent of the women said they knew that there is no legal status of second wife and that she does not have any rights to maintenance and inheritance. While earlier, modernists did not want to take notice of such complex evidence, Agnes (2000: 86–8) discusses the implications of simply enforcing monogamy for Hindus, finding that in some cases it caused a lot of resentment and disadvantages for women. At p. 88, she claims:

> So the progressive sounding provision of monogamy not only turned out to be a mockery but in fact even more detrimental to women than the uncodified Hindu law which recognized rights of wives in polygamous marriages. For instance, in a case for maintenance where the husband pleaded that since the woman was his second wife he was not entitled to pay her maintenance, the court took recourse to the uncodified Hindu law and held that since the couple is governed by the ancient Hindu Law (which permits bigamy) and not by the reformed code, the second wife is entitled to maintenance.[89]

Agnes (2000: 187) further notes that abolishing polygamy through compulsory registration of marriages seems to form the core of the controversy over the uniform civil code. As discussed in Chapter 8, she argues convincingly that the various draft bills produced by academics and women's groups have not been able to recommend viable solutions. Agnes (id.) claims that this is due to two opposing concerns, namely the desire to strengthen deterrent measures against male polygamists and to provide for the rights of women in informal relationships:

> A tilt towards the first option will increase state control over people's lives and will drastically affect the rights of women and children. A tilt towards the second option will render inconsequential the provisions of monogamy and compulsory registration of marriages .... The consensus seems to be governed more from a sense of middle-class morality and the Christian framework of marriage adopted by the liberals in India than a genuine concern for women's rights.

[89] The case reference cited here is *Anupama Pradhan v Sultan Pradhan* 1991 CrLJ 3216 Or.

In her concluding discussion, Agnes (2000: 207) argues that '[t]he principle of monogamy, which was modelled on the western and Christian doctrine was not suited to the cultural conditions of a custom-ridden, pluralistic Hindu society. So at one level the law was ineffective in curbing monogamy, but conversely it strengthened the patriarchal base by depriving women in informal relationships of their customary rights'. This suggests that modernist authors like Agnes are attempting to reconsider the positivist reform-centred approach and have begun to develop a multidimensional, more sophisticated view of polygamy and its legal control.

From a constitutional law angle, in view of the authority to make special provisions in favour of women under Article 15(3) of the Constitution, dominant modernist assumptions about the continued official condonation of Muslim polygamy confuse the debates about the extent of state intervention. Singh (1993: 124) argues that a uniform law should be introduced for all Indians, providing bigamy as a ground for divorce to the wife and the husband equally, irrespective of their religious affiliation. It is also argued by Singh (id.) that this kind of reform will arrest the prevalence of polygamous marriages (as though they were really prevalent) and will promote the desirable concept of monogamy. Bhattacharjee (1985: 128–41) goes further in his discussion, tackling the polygamous licence for Muslim husbands, but not for wives, as impermissible gender discrimination, violative of Article 15 of the Constitution. This author, a retired judge, seems to demand the right of polyandry for females, which appears to be no more than politically correct and fashionable gender rhetoric ignorant of social reality.

In fact, these debates are not new. Decades earlier, doubts about the wisdom of outlawing Hindu polygamy in blanket fashion began to be expressed, mainly to a chorus of dismay from more committed (and more blinkered) modernist observers. Partly relying on the views of the great scholar of *dharmaśāstra,* P. V. Kane, Derrett (1970: 309–10) argued that 'polygamy should be tolerated for some classes on purely economic grounds .... It is the health and happiness of Hindus that counts', while noting, at p. 310, that 'the rash abolition of polygamy in a euphoric moment is not working out satisfactorily'. Derrett therefore argued for carefully controlled polygamy, only to be brusquely dismissed by *Towards Equality* (1974: 107–8), which claimed that the usefulness of regulated bigamy 'gives a misleading impression of being in the interests of women and as it is likely to be advanced in the context of Muslim law also, it needs to be rebutted in full'. For good measure, the Committee added (id.): 'We are not aware of a sympathy for bigamous unions or an opinion in favour of them in the absence of a systematic survey'. However, even that report itself contains evidence that some women did not think that outlawing polygamy had been a useful legal measure.[90] Singh (1989: 62) also joined this

[90] Banerjee (1984: 286–7) claims that polygamy survived into the early part of the twentieth century but does not explain this statement. Singh (1993: 30) presents statistical research showing more polygamy among Hindus than among Muslims.

debate, agreeing with Derrett that careful regulation, involving polygamy on account of infertility or mental instability of the first wife, and in cases where 'the good sense and humanity of the husband and his family recoils from divorcing her or annulling the marriage would not only be in accord with traditional Hindu religious sentiment and practice, but also much more realistic'. Mahmood (1986: 117) also criticizes the abolition of polygamy:

> All these unhealthy trends, in my opinion, follow from the fact that, imitating England, we have simply abolished polygamy in blanket terms by one stroke of legislation with a pious hope that the new law would be faithfully followed by all Hindus, Sikhs, Buddhists and Jains.

Bedwa and Ullah (1992: 69) discuss the formal abolition of Hindu polygamy as evidence of legal reform, but complain about the limited effects of the new legal dispensation. In their view, despite stringent laws and strong public opinion against polygamy, some people still indulge in contracting second marriages during the subsistence of the first marriage because the wording of Section 494 of the IPC is such that it is very difficult to convict a person who commits this offence. The authors explain this reasoning by saying that the modern provisions are basically redundant for Hindu polygamists if they play their cards cleverly, and solemnize the second marriage with defective ceremonies, as 'under the section one can only be convicted if the second marriage is celebrated with proper ceremonies' (Bedwa and Ullah 1992: 96). They also point out that '[u]nder the present law a married man may keep a concubine or contract a second marriage with defective ceremonies, he will not be liable for conviction ... and will continue to enjoy the fruits of the lacunae of law' (id.).

This constitutes evidence that Indian lawyers (in this case, too, inspired by the work of Paras Diwan) have been giving misleading advice, since this is by no means the only way to look at the legal position on Hindu marriage solemnization. By carping on about the loophole under Section 7 of the HMA, Indian lawyers have created the impression that there is only one line of case law on Hindu polygamy,[91] when in effect there are at least two, and the ample use of presumptions of marriage is well documented, as discussed earlier. As we began to see, thankfully there is a growing realization among modernist commentators that polygamy and its legal abolition cannot simply be viewed in isolation. In the context of a moralizing debate about adultery, Qureshi (1978: 359–60) states:

Bhandari (1989: 89–90) reports that various forms of polygamy occur among the tribal Bhil and Gharasia groups.

[91] For example, Sharma (1994: 93) claims that unfortunately the doctrine of *factum valet* regarding presumption of marriage has been accepted as a recognized norm under the law except for prosecuting the male bigamist under Section 494 of the IPC, speculating that the judiciary may surreptitiously want to decriminalize polygamy. S. Singh (1990: 428–35) offers some suggestions for better enforcement of prohibitions against polygamy among Hindus.

> Now times have changed. Polygamy has become a story of the past. The new wave in our country wants equality between sexes. The modern woman wants to check the moral lapses of her husband, in the same way as the husband checks the wife. Therefore, a law should be passed which may be applicable to husband and wife, both. Adultery and all sorts of sexual gratification outside marriage should be forbidden. Moral lapses including remarriage of the husband should be stopped.

A reader who is aware of the concept of *zina* as a serious crime and sin in Islamic law will understand that Qureshi here merely rephrases traditional Muslim law arguments that the state should uphold Islamic morality, rather than underwriting Western laxity and 'freedoms'. However, all forms of adultery cannot be checked easily by legal intervention and supervision. Because it is often practised in secrecy, proving a charge is made extremely difficult and, in a patriarchal set-up, women tend to be morally blamed and victimized.[92] Qureshi (1978: 360) argues that since in every case some margin is left between technical proof and fact, this margin should be interpreted in favour of the spouse alleging adultery, unless some deceit or ulterior motive is shown. However, the author himself rightly warns that this may be abused by men claiming that the wife has been unchaste, so as to free themselves from her claims for maintenance, a familiar technique in South Asian laws. In such situations, the courts should indeed insist on strict proof in order to prevent the wife being thrown on the road without financial support.[93]

A related matter of particular concern, which is hardly ever raised in the literature, strongly reflects the 'conspiracy of silence regarding sexuality in India' as highlighted by John and Nair (2000a: 1). It is a fact that the prosecution of Hindu men for polygamy will probably drive them towards arranging informal liaisons with concubines rather than attempting to marry formally. The present analysis has provided some indications that this is a complex area of concern, on which much research needs to be conducted. If there was more real concern for the protection of Hindu women in informal marital arrangements, rather than just vocal ideological objection to polygamy, much more would probably have to be done to assist such women, who appear to be in a really vulnerable legal position. But Indian scholarship and law are clearly taking their time in addressing the legal issues of subaltern groups when it comes to sexual matters (John and Nair 2000b).

[92] It is relevant to point out here that traditional Islamic law was acutely aware of such problems of evidence and stipulated enormously strict rules about eyewitnesses before permitting punishments for *zina*. Details would take us too far here, but it should be noted that Pakistani law under its Islamic dispensation has not managed to control male abuse in this area of the law, and in effect still punishes women for male sexual immorality. The risks for women are especially grave when they have become pregnant, as even a recent case from Peshawar reported in *The Japan Times* of 25 May 2002 confirms.

[93] This particular issue is further discussed in Chapter 12. Sagade (1989: 336–45) contains a useful discussion on polygamy and women's right of maintenance.

In sum, one may therefore agree with Derrett and Agnes that the formal legislative abolition of Hindu polygamy in Indian law appears to have been partly counterproductive. While modern post-colonial India could hardly have chosen to ignore the pressures towards explicit legal control of polygamy for Hindus, legislative activism by itself was not sufficient to curb the perceived problem. In the reformist spirit of the 1950s, however, it was still believed that making law would have more or less instant positive consequences. The relevant legal facts have indeed been created; the HMA 1955 appears to outlaw Hindu polygamy in clear terms. Modernist and international opinion should thereby be satisfied about the Indians as good pupils of the Western civilizing model.

However, the matter did not end here, because the same Indian state that appeared to outlaw Hindu polygamy has formally continued to condone it for Muslims. Mindful of international opinion, no doubt, the modern Indian state has taken the politically correct path of officially prohibiting polygamy for the majority of Indians but has, as in other fields,[94] bowed to Muslim pressure to preserve the shariat as the personal law for Indian Muslims. It appears that this has seriously derailed the discourse about the extent of state control for Hindu polygamy. It is tempting to interpret this manifestation of legal pluralism as devious doublespeak by the state. However, the present analysis suggests that we should read this rather as an integral element of a purposeful, planned and conscious strategy, specifically the South Asian reassertion of indigenous legal postulates for the reconstruction of postmodern South Asian family laws. This indicates that the Indian state does not favour Muslim polygamists in any meaningful sense; it simply refuses to implement strict legal prohibition of polygamy for all Indians, partly because this is no longer seen as culturally and socially inappropriate for South Asia.[95] But of course, it is not possible to go back legally to the pre-1955 position (Derrett 1970: 441) and to reinstate Hindu polygamy.

The unique secular legal model of India, purportedly based on equidistance from all religions, should have been able to inspire more trust among analysts. But as we saw earlier, modernists find it difficult to appreciate the Indian concept of secularism because it involves explicit recognition of the role of religion in governance. In my view, rather than fussing over secularism, Muslim privileges, the risk of conversions, or demographic scaremongering, it would be more productive if scholars stopped worrying about Hindu domination (or the corresponding Muslim apprehensions of minority suppression) and got down to addressing the real issues of substantive justice that are posed by the legal regulation of polygamy in India. Publicly voiced fear of Hinduization merely masks the fact that India has always been, and will continue to be, a part of the world dominated by Hindu concepts in their various manifestations.

[94] But, as we shall see in Chapter 12, the Indian state has legislated on Muslim laws concerning post-divorce maintenance, in a manner that baffles analysts.

[95] In addition, there is an economic dimension to this issue, which we need to discuss further in Chapter 12.

What these concepts were and are remains subject to constant negotiation, as the present study shows from many angles.

Significantly, the legislature has not interfered further in the Hindu law on polygamy since 1955. There are no subsequent amendments, nor increase of penalties for violations of the law.[96] This demonstrates that criminalization of Hindu polygamy per se has inspired little enthusiasm and does not really dominate the agenda, as confirmed by the case analysis in the section on deficient penalization. While it is undoubtedly useful to have modernist provisions on the statute book to achieve a more gender-balanced protective framework for women in an androcentric environment, blindly technical and formalistic application of the modernist statute law can and will do a lot of damage in a society that remains largely traditional. The postmodern Hindu law regulation of polygamy has faced that particular conceptual and practical challenge, not entirely successfully as yet, but in a much more complex way than modernist scholarship has managed to understand.

Nevertheless, there is no need to become regressive and assume that it will be necessary to call for the reintroduction of some form of 'controlled' polygamy into Indian law. To do so explicitly would obviously be politically unwise and unthinkable for Indian lawmakers, since it would give rise to charges that India was returning to medieval value systems or the 'Hindu dark ages'. So the legislative prohibition of Hindu polygamy will stay in place, but how and to what extent will it be implemented in practice? This is not the only example in South Asian laws of modernist family law legislation that seems to say one thing and does something else.[97]

To understand the postmodern legal regulation of Hindu polygamy, it is helpful to go back to Derrett's comment of 1970, to the effect that 'the rash abolition of polygamy in a euphoric moment is not working out satisfactorily'. As the present chapter has shown, judge-led postmodern Hindu law on polygamy has meanwhile begun to regulate various modalities of polygamy, rather than merely enforcing and policing its legal abolition. Reflecting judicial creativity and sensitivity over social and economic distress among women and children, the Hindu law on polygamy has developed a notable postmodern quality: it neither discards tradition nor follows modernist demands for abolition. However, this has escaped the notice of most analysts, who only see male collusion everywhere and suspect that the judges, as men and as unelected male mouthpieces of patriarchal traditions, more or less secretly oppose the

[96] The contrast with other areas of the law, notably dowry prohibition and 'dowry murders' is quite significant (for details see Menski 1998b).

[97] A relevant case in point is Pakistan's Muslim Family Laws Ordinance of 1961, which is peddled as a modernist myth by Indian legal scholars and as evidence of Pakistan having radically modernized and reformed its Muslim family laws. For example, Agnes (2000: 196) asserts that Pakistan 'regulated polygamy' and even that it abolished the practice of 'triple *talaq*'. This is plainly wrong (see in detail Pearl and Menski 1998: 334–73). Such scholarly constructs unfortunately confuse debates about the impediments to reforming Muslim law in India.

official criminalization of Hindu polygamy. The complex postmodern manifestation of the Hindu law on polygamy confirms again that the most important guarantor of ultimate justice in Indian matrimonial law is not some type of modernist uniform legislation, but rather judicial supervision of justice on a case-by-case basis. This strongly resonates with the ancient Hindu concept of *vyavahāra* as an ultimate safety net for indigent individuals who perceive and experience problems with justice.

Looking back at this legal position of polygamy in Indian law, it comes as a surprise to find that most judges are so well focussed on the job in hand. It is possible that most women and children who suffer from the consequences of polygamy can actually expect a sympathetic judicial hearing, if the matter goes that far (Vatuk 2001). The present analysis of the Hindu law of polygamy offers further evidence that the postmodern Indian state is relying on people's sense of self-controlled order and is purposely restraining itself from playing an active role in the arrangements that Hindus wish to make among themselves and on their own terms.

Thus, rather than actively seeking out Hindu polygamists for punishment, the legal efforts of the postmodern legal order are concentrated on listening to the complaints of those individuals who feel victimized by the polygamous arrangements that men create. The postmodern Indian state appears to be happy to delegate jurisdiction over many matters to society and to act—rather in the manner of the ancient Indian ruler—as a watchdog over justice. In such circumstances, it becomes important to facilitate access to courts for individuals who need to make a bona fide complaint. Once that happens, the perceived judicial task, it appears, goes beyond application of the strict and formal letter of the law. The overriding concern becomes to find a just solution, so as to safeguard the social welfare and well-being of women and children, rather than to protect the positivistic certainty of legal concepts for the sake of following the modern West. This approach to legal regulation resonates with postmodern understandings of the 'rule of law' (Tamanaha 2001), but on terms distinctly reflective of traditional Hindu legal concepts that stress situation-specific justice. The postmodern Indian state pursues a contemporary variant of the ancient Hindu policy of constant flexible adjustment to new circumstances, as much to protect dharma in the form of local normative orders as to ensure its own legitimation and survival as a politically acceptable unit within a constitutional framework.

An important finding regarding the legal regulation of Hindu polygamy in India is, therefore, that the state cannot, in this field of law, suddenly adopt a different stance from that taken in marriage and divorce law and insist on being involved in all arrangements within society when it comes to polygamy. State law has to be internally consistent to be effective. It cannot construct a system of rules which amounts to virtual permission for do-it-yourself Hindu marriages and divorces, and then expect to police and punish all polygamous arrangements. Indeed, the courts should be there to assist women and children if polygamous arrangements cause them distress and disadvantage. The postmodern Hindu law on polygamy shows that it is not the state law's task to lay down binding statutory norms for everyone's private life. The law, more specifically the courts, will only be able to act as safety nets in cases of complaint, rather than fully monitoring the implementation of the law. The ongoing modernist discourse on polygamy in Indian law tends to overlook this recognition by Indian judges of the limits of state law. This calls for more critical, rigorous, and honest research that also recognizes the specificity of locality.[98]

The existing shallow analyses of Hindu polygamy demonstrate that most of the modernist suggestions by scholars and activists about how to protect women from the perceived ills of traditional Hindu society are not realistic remedies. Perhaps we should no longer be surprised at this stage of the present enquiry that India's judges have understood this better than scholars and have led the way towards postmodern legal regulation of Hindu polygamy.

Looking at the legal literature, in particular, it would appear that the male-dominated Indian courts were merely helping Hindu men in bailing them out of criminal prosecutions for bigamy. That is clearly not the full story. In reality, the implications of India's new gender awareness in law go beyond male-dominated agenda and must again be linked to fiscal concerns and to efforts to protect situation-specific self-controlled justice rather than pressing for the application of uniform legal rules. In relation to polygamy, too, postmodern Hindu law has focused on protecting the material interests of individual women and children caught up in polygamy. Thus, rather than underwriting the ideological axioms of anti-polygamy rhetoric and thereby in effect punishing women for becoming involved in polygamy, the postmodern Hindu law places concern for the social welfare of disadvantaged female claimants higher than ideological compliance with the expectations of Western modernity. The postmodern legal condition in South Asian laws, as the present chapter confirms, involves developing an economically focused, welfare-based safety net for claimants in society, in this case polygamously married women, recognizing the social presence of Hindu polygamy while not granting it formal legality. This sophisticated postmodern approach challenges the ideological demands of anti-bigamist rhetoric and emphasizes instead social welfare measures that could be of real benefit to the women concerned. Although this amounts to subtle legalization of Hindu polygamy,[99] there is otherwise little fault to be found with this approach.

[98] The lengths to which abuses could easily go is indicated by a study on devadasis and commercial prostitution in Mysore, in which Tarachand (1991: 6) argues that polygamy contributes significantly to commercial prostitution. On the other hand, Sen (2000: 96) begins to uncover important evidence that women could also creatively use male-centred marriage laws as an instrument against men whom they wished to leave.

[99] As shown in Chapter 9, the same argument applies to postmodern state policies towards the legal validity of child marriages. Here, too, despite ideological objections, the protection of the tangible interests of women and children is considered more important than obedience to dominant, metropolitan gender ideology.

11

Divorce

The complex subject area of Hindu divorce law is a huge topic to which a separate monograph could be devoted. It involves so many sub-issues relevant to the present debate that it will be necessary to focus on some aspects only.[1] The detailed analysis of traditional Hindu divorce law is complicated by the fact that there have been—and still are—two contradictory understandings of 'tradition' in this field. On the one hand, the dominant view among scholars has been that classical Hindu law did not permit divorce, mainly because it infringes the ideal of sacramental marriage, seen as the central foundation of Hindu family law.[2] At the same time, there is much evidence of the long-established existence of various ancient customary forms of divorce among Hindus. Practised in social reality, and in abundance, they have nevertheless been unable to gain full legal recognition within the socio-legal field of diversity that classical Hindu law represents. Clearly, this is a reflection of the ideological and largely scholar-led marginalization of Hindu customary law under British rule, which has had a significant impact on the modernist discourses about Hindu law reform.

While the British colonial regime hesitated to get involved in this touchy subject, it broadly accepted the axiom that Hindus have no right to divorce. However, while British India experienced timidity towards law-making in this area, several princely states introduced pioneering divorce reforms, making this remedy formally available to Hindus on specific grounds and in certain situations. By ignoring the existence of customary rights to divorce, colonial and modernist reformers claimed authority for the state and its laws in a space that was already occupied by other normative orders and was not a void, as claimed by Sanskrit elitists and modernist lobbyists. Eventually, the post-colonial construction of knowledge about a 'traditional' and 'religious' Hindu divorce law which simply did not permit divorce motivated reformers to demand wide-ranging grounds for divorce among Hindus. The Indian legislature moved cautiously, though, partly because during the 1950s divorce was also not accepted so freely in England, which continued to constitute a guiding model for reformers during that time.

[1] The related topic of restitution of conjugal rights is covered in the excellent study by Chandra (1998).

[2] Feminist analysis often suggests that Hindu women are treated virtually as property of the husband. That is clearly too simplistic, but serves powerful agenda.

The modernist agenda of the postcolonial state were focused on freeing Hindu men and women from the shackles of a traditional marriage law that seemed to tie spouses together not only in this life, but also for all lives to come. However, given that customary divorces were available to virtually all Hindus, the alleged restrictiveness of the old law led to confused modernist analysis over the pace and direction of Hindu divorce law reforms. Officially, it has concentrated on the effects of formal state intervention, viewing legal reform as liberating for spouses. However, quite significantly, the post-colonial Hindu divorce legislation also recognizes the presence of customary divorces among Hindus,[3] thus presenting a duality of processes and provisions which has been causing many practical problems, not only in India.[4] But more disconcerting for many modernists has been the reluctance and ultimate refusal of the Indian legislature to introduce full-fledged legal permission for divorce on the basis of 'irretrievable breakdown'. While this basic liberating tool of modern English divorce law has been treated as a desirable magic remedy and almost a golden 'holy cow', few analysts realized that the much-criticized unilateral instant Muslim *talaq* is actually based on the same reasoning: If a spouse (not just the man) feels that the marriage is finished, it should be terminated. But is it a healthy development that modern Indian law should support individual whims to the exclusion of wider social concerns?

There has been no clear thinking about this particular issue and rather too much ideological positioning, also in the context of uniform civil code debates. While there is no space here to analyse this aspect in detail, some critical comments are necessary at this early stage to illustrate the ideologically twisted nature and direction of modernist debates about Hindu divorce law. In particular, the deliberate and mischievous construction of Indian Muslim law as not allowing Muslim wives the right to divorce, while Pakistani law has clearly underwritten this right for a long time,[5] has legitimized modernist calls for Muslim divorce reforms in India, based on the claim that Indian Muslim law is

[3] This is hidden away in Section 29(2) of the HMA, phrased in such a way that it is easily overlooked. The general divorce rules, on the other hand, are found in Section 13 of the HMA.

[4] The matters debated here have crucial relevance to many people's lives today. For example, a young Gujarati Hindu man from the UK has been unable to marry his Hindu fiancée in London for years because the British authorities insist, quite wrongly, that his earlier customary divorce under Hindu law in India was not legally valid as it lacked evidence of 'proceedings'. Muddled and incomplete knowledge of Hindu divorce law, combined with legal centralist assertions, is here used to harass Asian 'immigrants', even when both intending spouses have been living in the UK for many years.

[5] India, Pakistan, and Bangladesh share the Dissolution of Muslim Marriages Act of 1939, under which Muslim women have made successful claims for divorce on the principle of marital breakdown. For details see Pearl and Menski (1998). This Act is interpreted much more conservatively in India than in Bangladesh and particularly in Pakistan, where a rich case law exists to support women's claims.

backward and virtually enslaves women in marriages. Such constructed images of backwardness could then be used to praise Indian lawmakers for modernizing Hindu divorce law, in the same breath as demanding further state intervention in divorce laws for all Indians. While significant reforms were introduced in Hindu divorce law in the HMA of 1955, the Hindu Marriage (Amendment) Act of 1964 and the Marriage Laws (Amendment) Act of 1976 went much further in the direction of facilitating easy divorce. It is at that point, during the late 1970s, that Professor Derrett wrote his famous *Epitaph to the Rishis* (Derrett 1978a), which warned in its conclusions that the modernist policy would have absolutely disastrous consequences for India and for Hindus, especially women.

It seems that Derrett was entirely right in being so critical. During the 1970s, dreadfully destructive Hindu case law began to appear, hailed by modernists as liberating, but soon more widely perceived as disastrous for social stability and for women.[6] It is highly significant that, since 1976, the Indian legislature has no longer allowed itself to be bullied into further rash legal action by various women's groups and other modernist forces, among which some legal textbook writers have been prominent. The failure of the Marriage Laws Bill of 1981 signals this frozen state of statutory Hindu law reforms on divorce. Subsequent efforts have been stymied, too.

In this area, the often painful first-hand judicial experience of applying modernist post-colonial laws has been a key ingredient for the genesis of postmodern thinking among the higher judiciary. In the 1970s and into the early 1980s, most Indian judges were liberal in granting divorces to almost anyone who cared to ask, ignoring at first the disturbing evidence that this law was mostly being manipulated by men to the detriment of women. Yet the judges realized during the 1980s that their own liberality in interpreting the Hindu law on divorce, which contributed to this process in no small measure, was driving Indian society towards ruin. The huge judge-made case law on 'cruelty' as a ground for divorce among Hindus offers probably the most convincing evidence that judicial reconsideration of modernist liberality and its social consequences in Indian conditions could not be in the public interest. Judges began to refuse divorce decrees where it was evident that the marriage was not finished, especially when it was the wife who expressed an interest in the continuation of the marital tie.

Contrary to my own initial suspicions about hidden Hinduization of Hindu divorce law, the judges have demonstrated that they are not in the business of reinstating traditional Hindu law (which at any rate allowed divorce, as everyone should have understood a long time ago), but that their main task is to find just solutions to the family problems brought before them. Moreover, the Indian judiciary has become immensely alert to the potentially disastrous economic and social consequences of a high divorce rate. Restrictive and only cautiously liberal application of the modernist divorce rules for Hindus in India today is therefore coupled with strong judicial activism about protecting

[6] An important modernist case is *N.G. Dastane v S. Dastane* AIR 1975 SC 1534.

the rights of women and children to maintenance (see Chapter 12). Abundant case law evidence demonstrates that the reconstruction process in Hindu divorce law is not some conservative backward-looking conspiracy of old men, many of whom are Brahmins, but a progressive, postmodern method of safeguarding socio-economic justice.

The present chapter follows the familiar chronological pattern of analysis applied throughout this Part and examines first of all the conflicting evidence about the nature of divorce in ancient Hindu law. Subsequent sections scrutinize the rather meagre reformist efforts during the colonial period and then concentrate in more detail on the modernist reforms of Hindu divorce law in the HMA of 1955 and in particular its subsequent amendments. The postmodern scenario, as indicated above, appears to involve a reappraisal of the value of marriage and of the role of divorce as a safety valve and an emergency remedy.

Traditional Hindu Concepts of Divorce

The discussion of Hindu marriage concepts in Chapter 8 brought out the wider dimensions within which Hindu concepts of marriage and divorce operate, as manifested over time in Hindu normative, textual statements and in social reality. In that context, the centrality of marital status in Hindu law became apparent. The close links between Hindu marriage and divorce are reinforced in the traditional literature with reference to perceptions and discussions about divorce. In the present context, too, a gradual transition from Vedic concepts to classical, late classical and postclassical assumptions about the role of women and the question of divorce is notable. In all of this, the *ṛta*/dharma context is ever-present but is rarely made explicit in the academic literature. While traditional authors knew of its existence and saw no need to mention it, modernists choose to ignore it.

Discussions about traditional Hindu divorce law remain often oddly skewed and quite confusing for readers who are not familiar with traditional Hindu concepts. While customary Hindu divorces have always been known and practised in certain circumstances, particularly among lower classes and castes, the dominant view in the academic and legal literature is to the effect that classical Hindu law did not permit divorce at all. Interestingly, the key issue here is the definition of 'law', more specifically of 'Hindu law', which most writing takes to mean only the scriptural tradition rather than customary laws as well. However, traditional Hindu divorce law has always been much more liberal and flexible in social reality than many writers admit. The apparent contradiction could be resolved by recognizing that divorce is evidently a violation of the shastric high-caste ideal of Hindu marriage as a *saṃskāra*, but has always been a part of Hindu social life as a whole. Most authors, however, prefer simple dogmatic statements relying on— and in turn reinforcing—the axiom that traditional Hindu law did not permit divorce, nor even knew such a concept.

Analysis of the profuse ancient textual sources clearly shows that the texts themselves reflect and contain a totally ambivalent picture. Conservative statements, to the effect that a married Hindu woman must put up with everything that the supposedly 'divine' husband throws at her,[7] are sitting irreconcilably side by side with radically 'modern' verses that encourage Hindu wives to terminate a bad or seriously defective marriage and to start a fresh life with another man.[8] Looking for a fixed Hindu law on the subject, scholars have made critical methodological mistakes, overlooking not only the internal complexity of Hindu textual sources in terms of time and space, but also the centrality of situation-specificity, and hence of *sadācāra* and the ideal model of Hindu self-controlled ordering (Chapter 3). Here again, therefore, particular selective scholarly constructions and distortions of classical Hindu law and its manifestations are evident, but it could not be said that this is exclusively a European-led process. We have been systematically taught, mainly by Indian feminists, among whom there are many expatriates, to view traditional Hindu divorce law as a system of rules that enslaves women and does not permit them the freedom and space to make decisions over their own lives. This constructed, strict image of Hindu 'tradition' (into which evidence of flexible customary Hindu divorce rules and women's agency does not fit, of course) was employed first to legitimise modernist reforms in the post-independence period, and continues today to buttress modernist calls for further 'liberalizing' changes to Hindu divorce law in India.

Nevertheless, much scholarly energy has been spent on debating whether and to what extent ancient Hindu law allowed divorce. The high ideal of the Vedic marriage did not, it appears, militate against termination of a marital tie if a marriage was defective in terms of procreative achievements. Since the major Vedic expectation appears to have been that a couple should have many children, if the husband was for some reason infertile, the wife in Vedic times would be expected to cohabit with another man for the sake of procreation, even while remaining formally married to the husband.[9] This was not evidence of divorce, therefore, but a sign that techniques of 'assisted reproduction' were being employed in ancient days to strengthen the family and activate the woman's procreative potential (Diwan 1980). Sharma (1993: 36) provides a sensible, balanced insight into the prevailing conflicting picture of ancient Hindu divorce law:

> In the Vedic literature there is no reliable reference to divorce and there is not much evidence of it in post-Vedic literature ... marriage is a holy and religious institution and is based on spiritual values. Therefore once the

[7] *Manusmṛti* 5.154 is cited as an androcentric injunction by Chandra (1998: 121): 'Though destitute of virtue, or seeking pleasure [elsewhere], or devoid of good qualities, [yet] a husband must be constantly worshipped as a god by a faithful wife'.

[8] These arguments may not be 'modern' where they concern the dominant concern of progeny rather than marital chastity. Excellent examples are now offered by Olivelle (2000) in his new translation of the four *dharmasūtra* texts.

[9] The resulting dharma dilemmas are analysed by Datta (1979). Such concepts linger on in the ambivalence surrounding levirate marriages among Hindus.

marriage ceremony is performed, it was considered irreligious to think of divorce or even separation.

Sharma (id.) emphasizes that according to various texts, for example the *Āpastāmba Dharmasūtra* both husband or wife would go to hell if the vows taken during the marriage ceremony are broken. The *Manusmṛti* suggests that *kanyādāna* can take place only once and that strict penances should be applied to spouses who forsake their life partners.

Details of those penances are clearly designed to shame the man, and similarly the woman, and thus reflect the social reservations about divorce among early Hindus. Sharma (1993: 37) claims that the indissolubility of the sacrament of marriage has been clearly explained in the Vedic literature. The ideal married life was found in monogamy for both sides,[10] with no mention of divorce anywhere. However, some of the *dharmasūtra* texts indicate that women must have abandoned their husband to produce a son with another man.

Women's position in marriage appears less safe. The *Manusmṛti* justifies a man abandoning a wife who does not bear children while the *Arthaśāstra* also mentions divorce (Sharma 1993: 38) and seems to support it (ibid.: 40). Sharma (1993: 39) quite correctly states, therefore, that 'in the ancient Indian literature there are contradictions regarding the views on divorce'. A fuller analysis would demonstrate rather weak textual support for Hindu divorce, as compared to the texts supporting indissolubility of marriage, but it could not be said that divorce was unknown. Divorce is linked to extraordinary circumstances, as Sharma (1993: 39) indicates:

> Normally the Dharmashāstras are against divorce and consider the sacrament of marriage as the most important and holy. Manu himself supports this view. He says that the husband and the wife must consider it their sacred duty to see that they maintain a life-long married life.

This is simply a classic restatement of the Hindu ideal. Texts like the *Manusmṛti* clearly indicate that after the consummation of the marriage, there should ideally be no divorce or separation between the spouses.[11] The result, over time, has been an exaggerated popular belief within India and outside that traditional

[10] For example, *Āpastambadharmasūtra* 2.11.12–14 (Olivelle 2000: 91) indicates that '[s]o long as his wife participates in religious rites and bears children, a man may not take another wife. If she is wanting in either of these, he may take another prior to establishing his sacred fires, for a wife who participates in the ritual establishment of his sacred fires becomes associated with the rites to which the establishment of the sacred fires is only supplementary'.

[11] It is possible to link this to the central role of the classical understanding of stages of life, and the ideal that a man should become a householder. In the context of a growing trend of male (and female!) renunciation, there was a risk that more young people, men and women, would not marry, and would seek short cuts to salvation (*mokṣa*) through celibacy.

Hindu law makes divorce impossible. This is reflected in many dogmatic statements about the alleged indissolubility of Hindu marriages. Nair (1978: 14) definitely overstates this because he does not make a distinction between 'high-caste' law and lower-caste customs when he writes that '[d]ivorce is unknown to customary Hindu law, because marriage is an indissoluble union between the husband and the wife. Incompatibility of temper, adultery, fornication, cruelty and incurable diseases were not grounds that called for divorce'. The above statement is marred by its careless use of 'customary', when 'traditional' seems intended and 'classical' would be better. Virdee (1972: 19) summarizes the traditional ideal position by saying that Hindu marriage as a sacrament, once performed with appropriate rituals, 'becomes irrevocable on the completion of the ceremony of taking seven steps by the couple'. Virdee (id.) also indicates that '[t]here is no evidence as to the practice of divorce as such during the Vedic and post Vedic periods', reiterating that the classic concept of Hindu marriage was that of an indissoluble union:

> It was a holy union of mind, body and soul of the spouses and, it was believed, that even death did not put an end to it, for the wife remained linked with her husband in soul after death in the next world. It was the highest duty of husband and wife to remain united in marriage and be utterly faithful to each other (id).

Such idealizing statements are by no means unquestioned.[12] Many texts point out certain circumstances in which a separation may be necessary in view of higher concerns. Thus, if there are no children, or the wife (and sometimes the husband) seriously misbehaves, then this may be a ground for changing the marriage partner.[13] Whether this is to be called divorce, or something else, has become a controversial topic. While suggesting that the concept of divorce did not exist, though in ancient India in certain circumstances a man could forsake his wife, Sharma (1993: 40) plays with words, claiming that the *smritis* do not consider it to be a divorce. There is a traditional right of forsaking an unfit husband or wife, but his did not provide for complete removal of the spouse from the household. Sharma (id.) explains that 'forsaking meant depriving one from the household duties and stoppage of all conversation. Thus, this could not mean divorce and the sacred sacrament of marriage remained indissoluble'.

[12] For example, the idea of a 'next life' in which a couple is still living together, is neither a binding Hindu dogma, nor probably even a widely shared belief. Firth (1997: 45–8) reports on a range of different perceptions about such issues among Hindus today. Weinberger-Thomas (1999) considers this issue in the context of sati.

[13] On impotent husbands, see *Nāradasmṛti* 12.11–13, *Manusmṛti* 3.4–11 and 3.204–205. Supersession is indicated as the most common remedy in *Manusmṛti* 9.77–83. *Arthaśāṣtra* III.15–18 seems to admit the possibility of divorce, and so does *Nāradasmṛti* 12.96–97.

The above chain of arguments refuses to accept the full impact of the social reality of divorce among traditional Hindus.[14] Virdee (1972: 27–32) examined the distinction between abandonment and supersession and, attempting a linguistic analysis, found a clear difference. The Sanskrit word for 'abandonment' is *tyāga*, renouncing contact with the wife, but this word can mean a number of things and the question remains whether a wife would be free to marry again after being abandoned.[15] Virdee (1972: 28) saw abandonment as a more or less temporary measure of punishment for an errant spouse, arguing that 'abandonment in any case did not amount to dissolution of marriage whereby the status of the husband and wife ceased to exist as such and the marriage-tie was severed at law'. Taking a strict view, Virdee (1972: 30) therefore agreed that 'divorce as such did not exist at *sastric* Hindu law'.

When it comes to 'supersession', this is more clearly a method of terminating the marital relationship for good, provided this is in accordance with the higher concerns of dharma.[16] Virdee (1972: 30–1) asserts that supersession under certain circumstances is justifiable:

> As the purpose of the Hindu *sastric* marriage is to perform religious rites and beget male progeny, if either of the two is frustrated, a man is entitled to take another wife .... The supersession had to be just and reasonable, and in the case of a sick wife who was virtuous and kind to her husband her consent had to be obtained. However, in practice husbands could supersede their wives without their consent and even against their wishes merely on the ground that the wife was of a harsh and disagreeable nature.

This seems to indicate that the textual ideals and social reality were not always matching. Virdee (1972: 31) emphasizes that a wife who was abandoned or superseded did not thereby lose her financial entitlements against the husband. This strengthens the view that from a strictly dogmatic perspective, there appeared to be no way out of a Hindu marriage.[17] Virdee (1972: 32) firmly concluded that according to the shastras a sacramental marriage cannot be dissolved, because the wife is a gift from the gods which cannot be revoked by an act of human beings. Sociologists like Kapadia (1972: 168) also link the sacramental nature of marriage and its irrevocable standing to reservations about divorce, but seem less stringent:

> ... marriage is said to be sacred [and] it is irrevocable. The parties to the marriage cannot dissolve it at will. They are bound to each other until the

[14] *Manusmṛti* 9.76 indicates that even if a husband has gone on a long journey, the wife should wait. *Arthaśāstra* III 4.24–8 mentions this, too.

[15] On *tyāga* see also Singh (1993: 37–8).

[16] On supersession in the ancient period, see Altekar (1978: 106–07) and Sharma (1994: 24–5). A good discussion is found in Larivière (1991).

[17] However, Parashar (1992: 116) argues that the *Parāsarasmṛti* and the *Devalasmṛti* also allowed divorce to women, using this reasoning to justify further modernist reforms.

> death of either of them; and the wife is supposed to be bound to her husband even after his death. This concept of marriage, that it is indissoluble ... means that the husband and wife after marriage have to adjust their tastes and temper, their ideals and interests, instead of breaking with each other when they find that these differ. It thus involves sacrifices on the part of both husband and wife as each is called upon to overcome the incompatibility of the other.

Kapadia (1972: 169) argues, therefore, that the requirement to compromise and adjust is hard work, but was expected in Hindu society and is supported by the law. Kapadia (1972: 181–2) examines further why the Hindu conceptual environment is hostile to divorce:

> Manu declared mutual fidelity till death as the essence of *dharma* for the husband and the wife because, according to him, man and woman, united in marriage, should constantly so exert themselves that they may not be disunited and may not violate their mutual fidelity. In spite of this ... Manu permitted supersession of the wife both in the absence of a male child and, theoretically at least, for her sharp tongue or rebellious nature. Supersession on the former ground is accepted by many as valid simply because *dharma* is the focal point of marriage.

Undoubtedly, the *dharmaśāstras* stress mutual fidelity and devotion to the spouse, especially for the wife. Kapadia (1972: 184) argues that the author of the *Manusmṛti* remained silent on the details of divorce because 'he also stood for a philosophy of marriage that was not consonant with such a step'. Singh (1989: 76) argues that '[a]ccording to traditionalists, divorce was unknown in Hindu law. Even today divorce is not a socially accepted norm among many sections' and looked upon with disfavour. Virdee (1972: 20) stresses that dissolution of marriage was not contemplated by the *shastra*, 'for it was un-*dharmic*, unrighteous and sinful'. Kapadia (1972: 183) emphasizes the initial difficulties of replacing a wife and allows a glimpse of the pernicious impact of relaxation of such strict rules:

> The privilege of superseding the wife was initially very restrictive both in its scope and exercise. It was justified on grounds of *dharma*. But recognition of this discrimination in favour of the husband developed in course of time into frequent assertion of his privileged position which neglected the approved reason for it: *dharma*.

This already allows a glimpse of the major problem which later reformists were going to face. The key issue would inevitably become how to balance easier divorce with protecting women against desertion by unscrupulous men. In ancient Hindu society, such interspousal problems were considered by reference to joint family concepts, which is clearly evident from how customary divorces operated—they tend to involve community elders and other family members, thus in effect *sadācāra*.

Diwan (1978: 15) was characteristically dogmatic on the indissolubility of Hindu marriages and claimed that because of this doctrine, the *dharmaśāstra* did not recognize divorce. He also asserted that 'any attempt to deduce from stray *smriti* texts the proposition that divorce was recognised by some *smritikars* is nothing but one's inability to comprehend the basic concepts that the *dharmashastra* propounded'. Such strong words are clearly not warranted. Where is it written that we have to assume that the *smṛtis* took only one view? What about unity in diversity? It is remarkable that this learned author refused to see the link with massive evidence of lower-caste customs of divorce, of which he himself provides the evidence at pp. 15–16:

> However, the *dharmashastra*'s adherence to the doctrine of indissolubility of marriage did not hamper the recognition of the people's need of divorce, and a large section of Hindus (*i.e.* the lower classes) did enjoy the right of divorce. This was under the custom which prevailed over the sacred law. Customary modes of divorce were easy. In some cases a marriage could be dissolved by mutual consent. Sometimes divorce could also be purchased. Very little formalities for dissolving a marriage were needed. Many a time it was purely a private act of parties. In some communities a forum was necessary—it was either a *panchayat* or a family council. Customary divorce was the privilege of the lower castes and higher castes seldom had a custom which permitted divorce.

The overall result of such a fragmented and piecemeal discussion should have been an explicit recognition that traditional Hindu law operated two concepts of divorce side by side. Singh (1989: 76) notes in this respect that '[c]ontrary to the general notion regarding the indissolubility of Hindu marriages, a large section of Hindus among the lower castes have traditionally practised divorce'. Such customary forms of divorce were recognized, both socially and judicially, and the most usual forms are divorce by mutual consent, unilateral divorce by the husband, or divorce by deed. Singh (id.) notes that '[u]nder customary law, there is no waiting period after divorce for remarriage. The other advantage of these forms is that they save both time and money which is generally lost in litigation; but since some of these forms are against public policy or morality, a divorce under customary law may be rejected by a court'.

Such customary divorces are frequently in use, however. Minattur (1980: 168) confirmed that while the right of a Hindu wife to obtain such a divorce may be much more restricted than that of the husband, in certain Hindu communities and among most tribal groups, it is possible for the husband and the wife to obtain a divorce without any recourse to court. The only requirement may be that some customary practices have been followed, for example making a declaration before the elders of the community or the headman of the tribe that the parties no longer wish to continue their marital relationship. This is also confirmed in *Towards Equality* (1974: p. 117):

> Usually customary divorces are through the intervention of the traditional Panchayats or caste tribunals. Therefore, in States where this has not been

> customary, the courts have not permitted Panchayats to take upon themselves the right to dissolve a marriage. Once the custom is proved, however, the courts will not interfere.

Virdee (1972: 32–6) also discussed this topic, admitting that Hindus in India are familiar with divorce because of its manifestation in custom. Since the shastra itself recognized custom (*sadācāra*) as a source of law, it was not possible (nor indeed desirable) to impose strict idealistic high-caste norms on everyone. Virdee (1972: 33) notes that also in custom, divorce is 'regarded as a concession to a husband rather than as a right' and highlights that divorce is known in many communities that are not of low standing, and is a practised custom even among some Brahmins.

Against this, the axiomatic official legal position on classical Hindu divorce law is authoritatively stated in the leading textbook on Hindu law (Desai 1998: 666) as a general principle of prohibition, but it immediately involves shastric and non-shastric Hindu law in contrast:

> Divorce is not known to the general Hindu Law. The reason is that a marriage, from the Hindu point of view, creates an indissoluble tie between the husband and the wife. Neither party, therefore, to a marriage can divorce the other unless divorce is allowed by custom.

It is important to examine briefly the terms used here. The reference to the 'general' Hindu law points us to the textual sources and links with the *saṃskāra* ideal, while the exceptional situation of custom is also indicated.[18] The resulting image is certainly not that of a uniform Hindu law, but at least a duality of possible approaches. Other commentators have used different language to create an impression that traditional Hindu law did not know divorce when it seems more appropriate to assume that it did not *want* to know about it. Qureshi (1978: 40) engages in the construction of Hindu-Muslim contrasts and claims that before the passing of the HMA, Hindu women were treated like chattels and were not given the right to ask for the dissolution of marriage. This serves the hidden agenda of portraying Muslim law as more advanced. Qureshi (id.) writes further that the sacramental union implies an eternal union for all lives to come, and hence a Hindu woman could not remarry.

Diwan and Diwan (2000: 23) explain that Hindus conceived of marriage as a sacramental union, a 'sacrosanct, permanent, indissoluble and eternal union', thus not as a contract, but as a tie which cannot be untied. They claim that the indissoluble nature of Hindu marriage is 'expressed by Manu' (id.) in a statement to the effect that the husband is declared to be one with the wife and neither by sale nor by repudiation can a Hindu wife be released from her husband. The authors therefore conclude that under Hindu law, divorce was out of the question, while under custom divorce has been recognized in some Hindu communities and tribes.

[18] Diwan and Diwan (1993: 167–8) discuss divorce by custom in some detail.

Other authors have been less hazy about Hindu customary divorces. Qureshi (1978: 32) notes that though divorce is not sanctioned among Hindus and by the traditional texts, it was always prevalent by custom. He provides ample evidence from various writings of observers and government anthropologists, as well as early cases, concluding that 'from the very beginning there was a custom among the Hindus under which they were allowed to divorce their wives' (ibid.: 34). Parashar (1992: 116) links the concept of customary divorce with that of folk marriage, which 'has the concept of a contract divorce as a logical corollary'. She also observes that among tribals, no ceremony is required for effecting a divorce, only a formal intimation. But was this informal permission to divorce the same for men and women? Kapadia (1972: 185) highlighted the issue of gender discrimination inherent in classical Hindu law, observing that allowing men to replace women was not necessarily a positive social development:

> The greatest tyranny of the male over the female lies in the privilege of supersession enjoyed by the Hindu husband. This tyranny could be minimized by prohibiting bigamy on the one hand and by allowing the superseded wife the opportunity for divorce on the other. Divorce alone will not better the position of women because a majority of them are economically dependent on men and it would be difficult for a divorced woman to find someone else to marry her .... Facilities for divorce would, however, usher in a new concept of marriage.

This chain of arguments indicates how making divorce available to Hindus, male and female, eventually came to be seen as progressive in itself during the twentieth century, especially as an act of liberation for Hindu women.

Reforms During the British Period

In view of the explicitly traditional and androcentric nature of English law in the eighteenth and nineteenth century, with much impact from older Roman law concepts,[19] it could not be expected that British colonial intervention would assist Hindu women in improving their socio-legal position.[20] Early British efforts in seeking to alleviate perceived social abuses and evils among Hindus focused on assisting widows to be able to remarry, rather than helping individuals, let alone women, to break up marriages. Noting that under the classical

[19] One particularly relevant issue was that women were treated as legal minors in virtually all respects, and a married woman had to accept the husband's right over her property, becoming a virtual chattel herself. Such traditional Romano-English concepts inevitably influenced the way in which colonial officers perceived Hindu women and their legal position.

[20] A useful discussion is found in Chandra (1998), who highlights the institutional sexism of Victorian England (p. 4), finds that English law was not an appropriate model of a civilized law for the Indians (p. 81), and compares the traditional Hindu wife to the Victorian 'angel in the house' (p. 122).

law, a Hindu widow was not allowed to remarry, Virdee (1972: 36) wrote that 'it was not until the passing of the Hindu Widows' Remarriage Act, 1856 that the harshness of this *sastric* principle was abolished by legalising the remarriage of widows'.

Chandra (1998: 122) shows that during the debates over the law on restitution of conjugal rights in connection with the *Rukhmabai* case, a Hindu woman who had repudiated her marriage (however unsatisfactory the match and the man), and was willing to go to jail rather than be forced to consummate an unwanted marital union, 'was projected as a threat to social well being'. When the British circulated some tentative proposals for the introduction of divorce to alleviate the perceived sufferings of Hindu women like Rukhmabai, the reaction was unqualified horror, as Chandra (1998: 122) documents:

> This was worse than the worst that the Privy Council could do in the event of an appeal in the Rukhmabai case. It confirmed the suspicion that the British policy of non-interference in the religious affairs of the ruled was not entirely trustworthy. The rulers, the *Hindi Pradip* observed, might as well admit that they aimed to Europeanize the Hindus and wipe out their religion.
>
> Fears got exaggerated in this state of agitation. They were fed by a deep-seated anxiety about female sexuality. Supposed to be insatiable, female sexuality was believed to require constant vigilance and control. Like the deification of the Hindu husband, attitudes to female sexuality and its controlling mechanisms also had a long unbroken tradition. For those socialized in this tradition, divorce was not only corrupting and anti-shastric, it also appeared—despite the wide prevalence of customary divorce—to be the negation of marriage. Considering that men, even without divorce, were not particularly constrained, the prospect of freedom it might give women was the only reason for apprehending chaos from the introduction of divorce.

As the public reaction was negative, the British realized that it would be dangerous to interfere in Hindu marriage and divorce law, and as Chandra (1998: 170) reports, 'inadvisable to proceed "too far in advance of the social and moral sentiments of the community concerned"'. Thus, the British 'had developed cold feet on the question of altering the existing law for fear of popular discontent' (Chandra 1998: 186) and no divorce reforms were introduced for Hindus during British rule.[21]

[21] The Christians of India were made subject to the Indian Divorce Act, 1869, with a restrictive divorce regime that favoured men and was for a long time criticised as outdated. Because of Parliamentary inactivity (and back-pedalling by some Church leaders) this outdated law was ultimately amended by activist judicial intervention in the High Court of Kerala (in *Mary Sonia Zachariah v Union of India* 1995(1) KLT 644 FB) and more recently also elsewhere. On the demands for further reforms and the Indian Divorce (Amendment) Bill 2000 see Ghosh (2001). The Parsi law, as

Virdee (1972: 36-37) showed that the Native Converts' Marriage Dissolution Act of 1866 provided an indirect way of divorce for converts to Christianity. When one of the Hindu spouses adopted Christianity, and the other refused to live with the spouse on that ground, a decree for restitution of conjugal rights or alternatively for divorce, could be applied for.[22] Divorce was also made available under the Special Marriage Act of 1872, which would have applied only to very few Hindus.

For Hindu law, Derrett (1978a: 5) reports that deviations from the Brahmanical ideal, as may be found even in the text of the *Manusmṛti*, were contemptuously dismissed by traditionalists as corruptions, thus refusing to accept that there could be a variety of views on the permissibility and extent of divorce among Hindus.[23] Lack of honesty about the manifest internal pluralism of Hindu divorce law did not create a climate of open debate in which the colonial powers might have made any impact.

However, in some of the princely states, it was possible to introduce some reforms to Hindu divorce law, even though there, too, orthodox resistance was felt. Kapadia (1972: 185) reports that the first legislation in respect of the dissolution of Hindu marriages was probably that enacted in Kolhapur State in the 1920s.[24] Derrett (1978a: 5–7) shows in detail how the significant Hindu law reforms in Baroda gently and carefully first made divorce on some grounds available to Hindus in 1931, and then more fully through the Baroda Hindu Nibandha of 1937. Derrett (1978a: 6) explains that the impact of the 1937 Act was first of all that customary divorces 'should still be valid though made "outside the court", provided that when made they were registered "in the court"'. But for those communities which had no such customs, actually a small minority, judicial dissolution of marriage became available for the first time on a number of grounds, as listed by Derrett (id.):

1. disappearing for seven years or more;
2. becoming a recluse;
3. changing his/her religion by conversion;
4. being guilty of cruelty so as to cause danger to (a) life, (b) limb, or (c) bodily or mental health so as to give rise to a reasonable apprehension of such danger;

earlier found in the Parsi Marriage and Divorce Act, 1865, also permitted divorce on certain grounds, but involved the Parsi panchayat in this process. Thus it could be seen as a formally regulated version of customary law.

[22] On this Act, see also an article by Derrett, reprinted in Derrett (1978b: 53–61), noting that divorce by consent had become the major feature of English divorce law.

[23] For example, Paras Diwan (1978: 15) was cited above to that effect.

[24] Kapadia (1972: 185) also wrote that in Baroda state an Act was passed in 1942, but that seems to be incorrect, given what Derrett (1978a) reports about the 1931/1937 reforms.

5. being guilty of desertion without reasonable cause for more than three years after cohabitation commenced;
6. being addicted to intoxicants for more than three years and thus unable to fulfil marital obligations;
7. committing adultery; or
8. marrying a second time during the lifetime of the petitioner.

Kapadia (1972: 186) notes that this enactment demanded fidelity on both sides, not only on one as before, while Derrett (1978a: 6) emphasizes that under the social conditions of India, most of the above grounds amounted to relief for the wife against an errant or deficient husband. Therefore, while in Baroda divorce could be obtained for desertion or adultery, as Derrett (1978a: 12) points out, 'in British India this was still far below the horizon'. Elsewhere, he highlights that the earlier traditional Hindu framework of reference militated against divorce and that late medieval Hindu rulers even punished spouses who failed to behave decently towards their life partner. Asking modern Hindus to put their house in order, Derrett (1970: 443) writes:

> The ancient jurists, who were wiser than you are, had all the experience of India at her best and her worst, and there is nothing new under the sun. They wanted litigation of this type entirely to be avoided. When the Peshwa was the effective ruler of Maharashtra he punished erring spouses with great severity.

While such traditional views will have survived to a large extent in society, towards the end of British rule and in the early post-independence period a number of local enactments were introduced to facilitate divorce among Hindus on certain fault grounds.[25] *Towards Equality* (1974: 118) claims that the ground for the HMA of 1955 had been prepared by the passing of the Hindu Married Women's Right to Separate Residence and Maintenance Act in 1946, which inter alia permitted a Hindu wife to separate from her husband on the ground that he had married again.[26] Following this, some of the states legislated on divorce for Hindus. The Bombay government passed the Bombay Hindu Divorce Act of 1947, permitting divorce on the grounds of impotency, lunacy, leprosy, desertion for four years, absence for seven years leading to a presumption of death, and bigamy (Kapadia 1972: 186). The close link with anti-bigamy laws is clearly evident from several enactments,[27] especially the Madras Hindu (Bigamy Prevention and Divorce) Act, 1949. Saurashtra, today a part of Gujarat state, but at that time still a separate entity, followed Bombay in providing opportunities for divorce, in the Saurashtra Hindu Divorce Act, 1952. Such

[25] Virdee (1972: 247) lists the relevant Acts during the British period.

[26] See to the same effect Singh (1989: 76).

[27] Sharma (1994: 89) reports that the Madras Marumakkathayam Act of 1932 made certain marriages in that part of India strictly monogamous. On Malabar divorces, see Derrett (1963c: 238–40).

piecemeal efforts led to the argument that India had not gone far enough in reforming its divorce regime in line with modern (and supposedly advanced) Western notions, so it became evident that uniforming divorce laws would be a major focus of post-colonial Hindu law reforms of the 1950s.

Modernist Divorce Reforms in Independent India

Modernist commentators have been claiming in blanket fashion that traditional Hindu law did not permit divorce,[28] thus seeking to legitimize comprehensive statutory intervention in this field. The National Committee for Women in *Towards Equality* (1974: 117), for example, still repeats the mantra that '[a]ccording to traditionalists, divorce was unknown in Hindu Law' but notes in the same breath, quite correctly, that '[e]ven today divorce is not a socially accepted norm among many sections'. That picture has been changing, perhaps a little too rapidly, as we shall see.

Given the flexibility and wide spread of traditional Hindu customary divorce law, however, one must ask why more and formally defined divorce grounds were actually introduced by the modern state law in the first place. Derrett (1963c: 138) observed that despite the passing of the HMA, 'the Act does not strictly *codify* the law, and the scope allowed to custom is extensive, if carefully defined'. Clearly, simple reliance on informal Hindu customary traditions was not considered good enough for the modernist image. The reformers wanted to portray themselves as modern and innovative, and needed to push for statutory reforms. This was made fairly easy with regard to divorce, provided one could maintain the fiction of the alleged absence of divorce in traditional Hindu law. However, given the massive evidence of Hindu customary divorces all over the country, this became a suspect, devious strategy. It appears that the legislators were extremely cautious not to come across as introducing, in statutory form, the traditional Hindu customs of divorce, but that is in effect more or less exactly what happened.

A major reason for the official reluctance to admit this must be that the traditional Hindu divorce customs are, from an elite perspective, tainted with low status, illiteracy, rural backwardness, and all that comes with it, including the sexual licentiousness that Chandra (1998) highlighted as such an important factor.[29] But an outrightly modern Western-style divorce regime would

[28] This approach is reflected, for example, by Derrett (1963c: 228), who succinctly claims that '[f]ormerly Hindu marriages were indissoluble by divorce except by caste custom'.

[29] Agnes (2000: 20-21) confirms that many communities in India today continue to practise customary forms of divorce, which were earlier more strictly linked to various social prohibitions or, in reverse, were avoided to acquire status through Sanskritization. Agnes (2000: 22) notes the absence of a strict sexual code and correspondingly, a wider scope for negotiating women's rights of divorce, remarriage, and property ownership, giving several examples. Sen (2000) reports rich details of relevant customary practices in colonial Bengal.

have been too revolutionary at that early stage, so an odd compromise was reached, which has not been noticed and analysed as clearly as could be, demonstrating that the hidden agenda of early Hindu divorce law reforms were quite successfully camouflaged by the modernist leadership.

The Hidden Agenda of Hindu Divorce Reforms

The post-colonial Hindu elite which eventually gave the new divorce law to all Hindus was deeply concerned to maintain an aura of progressiveness and modernity. At the same time, it could not—and probably did not even wish to—modify the existing rule systems too radically to bring about a legal revolution. The overall scheme of modernist reforms in relation to dissolution of marriages had to take account of the need for social stability, and it did so in various ways. This was explicitly recognized early on, with reference to *Arun v Sudanshu* AIR 1962 Or 65 (SB), where a devious husband was seeking to obtain nullity without satisfactory evidence. Derrett (1963c: 140) explains the underlying philosophy of the post-HMA legal position:

> There is not the slightest doubt but that whatever sympathy a judge may have for the difficulties of a particular spouse or couple, he will not facilitate their separation or divorce otherwise than in complete accordance with the policy of the HMA, which does not by any means provide for the termination of the duties reciprocally of a married pair to suit their personal claims or prejudices. It is of interest to the nation that marriages should be stable, and matrimonial relief is available upon that fundamental understanding.

Such statements have been replicated elsewhere.[30] They clearly balance the reformist claims of facilitating an individualistic free-for-all under the new Hindu divorce law. Scholars should have looked more carefully behind this emerging compromise of tradition and modernity in Hindu divorce law, analysing it in more depth. Instead, they were mostly blinded by their own revolutionary euphoria and legislative zeal. Had they looked and thought more carefully, they would have come up with a rather different analysis than the one we find in our present textbooks and academic studies.

In this regard, one must highlight in particular that Diwan and Diwan (2000: 27) still state that the fault theory of divorce came to Indian law from English law, as though the Hindus had no indigenous understanding of such matters many centuries earlier. This demonstrates that the scholarly and legal debates created and sustained the misleading perspective that Western modernizing influence and conceptual borrowing has been dominant in this process. This was systematically highlighted out of all proportion, as shown further below.

[30] For example, Derrett (1963c: 177) reiterates that 'the subsistence of marriages is the concern of the country and not merely of the spouses, and therefore in cases where there is any possibility of a reconciliation ... the court is under a positive duty (even on an appeal) to endeavour to bring about a reconciliation'.

In the literature and discussions on reforms to Hindu divorce law, the dominant theme is the introduction of statutory grounds of divorce for all Hindus through the HMA of 1955. Officially for the first time, so it is claimed, divorce was made available to all Hindus in India by Section 13 of the 1955 Act, which has since been amended several times to introduce more grounds for divorce, purportedly to free Hindu women, in particular, from the yoke of unwanted marriages. An impression has therefore been created that the legal reforms achieved and pursued something really significant and 'modern' that the ancient tradition either did not know or would not tolerate. In fact, this process of modernist law reform has been authoritatively portrayed as comprehensive copying from English law by leading legal textbook writers, thus giving a particular twist to the debates. Desai (1998: 68) describes the reforms of the 1950s as a modernist restatement and claims that divorce constitutes a fundamental departure from the traditional Hindu Law, which ruled out divorce by treating marriage as a sacrament. Desai also asserts, quite wrongly in my view, that a number of other Western concepts, such as restitution of conjugal rights, judicial separation, desertion, cruelty, and nullity of marriage were introduced by the HMA, arguing (id.):

> These concepts are borrowed from the English law and were unknown to the traditional Hindu Law. Further, to interpret the Hindu Marriage Act, the Indian Courts now look for guidance to the English law and freely cite English cases to expound the significance and meaning of these concepts. Thus, many Western values are being gradually introduced into the Hindu Marriage Law. In reality the law now is more Anglo-Hindu law than pure and pristine Hindu Law, as it is being further anglicized by the judicial process.

This clearly goes too far in asserting that so many aspects of modern Hindu law are just borrowed 'Western' concepts.[31] While the assertion about judicial borrowing from England may have been correct in the late 1950s,[32] it is certainly no longer appropriate in India's leading practitioners' handbook on Hindu law in the late 1990s. The crucial but semi-hidden influence of indigenous Hindu concepts was initially sidelined, tucked away in the almost embarrassed admission, found under Section 29(2) of the HMA, that customary divorces among Hindus who know such customs (and almost all do, even if they might not practise them) continue to enjoy the official legal protection of the state. Section 29(2) of the HMA is phrased in such a way that only specialists will understand its wide-ranging implications:

[31] Indeed, Derrett (1957: 268) saw a unique mixture of old and new, which posed important challenges to India's judges. Parashar (1992: 116) notes that '[t]he statement that divorce is an absolutely foreign idea to Hindu law was not accepted, in view of the prevalence of the practice in the lower social strata of the Hindu community'.

[32] Also Derrett (1957: 168) predicted that Indian judges 'will turn to existing Indian, English or American precedents in order to support the decisions which they feel it appropriate to give'.

> Nothing contained in this Act shall be deemed to affect any right recognised by custom or conferred by any special enactment to obtain the dissolution of a Hindu marriage, whether solemnized before or after the commencement of this Act.

Thus, the various forms of traditional customary Hindu divorce law have been explicitly saved by Section 29(2) of the HMA. It should not escape notice here that the common Hindu's detachment from the formal state law in daily life situations, when it comes to marriage and polygamy, as shown in Chapter 8 to 10 earlier, is neatly parallel to the scenario of a divorcing Hindu couple who agree that their marriage is at an end. They do not need to approach agents of the state. They, too, using local and caste-specific customary norms, may remain outside the official fora to make their own consensual arrangements. In Hindu social reality, such customary informal divorces had always been allowed for men and women, so that now the official legal requirement of formal divorce would create problems for some Hindus, especially women, who got caught in the undefined boundaries between formal state law and customary rules.

On the prominence of customary divorces, Virdee (1972: 33) notes that 'writers belonging to high castes attribute this to the low cultural level and high degree of illiteracy of tribes rendering the enforcement of the provisions of the Act both inexpedient and difficult'. However, these customs applied not only to primitive tribals, but much more widely than modernists wanted to admit.[33] Virdee (1972: 36) confirms that the HMA of 1955 'does not disturb the position which a customary divorce occupied before the enactment ... it must be proved as a fact that such customary dissolution of marriage was effected .... Where such divorce is obtained it is not necessary for the parties to have again to go before the court'. Pujari and Kaushik (1994, III: 310) confirm that '[c]ontrary to the general notion regarding the indissolubility of Hindu marriages, a large section of Hindus among the lower castes have traditionally practised divorce. These customary forms of divorce were recognised, both socially and judicially'. Customs of divorce by mutual consent are especially prevalent in the state of Bombay. At p. 311, these authors explain further:

> Usually customary divorces are through the intervention of the traditional Panchayats of caste tribunals. Therefore, in States where this has not been customary, the courts have not permitted panchayats to take upon themselves the right to dissolve a marriage. Once the custom is proved, however, the courts will not interfere.

[33] This is supported in a detailed discussion by Pujari and Kaushik (1994, III: 310–12). Rama Mehta (1975: 7) explains that she left rural women out of her research on divorce, since 'divorce in that group was and is still determined by caste customs rather than legislation. The village women in many ways were more free than their counterparts in urban India. Their personal lives were adjusted by caste ethics and mores, and if these permitted divorce, they were free to seek it and also remarry'.

> The courts ... have applied the strict test for the validity of such customs. When the existence of a custom was not proved, or where the custom could be regarded as running counter to the spirit of Hindu Law, or was against public policy or morality, courts have declared such customary forms of divorce as invalid.[34]

While much scholarly attention has been lavished on Section 13 of the HMA and the new grounds for divorce among Hindus, we see that in social reality, the customary law under Section 29(2) is at least as important as the new statutory regime. However, this crucial fact has been ignored in the literature. This dualistic approach to legal drafting and reformative technique of the Hindu divorce law stands therefore in quite remarkable contrast to the reforms of the Hindu law on marriage solemnisation, as found in Section 7 of the HMA, and yet it contains a similar cultural and legal message. As we saw in Chapter 8, the traditional Hindu law on solemnization of marriages remained in essence fully intact and was indeed preserved by the HMA in all its customary diversity. While this particular aspect of the customary and shastric Hindu law was merely put into statutory form, nobody would wish to argue (given the axiomatic argument that traditional Hindu law did not know divorce, and the status implications) that the new statutory divorce grounds under the HMA were perhaps also little else than the old Hindu law of customary divorces!

It is not possible to produce here a detailed analysis of the divorce rules introduced in Section 13 of the original HMA in 1955. However, it strikes me that the original collection of fault grounds is more or less directly derived from the traditional Hindu customary laws of divorce.[35] Nobody noticed this—and nobody wanted to know—since the principle of fault ground has allegedly been imported from English law, as asserted in the self-congratulatory fashion of modernists like Paras Diwan, as cited earlier. One must, however, be sympathetic to the dilemma of the modernist commentators and legislators. From a perspective that remains somewhat protective of traditional Hindu social values, despite wishing to reform them at the same time, it makes sense that there should have been no official admission that low-caste Hindu rules were here being smuggled into the modern Hindu law in the garb of modernist Western-style reforms. But that is what happened, at least initially. The original wording of Section 13 of the HMA 1955 was as follows:

> Divorce
>
> (1) Any marriage solemnized, whether before or after the commencement of this Act, may, on a petition presented by either the husband or the wife, be dissolved by a decree of divorce on the ground that the other party -
>
> (i) is living in adultery; or

[34] This latter paragraph is taken verbatim from *Towards Equality* (1974: 117–8).

[35] Derrett (1957: 268) speculated that 'the content of the Code itself will be a unique mixture of the traditional and the modern' and rightly predicted that the judges would find it difficult to interpret these new provisions.

(ii) has ceased to be a Hindu by conversion to another religion; or

(iii) has been incurably of unsound mind for a continuous period of not less than three years immediately preceding the presentation of the petition; or

(iv) has, for a period of not less than three years immediately preceding the presentation of the petition, been suffering from a virulent and incurable form of leprosy; or

(v) has, for a period of not less than three years immediately preceding the presentation of the petition, been suffering from venereal disease in a communicable form; or

(vi) has renounced the world by entering any religious order; or

(vii) has not been heard of as being alive for a period of seven years or more by those persons who would naturally have heard of it, had that party been alive; or.

(viii) has not resumed cohabitation for a space of two years or upwards after the passing of a decree for judicial separation against that party; or

(ix) has failed to comply with a decree for restitution of conjugal rights for a period of two years or upwards after the passing of the decree.

(2) A wife may also present a petition for the dissolution of her marriage by a decree of divorce on the ground, -

(i) in the case of any marriage solemnized before the commencement of this Act, that the husband had married again before such commencement or that any other wife of the husband married before such commencement was alive at the time of the solemnization of the marriage of the petitioner:

Provided that in either case the other wife is alive at the time of the presentation of the petition; or

(ii) that the husband has, since the solemnization of the marriage, been guilty of rape, sodomy or bestiality.

Thus, the formal Hindu divorce law introduced in Section 13 of the HMA looks like a typical state law, laying out a detailed set of rules. In the present case, these were made by an élite for itself, using a number of allegedly 'modern' fault grounds to permit any Hindu petitioner to seek divorce. Since the reformers were aware that the majority of Hindus knew and practised customary forms of divorce as and when necessary, which would often be agreed or granted on the same grounds as those listed under Section 13 of the HMA, it is unbelievable that the reformers should have envisaged that their modernist divorce reforms would liberate all Hindus. They were only looking at certain classes, and providing for themselves as a Hindu elite. Allowing certain individuals to litigate for divorce on certain grounds therefore served only specific agenda, not the nation.[36] At the same time, the modernist reforms were vigorously

[36] Virdee (1972: 42) picks this up when she argues that the introduction of Western-style divorce laws for Hindus in East Africa and in India had significant consequences. It did not really destroy Hindu marriage, as claimed by the

portrayed as an innovation for everyone, and of course they also supported the image of the benevolent, paternalistic state that offered all its citizens legal remedies in a crisis.

These supposedly new reforms of Hindu divorce law must also be seen and analysed in the wider context of other provisions found in the HMA which underpin the stability of marriages and are designed to prevent marital breakdown among Hindus. In particular, Section 9 and Section 10 of the Act are relevant in that respect. In Section 9, restitution of conjugal rights is provided for, allowing a spouse to ask the court to issue a decree of restitution, which would put the spouse under pressure to return to the matrimonial home, perhaps even to submit to sexual intercourse.[37] In Section 10, the HMA contains a large number of grounds for a decree for judicial separation, which has the effect that a spouse may be allowed to live separately from the partner, while the marital tie remains formally intact. Many of the grounds under this section are also found in Section 13, but desertion in Section 10(1)(a) and cruelty in Section 10(1)(b) were originally only grounds for judicial separation, and not for divorce. This means that the 1955 version of Section 13 of the HMA indeed facilitated divorce among Hindus, but it did so cautiously and somewhat reluctantly.

The case law under this new regime took some time to develop, evidenced for example by the fact that Derrett (1963c: 225–43) still had not much to write about the topic. But Indian lawmakers were soon made to realize that these supposedly modern legal reforms actually created a looming crisis, because in a patriarchal environment, they empowered strong individuals and scheming families to take disproportionate advantage of the new rules. In other words, the reformed Hindu divorce law allowed men to abuse the new rules for their own personal gain, helping them to discard women—and thus their responsibilities towards them—more easily than they could do in the 'old' system.[38]

traditionalists, but '[i]t may be more true to say that remedies have been provided for those to whom their sacrament is no longer meaningful'. Derrett (1957: 271) found it 'evident that Parliament has not legislated so far with the interests of the poor and illiterate citizens (*i.e.* the majority) in mind'.

[37] On the earlier history of this remedy, with an excellent discussion of colonial attitudes and input, see Chandra (1998), who finds at p. 209 that this remedy never helped women. In post-colonial India, several important cases have clarified that this remedy remains constitutionally acceptable, since the courts have been concerned to protect the home sphere from the 'bull in a china shop' effect of applying modern constitutional principles to Hindu domestic relations, rather than protecting individualism. For the relevant cases, see *T. Sareetha v Venkata Subbaiah* AIR 1983 AP 356, *Harvinder Kaur v Harmander Singh Choudhry* AIR 1984 Del 66, and especially *Saroj Rani v Sudarshan Kumar Chadha* AIR 1984 SC 1562.

[38] Qureshi (1978: 352) reports on the basis of surveys from north India that 99 per cent of divorces among Hindus are asked for by men.

Derrett (1963c: 140) began to pick up early warning signs and referred to a number of cases,[39]

> recently started by husbands who have never come to grips with reality, trumping up preposterous charges against their wives in the hope of marrying again. The courts must scotch these unhealthy efforts at an early stage and save the parties costs and loss of self-respect if their disputes come to be rehearsed in a court of appeal.

Hence, while it is undoubtedly true that the Hindu divorce law reforms gave more freedom to individuals, this freedom was soon widely abused. Offering Hindu women the chance to ask for divorce in a formal court, and thus liberating them in a sense, needs to be contrasted with significant evidence that most Hindu women did and do not favour divorce—or simply could not afford it. Furthermore, the state was eventually to become nervous about floods of Hindu divorce petitions by husbands, which may clog up court lists of pending cases for many years and contribute to the mounting arrears of unheard cases (Jain 1986: 51).

Modernists have continued to congratulate themselves on the successful introduction of permission for Hindu men and women to claim divorce, albeit under certain carefully defined conditions.[40] Sharma (1994: 38) comments from a triumphalist modernist perspective that '[i]n the light of social values and equality of sexes, the concept of marriage as a sacrament and an indissoluble union has been modified'. Since Hindu legal tradition had been perceived to be strict, not permitting divorce, the assumptions of the law reformers were to the effect that modernity was liberating spouses who wanted to get out of impossible marriages. Those claims must now be examined in more depth.

Modernist Representations of the Statutory Scheme

The full picture of Hindu divorce reform between the 1950s and the 1980s is rather too complex for the present chapter, but certain elements need to be highlighted here. For the present critique of modernist writing, as well as a fuller discussion of Hindu divorce law, the first important point is that the tepid scheme of the original Section 13 of the HMA was felt to be inadequate, so that further reforms were soon introduced. While more detailed research is required

[39] The case cited here, typically from the Panjab, is *Bhagwanti v Sadhu Ram* AIR 1961 Pun 181.

[40] Abuse of the procedures became an issue that modernists did not address sufficiently well. It is highly significant that not even a decade after his first tentative critical comments about the abuse by Hindu husbands of the new divorce law, Derrett's criticism (1970: 441–2) had become almost virulent. He even suggested introducing the death penalty for all those who supply false evidence and concluded that prison sentences for fomenters of matrimonial litigation would be most appropriate (ibid.: 443–4). This is discussed in greater depth later in the section on the psycho-social basis of postmodern Hindu divorce law.

to explain precisely why that was so, the underlying modernist pressures for recognizing marital breakdown as a ground for divorce are quite apparent. Specifically, two extra grounds for divorce were added to the scheme of Section 13(1) of the HMA by the Hindu Marriage (Amendment) Act of 1964. Divorce was now explicitly provided for where the other party had not resumed cohabitation for a period of two years after an earlier decree of restitution of conjugal rights or judicial separation. The new Section 13(1A) of the HMA provided as follows from 1964 onwards:[41]

> (1A) Either party to a marriage, whether solemnised before or after the commencement of this Act, may also present a petition for the dissolution of the marriage by a decree for divorce on the ground –
> (i) that there has been no resumption of cohabitation as between the parties to the marriage for a period of two years or upwards after the passing of a decree for judicial separation in a proceeding to which they were parties; or
> (ii) that there has been no restitution of conjugal rights as between the parties to the marriage for a period of two years or upwards after the passing of a decree for restitution of conjugal rights in a proceeding to which they were parties.

The effect of these amendments was to introduce an element of the 'breakdown principle' into Hindu divorce law, with quite negative consequences for women, a fact about which modernist analysis has been conspicuously quiet. However, as Derrett (1973; 1975c) eloquently showed, this new liberty for Hindu spouses came to be abused by men. Derrett (1981) highlighted this malpractice as the 'own wrong' problem,[42] created by Hindu husbands who simply engineered non-cohabitation for long enough to be able to plead for divorce under Section 13(1A) of the HMA. The Indian courts have from the start been under a statutory obligation to satisfy themselves in every case that a person petitioning for divorce or other matrimonial remedies under the HMA 'is not in any way taking advantage of his or her own wrong or disability for the purpose of such relief', as provided in Section 23(1)(a) of the Act. These procedural safeguards were in several early cases not properly observed by the courts, leading to the termination of marriages by unilateral repudiation of the husband. While Derrett (1981) was extremely critical of such decisions, in marked contrast Diwan and Diwan (1993: 164) have argued that if Section 23(1)(a) remains on the statute book, there will be hardly any petition in which divorce can be granted. This demonstrates that modernist pressure for the full introduction of the breakdown principle has not relented, while it is highly significant that India's judges have become more alert to this particular problem over time.

[41] This waiting period was reduced to a year by the Marriage Laws (Amendment) Act of 1976.

[42] A brief analysis of this is found in Menski (2001: 115–9).

Going back for a moment to the 1950s, we see that Altekar (1978: 364) had argued at the time of the Hindu law reform debates that Hindu marriage should continue to be regarded as a religious bond, normally indissoluble, but that it should also be recognized that in some cases the marital tie may need to be dissolved.[43] He advised stringent conditions, for example where a wife has been abandoned by the husband and was left hanging unless she converted to Christianity or Islam. This looks like a rescue mechanism for women who are punished for adhering to traditional Hindu values.

Sharma (1989: 18) claims that '[w]e accepted divorce grudgingly' in 1955 when Parliament enacted the HMA. Indeed, even women's activists have not been entirely convinced of the bona fide intentions of the new law. The Committee on the Status of Women (*Towards Equality* 1974: 116–24) discussed divorce reforms in considerable detail.[44] Its major final recommendation relates to calls for parity of rights for all Indian men and women in divorce.[45] The constitutional law angle is briefly raised by Singh (1993: 40–1), who claims that the introduction of divorce for Hindu men and women confirmed due respect for the Indian Constitution and the Fundamental Rights. This is not an argument that stands detailed scrutiny, however, since the articulate proponents of a uniform civil code have never been satisfied with the existing law.

Parashar (1992: 118) closely examines the debates about the introduction of divorce reforms for all Hindus and finds that it is 'doubtful that the dominant consideration for enacting them was to advance the rights of women'. Rather, she observes that the 'concern to safeguard marriages clearly overrides the concern (if any) of the government to provide women with equal rights or the conditions enabling them to exercise those rights' (id.). Kapadia (1972: 187) also observed that the modern reforms were not that open to easy divorce:

> The apprehension that the legislation makes divorce easy and consequently treats marriage lightly has obviously no foundation.

[43] Kapadia (1972: 188–9) observed that not only sonlessness, but also domestic disharmony would qualify as a ground for divorce.

[44] *Towards Equality* (1974: 116) sees monogamy and divorce as closely linked, since '[a] monogamous marriage without the right of divorce would cause great hardship to both parties to the marriage'. This statement was copied by Singh (1989: 75) and other authors, e.g. Pujari and Kaushik (1994, III: 309).

[45] In this context, *Towards Equality* (1974: 121) vigorously suggests reform to Muslim divorce law: 'We recommend immediate legislation to eliminate the unilateral right of divorce and to introduce parity of rights for both partners regarding grounds for seeking dissolution of a marriage'. There is no recognition of the fact that, at the same time, their calls for more relaxed Hindu divorce grounds would have the same negative effects as the supposedly inhuman and discriminatory *talaq* which they seek to abolish. Such confusions have continued to mar the debate. The issue resurfaces in the press from time to time, with inflated claims, catchy headlines, and much misguided information on Muslim law. For a recent example see Shefalee Vasudev's article 'Taming talaq' in *India Today* of 20 May 2002.

> The principle of divorce is alien to the social pattern in which Hindus have been living for centuries .... It is generally argued that if legislation is allowed to interfere with the sacrament of marriage, the institution of marriage will break down. This fear is unreasonable and unfounded.

Kapadia (1972: 188) further argued that the fear that the new divorce legislation would bring about chaos was unfounded, 'because it ignores the fact that legislation alone cannot change the social ideals of a community unless people are favourable to it'. He suggested that changes in people's attitudes can best be judged from studies in communities that allow customary divorce. As a social scientist, Kapadia (1972: 193) found that modernity brought about some changes in society:

> The new generation attaches importance to marital obligations on both sides, and if the husband fails to fulfil his obligations as a result of certain contingencies it should be open to the wife to ask for a dissolution of the marriage. What is pertinent here is the fact that these contingencies having been declared legal grounds for divorce have also been accepted as valid grounds by the people themselves. The law may thus be said to have provided for the satisfaction of new needs in the social *milieu*.

The literature offers no clear picture about the extent of acceptability of divorce among Hindus, but it seems fair to suggest that divorce has become more common among Hindus (Jain 1986). Similarly, Choudhary (1988: 164) found:

> There was a time when practically every one disapproved of divorce. The legislators who provided for it, the attorneys who filed petitions for it, the judges who granted it, and the men and women who got it, were all convinced that divorce is 'bad'. Inspite of this, the rate of divorce has been continuously increasing since the last one decade or so. Besides, it appears that the social reaction of the community to divorce has also changed. The morality of divorce is no longer questioned.

Mehta (1975: 7) discovered in her fieldwork that not only the legal provisions of the HMA, but also the overall socio-economic changes in society have enabled Hindu women to demand freedom from unhappy domestic situations. Mehta (1975: 5) notes that while divorce is still a minority phenomenon, the divorce rate in India is on the increase. Setting out to investigate the major problems 'faced by the Hindu women divorcees in Indian society' (p. 1), while also testing 'what remains of the family structure that promotes the traditional concept of marriage as an indissoluble union' (p. 158), she presented an intricate analysis that allowed clear distinctions to be made between lower-middle-class and upper-middle-class divorcees, whose experience differed significantly.[46] As Mehta (1975: 3) explains:

[46] One major finding of Mehta's excellent study is that most lower-middle-class women regretted having resorted to the law because as divorcees, they suffered economically and in status terms. Mitter (1992: 132) notes difficulties for women seeking divorce formally and asks how many women are strong enough 'to leap irredeemably into a space that society does not yet admit'.

> The upper middle-class women were found to be less subjected to the pressures of the caste-community, were better educated and more likely to have come from a western-oriented family. The lower middle-class women were more likely to be traditionally-oriented, less educated and more closely tied to the caste-community.

Mehta (1975: 1) perceptively indicates the ethical dilemma of the researcher in such intricately personal matters, since 'it would be indelicate, if not offensive, to ask them the reasons why their marriage had not worked or even about their life after separation'. But she found that her respondents wanted to talk about those very issues and thus devised a sophisticated indirect method of locating willing respondents, which proved highly successful. The research showed that 'the growth of feminine awareness is far more rapid than the liberalisation of society itself' (Mehta 1975: 5), a finding fully corroborated by Derrett (1978a: viii–ix), who analysed Mehta's material and found that women were putting up a fight for their rights and position in society (p. ix):

> Even in the upper-middle-class groups where women have, perhaps rashly, reacted against the old-fashioned ideas of their husbands, there is no suggestion that they were really undisciplined or promiscuous. They simply wanted their personal dignity and worth to be accepted. They deny that Sita is their model, yet they do not aim to have the casual relationships which they despise in Western woman.

Derrett (1978a: ix) draws an important conclusion from this for policy makers and reformers who wish to rush into making divorces still more easily available for Hindus:

> We must take account—and the judiciary must notice—a fact to which Rama Mehta draws repeated attention, based on her interviews with actual participants in this drama. The fact is that, for the Hindu woman, an unsatisfactory marriage ... is far better than no marriage at all. There is no place, even in new Delhi, for the divorced or separated Hindu wife, for whom remarriage is almost impossible, and for whom respectable male friendships are disappointingly hard to come by.

At the same time, as Mehta (1975: 168) concludes, 'women of both upper and lower middle-classes are not going to accept a domestic situation which lacks basic dignity' but are going to find that after divorce, 'the possibility of a woman to lead a life of gainful employment leading to economic independence is not bright. She is still dependent on the family and therefore her life is restricted and full of anxiety' (id.). Ultimately, as Mehta (1975: 169) ominously put it, '[i]n this confusion of modernity and tradition, present in India today, women were at a disadvantage'.

Singh (1989: 75) reports that the Census in 1961 indicated wide acceptance of divorce by villagers,[47] while the Census of 1981 gave 870,000 divorced

[47] The respective figures of acceptance given are: Muslims 6.06 per cent, Hindus 3.21 per cent, Buddhists 3.07 per cent, Jains 1.68 per cent, Sikhs 0.91 per cent and

or separated women, of whom 743,200 lived in rural areas. In a well-documented report, Jain (1986: 44) claims that '[m]arriage is no longer a sacred word and divorce no longer a dirty one' in India today, but also indicates that there are a number of negative consequences of growing marital breakdown, not the least for children of such marriages. Bumiller (1991: 37) reports that '[n]o matter what all the Indian magazines said about the increasing divorce rate among the middle class, the truth was that for women it was still considered shameful'.[48] Sharma (1994: 336) observes that more women are coming forward to file divorce cases against their husbands and most of them reached the family courts by themselves, as '[t]hey were not scared of divorce any more nor did they hesitate to explain their marital problems'.[49] The general trend is, so it appears, in the direction of more acceptance of divorce. Choudhary (1988: 18-19) sums up various research findings and claims that there have been significant changes:

> The untiring efforts of the social reformers and educationists in the second quarter of the twentieth century and the various legal enactments in the third quarter of the century have contributed a great deal in bringing about these changes. Besides, the increasing enthusiasm for higher education, particularly professional education, and the employment of women have played a vital role in affecting the values of males and females and changing the attitude towards marriage and divorce. These changes have not only contributed considerably to the breaking of traditional structure of Hindu marriage but also to the increase in the rate of divorce in our society.

Virdee (1972: 38) found earlier that the HMA had brought real and drastic changes in Hindu personal law and that the motive behind this enactment was 'to open the way towards a progressive society and to recognise the independence of women'.[50] But would people rush to divorce courts as a result of the

---

Christians 0.41 per cent. The main reasons advanced were adultery and barrenness. The 1961 census counted 817,000 divorced women, but such figures do not tell us about the number of actual divorces in the country, which remains unknown. Choudhary (1988: 309) notes that the proportion of women who remain in the state of 'divorcee' is higher than men, in both rural and urban areas.

[48] Mitter (1992: 103) reports on the case of a broken marriage where the father ultimately takes his daughter home and proposes a divorce, but the girl's mother would not accept this. Jain (1986: 51) shows the links with dowry deaths when she highlights that '[d]owry deaths have taught parents that a divorced daughter is better than a dead one'. Mitter (1992: 18) refers to marriage adverts in papers and the difficulties of advertising divorced wives: 'One cannot be too choosy when putting second-hand goods on the market'.

[49] This is also confirmed by Jain (1986: 48), while Mitter (1992: 159) gives the example of women who are afraid of going to court and fighting against their husband in a public forum.

[50] Virdee (1972: 36) also noted that the HMA 'recognises a utilitarian concept of law and therefore left customary Hindu divorces undisturbed.

new law? Dhagamwar (1987: xii) reports that in the five years between 1973 and 1977, only 1,118 persons approached the Pune district court for relief under various provisions of the HMA, a small and almost insignificant number. Dhagamwar (1987: 105) emphasizes the importance of legal education and awareness for women:

> If the woman knows about the ban on polygamy, about prohibited degrees of relationship, about minimum age of marriage, about the provisions of divorce, she may still not be able to take advantage of all she knows. But, if she does not know, she is in a still worse position.

Sharma (1989: 17) argues that it is now accepted that divorce is a necessity. It is not an antithesis of marriage, but rather strengthens the institution of marriage, since it offers a type of escape value for the release of undesirable tensions of marriage. Choudhary (1988: 1) argues more generally that some marriages are bound to fail and all societies have to devise methods for dealing with unsuccessful marriages; divorce is one of those ways. Choudhary (1988: vii) argues that '[t]hough divorce is permitted legally, yet socially it is still not highly appreciated' and indicates that the increase in divorce during the past two decades has led to larger acceptance of divorce as 'a reasonable, and at times desirable, alternative to an unhappy marriage' (ibid.: viii). Jain (1983: xxv) claims that '[t]he divorce court does not exist for the purpose of promoting the dissolution of marriage, but for the purpose of discharging the painful duty of dissolving them when all reasonable hope of reconciliation between the parties has failed'. This seems to confirm that stability of marriage remains a major consideration, as Jain (1983: xxv) reinforces:

> ... stability of marriage should be protected but at the same time, if circumstances exist which show that conjugal life is impossible ... then reality must be recognised and provisions should be made for terminating the bond of marriage ... Divorce is for a real matrimonial wrong. It cannot just be granted for trivial ups and downs of married life. It cannot be granted even where [the] court is satisfied that the marriage has completely broken down, or broken up, whichever way one puts it.

Thus, an intricate balancing act would have to be performed by the courts, seeking to weigh individualism against the needs of stability in society, freedom to divorce against commitment to one's spouse, not to speak of financial responsibilities and duties in relation to children. The critical period for these debates and their manifestations in further legislative activity and a rapidly growing case law was undoubtedly the 1970s.

The Reforms of the 1970s: Pushing the Limits

It is evident that allowing statutory divorce for Hindus created new pitfalls for Hindu women in particular. However, the reformative energies of the 1950s were not at all spent when it came to Hindu divorce law. While the abolition of polygamy was smugly celebrated as a fait accompli, growing dissatisfaction with the piecemeal and restrictive nature of Hindu divorce law became a huge source of irritation, frustration, and further reformative initiatives which have still not abated. For example, Diwan and Diwan (2000: 30) continue to argue vigorously for the full-fledged introduction of the breakdown theory of divorce, especially the principle of 'irretrievable breakdown', within the context of a uniform civil code. Modernist commentators have been expressing much dissatisfaction with the way in which the Hindu divorce law was developing during the 1960s and early 1970s. From a constitutional law perspective, Minattur (1980: 169) stated that the divorce provisions of the HMA 'maintain equality of the sexes in the matter of grounds for divorce', but then noted, at p. 171:

> In spite of the provisions for divorce in the Act of 1955, it is not often that recourse is had to them; this is because Hindu social values in general are opposed to the concept of divorce .... Whereas prior to 1955, divorce was considered absolute anathema by women of the higher castes, after the passing of the Act it is the women of the upper classes and higher castes as well as the rich and the educated in urban areas who petition the courts for divorce. Probably, the illiterate women in the rural areas do not even know that there are legal provisions for divorce apart from those enshrined in the customary law of certain communities or tribes.

Diwan (1978: 28) criticized that Parliament had not gone far enough and should have introduced the breakdown principle from the start and complained that 'the Hindu Marriage Act displays a strange conservatism, a strange faltering attempt at reform, a half-hearted endeavour to march with the time' (id.). Diwan (1978: 28–9) argued that the lower classes of Hindus always had a liberal divorce law, while conservatism prevailed 'mostly among the elite, the *purohits*, the ruling classes, and the *Vaishyas*. *Dharmashastras* have not been conservative. The Law Commission is as much aware of this as any one of us'. Interestingly, Diwan (1978: 29) asserted that ever since the British left India, the traditional flexibility had evaporated.[51] Such grumblings push and pull for more discretion for the individual to determine whether or not a marriage should survive or not. A slightly different modernist chain of arguments for further reforms was produced by Thomas (2000: 144), who pleads vigorously for self-controlled regulation of divorces:[52]

[51] It is possible to argue that some of that flexibility was in fact defined away by scholars like Diwan himself, who clearly exercised much influence on the literature.

[52] We saw in Chapter 8 that this author took a rather dim view of marriage. This is not without impact here, as among the many related points raised one finds that 'women must be freed from the tyranny of men, and the crux of that is found in the economic independence of women' (Thomas 2000: 150), so that an ideal society would be one in which inheritance laws grant sons and daughters equal shares, and all women follow the ideal Russian model of full-time work, which is supposed to lead to equality.

> The trouble about moralists is that they know too much of logic and too little of human nature .... They forget that there are sound human sympathies that stand in the way of frivolous divorces ....
>
> The existence of a particular piece of legislation does not mean that it should be taken full advantage of by all. Things that are lawful are not always expedient ... we will have to permit divorces in the hope that the law will be made use of only in those cases wherein the parties find it quite impossible to live together. And we have reason to believe that most married couples would stay together in spite of the most liberal laws regarding divorce.

Actually, Thomas (2000: 146) looked at America's guiding rationale that '[d]ivorce is the test of marriage' and 'fear of divorce is the beginning of matrimonial wisdom', concluding at p. 149:

> When all is said, the balance is struck in favour of free divorce. Imbeciles, idiots, criminals and lepers may rightly object to liberal divorce laws as they may not be able to keep the partner they secured by chance or cunning. But humanity as a whole is more important than the few defectives, and it is better that these should go without partners than that the whole community be contaminated by them.[53]

Thomas (2000: 150) suggests that some kind of self-restraint or self-controlled order should operate and that, '[i]n the present state of Indian society, the most liberal divorce laws would merely remain in the Statute Book without affecting society in any way. This is evident from the fact that among Muslims, to whom divorce is almost as easy as to Americans, there are very few actual cases'. A lot of issues are getting confused here.[54] Some writers have criticized the long time, effort, and expense involved in bringing about a divorce. Singh (1993: 5–6) argues vigorously that divorce is a necessary evil and 'a need-based social fact of our generation'. In typical modernist logic, Singh (1993: 6) therefore argues for speedier divorces, claiming that this would be good for women:

> ... the greater the time taken in disposing of petitions, the lesser will be the chances of re-marriage, especially in case of women. Therefore, if the interest of the society has to be preserved the women should be granted an expeditious divorce and allowed to remarry according to their volition before they pass their child-bearing age.

[53] Thomas (2000: 149) also argues that if marriages and divorces are left completely to the will of individuals, there is no need for legislation. Thus, in anarchist fashion, she asks mockingly: 'Why not mate and separate as we like and abolish the institution of marriage altogether and live in what is called free love?'. However, she admits that the concerns of children cannot be ignored.

[54] This argument overlooks the informal nature of Muslim divorce law in India, so that we actually do not know how many Muslim divorces occur. The author could have used comparison with Hindu customary divorces instead, but there are similar evidence problems.

Along similar lines, Sharma (1994: 177) comments that a woman gains nothing by fighting a divorce case when the husband thinks the marriage is broken down. Rather than turning women into mental and physical wrecks due to the stress and delay of divorce proceedings, divorce should be made easy and quick. At present, women are often too old for remarriage by the time a divorce case is decided. They should be saved the trauma of a divorce suit and would then stand a better chance to start a new life with a more compatible husband. Choudhary (1988: 115) concludes that '[t]he upsurge of divorce in recent years has been stimulated by a growing acceptance of the principle by the wives that divorce is a reasonable and at times desirable alternative to an unhappy marriage'. He notes that negative social sanctions have become less stringent,[55] as have the legal and economic constraints involved in obtaining divorces. This reflects a widespread recognition that further reforms to the divorce law should be made, overhauling the legal machinery, especially in terms of costs and delays. Choudhary (1988: 107) notes that divorce involves a lot of expenditure and can be a heavy burden, given that about a third of respondents spent well in excess of Rs 900 on the divorce suit. There is, however, no realistic prospect of state-funded legal aid for divorce in India.[56] Instead, a variety of social work organizations are now active in this field (Jain 1986), seeking to empower women in particular.

Towards Equality (1974: 118–9) examined the various grounds for divorce and argued for relaxations, especially the introduction of cruelty and desertion as grounds for divorce, so that the wife does not have to go to court twice over. Such suggestions put the emphasis on making divorce petitions easier in procedural terms. Choudhary (1988: 85–116) produces a detailed examination of divorce and remarks, at p. 90, that divorce litigation is widely misused:

> The real causes of divorce bear little relationship to the tabulations of divorce complaints as they appear in divorce suits. In general, the rule in such suits is that the legally *most effective* and *morally least accusatory* grounds are asserted in the suit. It is for this reason that legal accounts are so replete with apparently trivial grounds for divorce.

Srivastava (1978: 99) also points to the abuse of Hindu divorce law, observing that many suits are not genuine but involve 'vengeance for the sake of false prestige and honour or for artificially created family troubles and extra-marital considerations', while the fomenting intervention of lawyers often makes

[55] Chaudhary (1988: 49–84) produces a detailed examination of the causes of divorce, noting that the emerging structures are still largely undefined (p. 49) and that legal divorce cases do not necessarily reflect the reality of marital conflicts (p. 50).

[56] It may serve as a warning example that in England, £351 million was spent on legal aid in family matters including divorce in 1994–95, representing one third of the total expenditure on civil legal aid. Divorce is by far the most common type of family matter litigated. The government's expectation that settling divorces through mediation would be much cheaper is not seen as realistic, since such professionals would need to be paid, too. For relevant details see Douglas (1998: 159).

obtaining a divorce decree embarrassing even to those who win their case. Jain (1983: xxiv–xxv) observes that '[t]he number of cases relating to matrimonial offences has considerably increased and now parties do not try for reconciliation because they can get divorce easily and in shorter period'. Modernists were still not satisfied, however, and pushed for further reforms. Diwan (e.g. 1978: 29) in particular was extremely vocal in this context.

The result of efforts to update and modernize Hindu divorce law further is found in the Marriage Laws (Amendment) Act, 1976 (Act No. 68 of 1976). This was a complex reform measure with a multiple agenda, focused not only on providing extra grounds for divorce among Hindus, but also an attempt to harmonize various related laws, especially the HMA and the SMA.[57] This Act has been incompletely analysed so far, but Derrett (1978a) provides an early critique. Its many provisions cannot be discussed here in detail,[58] but two particular provisions need to be highlighted to pursue the present debate. These relate to divorce by mutual consent,[59] and divorce on the basis of cruelty and desertion. The 1976 Act added Section 13-B to the old provisions of the HMA to allow also petitions for divorce by mutual consent, thus reflecting a movement towards recognition of the breakdown principle. The new statutory provision reads as follows:

> 13-B. Divorce by mutual consent.-
> (1) Subject to the provisions of this Act a petition for dissolution of marriage by a decree of divorce may be presented to the district court by both the parties to a marriage together, whether such marriage was solemnized before or after the commencement of the Marriage Laws (Amendment) Act, 1976, on the ground that they have been living separately for a period of one year or more, that they have not been able to live together and that they have mutually agreed that the marriage should be dissolved.
> (2) On the motion of both the parties made not earlier than six months after the date of the presentation of the petition referred to in sub-section (1) and not later than eighteen months after the said date, if the petition is not withdrawn in the meantime, the Court shall, on being satisfied, after hearing the parties and making such inquiry as it thinks fit, that a marriage has been solemnized and that the averments in the petition are true, pass a decree of divorce declaring the marriage to be dissolved with effect from the date of the decree.

It should be noted that the time frame for petitions was also changed in the 1976 Act. It is now sufficient that the parties should have lived separately for only one year. Here, too, the interaction between Section 13 of the HMA and

[57] Agnes (2000: 208) complains about the Hinduization of the SMA.

[58] On the provisions relating to nullity for fraud under the new Section 12(1)(c) of the HMA see Menski (2001: 106–15).

[59] Jain (1986: 45) asserts that the turning point for divorce came in 1976 with the inclusion of mutual consent as a divorce ground, but is wrong that this applied only under the SMA.

Section 23(1) of the Act became a critical flashpoint, concentrated in the question whether the alleged marital breakdown needed to depend on the explicit agreement of both spouses until the time of making the decree. What if consent to the divorce petition was withdrawn at any point? More particularly, what if the wife reconsidered her earlier agreement to divorce, finding for example that she would face financial or other difficulties after the divorce? While earlier cases reflected a strong inclination towards the breakdown principle,[60] from about 1988 onwards the courts recognized that they needed to give more attention to the question of continuing consent. In *Sureshta Devi v Om Prakash* AIR 1992 SC 1904, the Supreme Court eventually held that consent to a joint divorce petition can be unilaterally withdrawn at any time, insisting that mutual consent to divorce must continue until the decree is passed. It appears that this decision took specific account of the need to protect women against agreeing to a divorce under various pressures.

A further important modernist innovation in the 1976 Marriage Laws (Amendment) Act concerned the possibility of divorce petitions on the basis of cruelty.[61] Under Section 10 of the HMA 1955, cruelty had only been a ground for judicial separation, but not for divorce under Section 13. This was now changed, following recommendations from many sides that this would be an appropriate modernizing measure. The provision itself seems innocuous enough.[62] While cruelty was retained as a ground for judicial separation, it now also figures in Section 13(1)(ia) , to the effect that:

> Any marriage solemnized, whether before or after the commencement of this Act, may, on a petition presented by either the husband or the wife, be dissolved by a decree of divorce on the ground that the other party has, after the solemnization of the marriage, treated the petitioner with cruelty.

This extremely brief reference to 'cruelty' was understood by virtually all commentators as a liberalizing measure and a virtual synonym for 'breakdown' of the marital relationship. Indeed, there is richly documented case law evidence

[60] For details see Menski (2001: 120–30).

[61] As noted by Derrett (1963c: 236), Uttar Pradesh made cruelty and desertion grounds for divorce many years before this was introduced for all Indian Hindus in 1976. The relevant Act is the Hindu Marriage (Uttar Pradesh Sanshodhana) Adhiniyam of 1962.

[62] The same goes for desertion, which also became a ground for divorce under Hindu law. Choudhary (1988: 8) portrays desertion as 'poor men's divorce', claiming that many desertions are never brought before any public agency, since many wives feel the stigma of being abandoned and prefer not to make the matter more public than necessary. Also, since divorces cost money, and many deserted women are financially unable to bear the cost of court proceedings, they avoid courts. While Choudhary observes that many of the consequences of desertion are similar to those of divorce, since the family may be permanently dissolved, the boundaries between formal divorce and customary divorces appear to be at issue here, yet this is again ignored in scholarly debate.

to demonstrate that 'cruelty' became a most popular ground for divorce during the late 1970s and early 1980s. The slightest fault or omission became a divorce ground, making extremely entertaining reading.[63] However, from the end of the 1980s onwards, judges began to express their disquiet about treating petitions on the basis of 'cruelty' as a virtual equivalent to application of the breakdown principle.[64] Here again, the judges began to reconsider the social effects of their earlier modernist inclinations and changed their tactics of dealing with divorce petitions on this ground, becoming much more restrictive as a result.

Scholarly opinion about the 1976 Act has been remarkably positive and reflects the fact that the Act implemented many modernist demands, including—so it was assumed—application of the breakdown principle, though this was not explicitly stated in the Act.[65] Singh (1989: 78) finds it heartening that divorce by mutual consent was introduced in 1976. Jain (1983: xxvi) notes that by introducing certain extra divorce grounds in 1976, the legislature has to some extent accepted the principle of broken marriage. Sharma (1989: 62) claims that the philosophy of divorce has shifted from 'offence' and 'fault' to 'breakdown' and notes, at p. 63, that punishment of the guilty spouse actually fell hardest on women. Jain (1983: xxiii) asserts that the changes brought about by the 1976 Act are revolutionary in character and have made the law of divorce more speedy and liberal, but at the same time the basic idea of reconciliation between the parties has also been preserved.

However, there is also significant evidence that modernist scholars remained dissatisfied with the legal reforms of 1976. Singh (1989: 77) notes that the interpretation of 'reasonable cause' for desertion or restitution of conjugal rights as made by the judiciary is unsatisfactory:

> Whenever conjugal rights have come into open conflict with the woman's right of equal opportunity in education or employment, the attitude of the judiciary has often been rather ambiguous ... the judiciary has either evaded the issue or thrown its weight on the side of the traditional view of the husband's authority—a reflection of judiciary's wallowing in male ambience, with very few streaks of its manumitting itself from the fetters of machismo.

Actually, these criticisms relate to a specific type of case law, namely disputes over the wife's right to work and to determine where the matrimonial home should be. These cases have not been systematically analysed so far.[66] They

[63] Agnes (2000: 190 n. 34) refers to some cases. For details see Menski (2001: 74–106).

[64] See in detail Menski (2001: 81-90). It is no longer appropriate to suggest, as Kusum (2000: 237) still does, that '[t]he concept of cruelty is fast expanding'. In reality, the courts have become much more restrictive since the late 1980s, a trend which Kusum has overlooked.

[65] Kusum (2000) provides a useful overview of the relevant issues and cases.

[66] Agnes (2000: 84–5) briefly discusses some of the relevant cases.

seem extremely relevant for understanding how changing gender relations have been assessed by India's judges, initially in petitions for restitution of conjugal rights, and later in divorce petitions. With a view to such cases, Singh (1989: 78) claims that '[i]n such a situation an enlightened judiciary can add life and blood to our Constitution by its emancipative interpretation, which stirs the dialectic and makes it more productive and progressive ... so far as women's rights are concerned'. The main concern here is women's rights, not the changing rules of Hindu divorce law.

Much scholarly comment remains critical of the fact that the breakdown principle was not more explicitly introduced into the HMA in 1976. Choudhary (1988: 11) writes that the 1976 legislation has brought about colossal changes, removing many of the shortcomings in the earlier legislation, but asks for more:

> Still a provision for every divorce on an irretrievable breakdown of the marriage would have been welcome, for, when the intrinsic love and affection has withered away, the empty shell of marriage should be exploded at the first available opportunity, without further bitterness.

These are phrases used by English judges during the 1970s, when English divorce law switched into adoption of the breakdown principle. Sharma and Nagpal (1992: 83) discuss the scope for the breakdown principle, note that it was not introduced in 1976, but highlight that the Law Commission made its seventy-first report recommending the introduction of breakdown as an additional ground. These authors complain, at p. 85, that in the absence of the full-fledged breakdown principle, the law developed so far is still in a rudimentary state. Diwan (1978: 43) vigorously argued for the introduction of irretrievable breakdown, submitting that India should unreservedly accept this principle as the basic structure of divorce. While his advice was that '[i]n the present state of social development probably the Soviet pattern would not suit', drawing from the English experience and making 'suitable modification to suit our conditions' (id.) were suggested at an early stage. Diwan and Diwan (1993: 165) went even further and demanded not only introduction of the breakdown principle, but the abolition of all other grounds:

> In our submission proliferation of the grounds of divorce will not serve any purpose. One wonders how long we will go on aping the West. We are introducing a very bad copy of English law of divorce. Best thing to do will be to have one single ground of divorce: irretrievable breakdown of marriage. We may also retain divorce by mutual consent. This will help in having a uniform law of divorce.

These are clearly radical modernist suggestions that propose following the rocky road of English developments, only to find that today, the substantive English law on divorce has become virtually irrelevant, and the courts are merely dealing with a few procedural hurdles and protracted fights over money and children (Douglas 1998). It is evident that modernist Indian writers put themselves in a dark corner, from which they did not want to emerge towards a brighter postmodern future. As we shall see in the next section, India's judges—and not the scholars—have seen the light and have consequently radically modified their methods of dealing with the question of marital breakdown, and its acceptability as a formal ground of divorce among Hindus.

Postmodern Hindu Divorce Law

The involvement of the post-colonial state through the judiciary constitutes a critical aspect of analysis in the field of Hindu divorce law, too.[67] Given that the modern Indian state has found it impossible to control entry into marriages through a comprehensive system of registration, it would have been totally unrealistic to devise comparable bureaucratic rules about compulsory registration and regulation of all divorces. In other words, a definite legal requirement for all Hindus to go through a formal court procedure in order to effect a legally valid divorce could not have been maintained.[68]

Post-colonial Hindu divorce law has therefore become an odd mixture of increased state intervention in the processes of divorce, manifested in legislative amendments until the mid-1970s and masses of reported case law on divorce, coupled with a remarkable and entirely consistent *laissez faire* approach when it comes to customary divorces. The boundaries between formal and informal divorces are clearly not defined, and nobody seems to want to tackle that particular aspect of the topic. The modernist debates have centred on expansion of the formal grounds for divorce among Hindus, with the ongoing push towards full-fledged acceptance of the uniform principle of irretrievable breakdown of marriage as a major, if not the only, ground for divorce.

However, recent case law confirms in abundance that the breakdown principle is certainly not seen by the higher judiciary as a useful tool of social engineering, but more as an insidious weapon frequently used by selfish individuals, usually unscrupulous men, against their wives. Thus, a remarkable gulf has developed between modernist scholars demanding easier divorce and judicial warnings of the negative effects of massive marital breakdown and its socio-economic consequences. As we shall see, the judges have been conscious of their task in having to develop rules for Hindu divorce law that remain

[67] Kusum (2000: 247) emphasizes the significant role played by the SC in filling gaps in statutory provisions and evolving the law 'so as to meet the ends of justice in a given set of circumstances'. However, she does not go beyond this in her analysis, merely noting that 'the past few years have witnessed a pragmatic approach by the court'.

[68] For details see Douglas (1998). This is now a mere formality in England, where indeed millions of couples neither marry officially, nor need the state to terminate their cohabitation arrangements. In the light of the Indian evidence, does this not ominously look like postmodern English recognition of 'customary' marriages and divorces?

appropriate to India and her people, rather than indulging in borrowing of trendy foreign concepts.

The fact that the views of modernist commentators and of India's judges have diverged more and more during the 1990s should have led to much more critical thinking than we find documented so far. While Dhanda and Parashar (1999) are beginning to consider the new postmodern scenario, they remain stuck in their own modernist grove, as does Agnes (2000). Kusum (2000), too, identifies the postmodern condition of Hindu divorce law, but does not go beyond modernist paradigms. Evidently, much work remains to be done in analysing the complex phenomenon of postmodern Hindu divorce law. The Indian Supreme Court, in particular, but also Parliament, have given resoundingly clear messages to the effect that full-fledged copying of Western models of divorce law into the Hindu system, or indeed any Indian system, is not an appropriate strategy for India. At the same time, the principle of breakdown as such, which is neither 'modern' nor 'Western', but a universal manifestation of defective human relations, is certainly not irrelevant in this field.

The balancing act between competing assumptions about the desirability of divorce among Hindus reflects that a central policy-making task has fallen to India's higher judiciary. As the present analysis demonstrates, far from operating in a vacuum or indulging in gerontocratic patriarchal games, India's judges have been engaged in constructing a postmodern Hindu divorce law that leaves plenty of room for ideological disagreements, but little scope for substantive criticism. Apart from the field of judicial intervention and guidance, it still looks as though the field of Hindu divorce law is muddled and undeveloped, but these are superficial impressions that appear misleading upon closer inspection. At first sight, though, it appears that there continues to be lack of appropriate development.

Backlash Phenomena: Refusing to Legislate Further

There are two significant backlash phenomena which require some analysis at this stage of the discussion, as they apparently create and underpin the modernist impression that Hindu divorce law is deeply deficient. First, it is evident that since the early 1980s the Indian legislature has become quite unwilling to introduce further legislative reforms to Hindu divorce law. This is documented here by bringing out several dimensions that need to be understood more clearly. The refusal to legislate further appears not only as conservative reluctance to introduce still more modern divorce regulations, but also constitutes a considered response, namely a refusal to be pushed by women's activists and other lobbyists into making supposedly modernist amendments that would actually damage many women's interests and involve the state in fiscally unsustainable claims and procedures for securing maintenance and other social welfare rights for women.[69] The postmodern Indian state is clearly unwilling

[69] My research has demonstrated that this implies a self-protective strategy by the state, rather than explicit concern for women. For details see Menski (2001).

to be steered by elitist feminist lobbying, no matter how eloquent the arguments.[70] Caution about further law-making is subtly advised by several experienced observers.[71] The financial implications of Hindu divorce law must be seen as closely linked to the more ideologically oriented arguments over grounds for divorce and the extent to which irretrievable breakdown should be the guiding principle. These aspects are further discussed in Chapter 12, while some further comment is presented here on the blockage of legislative initiatives.

Second, some modernist writers on Indian family law are now beginning to appreciate more openly that simply following Western models in divorce law, while the socio-economic conditions of India remain very different from those of the Euro-American world, does not achieve the major policy aims that reformers envisaged for all Indian women, not just Hindu divorcees. Much of this comes out in anguished comments, as we shall see later. Rather than claiming in modernist fashion that Hindu women need to be liberated and assisted by all possible means to become independent individuals, the emerging postmodernist thinking among scholars, too, appears to be returning to an appreciation of the social embeddedness of human relations, rather than plain individualism, recognizing that the stability of marriages is directly linked to stability in society, and that the maintenance of family-based networks and support systems may actually benefit most individuals. None of this is phrased in Hindu terms, but for those who know enough about the traditional concepts, the subtle messages in some of the scholarly comments contain a 'Hindu' layer of meaning.

It is evident that postmodern Hindu divorce law does not operate in a friendly social environment of consensual debate about the basic rules of society and the extent of individualism. Rather, we are in a conflict-laden war zone of ideological struggles over tradition and modernity, religion and secularism, male claims to dominance and female assertions of equality.[72] These are, precisely, everlasting manifestations of what the Hindus call the era of *kaliyuga*, in which vigilance is required to protect all individuals, and even justice itself. Certain basic human values of dignity and compassion were not automatically promoted by the modernist reforms of Hindu divorce law. Rather, those laws brought out the worst in people, both men and women, as horrified analysts

[70] Many of the leading feminist activists are trained lawyers and evidently know how to put an argument across with great persuasion.

[71] Notably, Kusum (2000: 250) cautiously concludes her discussion of the desirability of irretrievable breakdown as a divorce ground, saying that 'it is important that irretrievable breakdown of the marriage as a ground for divorce, if incorporated, should be applied with utmost discretion. In any case, each case needs to be viewed on its own peculiar facts and merits'.

[72] See similarly Agnes (2000: 167), who also identifies 'aggressive majoritarianism of recent times', in other words *hindutva*, as a negative factor.

began to discover once they started reading case reports instead of merely engaging in activist chatter.

The refusal of the Indian legislature to go beyond the modernist reforms of 1976 is clearly documented by the fate of the failed Marriage Laws (Amendment) Bill of 1981.[73] Choudhary (1988: 11) explains that to facilitate divorce when a marriage has essentially broken down, the 1981 Bill sought to introduce Sections 13-C and 13-D into the HMA, allowing for the application of the breakdown principle. Some details about this Bill are reported by Vijay Sharma (1994: 175), but certain aspects are missing from her account, as well as from what Kusum (2000: 247–8) reports. The Bill was apparently introduced in the Lok Sabha on 27 February 1981, proposing amendments to the effect that irretrievable breakdown should become a new ground for divorce. It was then referred to a Joint Select Committee, which asked for all kinds of opinions. Sharma (1994: 175) reports that the proposed amendment sparked off a keen debate among women, 'as it has far-reaching implications for women and society at large'. While questions have been raised in certain quarters whether it will be in the larger interest of women if divorce is made easy, simple, and quick, this does not answer the question why the Bill failed.

Sharma and Nagpal (1992: 84) complain ominously that owing to some pressure from some quarters the government dragged their feet, the Bill lapsed, and the proposal seems to have been shelved. This looks like a typical Indian scenario of muddled inefficiency, but there is more to this story. The real reason for the failure of the Bill is more fully explained by Sivaramayya (1993: 57–8), one of India's leading male legal writers before his untimely death:

> The women's organisations voiced their opposition to the Bill on the ground that many women in rural areas live apart from their husbands as they (husbands) go to cities for earning their livelihood; that unscrupulous husbands would be in a position to take advantage of such separation and get divorce. They pointed out that unless financial security of women after divorce is assured by means of a provision for a share in the assets acquired by the husband during the subsistence of the marriage, irretrievable breakdown of marriage would be inimical to the interests of women. Conceding the validity of the objections, the Bill was allowed to lapse. It is pertinent to point out in this context the position taken by the Committee on the Status of Women. The Committee ... recommended the ground, but considered it as one among the package along with the other more important proposal *viz.* on divorce, a woman should be entitled to a share (at least 1/3 in the property of the husband).

This helps to explain why the full-fledged application of the breakdown principle was manifestly shot down. It also indicates why female analysts are probably withholding such information. Women activists wanted this ground for divorce, but they also demanded that it should be coupled with fixed

[73] Jain (1983: xxviii) merely notes that the 1981 Bill was introduced; it was too early then to know what happened to it.

entitlements of married women to a share of the husband's earnings and property.[74] Hence, it is no surprise that the 1981 Bill never became law, and that it is so difficult to obtain detailed information about it. The hidden dual agenda of the modernists, once they came out into the open, forced the legislature to refrain from action. Such revolutionary amendments, which would have enormous economic consequences, could not be brought onto the statute book without much further debate, even if the points made by the reformist lobby were valid. This is quite apart from the predictable fact that most Hindu men probably would not want to give their wives an automatic share in the matrimonial property or in their earnings.[75] Not surprisingly, Sivaramayya (1993: 60) noted that the modernists felt they were back to square one and had to return to the drawing board. It began to make sense even to the modernists that unless divorce grounds are backed up by property rights and economic security, irretrievable breakdown of marriage should not be introduced, as confirmed by Kusum (2000: 250).

In the twenty years since the Bill failed it seems that no progress whatsoever has been made by the modernist lobbies in coming up with sustainable proposals for further reforms to Hindu divorce law. This is documented by Agnes (2000: 167–91), who examines in detail several of the proposals from the late 1980s and the 1990s. She finds that they all have to be dismissed for want of practicality and sometimes even basic common sense. Her analysis makes it quite evident that there is very little interest among reformers in divorce law. While much of the attention has been focused on polygamy and especially registration of marriages as a means to exercise more state control over society, the new focus of modernist activism is directed at property-related issues and domestic violence against women. Agnes (2000: 167) finds that in a highly politicized climate of debate overshadowed by the uniform civil code fiasco, there is a lot of political rhetoric, but little legal substance. Even the most recent recommendations by womens' groups and activist lawyers still harp on about making divorce available on the basis of the breakdown principle (Agnes 2000: 180–1). Of course, this had been proposed by the Law Commission in its Seventy-first report. However, as Agnes (2000: 180) continues:

> But due to opposition from various women's organizations, the issue was abandoned. The opposition from the women's organizations was based on the fact that the remedy may not suit the Indian cultural ethos and women will be worse affected by it. It will provide an avenue for husbands, after

[74] Nobody, as far as I know, has analysed the implications that such new rules about matrimonial property would have in middle-class families and among the lower classes.

[75] In my professional advice work, I have come across a significant number of newly married Hindu women (and South Asian Muslim women, too) who like to believe that on the day of their marriage, they automatically acquired half of the husband's property, if not more.

> years of marriage, to opt out on flimsy grounds and leave the wife and children in the lurch. While the opposition is valid, it is premised on an abstract theoretical basis since at the practical level, the remedy has already made a back door entry into the matrimonial statutes. Firstly, the ground of mental cruelty is used by the parties almost on the same footing as irretrievable breakdown of marriage.

While this is indeed a lot of political rhetoric, the author does not pick up that the case law on cruelty, in particular, has now taken on a postmodern shape and has been restrained by the judges in many recent cases.[76] However, a valid point is highlighted by Agnes (2000: 178) in relation to desertion and its disastrously negative economic consequences for many women. That issue is more usefully discussed in Chapter 12 and links very closely to customary divorces. The various recent reform proposals examined by Agnes (2000) are not otherwise relevant for the discussion of Hindu divorce law. The Married Women (Protection of Rights) Bill, 1994 was a private member's bill.[77] It was quite radical in its proposals regarding a wife's entitlement to all the property of the husband, without giving men reciprocal rights. The Domestic Violence to Women (Prevention) Bill, 1994,[78] too, contained a number of provisions seeking to protect the economic interests of women, but did not contain any new ideas or suggestions about divorce. It seems firmly established that the reformist energies on Hindu divorce law have been spent and the activist focus has turned to other issues outside the present field.

Modernist Despair and Postmodern Inklings

Palpable despair about the lack of progress in several aspects related to Hindu divorce law continues to be evident in some of the modernist writing. While this is not constructive, it pinpoints that there are simmering, unresolved tensions in Indian and Hindu society. However, most complaints relate to the 'bigger issues' of gender equality and the highly politicized uniform civil code debate, rather than niceties of grounds for divorce among Hindus. On divorce law itself, the only remaining grievance of modernists is that the breakdown principle has not been introduced as fully and openly as could be. Even that argument is tempered by the realization that facilitation of easier divorces has increased the risks that wives may be simply discarded.

[76] Some of these cases are discussed by Kusum (2000: 237–50), but she does not notice the postmodern development of the law on cruelty.

[77] This is printed in Agnes (2000: 225–7). It is Bill No. XXV of 1994, and was introduced by Ms Veena Verma of the Congress Party in the Rajya Sabha, India's Upper House, in May 1994. Agnes (2000: 185) records that the Bill was debated thrice between August 1994 and March 1995 and received much positive comment, but the government was reluctant to implement it.

[78] This Bill is discussed by Agnes (2000: 184) and the text is also provided (ibid.: 216–21).

For example, Vijay Sharma (1994: 363) writes in her conclusions that the HMA abandoned the sacramental concept of Hindu marriage and permits divorce to both spouses. She sees that '[f]reedom to put an end to an unhappy marriage is a step towards woman's freedom from hardships of unhappy marriage', but also notes that many Indian women are illiterate and economically dependent, so that 'freedom' all too easily turns into lack of support from anyone and consequent risks of destitution in a new 'feminisation of poverty'. This does not strike me as new at all in view of what the *shastras* advised about the need to protect women's entitlements from husbands and the joint family.

In the context of an article criticizing the lack of provisions for shelter of divorced women, Kusum (1991: 55) notes that 'the concept of indissolubility of marriage no longer holds true' and seems to suggest that this new legal insecurity for wives has not been matched with added economic safeguards. Here again, the concern is over economic issues, not divorce law as such. One of the leading socio-legal researchers of India, Vasudha Dhagamwar (1987: 118), has recognized throughout her academic work that law and society do not match neatly, thus running the risk of victimizing women. She is quite despondent:

> The truth, I hope, is clear by now. The new Hindu Law promises sex-equality to women. Our social values continue to deny it. Legal equality is translated into reality only when social factors obtain. These are, as yet, conspicuous by their absence .... The circumstances in which a woman can believe that she is a person, and that her sex is secondary, do not exist. The pressure upon her is to sink in her femininity and to regard it as a handicap. It is not a situation in which she can stand up and exercise the rights the Republic of India recognises as being hers.

Dhagamwar (1987: 118–9) therefore asks for 'a revolutionary change in our values', but sees law only as an aid or encouragement in this context. Choudhary (1988: 170) notes that society is still not prepared to accept divorce easily, remarriage is difficult, and adjustments after divorce are not easy to make. Choudhary (id.) argues:

> The traditional morality demands that partners stay in marriage. The modern morality states that one ought to "adjust to reality". The fact is that many couples are not able to do either of these. In the conflict situation there are many alternatives. People with "modern" values choose the alternative of divorce without necessarily having the idea of re-marriage in their minds. In consequence most of them ... are likely to have an emotionally shattering experience.

Shastri (1990: 12) argues that the modern reforms need to be rethought, but does not appear to see that different types of law are involved and that the picture is a little more complex than she imagines:

> Shastric Hindu Law was repealed by the various enacted laws favouring Hindu women and to undo the injustice done to them for ages. These

> enacted laws misguide the Hindu Society by emphasising that Hindu women enjoy high status and position, and have special rights more favourable in comparison to Hindu males. But the real position is very much illusive and gloomy ... one can wonder that despite constitutional guarantee of equality of sexes, Hindu women continue to be victims of exploitation and discrimination. Hindu Society looks at a woman, who seeks divorce, with dismay and disgust.

Realizing the problems of turning thousands of divorced women out on the street, Qureshi (1978: 346) proposes that '[t]he best way to avoid all these calamities is to discourage divorce. It may exceptionally be granted, only when it is extremely necessary. It should not become a regular feature, amounting to annihilation of innocent divorced wives'. Similarly, Sharma (1994: 178) summarizes the position of those who warn against making divorce yet easier:

> A divorced wife is looked down in the society. The Indian society being as it is, and the status of women being what it is, the time is not ripe for introduction of what may be termed as "khuli chhutti" from matrimonial bonds ... the marginalisation of women from education and employment, the lack of low cost housing, long and short stay women's homes and crisis centres and government subsidised women's hostel, maintenance and accommodation during the separation and post-divorce period pose very real problems .... It flings the door wide open for desertion and gives the right to divorce unilaterally after three years of separate living on the ground that the marriage has irretrievably broken down.

With reference to Lord Denning, who had warned about making divorce too easy, Sharma (1994: 179) argues that in Hindu society 'divorce should be granted only in exceptional cases', linking this reasoning to family courts and expectations of reconciliation. Sharma (1994: 363–4) shows that illiteracy and economic dependence on men is more prevalent among females living in villages, whose husbands may simply engineer a divorce petition, of which the wife may not even come to know. Therefore, it is argued that if divorce becomes easier, it will harm women, as it will provide a unilateral right of divorce to men. Sharma (1994: 364) argues, therefore, that protective mechanisms for women are needed first, and without such safeguards, irretrievable breakdown of marriage should not be introduced.[79]

There is thus a well-documented, growing realization among modernist scholars that the position of Hindu women would not be helped by more liberal divorce laws. Instead, economic measures linked to divorce need to be improved first. From this perspective, it makes sense that the introduction of pure 'irretrievable breakdown' as a formal ground for divorce has been shelved. The judges have developed their own activism in this field, acting in the wider public interest, not as male partisans in the gender wars that some modernist writers imagine. They are the ones charged with the difficult task of making Hindu divorce law work for women, rather than against them.

[79] This is exactly what Kusum (2000) and Agnes (2000) also suggest.

The current picture reveals not only a coexistence of formal provisions for judicial divorce and of customary informal processes of Hindu divorce law—which are much more widespread than we think and textbooks disclose—but also the critical coexistence of statute law and case law. Admittedly, this is hardly a new observation with reference to such a hybrid legal system as post-colonial Indian law. However, the critical point for the present discussion is that while most scholars have not read enough cases on Hindu divorce law before making their statements, judges have sharpened their tools by applying the breakdown principle in a large number of cases since the early 1990s, constructing in the process a postmodern Hindu divorce law which is significantly different from its modernist aberrations during the 1970s and early 1980s. The next section seeks to explore how and why this may have happened.

The Psycho-social Basis of Postmodern Hindu Divorce Law

While the judges themselves remain largely silent about why they have been engaged in the process of postmodern reconstruction of Hindu divorce law,[80] looking back to Derrett's seminal writing during the 1970s locates the key issues and provides some answers.[81] Derrett, at least when it came to divorce law, was not just a male chauvinist conservative, as the National Committee for Women in the 1970s so readily assumed in *Towards Equality* (1974), but was an emerging postmodern Hindu lawyer. When India's highest judges are today dropping hints in hotly contested divorce cases about the balance between individualistic freedom and social responsibility, and the competing claims of men and women, they are unlikely to record that they read Derrett's work in earlier times, but the same concepts, ideas, and principles as explained by the leading scholar of Hindu law in the twentieth century are shining through. That is not to say, however, that such knowledge needed to be taught or would have been picked up only from Derrett's work. These are ancient Hindu principles, which exist and can be applied as and when needed. The critical issue, it seems, is mental awareness of the existence of those concepts and principles, not any factual knowledge of precise rules of Hindu law.[82]

Derrett (1957: 274) was still too impressed with modernist assumptions about a gradual uniformity and secularization of all aspects of Hindu life when he predicted that '[c]astes which are still allowed special privileges, as of divorce by mutual consent, will voluntarily give them up, and in course of time the

[80] In the context of the uniform civil code debates, this has led to recent observations that '[t]he judiciary refuses to be drawn into finding a solution' (Dhavan 2001: 318). However, this does not mean that the judges will not construct substantive postmodern solutions for individual cases, while keeping out of the never-ending politics around legal uniformity.

[81] Derrett (1970: 391–7), in particular, focuses on the central role of judges in the development of post-colonial Hindu law.

[82] This is also what marks Chiba's (1986) 'legal postulates' as a critical input in all legal processes.

unification of Hindu communities will advance still further'. It was evidently too early, otherwise, to expect further comments on the development of Hindu divorce law, but modernist anticipations were strong at that stage. Derrett (1963c) was merely a technical legal textbook that dutifully recorded recent developments in statutes and cases, with very little comment on divorce law.[83] By 1970 this picture looks quite different. Derrett (1970) produced the first of several sharp critiques of modern legal analysis, realizing that the new Hindu divorce law had begun to take on some really pernicious characteristics. By the late 1960s, he had read enough awful cases to be unable to enjoy his dinner on certain days and, as a true polymath, he put pen to paper. Derrett (1970) antedates the formal emergence of Indian legal postmodernity by a decade or so, but the analysis produced at that stage clearly anticipates the emerging huge dangers for Hindu society and for Hindu women, in particular, of simply following modernist legal axioms.

Significantly, the final analysis in that book focused on the role of judges, who in the words of Derrett (1970: 394) are 'Indian citizens charged with the ancient powers of the King to guide, protect, encourage and restrain'. Derrett (1970: 395) suggests that 'when they are applying their minds to the merits and deserts of individuals, they are putting Hindu, or at least Indian, principles into effect'. Further, as he states at pp. 396–7:

> I see no reason whatever why Muslim judges, atheist judges, judges deracinated from their indigenous culture, and even judges who have sold their soul to the West should not be as able to apply Hindu principles to cases between Hindus as any judge who has been faithful to his *dharma*; for if they do not know what those principles are they can ask the Bar to tell them. And if they have reached the High Court Bench they are presumed to know not only how to find things out, but also to test the credibility of what is told to them.

Thus, the continued usefulness of Hindu law in the post-colonial scenario was not doubted.[84] More recently, Weinberger-Thomas (1999: 181) supports this stance, while elaborately criticizing the anti-traditionalist approach taken by authors like Vaid and Sangari (1991):

> It is my feeling that research undertaken on the basis of such presuppositions cannot help but be skewed from the outset. If one is to hope to understand

[83] Derrett (1963c: 225–43) is remarkably short on divorce, while the bulk of the work centres on various aspects of Hindu joint family law.

[84] Deliberations about research methodology appear in a number of recent studies. As a vocally modernist field researcher, Srimati Basu (2001: 17) asks herself at the beginning of her fieldwork: 'In what ways would my predominantly Hindu cultural upbringing impinge upon the research process, despite my self-proclaimed status as a card-carrying atheist?'. Weinberger-Thomas (1999: 86) clearly acknowledges that 'there is no such thing as a bare fact' and that 'writing a book is a subjective endeavour' (*ibid.*: 182) while she produces an excellent postmodern analysis of *satī*.

> a body of data from within the religious sphere, then one must, regardless of one's personal feelings on the subject, give belief systems full credit, so to speak, even if one ends up with conclusions of a very different order.

Derrett (1970: 397) argued roughly thirty years earlier that it would be most appropriate to seek guidance from indigenous principles, whatever those may be: 'In the innumerable situations where the law is not clear the presumption must be that native criteria are the right ones, and the burden of proof that standards from London or New York (or Moscow) are better than Indian standards lies on the one who asserts it'. Armed with such presuppositions, Derrett (1970: 432) emphasizes that '*dharma* does go on for ever, and the arm of *dharma* reaches through generations. The King cannot create it, nor can he destroy it; the most he can aspire to do is to find out what it is and apply it. And if he does this and protects the people he need do nothing else'. This is not only a neat statement on the relationship between classical Hindu law and modern state law, but provides also a working brief for India's judges. Derrett's reflections make the continued operation of these principles visible and thus, despite his own modernist inclinations, contributed an awareness of firm foundations to postmodern Indian judicial law-making, at a subconscious invisible level, but manifest and powerful nevertheless.

We have seen how the modernist amendments to the Hindu divorce law in 1964 began to introduce the concept of irretrievable breakdown by stealth,[85] allowing devious spouses to misuse this modern law to a sickening extent. Derrett (1970: 436) recounts in an appendix that after he had written his *Critique of Modern Hindu Law*, he received a number of judgments from Calcutta that deeply upset him:

> After reading them my first thought was "How can I take food in the houses of people who are behaving like this?" The craze for matrimonial litigation has increased by leaps and bounds; the misconduct of the parties reaches back into years past; ... the malaise from which modern Indian culture suffers in this respect can be traced right back to July 1955, when the Hindu Marriage Act was passed. Nowhere in the world ... does such rascality go on and in such a vile way. Doctors with multiple foreign degrees, professional men at the top of Hindu society, are shown behaving in a manner almost beyond disgust .... The time for laughing at Indian cunning and folly is over. The amusement of the Indian public is tiring. This is an illness and it must be diagnosed in any treatment which calls itself a *Critique*.

Derrett (id.) clearly states that '[t]he fears of *some* women that divorce laws would do more harm than good were justified. Much more harm than good has been done, and I must show why, and suggest how this can be stemmed. A labour of Hercules indeed!'. In a brilliant (and cruelly funny) psycho-social analysis, Derrett (1970: 437–40) explored this maldevelopment in modern Hindu

[85] In his numerous writings on this topic, Derrett also uses the image of a torpedo and a Trojan Horse.

society, arguing that young men and women were brought up in such a way that an unhealthy appetite for romance developed and 'capacity for companionship (which is the essence of love) gets little chance' (ibid.: 437). Further, closely linked to this, 'marital fidelity is so highly rated that it obscures all other factors' (ibid.: 439). The Hindu divorce litigation of the 1960s represented the worst of Hindu culture and character. Derrett suggests that the ancient Hindus were quite aware of such problems, and were familiar with abuses of forgery and perjury. Noting that the *smṛti* texts offered copious guidance on how to control and punish this, Derrett (1970: 440) observes:

> The forgery and perjury normal in litigation over land and other valuable property has now emerged in full force in matrimonial litigation. This kind of litigation shows Hindus at their worst .... *It is the duty of the ruler to protect them from this.* They must be protected from their own weaknesses. This was the attitude of the *shastra*, and it was right.[86]

Derrett's argument is that the strictness of the *shastric* divorce law was deliberate, seeking to protect Hindu individuals virtually from themselves, thus forcing spouses to accommodate, rather than separating or arguing over the possibility of marital breakdown, which was declared to be a non-option in principle. Derrett (1970: 441) observed that there was no hope of going back from the current mess, and that the judges would have to bear the burden of clearing up the confusions:

> The dreadful damage now being done to Hindu society by the way the HMA is working out was obviated, because the *shastrakaras* knew what they were doing. They knew the follies of their people.
>
> I do not think it is possible, politically or otherwise, to abolish divorce. Parliament cannot go back on the reforms it has made, because the genuine case of the oppressed spouse will crop up occasionally. There will be instances where divorce is imperative by any standard. It is up to the judiciary to cope with the cases as best they can.

Derrett (1970: 442) reserves some choice words for the abusers of the new legal procedures in Hindu divorce law. His substantive suggestion is that by some procedural means, those who foment divorce litigation, forge documents, and give false evidence, should be prosecuted for forgery. Further, although we cannot be sure whether he was really serious about this or not, Derrett (1970: 443–4) suggested the death penalty for litigation tricksters:

> I should be inclined to introduce the death penalty for all those who supply false evidence in matrimonial causes, were I not afraid that the tender hearts of the Supreme Court judges, who would not want to have any life (even the vilest) on their consciences, would acquit them on any pretext. Prison

[86] The present study has shown this to be the central element of assisted self-controlled order among Hindus, represented through the ruler's punishing rod (section on assisted self-control in Chapter 3).

> sentences for fomenters of matrimonial litigation would be appropriate, and it is high time that people stopped looking upon such people as charming aberrations or the like.

That was the last word in 1970, a damning indictment of the emerging evidence of maldevelopments in modern Hindu divorce law. Following the promulgation of the Marriage Laws (Amendment) Act of 1976, Derrett (1978a) produced a further analysis of Hindu divorce law, which is much more explicitly postmodern, though the term is not used. To start with, Derrett (1978a: viii–ix) discusses Rama Mehta's fieldwork on the impact of divorce on middle class Hindu women, and notes the marvellous fight being put up by Hindu married women, who deny the Sita model and yet follow it to a large extent.[87] Complaining vigorously that his advice was not heeded and that Hindu wives were made to pay a heavy price for modernity, Derrett (1978a: 185–6) presents a bleak outlook on the future:

> ... a marriage law which was professedly intended for the relief of suffering wives may quite as easily be used to browbeat, oppress, deprive and corrupt women! 'Philanderers' charter or not, the new marriage-law available to all the majority community is a means whereby vast numbers of women, whose fault is merely that they were married off into unsympathetic or unscrupulous families, will be put on the street with a few rupees a month and with a psychic trauma which no amount of 'freedom' will assuage. For however low their expectations might have been when they married, consummation of that marriage has anchored them psychically in that family, and cannot be simply washed out by litigation.

Here again, as the image of 'washing out' reinforces, the sexual dimension of matrimonial relations figures prominent. Derrett (1978a: 199) emphasizes (as he claims he has always done) that the core problem in the specific conditions of Indian society is the lost virginity of the divorced wife. Promising women freedom from oppression and individualistic independence, the modern Hindu divorce law threatened to throw millions of women out of marriages, potentially even against their wishes, without creating socio-economic conditions that would assist such women. Derrett (1978a: 197) therefore highlights that unlike English judges, the Indian judiciary has purposefully retained the duty to attempt reconciliation of the warring spouses, so that every case under Section 13 of the HMA has to be heard and judges can (even must) question the parties in person to ascertain the extent of the marital breakdown being alleged.[88] Still, as Derrett (id.) warns,

[87] This is another key example of 'overlapping consensus', so typical of Hindu conceptualizations and their fluid social application.

[88] Derrett (1978a: 199) emphasizes that such litigation does not only involve the two spouses and reports that '[t]he court must see them personally, and it must develop practice regulations and jurisprudence to detect the seeds of future harmony and fruitful cooperation in the consciousness of the spouses themselves that they have been manipulated by others, as poor pawns in others' games'.

> though India has retained the *search for reconciliation as a judicial duty* (in contrast to a mere lawyer's formality), the likelihood is that India, like England, will develop a divorce-production-line; ...
>
> ... India *did* retain the judicial duty, and it knew what it was doing. Conditions of marriage in India differ *toto caelo* from those in England, and that is what makes the difference.

The procedural conditions explain partly why and how India's judges became so experienced in balancing the conflicting expectations and claims of husbands and wives. In the late 1970s, the focus was still on arguments over the grounds for divorce, while during the 1990s the main concern shifted to financial arrangements in connection with divorce.[89] In Derrett's concluding comments, it is evident that modernist thinking still dominates his thought patterns and presumptions, but there are also indications of recognition that there is a continuing space and role for traditional concepts of law. Derrett (1978a: 206) offers some predictions about the direction of Indian laws and the continuing role of Hindu law in it:

> When a family-law jurisprudence and reconciliation practice have matured, the way will be much clearer for the Uniform Code, which, one cannot help agreeing, is more than simply politically desirable for the country. The *dharmasastra* will then be suitably parted from daily life, so far as the courts are concerned. Who knows? Its ethical element may undergo a renaissance and, free from the handicap that judicial knowledge could be taken of it and portions of it applied as if it were statute, it will be conveniently placed for scholarly research and spiritual investigation in a way that has been denied it for a century or more. The defensive, apologetic and 'white-washing' approaches will disappear, as they should.

This suggests that even the formal incorporation of Hindu law into a uniform national code, and thus its official disappearance as part of state law, would not wipe away the relevance of Hindu concepts as an aspect of life for the people themselves. Despite the polemic subtitle of his book as an *Epitaph for the Rishis* and its dramatic pronouncement of the formal death of Hindu law in 1976 as a result of introducing further reforms to Hindu divorce law, Derrett clearly predicted an ongoing future role for Hindu cultural concepts within the wider Indian legal framework. More specifically on women, Derrett (1978a: 206) concluded his study:

> In the new 'self-image' of modern Indian women we shall find an internal discipline, a spontaneous self-respect and well-founded prudence such as will make it possible, one day, for a thinker to compose a new *sastra*, a modern *stridharma* owing little to the old, and based on the achievements of noble Hindu women who, though tempted by easy-divorce statutes, developed a technique of getting the most value, emotionally and spiritually,

[89] This process began already during the mid-1980s, following the Shah Bano drama and growing realization that women and children required specific protection mechanisms.

> out of even the most unpromising partners and the most depressing living and working-conditions. These new standards will set the tone for the new 'people's justice' in India in which, as always, the judges reflect the habits, but not less the aspirations of their time.

While one could easily dismiss this passage as idle talk about 'noble Hindu women' and the like, a relevant dualistic legal message is hidden here. This needs to be brought out; it is pertinent (if not central) to the present analysis. First, it is Derrett's understanding that Hindu women—not men—through their capacity for adjustment, and for the sake of their own well-being and survival, will have to face the main burden of developing sustainable methods of coping with the strains and stresses of marital life.[90] This explicit recognition of women's agency in suffering is not a traditionalist allocation of gender roles, as modernist analysis assumes, but a reflection of social reality observed in Hindu divorce litigation. In case after case, as Derrett knew only too well (and I was soon to discover as well) Hindu women had to defend themselves and their most basic interests and needs in courtrooms before almost exclusively male judges and often a prying public. A Hindu wife who meekly claimed that she did not object to her own divorce and did not speak up when it came to money and children could not later blame the 'system'. Derrett realized that Hindu women had to learn to speak up in order actively to take part in shaping their own future, irrespective of all kinds of restrictions and difficult circumstances of life, including devious husbands who turned out to be litigation tricksters. There is not a word here about postmodern reconstruction, but the sage advice to India is that the voice of her women would need to be better heard to bring about a better future.

Closely related to this, and manifest in his final sentence as cited above, Derrett's second point of imminent relevance here is, again, that the Indian judiciary is the pivotal agent in this reconstruction process. We need not debate here why this should be so, it is a fact that the judges apply the law and make the decisions. However, Derrett is not just restating here what we know anyway, but is bringing out the centrality of the judicial input in this process. Only an open-minded judiciary that is alert to the needs of 'people's justice' could face that challenge. Themselves members of the elite, the judges would have to consider at all times the wider picture, the entire framework of reference, not just the narrow parameters of a particular case before them. This enormous challenge, as the next section shows, was indeed taken up by India's superior judges, leading to the formation of a decidedly postmodern Hindu divorce law.

Postmodern Judicial Activism in Divorce Law

In what is innocuously called modern 'divorce litigation', manifest abuses of human relations occur almost as a matter of course, are often dramatically played

[90] Derrett actually made that particular point in many of his articles and especially in Derrett (1970: 436–9) and Derrett (1978a: 198–200).

out before the court without shame or feelings of restraint, are fomented by lawyers for whom divorce has become a lucrative business (Jain 1986), and are facilitated by purportedly advanced formal legal mechanisms and procedures. By tightening up the entire process and restricting their earlier indulgence and willingness to be entertained by lengthy concocted stories of human misery or misogyny, the superior judges of India have become more efficient in handling divorce litigation. At the same time, they have also intervened in a restrictive but constructive manner in order to rebuild human relations and to restore visions of microcosmic balance, searching for justice in innumerable difficult situations. This occurs in various ways, buried under citations of Telugu poetry,[91] in comments about public policy and the public interest,[92] or even with reference to the Constitution.[93] Rarely does one find an explicit reference to Hindu concepts of sacramental marriage.[94] At any rate, such comments are not majoritarian reminders of Hindu power but moralizing appeals to self-controlled order in a messy family situation where the position of the woman is at risk. India's senior judges have had to be highly educated and extremely skilled social realists to do their job well, while academic writers and social activists, it seems, could afford to dream and speculate more freely about the ideal societies they would like to create.

Whether or not India's superior judges have been prominently influenced by Hindu concepts of appropriateness, or more by general ideas of justice, or modernist assumptions about human rights, may not be the right sort of questions to ask about the nature of Hindu postmodernity. At the end of the day,

[91] In *K. Omprakash v K. Nalini* AIR 1986 AP 167, at p. 170, it was held: 'The great Telugu poet Vemana said that the broken iron can be joined together, but not broken hearts. Parties have been living apart for long and their wedlock has now virtually become a deadlock. Chance of reunion had completely faded away. In these circumstances, we think it just and proper to grant a decree of divorce straightway'.

[92] In *Madan Mohan Manna v Chitra Manna* AIR 1993 Cal 33, the HC refused the husband a decree of divorce even though he was already living with another woman. Faced with a situation where the lawful Hindu wife still wanted her marriage, but not a *ménage à trois*, it was held at p. 38 that divorce decrees could not just be given to anyone according to whims and caprice, and 'the whole institution of marriage itself would be seriously shaken if such liberty is given to a person'.

[93] In several important cases, the SC has emphasized its duty to achieve 'complete justice' in accordance with Art. 142(1) of the Constitution. See *Chanderkala Trivedi v S. P. Trivedi* (1993) 4 SCC 232 and *Kanchan Devi v Promod Kumar Mittal* AIR 1996 SC 3192. On recourse to Art. 51-A of the Constitution and the concept of fundamental duties, see later.

[94] In *V. Shankar Ram v Sukanya* AIR 1997 Mad 394, Lakshmanan J dismissed the husband's appeal against a refusal of divorce on the basis of breakdown. It was held, at p. 406: 'The wife in her evidence says that she likes her husband and still wants to live with him. We do share the feelings of the wife expressed before us that a conservative Hindu Brahmin family girl would not prefer to be known as a divorcee ... in the society .... Both parties, in our opinion, have not crossed the point of no return'.

situation-specific justice, like the rule of law, seems devoid of content. It is a general principle that is applied to innumerable situations, in the search for appropriate solutions to conflicts that are unique to the case but demand an equitable result.[95]

The never-ending search for appropriateness is certainly most impressively reflected and documented in the recent case law on Hindu divorces and the writings of some leading analysts, starting with Derrett in the 1970s. Comparing the English and Indian approaches to reconciliation, Derrett (1978a: 200) had this to say on how Indian ideas of progress might shape up:

> The judiciary of India, however compassionate to spouses who have suffered intolerably from abominable domestic conditions, will be united *to a man* and *to a woman* in the view that reconciliation, on the lines I have adumbrated, is worth every possible effort and ingenuity, rather than that a woman should be cast on the world only for some lonely old widower or possibly unsavoury bachelor to take up as a matter of pity. The progress of Indian ideas is not towards more licence and more casual concessions to individual whims, nor is the progress of Indian law towards the utilising of law-courts for sustaining individual preferences at the expense of the country's higher needs.

It is crystal-clear today that the so-called liberality of the 1970s, coupled with an underlying assumption about the need to free Hindu spouses from the yoke of unwanted marriages, has almost completely been abandoned.[96] The postmodern genesis of Hindu divorce law, which occurred in the main only during the 1990s, can be illustrated by reference to petitions for divorce based on cruelty.[97] Whereas earlier, the slightest fault of the spouse and any number of small acts of cruel behaviour by the wife could serve husbands as a divorce ground,[98] Indian judges now often lecture couples, refusing many divorce applications with the almost flippant argument that there is a bit of cruelty in every marriage, and that people should learn to put up with the daily wear and tear of married life more patiently.[99] These are not judges expatiating on the

[95] I read Kusum's (2000: 150) comment that 'each case needs to be viewed on its peculiar facts and merits' not only as confirmation of the relevance of that particular legal approach (rather than slavish adherence to precedent), but also as a secular phrasing of basic Hindu principles of *vyavahāra*.

[96] Kusum (2000: 237) wrongly asserts that '[t]he concept of cruelty is fast expanding', whereas the postmodern evidence involves a contraction and a tightening up rather than an expansion.

[97] For details on such cases during the 1980s and 1990s, see Menski (2001: 74–106).

[98] For some time during the 1970s and 1980s, nullity petitions on the basis of fraud seem to have been an attractive alternative (for details see Menski 2001: 106–15). This loophole seems to have been plugged by postmodern judicial vigilance as well.

[99] In *Nirmala Manohar Jagesha v Manohar Shivram Jagesha* AIR 1991 Bom 259, Savant J held at pp. 266–7 that in order to constitute cruelty as a basis for a

vagaries of life, but highly skilled individuals who lecture the men and women before them,[100] educating today's Hindu public about standards of appropriateness, even if the term dharma is not outwardly expressed.

Another area of hotly disputed case law concerns cases on whether a particular marriage has irretrievably broken down, as evidenced by some fault of the respondent or even mutual agreement of the spouses. There is no space here to produce a detailed case analysis. Only some samples can be given to demonstrate the extent of postmodern reconstruction and the clarity of the postmodern vision which India's judges have already developed.[101] In the 1970s, the Supreme Court judiciary had still been impressed by modernist and individualistic pleadings in earlier cases like *N.G. Dastane v S. Dastane* AIR 1975 SC 1534, freely granting divorces on the basis of cruelty and breakdown, dishing out decrees almost as fast as the English courts. Since the late 1980s, however, the Indian Supreme Court has been instrumental in constructing a postmodern Hindu divorce law that allows divorce based on the breakdown principle, but only in certain exceptional circumstances, where this is deemed sensible.[102] It remains a fact that this is not a statutory ground, so the judges have a weapon to stop irresponsible unilateral pleadings of breakdown of the marital relationship.[103]

---

divorce petition, conduct 'must be more serious than the ordinary wear and tear of married life'.

[100] A judicial tutorial in Hindu divorce law was given to the husband of a young female lawyer in *Indira Gangele v Shailendra Kumar Gangele* AIR 1993 MP 59. The wife's attempts to build her own career had upset the husband, but that was not accepted as a ground for divorce. He was told, at p. 64, that 'divorce in this country is not granted merely because it is asked for'. The court had held earlier, at p. 63, that the times of Tulsidas, a medieval poet-saint, are over and that 'we are living in a country where equity is constitutionally guaranteed'.

[101] I discussed some of these cases elsewhere (Menski 2001: 119–30). Several of these cases are also identified as important by Kusum (2000: 247–50).

[102] An excellent early example of refusal to grant divorce on flimsy grounds is found in *K. Narayanan v K. Sreedevi* AIR 1990 Ker 151. The facts of the case demonstrated in cruel clarity that the husband was sacking his wife after the death of his mother—he did not need her elder-care services any more and had no interest in the marriage anyway. In contrast, at an earlier time when copying foreign models was still a fashion, Diwan (1978: 20) refers even to snoring as a ground for divorce in US law.

[103] In *Chetan Dass v Kamla Devi* AIR 2001 SC 1709, a Hindu husband had kept a Christian concubine, while the Hindu wife remained willing to keep the marriage alive on condition that he gave up his lover. The SC refused the husband divorce on the basis of breakdown, noting that he was taking advantage of his own wrong. If this husband were to make a reasonable financial offer to the wife, he might as yet purchase his freedom, but the case mentions nothing about such financial arrangements. Instead, at p. 1714, the learned judge attempts to make some comments about the need to preserve order in society, indicating that matrimonial conduct 'is sought to be controlled in the interest of the individuals as well as in broader perspective,

The postmodern element in this context is found in the fact that judges will grant divorces based on breakdown—but only on condition that the wife's complaints are being addressed, and her financial claims satisfied. In this respect the courts appear to follow Derrett's suggestions for a better system of Hindu divorce from the 1970s, listening to the wife, in particular. If she agrees that the marriage has broken down and there seems no hope of reconciliation, the focus switches to concern over her material well-being after divorce. A good example of this kind of judicial construction of postmodern Hindu divorce law is provided by the leading case of *V. Bhagat v D. Bhagat* AIR 1994 SC 710.[104] Here, a professional couple of mature age, the husband a senior SC advocate, had wasted eight years in litigation throwing wild allegations at each other, even before the Supreme Court. It was evident that the marriage could not be sustained. Despite the fact that 'irretrievable breakdown' does not exist as a statutory ground of divorce for Hindus, divorce was granted on that basis by the Supreme Court, with the clear admonition that this case was *not* to be taken as a precedent for the breakdown principle as an integral part of Hindu divorce law. My analysis of the subsequent case law shows that 'the dam which the Indian Supreme Court has erected against the continuous flood of breakdown arguments held up well' (Menski 2001: 132). It is evident that judicial thinking and action on Hindu divorce law has developed with greater consistency and clarity than scholars seem to appreciate.

The postmodern condition in this particular arena is clearly represented by the argument that it is socially undesirable that millions of Hindu marriages should be terminated because one of the spouses is unhappy with the marriage. Modernists need to note that the key argument is no longer—if it ever was—that Hindu marriages are sacramental unions which should not be broken in order to respect some form of Brahmanic tradition. That aspect of traditional Hindu culture was elevated by scholarship to such an exalted status that it actually damaged women. Postmodern Hindu law has definitely brought with it a traditionalization of the approach to divorce, but this was not done for the sake of tradition, but with the higher aim of supporting social welfare and social justice, especially for women.[105]

It is a measure of the growing sophistication of postmodern Indian and Hindu law that we are now beginning to see an explicit welding together of

---

for regulating matrimonial norms for making of a well knit, healthy and not a disturbed and porous society'. Hence, 'irretrievable breakdown of marriage' in circumstances shown by this case, could not be applied.

[104] This case, together with *Chanderkala Trivedi v S. P. Trivedi* (1993) 4 SCC 232, is also discussed by Kusum (2000: 249–50), but in her analysis these cases are only considered important as evidence of the application of the breakdown principle. This is merely an assertion of modernist assumptions, there are deeper layers of analysis that need to be brought out.

[105] In cases where wives seek to abuse the legal procedures, as was also evident in *V. Bhagat v D. Bhagat* AIR 1994 SC 710, the courts will not tolerate abuse either.

Hindu principles and directives of India's Constitution. There is evidence that the judges have been tempted to bring the new constitutional dharma, namely the Fundamental Duties under Article 51-A into the picture of Hindu divorce law. In particular, Article 51-A(j), which refers to the fundamental duty of every citizen 'to strive towards excellence in all spheres of individual and collective activity so that the nation constantly rises to higher levels of endeavour and achievement', has been used to remind erring spouses of their most basic duties, for their own good as well as that of the nation.[106]

While the formal refusal to introduce the divorce ground of irretrievable breakdown confirms a notable reluctance to rush through legal reforms for the sake of modernity, the creative and suitably restrictive application of that principle by the Indian higher judiciary balances what is still widely seen as a deficiency in commitment to modernity. We have solid evidence that the law has moved beyond the boundaries of tradition and modernity and is beginning to explore the new frontiers and limits of postmodern legal regulation of divorce law for Hindus.

It is evident from the foregoing analysis that the scholarly debates on this subject have largely remained stuck in modernist assumptions and have been unable, mainly because of ideological blinkers, to perceive and assess significant new developments. It is evident that many judges have crossed the ideological divides and have freed their minds to focus on thinking about appropriateness.

The present debates about Hindu divorce law, more than the discussions in the other chapters of this Part II, have brought out that there is another dimension of legal analysis that needs to be highlighted. By pretending and assuming that there is such a thing as an official Hindu law, which comprises a certain range of rules, modernist scholarship has also constructed a coexistent, less than official or second-rate, unofficial Hindu law. But the latter is not fully recognized as part of the formal Hindu law, though of course it is a part of it.[107] More significantly as an omission of scholarship, the symbiotic interaction between these levels of laws has been ignored, and Chiba's 'legal postulates' have not been factored into the analysis either.

An interesting challenge for future research on Hindu divorce law will therefore be to examine the interaction, in social reality and in law, between the vast field of Hindu customary divorces, still a world of its own, and the formally codified and judge-made Hindu divorce law. Perhaps we can one day learn to see, no doubt based on many years of intense fieldwork of the kind

[106] In *Sunil Kumar v Usha* AIR 1994 MP 1, it was held at p. 4 that it is now a constitutional obligation to renounce practices derogatory to the dignity of women, which is also part of Art. 51-A.

[107] This seems remarkably similar to the technique among positivist lawyers to state only certain formal rules as 'the law', while not telling the reader that informal deviations from that rule may also be part of the legal system. A rich collection of such evidence from a number of jurisdictions is found in Bainham (1998).

that Weinberger-Thomas (1999) indicates as useful, that there is a limitless complexity before us in which nevertheless there are certain things that make general sense. We may find, then, that not only the highly educated judges of the Supreme Court, but also humble citizens of India in their panchayats and through other forms of application of *sadācāra* and assisted self-controlled order, have been partaking in the construction of a culture-specific and situation-sensitive Hindu divorce law that carries definite characteristics of postmodern justice-consciousness. In the vast field of Hindu divorce law, too, modernist assumptions and postmodern reality do not match, and much rethinking needs to be done.

12

Maintenance Law

The critical importance of this area of the law for Hindu women and children has only recently been recognized by modernist scholars and lawyers. It seems that feminist scholars, themselves often privileged members of an elite group, could afford to focus on ideology and reformist agenda, while paying little attention to the material circumstances of impoverished women.[1] In this regard, there has recently been a definite shift in the understanding of the problem as a whole.[2] Feminist and modernist writing is now centrally concerned with the property rights and financial entitlements of all women, manifested in trendy phrases like the 'feminisation of poverty' (Agnes 2000: 187), and there has been growing recognition of the special predicaments of poor women within the 'subaltern' category.

The underlying core problem for understanding Hindu maintenance law in its traditional, modern, and postmodern manifestations is that within an androcentric, patriarchal framework of reference, Hindu women have always had a number of definite rights to maintenance, but these have depended on male cooperation and willingness to share resources. While Hindu women had defined rights and entitlements in principle, men (and often other women) would, in social reality, try and restrict, or even deny the claims of individual women. Hindu tradition definitely did not divest women of rights in this respect; rather it placed definite obligations on men to take responsibility and to look after women.

Of course, that is precisely where the ideological problems of many modernists and feminists are rooted. It seems that property rights and entitlements to maintenance were not granted to Hindu women as individuals in their own right, but arose as a result of links with men, either in the joint family context,[3] or as the wife or female relative of a Hindu male. While expressing indignation

[1] Agarwal (1994) is widely treated as a landmark study on women's rights, focusing attention on female entitlements to property in various forms. The earlier work of Gulati (1981) seems underrated, perhaps because it focused only on 'little' women and is centred on Kerala.

[2] For example, S. Basu (2001) reports on fieldwork with three sets of women in Delhi and provides instructive discussions on the entire field of women's claims to property entitlements.

[3] This category is vast and may include women as a daughter, wife, widow, unmarried or divorced sister or aunt, grandmother, or even concubine.

about this, feminist authors and modernist scholarship have failed to disclose that most Hindu men face potentially the same predicaments of conflicts between joint family status and individuality, entitlement to shares in joint family property, and legitimate claims to 'self-acquired property' as owned absolutely by an individual. In this respect, too, Hindu men and women are inevitably in the same boat, competing not only for space but also for authority in determining who can claim certain privileges in the allocation of resources.[4]

While the critical importance of marital status is immediately evident in the present field of enquiry too, particularly if we focus on women's entitlements to post-divorce maintenance, the subject is potentially much wider than what the term 'maintenance' suggests. In particular, it will be relevant to consider to what extent a Hindu woman's claims to a share in joint family property, dowry, and marriage expenses may be linked with the core question of post-divorce maintenance. These interconnected issues become relevant because a former husband may point to the existing property or financial entitlements of his wife from others to exonerate himself from further liability. Modern Hindu law in its gender-focused enthusiasm (Sections 24 and 25 of the HMA) has even gone as far as granting Hindu men the right to be maintained by the wife after a divorce. It is also necessary to point out that, unlike Western welfare states, the Indian state will not financially support individuals, male or female, who suffer marital breakdown.[5]

The centrality of marriage in Hindu law and the emphasis on formal marriage solemnization (Chapter 8) carries important consequences. A woman's claim to maintenance after divorce needs to be supported by evidence of her relation to the man through whom, or from whose estate, she wishes to claim. Effective financial protection of women and children is sought to be achieved

[4] It would go too far here to embark on a detailed explanation of Hindu property law, but readers need to be aware of the coexistence of basically four types of entitlements to property in Hindu law, two each for men and women. 'Male' property among Hindus may be a nominal and fluctuating share of the male sharers (coparceners) in joint family property, which is normally not defined by metes and bounds until there is a partition of joint family assets, or it may be a form of 'self-acquired property' of an individual, which he may dispose of as he pleases. Differences between the major school traditions of Hindu joint family law may create some intermediate forms, details of which do not concern us here. Conceptually parallel to this, Hindu 'female' property is either some form of (often entirely undefined) entitlement to maintenance of a Hindu woman from the joint family, or it is a woman's absolute property, for which the term *strīdhanam* (women's wealth) has been known since classical times. Muslims are therefore wrong to claim that their legal system was the first to give women separate property rights; that argument is only correct in relation to Jewish and Christian women, but not for Hindus.

[5] Thus, there are also no 'welfare mothers' as in the USA, where the availability of state support for single mothers led, over time, to significant changes in family patterns, which are now seen as problematic. Indian judges are clearly not unaware of such developments.

by holding men, primarily husbands and fathers, responsible for the maintenance of female family members, both within marriage and after its termination. This particular social welfare approach is based on ancient principles and implies an explicit recognition of androcentricity in Hindu law. It builds the consequent concentration of economic power and control in the hands of men into an idealized protective framework for divorced women. As a result, the Hindu joint family and individual men within it are held morally responsible for satisfying various claims to maintenance by women.

Undoubtedly, in this scenario Hindu women remain to a large extent dependent on the goodwill of men. However, the suggestion that this is a defining feature of Hindu law ignores the fact that large-scale economic dependence of women on men is evidently a universal phenomenon. Bargaining over the sharing of resources occurs everywhere, and it would be quite wrong to assume that only Hindu women had limited or no say in this context. Shastri (1990: 171) emphasizes in this regard that the concept of maintenance is an aspect of relations between parties by blood or by marriage or sometimes otherwise. Thus, an individual woman's claim must always be situated and contextualized in her specific family circumstances. When Anand (1992: 173–4) highlights that a divorced woman is often worse off than a widow financially and may lose everything that earlier secured her maintenance in terms of food, clothing, and shelter, this merely confirms a universal predicament of women, not a defining feature of Hindu law. The insecure legal status of a female claimant may only become an issue when the man against whom such claims are made has died or disappeared. This is a further universal problem for women, which will be worse when judges are inconsistent or simply insufficiently alert to the demands of gender justice.[6]

The present chapter follows the familiar diachronical pattern, examining first the vast field of traditional Hindu laws on maintenance for divorced or abandoned wives, seeking to ascertain to what extent Hindu women were effectively protected within the traditional framework. Interestingly, the colonial legal system did intervene, albeit late and in a rather gentle manner, providing important support mechanisms to indigent Hindu wives, initially through criminal legal provisions and later by specific enactments. However, these legal measures only had a limited supportive effect and primarily protected women's entitlements during the marriage.

In the post-colonial period, the liberalizing reforms to Hindu divorce law necessitated some thinking about corresponding provisions on maintenance for divorced Hindu spouses, found in Sections 24 and 25 of the HMA. However, it soon became apparent that these protective mechanisms were not good enough to safeguard the financial interests and entitlements of divorced Hindu wives. Rather than introducing further reforms to Hindu law in this field, the modern Indian state demonstrated its concern for the financial predicaments

[6] The ill-judged case of *Surjit Kaur v Garja Singh* AIR 1994 SC 135, which concerned a Sikh widow, has already been discussed in earlier chapters.

of all Indian divorced wives by reformulating the criminal law provisions so as to include 'divorced wife' under the legal definition of 'wife' in Indian law, as found in Section 125 CrPC 1973.

While attention during the 1980s has been focused on more polemical matters, namely the maintenance of divorced Muslim wives, as we saw in the *Shah Bano* case and its confusing aftermath,[7] it has not been widely noticed that the activist, socially aware Indian judiciary has also restructured the Hindu maintenance law to give it a decidedly postmodern shape. The progression of this protective law for divorced Hindu wives during the last two decades, from an initial state of confusion and rather unsatisfactory regulation to a fairly settled and stable position in the official law, is not a haphazard, accidental development, but a skilfully planned strategy to maximize social welfare and well-being despite limited state resources. Behind a smokescreen of idealizing statements about stability of marriage and society lies, therefore, a hard-nosed fiscal policy which, in a country of over a billion people, has to remain focused on self-controlled ordering within society, not on charity from the coffers of the state. Given that they operate in a secular framework, Indian judges do not express rules regarding maintenance as elements of Hindu law or some other personal law, but phrase their decisions in terms of assistance to needy individuals, public interest and 'complete justice' in its new constitutional avatar.

The Traditional Protective Framework

The present chapter, too, must take account of two possible scenarios relating to divorce and maintenance, depending on whether custom or the formal Hindu law applies.[8] In the former case, the likely expectation is that the woman will remarry, and another man will become responsible for her, while application of the more traditional sacramental concepts of Hindu marriage may be matched with continuing liabilities for the husband and prohibitions on female remarriage.

In the more common context of customary divorce arrangements, the position of the ex-wife regarding maintenance will not normally become a

[7] *Mohd. Ahmed Khan v Shah Bano Begum* AIR 1985 SC 945. Following riots and other manifestations of Muslim protest after the case, the government (hurriedly, it seems, but rather well-planned) introduced the MWPRDA of 1986, which allegedly denied Muslim divorced wives maintenance from the husband after the traditional three months of the *iddat* period. In reality the 1986 Act has done the exact opposite, granting Muslim women the right to be maintained by the ex-husband till her death or remarriage, as confirmed by a large number of cases which scholars have ignored, starting with *Ali v Sufaira* 1988(2) KLT 94. The political use of this Act by modernist lobbies needs to be critiqued further. Even the most recent writing on this topic is deeply misleading and shows that scholars are all too easily led astray (Vatuk 2001).

[8] Some of the writing (e.g. Gupte 2001) does not take sufficient account of the presence of the customary realm.

matter for courts, but is just as crucial for the woman. Since customary Hindu divorce law is characterized by the absence of generally binding fixed rules, a multitude of flexible situation-specific arrangements occur. Depending on the age and fertility status of the woman, in most situations, the customary expectation among Hindus would be that the woman would remarry and that the former husband has nothing more to do with her. It is only logical that the responsibility for a woman's maintenance should shift to the new husband. Where this is not the case, the woman will either have to survive independently and support herself, or she may seek the support of her natal family, claiming her traditional rights to protection under Hindu joint family law.[9] Shastri (1990: 172) argues in this regard that Hindu women as wives, daughters-in-law, widows, or daughters had no substantial rights of maintenance, but they could claim family support. Disputes were decided in the light of basic requirements by the so-called *panchas* of the male-dominated society.

One traditional guiding principle in the customary Hindu system of divorce is, thus, that the ex-husband will have no further obligations towards his former wife after the end of the marriage. However, in cases of informal marital breakdown under classical Hindu law, where the sacramental tie is assumed to remain intact, the husband's liability for maintenance will probably also continue. In the context of her discussion of different types of abandoning or superseding a Hindu wife, Virdee (1972: 31) clearly shows that such a wife retained her socio-economic status as a Hindu wife. Unjust abandonment was punishable, and a man guilty of such an offence was threatened with rebirth as a barren woman (ibid.: 32). In the context of a discussion about divorce, Sharma (1989: 88) explicitly points out that there are huge differences between the traditional Hindu law and the customary Hindu system, in effect 'there were two sets of laws in existence: one, which was applicable to the members of the higher caste; second, a large body of customs and usages applicable to the members of the lower caste'. Sharma (1989: 88–9) then proceeds to explain that such customary protective mechanisms for women did exist. Where divorce was pronounced by the local body of elders, and a verdict of guilt passed, the guilty party was to pay a sum of money, fixed by the panchayat, to the other party. Often this equated to payment of the expenses of the original marriage. Sharma (1989: 89) also argues that no rules developed to afford explicit protection to wives and children. Poverty is given as one reason (ibid.. 90), but a more important practical consideration is probably the ease of remarriage and, despite poverty, the greater economic independence of the wife as a co-earner in lower status groups, rather than a dependent homemaker without her own income.

[9] Depending on circumstances, the natal family may actually find it quite useful to have an extra pair of hands, or another husband will be found for the woman to pass on the burden of her maintenance. To the extent that more women partake in paid employment, such traditional patterns of thinking are being modified today. For example, a woman might not agree to another marriage so that she can have control over her own earnings.

Evidently, however, there was no general rule in the customary systems to the effect that a husband remained liable for the maintenance of his ex-wife. This significant difference between the two methods of determining post-breakdown obligations needs to be highlighted here. For obvious social welfare reasons, the principle followed by the post-colonial Indian state law seems to favour the approach of the traditional *shastric* system, in which the husband's liabilities do not end unless the ex-wife were to marry another man. The current guiding principle in Hindu maintenance law for women is in effect that the former husband remains liable for the welfare of his ex-wife until her death or remarriage. The law perhaps assumes that there may not be another marriage for the woman, and thus expects the ex-husband to maintain a wife who is no longer his wife, thus also reasserting sacramental notions of marriage. It seems, though, that the more important concern is the socio-economic welfare of the divorced wife.[10]

Beyond this general principle, it has been virtually impossible to detect or devise any specific law in this field, since so much has always depended on individual circumstances.[11] In traditional contexts, providing food and shelter would have been as meaningful as it is for many women today.[12] Various modernist arguments have been advanced to give a Hindu wife an automatic share in the husband's property, but such bargaining from elite perspectives has been largely infructuous and ignores the needs of less privileged women. Traditional scholarship on Hindu law and women has assumed a little too easily that Hindu women, either as widows or divorcees, face enormous barriers of remarriage. While not suggesting that such barriers do not exist, I must reiterate here that it is a reality, now also documented in detailed fieldwork by one of my doctoral students,[13] that Hindus actively pursue remarriage of women to protect their financial interests and status. Fieldwork confirms that both men and women will use the relevant customs in an extremely flexible manner.

In this field of interrelated claims to certain statuses and entitlements, definitional clarity remains a significant problem. Sharma (1990: 4) remarks that maintenance is a very wide term that would include all the necessities of a person. Sharma (1990: 3) emphasizes that 'Hindu law never denied maintenance to any of the members of the joint family', so that every individual was covered

[10] Further research is needed on this point. I found no detailed discussion in the existing literature, but we know that notions of sacramental marriage underpin the continuing liability of Hindu husbands.

[11] This is confirmed by Gupte (2001: 155), who writes that '[n]o mathematical precision can be suggested or laid down for amount of maintenance'.

[12] May (2001: 281) emphasizes that such concerns are often deliberately ignored in human rights debates, but that Asian scholars are aware of such issues.

[13] Livia Sorrentino Holden (2003) conducted extensive fieldwork in Madhya Pradesh and is about to complete her doctoral thesis, *Seeking Equity Through Custom: Divorce and Remarriage on the Woman's Initiative in Hindu Law*, at SOAS in the University of London.

in some form. Aggarwal (1988: 3–12) discusses the subject of maintenance law under old Hindu law and says at p. 4 that the various *smṛti* texts gave much attention to this topic. This is unsurprising, given that maintenance is so closely linked to property law. Agnes (2000: 14) argues that within a patriarchal family structure 'women's right to property was constrained', while Aggarwal (1988: 3) claims that the benevolence of traditional Hindu rules on maintenance had deep roots:

> ... the law of maintenance was so devised by the Great Sages and *Rishis* that it was inconceivable if any person more especially a woman, would go altogether unprovided for. The daughter, the wife, the widow, the mother and daughter-in-law were the particular beneficiaries, who had the special protection for their right of maintenance. All this is not surprising because maintenance was regarded as a duty, a duty of a Hindu, which is owed to his dependent relations and by which both, the person and property, were bound.

Similarly, Reddy (1999: 56) places the topic firmly into a Hindu joint family context and notes:

> The head of the Hindu family is bound to maintain its members, their wives and their children .... The wives were entitled during their marital life .... Even the widows of the members of the family were entitled to maintenance from their son ... or from the other relatives .... Unchastity on the part of Hindu widows disentitles them to maintenance .... The quantum of maintenance depended upon the status of family, the conditions and necessities of the members, the age, habits, wants and class of life of the parties.

This gives a good overview of the complexity of the potential claims by women against the joint family. Sharma (1990: 76) also explains this well, adding a significant point about the potential liabilities of a purchaser of joint family property:[14]

> Since in the social structure of Hindu society the joint family system occupies an important place, the law of maintenance has a special significance in Hindu law. All members of a joint family, whatever be their status and whatever be their age, are entitled to maintenance. The Hindu law has all along recognised that a Hindu has a personal obligation to maintain certain near relations, such as, wife, children and aged parents. Hindu law also recognises that the one who takes another's property has an obligation to maintain [the] latter's dependants.

[14] While this goes too far here in terms of detail, it is useful to point out that such rules reflect ancient awareness that senior men or the joint family manager (*kartā*) might simply disregard the claims of dependants and virtually divest them of their claims through sale or transfer of the family's property.

Agnes (2000: 14) highlights the basic inalienability of joint Hindu family property as a central element of the traditional Hindu concepts. Since family property could not be easily disposed of by way of sale, gift or will, this protected the maintenance entitlements of all those individuals who were not part of the property-sharing agnatic group called 'coparcenary', and therefore also protected women and their entitlements, a point that Agnes (2000: 15) fails to highlight, while she is concerned to claim that women 'did not have even the notional right of joint ownership'.[15] The modernist argument here is that the exclusion of Hindu women from the coparcenary constitutes evidence of gender discrimination. Against this, traditional legal writing emphasizes that through marriage a Hindu wife acquired important entitlements to claims against the husband and his property, which equate to a property entitlement.[16]

Regarding the basic rules of joint Hindu family law, Desai (1998: 313–4) explains that a joint Hindu family consists of all persons lineally descended from a common ancestor, and includes their wives and unmarried daughters.[17] However, according to this author, a daughter ceases to be a member of her father's family on marriage and becomes a member of her husband's family. This statement reflects dominant north Indian patterns and could not be said to be a feature universally shared and accepted by all Hindus.[18] Diwan and Diwan (1990: vii–viii) suggest that originally there was no concept of self-acquired property in Hindu law and hence emphasize the joint family context and the role of the manager (*kartā*):

> Every member of the joint family has a right to maintenance against the joint family property .... It was the duty of the *karta* to see that all reasonable wants of the members were satisfied. If the *karta* failed to fulfil his duty, the members could enforce it by legal action.
>
> Even with the emergence of the concept of self-acquired property and the coparcener's right of partition, maintenance did not lose its importance. Rather, the concept of maintenance further grew and developed. So far the

[15] Gupte (2001: 155) goes as far as saying that the right to maintenance of a Hindu widow amounts to a charge on the property of the husband.

[16] When it comes to the rights of Hindu widows, at any rate, the Indian SC has clearly taken this protective position, as *V. Tulasamma v V. Sesha Reddi* AIR 1977 SC 1944, confirms.

[17] In addition, in the *Mitākṣarā* joint family system, three generations of ancestors are also an integral part of the Hindu joint family.

[18] There are various intermediary understandings of the place of the married woman. In matrilineal communities there are different considerations for why the daughter's links with her natal family are not completely severed. Diwan and Diwan (1990: 35) state that '[a]s soon as a daughter is married she forfeits her claim to maintenance', but there is an obligation to maintain a widowed daughter if she is unable to obtain maintenance from the husband's estate or family. On north Indian patterns and their implications in daily life, S. Basu (2001) reports many interesting details.

> right was available against certain properties now it became available against certain persons also.

Diwan and Diwan (1990: 17) similarly argue that, whatever the cost, ancient Hindu law has always recognized the right of maintenance of all male and female members of the joint family. The guiding principle is that '[m]aintenance of the members of the joint family is the necessary concomitant of the concept of joint family (ibid.: 22) and '[a]ll have to be maintained out of the joint family chest' (ibid.: 17). Diwan and Diwan (1990: 17–8) further explain that the ancient Hindu law distinguished legal and moral rights of maintenance. Significantly, these are also gender-based:

> All members of the family including the illegitimate sons have a legal right to be maintained out of the joint family funds, ... a widowed daughter, and even a widowed daughter-in-law had a moral right to be maintained .... If during his lifetime the father or father-in-law did not perform his moral duty, the widowed daughter or widowed daughter-in-law could not enforce her claim in a court of law. But on the death of the father or father-in-law the right could be enforced against those who inherited the property. The same was the position of the concubine.

Aggarwal (1988: 3) confirms that on the death of a male Hindu who had the moral obligation to pay maintenance, this would often be transformed into a legal obligation enforceable against the property left by the deceased. The underlying principle, that the heir of the deceased takes the estate not merely for his own benefit, but also for the spiritual benefit of the person whose property he inherited, reflects joint family ideology. Singh (1993: 222) reiterates that the social structure of Hindu society with its concepts of joint Hindu family relates closely to the traditional Hindu law of maintenance. The familiar image used is that 'Hindu sages in clear cut terms ruled that maintenance of certain members of the family was a personal obligation', with Manu cited as an authority.[19] Similarly, Diwan and Diwan (1990: viii) claim that the Hindu rules regarding maintenance were laid down by ancient law givers such as Manu,[20] to the effect that '[t]he aged parents, a virtuous wife and minor child must be maintained even by doing [a] hundred misdeeds'.

Diwan and Diwan (1990: ix) emphasize the dharmic duty to maintain dependants, but do so in terms that go well outside the Hindu framework of reference. In essence, they argue that the maintenance of a male Hindu's aged parents, minor children, and wife were considered to be the greatest duty: 'If he faithfully maintained them, the gates of heaven were wide open for him and he could attain salvation. A person who made gifts at the cost of maintenance of his family was condemned'. Such images of gates and heaven are

[19] The same verse is also cited by Aggarwal (1988: 3) as a basic principle.

[20] At this stage of our analysis, it should not be necessary to explain or reiterate why this approach is highly questionable.

oddly placed in a discussion of ancient Hindu principles.[21] We saw earlier that Diwan tended to overemphasize the role of salvation (*mokṣa*) for Hindus and took a monotheistic view of religion. In the present context too, Christian and Muslim conceptual influences are evident. Diwan and Diwan (1990: ix) also discuss the conceptual transition from moral to legal obligation to maintain family members, but do so by producing a sweeping historical and cross-cultural statement rather than a deeper analysis of Hindu law principles. They argue that '[d]uring the period of equity and natural law the moral duty of maintenance was turned into a legal duty, and we find that during the period of Justinian the reciprocal duty of maintenance between the parent and the child was firmly established and the presence or absence of the agnatic tie was immaterial.[22] With particular reference to women, Diwan and Diwan (1990: 24–7) focused first of all on wives and widows, confirming that it is in principle unanimously agreed in the *shastric* literature that wives and widows of coparceners in a Hindu joint family have the right of maintenance from joint family funds. There will be more to say on the position of widowed daughters-in-law later. Regarding the rights of daughters, Diwan and Diwan (1990: 27–8) state categorically and with several examples that '[a]ll unmarried daughters in the family, are entitled to maintenance out of the joint family funds'.

Sharma (1990: 4) summarizes the traditional position on the daughter's right to maintenance from joint family funds as long as she remains unmarried. After marriage, in case she became a widow or was abandoned by her husband, she could again claim maintenance from her father. In principle, thus, a Hindu woman in difficulty could go back to her natal family and claim support from its resources.[23] However, such a general rule might tempt the husband's family to deny an ex-wife any form of support and to send her back to her parents or brothers, thus endangering the security and financial support flowing from marriage, which the traditional Hindu system supposedly provided to women, as well as challenging the sanctity of Hindu marriage. It appears that there is much evidence of a multilayered debate about such issues in the traditional context.

According to Sharma (1990: 4), under ancient Hindu law the persons who could claim maintenance could be put into two groups. The first group would be those 'whose claim of maintenance arose by virtue solely of relationship with, and irrespective of the possession of property by the person against whom the claim was to be exercised'. These would be all female family members, but also certain male members who were not included in the coparcenary. This seems to suggest that the responsibility for maintaining a Hindu woman remains in principle (at least partly) with her natal family and is thus not entirely

[21] They are also found in Diwan and Diwan (1990: 38).

[22] The authors seem heavily influenced by the historical determinism of Sir Henry Maine (1861) and the sequence of legal development as he imagined it.

[23] Sharma (1990: 4) also briefly discusses the position of the Hindu mother, which does not centrally concern us here.

transferred to the husband's family, of which the north Indian Hindu wife was supposed to become an integral part, as cited above. This means that patrilocal residence patterns for newly married Hindu spouses do not necessarily imply that the wife is forever removed from her natal family.[24] It is evident that the literature on this important point of detail is not clear, but perhaps it is simply wrong to expect universal agreement on such a crucial economic matter, given the many different types of family arrangement that might need to be made.

However, this particular issue becomes rather central to the present chapter and its focus on the right to maintenance of divorced Hindu wives. To reiterate, the key question is who should be responsible for the maintenance of divorced Hindu wives, the husband's family or the natal family? While the rights of Hindu widows under Section 14 of the 1956 HSA have been more or less securely settled,[25] concern of law reformers in India for the maintenance of divorced wives became the major focus of responsibility. More clearly than in the case of widows, divorced wives would be expected to leave the husband's joint family and they would then either need to establish an independent residence or might return to the protective fold of their natal family. While many modernist authors seem to work with misguided assumptions of autonomous individuality also in this field, the traditional framework of reference involved primarily the protective joint family context. In this regard, Diwan and Diwan (1990: 24–5) explain that 'the widow of a coparcener is entitled to maintenance out of joint family funds, even if she has been deserted by her husband, or she had been living separately from him without any justifiable cause'.

Here again, the general principle of joint family liability for the maintenance of a potentially indigent woman is applied. A Hindu widow can rely on an entitlement that relates back to the deceased husband. In that sense, a dead Hindu husband remains liable for the maintenance of his surviving widow, a reflection of the sacramental idea of Hindu marriage, which creates binding ties and obligations not only for Hindu women, but evidently also for their men. We still need to examine here, however, how traditional Hindu law viewed the liability of the husband if the spouses were to divorce or separate. This is not a straightforward enterprise, because most scholars, as we saw in Chapter 11 earlier, assume that divorce did not exist or was not permitted under traditional Hindu law.

Diwan and Diwan (1990: 39) state that maintenance of the wife 'is a personal obligation of the husband which attaches to the husband the moment he weds her', and arises out of the status of the marriage.[26] Similarly, Sharma (1990:

[24] The flexibility of actual arrangements and their personalized nature is emphasised by S. Basu (2001).

[25] The leading case on Hindu widows' rights to separate property, *V. Tulasamma v V. Sesha Reddi* AIR 1977 SC 1944, established that a Hindu widow has a 'pre-existing right'.

[26] Diwan and Diwan (1990: 39) add that 'where a custom requires that an immature wife should live with her parents, he still had an obligation to maintain her. Her parents maintained her only out of affection'.

77) writes that Hindu law imposed a personal obligation on the husband to maintain an obedient and faithful wife. Aggarwal (1988: 8) says that the wife is the central figure of the law of maintenance. The obligation to maintain a wife was personal in character and arose directly from the marital relationship (Gupte 2001: 153). Refusal to maintain a wife was considered to be an offence in the traditional law, as we saw.[27] Aggarwal (1988: 9) points out the corresponding duty of the Hindu wife 'to remain faithful and obedient to her husband, even beyond death'. The resultant claim to be maintained is emphasized by Aggarwal (1988: 10–1). It was not an empty formality exercised as a matter of concession, indulgence, or generosity, but a valuable spiritual and moral right, which flowed from the spiritual and temporal relationship of husband and wife. Shastri (1990: 171–2) reinforces this protective framework, which exists not only for wives:

> The establishment of such a relation, *ipso-facto*, provides a right to the wife to have maintenance from her husband, right to the daughter-in-law to have maintenance from her father-in-law in case of inability of the husband to maintain her and a right to the widow to have maintenance from the property of her husband or from those persons who are managing the affairs of the property of her husband.

This particular ground rule, which relates first of all to maintenance during the marriage, not after it, is only to be expected. Significantly, it reflects the androcentric orientation of Hindu law and the gendered allocation of duties within a Hindu marriage, giving women claims against men. The critical question is, however, what the extent of the Hindu husband's obligations would be in the case of breakdown of the marital relationship or even formal divorce. Here we are beginning to face again the conceptual muddles over the alleged unavailability of divorce for Hindus. The initial scholarly reaction would be that this topic is irrelevant since Hindu wives were not supposed to be divorced, which Chapter 11 earlier showed to be a myth, given the prominence of customary patterns of divorce among Hindus.

Sharma (1989: 83) writes that under the old Hindu law, the husband's liability to maintain the wife was absolute and personal, while the wife's first duty was to submit herself to his authority and to 'remain under his roof and protection'. Therefore, a Hindu wife is not entitled to separate residence and maintenance except for a justified cause. Sharma (id.) asserts that '[s]ince there was no divorce under the old Hindu Law, the law provided the *tyaga* (desertion or more appropriately, separation) of another under certain circumstances'. Kapadia (1972: 182) reports in the context of polygamy that according to

[27] Other individuals are less explicitly protected by family relationships, but they are also not left to fend for themselves. Aggarwal (1988: 4) emphasizes that a Hindu male was under no legal obligation to maintain his sister and stepmother. However, if such a male then inherited property from his father, he became liable to maintain such women.

Kautilya a second marriage was permissible when the first wife failed to bear a male child within eight to twelve years of marriage. Should the husband violate this rule, he shall give the wife various sums,[28] and also pay a fine to the government.

Sharma (1989: 83–4) similarly shows that Hindu wives were protected against desertion by unscrupulous husbands. An abandoned faultless wife was entitled to maintenance and the husband was ordered to take her back. In case of non-compliance, as a penalty, the husband was supposed to give a third of his property to the woman. However, when a husband was so poor that such a decision would cause hardship, he should at least provide the wife proper maintenance. Even an adulterous wife was to be maintained, but was given only minimal support in the form of a 'starving maintenance' (Derrett 1963c: 171). A wife living apart from her husband for no improper purpose might at any time return and claim to be maintained by him. Her right was only temporarily suspended while she was living apart from him. If she subsequently came back and offered to live with the husband, his refusal to take her back entitled her to demand separate maintenance. Such general rules appear to be designed to impress on both spouses that they should try and make a success of their marriage.

Agnes (2000: 15) notes that in the traditional system, the Hindu husband was bound to maintain the wife despite all her faults, including quarrelsome nature, neglect of the household, barrenness, and even adultery. The scale at which she had to be maintained would vary depending on the severity of her faults. The Hindu husband could marry again, but he was under a legal obligation to continue to maintain the first wife. Agnes (id.) also claims that in addition, the wife was entitled to 'supersession fee' and an equal share of the property, notably more than the third indicated by other authors.[29] Aggarwal (1988: 5) says that there was no hard and fast rule to determine the amount of maintenance. Refusal to maintain was considered an offence under Hindu law (ibid.: 6) and '[a]bandoning mother, father, wife or son, for no fault of their own, was punishable by the King', the obvious policy aim being to avoid immorality and destitution. With reference to the *Āpastambadharmasūtra*, Olivelle (2000: 67) points out in the context of penances that a Hindu husband who unjustly abandoned his wife has to show public repentance. Such rules, whatever their precise standing as 'laws', reflect a progressive social environment in which women are sought to be protected from destitution. Such texts clearly confirm that ancient social welfare measures among Hindus put the onus on males and on joint family property to protect women from destitution.

[28] The author mentions various forms of property, including *strīdhanam* and an adequate monetary compensation.

[29] She also mentions that Hindu women had the right to claim marriage expenses from the joint property in their natal home.

Still within the classical framework of reference, as indicated, there is hardly any comment on what should happen to divorced Hindu wives in terms of maintenance, given that divorce itself was considered anathema.[30] Sharma (1990: 25–47) discusses Hindu concepts of women's property in some detail and claims, at p.26, that the Hindu woman's inferior position persisted throughout the ages not merely in family and society, but also with regard to property rights.[31] The supposedly inferior and dependent position of women was linked to their alleged incompetence to perform solemn sacrifices and to read the Vedas. Thus, because of her dependent status, a Hindu woman's right to property was also treated with disfavour, 'as there was general reluctance displayed by the ancient Rishis or sages to allow females to hold property' (id.). Such assertions need to be severely interrogated, because they appear one-sided and dogmatic. Sharma is content to cite a large number of *smṛti* texts to make the point that women were systematically denied any role in sacrifices and in property ownership, but does not analyse her material further. This remains a myopic representation of a very complex reality.

Many writers comment on the concept of women's property or *strīdhanam* in Hindu law. Sharma (1990: 2) notes that classical Hindu law did not take the concept of the unity of husband and wife as far as traditional English law, in which the personality of the wife merged totally in that of the husband, and whatever property the wife held became that of the husband, clearly disadvantaging women in terms of property rights.[32] As Sharma (id.) highlights, 'amongst the Hindus, the wife was an equal and essential participator in all religious and secular ceremonies which a house-holder was required to perform .... She was the full owner of her stridhan'.[33]

However, Sharma (1990: 8) also notes that there was a general deterioration of female status, which 'started with Manu, the law-giver', who equated women with slaves and said that a woman should never be independent. This is one of the favourite slogans that feminist scholarship about Hindu law has been citing ad nauseam. It must suffice here to assert three points against such blind assumptions, which are not based on any rigorous scholarly methodology but ideological selectivity. First, verses of this kind represent only one perspective, while there are clearly several other views on the subject, often found elsewhere in the very same shastric text. It smacks of scholarly politicking that anti-women statements in the Sanskrit literature are simply interpreted

[30] Gupte (2001: 7) ignores customary Hindu divorces and thus misrepresents the legal position by claiming that divorce or dissolution of the marriage 'were totally alien to the Hindu Law'.

[31] On the position regarding supersession of a wife and the husband's obligations towards such a woman, see Sharma (1994: 24–5).

[32] Agnes (2000: 16–7) mentions Sir Henry Maine's awareness that Hindus had developed concepts of female property law before the Romans.

[33] This clearly contradicts the statements cited above regarding the prohibitions on women acting in a ritual capacity.

by modernist scholars as solid evidence of Hindu misogyny and systematic gender discrimination, while pro-women sentiments expressed in the very same texts are dismissed off-hand as romanticizing idealism and *hindutva*-style attempts to present Hindu tradition in a positive light.

Second, therefore, we must again re-examine our understanding of whether these texts are actually binding legal rules, or merely private opinion.[34] Third, even statements that seem to indicate quite clearly the dependence of women on men at all times can—and in my view must—be read and interpreted as meaning, in social reality, that Hindu men were traditionally under strict and permanent obligations to protect and maintain the women in their family. This being the basic principle, all the rest is of necessity a matter of *sadācāra*, sorting out the most appropriate practical methods in the given circumstances of any case. The links with concepts of property law are emphasized by Sharma (1990: 3):

> The importance of maintenance in Hindu law, particularly of the Hindu females, can be understood only in the context that the Hindu female has very limited right to hold any property. Although Hindus recognised the concept of 'stridhana' [the] quantum of property was minimal. Most of the 'Stridhana' that she acquired and held were gifts made to her at the time of her marriage and occasionally thereafter.

The law on *strīdhanam* is said to be 'the least settled branch of Hindu law' (Sharma 1990: 9) and an examination of the textual evidence would appear to suggest that a narrow definition of *strīdhanam* prevailed (id.):

> ... as a rule it is only gifts obtained by a woman from her relations and her ornaments and apparel that constitutes her stridhana and only those gifts from strangers which are given to her before the nuptial fire and according to some sages, presents made at the bridal procession .... But neither gifts received from strangers at any other time nor her acquisition by mechanical arts would constitute her stridhana.

Agnes (2000: 15) typically portrays the rules on *strīdhanam* as though they had been laid down by ancient lawgivers:

> Continuing the tradition set by Gautama, Manu laid down six forms of stridhana consisting of gifts by relatives on various occasions: (i) gifts before the nuptial fire ...; (ii) gifts during bridal procession, while the bride is being led from her natal residence to her husband's house ...; (iii) gifts of love from father-in-law and mother-in-law ... and gifts made at the time of obeisance at the feet of elders ...; (iv) gifts made by father; (v) gifts made by mother; and (vi) gifts made by brother. A dictate of Manu which empowered

[34] Professor Werner Knobl at Kyoto University, a specialist of Vedic Sanskrit, suggested in a helpful conversation that scholars of any discipline need to be more alert about the distinction between Sanskrit texts as 'descriptive' or 'prescriptive'. This is undoubtedly a most relevant point for Hindu lawyers.

> a righteous king to punish as thieves, the relatives, who appropriated the property of a woman, is quoted in all the later smritis with approval.

Agnes (2000: 16) also mentions that later texts laid great emphasis on this topic and discussed it in detail. Sharma (1990: 14—7) examines *strīdhanam* according to medieval texts and concludes that two interpretations developed, the technical and the non-technical, which led to doubts and ultimately the judicial creation in Anglo-Hindu law of the concept of property held by a Hindu woman during her lifetime, or the 'limited estate'. Specifically on *strīdhanam*, Agnes (2000: 17) shows that the *Mitākṣarā* in the twelfth century expanded the category of women's property and 'every category of property was brought under the scope of stridhana and the woman was granted exclusive ownership over it'. The *Dāyabhāga* as dominant tradition in Bengal and parts of Assam allotted women as widows, daughters, and mothers a defined share in the family property (id.). S. Basu (2001: 75) notes that daughters in this system can acquire far larger portions of property than elsewhere in India.[35]

In the traditional Hindu system, thus, a woman had not only certain limited rights to property ownership in a personal capacity, but in addition had several concurrent claims to maintenance against her own and the husband's family. Even though divorce was not supposed to exist, it is evident from the literature as a whole that it occurred on a large scale within the customary system, which tended to exonerate the ex-husband by expecting the woman to seek protection in another marital arrangement or her natal family. However, in the formal Hindu law, the strength of the sacramental concepts of marriage protected the Hindu wife (and also the widow) by placing an obligation on the husband or those who took his property after his death to maintain the woman.

Given the limited extent of individual property rights for Hindu men as well as women, a finding that traditional Hindu women were dependent chattels is not reflective of the real situation within the classical system. Indeed, Agnes (2000: 203–4) confirms in her conclusions:

> While examining the patriarchy located within the parameters of Indian feudalism of the smriti and post-smriti period, it is evident that despite the negative dictates, there were certain protective measures built into laws and customs, which granted women certain significant rights over property. While these rights do not meet the modern concept of equality, they were governed by a notion of equity.

In principle, thus, Hindu women's entitlements to financial support and limited property rights existed and were protected within the traditional patriarchal framework. This operated on the basis of self-controlled ordering, probably

[35] Diwan and Diwan (1990: 31) state that there is no difference between the two schools regarding the liability of those who succeed to a person's estate to maintain the dependants of the deceased and that this aspect of the law is now covered under Sections 21 and 22 of the HAMA.

with minimal interference from the state. In practice, of course, as indicated earlier, individual women might not be able to claim their due entitlements against competing individuals, who might be male or female.

THE LULL OF THE BRITISH PERIOD

With regard to maintenance law, the colonial period represents a remarkable lull in reformist and modernist energies.[36] The financial arrangements between Hindu spouses in various situations were not a subject that the colonial rulers would want to be involved with. These were matters of private law, best left alone within the framework of the 1772 Declaration by Warren Hastings that virtually guaranteed continuation of the Hindu personal law.[37]

Vijay Sharma (1994: 235) writes that during the British period, the prevalent judicial view became that under Hindu law, maintenance of a wife by her husband was a matter of personal obligation. It was understood that this permanent, continuous obligation arose from the marital relationship itself, irrespective of whether the husband possessed any property or not. However, there were also certain limitations on the wife's right, relating to obedience, as seen in the previous section.

Sharma (1990: 17–25) comments on the legal position of *strīdhanam* during the British colonial era, showing that the *Mitākṣarā* interpreted the term liberally and included every kind of woman's property, while the *Dāyabhāga* restricted this concept to property over which a woman had absolute power of disposal. This was a most difficult subject for the British judges. In the light of their own cultural background and experience, the judges veered towards a restrictive interpretation of Hindu women's right to property. Sharma (1990: 85) clearly indicates that 'the English judges could not believe that the Hindus had been so advanced in the olden days that they gave absolute right over property to their women ... whereas in England ... the husband was the sole owner of all the property'. This observation helps to explain why there is so little to say about this particular period. The English system of marriage during colonial times would hardly have brought any advantage for a Hindu wife, who might be envisaged as chained to a sacramental marriage, but at least she had her own legal personality and rights to own property.[38] As Sharma (1989: 360–1) highlights, in England under common law, and until the Married

[36] Gupte (2001: 5) makes the general observation that '[d]uring the British rule the progress of Hindu Law was stalled purely for political considerations. The efforts for changes in personal law were never positively encouraged and the steps taken in that direction were slow, halting, and reluctant'.

[37] However, the work of Pamela Price (1979; 1989) and other historians of colonialism shows that family arrangements among ruling families were perceived as having a public dimension.

[38] Such observations are also reiterated and discussed by Chandra (1998: 4–6).

Women's Property Act of 1870, a married woman lost her legal existence and her rights to her own property by the fact of marriage.[39]

Sharma (1990: 4–5) makes the more general point that through their application of Justice, Equity and Good Conscience,[40] the courts in British India imported some English concepts on the subject and gave legal recognition to the moral obligation of husbands to maintain their wives. This reflects a formalization of Hindu law through Anglo-Hindu case law and indicates that awareness of the legal, rather than purely moral, nature of certain rights for Hindu women was growing.

While earlier traditional Hindu law and Anglo-Hindu law had focused on the widow and her rights, more legal attention was gradually given to the economic protection of the Hindu wife, even within marriage. This particular protective framework, it seems, was first developed within the general criminal law, seeking to force men to fulfil their obligations in terms of maintenance and support for family members, particularly wives and children. From a traditional Hindu law perspective, one can read this as an official reminder that certain customary obligations have to be fulfilled, a form of 'assisted self-controlled order' (see Chapter 3). The relevant provision in this regard is Section 488 of the CrPC of 1898. This Act belongs to the sphere of the general law and thus pertains to all communities.[41] The protective provision is found in Section 488(1):

> 488. Order for maintenance of wives and children.-
> (1) If any person having sufficient means neglects or refuses to maintain his wife or his legitimate or illegitimate child unable to maintain itself, a Magistrate of the First Class may, upon proof of such neglect or refusal, order such person to make a monthly allowance for the maintenance of his wife or such child, at such monthly rate, not exceeding five hundred rupees in the whole, as such Magistrate thinks fit, and to pay the same to such persons as the Magistrate from time to time directs.

Various provisos under this section allowed a wife, including a wife whose husband had taken another wife or wives, to refuse cohabitation with the husband and yet to claim maintenance from him. There is much evidence that this particular protective provision was challenged and bypassed particularly by

[39] Sharma (1989: 361) shows that equity provided some relief to such wives under the English system.

[40] This arises as a gap-filler, when it is presumed that there is no law that governs the matter, and the judges thus have to decide in accordance with general principles of fairness and justice. On this concept see in particular Derrett (1978d), who shows that application of this technique resulted in the importation of much Roman law into the Anglo-Indian system. This, too, could not be conducive to the protection of Hindu women's rights.

[41] Derrett (1963c: 169) saw this provision as beyond the scope of his study, presumably because it was not a matter of Hindu law, but of general law.

Muslim men, who might simply respond to a wife's claim for maintenance under Section 488 CrPC by divorcing her through an instant *talaq*.[42] Authors seem unaware that many Hindu husbands would have had a similar option within the large sphere of customary law. The practical effect would be that Hindu wives, too, would hesitate to litigate over financial entitlements, preferring instead to negotiate their claims informally. As a result, we do not seem to know how effective this particular legal provision was for Hindu wives in earlier times.[43] Aggarwal (1988: 11) indicates that the rights of the Hindu wife were gradually starting to attract more attention of the legislature, with an initial focus on the rights of widows rather than divorced wives. In particular, the Hindu Women's Right to Property Act, 1937 was introduced to confer upon the Hindu widow a right of succession in respect of non-agricultural property. But still the right of maintenance was held as subsisting.[44]

Agnes (2000: 206) claims that during the nationalistic struggle, there were certain attempts to protect women's rights, but this legal intervention brought only marginal respite. The primary aim of the Hindu Women's Right to Property Act, 1937 was to restore property rights 'subverted through the legal precedents set by the Privy Council'.[45] In other words, because the PC had disregarded and defined away the traditional rights of a Hindu widow after the death of her husband, legislation was needed to rectify the position. Gupte (2001: 154) confirms that the traditional shastric law received statutory recognition through the 1937 Act. By creating the concept of the 'limited estate', it sought to strengthen the claims of widowed Hindu women. Pujari and Kaushik (1994, III: 284) show that the 1937 Act made the widow less dependent financially during her lifetime, but stopped short of giving her full property rights, since this was only a life estate.

In Section 3(2) of the Act, a Hindu widow was given the same interest in the joint family property as the deceased husband had held prior to his death. In Section 3(3), it was provided that '[a]ny interest devolving on a Hindu widow under the provisions of this section shall be the limited interest known as a Hindu woman's estate, provided however that she shall have the same right of claiming partition as a male owner'. Thus, a widowed Hindu woman was not made a full-fledged coparcener in the husband's joint family, but at least during her lifetime, her legal position as an individual entitled to enjoy a share of

[42] For details see Pearl and Menski (1998: 203–4) and Mahmood (1986: 82–3).

[43] Fieldwork-based evidence from Delhi of how Indian women today handle such problems is provided in the excellent study by S. Basu (2001).

[44] Diwan and Diwan (1990: 34) refer to an old controversy, resolved by the PC in *Prithee Singh v Rani Raj Koer* (1873) 12 BomLR 238 (PC), over whether a Hindu widow was entitled to maintenance only if she continued to live with the husband's family. It was held that she was entitled to such maintenance unless guilty of unchastity or disreputable actions.

[45] The text of this Act is found in Derrett (1963c: 626–28). For some details, see also Diwan and Diwan (1990: 27).

the joint family assets was firmly secured and supported by the formal legal system.[46]

Aggarwal (1988: 11) further reports that specifically the Hindu woman's right to maintenance received statutory recognition when the entire law on the subject was consolidated and codified by the Hindu Married Women's Right to Separate Residence and Maintenance Act, 1946.[47] This Act, as a remedial measure, was conceived specifically for the benefit of married Hindu women who suffered from several disadvantages under the earlier law.[48] Under this Act, one of the grounds for a Hindu wife to ask for separate residence and maintenance from her husband was if the husband had married again, or kept a concubine in the house or habitually resided with a concubine. Sharma (1989: 85–6) discusses this problem for a Hindu wife in the traditional system and argues that the 1946 Act liberalized the law in favour of married women. While several authors suggest that the 1946 Act focused on the Hindu wife's right to separate maintenance, particularly where the husband had taken another wife, remedies are provided also in several other situations, which are left quite open-ended.[49] It is evident that the 1946 Act sought to assist Hindu wives in financial terms, while retaining the marital tie itself. The substantive provisions are found in Section 2:

> 2. Grounds for claiming separate residence and maintenance.-
> Notwithstanding any custom or law to the contrary, a Hindu married woman shall be entitled to separate residence and maintenance from her husband on one or more of the following grounds, namely,-
> (1) if he is suffering from any loathsome disease not contracted from her;
> (2) if he is guilty of such cruelty towards her as renders it unsafe or undesirable for her to live with him;

[46] For some details on the law and relevant cases see Derrett (1963c: 253–7). On the consequences for women as managers, see ibid.: 260–1.

[47] This is Act 19 of 1946, which came into force on 23 April 1946. The full text is found in Derrett (1963c: 629–30). The Act is also discussed by Sharma (1990: 5). It was superseded in India by certain provisions of the HSA and the HAMA of 1956. Gupte (2001: 154) argues that there was a clear-cut progression from the 1937 Act to the 1946 Act, and beyond that to the reforms of 1956. Details of the law are discussed in Diwan and Diwan (1990: 40–8).

[48] In Chapter 10 earlier, in the context of polygamy, Derrett (1978a: 11) was cited to the effect that women's opposition to polygamous arrangements needed to be strengthened. It was not acceptable that they should have to endure the husband's polygamy as well as suffer financial disadvantage.

[49] It is interesting to note that this set of provisions, particularly the last one, looks very similar to the grounds offered to Muslim wives in the Dissolution of Muslim Marriages Act of 1939. This Act sought to support the claims of Muslim wives for divorce a few years before the 1946 Act was passed. Significantly, the 1939 Act made no specific provisions for post-divorce maintenance and only concentrated on grounds for divorce. For other agenda related to this enactment, as well as the text of the Act itself, see Pearl and Menski (1998: 301–13).

(3) if he is guilty of desertion, that is to say, of abandoning her without her consent and against her wish;
(4) if he marries again;
(5) if he ceases to be a Hindu by conversion to another religion;
(6) if he keeps a concubine in the house or habitually resides with a concubine;
(7) for any other justifiable cause;
Provided that a Hindu married woman shall not be entitled to separate residence and maintenance from her husband if she is unchaste or ceases to be a Hindu by change to another religion or fails without sufficient cause to comply with a decree of a competent Court for the restitution of conjugal rights.

In addition, regarding the amount of maintenance, Section 3 of the 1946 Act provides that the court shall determine the amount to be paid by the husband to the wife, 'and in doing so shall have regard to the social standing of the parties and the extent of the husband's means'. This clearly leaves the quantum of any maintenance to be decided from case to case. Derrett (1963c: 173) indicates that '[t]here was a difference of opinion whether that Act declared the existing law or was innovative, but this is now of academic interest only as the Act of 1956 totally supersedes it in India'. One may ask, though, whether this Act was an attempt to test the waters for a fuller reform of Hindu matrimonial law. The only point that seems to be raised in opposition to the 1946 Act is that it encouraged Hindu men to bring suits for restitution of conjugal rights to defeat a wife's claim for separate maintenance, as noted by many scholars.[50]

Maintenance Law in Modern India

The past few decades have seen a virtual explosion of interest and legal cases in this field. All property-related questions of Hindu matrimonial law now have a much higher profile than they had when Professor Derrett was writing his major studies on Hindu law.[51] In recent scholarship, detailed legal analysis seems to have been complicated by the fact that maintenance law can be found both under the secular provisions of the CrPC, now of 1973 rather than 1898, and the modern Hindu law as embodied in various provisions of the HMA 1955, and the HAMA and HSA of 1956. In addition, for Indian law as a whole and with significant distraction effects for a highly politicized range of debates over legal uniformity, in particular, the MWPRDA of 1986 has entered the picture. While this Act is not directly relevant here, given that it concerns only Muslim wives in India, it will become evident in the present analysis that the provisions of this particular Act are really no different from the general law,

[50] For details see in particular Chandra (1998), Agnes (2000), and Kusum (2000: 239–42).

[51] Derrett (1963c: 244–492) focused in detail on the complex areas of joint family and succession law.

and must be seen in the wider perspective of the emergence of postmodern Indian laws on the maintenance of divorced wives.

Modernist Arguments for Law Reform

Much of the modernist writing remains critical of the allocation of gender roles among Hindus in relation to maintenance, and many authors seem to imply that Hindu marriage as the central social institution is nothing but an exploitative system that disadvantages women. A large collection of such statements could be provided here, but the arguments would soon become repetitive. For example, Sharma (1990: 1–2) highlights the gender inequality in this field:

> With the passage of time and the advancing march of the civilization people began to recognise that it was somewhat inequitable that the husband should be at liberty to pick all plums from the tree of marriage and the wife should be left only with stones. The legislature accordingly proceeded to enact a number of measures with the express object of emancipating married women from the liabilities which the Hindu law attached to them with the object of enlarging their rights.

Sharma (1990: 47–51) discusses in some detail the debates in the Hindu Law Committee around the time of independence, emphasizing the continuous agitation by Hindu women for enlargement of their rights: 'It had become necessary to set up a new social order where the women should be given a place of honour and equality with their male counterparts in every other respect' (ibid.: 51). Such vague statements do not specify the exact nature of women's expectations, although it seems that the focus is on equal property rights. At the same time, authors cannot help noting that the traditional Hindu law supported and protected the claims of women in various ways.

Modernist critics tend to be unwilling to admit this. Anand (1992: 174) notes that the only redeeming feature of male domination is that men are bound to maintain their wives and children. Sharma (1990: 7) argues that, on the whole, the codified Hindu law is a remarkable experiment of blending the old with the new, although there is further room for improvement. Singh (1993: 222) suggests that the Hindu law relating to maintenance has followed a movement towards equality of obligation, reflected in the Indian Constitution.[52] In typical modernist fashion, Aggarwal (1988: 11–12) writes that the post-colonial law even went as far as abolishing gender distinctions among Hindus:

> After the attainment of Independence, the entire perspective changed, the nature of old human values assumed a new complexion and the need for emancipation of womanhood from feudal bondage became all the more imperative .... In pursuance to these social pressures it was necessary to set up a new social order ....

[52] Gupte (2001: 153) observes that in the classical Hindu law, there was no reciprocal obligation of the Hindu wife to maintain the husband, while Anand (1992: 174) notes that modern Hindu law made women liable to maintain men in certain circumstances.

Aggarwal (1988: 12) claims that the HSA of 1956 fulfilled the need of the hour and was widely acclaimed by the people, because now the Hindu wife was no longer left to the mercy of the husband. This is an emotionally charged way of saying that the traditional moral obligations of the Hindu husband and other males had now been turned into legal obligations. To what extent this really protected women is quite a different matter.[53] The official law was certainly weighted in favour of women, thus educating society towards reconsidering women's entitlements. Familiar modernist thinking about the progression from custom to law and the need for codification of legal rules are apparent features in such discussions, even if not explicitly mentioned. Reformers also clearly looked to English law, as Sharma (1989: 65–82) confirms.[54]

Singh (1989: 86) argues that the obligation of the Hindu husband to maintain his wife arises not out of any manifest or implied contract, but from the status of the marriage itself.[55] Instead of making such explicitly pro-women rules work for the benefit of more women, modernists have engaged in politicized challenges to the institution of marriage itself as a form of gendered oppression. In this way, the existence of limited rights of the Hindu wife has become a favourite argument among modernists for demanding further reforms, buttressing claims that there needs to be total equality, demanding a transition from status to contract in the process of modernization.[56] However, traditional Hindu marriages clearly incorporate contractual elements, which are even expressed ritually during the solemnization of the marriage (Chapter 8). Indeed, in the context of his discussions about maintenance, Aggarwal (1988: 248) considers the conceptual background of Hindu marriage and detects not only sacramental but also contractual elements:

> ... marriage is considered to be a sacred union between the man and woman having pious duties and obligations towards each other. The persons who choose to enter the sacred bonds of marriage are obliged to conduct themselves to one another so that they fulfil the vows and promises which they have made to each other at the time of marriage. Heaven itself is made a party to the contract of marriage and the consent of individuals pledged to each other is ratified and consecrated by a vow to God.[57]

[53] For example, in *Dinkar Bandhu Deshmukh v State* AIR 1970 Bom 438, it transpires that a Hindu widow who insisted on farming some of the agricultural land of the husband's joint family was killed, together with her helpers.

[54] Sharma (1989: 83–93) discusses Hindu law principles of maintenance.

[55] This argument is supported by Gupte (2001: 153). Singh (1989: 86) also highlights that the right to maintenance forms a part of the personal law and therefore is not uniform.

[56] The ideas of Sir Henry Maine (1861) remain evidently influential through such assumptions.

[57] Again, here is a significant theistic slant, as though all Hindus had one God in front of whom the marriage is solemnized and contracted.

With regard to the present debate, an important issue is that a married woman's expectations of a certain level of maintenance within the marriage (and potentially after it) will crucially depend on the economic standing of the husband and his family.[58] Evidently, for this reason too, the selection of Hindu marriage partners focuses not only on personal characteristics of the spouses, but also takes account of the economic circumstances of the husband and his family. As Sen (1998) argues convincingly from an economist's perspective, this explains to some extent why Hindu families may be so concerned to place their daughter in a 'good' family that they will voluntarily pay a large dowry in the first place.[59] Saxena (1993: 74) discusses the issue in terms of allocation of gendered roles, but sees this as normal:

> A woman's financial dependence on her husband in the Indian social set up and consequently her secondary status in the family is considered neither extraordinary nor peculiar, but quite natural and common. Ordinary customs of our society expect a man to establish a matrimonial home, being the wage earner and the woman to assume the domestic responsibilities .... The term maintenance includes not merely food, clothes and residence, but also things necessary for the comfort and status in which a person entitled to be maintained can reasonably be expected to live.

However, Saxena (1993: 84) then compares a married woman to a bonded labourer in the home, complaining that it is time that married women should be given their rights and privileges in law, of which they have been robbed. The key argument of this author appears to be that injustice is being perpetrated on women in the name of duty. The modernist call is for adequate recognition of unpaid housework, although this is not clearly stated, while the argument is generally phrased in constitutional law terms. This also confirms that during the 1990s, the reformist pressure for further legal intervention in the relationship of husband and wife has not waned. But the focus now is on equal property rights for women rather than discretionary entitlements to maintenance for wives during the marriage or after it. The unspoken larger agenda is quite clearly that a married Hindu woman should, from the date of the marriage, be given an automatic share in the husband's property, in fact up to a half of his property, rather than just a vaguely circumscribed right to support and maintenance. We have already seen with regard to debates about divorce reforms (Chapter 11) that such far-reaching claims of legal restructuring have, since the 1970s, led to an almost total stalemate in the legislative field, while the

[58] Such arguments disregard the very significant contribution, whether paid or unpaid, that married women make to the household and its economy. In addition, as S. Basu (2001: 102) confirms, it is now well-established that a woman's earning power has become a significant consideration in marriage arrangements.

[59] The expectation that payment of a dowry should secure the bride a good and prosperous future is also strongly reflected in the evidence collected by S. Basu (2001: 103).

often frenzied activities of modernist lobbyists seek to push the boundaries further.

Legal Reforms of Hindu Maintenance Law

In the reform-oriented atmosphere of the 1950s, however, the scenario was still rather different. While there seems to have been no contentious debate over Hindu women's rights to maintenance, given that it already existed within the traditional system, vigorous disagreements over the extent of property ownership by Hindu women are recorded. Much of this goes beyond the ambit of the present chapter, which seeks to focus mainly on the entitlements of divorced Hindu wives to maintenance, but cannot ignore the wider field.

Singh (1989: 88) merely restates the traditional position when she says that under Hindu law, the claim of the wife does not depend on the husband's economic position, but 'her right is absolute and the husband cannot claim inadequate means to deny maintaining her'. But despite such a right in principle, a Hindu wife may lose her right to maintenance if she deviates from the path of chastity. Singh (id.) claims that even a single lapse may affect her right detrimentally. Derrett (1963c: 168–9) restates the basic principles:

> The wife's right to be maintained by her husband is an important result of the marriage and a principal matter to be attended to in a decree for nullity, judicial separation, or divorce .... The wife, whatever her conduct, is entitled to maintenance by her husband, irrespective of whether he possesses property of any particular kind and independently of any distinct demand for it.

Vijay Sharma (1994: 233–80) offers a detailed discussion on the rights of maintenance to women in the matrimonial home. She confirms, at p. 233, that the fundamental basis of claims to maintenance lies in the marital tie, since the conjugal relationship carries with it an inherent obligation of the Hindu husband to protect the wife and to provide for her maintenance.[60] It is also stated

[60] Anand (1992: 181–3) reports on a number of decisions, from all over India, in which women won the right to maintenance despite the husband's claims that she was not properly married to him. The courts have become more alert to this abusive strategy and now apply a presumption of marriage more readily than before to protect the woman (Diwan and Diwan 1990: 98–102). It is relevant to note here specifically that child marriages are valid marriages also for the purpose of securing maintenance to the wife. In *Panchada Chitti v Panchadi Mahalakshmi* 1976 (2) *AnWR* 45, a child marriage had remained unconsummated and the husband had abandoned the wife, but remained liable for her maintenance. Anand (1992: 184) argues that simpler ceremonies of marriage should be recognized as creating valid marriages, and thus securing rights to women. Previous chapters showed that the issue is much more complex, and that the courts have become increasingly aware of this aspect of Hindu matrimonial law. Diwan and Diwan (1990: 100) rightly refer to *Sumitra Devi v Bhikhan Choudhary* AIR 1985 SC 765 (though they wrongly spell the husband's name) as providing a protective mechanism for Hindu wives.

that whenever there is a breach of this obligation, the law should come to the aid of the neglected wife. This assumes that a wife will actually go to court, rather than seeking to secure her entitlements through informal negotiations with the husband and within the family. As we saw earlier, the formal legal system will tend to emphasize the obligations of the Hindu husband arising from a sacramental marriage, while the customary system may actually exonerate the ex-husband and even give him some form of compensation for allowing the wife to go. Significantly, Sharma (1990: 3) emphasizes the need, in the current economic set-up, to retain a system of maintenance that is not based on gender equality, but on explicit recognition of differential statuses since 'the constitutional equality of sexes is not reflected in the factual economic equality of sexes. Only a small number of women are economically independent .... Thus, there seems to be no alternative but to retain [the] husband's obligation to maintain his wife'.

The new Hindu law of the 1950s, by introducing a number of grounds for divorce and by outlawing polygamy, also significantly changed the economic relationships between Hindu spouses, although this was at first insufficiently well recognized.[61] The new law forces a childless couple into divorce, and thus might deprive an infertile woman of the joint family protection that the traditional law gave her, while the husband would find it comparatively easier to remarry. The new law also divests concubines of various forms of protection known under the traditional law.[62]

Significantly, Sharma (1989: 17) notes that in at least two respects, the relationship of the parties to a Hindu marriage continues after divorce: firstly, in relation to maintenance payments, and secondly with regard to children and their custody, maintenance, and education. Sharma (1989: 19) also observes that '[t]he resistance put to the introduction of divorce, it seems, was mainly focused on its aftermath in relation to the hardship caused to women' and argues, at p. 21, that the escalating divorce rate makes it necessary to take a further look at the post-divorce arrangements for women and children. Sharma (1989: 31) notes further that the liberalization of divorce grounds was not followed up with activist attention to post-divorce problems.

The major focus of the legal reforms in the 1950s, more or less directly in relation to maintenance, concerned four areas. First, the traditional entitlement of a Hindu wife to maintenance from the husband during the marriage was statutorily guaranteed and strengthened in Section 18 HAMA 1956. Second, the pre-existing right of a Hindu widow to a share in joint family property was secured and significantly improved by introducing Section 14 of the HSA 1956. Third, the tenuous financial position of Hindu wives who have to go to court to secure their financial entitlements was strengthened by certain provisions in

[61] The new law did not, however, as Desai (1998: 68) claims, have the effect that Hindu men and women are now treated absolutely equally in terms of succession.

[62] The legal position of a concubine is briefly covered by Diwan and Diwan (1990: 29).

Section 24 HMA 1955 to support women during the pendency of litigation. Finally, the right of divorced Hindu wives to maintenance was reinforced in Section 25 HMA 1955. These provisions are each briefly discussed in turn below.

With regard to the Hindu wife's entitlement to maintenance during the marriage, there should be no dispute in principle, given the existing protective framework of the traditional Hindu law. Self-controlled order, which clearly is an ideal in this field too, should take care of such matters, but often does not effectively assist a Hindu wife, especially if she does not assert her claims and suffers in silence. It may become critically important for a Hindu woman to be able to establish her status as a 'Hindu wife'.[63] The statutory law and the courts have made every effort to assist Hindu women in their rightful claims for maintenance from the husband during the marriage. In this regard, the legislative support mechanism under Section 18 HAMA 1956 provides as follows:

> 18. Maintenance of wife. -
> (1) Subject to the provisions of this section, a Hindu wife, whether married before or after the commencement of this Act, shall be entitled to be maintained by her husband during her lifetime.
> (2) A Hindu wife shall be entitled to live separately from her husband without forfeiting her claim to maintenance, -
> (a) if he is guilty of desertion, that is to say, of abandoning her without reasonable cause and without her consent or against her wish, or of wilfully neglecting her;
> (b) if he has treated her with such cruelty as to cause a reasonable apprehension in her mind that it will be harmful or injurious to live with her husband;
> (c) if he is suffering from a virulent form of leprosy;
> (d) if he has any other wife living;
> (e) if he keeps a concubine in the same house in which his wife is living or habitually resides with a concubine elsewhere;
> (f) if he has ceased to be a Hindu by conversion to another religion;
> (g) if there is any other cause justifying her living separately.
> (3) A Hindu wife shall not be entitled to separate residence and maintenance from her husband if she is unchaste or ceases to be a Hindu by conversion to another religion.

These protective provisions are self-explanatory. It is remarkable how closely they relate to the Hindu Married Women's Right to Separate Residence and Maintenance Act of 1946, cited earlier in this chapter at pp. 503–4. While Section 19 of the HAMA 1956 secures maintenance rights for a widowed daughter-in-law, Section 20 of the same Act focuses on the maintenance of children and aged parents.[64] Shastri (1990: 175) argues that the term 'maintenance' is

[63] Chapters 8 and 10 already examined the risks to the status of the Hindu wife by a restrictive interpretation of Section 7 HMA.

[64] These particular provisions are not centrally relevant to the current discussion but indicate that Hindu law has traditionally recognized the obligation to look

still not properly defined and remains to be determined in the light of family circumstances, as though it was a problem that the facts and circumstances of a case should be taken into account. Shastri (1990: 172) claims that the law relating to maintenance has been radically changed by the HAMA and that 'new values have been substituted in place of the old and ineffective traditions', but offers no substantive evidence for such assertions.

Case law under Section 18 HAMA has firmly established that a Hindu wife, on account of the sacramental-cum-contractual relationship of the Hindu marriage, is entitled to maintenance from the husband.[65] This also means, interestingly, that a Hindu wife who is party to a polygamous marriage will be covered by this protective section. Her marriage may be void under Section 5(i) and Section 11 HMA 1955 but she is still a 'Hindu wife' for the purposes of the 1956 Act.[66] However, if such a woman were to litigate under the secular Indian law, her claim to maintenance would be refused.[67] This has given rise to the argument that the protective pro-women mechanisms of the modern Hindu law should be extended to all Indian wives under the provisions of Section 125 of the CrPC 1973 (Sagade 1989: 342–4).[68] The courts have become more alert to the potential for misuse by husbands of allegations that the wife is not party to a valid marriage.[69] This shows that Hindu wives in India, at least in this regard,

---

after the elders of the family. An important case on the obligation of Hindu daughters to maintain their parents, decided under Section 125 of the secular CrPC of 1973, is *Vijaya Manohar Arhat v Kashirao Rajaram Sawai* AIR 1987 SC 1100. This means that more recent efforts in Singapore, for example, to promulgate the Maintenance of Parents Act of 1993 (Harding 2001: 207) are not new at all, and are not unique to Confucianism or to Singapore, but are part of a wider cultural manifestation of 'Asian values'.

[65] Derrett (1963c) could not yet report on many cases during the 1960s. Menski (2001: 261–3) discusses some significant cases on this issue. See also Reddy (1999: 56). Singh (1993: 219–51) offers a wide-ranging discussion on various aspects of divorce and maintenance. Diwan and Diwan (1990: 47–8) emphasize that the facts and circumstances of individual cases remain crucial, especially when it comes to Section 18(2)(g). Thus, in *Sobha v Bhim* AIR 1975 Or 180, it was held that heavy drinking of the husband by itself was not a ground for separate maintenance unless cruelty was made out.

[66] This was firmly established in *C. Obula Konda Reddy v C. Pedda Venkata Lakshamma* AIR 1976 AP 43.

[67] An important case on this subject is *Yamunabai v Anantrao* AIR 1988 SC 644, which held that the expression 'wife' means 'legally wedded wife' and thus excludes a polygamously married Hindu wife. Kusum (2000: 257) notes this, but fails to point out that a Hindu wife who is unsuccessful under the secular section 125 CrPC 1973 could seek remedies as a 'Hindu wife' under s. 18 HAMA 1956.

[68] Modernists would challenge this as 'Hinduisation' and would raise warnings about *hindutva* and imposition of majoritarian values.

[69] For details on the new activism in Hindu maintenance law and relevant cases, see Menski (2001: 261–75).

are better protected under Hindu law than in the corresponding secular framework of rules.

Regarding the Hindu widow's position, we saw that under traditional Hindu law, a widow had not only definite entitlements to maintenance from the husband's family,[70] but was also allotted the deceased husband's share in joint family property as a 'limited estate'. This legal position was strengthened by the Hindu Women's Right to Property Act of 1937, as discussed earlier in this chapter. A Hindu widow could enjoy this property during her lifetime but could not normally alienate it, since the property was, after her death, supposed to revert to the coparcenary.[71] This pre-existing right of a Hindu widow to a share in joint family property, secured and significantly improved by the 1937 Act, was further strengthened by the introduction of Section 14 HSA 1956. This particular legal reform brought a real revolution in terms of the extent of the widow's right over such property, which was now upgraded from a 'limited estate' or 'life estate' to a form of property owned by the widow absolutely, making it in a sense a category of *strīdhanam*. This, of course, had the consequence that widows could now sell or otherwise alienate such property as they pleased, which obviously did not find favour with many joint families and led to enormously complex litigation, on which a whole book could be written. The relevant section is Section 14 HSA 1956:

> 14. Property of a female Hindu to be her absolute property. -
> (1) Any property possessed by a female Hindu, whether acquired before or after the commencement of this Act, shall be held by her as full owner thereof and not as a limited owner.
> *Explanation.* In this sub-section, 'property' includes both moveable and immoveable property acquired by a female Hindu by inheritance or devise, or at a partition, or in lieu of maintenance or arrears of maintenance, or by gift from any person, whether a relative or not, before, at or after her marriage, or by her own skill or exertion, or by purchase or by prescription, or in any other manner whatsoever, and also any such property held by her as *stridhana* immediately before the commencement of this Act.
> (2) Nothing contained in sub-section (1) shall apply to any property acquired by way of gift or under a will or any other instrument or under a decree or order of a civil court or under an award where the terms of the gift, will or other instrument or the decree, order or award prescribe a restricted estate in such property.

This convoluted wording has given rise to much criticism, even from SC judges, but behind this wall of words is a clear-cut, effective reform of Hindu law on

[70] Diwan and Diwan (1990: 54) clearly refer to the well-known obligation of the joint family in traditional Hindu law to maintain the wives and widows of coparceners, so that a widowed daughter-in-law could claim maintenance against the joint family property.

[71] The technical term for this group of males in the joint family context is 'reversioners', those to whom the property reverts on the widow's death.

women's property. While this section confirms that all forms of *strīdhanam* qualify as the absolute property of a Hindu woman, the new law also covers all other kinds of property 'possessed' by a Hindu woman.[72] It became inevitable that this term should be subject to critical scrutiny. Did a Hindu wife 'possess' some item of property given to her in lieu of maintenance, on the explicit understanding that it would revert to the joint family after the widow's death? After some initial bad decisions during the 1970s, the Supreme Court of India virtually apologized and held firmly in *V. Tulasamma v V. Sesha Reddi* AIR 1977 SC 1944, that a Hindu widow's right to property was a pre-existing right of which the widow could not be divested.[73] Her 'limited estate' therefore became transformed on 17 June 1956, the commencement date of the HSA, into full and absolute ownership. Sharma (1990: 27) explains correctly that the main object of the new law was to enlarge the Hindu widow's 'limited estate' into full ownership, turning it into an absolute estate.

Sharma (1990: 27) claims that the HSA of 1956 was 'undoubtedly a piece of social legislation which fulfilled a long felt need of the nation and was widely acclaimed by the entire people'. However, this is not quite what the judges thought. Aggarwal (1988: 12) cites Bhagwati J, who in *V. Tulasamma* AIR 1977 SC 1944, at p. 1946, criticized the convoluted wording of Section 14, saying that '[t]his is a classic instance of a statutory provision which, by reason of its inapt draftmanship, has created endless confusion for litigants and proved a paradise for lawyers'. This important case also contains a detailed discussion of the Hindu law on maintenance. It was ultimately held, at p. 1979, that any allotment of property to a Hindu widow in lieu of maintenance was 'merely in recognition of her right to maintenance which was a pre-existing right'. This Supreme Court judgment therefore firmly protects Hindu widows against predatory reversioners. The case law under this section virtually exploded during the 1970s, but the topic is not central enough for the present debate to warrant detailed discussion.[74]

[72] Derrett (1963c: 122 and 126–7) focuses merely on the effects of adoption, while Derrett (1963c: 325) assumes that some Hindu women's interests were turned into absolute ownership by Section 14 HSA, and such female owners are then entitled to demand partition, as though they were coparceners. While only a passing reference to 'possessed' is found in Derrett (1963c: 368), a detailed discussion (ibid.: 424–42) can be located under 'limited estate', with innumerable case citations. Derrett (1963c: 424) emphasizes that the former limited estate of female heirs was now, bar a few exceptions, largely dead.

[73] For an indication of the discussions and some case references see Menski (2001: 332–9).

[74] Derrett (1963c: lxxxix) predicted that all the problems arising from the 1937 Act would have been forgotten by the 1980s, but that seems too optimistic. Many cases continue to arise, even if there is no hope of success, as in *Partap Singh v Union of India* AIR 1985 SC 1695, where a Sikh male unsuccessfully pleaded gender discrimination in reliance on Articles 14 and 15(1) of the Constitution.

The tenuous bargaining position of Hindu wives, who may have to go to court to claim their pre-existing entitlements in terms of maintenance against recalcitrant husbands, was strengthened by two sets of provisions in the HMA of 1955.[75] First, in Section 24 HMA 1955, the wife was granted additional protection in terms of maintenance during the pendency of the litigation (*pendente lite*). This would often be crucial for a wife who has no financial means of her own to support herself (and maybe several children) during a protracted court battle. Such a woman might not have the money for lawyers' fees, in the first place, thus impeding her access to court. An intricate combination of legal aid and additional financial support from the husband was therefore provided in this beneficial section:

> 24. Maintenance pendente lite and expenses of proceedings. -
> Where in any proceedings under this Act it appears to the court that either the wife or the husband, as the case may be, has no independent income sufficient for her or his support and the necessary expenses of the proceeding, it may, on the application of the wife or the husband, order the respondent to pay to the petitioner the expenses of the proceeding, and monthly during the proceeding such sum as, having regard to the petitioner's own income and the income of the respondent, it may seem to the court to be reasonable.

Aggarwal (1988: 247–87) produces a detailed analysis of this issue and emphasizes at p. 249 that Parliament was aware that a party to a marriage may not be financially sound and may thus require support *pendente lite* to be able to make rightful claims through a court of law. This is clearly a measure designed to facilitate access to courts and could be seen as a legal aid strategy. However, unlike most Western legal systems, in Indian law this does not mean that the state will bear the wife's costs in the form of legal aid.

Case law under section 24 originally reflected male-centred bias, as documented in several decisions that were socially totally inadequate.[76] It is quite clear that since the 1980s, judicial activism has come to the assistance of Hindu wives also under Section 24 HMA. To an extent, this necessity to protect wives during the pendency of litigation, and to assist them in litigating in the first place, reflects that the traditional support mechanisms for Hindu women are not fully effective and are not reliably implemented in social reality. However, one should not overlook the considerable bargaining power that Hindu women

[75] Sharma (1989: 90–1) explains Sections 24 and 25 HMA 1955. Derrett (1963c: 177) sees Section 24 HMA as an important feature and reports at this early stage that the various Indian High Courts disagreed mainly over procedural issues, but not the principle.

[76] Some early case references are found in Derrett (1963c: 177). Examples of bad cases are *Akasam Chinna Babu v Akasam Parbati* AIR 1967 Or 163 and *Bankim Chandra Roy v Anjali Roy* AIR 1972 Pat 80. These cases were severely criticized in *Monoj Kr. Jaiswal v Lila Jaiswal* AIR 1987 Cal 230, which took account of the predicament of the Hindu wife and of children affected by such litigation.

may use in informal negotiations. Based on the views of one particular woman from Delhi concerning entitlements to property from the natal family, rather than claims against the husband, S. Basu (2001: 155) argues that '[h]er vision of property distribution vividly shows how women may be practically or emotionally unable to be free of constitutive ideology, yet able to negotiate solutions that optimize their needs rather than becoming passive martyrs of custom'.

Clearly, going to court is not the only avenue open to a woman who is being deprived of pre-existing rights and due entitlements. In fact, as S. Basu (2001: 186) reports from her fieldwork,[77] the formal law is not really trusted by many women, so that litigation is avoided as far as possible, both when it comes to divorce and to property matters. S. Basu (2001: 11) therefore warns against the 'overdetermination of law as an ideological apparatus' and argues that over-reliance on law for bringing about social change is fundamentally problematic. When Basu (2001: 156) advises instead that intelligent use and virtual celebration of 'the spaces of discursive leakage' would empower women more than recourse to formal laws, this is more than a matter of finding optimal compromises. It also reflects an emerging postmodern awareness that formal legal provisions by themselves are not good enough to assist women in making their rightful claims heard and implemented.

Finally, in addition to assisting Hindu wives during the period of litigation, the right of divorced Hindu wives to permanent maintenance or alimony was reinforced in Section 25 HMA 1955:

> 25. Permanent alimony and maintenance. -
> (1) Any court exercising jurisdiction under this Act may, at the time of passing any decree or at any time subsequent thereto on application made to it for the purpose by either the wife or the husband, as the case may be, order that the respondent shall, while the applicant remains unmarried, pay to the applicant for his or her maintenance and support such gross sum or such monthly or periodical sum for a term not exceeding the life of the applicant as, having regard to the respondent's own income and other property, if any, the income and other property of the applicant and the conduct of the parties, it may seem to the court to be just, and any such payment may be secured, if necessary, by a charge on the immoveable property of the respondent.
> (2) If the court is satisfied that there is a change in the circumstances of either party at any time after it has made an order under subsection (1), it may, at the instance of either party, vary, modify or rescind any such order in such manner as the court may deem just.
> (3) If the court is satisfied that the party in whose favour an order has been made under this section has remarried or, if such party is the wife, that she has not remained chaste, or, if such party is the husband, that he has had sexual intercourse with any woman outside wedlock, it shall rescind the order.

[77] Holden (2003) confirms this, too, for women in rural Madhya Pradesh.

Aggarwal (1988: 288–308) provides a detailed discussion of developments under Section 25 HMA, emphasizing that this is virtually a code in itself. Derrett (1963c: 182) confirms that at an early stage the Indian courts were still looking to guidance from English law, especially in cases concerning discretion 'in withholding alimony from a guilty wife if she has means'.[78] Obviously, both spouses would try to hide assets, and in many cases the courts would have to engage in intricate detective work. Sharma (1989: 143–203) notes in her detailed analysis, at p. 192, that problems of enforcement become compounded due to the adversarial nature of divorce proceedings.[79] Clearly, it is not a simple matter for women to use the above protective provisions, which are not free-standing, but linked in most cases to divorce, certainly when it comes to Section 25 HMA.[80]

Regarding the quantum of maintenance that a Hindu wife may expect, it is impossible to be definite, since everything depends on the facts and circumstances of individual cases. Derrett (1963c: 170) writes that '[t]he amount of maintenance is affected by the wife's conduct ... the relations between the spouses, and by the standard of living of the family, their income, or, when the husband is separated, his income, the woman's reasonable needs, and by her possession of independent means'. Much has been made of the issue of unchastity, often giving rise to utterly ridiculous claims by husbands that their

[78] Interestingly, Derrett (1963c: 182) points out that 'a general rise in the standard of living will be taken into account' and refers to *Saraswati v Rupa* AIR 1962 Or 193.

[79] Another related area of practical importance in litigation, closely linked to 'dowry' problems, but almost totally unexplored by legal writers so far, is found in Section 27 HMA concerning disposal of property and especially wedding presents. Derrett (1963c: 183–4) briefly discusses this contentious issue, which also occupies courts in the UK today in a growing number of 'dowry disputes'. Sharma (1989: 381–7) contains a useful analysis and reports, at p. 382, that Section 27 empowers the court to make decrees 'with respect to any property presented, at or about the time of marriage, which may belong jointly to both the husband and the wife'. The underlying purpose of this provision is that, when a Hindu marriage breaks down, the interest of the wife in various forms of moveable property (often prominently gold jewellery) should be protected from predatory actions by the husband and (as is quite often the case) the mother-in-law. Important cases, which link with *strīdhanam*, have now firmly established that the Hindu wife has absolute ownership rights over property given to her. *Vinod Kumar v State of Haryana* AIR 1982 P&H 372 FB, which held in effect that women are owned by men, was firmly overruled in *Pratibha Rani v Suraj Kumar* AIR 1985 SC 628. This position was reiterated in *Rashmi Kumar v Mahesh Kumar* (1997) 2 SCC 397. In practice, though, conflicting claims are difficult to unravel and much depends on family arrangements and the intentions of those who gave the property in the first place.

[80] In fact, if a divorce petition has been dismissed, the wife's claim to maintenance under Section 25 HMA must fail, as Kusum (2000: 255) demonstrates with reference to *Chand Dhawan v Jawaharlal Dhawan* (1993) 3 SCC 406. In such cases a wife can claim maintenance under Section 18 HAMA instead.

wives were now linked to another man. In the context of divorce litigation, Chapter 11 confirmed that Hindu husbands would not hesitate to advance unbelievably false claims to defeat the wife's claim to maintenance. V. Sharma (1994: 178) also correctly notes that '[d]espite maintenance orders passed by the courts in favour of women, men often refuse to pay maintenance'.

Diwan and Diwan (1990: 25–6) indicate some general principles outlined by the courts, the main rule being that a claim to maintenance by a female cannot be defeated by alienation of that property (ibid.: 26). While courts have had to be alert in spotting male attempts to defraud women, they have also had to find the right balance at the other extreme, protecting men from exaggerated and exploitative claims by women. Diwan and Diwan (1990: 120–1) note that '[t]he idea behind the maintenance provisions is to help destitute wives in real need and not to give them a weapon to fleece and exploit husbands'. Generally speaking, as Derrett (1963c: 172) reports, the amount awarded 'may fluctuate with the fortune of the husband and the wife is entitled to apply for an enhancement, just as the husband may apply for a reduction'.[81] The general early trends, supported by case law, were as follows (id.):

> Where nothing operates to diminish the amount, a wife can expect one-fifth or upwards of one-fifth of her husband's income. But in a case where a husband married a wife of a more expensive standard of living than his own, he would normally be expected to keep her on the scale to which she was accustomed. Equity will normally secure that the husband is not exploited by his wife's refusal to live with him, and that she is not impoverished by his neglect. The result may in such cases be a higher proportion than one fifth. A man who has one wife and no children to support may be ordered to pay as much as a third of his income.

Derrett (1963c: 174) emphasizes that the Hindu wife's right to maintenance does not cease at her husband's death. The widow becomes a statutory dependant with claims on the husband's estate. Hence, whether dead or alive, the Hindu husband serves as a protective shield for his wife through the principle that the marital relationship legitimizes her claims to maintenance.[82] Within the modern legal set-up of the Hindu personal law, this is a powerful support mechanism for Hindu wives, but the traditional moral as well as modern legal claims may still not result in meaningful support for the Hindu wife if she does not assert her claims. In extreme situations, the general criminal law of India may come to the rescue of Hindu wives who failed (or were not allowed) to negotiate their entitlements informally within the family context.

[81] Reference is made to early cases like *Subbarayayudu v Papayamma* AIR 1957 AP 865.

[82] The issue of inflation and the courts' duty to take account of it has become a more prominent aspect in several important cases since the 1970s, under the HMA as well as in litigation under section 125 of the CrPC of 1973, as shown by *Bai Tahira v Ali Hussain Fissalli Chothia* AIR 1979 SC 362.

Secular Reinforcement: The Criminal Procedure Code

We saw earlier that the old provisions of Section 488 of the CrPC of 1898 were replaced in the restructured Section 125 of the CrPC of 1973 with more stringent rules regarding maintenance of all divorced Indian wives.[83] Being part of the general law rather than Hindu personal law, this Code is not directly relevant to a discussion of Hindu women's entitlements to maintenance, but as an alternative remedy, it does have some importance. In particular, the new provision is to some extent symbolic, strengthening the bargaining position of wives who might threaten a recalcitrant husband with litigation under the general criminal law.

In essence, Section 125(1) of the 1973 Code provides, at first sight, that husbands of any community have to maintain their wives.[84] That was also the old position under the 1898 Code, which had covered married women, but not divorced wives. This approach reflects customary traditions within an androcentric framework of reference. However, the new Indian CrPC of 1973 adds in an innocuous explanation in Section 125(1) under paragraph (b) that 'wife' 'includes a woman who has been divorced by, or has obtained a divorce from, her husband and has not remarried'. This is a significant legal change, an innovation which has led to much controversy, mainly in relation to the rights of divorced Muslim wives to maintenance beyond the traditional three months of the *iddat* period.[85] While the dominant view among Indian Muslims, and more so those who write about them,[86] has been that the divorcing husband has no further obligations to his ex-wife after the expiry of the *iddat* period, Section 125(1) of the 1973 Code clearly conflicts with this as far as Muslims are concerned. However, also among Muslims, there is some recognition of the fact that a divorced wife should not simply be left to fend for herself, though the customary pattern has been to expect a divorced Muslim wife to return to her natal home.[87]

[83] For a brief discussion of the older law and early cases, see Menski (2001: 250–3).

[84] The relevant parts of Section 125 of the 1973 Code are cited in Menski (2001: 254–5). Diwan and Diwan (1990: 95–6) reprint the section and discuss the Code in detail (ibid.: 95–197).

[85] For details on the traditional Muslim position, see Pearl and Menski (1998: 182–3).

[86] Vatuk (2001: 227) notes that the literature on the subject is 'largely anecdotal and highly polemical'.

[87] This is certainly the case in Pakistani Muslim law, which has been avoiding discussions of this issue, going along with customary norms that expect divorced Muslim women to return to their natal families. For a detailed analysis of Muslim women's rights to post-divorce maintenance in India, see Pearl and Menski (1998: 201–22). Specifically on the relevant Indian law, see Menski (2001: 256–61 and 275–89). Muslims anywhere need to recognize that it is blatantly un-Islamic to force a woman who has legal entitlements to maintenance against men to fend for herself,

For Hindu wives, the significance of this change of terminology lies in the fact that sacramental notions of Hindu marriage have been strengthened and re-imported even into the secular CrPC of 1973. Predictably, this has led to politicized bickering from modernists, who are refusing to recognize openly that this was actually a beneficial reform for women. Since this Code re-enforced the traditional legal rule that a Hindu husband would be liable for maintaining his wife, modernist scholarship has only cautiously welcomed this legal change, putting ideology above the material interests of impoverished Hindu wives. For example, Singh (1989: 87) complains that the new Code continues to reflect the old patriarchal attitudes towards women, and is particularly critical of the fact that the obligation to maintain under the CrPC continues to be that of the man alone.[88] It is argued (id.) that in view of modern expectations regarding gender equality, it is irrational to place the obligation to maintain only on the man:

> However miniscule the number may be, there are today women economically independent who can not only look after themselves but also their husbands and children. Similarly the duty to look after indigent parents cannot be restricted only to sons. As a matter of fact the exclusion of daughters from the obligation may be used as an argument to deprive them of their share in the father's property.

This is a typical elitist form of reasoning which overlooks the concerns of poor Hindu wives, pushing gender equality buttons in a status game, rather than thinking about social relevance for the majority of Hindus. Such myopic arguments tend to ignore Supreme Court judgments, in this case *Vijaya Manohar Arhat* AIR 1987 SC 1100. However, modernist criticism is also productive, in that it highlights the complex ways in which the field of Hindu maintenance law and concern for the protection of divorced Hindu wives have become interlinked with several other areas of the law.[89] Reformist authors like Singh (1989) clearly place the agenda of sexual equality and elitist perspectives above any immediate concern for desperately poor Hindu wives.[90] Such writers also

exposing her to the risk of illicit sex (*zina*). Still, the current policy in Pakistan and Bangladesh is to put the burden on the natal family or the woman herself, while the *Shah Bano* case and the MWPRDA of 1986 in India place an obligation first of all on the former husband.

88 This is not in fact totally correct, as Hindu daughters have an obligation to maintain their parents, as established in *Vijaya Manohar Arhat* AIR 1987 SC 1100.

89 This is also one of the starting points for S. Basu (2001) in her research on how Hindu women negotiate property entitlements vis-à-vis their natal families.

90 Singh (1989: 87) refers to *Towards Equality* (1974), which recommended further amendment of the law to provide for an obligation of economically independent married women to maintain their dependent husbands, to share with such husband the duty to maintain their children, and to share with brothers the duty to maintain their indigent parents.

refuse to see the socio-economic urgency and the wider fiscal dimensions of such welfare measures and seem only focused on gender ideology.[91]

The 1973 Code sought to counteract the increasing plight of divorced women of any community in India.[92] Not surprisingly, there has been much litigation over financial entitlements.[93] As a result, however, India has today an eminently sensible post-divorce maintenance law, found both in the realm of general law and personal laws. This protective legal framework does not, above all, involve the state in any welfare expenditure and thus in essence places the onus concerning maintenance of divorced wives squarely on the former husband, irrespective of religion.[94] While recent attention has focused on Muslim law and to some extent on Christian law reforms, well-documented heated debates about Hindu law reforms took place already in the 1940s and especially during the early 1950s, but they have been superseded by new concerns.[95]

Recent scholarship is still grumbling over the new provisions. Diwan and Diwan (1990: 4) argue generally that despite some good intentions, the law is still far from satisfactory. Singh (1989: 87) welcomes the extension of maintenance provision to divorced wives and argues that the relevant provision of the CrPC of 1973 has the advantage of delivering a speedy and cheap remedy.[96]

[91] Exhaustive coverage of the entire field is provided in Aggarwal (1988: 312–466). I have argued recently (in Menski 2001, Chapters 4 and 5) that these pro-women provisions must also be interpreted as self-protection on the part of an impoverished state, which could not possibly take on such onerous liabilities as part of a social welfare strategy. The postmodern Indian state needs the input of the patriarchal set-up to implement family-based social welfare measures.

[92] Sharma (1989: 204–49) provides a detailed analysis of Section 125, emphasizing its main objective to avoid vagrancy and destitution. Vijay Sharma (1994: 234) suggests that the 1973 Code has been incorporated 'to provide a speedy relief for maintenance to [the] wife irrespective of her religion'. Sharma (1989: 241) argues that where a wife receives relief under Section 125 of the 1973 Code in full and final settlement, her right to maintenance is extinguished and she cannot claim under Section 24 HMA as well.

[93] For a detailed discussion, see Diwan and Diwan (1990: 95–197).

[94] The famous case of *Mohd. Ahmed Khan v Shah Bano Begum* AIR 1985 SC 945, known as the *Shah Bano* case, did not involve any new legal issue, but demanded the imposition of a uniform civil code, leading to riots and the 1986 Act. For details see Menski (2001: 256–61 and 275–89).

[95] Some details on the older debates are found in Derrett (1957; 1970). Agnes (2000) demonstrates quite clearly that, more recently, the concern of women's activists and reformers has shifted to claims for women's property rights rather than entitlements to maintenance.

[96] Many authors reiterate this particular aspect. For details see Asif (1991: 1), who also points out that interim maintenance is available to an indigent wife under Section 125 CrPC 1973, as confirmed in *Savitri v Govind Singh Rawat* AIR 1986 SC 984, at p. 986.

The idea is to prevent starvation and vagrancy, which are linked to petty crimes and prostitution.[97]

Towards Equality (1974: 363) called in the summary of recommendations for the removal of the ceiling of Rs 500 for maintenance under the Code. Singh (1989: 87) also criticizes this low upper limit, saying that 'it seems unjustified to limit the total amount of maintenance for all dependent persons to Rs 500 per month'. Diwan and Diwan (1990: 11) question the ceiling of Rs 500 on the ground that in line with inflation, this should now be Rs 4500, and the limit should be removed altogether. Sharma (1994: 274) also concludes that the protective mechanisms are not good enough and that the maximum amount of Rs 500 may not be sufficient in all cases according to the needs of the wife and the status of the families concerned:

> It is, therefore, submitted that legislative cognizance is to be taken of the devaluation of the rupee and escalation of living cost, by raising the maximum allowance for maintenance from Rupees 500 to Rupees 1500 or to do away with the ceiling thereby giving a free hand to the court to use its judicial discretion in its full amplitude.[98]

Singh (1989: 89) emphasizes absolute equality, noting critically that while the legal reforms of the 1950s exhibited some awareness of gender equality, the 1973 Code 'reverted again to the 19th century concept which regards woman as only a dependent'. Sharma (1989: 207–8) observes in a more constructive manner that the 1973 Code imported a legal fiction to create an artificial relationship of husband and wife only for the purpose of maintenance after divorce. That is clearly another way of saying that this Code is not simply evidence of *hindutva* or a superimposition of majoritarian values, as it is now called in the fashionable literature, but a sophisticated legal mechanism to protect the rights of women.

Sharda (1988: 51) discusses the rights of minor children under the CrPC of 1973 and argues that the Code remains unclear regarding the obligation of relations other than the parents to maintain minors, and there are no provisions applicable to a widowed minor daughter or daughter-in-law. Such arguments by lawyers reflect a desire, common among black-letter practitioners, to plug all legal loopholes and to legislate for each and every possibility in protective statutes, rather than relying on processes of self-controlled order or

[97] Asif (1991: 1) emphasizes that '[t]he provisions are designed to prevent vagrancy and provide a summary and speedy remedy .... They are meant to unburden the society of destitute married or divorced women'. Asif (1991: 2) cites V.R. Krishna Iyer, who emphasized in a judgment involving Muslims from Kerala that 'no civilized State can relax its duty in this regard and so this humane law deserves to be enforced sternly in a country and at a time when the paramount law of the land breathes the air of social justice'.

[98] The ceiling was in fact removed in 2001, but this amendment has remained virtually unknown.

judicial creativity in applying equitable rules. Surely, when a divorced wife has children to look after, this must be taken into account by the courts.[99]

Several relevant procedural issues have been raised. Asif (1991: 1) notes that litigation on maintenance by discarded wives and children against their husbands and guardians is adding to the explosion of litigation in India. She also mentions the issue of endemic delays, besides the cost of litigation. All of this supports the argument that such litigation should be avoided or reduced as much as possible and that self-controlled negotiation is preferable to formal litigation. As will be seen in the next section—the subsection on postmoderms in judicial social engineering—judges are now increasingly ready to punish litigants for being obstructive and uncooperative.

Gupte (2001) focuses in detail on the role of the new family courts, about which much more research needs to be conducted, as Vatuk (2001) also argues. In the context of litigation under the Family Courts Act, counselling and informal negotiation are to be strengthened. Asif (1991: 1) makes the valid point that Section 7(2)(a) of the Family Courts Act, 1984 proposes the transfer of jurisdiction over maintenance claims under Section 125 of the CrPC to the family courts, basically to ensure that civil and criminal aspects of a litigation are amalgamated to avoid duplication of proceedings. Diwan and Diwan (1990: 6–10) discuss the 132nd Report of the Indian Law Commission on Section 125 of the CrPC and find, at p. 10, that most of these recommendations cannot be faulted and should be implemented.[100]

Sharma (1990: 7) neatly summarizes the relevant legal protection mechanisms regarding maintenance for married and divorced Hindu wives, identifying five headings: (1) claims under the Hindu joint family system; (2) claims to maintenance from the husband (who has a personal obligation in this regard towards her) during the subsistence of the marriage; (3) claims to separate maintenance if she has a valid cause; (4) maintenance 'pendente lite' and permanent maintenance in matrimonial proceedings; and (5) a claim for maintenance against the husband under Section 125 of the CrPC, 1973. To the extent that any law made by the state can meaningfully exercise control functions, it seems that there is little else that the Indian state can now do. The practical challenge clearly lies in the field of implementation, especially in providing support to Hindu women in voicing their rightful claims to maintenance if the men closest to them do not want to listen.

[99] This has indeed been the case since the mid-1970s, as a long line of cases demonstrates, for example *Baboolal v Prem Lata* AIR 1974 Raj 93 and *D. Thimmappa v R. Nagaveni* AIR 1976 Kant 215. It would go too far here to provide further details.

[100] The text of the Law Commission Report is provided by Diwan and Diwan (1990: 307–45).

The Postmodern Condition of Maintenance Law

While practising lawyers seem quite content with the legal position reached in this important area of Hindu law, significant dissatisfaction and vocal dissent over the direction of legal change in the present field is reflected and documented in the modernist literature. Despite admitting that significant achievements have been made, many writers (as we saw) are deeply dissatisfied with the continuing androcentric scenario, in which women remain dependent on men's goodwill and cooperation for securing maintenance. The clarion call is for separate female property rights, to be given upfront to a woman at the time of the marriage, or alternatively at birth, thus seeking to strengthen female autonomy.

However, such reformist agenda privilege Western-style individualism and assumptions of equality over traditional Hindu patterns of interlinked, symbiotic, and ideally equitable human relations. At the same time, modernists have to admit that the relevant Indian statutes and the courts have provided an explicitly protective framework for Hindu wives, and really for all Indian wives. Still, such pro-women approaches should not blind us about the underlying agenda for such generosity. Rather than seeking to protect women and children in terms of gender equality and anti-discrimination guarantees in the Constitution, it would appear that the postmodern Indian state, through an intricate combination of statute and case law, has devised a method to create a sustainable social welfare system for divorced and abandoned wives without having to pay the welfare bill itself, i.e. from public coffers.[101] By re-invigorating pro-women rules from traditional Hindu law and extending them to all Indians, the state is not engaging in Hinduization or the return to some medieval patriarchy, but is creatively employing selected and useful elements of indigenous tradition to construct a viable socio-economic system for the future. Reminding men of their traditional obligations, given that they continue to dominate and control the material resources of society, continues to put the burden for maintenance of women and children on them and thus reflects the symbiotic, multi-stranded socio-economic power relationships that exist in society.

While modernist scholarship is now at least beginning to recognize these new developments, as we shall see later, the tone used by most critics remains hostile and unduly critical, thus reflecting that modernist understandings of the innovative postmodern developments in Indian maintenance law remain incomplete and seriously deficient.

[101] Naturally, when it comes to desertion, i.e. a spouse simply disappearing in the sea of Indian humanity, or even moving abroad, any state legal system would find it difficult to locate individuals and to enforce the rightful claims of those who are left high and dry. In such circumstances, the family-centredness of maintenance claims might protect individuals, provided there is a wider family.

Modernist Critiques of Maintenance Law

Many modernist writers, it seems, are not happy with the existing state of the law and have voiced vigorous criticism on several aspects.[102] Some writers address more practical issues, while most comments allude to bigger political issues in terms of gender equality, legal uniformity, and giving full-fledged property rights to all Hindu women from birth and/or on marriage. Ideological arguments tend to prevail over full reflection on the current state of the law and considerations of economic viability and practicality.

Sharma (1994: 338) notes the complaints of women that maintenance decrees are painfully low, given the rising cost of living. However, a few of her female respondents did not even claim maintenance since they were in gainful employment or came from a prosperous family.[103] In this field, it seems that someone will always complain that his or her slice of the cake is not big enough, but there are other concerns as well.[104] Qureshi (1978: 346–7) states, in the light of the realization that allowing too easy divorce will disadvantage a growing number of women, that there is no concrete financial support for a divorced woman other than alimony. Thus, especially the condition of poor women becomes potentially pitiable. He bemoans that divorced women have been compelled to take up manual labour, and 'easily fall prey to polished and refined rascals in disguise' (id.), an elegant reference to prostitution. Surprisingly, Qureshi (id.) further asserts:

> The various High Courts and the Supreme Court of India should be empowered to make an order for maintenance in favour of either wife or husband after a decree of divorce, nullity of marriage, judicial separation or restitution of conjugal rights, or after a finding of wilful neglect.

This reasoning seems factually incorrect, since the reformed Hindu law, as discussed earlier, provides plenty of scenarios in which a Hindu wife may claim maintenance. Sivaramayya (1993: 60) also complained that the protection mechanisms for Hindu women are not sufficient, warned that 'irretrievable breakdown' should not be allowed as a ground for divorce,[105] and pointed out the practical difficulties faced by wives:

102 It often seems that being critical and producing a critique are being confused and conflated.

103 S. Basu (2001) produces detailed evidence to the effect that women may not voice their legitimate claims in order to maintain good relations with others, especially in their natal families.

104 In connection with post-divorce maintenance, one often finds concern on the part of the woman to distance herself from the former husband and to refuse all links. However, if this becomes financially detrimental, what approach should be chosen?

105 Sivaramayya (1993: 61) asked pointedly whether 'irretrievable breakdown' would become a gateway for women's liberation, or in fact a tool for oppression.

> ... even after a wife or a divorced wife secures a decree, after some years the husband or the former husband contumaciously stops payment of the amount and the woman is forced to approach the court once again. It may be recalled that [the] 73rd Report of the Law Commission recommended that erring husbands, who contumaciously stopped payment of maintenance to their wives, should be punished with 6 months rigorous imprisonment. This Report has not been implemented as yet.

Qureshi (1978: 348) seems to express much ill-thought sympathy with husbands when he writes that '[t]here is always a problem of enforcement of maintenance order passed by the court, since the husband has rarely any money or property available for maintenance'. That is not the evidence one gets from reported decisions. Qureshi (1978: 381) advises, in view of prevailing social conditions, that a divorce decree should be withheld unless proper financial arrangements have been made. While this may sound sensible at first sight, common sense as well as the experience of the most recent English legal developments (Douglas 1998) clearly suggest that this is definitely not a viable approach. Once a marriage has broken down, some couples may indulge in protracted court battles over everything they can think of, which is ultimately only to the benefit of lawyers. For most Hindu women, courts will not even be accessible, and their marital status is not decided by a court decree, but by social norms and social reality as sanctioned by the family or local body of elders, in other words, by something akin to *sadācāra*.

Some academic writing draws links between the increased liberality of divorce laws and the consequent risks for women of just being thrown out of the marriage and the matrimonial home, as well as being divested of maintenance entitlements. In a discussion of the failed Marriage Laws (Amendment) Bill of 1981, Sharma (1989: 32) points to some proposed safeguards for the divorced wife. Clause 13D of Section 2 of the Bill provided that the wife would have the right to oppose a petition for divorce on the ground that it would result in 'grave financial hardship' to her. However, the effectiveness of such a safeguard is immediately questioned by Sharma (1989: 33) herself, arguing that in such situations, merely refusing a divorce decree because the court does not have the powers to order proper protection for the wife in terms of finances and accommodation, is hardly a good option when the marriage is actually finished.[106] Sharma (1989: 34) therefore argues for a new divorce law, 'which successfully and efficaciously deals with post-divorce problems .... Our future policy of healthy divorce entirely depends on how we resolve these

[106] If English experience in this field can teach Indian lawyers anything, it strongly reinforces the futility of attempts by wives to oppose a divorce on grounds of economic or other hardship. Douglas (1998: 167) confirms that in English law, applications to that effect are hardly ever successful. Many of those failed applications were actually made by Hindu wives under English law (and an assortment of Mediterranean women), arguing that for them, to be divorced constituted in itself grave hardship and a crushing social stigma.

post-divorce problems'. Sharma (1994: 349) also notes that the law has not been perceptive enough about the needs of women and contains plenty of loopholes. She mentions in particular that there is lack of protection for deserted or separated women who may be forced to take refuge in their parental homes, since a separated woman is only entitled to maintenance from her husband. This is another semi-hidden argument for granting an automatic share in the matrimonial home to the wife, as well as giving her a virtually permanent right to reside in the matrimonial home.

Such comments reflect growing recognition among scholars that modernist clamouring for more and more grounds of divorce, and in particular the full-scale introduction of the principle of 'irretrievable breakdown', posed immense dangers to the financial interests of Hindu wives. Sharma (1994: 364) suggests that the government should first review the existing laws for the protection of married women and should ensure that certain fundamental changes are made to give an equal status to women in the matrimonial home, so that they have at least adequate financial and other means to meet their day-to-day requirement. Consequently, Sharma also argues (id.) that '[i]rretrievable breakdown of marriage should not be introduced without such safeguards'. Mitter (1992: 125) observes more generally that, following the liberalization of divorce laws, with divorce becoming a feasible alternative for more than just the Westernized elite, lower-middle-class women still find seeking divorce very risky. Both in social and financial terms, such a woman is likely to experience restrictions and isolation in a society 'that may no longer repudiate but cannot yet integrate her'.[107] The continuing social ambivalence about the status of divorced Hindu women, in particular, motivated Sharma (1989: 61–2) to note a significant change in the position of the wife as a result of legal reforms:

> The public stigma formerly attached to divorce has gradually been diminished by familiarity. The legal purpose has changed from punishment of the "guilty party" to equitable and expeditious dissolution of a marriage irretrievably broken. Earlier, the wife, who was mainly a consort, kept in her husband's home for purposes of companionship and propagation, has now become a social person, quite equal with her husband, thoughtful of civic and public affairs and interested in broader things of life. In short, we can say, that the position of married woman has progressively changed "from Chattel to Challenger".

This seems to suggest that the reformed Hindu law has contributed to social advancement of women as well as to marital breakdown. Modernist analysis suggests that the unacceptable alternative on both counts would be for women to remain chained in marriages and dependent on men's goodwill. Modernization, from that perspective, involves freedom for the woman to decide as she thinks fit, and to make rightful claims for herself, rather than always defining

[107] Detailed illustrations of this scenario are provided by Jain (1986) and in the fieldwork-based study of Mehta (1975).

herself through others. The problematic of the resulting individualization is rarely addressed by modernists.[108]

A different aspect, precisely the final issue in the above quote about the wife becoming a challenger—rather than a friend, as appears to be the Hindu ideal, while feminists see only the chattel aspect—and making claims that others find unreasonable, has elicited à stringent critique from Mahmood (1986: 127) about the insurance offered to divorced wives by the new maintenance regime. It is useful to quote this important comment in full:[109]

> Under our modern personal law enactments there is not as much stress on the mutual obligations of the married couples as on the rights of divorcees. Particularly, women who have been divorced [or have obtained divorce on their own initiative] are provided with all sorts of legal reliefs under the civil and criminal laws of the country. To use Justice V.R. Krishna Iyer's terminology ... our "functionally sensitised" judiciary is gradually turning divorce into a sort of an insurance deal offering far more lucrative benefits than available in marriage. In return for the social and economic security offered to women through marriage, our traditional laws imposed on them domestic responsibilities and an obligation to respect all reasonable wishes of the husband. The modern Indian laws of divorce, as judicially interpreted, absolve divorced wives of all these obligations without depriving them of the benefits that were available to them in married life. The only constraint that these laws impose on divorced women is a forced celibacy; "unchastity" being fatal to the privilege of being maintained by the former husband.

Mahmood (1986: 127–8) continues this attack on the excesses of modernity in the field of divorce law and maintenance:

> Under the Hindu Marriage Act a wife can sue her husband for divorce at his cost, draw maintenance from him during the pendency of the case, and after attaining the desired divorce, burden him with a "permanent alimony" for herself. Though the Act effects a two-way traffic in this respect and theoretically an indigent husband can seek alimony from his affluent wife, in practice Hindu husbands do not stoop so low—and so perhaps such an order in favour of a husband has never been passed by any court. These reliefs are granted to wives even if they are the divorce-seekers or have—by their conduct—forced the husband into seeking a divorce.

Evidently, this can be read as male backlash to the perceived excesses of pro-women maintenance laws and must also be understood in a specific Muslim context. However, Mahmood's deep critique goes beyond communal politics,

[108] An instructive exception is provided through the field research conducted by S. Basu (2001), who examines to what extent women who claim property rights are seen as the stereotypical uncaring and greedy sister (ibid.: 5 and 9).

[109] The hidden agenda here is vigorous protest over *Mohd. Ahmed Khan v Shah Bano Begum* AIR 1985 SC 945, and the consequent legal position that Muslim wives should be entitled to maintenance until death or remarriage. The author is notably careful to phrase his critique in general terms.

as he warns of men being taken advantage of by unscrupulous women, hardly a modernist argument, but a point that modernist analysis needs to answer, for simply turning tables in adversarial fashion cannot be a viable solution for the future of any civil society.[110] Qureshi (1978: 347) also tackles the perception of unfairly overburdened men, using arguments that are dressed up to protect the wife by looking at English models:

> The courts should have regard in every case to the wife's potential earning capacity if she is not working at the time of the application, as well as to her capital. While accepting that a wife who leaves the house with young children, or incapacitated by age or illness, is entitled to look for maintenance to her husband, wives with no young children, or who have worked regularly during the married life together, or before the marriage, when the separation follows not long afterwards, should be expected to make some attempt to support themselves after the breakdown of the marriage. The standard of living enjoyed by the wife before marriage, her age and the position she has occupied in the community must also be taken into account, while considering the cases of maintenance.

However, such recourse to comparisons with English law needs to be critically examined and placed into a wider context. English law, mainly during the 1970s, could afford to argue in modernist, individualizing tones that divorced wives should not be made dependent on the ex-husband and should be freed from the bonds of a broken relationship. However, this chain of arguments was underpinned by the state's willingness (and, it was thought, long-term capability) to foot the social welfare bills that broken marriages brought with them. More recently, however, it has become evident that these hugely mounting welfare expenditures, including an exploding legal aid budget, are not a sustainable burden for the state. As a result, English judges are now under an explicit obligation to work out an equitable balance between the claims of the spouses, so that the state will not be burdened with welfare payments. England has learnt the hard way that letting men off the hook when it comes to post-divorce maintenance arrangements for ex-wives cannot be good for the state and its coffers. Traditional Hindu law experts warned much earlier of such misguided experiments with individualism, as Derrett's work shows, but there is clearly today much colonialism-inspired modernist reluctance to accept that developments in Asian jurisdictions can provide us with sage advice.[111]

[110] We saw earlier that Diwan and Diwan (1990: 120–1) also expressed concern about men being fleeced and exploited.

[111] Modernist literature (e.g. Rajan 1998), as we saw, simply refutes the potential of Hindu tradition to provide equitable support to women, minorities, and other subalterns. Significantly, a recent study of the use made of foreign laws by courts in various jurisdictions finds that more judges are beginning to recognize the usefulness of foreign laws (Drobnig and van Erp 1999: ix). However, there are significant language barriers, as well as reluctance to borrow from certain jurisdictions, with a

It is evident that a system of state-sponsored welfare payments would not be a feasible way of dealing with problems of maintenance for ex-wives and children in Indian law. India's judges knew this, and hence did not fall into the modernist trap of seeking to 'free' women so that men could shift burdens to others. For the present debate, this means that an official maintenance law that does not grant a former wife an automatic ongoing entitlement, as Qureshi (1978, cited above) suggests, would in social reality withdraw very crucial protection from many women who desperately need this kind of support, in material terms as well as a bargaining tool. The modernist argument that after the breakdown of the marriage there should be a 'clean break' rather than continued financial dependence by the ex-wife on the former husband, only works well for elite people with their own assets, but not for millions of disadvantaged women who need every paisa or handful of rice they can get from the former husband. Whether Indian men like this or not, the 'traditional' rule that husbands remain liable for the maintenance of any wife they married, even after the breakdown of the marital relationship, is an appropriate element in India's postmodern regime of maintenance law. It holds men, as the major controllers of property, accountable for the welfare of all those who depend on family relationships for sustenance.

Modernist scholarship has neither considered in depth the impact of the customary systems of divorce law, as we saw in Chapter 11, nor has it paid attention to the significant implications that such informal settlements will have on the rights of most Hindu women to maintenance. Here again, the symbolic value of supportive legislation, even if it relies on traditional norms, must not be undervalued. There is not only one message in such traditionalized laws, but two. The basic message that the current Indian and Hindu divorce law gives to the people at large is that husbands remain liable for the maintenance of their ex-wives until death or remarriage. This is a matter of tradition, *as well as* of contemporary practice. Modernist scholarship is fundamentally misguided when it one-sidedly opposes this basic normative framework, which crucially legitimizes and underpins the informal claims that Hindu women may be able to make in bargaining processes.

Some writers are beginning to recognize this, seeing that Hindu women (and really all Indian women) are able to explore and expand the scope for what S. Basu (2001: 10) refers to, albeit specifically in the context of succession law, as underutilized 'pockets of equity'. Hindu women in India today need the reference back to the traditional dharmic obligations of the Hindu husband and his duties in accordance with traditional concepts of marriage to buttress their forever contested, current claims to maintenance against competing arguments.

---

preference for looking towards Western liberal democracies (ibid.: 143). Here again, it is confirmed that few lawyers would want, or indeed be able, to make use of Indian laws.

Modernist scholarship takes a rather one-sided approach when it insists that Hindu women remain tied, even by the modern state law, into traditional androcentric linkages from which they have great difficulty in extricating themselves to become sovereign individuals. Modernism struggles with the realization that 'tradition' is also part of the present. Agnes (2000: 215) complains that in India, the rights of married women and divorcees have continued to be confined to a right of maintenance. She argues that discussions of family law reforms need to be situated within the context of economic structures; otherwise women's rights will continue to be illusory. This particular modernist line of reasoning clearly implies that demands for property rights of women are now a more prominent focus for reformists than the area of maintenance law.

But the issues raised go much deeper. Agnes (2000: 206) recognizes that it is not a simple matter for the law reformers to promote a fundamental restructuring of economic relations among Hindus. The familiar complaint (id.) that the law did not pay sufficient attention to securing women's rights to maintenance is only one part of the message, as is evident from the argument that the HMA introduced divorce, but 'did not provide for any economic security for divorced women except the right of meagre maintenance'.[112] Agnes (2000: 206–7) therefore argues more elaborately, but still not disclosing the main point:

> The concept of maintenance could provide safety only within a feudal property structure where property is inalienable and marriages are indissoluble. The large-scale destitution of Hindu women after divorce in the post-reform phase seemed as though Hindu women had bartered the right of residence and economic security, to the right of divorce and consequent destitution.

Hence, Agnes (2000: 207) bitterly complains that the HMA 'turned out to be a poor imitation of the *English Matrimonial Causes Act.* Based on the concept of formal equality, the Hindu law was stripped of all its protective measures. The traditional right of maintenance was now even extended to husbands, a concept unheard of under either the scriptural or customary Hindu law'.[113] Such scathing comments indicate that modernist analysis may at last begin to recognize that insistence on formal equality may well be counterproductive for women.

The argument advanced by Agnes (2000) that women should be given larger rights than merely entitlements to maintenance remains partly hidden,

[112] The complaint that maintenance decrees tend to be insufficient is reiterated by Jain (1986: 51): 'Maintenance laws often let the husband off very lightly; and even in cases where the judge has stipulated an amount to be given to the wife, it is just a pittance'. A husband may also simply ignore the court verdict, as happened in *Jai Singh v Khimi Bhiklu* AIR 1978 HP 45.

[113] It is evident that modernist commentators are split on how to assess this particular provision. While Agnes, cited in the next section, is critical of this type of gender equality, others were full of praise.

but is not actually new at all. It arose prominently in the 1970s when the Committee on the Status of Women (*Towards Equality* 1974) examined the entire field of family law and made a wide-ranging set of recommendations for further legal reforms. These evidently influential comments inspired much modernist clamouring for further reforms. However, as Sivaramayya (1993: 60–1) pointed out, the proposal made by the Committee, to the effect that on divorce a woman should be entitled to a share in the assets of her husband, is yet to be considered seriously either by the Law Commission or by the government.

An extended discussion of a number of more recent reform proposals raises many pertinent points. In her critique of the Bill produced by the National Commission for Women in 1994, Agnes (2000: 183) notes that it 'leaves no legal avenue for a deserted woman to apply to the courts for remedies of maintenance, custody of children, right of residence in the matrimonial home etc. unless she is willing to dissolve the marriage either by divorce or annulment'. Agnes (2000: 178–9) clearly identifies that in the absence of separate female property rights, a major problem for women remains maintenance after divorce, writing at p. 179:

> Since enforcement of maintenance orders is one of the major hurdles faced by women, the draft ... suggests that the husband should be required to make a voluntary disclosure of his assets and income immediately after a petition for divorce is filed by either of the spouses. Thereafter, he must deposit three months' maintenance for the wife and children. The amount must be calculated by dividing the income in equal shares between the husband, wife and minor children. The draft also stipulates that matrimonial courts should have the power to award lump sum maintenance, property settlements and salary attachments.

It appears that various women's groups and other activists have been busy calculating shares and carving up other people's property in their imagination, but forgot to address the question whether the various reform proposals are realistic for Indian women and good for the nation as a whole. Agnes (2000: 184–6) also comments on a private member's bill of 1994, the Married Women's (Protection of Rights) Bill of 1994,[114] which militantly proposed to grant instant rights to married women over the husband's property, but not vice versa. This draft covers a comprehensive sweep-up of all kinds of property, as Agnes (2000: 185) shows:

> The Bill grants the wife the right to live in the house of her husband, whether owned by him or by members of his joint family, the right to food, clothing and other facilities, the right to an equal share in the property of her husband and the right to be consulted in matters of family business and other financial transactions regarding the husband's property.

Much of this is not in fact new, given the existing law and the principles of Hindu marriage law, but the proposal to give an equal share to the wife in the

[114] This is printed in Agnes (2000: 225–7).

property of the husband was smuggled into this draft and constitutes a huge innovation. Agnes (2000: 185–6) reports that this Bill was debated and partly opposed between August 1994 and March 1995, inter alia by glorifying arguments about wives as Hindu goddesses who do not need explicit financial support. It is clear that such radical proposals upset the guardians of patriarchal society and could not possibly be implemented as law by the state. Agnes (2000: 186) reports that the law minister opposed the draft, saying that '[w]e cannot insist that a husband must give fifty per cent of his property to his wife. The women's movement in India is different from the west. We cannot really think that women will be better only by making legal provisions'. Issues of taxation and the problem of the various personal laws were also raised. Agnes (2000: 186) claims therefore, polemically sidelining the issue, that '[w]hen reforms cause a dent in the economics of patriarchy, perhaps it is easier to stall them off by communalizing the issue', but she is not willing to admit that the proposed reforms perhaps simply went a little over the top in promoting individualism at the cost of symbiotic cooperation.[115]

Agnes (2000: 187) also observes that a shift from marriage as a mechanism to control sexuality towards marriage as an economic contract is visible in the various drafts by women's organizations. As in labour legislation, it should be accepted that the weaker partners need additional statutory protection. There is also increasing recognition in the development discourse that there is a link between divorce or desertion and the destitution of women.[116] Agnes (id.) notes again that '[w]omen's rights to shelter in their matrimonial home and the right to a share of matrimonial property upon divorce are emerging as concrete strategies of tackling the issue at hand'. Significantly, and much to her credit, Agnes (2000: 188) notes a lacuna in the existing drafts as far as less privileged women are concerned and rightly warns about the innocuous term 'spouse', which can so easily be used to put obligations on women that even the traditional Hindu law did not impose:

> The drafts are based on either of the two premises: (i) Women as a class are non-working spouses and their only contribution is unpaid domestic labour, or (ii) Men and women are equal partners and hence their rights, duties and responsibilities are equal and of a similar nature. A third category of women, who are the sole providers of their families, are invisible in this debate. The recommendations do not protect these women who shoulder the double burden as wage earners and home makers. The implications of introducing the concept of joint family property and equal right to matrimonial home and maintenance etc. using a gender neutral term spouse would be detrimental to the rights of these women, most of whom belong to the marginalized sections of society. The concerns of this large category of women are not reflected in any of the drafts.

[115] Agnes is less restrained when it comes to some other criticisms in the course of her discussion, as we also saw in some earlier chapters.

[116] This is where the newly fashionable term 'feminization of poverty' appears.

Agnes (2000: 188) concludes that a sustained campaign focusing on specific issues to pressurize the government into introducing reforms is lacking because the issue has become politicized and is submerged in other agenda. Noting that '[w]omen's rights seem to be lost in the larger controversy around [the] Uniform Civil Code which today, has become a political question',[117] she is not willing to admit that feminist reformists overcooked their goose. However, rather than making grand demands, she now advises a cautious reformative approach, bringing in small and specific reforms through concentrated campaigns. This reflects a notable modernist disillusionment, which is also apparent when Chandra (1998: 210) concludes that there is no reason for undue optimism when it comes to reforms that challenge patriarchal domination. In her concluding comments, Agnes (2000: 215) reiterates the major modernist, feminist agenda:

> There is a need to locate property at the centre of matrimonial law reform, if adequate solutions to the trend of poverty and destitution of women have to be evolved. Since patriarchy is reinforced through economic structures, be they feudalism, capitalism or post-capitalism, a solution to the oppression and destitution of women would have to be found primarily in the context of the economic structures and the state responsibility towards women within these structures. It is towards these directions that efforts of family law reform need to be forged.

It seems that the rather satisfactory current state of maintenance law for divorced Hindu wives has freed modernist energies for the next stage of assault on gender inequality. The focus now is on safeguarding the wife's automatic right to a share in the husband's property, which would involve a fundamental restructuring of property relations among Hindus. This may be well and good for rich women, but what about the poor wife who has no hope of any financial benefits from the husband?[118] Again, the modernist arguments are too much focused on the concerns of upper class women and too little interested in the real benefits for the average Hindu wife. A tough law on post-divorce maintenance is actually a device to keep marriages going, even if they are not a bed of roses. The modernist arguments push for privileging women to the extent that they can claim property rights merely on the basis of marriage. That is perhaps not a feasible system of making marriage arrangements in any society, and modernists had better recognize that. However, to the extent that their underlying agenda remain focused on the argument that marriage is a patriarchal institution for the suppression of women, there is no hope of coming to any agreeable solutions that would satisfy radical modernism and the

[117] On the uniform civil code debate, see Sathe (1995), Menski (2001, Chapter 6), and Larson (2001).

[118] S. Basu (2001) suggests on the basis of her fieldwork that even for poorer women, the value of dowry and presents received from their natal family never approaches the value of male shares.

establishment-oriented views of India's society, which like almost all human societies, continues to be dominated by androcentric notions.

The above arguments about increased property rights for women expect the state to assist women, and yet do not discuss to what extent the state has been seeking to achieve pro-women social welfare objectives. Stressing that the issue of the matrimonial home assumes great importance when a marriage breaks down, Kusum (2000: 234) reiterates correctly that there is no provision in Indian law that explicitly guarantees a Hindu wife the right to stay in the matrimonial home. She argues therefore that the concept of matrimonial home and its division after separation need to be clarified, more so in the light of recent rulings (ibid.: 235).

Modernist scholarship clearly remains deeply distrustful of the state. Several writers note that modern state law continues to be based on the same patriarchal presuppositions and traditional social norms that modernist activism has been seeking to combat. The problem for scholarly analysis has been that such feminist distrust of the state clouds the understanding of legal achievements and does not facilitate a full discussion. For example, Kusum (2000: 231) notes initially that '[n]ew dimensions have been added to various statutory provisions by liberal interpretation or by invoking principles of justice, equity and good conscience so that meaningful justice is imparted'. She then cites several older and inadequate cases on marriage solemnization which have been bad for women,[119] but does not mention that in many more recent decisions a presumption of marriage was applied, explicitly to assist and protect women.[120] When it comes to maintenance, too, Kusum (2000: 257) notes that the courts' activism in awarding damages to women has been positive. Still, judicial activism and discretion seem not to be fully accepted, as Kusum (2000: 268) indicates when discussing the impact of using Article 142 of the Constitution of India in terms of achieving 'complete justice':

> The article is capable of being stretched to any length in order to do 'complete justice'; and the court of late has been very generous in invoking this article. In the process there have been some judgements which have a potential of negative fall-out, but it needs to be conceded, that subjectivity and personal opinion of the judge cannot be completely extricated from the process of decision-making.

An undercurrent of fears that the state law cannot be completely trusted is evident from such statements. Agnes (2000: 169–70) clearly recognizes that

[119] Chapter 8 discussed this issue in detail, demonstrating the use of presumptions of marriage in cases that were not criminal prosecutions of husbands. Agnes (2000: 87) still complains that crafty husbands can use the loophole of marriage solemnization to evade responsibilities for their wife's maintenance and does not provide a balanced account at this point.

[120] However, Agnes (2000: 174) clearly recognizes the important role of presumptions of marriage.

insistence on complete state regulation in this case that without a certificate of marriage registration, there could be no claim for maintenance would be bad for women and children. Agnes (2000: 181) notes that in litigation on maintenance, 'husbands will find myriad ways to wriggle out of their economic responsibilities'. That is hardly unique to tradition or to Hindu law, and the same observations could be made for any legal system, confirming that such statements are little more than political rhetoric.

Agnes (2000: 178) highlights the problem of desertion and its disastrously negative economic consequences for many women. Yet if India weighted the laws of maintenance too much in favour of women, more Hindus might start following the modern Western pattern of unmarried cohabitation, which is evidently largely due to the fact that men and women in England have become wary of the formal legal ties of marriage and the potential legal difficulties of untying the knot. The feminist and modernist critiques of Hindu maintenance law are clearly too focused on individualism and take too little account of the socio-economic realities of India.[121] As we shall see below, the Indian judges have taken a remarkably wider view of such intricate matters.

Postmodernity in Judicial Social Engineering

In this final section, we see postmodern Hindu law on maintenance in action, constructed by India's superior judges,[122] who have clearly realized from the human misery displayed in front of them all the time that an activist approach was needed to secure Hindu women better implementation of their pre-existing traditional rights to maintenance. There is a clear progression in this field from paternalistic indulgence of male chauvinism towards almost militant reminders to Indian men that they cannot simply discard women and children at will, leaving others to care for their social and economic welfare.

As discussed in the previous section, it is not difficult to understand why modernist Indian scholars, arguing from their ivory towers, do not perceive more clearly that the needs of millions of potentially near-destitute Hindu wives and other Indian women have been at the centre of concerns among Indian judges. The evidence for this is found in the case law, which most modernist scholars and journalists have simply not read, so that it has remained easy for a few fashionable publications to misguide everyone about the true extent of judicial activism in Indian maintenance laws. A search for relevant judicial

[121] Singh (1989: 157) notes that in India, law has a different role to play than in the West where, generally speaking, law follows public opinion: 'In India, on the other hand, law should mould public opinion, remove traditional attitudes and foster new values'. This modernist approach does not account for the possibility that the law might reinforce tradition for the sake of protecting weaker sections.

[122] Too little is known about how lower courts decide such matters, mainly because their decisions are not reported. A detailed study of Bangladeshi family court cases (Monsoor 1998) confirms that it takes time for judicial activism at superior level to filter downwards, and that local judges may resist change.

statements would yield rich rewards. Already during the early beginnings of judicial activism in the late 1970s, with specific reference to Section 125 of the CrPC 1973, it was held by Krishna Iyer J in *Ramesh Chander v Veena Kaushal* AIR 1978 SC 1807, at pp. 1809–10, with particular focus on the constitutional dimension:

> This provision is a measure of social justice and specially enacted to protect women and children and falls within the constitutional sweep of Article 15(3) reinforced by Art. 39. We have no doubt that sections of statutes calling for construction by courts are not petrified print but vibrant words with social functions to fulfil. The brooding presence of the constitutional empathy for the weaker sections like women and children must inform interpretation if it has to have social relevance. So viewed, it is possible to be selective in picking out that interpretation out of two alternatives which advances the cause—the cause of the derelicts.

This is vintage Krishna Iyer, somewhat verbose and complex, but it gets across important social messages of fundamental importance to the Indian state and not just any particular community or group of people. I vividly recall that, at the time of his retirement, Derrett (1981: 15–6) was especially full of praise for the decision by Sathiadev J in *Soundarammal v Sundara Mahalinga Nadar* AIR 1980 Mad 294, which called for a rethinking of judicial policy towards Hindu men who simply abandoned their wives and left them to fend for themselves. After *Soundarammal*, there was for many years what I have called 'embarrassed silence' (Menski 1994), until by the mid-1980s judicial activism in maintenance law seemed to take off. Overshadowed by the public focus on Muslim law, there has been a parallel process of activization of Hindu maintenance law, which has hardly begun to be noticed by scholars. Earlier, in the context of debates about adultery and allegations of unchastity, Qureshi (1978: 360) clearly saw the problem that a wife may be mischievously deprived of maintenance entitlements by fake allegations of unchastity:

> ... in the case of unchastity, the court should adopt a very strict standard of proof because withholding the right of maintenance means literally throwing a woman on the road without means of support. If the wife has no source of income for her maintenance, she may be constrained to adopt improper means of earning her livelihood. Therefore, charge of adultery should strictly be proved in case of maintenance claims.

Postmodern Indian maintenance law has clearly taken such economic concerns on board, even though it remains correct to argue that access to courts constitutes a first hurdle for many women.[123] However, given the traditional claims that married Hindu women have against their husbands, it should not even be necessary to go to courts; informal negotiation should yield equitable deals for women. The notable recent judicial strictness with men who oppose

[123] See now Vatuk (2001) on Muslim women and access to family courts in Chennai.

the maintenance petitions of their wives and former wives can therefore also be interpreted as a strategy to direct Indians back to traditional methods of dispute settlement and informal negotiation of an individual woman's claim in the light of her specific circumstances. Modernists often forget in this respect that a woman who needs to negotiate her maintenance entitlements and future economic position will normally not be facing these negotiations on her own, but will be supported and often represented by men.[124] While it remains legitimate to ask why women's voices are not better heard, it could not be claimed that the traditional social framework totally disempowers women when it comes to financial arrangements.[125]

In addition to discouraging litigation in the first place, it is certain that the Indian state—prominently personified by the judges—realizes that it does not have the means to pay welfare handouts to divorcees and other victims of broken marriages. As we saw, it therefore became a matter of fiscal policy to restrict litigation,[126] to put men under strictly defined traditionally-gendered obligations, and thus to force Hindu society to address the problem within the informal social realm rather than in the formal courts, while retaining the official image of a modern legal system based on gender equality under the constitutional banner of 'complete justice', which is of course also a hidden reference to dharma.[127]

One consequence of this policy approach is that it forces most Hindu women to fall back on traditional compromise strategies to ensure survival and discourages formal litigation. However, women whose rightful claims are being disregarded will be given a sympathetic hearing, as several recent studies have noted. Research on divorced Hindu women clearly shows that economic factors force many women to remain in unsatisfactory marriages.[128] This would probably not be any different if Hindu women were given separate property rights from birth or at the time of marriage, unless there was a lot of property to claim. The problem lies primarily in widespread poverty, not in the nature of Hindu property rights per se. In other words, economic realism and plain necessity will continue to force spouses to make compromises. From

[124] Holden (2003) argues that, as a result, speaking of women's agency needs to be balanced with evidence that the males in a woman's natal family may be negotiating with the former husband, with or without the involvement of a panchayat.

[125] S. Basu (2001) reports interestingly on various strategies employed by women to hide assets from men and other family members.

[126] The Supreme Court of India, in *V. Bhagat v D. Bhagat* AIR 1994 SC 710, prevented the warring parties from wasting any further judicial time in a remarkable judgment that has many layers of meaning.

[127] A little later, the reformist eyewash of the Hindu husband's right to be maintained by his wife will be examined.

[128] On details see Dhagamwar (1987) and S. Basu (2001). Significant evidence that many divorced Hindu women regret having opted for divorce is found in Mehta (1975).

modernist perspectives, this will obviously be seen as negative, while the stability of marriages—and thus precisely the never-ending process of working out viable compromises in married life—as a foundation for social peace and well-being of the nation as a whole is being emphasized by India's postmodern judges. They are clearly the key thinkers in the dynamic field of Hindu maintenance law and they have not been afraid to voice some of their opinions. On the issue of social peace, the minority judgment in *Pratibha Rani v Suraj Kumar* AIR 1985 SC 628, at pp. 650–1, argued against use of stringent penal provisions in family litigation:

> Entertaining complaints of the irate wife or husband against the husband or wife without even an allegation of a specific and separate agreement constituting entrustment of the property ... would have disastrous effects and consequences on the peace and harmony which ought to prevail in matrimonial homes.

Similar arguments have been made about importing constitutional law into the family home in the context of restitution decrees, using the image of a bull in a china shop.[129] However, Kusum (2000: 237) is scathing in her reaction to the judge in *Pratibha Rani*, as cited above:

> While one appreciates the judge's concern for peace and harmony in matrimony, it needs to be noted that criminal law or other matrimonial litigation enters the matrimonial home only after peace and harmony has departed. The majority judgement is more in consonance with present-day reality, when greed for dowry is on the rise and wives are being tortured, harassed, killed or driven to death on this account. The court has made it explicit that the husband who withholds or uses the wife's stridhana without her consent 'takes a clear risk of prosecution under article 406 of the IPC'.

India's judges have evidently thought about the nature of modern maintenance laws, which cannot be based on state-financed input. They have consequently rejected that method of legal support for women and children, for fiscal rather than ideological reasons (Menski 2001). Further, regarding traditional Hindu law concepts, the judges have not rejected tradition in a modernist fashion, but are seeking to build it creatively into the most recent case law. Some authors are beginning to see this as well. Aggarwal (1988: 6–7) makes reference to *Kesarabai v Haribhau* AIR 1975 Bom 115, in which judicial awareness of the links between past and present and the interlinkedness of individual and society was indicated at p. 117:

> The system of Hindu law, as [it] came to be handed down to us, cannot be treated merely as a system of a religious or personal law. It has always been and has all the incidents of a purposeful and pragmatic law of social growth and development. There were principles present to the mind of the

[129] For details see Chandra (1998: 207–8) and *Harvinder Kaur v Harmander Singh* AIR 1984 Del 66.

> earliest law-givers that appear to be now statutorily recognized even in the present legislation .... In the institutional set-up, there is eminent effort to uphold the balance between individual interest and social good.

Significantly, the confused image of ancient lawgivers is surfacing here as well, but the pre-eminence of social balance is duly emphasized, albeit in secular language, and between the lines the principle of *sadācāra* may be detected. In this case, a Hindu wife was successfully seeking separate maintenance and the right to live separately because her husband was living with a concubine. Some thirty years later, Agnes (2000: 87) discusses the particular predicament of the Hindu wife who is party to a polygamous marriage and is at risk of being divested, finding (ibid.: 88) that the Indian courts will indeed protect the woman in that situation. Rather than being discriminatory against women, the postmodern Hindu law therefore explores gender equity by insisting that the traditional privileges of men must be reflected in larger obligations.

The issue of gender equity can also be instructively debated in the context of modern Hindu law rules, as found in Section 24 and Section 25 HMA, to the effect that a Hindu husband may seek maintenance from the wife. Qureshi (1978: 347) evidently liked the idea of gender equality and suggested that '[i]t should also be provided in the Uniform Civil Code that the husband is given an equal right with a wife to apply to the courts for maintenance. The courts should have discretion to decide, in what circumstances a wife should be required to make provision for him'. As a general rule, this seems a gender-neutral interpretation of 'spouse', as demanded by modernists. However, not even the modernists are totally happy with that legal position. Kusum (1990: 403–4) comments:

> The idea of a wife paying maintenance to the husband is not very popular as yet since it has always been the man's role to earn and maintain the family. Now with the changing times, however, there are changes in these age old concepts as well. Recognising this change, the Hindu Marriage Act 1955 made this revolutionary provision whereunder a husband has an equal right to claim maintenance from a wife as she has from him. This is the only Indian statute providing for maintenance to husbands.

The Indian courts have responded vigorously, slapping down the devious claims of some Hindu men who risked potential loss of status and reputation in society (*izzat*) to go to court claiming maintenance from their wives or tried other devious means to defraud their wives. In *Vinod Kumar Kejriwal v Usha Vinod Kejriwal*, AIR 1993 Bom 160, a devious husband was hiding his assets and making baseless allegations about the wife's unchastity, but was punished financially by an alert HC. In *Kanchan v Kamalendra* AIR 1992 Bom 493, a husband had successfully claimed maintenance from the wife, but on appeal he was sternly reminded that a mentally and physically able-bodied male has an obligation to maintain himself and his family. It was held at p. 494 that to hold otherwise would promote idleness and is opposed to the spirit of Section 24 HMA.[130]

Researchers seem even less convinced today that this placative emphasis on gender equality was useful. Agnes (2000, Chapter 6) describes it as a stilted effort at gender justice. Speaking of the 'perverse logic of equality' in the rule that a Hindu husband could ask to be maintained by his wife, Agnes (2000: 83) argues further that the concept did not exist in traditional marriage laws in India, was introduced for the first time under the HMA and was based on the Western notion of formal equality.

Kusum (1990: 404) seems more radical and significantly notes that '[h]ow many husbands would really want to go to court and seek maintenance from wives is a different matter, but the law should surely make a provision to meet such situations'. She also cites a case from Kashmir, *Lalit Mohan v Tripta Devi* AIR 1990 J&K 7, in which a Hindu husband successfully claimed maintenance against his wife. This husband had been the victim of an accident which caused a head injury, so that he lost his mental balance. The marriage broke down and the wife obtained a decree for divorce. The husband's appeal against the divorce failed, but he was granted maintenance from the wife. He had asked for Rs 500 per month, but was given Rs 100 per month and Rs 500 as litigation expenses. R.P. Sethi J was quite proud of the achievements of modern Indian law in promoting gender equality and held, at p. 10, that it was a revolutionary provision, which did not exist in any of the Western countries.

In their postmodern desire to find justice and appropriate solutions to family problems brought before them—and to discourage such litigation at the same time—India's superior judges have been quite candid about the financial dimension, awarding in some cases huge sums of money to women who might not even need it, but whose ex-husbands certainly could afford to share their wealth. At the same time, they have been telling poor litigants that they will have to survive as best they can, since 'where the husband happens to be an indigent person or becomes an indigent person, it is a misfortune that has to be shared by the wife also', as held in *Sivankutty v S. Komalakumari* AIR 1989 Ker 124.

Significantly, Anand (1992: 184) argues that the courts must be enabled to grant compensation, and not just maintenance, to women who are duped by men. In fact, Anand (1992: 185) goes further and argues that because the law of post-divorce maintenance ties the woman uncomfortably to the former spouse, relationship with whom was no more possible, the law of maintenance should be construed as a law of compensation. This has begun to be considered by some judges. Anand (1992: 184) also argues that the emphasis ought to shift from periodic payments to one lump-sum payment, thus avoiding problems over the refusal of husbands to honour their obligations at any time after the court hearing. Kusum (2000: 257) argues:

[130] For relevant details of such cases and quotations of the key statements, see Menski (2001: 263–5).

> Divorce or separation has a traumatic effect on the spouses but the repercussions are more serious for the wife because of her weaker economic and social position. Judicial sensitivity to the emotional, physical, mental and economic problems of wives is indicated in several judgements during the past few years where damages or compensation has been awarded to aggrieved wives. Though the judicial process cannot restore the emotional damage, it can to some extent, mitigate the financial problems.

Kusum (2000: 257) also indicates that compensation was ordered in cases where husbands duped women into a marriage.[131] She also helpfully reports on a case in which Supreme Court judges severely criticized the husband, and punished him financially, for harassing the wife in various ways.[132] Kusum (2000: 258) reports that the Supreme Court expressed deep anxiety and concern that the wife should be adequately compensated for the mental agony, strain and stress that she had undergone as a result of the allegations against her. Indeed, relatively generous financial terms were agreed for the wife. A court-induced settlement produced an order under which the husband agreed to deposit Rs 30,000 as ordered by the HC. In addition, as Kusum reports (id.), the appeals against conviction for defamation were compounded on the husband paying another Rs 100,000. There is a significant element of public education in this case, reminiscent of the advice which Derrett (1970: 441–2) gave about handling obnoxiously litigious husbands. Kusum (2000: 258) reports from the decision in *Mukund Martand Chitnis,* at p. 1806:

> The husband was also required to tender an unqualified apology in the court within one week for the mental strain and stress caused to the wife on account of the various defamatory allegations made against her. As aptly remarked by the court: '[T]his should prove to be an eye-opener to those who believe that they can get away by casting aspersions on a woman to serve their ends and silence her'.

Recently, the Supreme Court of India has also begun to be more alert to cases of fraudulent marriage arranged by overseas Indians, and has been pursuing such husbands vigorously, giving clear signals that they would be penalized financially.[133] All of this must be seen within the wider context of India's postmodern welfare state. Singh (1993: 219) notes in this respect, with some satisfaction:

> Today the concept of welfare state regulates every aspect of life of its citizens. The state felt it necessary to remove the servile condition of women and to provide for them certain protections against masculine tirade. Today's woman has come to have better acceptability and respectability, better status

[131] The cases cited by Kusum are *Bodhisattva Gautam v Subhra Chakraborty* AIR 1996 SC 922 and *Ranjit Kumar Bhattacharya v Sabita Bhattacharya* AIR 1996 Cal 301.

[132] The case is *Mukund Martand Chitnis v Madhuri Chitnis* AIR 1997 SC 1804.

[133] See *Neeraja Saraph v Jayant Saraph* (1994) 6 SCC 461.

> of equality with men, better rights and privileges, in all the spheres of Indian life—social, economic and political. In this upgradiation of status of woman and recognition of her legitimate place in the family and in the society as a whole, the law has played a great role and it has acted as an instrument of change.

Much earlier, Ross (1961: 72) noted perceptively that '[a]lthough giving alms is part of the religious duty of Hindus, to be the recipient of public charity is considered to be a calamity'. However, there is clear awareness among India's judges that Hindu wives who claim post-divorce maintenance and other entitlements are not asking for charity, but for justice and implementation of their due rights. Skilfully constructing a postmodern protective legal framework for Hindu wives with particular reference to post-divorce maintenance, India's judges have grasped the nettle in a much more efficient manner than modernist analysis, which remains myopic also in this field.

It is thus evident that economic pressures propelled the Hindu law of maintenance, and with it the entire Indian legal regulation in this particular field, into a decidedly postmodern scenario, in which the state formally watches over flexible, local, and situationally-conditioned solutions, but primarily expects social processes to take care of the welfare of women, children, and elderly people.[134] The most significant development in this field is not, as politicized scholarship tends to assume, the *Shah Bano* controversy of 1985, but rather the 'quiet reforms' from as early as 1973, when India's old colonial CrPC of 1898 was reworked. This patriarchal colonial law had protected the maintenance rights of wives only during marriage, so that a devious husband in newly independent India could now simply divorce his wife with ease under the modern provisions of the HMA 1955 and then refuse all further responsibility for her. By adding 'divorced wife' to the definition of 'wife', Section 125 of the secular CrPC of 1973 ushered in a postmodern revolution which evidently took time to make itself felt. The present analysis of this particular legal topic confirms that modernist Indian lawmakers have learnt some crucial lessons during the past few decades, mainly about the limits of law in society.[135] Postmodern Hindu law in this field now reflects the realistic recognition of a need for the formal state law to rely on social support mechanisms from within the family to make up for the lack of a welfare state system in India. Modernity, in this field, has simply proved too costly for the state.

[134] Similar developments can be observed in Chinese law, and also in Singapore, where Confucian values of filial piety and correct social behaviour have been invoked for a new law in 1993 regarding the maintenance of parents (Harding 2001: 207).

[135] Such lessons are going to be more difficult to accept in the vast field of Indian constitutional law (but see already Menski 1996b). The warning signs have been there since long. Arun Shourie (2001: 198) now identifies 'grievance-mongering' through inflated expectations of the law as a major problem for the postmodern Indian state.

Part III

Concluding Analysis

13

Postmodernity and Beyond

The present study has examined the theoretical and historical development of Hindu law from a postmodern approach that critically deconstructs its modernist distortions. Hindu law can no longer be read as an isolated case study of an 'oriental' legal system undergoing a unilinear process of modernization that leads to its eventual supersession. The evolution of Hindu personal law since independence suggests that a substantial portion of the world's population has gently and silently rejected modern Western, state-centric notions of law as unsuitable for their respective conditions of life. Hindu law today retains culture-specific elements which effectively resist globalizing pressures and create space for a future that most modernists would deny to indigenous Asian and African legal systems. The findings of the present study carry important implications for the study of Hindu law itself, as well as highlighting the gradual metamorphosis of law into a broader, multidisciplinary field of scholarly inquiry.

The central challenge of this study has been to enable lawyers as well as non-lawyers to make sense of Hindu law as a major legal system in past and present times. This has been a difficult task, not only because of interdisciplinary complications and specific technical terminologies, but also because of the nature of Hindu law itself. The deconstructivist analysis of this study has shown that Hindu law is not neatly laid out in codes, as we are still constantly told. Ancient Hindu law was primarily located in natural law presumptions and in social environments which may or may not take account of the formal state law that may exist on certain subjects, but not on many others. Law as a phenomenon is much more than the positivist state law of dominant Western theories. In particular, the model of tripartite legal structure proposed by Chiba (1986) proved useful as an analytical tool.[1] While official law does not represent the whole field of law, it became evident from analysis of Indian case law that custom and Hindu cultural concepts continue to play a critical role in the evolution of Hindu jurisprudence. There is a need for current research to investigate such important aspects of Hindu law more thoroughly, rather than succumb to simplistic modernist accounts of formal textual prescription and traditional rigidity. Hindu law must be understood as a complex living system

[1] To recapitulate, Chiba (1986) distinguished 'official law', 'unofficial law', and 'legal postulates' and argued that their constant interaction creates 'law', thereby challenging the dominance of positivist thinking that law is only what the state says it is.

with many intangible and invisible elements, rather than a single, tangible fossilized relic.

Arguing that Hindu law in India today has reached a condition of postmodernity,[2] this study has challenged not only core assumptions of legal modernity, but also traditional and modernist perceptions and constructions of Hindu culture and Hindu law, as well as dominant ideas about law itself. Hindu law is a classic example of a non-Western legal system that refuses the primacy of state-centred approaches to law. Law, from a Hindu perspective, is primarily concerned with natural law ideals, emphasizing self-controlled ordering at all levels and in all situations, a cultural message that Indian law has constructively employed.

The present study has demonstrated in detail that modernist assertions about the displacement of Hindu law are not based on solid research, but arise from ideological presumptions about the innate superiority of formal, supposedly Western legal models. The modernist discourse expected unidirectional assimilation to dominant Euro-American lego-cultural norms and models. In effect it demanded de-Hinduization through abandoning of Hindu customs, traditions, and religion and the adoption of secular, modernist law reforms. However, the modernist discourse, in distorting both the representation and actual structure of Hindu law, itself eventually fell to its own civilizing sword. Slowly, but surely, the modernist process of reform reached a stage where its protagonists and enforcers, particularly the higher judiciary, recognized that Hindu law does not fit into the straightjacket of 'religious' and 'secular' binaries. It has always been both, and continues to make creative use of its internal plurality to maintain dharma. Indian judges, as the most eminent representatives of the state, have recognized that to maintain a blind adherence to modernist axioms, and dismiss tradition in all its ugliness, would not ultimately be conducive to achieving socio-economic justice, the fundamental goal of the Constitution. In order to govern the vast majority of India's more than one billion people justly and effectively, Hindu law must be actively integrated into processes of making and implementing law. As a result, Hindu law has continued to play a central role as an Indian personal law and its concepts have arguably become embedded and interwoven within the wider superstructure of Indian law.

Demonstrating that certain traditional conceptual elements of Hindu law have remained relevant for the reconstruction of Hindu law during the post-independence period, the present study was able to show with reference to statutes and case decisions how the resuscitation and unexpected growth of Hindu law in post-colonial India occurred. Without essentializing Hinduness, adopting a socio-legal approach, it has been possible to explain how ancient Hindu key concepts in their contemporary incarnations have contributed to

[2] This explicit emphasis on Indian Hindu law is necessary, since there are many other types of Hindu law in the world, none of which seems to have reached a postmodern condition in quite the same way.

the genesis of postmodern Hindu law. Rather than being abandoned for the achievement of a modernist agenda, Hindu law has experienced a process of conceptual remoulding through the justice-conscious actions of an activist judiciary. In turn, it has metamorphosed into a sophisticated legal system that has moved beyond the discursive axioms of 'tradition' and 'modernity' into a condition of postmodernity.

These findings, undoubtedly polemical,[3] raise numerous questions for the study of Hindu law, Indian public law, and Indian family law. Theoretically, they also contribute to the emerging debates in comparative jurisprudence and ethnic minority legal studies. Five issues for critical reflection are examined in turn below: (1) the imperative to study Hindu law from a postmodern perspective as an evolving conceptual entity and a living legal system, rather than in modernist terms as a fixed textual code; (2) the need to analyse the manifestations of postmodernity in the wider system of Indian law; (3) the utility of deconstructing modernist discourses of law in understanding non-Western legal systems; (4) the need for a critical re-assessment of dominant concepts of law, particularly given current debates about the globalization of laws; and (5) the implications of such shifting understandings of law for an increasingly visible, relatively ignored facet of globalization, namely the transplantation of non-Western communities to Euro-American jurisdictions as a result of global labour and migration flows.

Transcending Tradition and Modernity in Hindu Law

The diachronical history of Hindu law examined in this study suggests that it must be viewed both as an ancient, constantly evolving conceptual entity and a living legal system, rather than as a positivist system of regulation based on fixed textual codes. Chapters 3 and 4 showed traditional Hindu socio-cultural (and hence legal) structures as premised on the supremacy of self-controlled ordering, encapsulated in the idealized term of dharma. This method of microcosmic ordering, which need not even involve any visible processes of dispute settlement, as the concept of 'satisfaction of the individual's conscience' (*ātmanastuṣṭi*) demonstrates, was explicitly dismissed by Lingat (1973: 6) as not legal. This study has illustrated with reference to past and present case law material that such basic Hindu concepts are in fact centrally relevant to understanding the Hindu system of legal regulation. The ideal is that there should be no need for formal legal processes to ascertain dharma. Self-reflective contemplation should be sufficient to make individuals do the right thing at any time, which remains the simplest general paraphrase of dharma.

[3] Peters and Schwenke (2000: 829) emphasize that the historical situatedness and the research environment in which we write influences legal study and that 'heightened reflexivity comprises an awareness of the relationship between one's research and the *Zeitgeist*: the comparatists' themes, goals and approaches are shaped by broad intellectual or theoretical trends or movements, by societal developments and the political climate'.

The next level of ascertaining self-controlled order or dharma, namely satisfaction of peer expectations or group norms (*sadācāra*) has widely been treated as 'custom'. This central element of traditional Hindu law became formally and legally marginalized once the British obtained control of Hindu legal administration, though without ever managing to remove this important aspect of Hindu practice from the legal scene. Even today, customary law remains a vital aspect of Hindu law for many citizens of India, and even for overseas Hindus. Closer analysis shows that custom has resurfaced in statutes and cases as an integral element of postmodern Hindu legal ordering. Recognition of legal diversity is a systemic part of Hindu legal philosophy, while uniformity of legal rules is treated as a manifestation of injustice. To that extent, it could be said that the ancient Hindus were postmodern without having experienced what we perceive as modernity.

However, this and other characterizations of the nature of Hindu law continue to be contested in various ways. Despite the writings of Derrett (1968b) and others, our understanding of the ancient Sanskrit texts remains unclear. To what extent should they be seen as legal texts? But how can we find universally acceptable answers to such questions, given the absence of agreed definitions of law in the first place? As highlighted throughout this study, images of ancient, divinely given codes offer some Hindus evidence that their cultural system is not only ancient, but also legally authoritative in the highest sense.[4] But to what extent is there some truth in the assertion, prominently made by a group of American specialists, that some of the later *smṛtis* were indeed legal texts written by jurists for lawyers? On this point, I have to criticize my Indological colleagues rather than modernist lawyers and social scientists.

Few scholars are prepared today to undergo the hardship of producing critical editions and readable new translations of ancient Sanskrit texts.[5] Such authors are far too experienced not to be aware of the complexity of the subjects they cover. However, while one must admire such Indological scholarship, serious doubts remain over the modernist (mis)representations of Hindu law. My main criticism is that Indological scholars miss the point when they characterize dharma as 'law' as understood in common parlance and in positivism-focused legal circles.[6] In fact, the concept of dharma as 'self-controlled

[4] But Hindus then pay the price for asserting that their legal system is religious law by finding it dismissed as 'traditional' and unsuitable for the modern age.

[5] I refer in particular to three recent projects of textual edition and translation, Larivière (1989) on the *Nāradasmṛti*, Olivelle (2000) on the *dharmasūtras*, and Rocher (2002) on the *Dāyabhāga*.

[6] Indologists claim to know this, but the large number of casual references made to the 'laws of Manu' and continuing use of positivist language by many writers demonstrates that claim and reality do not coincide. The main damage was apparently done by Bühler's (1975) translation of the *Manusmṛti* as 'The Laws of Manu', but it did not help that Doniger (1991) retained the same title. More recently, Domenico Francavilla, the young Italian translator of Lingat's (1973) *The Classical Law of India* agonized over the choice of an appropriate Italian title that will not

order' carries definite anti-positivist legal messages—it seeks to avoid state law. Chapter 3 showed that classical dharma was centrally concerned with self-controlled order and ideally requires no formal legal intervention. The need for law is treated as evidence of decay and decline in moral standards. This seems quite akin in outlook to Marxist idealizing about the ultimate withering away of legal superstructures. But early Hindu assumptions were already developed at a time when formal superstructures were not yet in existence.[7] In that sense, dharma not only precedes but virtually pre-empts law. To suggest that the ancient Sanskrit texts are law books of some kind, thus, distorts the important cultural and legal messages that ancient Hindu law contains. They are indeed important normative texts (Olivelle 2000: v), but that does not make them law books in the Western positivistic sense of the term.

However, Larivière (1989) asserted that the *Nāradasmṛti* represents Hindu jurisprudence par excellence, treating the concept of *vyavahāra* as 'law' and as a purely secular process described in a Hindu law code. While many Hindus will find it quite agreeable that an American professor should underwrite claims that the ancient Hindus had codes of law, even if just of procedural law, I disagree. Precisely here, secular modernist assumptions about the nature of 'law' are rather violently interfering with the internal perceptions on which the ancient Hindu textual sources themselves are built. Superficially, indeed, formal legal processes of dispute settlement can be perceived as secular legal phenomena and as 'law'. My argument is most definitely not that the ancient Hindus had no awareness of 'law' and legal processes: Hindu law is focused on self-controlled order *as well as* the processing of disputes, but these both seek to avoid creating space for litigation as a secular activity.

If one takes a purely secular approach, what then has happened to the idea of the primacy of self-controlled ordering? More specifically, where is dharma in this equation? Why has it become invisible though it still exists, even if only as the desirable end result of dispute settlement processes? The concept of dharma is surely not absent altogether, but Larivière's approach has indeed

create misleading expectations about Hindu 'law'. The subtitle of Olivelle (2000) indicates that the *dharmasūtras* are sold to the public as 'law codes', probably a marketing device by the publishers: a law book would surely sell better than a book of cryptic sayings by old men. Olivelle himself does not take the view that dharma is just law, but then the language we use should carefully reflect such knowledge. For an appropriately cautious recent example of treating *smṛti* texts as 'instructing', non-binding guidance rather than legal prescription, see Arp (2000).

[7] This may be wrong, since there is a distinct possibility that the learned people who created the relevant Sanskrit verses about the decline of self-controlled order (Chapter 3) might have been engaged not only in social criticism, but more specifically in critique of early rulers and their abuse of powers. The ancient Greeks were not unique in exploiting legal and political powers; we know what their early philosophers thought about that. For ancient India, the image of general decline in the *kaliyuga* suggests an element of shoulder-shrugging resignation, as ideal standards were simply not met, and could not ever be met, given the exigencies of life.

outlawed it in the sense that Ugo Mattei identifies,[8] so that dharma is now considered irrelevant for the lawyer, while the focus falls on the legal technicalities of dispute settlement. However, the deeper purpose of disputation and settling disputes, as processes of ascertaining dharma, is to protect macrocosmic and microcosmic order, not just to decide disputes. The fact that ancient authors were more or less silent about dharma in this context merely confirms that they took the underlying concepts as known, not that they were superseded.

This means that *vyavahāra* cannot properly just be read as 'civil law'. It is first of all a tool of dharma, a technique to bring about order and balance with minimal interference from outside agents, such as judges and the state. The concept of *vyavahāra* may look secular to an outside observer. But from an insider's perspective, it is not only religious, in the broad sense in which everything in the Hindu cosmic vision could be said to have a religious dimension (Menski 2002), but is at the same time also social, legal, and everything else that may be relevant in any specific scenario of dispute settlement. A diversity-focused, postmodern interpretation of this ancient concept confirms therefore that, long before the current postmodern age, ancient Hindus were able to handle plurality and interdisciplinarity in a way that reflects the integrated and central nature of dharma as self-controlled ordering rather than technical 'law'. Rather than being treated as skilfully constructed manuals for ancient litigators, texts like the *Nāradasmṛti* should therefore be read as expressions of concern for the protection of this dharmic self-controlled order.

Other American Sanskritists working on law-related texts appear to follow Larivière's lead in portraying certain later *smṛti* texts as legal documents. Such conceptual errors are exacerbated when Rocher (2002: 4) now asserts that '[w]hat is understood as "law" in the West is expressed in Sanskrit by the terms *vivāda* and *vyavahāra*, the former corresponding to substantive law, the latter to legal procedure'. These two Sanskrit terms do indeed relate to disputation or litigation, more or less formal processes of dispute settlement, but this is hardly a full equivalent of 'law' in its Western sense. Such scholarly misrepresentations of concepts of Hindu law as 'law' lull readers into a false sense of certainty and create a misguided view of the nature of Hindu law. The way in which Rocher (2002: 4) describes how the texts 'determine who can sue whom and in what form, and lay down the rules on how persons who are sued ought to present their defense' creates the impression that fixed formal rules, rather than situation-specific informal suggestions for solutions to dharmic problems, were produced in the shastric literature. Such comments show that positivist blinkers have continued to affect the work of Sanskritists, resulting in potentially disastrous distortions of the nature of Hindu law and its sources. This, in turn, makes it easy for others to say that this ancient law is now defunct and virtually irrelevant (Galanter and Krishnan 2001). Contrary to their own presuppositions, therefore, the American scholars of Hindu law are producing

[8] See Mattei (2001: 254–5), cited in the last section of this chapter.

highly relevant material for the postmodern analysis of Hindu law, rather than just documents of antiquarian value. But what they are presenting to us is not 'the law' as it ever was, but specific samples of ideas about certain key concepts and processes. Such research is successful in uncovering some building blocks of traditional and post-classical Hindu law, but misrepresents legal processes in Hindu law.

It is remarkable that the pitfalls of such positivist reductionism are also strongly reflected in scholarship on Hindu law produced by Indian legal scholars. As we saw, the whole field of Hindu law was fundamentally redefined through legalistic, modernist interventions during the colonial period, creating the 'monstrous hybridity' of Anglo-Hindu law. Among lawyers (and large sections of the general public, too) Hindu law as a term was thereafter no longer used for the holistic entirety of what Hindus perceive as dharma, but became restricted to formal rules based on textual authority, judicial decisions and high-caste normative assumptions.[9] The result has been, as we saw particularly in Part II, the creation of strange academic half-truths, such as the claim that Hindu law does not know divorce, while in social reality customary divorces remain widespread.[10]

This split consciousness is strongly reflected in current legal scholarship, which continues to cling blindly to modernist discourses about law. The wide field of Hindu law has, since colonial times, been divided into Hindu law proper, i.e. rules based on textual sources and Sanskritic conceptualizations, and 'custom'. The latter is either not treated as law at all, or only recognized grudgingly when a claimant insists that habitual action, or simply the action followed in a particular scenario, should qualify for legal recognition under 'customary law'. Many references to 'Hindu law' therefore cover only a thin segment of reality and readers are not often told about this. The neglect and contempt of Hindu customs by much of legal scholarship and practice has not only done enormous social damage,[11] it has also created a widening gulf between the formal, official Hindu law and unofficial Hindu socio-legal realities. We have had many occasions in this study to observe such discrepancies.

The ancient *smṛti* texts as a source of legal authority were formally deprived of legal standing and are presumed to have become more or less legally

[9] In addition, for many social scientists, Hindu law became reduced to certain obnoxious placative rules, such as the 'law' relating to women, who should at all times be dependent on men.

[10] Certain claims of this type have been shown to be false. For example, the assumption that all Hindu marriages must include a *saptapadī* ritual, which would mean imposition of high-caste values on all Hindus, is clearly not underwritten by the current law as found in Section 7 HMA 1955 (see Chapter 8).

[11] This was illustrated in the case of the Tamil self-respecters (*Deivaini Achi* AIR 1954 Mad 657) who found their marriages legally de-recognized, and occurred as late as 1994 in *Śurjit Kaur v Garja Singh* AIR 1994 SC 135, depriving a Sikh widow of her due entitlements to property.

irrelevant when statutory interventions codified modern Hindu law, especially during the 1950s and until 1976.[12] Superficially, it may appear that all the traditional elements of classical Hindu jurisprudence have been superseded by modernizing developments, so that observers like Galanter can simply assert the irrelevance of Hindu law.[13] In addition, knowledge acquisition of traditional Hindu topics has systematically been suppressed through Indian and other education systems, so that students are fed on modernist diets, individuals are indoctrinated as subjects of a positivist state, and teachers are almost everywhere unable, unwilling, or even afraid to bring traditional Hindu law into the academic picture. This is modernist social engineering through education, a process of deliberately promoting the withering away of a branch of knowledge that is actually central to developing self-awareness among those people who consider themselves Hindus. Perhaps it is not explicitly the job of schools and academia to produce order-conscious and socially responsible individuals who can think on their own, can solve problems, and who are aware of justice, but all of these elements would appear to make not only a good Hindu, but also a versatile lawyer and a decent human being. Denying validity to traditional Hindu law as a subject of knowledge damages global knowledge structures.[14]

In a climate of widespread hostility and ignorance, even among scholars, the academic analysis of Hindu law has been impeded and has become thin.[15] In India too, modern scholarship has marginalized Hindu law, declaring it irrelevant to our day and age, opposing it as reactionary, misogynist, and representing everything that an unsatisfactory past and 'tradition' stand for. Such obvious political interferences have driven away potential researchers and have further contributed to the paucity of knowledge on Hindu law. Frustration is evident when Olivelle (2000: v) notes:

> Normative texts have had a bad press lately among scholars. Some argue that these sources are unreliable and worthless for historical purposes,

[12] Hence, Rocher (2002: vii) emphasizes that his aim in re-translating the text of the *Dāyabhāga*, since it is no longer a direct legal authority, is academic rather than practice-relevant in a legal sense.

[13] Derrett (1970: 400) indicates criticism of Galanter's early views, which have not been modified, as Galanter and Krishnan (2001: 285–6) demonstrate through their renewed assertions, which do not answer the question that Derrett raised more than thirty years earlier.

[14] Bhambhri (1998) critically notes that social science in India has now accepted the Western intellectual agenda, a process promoted by funds from outside the universities. I found this confirmed in leading Indian institutions of legal education.

[15] Scholarship on Hindu law remains at preliminary levels of observation and analysis (Sivaramayya 1988; Singh 1990; Dhavan 1992). Mansfield (1993) appears to have been influential, as the bibliographical overview in Larson (2001: 349–50) confirms. Interdisciplinary work remains undeveloped (see earlier O'Flaherty and Derrett 1978). Dhagamwar (1992) provides an excellent model of socio-legal analysis.

> proposing instead the use of archaeological, inscriptional, and art historical materials for historical reconstruction. Clearly, these are invaluable sources for any study of India's past. But I think the dismissal of normative texts is unwise and unwarranted and betrays a singular ignorance of these documents. Many scholars unfortunately derive their knowledge of these texts through secondary sources, which often flatten the intellectual landscape and describe these documents as presenting a uniform code of conduct. The divergent views and dissenting voices are silenced. The reality, as anyone who undertakes a close reading of these documents can see, is very different.

While I have cautioned above against reading too much formal law into the ancient Hindu texts, I am definitely not denying that the Hindu cultural texts are legally relevant. But they are neither the law itself, in the sense of codes, nor even a dominant source of law. Instead, as Olivelle indicates, they are *one* potential support mechanism for ascertaining dharma, reflecting a conceptual understanding of law that differs significantly from modernist and positivist assumptions about the nature of the state, law and order, and justice. All of these, in the cosmic vision of the traditional Hindu system of thought, are more or less invisibly linked to macrocosmic order, the conceptual core of Hinduism, which has remained carefully protected from making ambitions uniform for any one sect or group of Hindus throughout times.[16] State law has always been merely a servant of Hindu legal order, a marginal force in view of the primacy of internal self-control. Hindu philosophy admits that it is virtually impossible to find the ultimate Truth,[17] which did indeed lead many ancients to nihilism in the form of *saṃnyāsa* and other methods of renunciation from worldly affairs, including the refusal to marry or to maintain a marital relationship.[18]

Unacknowledged for various reasons, there has always been an inherent tension in Hindu philosophy between uniformity and plurality, based on the conceptual links between the uniforming principle of *ṛta* and the infinitely plural element of dharma. In this constant struggle at all levels of mental and physical activity, *ṛta* and its dharmic tentacles seem to pull all Hindus, whatever their position, towards awareness that, at the end of the day, there is only

[16] Hence, even today, there can be no agreement over 'Hindu', nor over *hindutva* and A.B. Vajpayee, the Indian prime minister (cited in *India Today* 20 May 2002), is quite rightly critical of the political use made of the concept.

[17] We know in particular that the ancient quest of Hindus for ultimate truth (later, it seems, diverted into the more easily manageable search for individual salvation) encountered all the time the basic problem of *neti neti*, namely that the Absolute 'is not this, and is not that'.

[18] This is an issue not only for men, but also for women, as the powerful story of princess Mirabai demonstrates. It is now mainly interpreted as a story about individual devotion (bhakti) to a chosen god. However, other layers of meaning, namely social protest and opposition to the dominant male framework are equally powerful.

one big but unknowable Truth which links everything and everyone together.[19] At the same time, inherently complementary in principle as well as contradictory in practice, the unlimited diversity and differentiation of dharma makes for observations of total, messy diversity, in which differentiations of gender, caste, and other status markers blur the underlying picture of uniformity. Such creative conceptual tensions, irresolvable in principle, have been too narrowly perceived as negative by a modernist scholarship that treats traditional Hindu law as static, rigidly hierarchical, and focused on the systematic exclusion of women, low-caste Hindus, and others. Since the sea of Hindu cultural texts allows everyone to pick and choose those elements that suit specific conditions or arguments, there cannot indeed be any agreement on anything. Unsurprisingly, widespread confusions persist over the assessment of Hindu law as a culture-specific entity and a conceptual and real system of legal regulation that rightly claims to be different (Shourie 1993: 9–17).

The process of adjusting law to the people's needs is also not an unfamiliar concept for Hindu law, given that it is not based on positivist presumptions. A despotic ancient Hindu ruler could not simply terrorize his people through his own dictates and hope to survive for long. Hindu law allows such a ruler to be killed by his own people to protect dharmic order. The ruler's dharma is to respect the concerns of his subjects, not to lay down the law for them. Traditional Hindu law and personal law regulation were securely established long before Muslim rulers attempted to intervene in Hindu self-regulatory processes.[20] The new rulers realized that it would be best to continue the old system, in which different laws for various groups of people within the realm would prevail, while keeping a semblance of 'official law' at the top. This reflects political expediency, but also a culture-specific understanding of Hindu law on the part of Muslims, who face similar conceptual problems. The British

[19] One may compare the problems that monotheistic religions created for themselves and their followers by insisting that the identity of the Absolute is known—but He (about whose gendered identity Christianity is not absolutely sure, while Muslims insist that God is male) must not be pictured. Thus epistemological traditions that insist and depend on assertions that God is known still do not permit believers to know 'the full story'. In either case, there will then also be limits to absolute legal authority, important safeguards against terrorism directed at one's own people in the name of religion.

[20] It is quite wrong to assume that colonial rule produced the personal law system of the subcontinent. Personal laws pre-existed colonial rule everywhere, and merely assumed a new form following colonial intervention. Yet modernist discourses continue to distort our knowledge of Indian legal history. Corbridge and Harriss (2000: 25 and 31) categorically deny that pre-colonial India had anything resembling a 'civil society' and also claim, at p. 180, that the British introduced separate laws for Hindus and Muslims in their realm. Parker (2001: 184) faithfully reports that '[t]he established historiography of Anglo-Indian law places the origin of the "personal laws" in Warren Hastings's Plan of 1772'. This is a classic case of myopia among colonial historians, as well as a device to declare the earlier past irrelevant.

were apprehensive about upsetting their colonial subjects through interference in their religious and social rule systems and somehow knew they could not abolish Hindu law. Hence, neither Muslim nor European colonization and the subsequent top-down modernization of independent India have been able to dislodge Hindu law. Baxi (1986a: 216–7) notes:

> Colonization processes superimposed "Western" legal norms, institutions and culture. Even so, most social life still continued to be under the domain of people's law. In these societies, even after independence and despite massive reassertion of Western legal culture, many vital areas of social life continue to be governed and dominated by non-state legal systems (NSLS), which as often complement as contradict the SLS.

The above observations reflect the latent power struggle between state law and people's law in India. Ambedkar's modernist radicalism in the 1940s and early 1950s assumed a little too brashly that one could simply do away with 'Hindu tradition' through legislation. Not surprisingly, he was defeated and resigned in disgust. The underlying conceptual problems go much deeper than academic focus on the clash of prominent legal personalities has cared to investigate. The critical question is whether positivist state laws can actually abolish an entirely different category of law, such as concepts and principles of *ṛta* and dharma. The answer to that must be in the negative. Hence, any state that attempts to reform its people's cultural and religious traditions will generate not only protests, but also a certain level of legal pluralism and of non-compliance.[21]

If concepts like *ṛta* and dharma do not lend themselves for legislative abolition, can their consequences be challenged by state law? Here the official answer must be in the affirmative, because the state law must formally uphold its own claims to supremacy in order to buttress a desired model of 'rule of law'. But this works only as long as the analyst applies standard legal positivist assumptions. It makes no sense from the analytical perspective of legal pluralism, or Chiba's (1986) model of the interactive coexistence of 'official law', 'unofficial law', and 'legal postulates'. No amount of official law-making will render the other aspects of law irrelevant.

We saw that in post-colonial India neither Ambedkar's purely secular approach nor Gandhi's model of return to Hindu values, concepts, and processes were chosen. Instead, a messy compromise was decreed, replicating the ancient shastric duality and doublespeak of texts and customs, leading to a contest between central state legislation and local norms. Post-colonial India

[21] The romantic modernist notion that legal transplants function without problems has been insufficiently challenged. Turkey's continuing struggles to defend secularism and enforce secular family laws are contested (Yilmaz 1999; Örücü 1999b). Ethiopia rejected an imposed codified legal system. Japan and Thailand adopted foreign rules, but translated them into their social environment. Tanase (2001: 190) notes for Japan that '[a]n eventual victory of the law is not so certain'.

was neither going to be modern nor traditional: it would have to find a myriad of middle paths. Seen from this perspective, there is a compelling internal logic underpinning the eventual process of moving beyond tradition and modernity.

For a while, though, it looked as though modernism had won the day. Reformist projects were still promulgated in the mid-1970s, but in India this process came to a halt in the early 1980s. In various areas of constitutional law and family law, the legislature and the judiciary realized that social justice for around a billion people could easily be guaranteed on paper, for example in the Constitution of 1950, but would not be achieved in social reality by state intervention alone. It seems that post-colonial Indian lawmakers and policy planners rediscovered the concept of 'self-controlled order' and began to integrate the role of 'the people' more explicitly into legal planning. In this model, every individual citizen would have to contribute, giving his or her best to the collective effort of nation building and maintaining a viable legal system. The result has been that the purportedly modern Indian state became a postmodern manifestation of the ancient Hindu system of ruling.[22]

All of this demonstrates that the Hindu spirit within the legal system did not evaporate or vanish, as widely anticipated, but rather reasserted its presence. Significantly, during Indira Gandhi's Emergency, the Indian Constitution was embellished with a new Article 51-A on fundamental duties through the 42nd amendment in 1976, and India's superior judges began to talk more openly about duties, not in terms of dharma but in secular language to the same effect. Article 51-A reads like the idealizing edicts of Emperor Aśoka, admonishing all citizens to abide by the laws of the country and to protect its institutions, but to rely on self-controlled order first. India's postmodern dharma is encapsulated in some key portions of Article 51-A, which suggest the citizen's obligation:

> ...
> (e) to promote harmony and the spirit of common brotherhood amongst all the people of India transcending religious, linguistic and regional or sectional diversities; to renounce practices derogatory to the dignity of women;
> (f) to value and preserve the rich heritage of our composite culture;
> (g) to protect and improve the natural environment including forests, lakes, rivers and wild life, and to have compassion for living creatures;
> (h) to develop the scientific temper, humanism and the spirit of inquiry and reform;
> (i) to safeguard public property and to abjure violence;
> (j) to strive towards excellence in all spheres of individual and collective activity so that the nation constantly rises to higher levels of endeavour and achievement.

[22] The heavily contested phenomenon of Indian 'public interest litigation' makes an appearance at this stage, demonstrating that the relevance of Hindu legal concepts is not restricted to the sphere of family law.

The above 'excellence in all spheres of individual and collective activity' under the last heading constitutes a secular rephrasing of dharma, which clearly remains valid today. In a deep national crisis, Indira Gandhi's multilayered technique to invoke an Emergency forced both Indian constitutional law and the various family laws to re-integrate traditional Hindu concepts of self-controlled order and of assisted self-control, precisely dharma and *daṇḍa*, without saying so explicitly. Such developments confirm the resilience of all South Asian socio-cultural traditions as legal building blocks of antiquity to be recycled from time to time. Despite constructing an elaborate Constitution with bricks from all over the world, even Japanese law (Shourie 2001: 143) and outwardly following the path of modern, Western-style legal regulation, Indian lawmakers have also retained the tool boxes of the ancient law. To that extent, the postmodern Hindu legal developments analysed in this book reconfirm the place of certain South Asian cultural axioms in today's world.

Hence, the pluralistic basis of traditional Hindu law rings postmodern bells. Modernism and legal positivism as methodologies, and especially legal centralism as a technique to segregate 'law' from other aspects of life, have all failed to account for the fact that Hindu legal concepts in their diachronical complexity are alive and well in Indian and Hindu law today. They were not simply replaced as 'indigenous traditions' by British colonial interventions or the modern Indian state: Hindu law will remain a central element of Indian laws. Today, within a pattern of personal law plurality, combined with a culture-specific general law, the various Indian and Hindu family laws have metamorphosed into their own specific postmodern conditions rather than remaining stuck in some ancient or colonial pattern. The challenge for analysts of any hue is to recognize the resulting forms of legal pluralism and of postmodern diversity in Hindu law.

Postmodernity in India's Legal System

The complex processes of Hindu law reconstruction in India reflect a parallel postmodern, seemingly paradoxical, re-traditionalization of the entire Indian legal system. This process should not be understood as following tradition or even *hindutva*, as is widely feared by modernists,[23] but as the application of traditional notions of legal regulation to bring justice for the hundreds of millions of common citizen that little closer within reach (Menski 1996b). According to visible postmodern developments within the Indian legal system as a whole, justice is now recognized not as some universal phenomenon, but as a situation-specific element that needs to be ascertained and confirmed all the time, from case to case. The Indian judiciary, having realized that making wonderful laws, by itself, may help promote justice and equity, but cannot implement

[23] As members of various elites, modernists are actually seen to be rather conservative in their resistance to the pluralizing implications of postmodern developments.

them through the act of legislation alone, has spearheaded and pioneered new techniques that are now subsumed under 'judicial activism' and 'public interest litigation'.

We have seen that as a huge jurisdiction, Indian law faces specific problems of application which are not new at all, but have gained new relevance in today's world of globalizing pressures. To remain relevant to all Indians rather than just a tiny privileged elite,[24] Indian law had to retain its non-metropolitan spirit and could not just be modernized by transplants from abroad. Over time, this has had the effect that some critical legal provisions, such as the official criminalization of Hindu polygamy, are applied in social reality in direct derogation of what the official law appears to say (Chapter 10). This was virtually inevitable, given that the core concepts of Hindu culture, particularly *ṛta* and dharma, have remained central concerns in terms of maintaining order, while the Indian state law upholds the image of secular modernity. Rather than blindly applying black-letter statutes and case precedents in modernist fashion, however, postmodern Hindu law is more concerned about situational justice and equity, rather than rigidly fixed legal models.

It seems fair to say that the formally legislated law has become relativized under the influence of a postmodern recognition of socio-legal realities. It is now seen as one of many elements in a complex socio-legal field, rather than claiming to be the dominant force. We found that this process of relativizing state law is not documented in so many words. Generally, the formal claim of the 'rule of law' is maintained and legislators would not admit that their rules will not actually be followed. However, the present study has found several instructive examples of purposeful legislative silence in Indian and Hindu family law.[25] Some modernist observers are therefore questioning the point of having any law at all (Dhagamwar 1992), while the main problem seems to lie in the unwillingness of modernists to accept and understand the postmodern nature of Hindu law and its impact on Indian laws as a whole.

Various approaches to a deeper analysis of postmodern Hindu legal developments are possible. It is useful to remember that the starting point of

[24] Such elite law-making is found in *T. Sareetha v Venkata Subbaiah* AIR 1983 AP 356. A south Indian film star wanted to get rid of her rustic husband once she became famous. Modernist commentators have not disclosed such relevant social facts but complain about the androcentricity of the Hindu law on restitution of conjugal rights (Chandra 1998: 207–8).

[25] India's child marriage legislation keeps silent about the consequences of marrying children below the stipulated minimum ages, leaving judges to apply and interpret the law. This was evidently done on purpose, to allow society to find the right balance, while educating the public towards gradual acceptance of higher marriage ages (Chapter 9). The activist AP Chief Justice in *Panchireddi Appala Suramma* AIR 1975 AP 193, was overruled and shown to be wrong in *Pinninti Venkataramana* AIR 1977 AP 43 FB, which held that child marriages in violation of the state's law cannot be declared legally void in view of social realities and the need to protect women and children.

state intervention in the traditional Hindu legal system was the threat of punishment and retribution, but only when self-controlled ordering did not function. State law was not supposed to come into play automatically, acting only as a support mechanism for assisted self-control. Precisely this kind of need for law exists today. Individuals, male and female, albeit with different means at their disposal to assert their contested positions, still have a propensity to be selfish and greedy, as the ancient *smṛtis* observed for the *kaliyuga*. The classical Hindus realized that the need for assisted self-control, rather than the idealistic self-governance model of pure dharma, would be the operative pattern in human life for all times to come (Chapter 3). Since the mythical 'Golden Age' never seems to materialize, the Hindu principles of assisted self-control are still as necessary and central in social reality as ever. We also saw that the world, and not just India or Hindu society, remains an androcentric place in which granting space to 'the other' poses a daily challenge, not only for those who have to fight for survival. Wealth, social status, and modernist education have provided no brakes on moral corruption and selfish deviousness; in fact they raised even greedier expectations, as trenchantly observed much earlier (Derrett 1970). Indian judges have direct experience of this, in its most cruel manifestations, being for example faced with one dowry murder after the other, virtually crying out in agony themselves that they can hardly bear the responsibility of having to decide such cases.[26] The judges are evidently aware that they are needed to protect the legal system as a whole against selfish anarchy, the 'shark rule' (*mātsyanyāya*) of the ancient law.

It could be argued, therefore, that something has gone seriously wrong within Hindu society in terms of internal self-control, otherwise there would not be so many cases. The practice-focused chapters of Part II demonstrated in detail how easily the official law may be abused by selfish individuals. Does this mean that the central Hindu concept of self-controlled order is no longer strongly enough present in the minds of the average Hindu today to facilitate invisible automatic processes of self-control?[27] It is indeed incredibly romantic to assume that such a paradise-like state ever existed: the present study firmly suggests that the model of self-controlled order has validity primarily as an ideal that everyone should strive for. It may well be that because of positivist indoctrination, originating in the colonial period and extending to the present, the primary place of social self-control is no longer fully appreciated. Instead, individuals have been taught to be enterprising and selfish, and perhaps to

[26] In *State of Himachal Pradesh v Nikku Ram* AIR 1996 SC 67, the judge expresses his disgust over dowry murders: 'Dowry, dowry and dowry. This is the painful repetition which confronts, and at times haunts, many parents of a girl child .... Greed being limitless, the demands become insatiable' (p. 67).

[27] The simple answer is found in the ancient textual statements that emphasize the need for 'assisted self-control' and the threat of punishment: Since the end of the 'Golden Age', people have always been lacking in self-control—it is simply part of the human condition.

look towards the paternalistic state for all kinds of support. Self-controlled ordering does not seem to matter as much as before and it may appear that notions of individual vigilance and scrupulousness in 'doing the right thing' have slackened,[28] while an overambitious state with its placative formal laws can never exercise full control. Perhaps such a state reaps the bitter fruits of its own exaggerated claims to domination and supervision which, if not effectively executed, must lead to massive disappointment and ultimate disregard for formal state law, creating considerable legal insecurity. At the same time, the realization that the informal non-state legal systems have remained part of the equation allows for a relaxation of the expectation that the state law alone should be governing the social and legal field.

Such intricate balancing acts have escaped the notice of many observers. Modernist discourse on India's legal crisis often degenerates into a dismissal of the entire Indian scenario as a bottomless pit into which one had better invest as little as possible. One should avoid such one-sided dramatization of deprivation and crisis. As Baxi (2003) claims, it has merely given rise to the production of indifference among scholars.[29] The most recent *India Briefing* (Ayres and Oldenburg 2002) paints a more positive and constructive picture, highlighting that India is a major industrial nation, rich in all kinds of resources, and a functioning democracy despite many doubts. Modernist analysts are now beginning to realize that grand gestures of large-scale reform will not be productive, emphasizing instead a 'law of small things'.[30]

Particularly in huge jurisdictions like India, an official state legal system can only realistically claim to preside over all legal processes in an abstract or formal sense. With over a billion citizens, it becomes practically impossible to claim that state law is capable of regulating the day-to-day reality of people's lives.[31] In such conditions, reliance on 'traditional' informal, localized self-controlled ordering becomes a self-protection mechanism for the formal law and constitutes a critical element of postmodern legal and political

[28] Sarkar and Butalia (1995), N. Rajan (1998), and R.S. Rajan (1999) vocally oppose suggestions that recourse to Hindu tradition could produce just outcomes. From a policy perspective, Shourie (2001: 403) advises a re-balancing of expectations: 'Given the circumstances in which the country is placed, I feel that the balance needs to be tilted from the individual towards the community, from rights of the individual towards his obligations'.

[29] However, it is not good enough for scholarship to make politically correct statements. Scholars can and should be more actively involved in analysing constructive solutions to perceived problems.

[30] Popkin (2001: 333–4) envisages a legislative and a judicial role in small-scale change. Chandra (1998: 209–10) concludes that 'the experience of a hundred and fifty years of legislative effort to remove certain social practices, such as child marriage, and promote others, like widow remarriage, warns against undue optimism'.

[31] It is highly significant that recent theoretical scholarship vigorously questions the idea that law simply 'mirrors' society. See in detail Tamanaha (2001) as well as Nelken and Feest (2001).

reconstruction. The formal state law must still concern itself with giving the right signals about the broader principles of law to the population as a whole. Postmodern states everywhere in South Asia now realize that they cannot perform the various large-scale functions they claimed to exercise.[32] The modern state manifestly took on too much, and now has to admit this.

The resulting gap points to a need to engage in private and public postmodern re-education about the value of self-controlled ordering. While the state continues to offer a formal hierarchical framework for dispute settlement and adversarial claims, the deeper message of India's postmodern state law seems to be that it does not want to be used. Contemporary postmodern Hindu law operates, then, on the basis of a reworked symbiosis of central state law and local legal orders, within an overarching higher order.[33] In such a scenario, the focus of postmodern analysis cannot remain fixated—as inevitably happened within modernist paradigms—on the alleged ineffectiveness of the state and its legal machinery.

Postmodern analytical methodology in the field of law recognizes the creative potential and freedom provided by the collapse of the modernist claim to absolute governance, which gives added space to those flexible social forces which have always demanded a legal role. This is not evidence of loss of legal authority, or of a meek surrender to tradition, but reflects a pluralist understanding of law and its operation in postmodern conditions. An intellectually alert postmodern analysis of Hindu law offers helpful conceptual tools for explaining the troublesome image of apparently wayward Indian lawlessness as a crisis of modernist governance, rather than an illness of the traditional social environment. It is manifestly dishonest to blame 'the people' when in fact the state law cannot fulfil its self-set tasks. The elitist trend in India to blame the demographic mass for 'lawlessness' in the countryside is a diversionary technique of the ruling upper stratum, as identified by Bardhan (1984). The sick unit, it seems, is not Indian society but the state's formal law, which had earlier become an instrument of exploitation for privileged groups and lost touch with the needs of 'little' Indians.

The postmodern analysis presented in Chapters 8–12 clearly shows that modern state law has often had to admit its incapacity to sustain viable solutions. The clearest example of planned non-involvement by the state comes from the law on marriage solemnization. While modernists like Diwan and Diwan (1993) vigorously proposed compulsory registration of all marriages to achieve control over polygamy and other perceived abuses, reformists do not seem to realize that such large-scale legal restructuring amounts to a significant

[32] Much could be said about Pakistan and its ongoing process of rethinking Islamic legal foundations. Pakistani judges have recently come up with conclusions about Islamic law that mirror postmodern developments in Hindu law.

[33] Somehow, it seems easier to understand and accept this for Islam and Christianity, but it is also an integral feature of Hinduism and other less formal religions in Asia and Africa.

shift of legal authority from local communities to the state, away from a pattern of self-controlled ordering towards bureaucratic supervision. Unsurprisingly, in Hindu law, it is still the local community, and not the state, that controls supervision of legal statuses.[34] Modernists continue to propose a shift towards direct, bureaucratic state control, which shows that they have not thought about the social implications.[35] In a postmodern scenario, this tension resurfaces in every area of law and positivist claims remain as strongly challenged as ever.

Such debates over the extent of bureaucratic state control are closely linked to growing awareness about the crisis of modernist welfare state ideology and practice worldwide. Van Creveld (1999: 361) observes that '[i]n both Europe and the United States—to say nothing of developing countries—the expansion of state-directed welfare led to an equally great growth of the bureaucracy'. The costs of bureaucratic growth have certainly been a consideration in India's fiscal planning, preventing rosy predictions of a full-fledged welfare system. A country that cannot even organize its registration of births and deaths, let alone legal control of marriage registration and divorce, will find it impossible to aim for bureaucratic perfection. Van Creveld (1999: 362–3) argues that an important factor which drove the modern welfare state to the breaking point was its own success, since 'the various programs had been designed to assist weak population groups such as the elderly, the sick, and, later, single mothers; however, it soon turned out that the greater the benefits offered, the larger the number of those entitled'. Consequently, there had to be cutbacks. By the late 1980s, apart from elementary and secondary education, the dream of using government to 'lift up' the masses was clearly in ruins everywhere (Van Creveld 1999: 365).

Despite specific constitutional guarantees, India has not even been able to provide primary education for all young children. In view of the worldwide crisis of the welfare state, Indian policy makers have wisely decided not even to start making ambitious plans and exaggerated promises. This, too, is part of India's 'fractured modernity' (Corbridge and Harriss 2000: 238). The state becomes not a bountiful provider of goods and services, but an arbiter in the contested distribution of scarce resources.[36] In the governance of India, such issues of basic justice will inevitably remain crucial. Closely linked to basic needs

[34] However, the postmodern Hindu law model retains indirect state supervision. Disputes over the validity of a Hindu marriage, for example, can be brought to the courts under section 7 HMA of 1955.

[35] As noted, Agnes (2000: 169–70) realizes that compulsory marriage registration would adversely affect women and children. She discusses various reform proposals, but still within modernist paradigms (ibid.: 172-182).

[36] This is pinpointed by Shourie (2001: 403), a prolific writer and now a government minister: 'A thousand goals are desirable; each of us would want to secure a thousand things for our citizens – especially in a country like India, scarred as it is with so much deprivation. But not all goals can be pursued simultaneously, not even those things which all of us would agree are bare essentials'.

debates and the growing scarcity of even the most essential resources, like clean drinking water, are matters of equality, caste and gender-based discrimination, but such ideological issues must take second place after concerns for bare survival, a lesson that many modernists have yet to learn.

Distress over limited resources, in particular, has propelled the emergence of an activist Indian judiciary, willing to take guidance from anywhere and not fixated by historical linkages to English law. The activist centre for postmodern Hindu legal developments now lies clearly within the realm of the judiciary. While legislative activity in Hindu law has virtually come to a standstill,[37] the centre of postmodern Indian law-making has during the early 1980s shifted to the courts, where it has firmly stayed (Shourie 2001; Sathe 2002). Evidence of the key role of judges is difficult to fathom though, and detached interpretation of judicial activism has been disrupted by unhelpful interjections to the effect that judges, as undemocratically appointed office holders, are not suitable—and cannot be trusted—as ultimate arbiters of justice. Such comments indicate a positivist hankering for power through legislatures. However, at the end of the day, everywhere, judges are needed to apply the rules that may, or may not, exist to solve problems brought before them.

Significantly, what has emerged in postmodern Indian law is a new form of Justice, Equity, and Good Conscience. Discarding blind reliance on 'precedent', postmodern judicial methods constitute what Derrett (1970: 12) earlier called 'an alternative intellectual system', which is not going to be subject to blindly positivist legislative domination. Judges will tend to speak about law rather than morals or their own values when they explain their role, as they do from time to time.[38] Building constructively on important structures provided by the legislature, some Indian judges have gone well beyond legal technicalities.

The Indian personal law system in its postmodern formation, and especially Hindu law within it, demonstrates that progressive, socio-economically sensible and sustainable legal developments can be reproduced within a traditional framework of reference and in a formally fragmented legal system of different personal laws. Unlike most modernists, postmodern analysts are not blinded by ideological reservations about the personal law system, realizing that uniform law has no exclusive patent for modernity, innovation, and 'the truth' about legal progress. Legal systems everywhere will have to strive hard to develop cost-effective and justice-focused systems of self-regulation. The debate will go on. While it remains important to use law, as S. Basu (1999: 281)

[37] We saw that Hindu law reforms stalled dramatically after the failed Marriage Laws (Amendment) Bill in 1981, with little activity since, despite a plethora of proposals (Agnes 2000).

[38] One of the most recent examples of judicial pontifications about justice (Yadav 2001) makes the point that '[w]e being the upholders of value in society are under legal obligation to maintain equilibrium between the rich and the poor, the elite and the non-elite groups of the people'.

reminds us with reference to Carol Smart's important earlier work, the purported dangers of 'tradition' need to be re-assessed in the light of methodological advances in comparative jurisprudential analysis. If 'tradition' remained at various levels an integral part of modernity and its post-colonial and postmodern reconstructions, it cannot be so easily dismissed as irrelevant or simply dangerous.

Hindu law clearly has the inherent potential to fall back on informal indigenous cultural concepts of law-making and dispute processing. In many other jurisdictions, there seems to be no recorded cultural tradition of self-controlled order. Modernist positivism has so deeply uprooted social processes that a postmodern reconstruction as in Hindu law seems virtually impossible.[39] However, in Asian contexts, there are quite different conditions. Baxi (1986a: 216) emphasized that '[t]he precolonial Asian societies were principally governed by the non-state law' and cryptically wondered, without giving an answer, whether Hindu law in India has moved from dharma to law, and back (Baxi 1986a: 217). This hits the nail on the head, but are we prepared to accept that those traditional legal systems and their methods remain useful today?

India's experience of a strengthened personal law system, rather than its abolition, demonstrates that age-old and yet contemporary experiences of negotiated norm-finding in the interface between state laws and other normative orders remain relevant today. Not only in terms of economics, justice and well-being cannot be guaranteed by exclusive reliance on global positivist models.[40] International conventions and legislative enactments do not feed people in their villages, and Indian judges clearly know this. It follows that if members of society are willing to tolerate their own local arrangements, the state law should not pretend that it has an obligation to interfere. The ever ready assumption that formally uneducated rustics 'suffer' from their customary legal arrangements is highly questionable: such people would not operate such rules if they were really so bad. Often, modernist intervention tends to be more concerned with following international political correctness than achieving locally sustainable arrangements for real people. The postmodern Indian legal system recognizes that sustainable solutions lie not in top-down legal models that intervene in people's daily lives, but in reminding individuals of the primacy of self-controlled ordering. The key message remains, therefore, that state law should be avoided.

Modernists will continue to object that the disadvantaged position of women and other subalterns in this postmodern scenario warrants deep

[39] Douglas (1998) shows for England that attempts to take lawyers out of the divorce process and to replace them with mediation personnel have been a failure. It appears that one modernist method has replaced another, but the underlying socio-cultural symptoms have not been tackled.

[40] Sayyid (1997: 132) notes that globalization does not alleviate poverty. Kaviraj (1999: 22) warns that legal globalization does not necessarily result in greater equality but wider disparity.

concerns over justice.[41] Since it is an almost axiomatic modernist presupposition that traditional legal systems such as Hindu law are bad for women, children, and low-caste people, such objections will not be silenced. But while the voices of Hindu women and children may not be adequately heard in local bargaining processes, a solution to such problems is not found by abolishing the allegedly discriminatory traditional system, but by making it work better, especially providing a forum to unheard voices. In this context, removal of existing barriers of access to courts needs to be further examined, but in the postmodern scenario of Hindu law it is clearly not perceived as ideal that courts should be used for every dispute.[42]

Postmodern Hindu law makes intelligent and creative use of traditional elements. For example, although low-caste status is no longer supposed to exist, given the formal abolition of caste, judges remain aware of such distinctions and explicitly discriminate in favour of women and others who need special assistance. This confirms that modernists' offhand dismissal of Hindu law as a traditional religious system marked by gendered patterns of oppression has been a grave mistake. Our analysis of case law material confirms that the reworked traditional model is capable, also within an androcentric framework, to balance the scales in favour of women and other groups who need special support to redress manifest imbalances.[43] Processes of dispute settlement are clearly weighted in favour of certain groups,[44] and it is no surprise that the privileged sections are complaining vigorously that unfair advantages are being given to others.

It is not only intrinsically against the nature of Hindu law to be portrayed as a uniform law, it is also not a viable method of keeping an extremely diverse

[41] Significantly, Spivak (2000) now writes about the New Subaltern in a global context.

[42] Strong proof comes from explicit recognition of customary Hindu divorces. Further, punishing litigiousness is an ancient strategy, which has begun to be used by Indian judges who may now award punitive damages against husbands who harass their wives through litigation (Kusum 2000: 257–8).

[43] The most persuasive case study in this respect comes from the Hindu law on maintenance for wives (Chapter 12), which allows claims under the traditional law as well as modern Hindu law provisions and criminal law. Direct access to the SC and HC has explicitly been guaranteed in the powerful judicial review mechanisms of Article 32 (for the SC) and Article 226 (for the HC).

[44] This does not mean to say that everything works perfectly. Vatuk (2001: 232) observes that even women who manage to approach a court are put under pressure to change their pleadings: 'A legal discourse of "rights" is thus transformed into a discourse of "welfare", whose defining terms are set, not by the woman herself, but by her counselor, her advocate, the judge, and, in the last analysis, by the realities imposed by the society within which she lives'. The same could be said of other types of litigation in which professionalisation of justice has tended to suffocate the voice of the complainant.

nation together by enforcing uniformity.[45] In this respect, too, India is like a microcosm of the whole world. While it is often argued that the coexistence of general and personal laws perpetuates inequality, and that India should therefore have a uniform civil code,[46] India has stuck to the principle that the personal law system remains useful but that social and historical imbalances need to be redressed. The resulting policies of 'protective discrimination' have created intense resentment. As elsewhere, political dispute has focused on the extent of such reservations rather than the principle, which is now felt to disadvantage those who were historically privileged.[47]

The Indian state's evident lack of enthusiasm for imposing a uniform law on every home has gradually become more evident during the 1980s and 1990s. The resulting 'soft state', unlike the Western legal centralist type, is not primarily focused on becoming the maker of universally binding legal rules for all citizens. It merely provides a framework for adjudicating conflicting claims brought to the law courts, instead of laying down the law. This is still a form of 'rule of law', but of a significantly different type than in Western legal systems—it is in fact the old Hindu law model. In the area of family law, postmodern Hindu law now re-emphasizes traditional interlinkages between individuals and the family. Principled objections to that approach are raised by those modernists who assume that individualism is the most desirable human condition (Rajan 1998). On the other hand, as Derrett (1963c: 177) emphasized with reference to *Jivubai v Ningappa* AIR 1963 Mys 3, 'the subsistence of marriages is the concern of the country and not merely of the spouses'. Therefore, where it is still possible to save the marriage, the court is under a positive duty, even on appeal, to attempt reconciliation.[48]

It is academically inadequate to view such reasonings in Indian law only as some dangerous form of Hinduization. It is dishonest to treat this simply as evidence of politically unacceptable Hindu fundamentalism, the bogeyman of modernist scholarship on South Asia. The major motivating factor has clearly been the search for various aspects of appropriate justice for a billion people,

[45] Sunil Khilnani (1997: 207) concludes that 'ultimately, the viability—and most importantly, the point—of India's democracy will rest on its capacity to sustain internal diversity, on its ability to avoid giving reason to groups within the citizen body to harbour dreams of having their own exclusive nation states'.

[46] Dhagamwar (1989) remains the most activist attempt to raise the agenda in favour of uniformity. Menski (2001, Chapter 6) shows that postmodern legal developments have overtaken the reformist bandwagon, achieving virtual uniformity of laws while retaining the personal law system. Significantly, modernist scholars still see and criticize only the continuation of personal laws.

[47] In principle, the experience of the dilemma itself is similar to that in the USA with its 'white backlash'. One can predict that India will not be able to turn her back on reservation policies altogether.

[48] Efforts by judges to avoid American conditions of massive marital breakdown were documented in Chapter 11 earlier.

and not a desire to return to some imagined glorious Hindu past or *Rāmrājya.* Simplistic sloganeering cannot replace the necessarily arduous search for justice. Comparative legal analysis indicates that postmodern Hindu and Indian law are no longer simply a form of Anglo-centric elite law, as they were to some extent until the 1960s, made by the leaders of society for themselves and their offspring.[49] Indian laws have now matured into a form of legal regulation that respects more explicitly the inherent plurality of differential needs in local societies. Postmodern Hindu law applies a variety of interlocking techniques instead of modernist dogma and is not afraid to innovate. Quite in line with general assumptions about postmodernity, Indian and Hindu laws must therefore be seen today as intricate compromises, not some neat final solution.

Whatever angle we choose to analyse postmodern Indian legal developments, therefore, the essence of the observation remains the same: This elephant is a historically conditioned, culture-specific entity with its own identity. Like a massive untrained pachiderm, Hindu law is not likely to react with swift and direct obedience to any intervention from outside. The Indian elephant called 'postmodern Hindu law' defies absolutist state control and will amble along its own, self-chosen path, which is not as predetermined as 'tradition' is supposed to dictate. Contrary to modernist representations, tradition itself is internally plural and inherently flexible, and thus full of creative potential for future reconstruction and perceptive reinvention.

In Indian law, the officially recognized legal position of Hindu law remains unsatisfactory for all those who refuse to grant space to Hindu law and other personal laws.[50] Such inherent conceptual conflicts are reflected also in the Constitution of 1950, which is itself a complex compromise between competing claims. The Indian Constitution has been honoured in systematic breaches, as the state itself cannot fulfil most of its modernist promises.[51] Social inequality, as well as inequality before the law, have in practice not been wiped out.[52] Modernist observers tend to decry this, pointing also to local violations of the official law, such as cases of murder through village justice, with no involvement of the state at all (Chowdhry 2000). However, is this simply evidence of lawlessness, or of complex socio-legal pluralism in action? Chowdhry (2000: 334) observes that in this way 'a successfully forged alliance between cultural codes, honour and violence justifies the violence and results in a broad complicity that cuts across social groups, gender and age'.

[49] See Derrett (1970: 420–4). This also goes for the Dowry Prohibition Act of 1961 and amendments to the HMA 1955 in the Hindu Marriage (Amendment) Act, 1964.

[50] A recent important case on this matter is *Ahmedabad Women Action Group (AWAG) v Union of India* JT 1997 (3) SC 171 and AIR 1997 SC 3614.

[51] The state, through its bureaucrats, is also the biggest violator of legal norms, as is especially apparent from many public interest litigation cases.

[52] Dhagamwar (1992: 9–10) confirms that for most rural Indians the Constitution and its rules have remained remote.

Such evidence does not justify entirely negative assessments, although one must appreciate that modernists find self-controlled order of this kind hard to accept. Not just Hindu law but the entire Indian legal system appears to have metamorphosed into a plurality-conscious, situation-specific, relativity-fixated network of rules that different interest groups and powerful individuals seem to manipulate almost at will—as they have always done.[53] While no state legal system in the world could claim to be totally effective, and only a despotic police state would make those claims in the first place, Hindu law has always privileged negotiated settlement in a domain that lawyers curiously and quite wrongly refer to as the 'extra-legal' sphere. Dismissing the current Indian state as an inefficient specimen of modernist governance simply avoids addressing the complexity of the postmodern legal problematic that the present study has identified for Hindu law.

The emergence of postmodern Hindu law in India has several important implications for the interdisciplinary analysis of South Asian and Hindu law developments, and it affects the conceptual understanding of law itself in a global context. If the story of postmodern Hindu law is actually as ambivalently positive as depicted here, what implications does this have for further legal developments in India, and for the future of personal law regulation in that country, in fact in the world? Equally important would be the question, addressed further later, whether uniform legal regulation of family laws in the now increasingly multicultural states of Europe and the Americas can be defended in the long run as conducive to justice.

In this postmodern phase, it is becoming evident that purportedly universal models have not been found useful in India, while some aspects of ancient Hindu tradition are proving more appropriate to achieve a semblance of justice. The evidence of postmodern Hindu law constitutes a culture-specific Indian manifestation of the current global search for the ideals of natural justice. If this incontrovertible contemporary evidence of Hindu law's reconstruction and re-traditionalization as a form of postmodernization can teach us a general lesson, it would be the old story that law is not only made by the state, but also by the people who apply such rules and attempt to live by them.

Examining Hindu marriage law (Chapter 8), the purported abolition of child marriages (Chapter 9) and the formal outlawing of Hindu polygamy (Chapter 10), we found that modern state law has evidently had to leave space for the application and recognition of traditional Hindu concepts, be it through explicit legal exemptions, or various methods that have allowed the formally codified law to remain practically ineffective, while retaining some educative functions. Thus, Indian child marriage law continues to uphold the legal validity of under-age marriages in an apparently self-contradictory effort to protect the (mainly female) child's best interests. While this makes sense from a postmodern socio-cultural perspective, the formal expectations of legal

[53] To that extent and at that level too, there is continuity between the traditional system and postmodern Hindu law.

positivism are not met: leeway for legal disobedience is built into the formal legal framework. Legal modernity has been used to shelter recognition of traditional normative standards that will, as the lawmaker knows, continue to operate in society. In other words, Indian law-making contains rich evidence of post-positivist self-doubt and of informal recognition of the 'extra-legal' sphere.[54]

That law, in its Hindu manifestations as well as elsewhere, should remain in various postmodern scenarios more than just a reflection of the respective state law is not new, but represents a shift away from the oppressive domination of legal positivism. Ehrlich (1913) had argued earlier that the 'living law' is never just state-made law on its own. The basic assumption of the historical school of jurisprudence, that law and society anywhere need to work in harmony to achieve good law, is vindicated by the present postmodern analysis of Hindu law. Overlooking what Chiba (1986) called 'legal postulates' is not useful for a deep analysis of Asian and African legal systems, and indeed for any legal analysis, 'culture' and 'tradition' need to be reconsidered as integral elements of postmodern legal reconstruction.

These must be depressing conclusions for modernists. Instead of a universalizing 'rule of law', we now have in postmodern Hindu law what was so desperately trying to be avoided, namely a remodelled rule of dharma. The present analysis shows that Hindu law, and with it the personal law system, are so strongly entrenched in postmodern India that they will not be dislodged by positivist interventions.[55] Rather than seeking to undermine and abolish well-established systems like the Hindu personal law, postmodernist analysis needs to become more constructive, recognising that personal law regulation may actually be a suitable model for the entire world.

POSTMODERN HINDU LAW AS NON-WESTERN MODEL JURISPRUDENCE

Faced with strong evidence of systematic postmodern legal reconstruction in Hindu law, the time has now come to realize that this is not a freak development or an accident of history, but part of a wider postmodern pattern in non-Western jurisdictions, searching for sustainable solutions to complex socio-legal problems in conditions of massification. Indeed, it may be argued that perhaps the time has now come for countries of the South to assert themselves more clearly against the dominant state-centred models of the North, to openly pursue their own flexible methods rather than simply pretending to follow the West.

[54] The key concept of *sadācāra*, 'model behaviour', as the practically most important source of dharmic order, was discussed in detail in Chapter 3, the section on Dharma and Classical Hindu Law.

[55] Menski (2001) shows that meanwhile a variant form of legal uniformity has been achieved by postmodern Indian legal developments that seek to harmonize the provisions of the various personal laws.

We saw that new uniformizing pressures of modernist positivism now come from international legal institutions and their representatives. At the end of the day, there may be little real difference between following international standards of human rights and indigenous values of equitable justice. One senses, though, that it is a matter of pride for most Western observers as well as many members of the Indian elite, including some judges, to be seen to be following Western 'rule of law' models based on equality and uniformity rather than indigenous traditions of relative justice. The 'traditionalist' label is not desirable for most analysts, and the taint of traditionality inevitably attaches to postmodernism as well.

Apart from analysing the conceptual details of Hindu law, it was necessary to examine as well the 'bigger picture' of Indian law in the world today, not only as a legal system in its own right; but as a pluralistic model for all non-Western legal systems, if not the world, as is now beginning to be realized.[56] It is evident, and more widely accepted today within a postmodernist framework of reference, that non-Western legal systems in various hybrid forms will remain part of the global picture for all times to come.[57] This has even given rise to new terminologies of hybridity,[58] while the prominent but simplistic

[56] While Freed (1998) suggests in typically blinkered fashion that the interaction of the US states is a useful model for global international legal regulation, Rajeev Dhavan (2001: 320) points out that India's quest for pluralistic secular legal regulation looks like 'devising a Constitution for the world'. This challenge is picked up by Popkin (2001: 331), who raises in his conclusion 'the provocative possibility that, instead of religious India becoming more like the secular United States, the United States might eventually become more like India'. As I wrote this, reports appeared that the Ninth Circuit Court of Appeals in the USA had ruled by a majority of two to one that it was unconstitutional to ask school children to recite the American Pledge of Allegiance by vowing fealty to one nation 'under God' (*Daily Yomiuri* 28 June 2002). This new challenge to the interpretation of the 'Establishment Clause' in US law remains subject to appeal. This is significant because it highlights that the Indian form of secularism, as equidistance from all religions (Larson 2001), needs to be better understood as a potential model for handling religious pluralism and its legal implications.

[57] This was also suggested earlier by Chiba (1986), a pioneer of legal postmodernism, through his powerful critique of Western 'model jurisprudence' and its false claims to universality. More recently, reviewing a collection of essays (Morigiwa 1998) that centres on Asian alternatives from an East Asian perspective, May (2001: 270) emphasizes that a uniform global legal culture cannot develop because various conflicting and competing worldviews continue to be in existence, so that Kant's 'citizen of the world' remains a nice fiction from a Eurocentric universalizing perspective, but no more.

[58] Harding (2002: 53) suggests that 'Westernistic' might describe the emerging legal systems in South-East Asia better than 'Western' or 'post-Western'. 'Westernistic' seems also suitable because it reflects the ambition of an impression or a wish, rather than attempting to prescribe a particular legal reality. However, this term still reflects Eurocentrism.

model of 'reception' of certain advanced legal systems in Asia, Africa, and South America is now an 'old hat'. In fact, Euro-focused postmodernism is not as 'modern' as is widely assumed.[59] King (1995: 120–1) writes that,

> ... the Eurocentrically defined cultural conditions of a so-called post-modernity – irony, pastiche, the mixing of different histories, intertextuality, schizophrenia, cultural chasms, fragmentation, incoherence, disjunction of supposedly modern and pre-modern cultures – were characteristic of colonial societies, cultures, environments on the global periphery (in Calcutta, Hong Kong, Rio or Singapore) decades, if not centuries, before they appeared in Europe or the USA.

The current postmodernist environment in a legal context is characterized by its explicit emphasis on plurality and difference rather than uniformity, which has enormous implications for legal scholarship as a whole, particularly for comparative law and the study of foreign legal systems. Peters and Schwenke (2000: 801–2) helpfully summarize the complex term of postmodernism:

> Post-modernism is a highly ambiguous term, whose meaning depends on the discipline ... in which it is used, and on the prior notions of "modernism" and "modernity". Roughly speaking, post-modernist thought considers as basic the experience of plurality and difference. It points out that there are highly diverse forms of knowledge, systems of morality, personal plans of life and behavioural patterns. Post-modernist theory welcomes these heterogeneous positions and finds their discordance absolute. It protests against the totalising monopolisation of certain types of rationality and against universalist concepts that raise false allegations of absoluteness.

Postmodern perspectives suggest that legal scholarship needs to look with more vigour for evidence of legal pluralism and of opposing trends to Euro-American globalization (Legrand 1996). These tend to manifest in complex processes that involve reconstruction of non-Western laws by reference to indigenous norms and values, whatever these may be in detail.[60] This process may not simply be attenuated, as has been placatively assumed,[61] but may

[59] See also Morley (1996). This debate also appears still too Eurocentric in language and thinking. It overlooks the possibility that 'colonial' societies may have developed typical elements of postmodern thinking well before colonial times. As new research findings suggest, this was perhaps based on much intercultural communication among early traders and other migrants, including many itinerant scholars.

[60] Indeed, Glenn (2000) observes a number of globalizations in his detailed analysis of legal traditions, especially Muslim assertions of plurality.

[61] Galanter and Krishnan (2001: 285) simply reiterate, relying on Galanter's earlier assertions, that 'there is no evident support for the restoration of traditional Hindu law' and suggest that 'there is at least a slight leaning toward dissolution of the personal law system in favor of uniform territorial law, together with a "secularization" or de-sacralization of the law of the largest community, and there is no indication of any inclination to devolve the administration of personal law to the

actually grow in the future.[62] Yet such research goes seriously against the grain of modernist ideologies. So far, the signs are that Western hubris, purported overload of information within national legal systems, and lack of knowledge about Hindu law or modern Indian law impede and prevent processes of free-flowing exchange in the global arena, even within Euro-America.[63]

A closely related problem remains that, for various ideological reasons, cross-cultural legal exchange is supposed to occur only in the direction of modernization, which seems to imply westernization, if not Americanization.[64] Hindu law would, in such a developmental model, eventually be submerged in this imagined modern global legal order and there would be no need for a book on the concepts of traditional Hindu law and their modern and even postmodern manifestations. But that is wishful thinking, clearly demasked now in the light of postmodernist realization that plurality and diversity are there to stay, and that Hindu law has partly achieved what modernists have declared to be impossible.

Hence, scholarly observations to the effect that modernizing, globalizing legal trends are all-pervasive are arguably not a faithful reflection of legal developments as they occur in reality all over the world.[65] These are merely ideologically grounded assertions of the superiority of modernity and

---

religious communities' (ibid.: 286–7). All of this reflects wishful thinking rather than a faithful summary of the current position of Hindu law and deliberate stalling of any progress in research on Hindu law.

[62] On social welfare in modern Indian family laws as an aspect of fiscal policy, see Menski (2001).

[63] The collection of country reports by Drobnig and van Erp (1999: 333) highlights that US lawyers are drowning under masses of domestic law and have no time for foreign laws. The same could be said about Indian lawyers, of course.

[64] In a massive volume of comparative law essays published in Japan (*Towards Comparative Law in the 21st Century*, 1998), one senior American lawyer suggests that comparative law teachers 'should be the leaders in international legal harmonization for a number of compelling reasons (Freed 1998: 1071), while a more deeply considered approach to rule of law, legal culture and modernity leads Friedman (1998: 1086) to presume that there is 'a general *legal* culture of modernity'. Friedman (1998: 1088) also asserts that '[t]he idea of the rule of law, and the notion of fundamental human rights in general, seems to be spreading rapidly throughout the world. These concepts originated in the West, and were elaborated by Western thinkers'. Friedman hence portrays a 'transition from culture to technology—a technology of modernity' (id.), but expresses some doubt over the extent of this development.

[65] Friedman (1998: 1083) admits this, too, when he writes that '[c]learly, each legal system is and remains unique. Each bears the marks of its history. Every country has its own problems, and its own solutions. This is true even of members of the same "family" of legal system'.

rationality.[66] In stark contrast, plural legal reality is visible in abundance almost anywhere, provided analysts are prepared to remove their blinkers.[67] Like many other non-Western legal systems, Hindu law is not only alive and well, but has, unbeknown even to many contemporary observers in India, not remained at some dark stage of traditionality or irrationality that would make it unsuitable for today's world. Rather, like all legal systems, Hindu law has dynamically grown and has now metamorphosed into a postmodern legal system that clearly confounds critics, enemies–and indeed many Hindus as well.[68]

My specialist position as one of very few scholarly experts on Hindu law outside India allows me to claim with some force that it remains necessary for outsiders to explain, also for the benefit of today's Indians, how they may learn to see the wood for the trees.[69] This is not Hinduizing indoctrination, but postmodern comparative legal scholarship in action, which is as yet not properly understood and continues to face ideological rejection as a politically incorrect activity.[70] Arguing from within Hindu law perspectives, as I have attempted to do throughout, allows us to re-examine our notions of who are the legal 'others', in a fashion that radically upsets traditional modernist assumptions about legal development. In that respect, postmodern Hindu law

[66] In the context of debates about the future of human rights, Baxi (2002: vi) argues for recognition of pluralized authorship and refutes the assumption that human rights are the '*gifts of the West to the Rest*'.

[67] I cited the instructive methodological discussion by Weinberger-Thomas (1999: 181–3) about the researcher's dilemma in situations where one's personal ideology and the observed facts do not comfortably match. This is not only an issue in 'hot' topics like satī but evidently in all academic work.

[68] In fieldwork conducted in India on a variety of issues, over two decades, I have repeatedly found that supposedly illiterate Indians seem to have a clearer understanding of certain aspects of Hindu law than formally trained lawyers, whose educational experiences somehow created blinkers that villagers do not have. Strong indications of this surfaced in my fieldwork in Kerala (Menski 1986a; 1986b).

[69] Derrett's writing shows in many places that he, too, laboured to hold up a mirror to Indians, aware that '[p]ontifications from a professor in London are hardly likely to hasten matters' (Derrett 1970: 439). His sarcastic critique of how elite representatives of Indian law, lawyers, judges, and scholars, deal with Hindu law (Derrett 1970: 399–400) remains valid today. Pompous speeches about Indian law are still being made in prestigious back-slapping exercises in London and elsewhere, cultivating pristine common law connections rather than taking account of messy current legal realities.

[70] Presenting the idea of postmodern Hindu law to Indian law schools has sparked off some defensive comments, which are highly significant for assessing the parlous state of Indian legal education. In one case, a young law lecturer's reaction to postmodern Hindu law was that 'these are things we do not want to know about'. That snappy comment says it all: Legal modernization in India is authoritatively perceived as linked to de-Hinduization and internationalization, not to thinking about law and society in their culture-specific Indian environment. The growing perception of a deep crisis in Indian legal education is not surprising, therefore.

is clearly an alternative model to the dominant Western 'model jurisprudence' identified by Masaji Chiba (1986), because it acknowledges legal plurality and diversity at all levels. The critical methodological instrument for conceptualizing all pluralistic legal models seems to be found in an interactively balanced (rather than exclusively dominant) recognition of legal positivism.

If, as Chiba (1986) suggested, law is always a combination of several elements in productive interaction, a more cautious approach to our understanding of 'official law', without leading to the exclusion of other legal elements and inputs that do not derive their legitimacy directly from the state, seems to be the key element of postmodern legal analysis and its inherent pluralism. This also implies that 'religion', however defined, is never far removed from such comprehensive legal analyses and 'the very notion of the separation of public and private realms, repeated by so many legal and social theorists, is completely suspect' (Tamanaha 2001: 67). To understand such reasoning, and to deconstruct what we seem to know about any one legal system, requires a strange mix of commitment and detachment, and enormous effort. Peters and Schwenke (2000: 832) seem to underplay the role of ideology, but observe pertinently that being a postmodern comparative lawyer is not easy:[71]

> At all stages of comparative research ... the real problems are not moral or cultural blindness, ethnocentricity and legal imperialism, but the lack of full knowledge and understanding of foreign legal rules and cultures. Comparativists have – pure and simple – an incomplete knowledge of many hard facts. They must know something about the historical, social, economic, political, cultural and psychological context which has made a rule or proposition what it is. Because thorough knowledge needs hard and extensive study, excellent language skills, good libraries, long experience, probably knowledge of life and legal practice within the foreign system, it is rarely acquired.

This is a huge methodological and intellectual challenge, which anybody working on comparative law would find daunting. It had to be faced here, too. As I demonstrate, an open-minded, interdisciplinary approach is helpful in this context, but raises in turn its own problems when it comes to presentation of the findings, because one ends up speaking in a variety of specialist languages and tends to fall between disciplinary stools. However, at the end of the day, there is no doubt that traditional modernist and Eurocentric legal analysis and methodology would have failed to produce a comprehensive analysis of Hindu law in today's world.[72] Authoritative, doctrinal legal textbooks (e.g. Desai 1998)

[71] This echoes Legrand's (1996: 239) prominent rhetorical question, '[w]ho ever claimed that comparative legal studies should be easy?'. Legrand himself answers this in postmodern terms by emphasizing the need to cultivate 'a proclivity on the part of the comparatist towards an acknowledgement of 'difference'' (id.).

[72] Weinberger-Thomas (1999: 181) eloquently critiques such modernist scholarship, observing that 'research undertaken on the basis of such presuppositions cannot help but be skewed from the outset'. Peters and Schwenke (2000: 820)

cannot produce such deep analysis either. Recent modernist critiques like Agnes (2000) tend to lack depth and detail, apart from a commitment to objectivity.[73] Most modernist writing remains mired in unproductive polemics. It is time to break those vicious circles, knowing that this, too, is ultimately an impossible task, because the writing on which one wants to improve continues to exist and will still be circulated for many years to come.[74] Rather than falling victim to postmodern nihilism or throwing in the towel,[75] however, regional law experts have only themselves to blame if their field of study does not progress as well as they hoped.

Modernist critics, whether men or women, sit at the same high table as legal positivists, who tend to be mostly men, when it comes to evaluating 'the other'. Both groups—each with its own rationale—haughtily dismiss from their elevated perspective all kinds of non-Western ideas and laws as irrelevant for our days, and have declared them especially bad for women, children, and minorities, as though modern laws had no problems with justice. Although the colonial times are said to be over,[76] far too many lawyers continue to fantasize about migration and reception of certain laws,[77] and thus continue to dream about their legocentric powers of law-making, imagining what the world would be like if they had the power to call the shots. A growing number of women

---

emphasize that 'there is always a *Vorverständnis*', in other words, premises which we apply even unconsciously, and which constitute a degree of inevitable interference.

[73] Agnes (2000) explicitly designed her study as a modernist reassessment (she uses the word 'rescrutiny' at p. 1) of women's rights and family law reforms in India.

[74] An example of such self-perpetuating citation policies is found in Larson's bibliographical note (2001: 349–50), which relies a little too much on the old 'standard' works.

[75] Harding (2001: 200) raises this possibility in view of the baffling, powerful image of a 'Thai buddhist monk using the internet to move shares around in order to make profits for his monastery to do good works'. This fits in with recent evidence that Hindus can now order the performance of prayer rituals in distant temples by internet, will receive an email confirming completion of the ceremony, and a parcel with *prasād*, blessed offerings. A more negative media image is found when scruffy Hindu sages make televised appeals for their own *hindutva* politics.

[76] Nandy's (1983) incisive analysis of the colonialism of the mind applies here, too.

[77] The most recent example is the currently debated plan, following the Bonn Agreement of 2002, to make Afghanistan adopt a 'rule of law' model to promote national cohesion and inter-ethnic cooperation. Given the large input of human rights lawyers in such projects, there should be more concern about complaints by the Afghanis that such foreign intervention implies new forms of legal colonialism in post-conflict scenarios of reconstruction. An existing legal system is clearly in place, based on Islamic law rather than any formal Constitution. As in Turkey (Yilmaz 1999), formal reception of new laws and their implementation would produce at least two quite distinct, yet interrelated stories of the shape of the new law.

among such modernists and legal positivists have added more spice to gender debates, but it has not solved any problems, as law itself continues to be a patriarchally oriented phenomenon the world over. A reformist agenda that seeks to eradicate patriarchy or the division of genders merely leads itself *ad absurdum* and leaves a bad taste in the mouth.

This book was never intended to be a delicious serving of romanticized, easily digestible *khichri* about Hindu law. The present analysis challenges various forms of modernism as well as certain brands of *hindutva*. As indicated, I am fully aware that writing a critical analysis of this type is not going to get rid of idiosyncratic hostilities, even if they are clearly shown to be little else than politicized constructions. It has been necessary to be harsh at times in view of the need to highlight the starkness and depth of our collective ignorance and stubbornness.[78] By arguing for a more open acknowledgment of the global reality of pluralism and of legal diversity, the present concluding analysis seeks to encourage further scholarship on non-Western laws and their continuing role in the global context as well as asserting the presence, against all authoritative predictions, of postmodern Hindu law.

Deconstructing Modernist Discourses of Non-Western Laws

Positivism-centred modernist legal scholarship has at various levels systematically challenged and attempted to delegitimize non-Western laws such as Hindu law. The claim that such traditional laws, and particularly customs and religion, should have a rightful place in legal analysis and practice is still widely denied today. Positivist and modernist pressures forcefully suggest that the only viable route of development in a rapidly globalizing world involves following so-called rational, secular Western models, shedding indigenous and local cultural, religious, and legal traditions as fast as possible (Rajan 1999). However, as the present study confirms in detail for Hindu law, such attempts to assimilate non-Western legal traditions to modern, Eurocentric models are not achieving their more or less hidden aim of wiping out the allegedly backward elements of non-Western cultures, religions, and traditions.

Modernist, positivism-centred scholarship has begun to notice the metamorphosis of 'traditional' laws into postmodern legal constructs, but remains

78 As we saw, the aftermath of the famous *Shah Bano* controversy over a divorced Indian Muslim wife's right to maintenance from the ex-husband has thrown up a wildly confused and irritatingly misinformed discourse, whose underlying devious purpose is to contrast the dutifully modernized Hindu law and India's secular legal system with the recalcitrant and stubbornly traditionalist Indian Muslims. This is not the right place to launch into a specific critique of this issue, but the scholarly web of lies and misinformation around the MWPRDA of 1986 is almost unbelievable. Recent legal writing on the issue seems to derive from local newspapers (Larson 2001: 338), while relevant case law, which has existed in abundance from various High Courts since 1988, remains almost totally ignored (see Menski 2001, Chapter 4).

unconvinced that this is a healthy development. Continuing to claim the moral high ground, modernists generally refuse to accept that any meaningful progress in terms of justice and protection of individual rights may be made in this way. In the *Shah Bano* case and its aftermath (see n. 78 above) modernist scholars in conjunction with journalists seem to be actively hiding the truth, because such new postmodern developments ruin their ideological house of cards and vested interests.

Given such troubling difficulties in defining and operationalizing law, it is too ambitious to expect that many Western legal scholars should pay focused attention to non-Western laws within the global legal scenario.[79] While non-lawyers encounter their own specific difficulties of access to 'foreign' legal materials and concepts, lawyers face enough challenges in working within their own large, technically complex national fields of knowledge and expertise.[80] In addition, it appears that lawyers cannot even agree on what 'law' is, let alone on how it should be used.

In view of such problems, it is remarkable how easily other social scientists have been impressed by lawyers' claims that, unlike the allegedly messy social sciences, theirs is a special field of securely fixed knowledge and expertise that is somehow segregated from other forms of knowledge. The image of law as something heavy, complex, and fixed to near perfection is lurking everywhere. For example, picture all those continental law students walking around with huge tomes of commentaries on all kinds of legal codes. They carry the law in their arms, and may even be convinced that this is all the law they need to know. These are not merely polemical snipes at lawyers. Such popular images and assumptions constitute hard and significant evidence that legal centralism exerts its pervasive influence everywhere and keeps non-lawyers at bay in the process as well.

[79] For example, Harding (2001: 199) complains about the neglect of South-East Asia, but also notes with some surprise that recently the Law Faculty of the National University of Singapore 'has introduced the study of Chinese and Indonesian law, a development almost unthinkable about 15–20 years ago' (ibid.: 205 n. 11). In Japan, the *Daily Yomiuri* of 25 June 2002 reported that in a new wave of Chinese education, some children are now being taught about Confucian sayings in an effort to counterbalance modernist consumerism. May (2002: 270) notes that 'Asian alternatives' deserve a higher profile and complains about lack of coverage on Hindu law in a recent comparative study of Asian laws.

[80] Drobnig and van Erp (1999: ix) emphasise that more judges are now beginning to recognize the usefulness of comparative law. However, often the judges depend on lawyers' expertise rather than their own resources. Örücü (1999: 256) points out that in English law, evidence of foreign law is treated as a matter of fact, to be provided by experts. Thus it becomes critical whether legal practitioners have any knowledge (or even awareness) of such foreign laws as may be relevant. Indeed, there will often be much argument over whether a foreign law should be considered at all. This complex issue is of growing importance, given the many questions about 'ethnic minority laws' that are now being raised worldwide.

But as long as lawyers themselves are not even feeling safe within their own intellectual environment, and to the extent that postmodernism increases rather than decreases the perceived problems of overload and fluidity of knowledge, most lawyers will not even want to step out of their cocoon to research and analyse 'foreign' legal systems. This becomes even more difficult if it involves learning new languages and studying different histories and cultural models. Yet not only trained lawyers can make sensible contributions to legal debates about comparative law, jurisprudence and 'foreign' legal systems. Peters and Schwenke (2000), cited in the previous section, argued that a postmodern scholar needs to be familiar with virtually every academic discipline that could be related to law, a tall hurdle, which few would wish to attempt. This raises the question whether non-lawyers are not perhaps better equipped to write about postmodern legal theory than technically qualified lawyers.

Many lawyers tend to resist interdisciplinarity, thus constituting another self-imposed barrier against adoption of postmodern techniques and methodologies. Despite some earlier debates, legal centralism has only been challenged quite recently, 1986 being a key year by some coincidence.[81] The practical application of such theoretical reorientations is still seriously undeveloped.[82] We seem to know a lot about theories, but applying them in practice involves a further level of commitment.[83] Positivist legal myths continue to dominate lawyers' thinking as well as public thought, and influence those non-lawyers who attempt to think or write about law (Pandey and Pathak 1995). At the same time, comparative analysis shows that pure legocentrism and Western-style positivist 'model jurisprudence' represent hollow claims. Wherever we look, legal positivist analysis on its own is not able to handle the pluralistic challenges that continue to arise now all over Asia and Africa. It is not new, as

[81] I am not saying that earlier times did not generate similar debates, far from it. But scholarly writing on this topic which may be accessed fairly easily today dates mainly from the late twentieth century. The earlier, pioneering study by Hooker (1975) is now seen as exclusively concerned with describing and analysing 'weak' legal pluralism (and thus really a specific form of positivism) in the colonial and post-colonial context, while Griffiths (1986) expands that model into 'weak' and 'strong' forms of pluralism and Chiba (1986) constructs his 'three-level structure' of law. Notably, in Britain at the same time, Poulter (1986) produced a pioneering study which tried to maintain a liberal façade, but actually denied the legitimacy of the presence of legal pluralism in an effort to protect 'English core values'. There is more to say about this in the last section of this chapter.

[82] For example, Griffiths (1986) does not go beyond constructing a theory of 'weak' and 'strong' legal pluralism and declines the chance to provide empirical illustrations. Tamanaha (2001: 248) refers to more recent work by Griffiths on the legal regulation of euthanasia as a case study of legal pluralism.

[83] In this respect, the relationship between legislation and its implementation, which is hardly as automatic as many 'black letter' lawyers assume, offers an instructive parallel.

Tamanaha (2001) reiterates, that law is a matter of social convention. Recognition of that principle should mean acceptance that the theoretical and practical experiences and challenges of diversity-conscious legal regulation in many different countries and cultures, often in conditions of much adversity, are just as valid as the supposedly superior Western 'model jurisprudence'.[84]

The reluctance of lawyers to address legal plurality in its global manifestations is evident in several other ways. Various techniques to reduce this plurality of legal systems by redefining categories have been employed, so that the global impression of the dominance of Eurocentric perspectives and concepts may be maintained.[85] However, global demographic realities suggest that various non-Western legal systems, including prominently Hindu law, will remain theoretically and practically relevant. Over a billion Indians, another overspilling billion of Chinese, as well as other large populations in Asia and Africa, will never turn into Europeans. Rather, it seems now that Europeans and North Americans should learn more about—and from—other parts of the world, also when it comes to law.

However, 'mainstream' lawyers are frantically busy with defining away this legal non-European 'other' in various questionable ways.[86] The persistent British-dominated practice to subsume Indian law and many other colonially linked Commonwealth laws under the 'common law' label, while the French are keen to highlight their own civil law family of ex-colonial systems, speaks volumes about post-colonial connections, since these are not relations between equals.[87] An even more invidious consequence is the perpetuation of myths

[84] May (2001: 281) cites a Korean law professor who, in an otherwise bland article observes that '... we must bear in mind the national and regional particularities in promoting and protecting human rights. In a country where the majority of people is poverty stricken, the major and primary aspirations of the people in that country is to live like a human being, free from hunger, with shelter to protect themselves from the cold, and minimum medical care to ward off disease'. Such comments are also relevant to India, where socio-economic realities and constitutional promise often do not go together.

[85] An example that is only recently beginning to attract some attention is the placative labelling of South American laws as 'civil law', as though that was the whole story. South America and most of Africa too, would not even figure in the now widely criticized methods of grouping legal systems in 'families of law' (e.g. David and Brierley 1978), which have tended to marginalize non-Western legal systems. The planned OUP Encyclopedia of Legal History (a total of eight volumes, scheduled to appear in 2006) attempts to take account of cultural diversity in legal histories and aims to be fully comprehensive.

[86] May (2001) observes a significant level of Eurocentrism among leading legal writers. Currently, China is taught about the usefulness of common law models, as though there was a new colonial race.

[87] Örücü (1999: 294 n. 208) mentions occasional references to the laws of Ireland, South Africa, and India, and other Commonwealth countries, but these are not used as legal authorities for English law.

about Indian law being just some inferior form of English law, so that the very basis for the recognition of legal systems like Hindu law is withdrawn and flatly denied.[88] This is not only due to colonial hangovers.[89] In such contexts, a public impression is created that Hindu law is merely a matter of religion, which in our secular age is supposed to have no future.[90] From that angle, Hindu law is not even perceived as law any more. The same practical effect is achieved by fashionable versions of human rights law. It is amazing that lawyers and others have been getting away with such deficient methodology and oversimplifying arguments for so long. It appears that the media have a lot to answer for, because they create platforms for the strangest of things for curiosity value.[91]

In view of such widely distorted images of what Hindu law involves, we need not be surprised that expertise in such traditional laws is not present among lawyers, but may be found among historians and other socio-cultural area specialists. Which serious lawyer would want to deal with sadhu law?[92] Even if some non-lawyers may be motivated to spend precious research time on such 'religious' phenomena, their involvement raises new questions about how such observers will make sense of internal debates among lawyers. The fact that modernist ideology and assumptions about legal positivism are so closely linked, and constantly reinforce each other, needs to be highlighted. It

[88] When I introduce myself as someone who teaches Indian law, the response is often that I must be a legal historian who teaches English common law as applied in India. Indian law, so goes the popular myth, is basically a corrupted form of English law. Galanter and Krishnan (2001: 271) still write as though the Westminster model was operative in India. If scholars peddle such myths, how can one blame the wider public for being wrongly informed?

[89] Such myths are found in Japan, too, where the popular image of Hindu law is linked with bearded old men in funny clothes who somehow seek to intervene in the running of their country, now by televised appeals to religion.

[90] As noted, agreeing that their system is 'religious', Hindus are helping others to dismiss their conceptual and normative systems as 'traditional' and legally irrelevant. The Indian press constantly feeds exaggerated religious images, making it difficult just to blame foreigners for misrepresentations. For example, the *New Indian Express* (Bangalore edition, 13 March 2002) described Govardhan Puri Shankaracharya Swami Adhokshajananda Devtirth, a senior Hindu priest, as 'Hindu pontiff'. Such assertions appear with great regularity in popular and academic writing.

[91] I was in India in early 2002, when some *Paramahamsa* tried to blackmail the Indian government into constructing a Hindu temple in Ayodhya and proclaimed on television that he would fast until death if his wish was not complied with, because he represented some higher order. The television commentator asked the local collector and others what they thought should be done, only to be told: '*Marne do*' (Let him die). As far as I know, the old man retracted and still lives. But was this a legal process, or an example of legal drama, or just another media spectacle?

[92] By this I mean here rules stipulated by old, supposedly wise and learned men, who appear from nowhere, especially in televised serials, shout symbolic phrases and demand to be heard because they claim to represent 'revelation' and 'truth'.

seems that many social scientists remain blissfully unaware of such links. One may wonder who educates (or rather misleads) whom here. It is evident that the entire discipline of Indian law, and not just Hindu legal studies, is not sufficiently well linked with other academic enquiries into contemporary South Asian cultures, societies, economies, and political systems. As a result, some persistent misapprehensions reflect more than just lack of interdisciplinarity.[93] On the other side, because most Indian lawyers are not well educated about socio-legal issues, they have not been able to contribute significantly to such debates.[94]

In addition to ideological and subject barriers, a major problem for comparative legal research in a global context today remains lack of relevant knowledge. Without access to Sanskrit and other ancient languages, it is virtually impossible to reassess for oneself what the traditional Hindu textual sources may have been saying about what we might call 'law'.[95] Given that the definition of 'law' itself remains contested, enormous risks of distortion and misrepresentation persist.[96] Colonial intervention exerted its own distorting influences. The pioneering nineteenth century European translations of Hindu cultural texts are often quite misleading on legal issues and are in urgent need of revision.[97] The study of Hindu law has also suffered as a result of the pressures exerted by modern political correctness, directed against all forms of religion and traditional cultures. Hostile ideological premises have meant that studying Hindu law is now widely seen as a regressive activity.[98] This denial of legitimacy

[93] Guha (1997: 24–30) attempts to analyse the colonial order in relation to ancient Hindu concepts like *daṇḍa*, 'which was central to all indigenous notions of dominance' (ibid.: 28), but merely represents this as a convenient tool of suppression, ignoring the conceptual framework of 'assisted self-controlled order' which has been discussed in detail in the relevant section in Chapter 3.

[94] A notable analytical exception is Baxi (1986b), pointing to some useful early studies. There has not been much progress since, but a lot of politicking, as a survey by Pandey and Pathak (1995) shows.

[95] Bronkhorst (2001: 167) emphasizes that the modern Western scholar, even after many years of Sanskrit training, will never be able to catch up with the traditionally trained Hindu pandit.

[96] For a start, there is no precise Sanskrit equivalent of the term 'law' as positivist state law, so that the Mughal *qanūn* (state-made law) would later appear to fill a conceptual gap.

[97] Olivelle (2000: v) argues that '[t]he time is ripe ... for a new set of editions and translations using not only current scholarship but also accessible English'. Menski (1984) contains a detailed analysis and new translation of all ancient key texts related to Hindu marriage.

[98] This is strongly reflected in much feminist legal writing. Dhanda and Parashar (1999) studiously ignore Hindu law, while Sarkar and Sivaramayya (1994: 1) are more explicitly negative about the oppression by the two major religions of India. Parashar (1992) focused on discrimination against women by the personal laws, but has since reconsidered some of her views.

to Hindu legal studies illustrates how quickly and conveniently modernists forget that laws virtually everywhere seem to be gerontocratic and androcentric tools of power and resource allocation in society.

While modernists want to reconstruct the world as they think fit, the impossibility of cutting out religion or culture from South Asian lived experiences need not be discussed here.[99] While more readily accepted for Muslims and Islam today, from a Hindu law perspective too, explicit recognition of the role of religion, culture, and tradition cannot be denied. Whether the modern 'West' likes this or not, the 'East' has different ways of looking at the world. Derrett (1968b: 557) captures this well:[100]

> In Europe it is accepted ... that you are not free to do what you believe religion teaches you to do, but only what the State allows you to do. In America and Australia the same formula ... prevails. You can have what beliefs you choose, provided you do not act upon them in a manner contrary to that determined by the legislators (who may have any or no religion); and nice difficulties constantly arise, especially where the majority think it proper that everyone should do something which a religion forbids.

Equally damaging as pompous attempts to declare religion, culture, and tradition as extra-legal and irrelevant is the modernist technique of not giving due credit to non-Western laws for getting things right, whenever that happens, as it does. Recent studies on the colonial system in India, focussing on the hegemonistic and universalizing claims of the metropolitan lawmakers (Chandra 1998), show that during the early colonial period the British could not quite fathom that traditional Hindu law should know rules that allow women property rights. The colonial masters promptly proceeded to restrict such rights, which led eventually to the Hindu Women's Right to Property Act, 1937, in which Hindu widows were given something by state law that their traditional law did not actually deny them.

Current discourses about non-Western laws in various fora and in much of the modernist literature demonstrate that old prejudices about different civilizations and their comparative value are as strong as ever.[101] As a result,

[99] Some modernists still purport to claim that one can have no religion. For example S. Basu (2001: 17) portrays herself as a card-carrying atheist feminist.

[100] See also Derrett (1978a: 200) on the Indian concept of progress as different from Western ideas.

[101] Issues that keep coming to the fore are 'honour killings', female 'circumcision' for many African women, and consent in marriage. While all of these problems pose real challenges and endanger some women, the issues are used as tools to denigrate everything non-Western as primitive, misogynist, and inherently discriminatory. The question of consent in marriage, now under the catchy heading of 'forced marriages', serves to legitimize immigration-related agenda and controls in Britain and the European Union. It also serves as a tool to teach 'immigrants' (often third-generation British citizens) that they should adopt the values of their host country by marrying among themselves, rather than 'importing' spouses. Human rights arguments are here selectively used to deny certain human rights.

dishonestly biased and often excessively polemical debates highlight only the negative side of complex non-Western realities and discuss only positive Western elements.[102] It is blatantly dishonest to behave as though only non-Western systems had problems with justice. Such biased assumptions then legitimize legal intervention from outside or from above, claimed to be necessary because somehow internal mechanisms and legal traditions are not equipped for the task. Legal theory here becomes, all too quickly, a willing handmaiden for colonialist and other hegemonic interventions.

Reservations about the *fides* of Indian law are by no means unique to Western observers. A leading modernist legal scholar, Kusum (2000: 268) concludes her assessment of fifty years of Supreme Court activity on a highly ambivalent note, writing that 'there have been some judgements which have a potential of negative fall-out, but it needs to be conceded, that subjectivity and personal opinion of the judge cannot be completely extricated from the process of decision-making'. Kusum seems unwilling to acknowledge that the judges have actually achieved far more than the legislators, and have occasionally gone well beyond the parameters imagined by scholars. Such ambivalence is also apparent when perfunctory references to Hindu tradition or classical Hindu law are made in textbooks and other studies today.[103] Recent doctoral candidates still indicate wholly well-intentioned plans to copy just a few details from older works, hoping to capture the essence of something that could be treated as 'traditional' Hindu law. Dangerous stereotypes are thus being perpetuated in the name of efficient scholarship. The ghosts of the 'laws of Manu', as we saw ad nauseam, still haunt Hindu women and scholars, preventing clear thinking. The remedy lies not in burning old books, but in refining current scholarly techniques to incorporate postmodernist approaches into legal analysis.

The particular issue of 'essentializing' and stereotyping has become a rather vexed subject, with much abuse and scholarly politicking. It is evident that a false dichotomy between tradition and modernity has been constructed and that existing debates are to some extent fruitless (Baxi 2002). Modernists routinely accuse traditionalists of essentializing tradition, religion, Hinduism, and Hindu law. In truth, modernists and feminists are equally prone to the risks

[102] This is another instance of 'overlapping consensus'. The critical question, simply put, is whether the glass one sees is half empty or half full. Ideologically motivated, blinkered analysis will presume that the cup of legal abuse is never half-filled when it comes to 'civilized' Western laws, whereas it is almost filled to the brim in non-Western legal systems.

[103] Many Indian authors have problems with 'tradition' in its various forms, and therefore now with postmodernism. Agnihotri and Mazumdar (1995: 1869) struggle to defend their modernist positions against postmodern challenges, portraying regressive appropriations 'by forces inimical to the goals of the women's movement'. Such reasoning is really a violent form of conservative academic censorship.

and temptations of stereotyping and using abridged versions of traditional Hindu law. As we saw, even the most intricate use of language may not manage to verbalize the limitless plurality of Hindu law, while the real challenge seems to lie in the application of postmodern awareness. How can one's work and words adequately reflect postmodern realities in all their complexity? Postmodern methodology suggests that this itself is an impossible aim. So we can only, like the ancient Hindus in their quest for self-controlled order, try our best.

What, though, are feminists and others doing if they insist, by reference to Manu and other ancient sources of alleged legal authority, that Hindu women are at all times subject to men's control and supervision? Ripping one verse out of an old text, presenting it as evidence of a whole legal system, is scholarly fraud and a form of feminist law-making in its most dangerous avatar. Leading women are in this way telling their subaltern sisters that they are in need of help, while elitist scholars are somehow above most of such restrictions, but may still feel the pinch, for example when it comes to claiming property rights. It is hard to understand how such placative feminist restatements of traditional Hindu women's dependent status may be creatively used for a strategy of empowering women. All too often, the feminist activist highlights her own role, and frequently that of her organization, in rescuing her less fortunate sisters from male oppression. This particular choice of feminist-cum-modernist methodology further disempowers women as a class and makes them dependent on the state's benevolence and modernist lobbying.

Through her specific methodological approach, agonizing over various reform proposals in family law of the 1990s, Agnes (2000) clearly demonstrates that feminists and modernists are today seriously baffled by the emerging postmodern scenario. While some writing has begun to capture evidence of legal advances,[104] most authors remain blinded by manifest legislative stubbornness, which is at times caused by excessive demands from feminist lobbyists rather than conservative back-pedalling.[105] As Arun Shourie (2001: 198 and 239) has observed with regard to certain areas of constitutional law, in India today we must be aware of an unduly prominent culture of 'grievance mongering', a form of unconstructive moaning. This familiar syndrome, again, confuses critique with criticism. Irrespective of whether it is perpetrated by lawyers or non-lawyers, it is not conducive to clear-headed thinking about the public interest in its widest sense, and about the place of Hindu law.

[104] Parashar (1992: 137) complains that the modernist reforms did not go far enough and were not even designed to be effective; they are limited and were watered down.

[105] No lessons seem to have been learnt from the *Shah Bano* agitation by modernists, still miffed that a separate personal law enactment was made for Muslims. At the same time, there is a blatant refusal to see that the public protests resulted in giving Muslims the separate law they wanted, but on terms determined by the government's fiscal and social welfare concerns (Menski 2001, Chapter 4).

Postmodernist Challenges to the Concept of Law

The critical reassessment of modernist representations of Hindu law attempted in this study also points to deep-seated deficiencies in scholarly understandings of law as a phenomenon. While some jurisprudential writing is now beginning to talk of post-postmodernism,[106] it is still important for lawyers to understand the theoretical and practical implications of postmodernism, as discussed earlier in the second section in Chapter 1. Most lawyers worldwide go through law schools without being challenged to think deeply about the nature of law. The result is that lawyers tend to become brainwashed legocentrists, to whom Legrand (1996) scathingly refers as 'technicians' of the national law rather than skilful comparative lawyers. Even if the supervening aim was more nobly the chance to work for the human rights of others, there is no guarantee that law schools prepare such idealists for asking relevant questions about their own roles and the perceptions of their 'clients'. While one must admit that all kinds of lawyers are needed, it is difficult not to be polemical about the lack of sensitivity for diversity and legal pluralism in legal education.

Plurality-focused postmodernist legal analysis, it seems, has been deeply disturbing for many sections of the legal establishment, because it unashamedly questions cherished beliefs and myths among lawyers about their own importance. Particularly, it challenges the ideology of legal centralism, dragging law firmly back into an intricate network of interdisciplinarity, rather than giving it separate and dominant status. Further, postmodernism questions how laws are constructed. It challenges certain practical legal axioms, such as the Westminster-style claim that legislatures alone are empowered to make laws,[107] while judges just apply given rules, or the supremacy of precedent over the desire to find justice in accordance with the facts and circumstances of a case. Postmodernism, thus, inevitably intervenes in legal debates at various levels, but does so often on the 'wrong' side, challenging in particular the certainty that doctrinal, 'black-letter lawyers' value so much that they often worship it in print. While doctrinal lawyers (who might not be modernists, of course) continue to emphasize objectivity and certainty, postmodern analysts of various descriptions have introduced troubling references to subjectivity and the socially constructed nature of all rule systems. Postmodern thinking also

[106] Peters and Schwenke (2000: 829) note that a 'post-post-modernist approach to comparative law will retain the (self-) critical impetus of the post-modernist critique, reject the postmodernist assertion that objectivity is not attainable in comparative law, and synthesise old and new demands for interdisciplinarity and thoughtful hermeneutics'.

[107] This claim is still being made for India by Galanter and Krishnan (2001: 271), writing of a 'Westminster-style parliamentary system' to assert the comparability of Israel and India.

upsets lawyers because it makes them realize that they may have acquired certain types of knowledge, but not others.[108]

Digging a little deeper, postmodern analysis finds that there is simply no universal agreement on the nature and concept of law itself. Modernist assumptions privilege what is called 'legal positivism', the view that law is law because a political (and hence legal) authority says so.[109] That explains partly how various forms of abuse of political and legal powers remain attractive to dictators large and small all over the world. The most recent writing on jurisprudence tells us, yet again, that even to ask 'What is law?' is wrong and misleading.[110]

Through the pluralising experience of postmodernism, certainty-focused legal scholarship has become somewhat unsure of itself, while the search for justice continues.[111] However, gone are the days when 'law' was simply the word of the ruler, when Austin's maxim was itself 'the law', precedent was the dominant rule, and judges did not make law.[112] It is increasingly recognized now that pure positivism is not sufficient to explain the totality of legal phenomena, but have lawyers not known this all the time? There is indeed a paradigmatic shift of understanding about law, part of which can be located in

[108] Riles (2001: 3) identifies 'a certain ubiquitous angst about the disciplinary identity of comparative law today...and a sense of being at a loss about the way forward'.

[109] The classic text, after John Austin's work (1913), is taken to be Hart (1961), now Hart (1994). H.L.A. Hart seems treated like a god in many universities, including Indian law schools, but wrote some rather nasty things about primitive societies that, according to him, have no law. How, then, can this be a universally valid theory of law? Tamanaha (2001) aims to improve on this project through his approach of 'socio-legal positivism' (p. 151), but in my view he does not succeed in presenting a credible universal theory, since he again claims that there might be societies without law (p. 201), and is too busy opposing legal pluralism, custom, and religion.

[110] Simon Roberts (1979), in an important study that has been out of print in English, but is available in German and Japanese, argued this a long time back. From a Hindu law perspective, Roberts seems to be talking about rough equivalents to dharma and *sadācāra*. Tamanaha (2001: 211–4) also begins to talk about 'order', without any apparent realisation that he may be circumscribing what Hindu philosophy has said on this theme thousands of years ago.

[111] There seems to be little disagreement that a focus on justice should be of central importance to any legal activity, but positivist theories of law, emphasizing power rather than justice, systematically undermine this and hence cloud the view for the relativity of perceptions about justice.

[112] A growing number of writers now admit that this is a myth and that judges have always made law in some form, and do so more openly now. Chen (1999: 54) acknowledges the importance of judicial law-making in Australia, but also in much wider general terms, to the effect that '[t]here is no doubt that strict legalism has gone and is now a thing of the past. It is now well recognised that judges do make law. It is also recognised that the doctrine of precedent is as much an attitude of mind as it is a legal doctrine'.

postmodernist theorizing. Still, young lawyers are constantly being pulled back from the brink of postmodern subjectivity by being made to learn about H.L.A. Hart, whose work represents a celebration of positivism and the Eurocentric assertion that 'law' rules the civilized world, while some 'primitives' have not even reached a level of organization that involves 'law'.[113] Despite the current lip service to increased sensitivity about discrimination of various types, it is remarkable how easily most lawyers swallow and uncritically adore such intellectual leadership. As Tamanaha (2001: 151) dares to suggest in a scholarly act of patricide, Hart's theory of law is really quite parochial, and not universally valid.

Hence, there is clearly much more to law and legal theory than Hart and others have been prepared to discuss. Scholars, too, want life to be easier, if only for their readers.[114] Tamanaha (2001: 150–1) roundly dismisses Hart's approach of identifying 'a single concept of law—*the* concept of law'. But how do we replace and reconfigurate such a central singular concept without leaving a huge void? Tamanaha (2001: 151) suggests in his analysis that '[d]iscerning the core features of state law is a worthy and monumental task. But it does not provide a suitable foundation for a general jurisprudence, because it is too narrow to account for the complex presence of legal phenomena, especially in (but not limited to) non-Western countries'. This line of reasoning clearly acknowledges the existence of legal pluralism, but Tamanaha does not like that concept, inter alia because he sees it as tainted by its closeness to social sciences and particularly its prodigious use by legal anthropologists (Tamanaha 1993). Seeking to preserve the field of law for lawyers, claiming legal pluralism back for jurisprudence, as it were, and retaining a positivist label, Tamanaha (2001: 151–2) proceeds to develop his own theory of law, which is attractively characterized as socio-legal positivism:

> Socio-legal positivism recognizes that law is a human social creation. Law is whatever we attach the label 'law' to. It will be unflinchingly conventionalist in the identification of what law is. If law is attached by usage to more than one phenomenon, rather than picking one to serve as the standard by which to evaluate the others, socio-legal positivism will accept that there are different kinds or types of law, each with its own characteristic features.

However, this seemingly pluralistic approach is not fully carried through to its logical conclusions. Tamanaha's analysis remains basically hostile to customs and religion, as he is not prepared to go all the way in accepting various forms

[113] Tamanaha (2001: 150) acknowledges that 'Hart's privileging of state law is ethnocentric', but does not seem to think that this is a major problem.

[114] Misguided attempts by specialists on Hindu law to make the reader's life easier by translating dharma as 'law' or stipulating other simple parallels were discussed in the first section of this chapter. Given the loaded nature of the term 'law', serious distortions are inevitable, and we are ever so subtly taught to read Hindu law as if it was a Western-style legal system.

of law that potentially pose a direct challenge to positivist norms. Tamanaha also does not fully answer the question how, for example, ethnic minority customs could be factored into his system of 'new legal pluralism' grounded in socio-legal positivism, though he is evidently aware of this issue. At the end of the day, this new legal theory appears as a repackaged form of positivism, based on the liberal idea that people anywhere in the world should decide for themselves if what they are doing is 'law'. But who finally decides such questions? And does it even matter what is officially decided, given that so much of law, not just in Hindu law, is manifestly located in the realm of the informal and the unofficial, virtually beyond the reach of the state?

The potential for conflicts over definition and boundaries seems seriously underplayed in this kind of theorizing. Tamanaha does not address the critical issue that in certain legal cultures, like traditional Hindu law, there is not even an equivalent term for 'law' in our Western sense. Examining the scholarship on Hindu law and other non-Western legal systems, especially African laws (Menski 2000a, Chapter 5), one may become quite pessimistic about the future of such incomplete postmodern analysis. How will Tamanaha's model of law ensure that the voices of the subaltern, however defined, will be taken account of?[115] What actually, at the end of the day, is law if it can be anything people say? Tamanaha's most recent attempt to improve on Hart's analysis looks impressive, but does not offer much help, particularly to specialists of non-Western legal systems.

Other recent jurisprudential scholarship is more explicitly postmodern. For example, Cotterrell (2000) uses the image of 'Pandora's box', from which law teachers and analysts may freely help themselves. This is a sensible way of writing about the challenges of postmodernist methodologies and the plurality of concepts and understandings, but this, too, only increases the lawyer's woes about legal insecurity. Depending on one's perspective, current jurisprudence could therefore be said to experience total freedom or, rather more likely, considerable turmoil, searching in the fast-moving postmodernist whirlpool for the lost security of law as a positivist given.

Not only since postmodernism appeared on the scene do we know that all legal systems are tools of power, and thus potentially the most cruel means of suppression. Earlier, Hans Kelsen watched in disgust and surprise as his beautiful theoretical house of cards about 'pure legal positivism' was torched by Pakistani political expediency.[116] That experience sent some shock-waves especially through the Commonwealth circles of legal thinkers and writers, as

[115] On this, see Spivak (1988). Based on field experience, I would argue that the subaltern can speak, but often do not care or dare to communicate their thoughts. This raises further questions about the nature of law, which may be purposely kept invisible, well beyond the reach of formal and often interventionist legal analysis.

[116] Kelsen (1945: 19) saw law in purely positivist fashion as a coercive order and thus produced a famous theoretical study. Faced with Pakistan's abuse, he claimed to be surprised and misunderstood, though one could have foreseen the problem.

though there had been no atrocities in the name of the law before. However, what sticks prominently in the Western mind is not the fact that a leading Western legal theorist so obviously forgot to build reality into his cleverly constructed legal theory and thus deserves full marks only in terms of academic creativity. Rather, it is the fact that this abuse of Kelsen's doctrine occurred in Pakistan,[117] reinforcing the common assumption that 'undeveloped' legal systems of the East are prone to such abuses of the cherished 'rule of law'.[118] Specifically on this key concept, Tamanaha (2001: 98) notes, in preparation for his argument that law has no essence:

> Judging from the frequency with which it is referred to ... the idea of the rule of law is the dominant legitimating slogan of law at the close of the twentieth century. Although there are competing versions of what this notion entails, its core characteristics can be stated without much controversy. In the narrowest terms, it means that the government rules through law, and that the government is itself under the law.

Tamanaha (2001: 98) therefore correctly finds that 'the rule of law, as formulated, is substantively empty' and reiterates later (ibid.:193 and 204) that law has effectively no essence. This raises again the spectrum of the Kelsen problem, namely anything that a government declares to be 'the law' thereby gains automatic legitimacy. The 'rule of law' model clearly also covers tyrannical regimes that rely on legal modernity to legitimize their hold on power and resources. It appears that Tamanaha's new approach to legal positivism seeks to evade this problem by stipulating that a better definition of law would be one according to which the conventions of a particular society determine what the law is.

Any reassessment of the dominant concepts of law, therefore, invariably drags legal theorists back to old debates on the nature of law, as well as highlighting the deficient understanding of comparative law in a globalizing world. Comparative law must no longer masquerade as cultural imperialism. There is much work to be done in debates about law and legal theory in the world at large, linked with those about law in India and the more specific discussions within Hindu law scholarship.

If modernists believed in the power of law to bring about desirable reforms in society, they now stand deprived of the seemingly safe network of agreed definitions of law, as well as challenged by feminist analysis (not to

[117] Indeed, a favourite adjective among journalists writing about Pakistan continues to be 'lawless', thus deliberately perpetuating images of a kind of Wild East, in which the rule of the gun dominates.

[118] Tamanaha (2001: 61) expresses this well when he highlights that the methodological approach of historical evolutionism creates a powerful stereotype, leading to the 'common notion that primitive (or non-Western) society stands in relation to modern (or Western) society as a child does to an adult. It feeds and reinforces the sense of the West that it represents the high point towards which history has aimed'.

speak here of ethnic and other minorities, who still have less of a voice) for abusing legal powers to weight the legal scales in subtly biased ways that blindfolded justice is not supposed to notice. For a start, we did not need postmodernism to tell us that all legal systems, even the matrilineal ones, are more or less patriarchally focused.[119] State legal systems have their own internal psychologies and mechanisms for functioning, reflect androcentric patterns and reinforce them, which means that such laws may not be useful tools for promotion of gender equity, let alone equality. Not surprisingly, feminists now struggle with the argument that modernizing legal reforms almost everywhere still deliver women into the hands of male-dominated justice systems made by almost exclusively male legislatures and judiciaries. But this is a global legal predicament, not an issue unique to Asia and Africa, nor to Hindu law.

Partly as a result of such uncomfortable realizations, modernist law reform by itself is everywhere no longer seen as a panacea. In a postmodern climate, the previously exalted status and power of legislatures is being questioned from many angles.[120] Legal centralism, as John Griffiths (1986: 4–5) so forcefully argued, is indeed a myth, while legal pluralism is an all-pervasive fact. Relying on Griffiths (1986) and particularly on Masaji Chiba's (1986) instructive model of the tripartite structure of law, globally relevant conclusions about the nature of law as an inherent pluralistic and diverse phenomenon with innumerable culture-specific characteristics also make sense when one studies Hindu legal developments. But they are far more difficult to reconstruct for non-specialists who only studied their own national legal systems and already face difficulties in using the law of neighbouring countries.[121] Recent legal writing (Tamanaha 2001) may make perfunctory reference to Chiba's work, but does not appear to apply his model. Paying lip service to 'great names' is not enough in jurisprudential analysis. Unlearning standard myths about law remains apparently a painful and much slower process than adopting new theories.

All of this does not lead to a scenario in which the state is absent or irrelevant. Parekh (1996: 49) rightly concludes that 'it is too early to write the obituary

[119] On *Dalitbahujan* assumptions about more equitable gender balances see Ilaiah (1996). Tamanaha (2001: 43–4) shows how feminist legal theorists, in particular, view law as a gendered construct, emphasizing that '[t]he essential "maleness" of law is reflected in everything from the "reasonable *man*" standard, to the adversary system, to the public/private distinction that perpetuates male domination within the family, to predominantly male judges and legislators, to "masculine jurisprudence" which emphasizes separation over connection and caring .... Patriarchal law thus mirrors patriarchal society, ignoring and suppressing women's interests and values'.

[120] Nandy (2002: 36–60) re-examines images of the state and observes that overemphasis on the state's role as protector and liberator of society has unleashed dangerous processes that require fresh analysis.

[121] For excellent case studies on the extent of use made by judges of foreign laws, see the contributions collected by Drobnig and van Erp (1999).

of the modern state'. Rather, postmodernist legal analysis involves a cutting to size of positivist claims that the 'rule of law' can achieve miracles and provide sustainable solutions for problems over justice anywhere in the world. To that extent, 'law' is partly receding, taking a place in a collectivity of relevant factors, rather than 'lording it' over all others. While some lawyers will resent this as a reflection of loss of status and power, many others will understand that a more democratic and socially constructive role of law in a postmodern environment actually opens up numerous new possibilities for creative lawyering and for a deeper understanding of the multiple roles of law. Postmodernism does not challenge law itself, but questions anew why and how law and legal processes continue to be widely misappropriated by certain dominant interest groups all over the world. What has happened to considerations of the wider public interest, even benefit for the universe or, if we prefer a more secular expression, the good of the global community? General appeals to the 'rule of law' are manifestly not sufficient safeguards for justice in a globalizing era.

Hindu Law, Postmodernity, and Globalization

The findings of the present study suggest that detailed knowledge of Hindu law will remain relevant not only in India, but wherever Hindus have settled in the world. This is partly due to the nature of Hindu law as a personal law, which moves with the migrant as some kind of 'cultural luggage'. Modernist discourses are clearly also inadequate when it comes to understanding the legal implications of large-scale migrations of Asian and African people around the world, particularly to the Euro-American honeypots. While lawyers have focused on the globalization of law as understood in the formulation among states worldwide of legal systems conforming to United Nations and World Trade Organization treaties, relatively little attention has been devoted to the legal implications of the globalization of labour and migration. Most modernists do not even accept the need to research such a subject, while positivist lawyers tenaciously argue that there is nothing to study for them, because these are matters of anthropology, not law. Postmodern legal developments suggest, however, that subject-specific boundaries are being crossed everywhere, and that pluralism-focused interdisciplinary analyses will be able to make constructive contributions to worldwide debates about globalization as a pluralizing, rather than uniforming, phenomenon.

My view has been for many years that diasporic migration inevitably creates new legal hybridities that need to be understood by jurisprudential scholarship. This final section focuses on the implications of postmodern legal pluralism among Hindus, who are now living in virtually all parts of the world, experiencing individually and as communities that globalization does not just mean assimilation to Euro-American models. It is my main argument here that the postmodern Hindu law developments in India carry important lessons for the gradually pluralizing states of Europe and North America which, due to the globalization of migration flows, are now being influenced ever more by Asian and African legal concepts and are under growing pressure to recognize aspects of such laws.

In short, rather than assuming that the new migrants from Asia will just assimilate to their 'host' country and its laws, open-eyed postmodern scholarship needs to be prepared for finding rejection of the axiomatic superiority of Western models,[122] as well as a cautious distance to traditional Asian and African concepts.[123] The latter remain, however, the major basic building blocks for postmodern reconstruction. The result everywhere, as fieldwork and some new studies show,[124] has been the informal emergence of ethnic minority laws. For Britain, this may be encapsulated in the term *angrezi* dharma, a form of dharma unique to British Hindus. This is a meaningful concept which underpins postmodern British Hindu law, a legal system that according to positivist theory is not supposed to exist.[125]

It is evident that the modernist resistance against dealing with any matters of personal laws in Western legal systems remains immensely strong, often on

[122] This is closely linked to the rejection of racism, since the false dichotomy of Western and non-Western laws not only assumes that Western law is inherently superior to non-Western laws, but also that whites are more human than others. This raises a number of unsavoury implications, which cannot be explored here. It is evident that Indians in the West experience first-hand that Western legal systems have only achieved equality on paper. Careful reading of jurisprudential work teaches that no legal system in the world actually achieves equality (Dahrendorf 1969; Kelly 1992). With specific reference to British Asians, Ballard (1994: 5) importantly observes that British Asians assimilate 'on their own terms', which challenges modernist assumptions about the cutting of roots, identifying instead confident counter-assertions of ethnic superiority when adherence to one's cultural values and forms of behaviour is seen to be more sophisticated than assimilation to English norms.

[123] This distance is often increased because residence abroad means that the familiar cultural environment has suddenly vanished and become remote. Individual migrants may take some time to realize how little they used to think about their own traditions, but they know probably still less about the cultural minutiae of the new home. This contested space, never just a vacuum, is then gradually filled by new constructs like British Hindu law (*angrezi* dharma).

[124] The reconstruction of officially informal personal law systems in virtually all countries of Europe and in North America is well under way, but there is much resistance among the legal establishment against accepting the new evidence. For Britain, Pearl and Menski (1998) introduced the concept of *angrezi* shariat, now also acknowledged in Germany (Rohe 2001: 221), while a study by the Friedrich Ebert Stiftung, *Islamisches Alltagsleben in Deutschland* (Lemmen and Miehl 2001) confirms the unwillingness to debate such issues publicly and is wary of the resulting 'judicialization' of such matters because this bypasses, to a large extent, public debates. Verma (2002) is a new study on Panjabi migrants in Canada and the reconstruction of their communities.

[125] According to Chiba (1986) it is therefore a classic case of 'unofficial law'. But this is never a static given and the process of gaining formal recognition is well under way by now.

the ground that personal laws imply backward, medieval standards, with negative implications for human rights. However, there is no point denying that personal laws and their role as 'cultural baggage' of immigrant communities are making an increasingly relevant input to postmodern legal analysis. If lawyers, in particular,[126] thought for a long time that Asian and African migrants settling in Europe or North America would just assimilate to the legal systems of the host countries, they made a huge conceptual error and miscalculated the internal strength of personal laws, which have been totally ignored in many countries, or redefined as 'ethnic minority customs' in others.[127] Rather than being stuck in the realm of allegedly static 'religion', 'tradition', or 'culture', everywhere in the world various 'ethnic minority' groups are actively engaged in reconstructing their own culture-specific forms of personal laws, mostly outside the formal legal systems of the host jurisdiction.

In a globalizing world, rather than everyone learning English or adopting American law to do business and get on in life, the majority of people (who demographically quite clearly live in Asia) will eventually make Euro-Americans realize the need to learn about non-European languages, cultures, and laws. Failure to do so will not be conducive to business, and bad for international peace at a global level and community relations in the local sphere. As we saw, the impending collapse of modernist debates about legal uniformity worldwide is powerfully reflected in the futile politicized debates over the uniform civil code in India. Significantly, Ugo Mattei (2001: 254) suggests that positivism itself may be the key problem for our lack of understanding for legal plurality and complexity:

> ... legal positivism is *the enemy* of understanding in the law. It is a reductionist perspective that artificially excludes from the picture the deeper structure of the law (things like legal culture, language of legal expression, revolutionary moments and so on) as well as (in typical postmodern style) the decorative, and symbolic elements of it. Positivism, as a consequence, is unmasked as an inherently formalistic approach, in the sense that form prevails over structure in determining the law's domain. It *outlaws* (considers outside the law) deeper structural aspects.

A large number of examples could be given from all kinds of inter-cultural contexts, showing that most legal scholars are quick to 'outlaw' ethnic minority legal matters and are too conservative when they expect the eventual

[126] With few exceptions, anthropologists seem to be no better at observing social realities, since they wear the same blinkers as their legal and other scholarly colleagues.

[127] This term was coined for Britain by Poulter (1986) in a pioneering study that is highly regarded by modernist lawyers. Poulter systematically applied legal centralist concepts and his methodology denied ethnic minorities the agency to reconstruct their own hybrid legal systems. For a pluralist critique of this approach, see Menski (1988; 1993a).

assimilation of non-European migrants. Friedman (1998: 1088) makes the general points that in this age of immigration, 'legal cultures run the risk of colliding with each other' and that '[t]his kind of culture clash is also a strain on the notion of the rule of law'. He then takes the example of polygamy among Muslims living in Italy to argue (id.) that '[t]he Moslem living in Italy will find it easier to adapt to Italian technology than to Italian culture, including legal culture. Convergence will take place—but it is slow and painful at times. It will, of course, be easier for his children'.[128] Here, too, assimilation over time is clearly expected.

It seems that comparative lawyers, too, have their own agenda, hiding behind clever language in an ongoing debate over whether their goal is '*solving*, rather than simply analyzing, the problem of difference' (Riles 2001: 15). Indeed, the problem is whether difference itself is actually the problem. Does not the modernist opposition to difference create a climate of war on plurality and diversity, notwithstanding loud proclamations of human rights principles? There is currently still a notable reluctance, if not outright refusal in Europe and North America, to discuss such issues of social and legal pluralism more openly.[129] Uniformizing pressures remain powerful everywhere, despite strong evidence that the key to a harmonious future lies in acceptance of ethnic diversity and the crossing of borders, rather than dogged focus on uniformity and nation-state agenda.[130]

Such conceptual matters concern academics and common people everywhere. Like all humans, Hindus anywhere in the world have to make sense in their everyday lives of the conflicting expectations and contradictory pulls of different normative orders and legal systems.[131] As the present study showed in detail, the process of finding appropriate solutions takes place, first of all, in the individual mind, as the ancient concept of *ātmanastuṣṭi* as the primary source of dharma confirms. From this perspective, Hindu law is a mental construct, a psychological rather than a legal phenomenon. Even at the community level, adjustments will occur more or less invisibly to outsiders and a wider public. In diaspora, for various reasons, it is rare for disputes among Hindus to be litigated before the official courts of the Euro-American realm. Because

[128] Poulter (1986) argued to the same effect about the impact of British education on the new generation.

[129] The fate of the so-called 'Parekh Report' on the future of multi-ethnic Britain (Parekh 2000) is highly significant. It was viciously attacked for asking uncomfortable questions about the meaning of 'Britishness' today.

[130] Among social scientists specializing in South-East Asian studies, the importance of crossing borders in social reality and academic methodology is now receiving more attention in border-land studies (Horstmann 2002).

[131] Unpublished research by my student Eric Bakilana, an African from Tanzania, begins to show that evidence of East African Hindu laws and their informal operation today can be collected in abundance if we spend enough time on local fieldwork.

almost all these cases have remained unreported, this is a most difficult field to research.[132]

While it is not a major purpose of the present study to make a contribution to the emerging debate on ethnic minorities and legal regulation in Europe and elsewhere, it would be irresponsible scholarship not to relate the findings of the present analysis to the currently emerging worldwide debates about 'ethnic minority laws'.[133] A detailed study about this issue in relation to English law discloses grave and persistent problems over human rights implementation within a system of uniform legal regulation which purports to be colour-blind and neutral towards culture, when it is in fact neither (Jones and Welhengama 2000). If the evidence from major non-European countries and jurisdictions such as India directly conflicts with the modernist principle of uniform legal regulation, does this not hold any lessons for the world as a whole? Whenever there are socially and culturally distinct groups of people, whether we treat them as 'ethnic' groups, 'communities', or 'minorities', their normative orders will tend to diverge in important details from those of the uniforming, official state legal system. In daily social reality—but significantly not in law—these 'ethnic minority laws' will prevail over the norms set by the state, as Hindu principles are asserting themselves over modernist rules in current Hindu law developments in India. However, what is re-emerging in the diasporic context is not Hindu, Muslim, or African legal tradition in itself, as rigid tradition, as is often alleged. In reality, certain elements of those legal systems are being reconstructed into new hybrids.[134] The finer balancing of such conflicting forces depends to a large extent on the nature of the respective state and the local participants. In every case, though, as the findings of the present study suggest, the results are culture-specific and situation-sensitive, new hybrid forms of Hindu law, which are undergoing constant change and require much more detailed study.

It is relevant to provide some glimpses here to illustrate the nature of the new postmodern hybridities. In the 1960s and 1970s, some Hindu families in Britain found to their dismay that their daughter or sister could simply be abandoned by a Hindu husband if the marriage had not been formally registered according to English law. The women and their families had no remedies under English law because there had only been a Hindu wedding in the UK.[135] After just a few early cases of this kind, none officially reported because of the element of shame involved, there was a rapid adaptation process among Hindus

[132] For a pioneering survey in relation to English law, see Pearl (1986).

[133] My introduction in Jones and Welhengama (2000: xiii–xxii) outlines the difficulties faced in this new field of academic and practice-related legal study.

[134] For Hindus in Britain, see in detail Menski (1987; 1991a; 1991b; 1993a).

[135] Of course the problem only arose if the Hindu marriage had taken place in the UK, since a Hindu marriage solemnized under Hindu law in India should be recognized by English law under the rules of private international law.

in Britain. The core legal message, to the effect that official legal registration of a marriage before a British registrar is necessary to achieve legal validity, was in this way successfully transmitted by the official legal system.

But this did not mean that British Hindus would now only marry under English law and abandon the legally irrelevant Hindu wedding in Britain. Instead, Hindus started marrying twice, first in a registered ceremony, then through Hindu ceremonies, keeping these two elements quite distinct and separate at first.[136] The earlier practice among British Hindus was to treat the 'English' ceremony of marriage virtually as an engagement, while the couple was only expected to cohabit, maybe months later,[137] after the Hindu wedding, which for the spouses and the community counts as the marriage (Menski 1987). Here, as in postmodern Hindu law in India, the community norms are seen to prevail over the official law, but the latter (now not Indian, but English law) remains unaware of such emerging legal pluralism among Hindus.[138]

British Hindu practice has meanwhile been further modified, to the effect that the preferred method of marriage arrangements now is to select a suitable weekend and to combine the registered ceremony with all the major religious and social functions (Menski 1991a; 1993a) into one big celebration. This socially and economically sensible strategy also avoids the earlier risk of nullity petitions among Asian couples, which were remarkably frequent in the 1970s, but have now subsided.[139] After a weekend of celebrations, getting married twice over, the earlier legal insecurities over the status of the spouses, and their very delicate personal relations to each other,[140] have now been refigured into a complex network of rules about how to fully legalize a Hindu marriage which are unique to British Hindus. Currently, a yet more intricate process of intertwining the Hindu marriage ceremonies and the registration process can be observed when, in many cases, the English legal ceremony

136 It appears that the explicit purpose was to 'pin down' the husband by this official legal tie, without allowing him to consummate the marriage. Arranging this sequence the other way round would still entail risks for the woman of being abandoned by an unscrupulous male.

137 This gave rise to many nullity petitions in English law among Hindus and Sikhs during the 1970s and into the 1980s.

138 Meanwhile, English law has had to learn some important lessons and is also beginning to gain first-hand experience of the postmodern reconstruction processes among ethnic minorities. In *Chief Adjudication Officer v Bath* 2000 [1] FLR 8 (CA), a Sikh case in which the couple had married only in a *gurdwara* in London thirty-five years ago, the English Court of Appeal had to recognize the widow's pension claims to avoid blatant injustice. See also *Gereis v Yagoub* [1997] 1 FLR 854, which indicates growing readiness of English judges to consider legal pluralism.

139 See e.g. *Kaur v Singh* [1972] AllER 292 CA.

140 In *A v J* [1989] 1 FLR 110, after their registered wedding, the spouses were evidently confused about the nature of their relationship and the marriage broke up as a result.

becomes a sub-ritual of the Hindu wedding.[141] This constitutes evidence of postmodern reconstruction of law in the field of Hindu marriage solemnization in Britain.[142] Stubborn unwillingness among scholars and bureaucrats alike to take official notice of the unofficial operation of personal laws among Asian and African immigrant groups and their descendants in Europe has thus led to important changes within the socio-legal fabric of those communities. Ballard (1994) captured this especially well, without writing explicitly about the reconstruction of Asian personal laws in Europe.

As we saw, evidence from India and other countries is now beginning to demonstrate that personal law systems can be more than modern, have enormous capacity to adjust to new circumstances, and can be immensely helpful to women and children, whose basic human rights might be less well protected by a modernist, uniformizing, secular, rights-based model of law.[143] The Indian pattern of concurrent operation of personal laws as part of a nation state's legal system confirms that all kinds of ethnic differences may be treated as legally relevant without endangering a state's viability and stability. The pluralistic Indian model, despite ugly predictions, has worked and continues to function well, even achieving model character on a global scale (Larson 2001). While the personal law system is made to look like a remnant of tradition and appears like a technique of discrimination on the basis of religious difference, the culture-specific Hindu response to such allegations of discrimination has been to say that if everyone is different, all are ultimately equal.[144]

Working constructively and trustfully within a socio-legal conceptual framework, rather than refusing to acknowledge postmodern legal realities, has other important consequences for global legal scholarship today. It helps to strengthen the largely silenced claims of Asian and African laws to be recognized as members of the global community of legal systems. It demonstrates that in the global arena of legal discourse, the voices of Hindu law and other 'Oriental and African' legal systems have long been neglected and need to be given more attention. It is only too evident that much can be learnt from Asian and African legal experiences, past and present, even if modernists remain reluctant to admit that one can benefit from supposedly 'backward' systems of law, and even demand a totally new law (Sangari 1995) without telling us what that would be like. As we saw, one expects perhaps too much from legal centralists in terms of conceptual flexibility and acceptance of 'the other'. However,

[141] This is not only a mental assumption, but becomes a physical fact when the formal registration of the marriage takes place in the same location as the Hindu solemnization.

[142] For details on this process, see Menski (1991b).

[143] This reasoning clearly impressed the court of appeal in *Chief Adjudication Officer v Bath* 2000[1] FLR 8 [CA].

[144] This argument of 'new equity' is also proposed in Australian scholarship (Castles 1994).

there is hope, as Rudolph and Rudolph (2001: 56) indicate in their debate on the Indian uniform civil code:

> The liberal and progressive dream that it is the fate of difference to fade, and for humanity increasingly to repair to a common mold, and the additional dream of rationalists that it is the fate particularly of religion to fade away in face of the triumph of modern science, have receded in the last two decades not only in India but the wider world .... Whether regarded as benign or malign, identity formation, in the form of religiously based personal law, seems to be alive and well.

Such conclusions are fully supported by the present study. The postmodern condition of Hindu law, which the present analysis has presented in detail before a multidisciplinary historical backdrop, clearly offers us critical conceptual and methodological tools for further detailed analytical studies of Hindu law, comparative law, legal theory, and the emerging field of ethnic minority legal studies in the globalizing era of the twenty-first century.

Table of Cases

India

England

List of Statutes

Note: italicised page numbers indicate where a statute is cited verbatim

India

England

Pakistan

Singapore

Bibliography

Abraham, C.M. (1999). *Environmental Jurisprudence in India.* The Hague: Kluwer Law International.

Agarwal, Bina (1994). *A Field of One's Own: Gender and Land Rights in South Asia.* Cambridge: Cambridge University Press.

Agarwala, S.N. (1962). *Age at Marriage in India.* Allahabad: Kitab Mahal.

Aggarwal, S.N. (1988). *Commentary on the Law of Maintenance.* 3rd rev. ed. Allahabad: Orient Publishing.

Agnes, Flavia (1995). 'Redefining the agenda of the women's movement within a secular framework'. In: Tanika Sarkar and Urvashi Butalia (eds): *Women and the Hindu Right: A collection of essays.* New Delhi: Kali for Women, pp. 136–57.

____ (1997). 'Protecting women against violence? Review of a decade of legislation, 1980–1989'. In: Partha Chatterjee (ed.): *State and Politics in India.* Oxford: Oxford University Press, pp. 521–65.

____ (2000). *Law and Gender Inequality: The Politics of Women's Rights in India.* New Delhi: Oxford University Press.

Agnihotri, Indu and Vina Mazumdar (1995). 'Changing terms of political discourse: Women's movement in India, 1970s–1990s'. *Economic and Political Weekly,* Vol. 30, 22 July, pp. 1869–78.

Agrawala, Raj Kumari and A. Ramanamma (1994). 'Women and the family law.' In: Lotika Sarkar and B. Sivaramayya (eds): *Women and Law: Contemporary Problems.* New Delhi: Vikas, pp. 248–69.

Agrawala, S.K. (1985). *Public Interest Litigation in India: A Critique.* Bombay: Tripathi and Indian Law Institute.

Ahmad, Imtiaz, Partha S. Ghosh, and Helmut Reifeld (eds) (2000). *Pluralism and Equality: Values in Indian Society and Politics.* New Delhi: Sage.

Ahuja, Sangeeta (1997). *People, Law and Justice: Casebook on Public Interest Litigation.* Vols I–II. London: Sangam Books.

Ali, A.F. Imam (1992). *Hindu-Muslim Community in Bangladesh: Caste and Social Structure.* Delhi: Kanishka.

Allchin, Bridget and Raymond Allchin (1982). *The Rise of Civilization in India and Pakistan.* Cambridge: Cambridge University Press.

Allott, Antony N. (1980). *The Limits of Law.* London: Butterworths.

Altekar, A.S. (1958). *State and Government in Ancient India.* 3rd rev. & enl. ed. Delhi: Motilal Banarsidass.

—— (1978). *The Position of Women in Hindu Civilization.* Delhi: Motilal Banarsidass.

Anagol-McGinn, Padma (1992). 'The Age of Consent Act (1891) reconsidered: Women's perspectives and participation in the child marriage controversy in India'. *South Asia Research*, Vol. 12, no. 2, pp. 100–18.

Anand, A.S. (2002). *Justice for Women: Concerns and Expressions.* Delhi: Universal.

Anand, R.D. (1992). 'Let the maintenance jurisprudence have a heart'. *Panjab University Law Review*, Vol. 39, no. 1, pp. 173–85.

Anderson, Benedict (1991). *Imagined Communities: Reflections on the Origin and Spread of Nationalism.* Rev. ed. London and New York: Verso.

Anderson, P. (1998). *The Origins of Postmodernity.* London: Verso.

Arp, Susmita (2000). *Kālāpāni: Zum Streit über die Zulässigkeit von Seereisen im kolonialzeitlichen Indien.* Stuttgart: Franz Steiner Verlag (Alt- und Neu Indische Studien, 52).

Ashcroft, Bill, Gareth Griffiths, and Helen Tiffin (1998). *Key Concepts in Post-colonial Studies.* London and New York: Routledge.

Asif, Zaheda (1991). *A Treatise on the Law of Maintenance (with Case Law up to 1990).* Bangalore: Lawyers' Law Book.

Augustine, P.A. (1991). *Social Equality in Indian Society: The Elusive Goal.* New Delhi: Concept.

Austin, Granville (1999a). *The Indian Constitution: Cornerstone of a Nation.* New Delhi: Oxford University Press.

—— (1999b). *Working a Democratic Constitution: The Indian Experience.* New Delhi: Oxford University Press.

—— (2001). 'Religion, personal law and identity in India'. In: Gerald James Larson (ed.): *Religion and Personal Law in Secular India: A Call to Judgment.* Bloomington and Indianapolis: Indiana University Press, pp. 15–23.

Austin, John (1913). *Lectures on Jurisprudence.* London: John Murray.

Ayres, Alyssa and Philip Oldenburg (eds) (2002). *India Briefing: Quickening the Pace of Change.* Armonk, NY and London: M.E. Sharpe.

Bagga, V. (ed.) (1978). *Studies in the Hindu Marriage and the Special Marriage Acts.* Bombay: N.M. Tripathi.

Bainham, Andrew (ed.) (1998). *The International Survey of Family Law 1996.* The Hague, Boston, and London: Martinus Nijhoff.

Baird, Robert D. (ed.) (1993). *Religion and Law in Independent India.* Delhi: Manohar.

Bakshi, P.M. (1999). *Public Interest Litigations.* New Delhi: Ashoka Law House.

Ballard, Roger (ed.) (1994). *Desh Pardesh: The South Asian Presence in Britain.* London: Hurst & Company.

Banerjee, A.C. (1984). *English Law in India.* New Delhi: Abhinav.

Banerjee, Ashish (1990). 'Comparative curfew: Changing dimensions of communal politics in India'. In: Veena Das (ed.): *Mirrors of Violence: Communities, Riots and Survivors in South Asia.* Delhi: Oxford University Press, pp. 37–68.

Banerjee, Tapas Kumar (1962). *History of Indian Criminal Law*, Calcutta: Riddhi.

Bardhan, Pranab (1984). *The Political Economy of Development in India.* Oxford: Basil Blackwell.

Barrett, M. (1991). *The Politics of Truth: From Marx to Foucault.* Cambridge: Polity Press.

Basu, Monmayee (2001). *Hindu Women and Marriage Law: From Sacrament to Contract.* New Delhi: Oxford University Press.

Basu, Srimathi (1999). 'Cutting to size: Property and gendered identity in the Indian higher courts'. In: Rajeswari Sunder Rajan (ed.): *Signposts: Gender Issues in Post-independence India.* New Delhi: Kali for Women, pp. 248–91.

____ (2001). *She Comes to Take her Rights: Indian Women, Property and Propriety.* New Delhi: Kali for Women.

Baumann, Martin (1998). 'Sustaining "little Indias": Hindu diasporas in Europe'. In: Gerrie Ter Haar (ed.): *Strangers and Sojourners: Religious Communities in the Diaspora.* Leuven: Peeters, pp. 95–132.

Baxi, Upendra (1980). *The Indian Supreme Court and Politics.* Lucknow: Eastern Book Company.

____ (1982). *The Crisis of the Indian Legal System.* New Delhi: Vikas.

____ (1986a). 'People's law in India—the Hindu society'. In: Masaji Chiba (ed.): *Asian Indigenous Law in Interaction with Received Law.* London and New York: KPI, pp. 216–66.

____ (1986b). *Towards a Sociology of Indian Law.* New Delhi: Satvahan.

____ (1990). 'Reflections on the reservations crisis in Gujarat'. In: Veena Das (ed.): *Mirrors of Violence: Communities, Riots and Survivors in South Asia.* Delhi: Oxford University Press, pp. 215–39.

____ (2002). *The Future of Human Rights.* New Delhi: Oxford University Press.

____ (2003). 'Global development and impoverishment'. In: Peter Cane and Mark Tushnet (eds): *The Oxford Handbook of Legal Studies.* Oxford: Oxford University Press (forthcoming).

Baxter, Craig, Yogendra K. Malik, Charles H. Kennedy, and Robert C. Oberst (1993). *Government and Politics in South Asia.* 3rd ed. Boulder: Westview Press.

Bayly, Susan (1999). *Caste, Society and Politics in India from the Eighteenth Century to the Modern Age.* Cambridge: Cambridge University Press.

Bedwa, P.C. and Izzat Ullah (1992). 'Conditions of Hindu marriage'. *Panjab University Law Review*, Vol. 39, no. 1, pp. 60–82.

Berreman, Gerald (1994). 'Himalayan polyandry and the domestic cycle.' In: Patricia Uberoi (ed.): *Family, Kinship and Marriage in India.* Delhi: Oxford University Press, pp. 257–72.

Bhabha, H.K. (1994). *The Location of Culture.* London: Routledge.

Bhagwati, P.N. (1993). 'Religion and secularism under the Indian Constitution'. In: Robert D. Baird (ed.): *Religion and Law in Independent India.* Delhi: Manohar, pp. 7–21.

Bhambhri, C.P. (1998). 'Globalisation and social science'. *Economic and Political Weekly,* Vol. 33, no. 1–2, 10 January, pp. 17–19.

Bhandari, Bhagwat (1989). *Tribal Marriages and Sex Relation.* Udaipur: Himanshu.

Bhandarkar, R.G. (1983). 'History of child-marriage'. *ZDMG,* Vol. 47, pp. 143–55.

Bharucha, Rustom (1998). 'The shifting sites of secularism: Cultural politics and activism in India today'. *Economic and Political Weekly,* Vol. 33, no. 4, 24 January, pp. 167–80.

Bhatia, K.L. (ed.) (1990). *Judicial Activism and Social Change.* New Delhi: Deep & Deep.

Bhattacharjee, A.M. (1983). 'Supreme Court on bigamy'. *AIR* 1983, Journal section, pp. 25–8.

____ (1994). *Hindu Law and the Constitution.* 2nd ed. Calcutta: Eastern Law House.

Bhattacharyya-Panda, Nalini (1995). *The English East India Company and the Hindu Laws of Property in Bengal, 1765–1801: Appropriation and Invention of Tradition.* Oxford: Unpublished PhD thesis.

Bleiker, Roland (2000). 'The "end of modernity"?'. In: Greg Fry and Jacinta O'Hagan (eds): *Contending Images of World Politics.* Basingstoke and London: Macmillan, pp. 227–41.

Bonnan, Jean-Claude (1999). *Jugements du Tribunal de la Chaudrie de Pondichéry 1766–1817.* Vol. I: 1766–1791, Vol. II: 1792–1817. (Publications du Département d'Indologie 88.1,2). Pondichéry: Institut Français de Pondichéry—École Française d'Extrême-Orient.

Bose, Sugata and Ayesha Jalal (1998). *Modern South Asia: History, Culture, Political Economy.* London and New York: Routledge.

Bowen, Paul (ed.) (1998). *Themes and Issues in Hinduism.* London and Washington: Cassell.

Brown, Judith M. (1990). *Modern India: The Origins of an Asian Democracy.* Oxford: Oxford University Press.

Bühler, Georg (1975). *The Laws of Manu.* Reprint. Delhi: Motilal Banarsidass.

Bumiller, Elisabeth (1991). *May You Be the Mother of a Hundred Sons.* New Delhi: Penguin Books India.

Caney, Simon and Peter Jones (eds) (2001). *Human Rights and Global Diversity.* London and Portland, OR: Frank Cass.

Chadha, Prem Nath (1974). *Hindu Law.* 4th ed. Lucknow: Eastern Book Company.

Chaitanya, Krishna (2000). 'Man, nature and cosmos in Vedic India'. *The Ecologist,* Vol. 30, no. 1, January–February, pp. 21–4.

Chakrabarty, Dipesh (1992). 'Postcoloniality and the artifice of history: Who speaks for "Indian" pasts?'. *Representations,* Vol. 37 [Special Issue], pp. 1–26.

—— (2000). *Provincializing Europe.* Princeton, NJ: Princeton University Press.

Champappilly, Sebastian (1988). *The Christian Law.* Ernakulam: Continental Publishing Co.

Chanchreek, K.L. (ed.) (1991). *Dr. B.R. Ambedkar (1891–1991). Patriot, Philosopher and Statesman. Vol. 1: Fight for the Rights of the Depressed Classes. Vol. 2: Role in Framing India's Constitution.* Delhi: H.K. Publishers.

Chander, Shailja (1992). *Justice V.R. Krishna Iyer on Fundamental Rights and Directive Principles.* New Delhi: Deep & Deep.

Chandra, Sudhir (1998). *Enslaved Daughters: Colonialism, Law and Women's Rights.* Delhi: Oxford University Press.

Chapman, Graham P. (2000). *The Geopolitics of South Asia: From Early Empires to India, Pakistan and Bangladesh.* Aldershot: Ashgate.

Chatterjee, Bishwa B., Sheo Swarath Singh, and Dharam Raj Yadav (1971). *Impact of Social Legislation on Social Change.* Calcutta: Minerva.

Chatterjee, Chanchal Kumar (1978). *Studies in the Rites and Rituals of Hindu Marriage in Ancient India.* Calcutta: Sanskrit Pustak Bhandar.

Chatterjee, Heramba (1972–74). *The Social Background of the Forms of Marriage in Ancient India.* Vols I–II. Calcutta: Sanskrit Pustak Bhandar.

Chatterjee, Krishna Nath (1972). *Hindu Marriage—Past and Present.* Varanasi: Tara.

Chatterjee, Partha (ed.) (1997). *State and Politics in India.* Oxford: Oxford University Press.

Chatterjee, Partha and Pradeep Jeganathan (eds) (2000). *Community, Gender and Violence: Subaltern Studies XI.* London: Hurst & Co.

Chaudhury, Rafiqul Huda and Nilufer Raihan Ahmed (1981). *Female Status in Bangladesh.* Dhaka: Bangladesh Institute of Development Studies.

Chekki, D.A. (1968). 'Some aspects of marriage among the Lingayats'. *Man in India,* Vol. 48, pp. 124–32.

Chen, Jianfu (1999). 'The use of comparative law by courts: Australian courts at the crossroads'. In: Ulrich Drobnig and Sjef van Erp (eds): *The Use of Comparative Law by Courts.* The Hague: Kluwer Law International, pp. 25–57.

Chiba, Masaji (ed.) (1986). *Asian Indigenous Law: In Interaction with Received Law.* London and New York: KPI.

_____ (ed.) (1993). *Sociology of Law in Non-Western Countries.* Oñati: Oñati International Institute for the Sociology of Law.

Choudhary, Jagdish Narain (1988). *Divorce in Indian Society.* Jaipur: Printwell.

Chowdhary, Manjaree (1998). 'Miles to go: An assessment of the enforcement hurdles in the implementation of the anti-dowry law in India'. In: Werner Menski (ed.): *South Asians and the Dowry Problem.* Stoke-on-Trent: Trentham Books, pp. 151–62.

Chowdhry, Prem (2000). 'Enforcing cultural codes: Gender and violence in northern India'. In: Mary E. John and Janaki Nair (eds): *A Question of Silence? The Sexual Economies of Modern India.* London and New York: Zed Books, pp. 332–67.

Cohn, Bernard S. (1997). *Colonialism and Its Forms of Knowledge: The British in India.* Delhi: Oxford University Press.

Colebrooke, H.T. (1984). *Dāyabhāga and Mītākṣarā: Two Treatises on the Hindu Law of Inheritance.* Reprint. Delhi: Parimal Publications.

Connor, S. (1997). *Postmodernist Culture: An Introduction to Theories of the Contemporary.* 2nd ed. Oxford: Basil Blackwell.

Corbridge, Stuart and John Harriss (2000). *Reinventing India: Liberalization, Hindu Nationalism and Popular Democracy.* Cambridge: Polity Press.

Cotterrell, Roger (1989). *The Politics of Jurisprudence: A Critical Introduction to Legal Philosophy.* London: Butterworths.

_____ (2000). 'Pandora's box: Jurisprudence in legal education'. *International Journal of the Legal Profession,* Vol. 7, no. 3, pp. 179–87.

Dahrendorf, Ralf (1969). 'On the origin of inequality among men'. In: André Béteille, (ed.): *Social Inequality.* Harmondsworth: Penguin, pp. 16–44.

Dammann, Angelika (1993). *Die joint Hindu family: Darstellung und Bedeutung dieses Institutes für die moderne indische Gesellschaft.* Frankfurt: Peter Lang.

Das, Veena (ed.) (1990). *Mirrors of Violence: Communities, Riots and Survivors in South Asia.* Delhi: Oxford University Press.

Dasgupta, Ramaprasad (1973). *Crime and Punishment in Ancient India.* Varanasi: Bhartiya.

Datta, Bhakti (1979). *Sexual Ethics in the Mahābhārata in the Light of Dharmaśāstra Rulings.* London: Asia Publications.

David, René and John E.C. Brierley (1978). *Major Legal Systems in the World Today.* London: Stevens & Sons.

Day, Terence P. (1982). *The Conception of Punishment in Early Indian Literature.* Waterloo, Ontario: Wilfred Laurier University Press.

Derrett, J.D.M. (1957). *Hindu Law Past and Present.* Calcutta: A. Mukherjee & Co.

_____ (1958). 'Factum valet: The adventures of a maxim'. *International and Comparative Law Quarterly,* Vol. 7 April, pp. 280–302.

____(1961). 'J.H. Nelson: A forgotten administrator-historian of India'. In: C.H. Philips (ed.): *Historians of India, Pakistan and Ceylon.* London: Oxford University Press, pp. 354–72.

____(1962). 'Law and custom in ancient India: Sources and authority'. *Revue Internationale de Droit de l'Antiquité,* Vol. 9 [3rd Series], pp. 11–32.

____(1963a). 'The discussion of marriage by Gadādhara'. *Adyar Library Bulletin,* Vol. 17, pp. 171–99.

____(1963b). 'Divorce by caste custom'. In: (1963) 65 *BomLR,* Journal section, pp. 161–9.

____(1963c). *An Introduction to Modern Hindu Law.* London: Oxford University Press.

____(1966). 'The definition of a Hindu'. *Supreme Court Journal,* 1966(2), Journal section, pp. 67–74.

____(1967). 'A round-up of polygamous marriages'. In: (1967) 69 *BomLR,* Journal section, pp. 84–93.

____(1968a). 'Hindu law'. In: J.D.M. Derrett (ed.): *An Introduction to Legal Systems.* London: Sweet & Maxwell, pp. 80–104.

____(1968b). *Religion, Law and the State in India.* London: Faber & Faber.

____(1970). *A Critique of Modern Hindu Law.* Bombay: N.M. Tripathi.

____(1973). 'Hindu matrimonial freedom, child marriages and Muslim divorce reform: Some notes'. In: (1973) 75 *BomLR,* Journal section, pp. 29–34.

____(1975a). *Bhāruci's commentary on the Manusmṛti.* Vols I–II. Wiesbaden: Franz Steiner Verlag.

____(1975b). 'The Indian Civil Code or Code of Family Law'. In: Narmada Khodie (ed.): *Readings in the Uniform Civil Code.* Bombay: Thacker, pp. 21–38.

____(1975c). 'Matrimonial freedom: A step "forward" in Bombay'. In: (1975) 77 *BomLR,* Journal section, pp. 8–10.

____(1977). *Essays in Classical and Modern Hindu Law.* Vol. 3. Leiden: Brill.

____(1978a). *The Death of a Marriage Law: Epitaph for the Rishis.* New Delhi: Vikas.

____(ed.) (1978b). *Essays in Classical and Modern Hindu Law.* Vol. 4. Leiden: Brill.

____(1978c). 'Family arrangements in developing countries'. In: J.D.M. Derrett (ed.): *Essays in Classical and Modern Hindu Law.* Vol. 4. Leiden: Brill, pp. 258–84.

____(1978d). 'Justice, equity and good conscience in India'. In: J.D.M. Derrett: *Essays in Classical and Modern Hindu Law.* Vol. 4. Leiden: Brill, pp. 8–27.

____(1979). 'Unity in diversity: The Hindu experience'. *Bharata Manisha,* Vol. 5, pp. 21–36.

____(1981). 'When is an "own wrong" not a wrong?'. *MLJ* 1981(1), Journal section, pp. 13–16.

Derrett, J.D.M. and T.K.K. Iyer (1983). 'Hindu family law'. *International Encyclopedia of Comparative Law.* Vol. 4, ch. 11, Tübingen: J.C.B. Mohr (Paul Siebeck) and Martinus Nijhoff Publishers, pp. 80–97.

Derrett, J.D.M., G.D. Sontheimer, and Graham Smith (1979). *Beiträge zu indischem Rechtsdenken.* Stuttgart: Franz Steiner Verlag.

Derrida, Jacques (1978). *Writing and Difference.* (Translated by Alan Bass). London: Routledge and Kegan Paul.

_____ (1981). *Dissemination.* (Translated by Barbara Johnson). London: Athlone.

Desai, Kumud (1993). *Indian Law of Marriage and Divorce.* 5th ed. Bombay: N.M. Tripathi.

Desai, Satyajeet A. (ed.) (1998). *Mulla Principles of Hindu Law.* 17th ed. Vols I–II. New Delhi: Butterworths.

Desai, Sunderlal T. (ed.) (1982). *Mulla Principles of Hindu Law.* 15th ed. Bombay: N.M. Tripathi.

_____ (ed.) (1990). *Mulla Principles of Hindu Law.* 16th ed. Bombay: N.M. Tripathi.

de Souza, Alfred (ed.) (1980). *Women in Contemporary India and South Asia.* New Delhi: Manohar.

Despande, V.S. (1993). 'Monogamy in India.' In: Kusum (ed.): *Women—March Towards Dignity: Socio-legal Perspectives.* New Delhi: Regency, pp. 22–33.

Dev, Bimal J. and Dilip Kumar Lahiri (1983). *Lushai Customs and Ceremonies.* Delhi: Mittal.

Deva, Indra and Srirama (1979). *Growth of Legal System in Indian Society.* New Delhi: Allied Publishers.

Devadasan, E.D. (1974). *Christian Law in India.* Madras: DSI Publications.

Devasia, Leelamma (ed.) (1990). *Women in India: Equality, Social Justice and Development.* New Delhi: Indian Social Institute.

Dhagamwar, Vasudha (1974). *Law, Power and Justice: The Protection of Personal Rights in the Indian Penal Code.* Bombay: Tripathi.

_____ (1987). *Women and Divorce.* Bombay and New Delhi: Somaiya.

_____ (1989). *Towards the Uniform Civil Code.* Bombay: N.M. Tripathi.

_____ (1992). *Law, Power and Justice: The Protection of Personal Rights in the Indian Penal Code.* 2nd ed. New Delhi: Sage.

Dhanda, Amita and Archana Parashar (eds) (1999). *Engendering Law: Essays in Honour of Lotika Sarkar.* Lucknow: Eastern Book Co.

Dhar, P.N. (2000). *Indira Gandhi, the 'Emergency' and Indian Democracy.* New Delhi: Oxford University Press.

Dhavan, Rajeev (1992). 'Dharmasastra and modern Indian society: A preliminary exploration'. *Journal of the Indian Law Institute,* Vol. 34, no. 4, pp. 515–40.

_____ (2001). 'The road to Xanadu. India's quest for secularism'. In: Gerald James Larson (ed.). *Religion and Personal Law in Secular India: A Call to Judgment.* Bloomington and Indianapolis: Indiana University Press, pp. 301–29.

Dhawan, S.K. (1991). *Dr. B.R. Ambedkar: A Select Profile.* Delhi: Wave Publications.

Dirks, Nicholas B. (1987). *The Hollow Crown: Ethnohistory of an Indian Kingdom.* Cambridge: Cambridge University Press.

Diwan, Paras (1978). 'Divorce structure of the Hindu Marriage Act, 1955 and Special Marriage Act, 1954'. In: V. Bagga (ed.): *Studies in the Hindu Marriage and the Special Marriage Acts.* Bombay: N.M. Tripathi, pp. 15–55.

____ (1979). *Modern Hindu Law.* 4th ed. Allahabad: Allahabad Law Agency.

____ (1980). 'Technological niyoga and nirodh and social engineering through law'. *JILI,* Vol. 22, no. 4, pp. 445–65.

____ (1982). *Modern Hindu Law.* 5th ed. Allahabad: Allahabad Law Agency.

____ (1983). *Family Law: (Law of Marriage and Divorce in India).* New Delhi: Sterling.

____ (1984). *Customary Law.* Chandigarh: Publication Bureau, Panjab University.

____ (1985). 'Hindu Law'. In: *ASIL* 1985. New Delhi: ILI, pp. 99–135.

____ (1987). 'Hindu Law'. In: *ASIL* 1987. New Delhi: ILI, pp. 291–311.

____ (1989). 'Hindu Law'. In: *ASIL* 1989. New Delhi: ILI, pp. 213–25.

____ (1993). *Private International Law.* New Delhi: Deep & Deep.

Diwan, Paras and Peeyushi Diwan (1988). *Modern Hindu Law.* 7th ed. Allahabad: Allahabad Law Agency.

____ (1990). *Law of Maintenance in India.* New Delhi: Deep & Deep.

____ (1991). *Muslim Law in Modern India.* 5th ed. Allahabad: Allahabad Law Agency.

____ (1993). *Modern Hindu Law.* 9th ed. Allahabad: Allahabad Law Agency.

____ (1994). *Women and Legal Protection.* New Delhi: Deep & Deep.

____ (1995). *Modern Hindu Law.* 10th ed. Allahabad: Allahabad Law Agency.

____ (2000). *Family Law.* 5th ed. Faridabad: Allahabad Law Agency.

Docherty, T. (1993). *Postmodernism: A Reader.* London: Harvester Wheatsheaf.

Dogra, Ramesh Chander and Urmila Dogra (2000). *Hindu and Sikh Wedding Ceremonies with Salient Features of Hindu and Sikh Rituals.* New Delhi: Star.

Doherty, J., E. Graham, and M. Malek (1992). *Postmodernism and the Social Sciences.* London: Macmillan.

Doniger, Wendy (1991). *The Laws of Manu.* London: Penguin.

Dosse, F. (1999). *Empire of Meaning: The Humanization of the Social Sciences.* (Translated by Hassan Melehy). Minneapolis: University of Minnesota Press.

Douglas, Gillian (1998). 'England and Wales: "Family values" to the fore?'. In: A. Bainham (ed.): *The International Survey of Family Law 1996.* The Hague: Martinus Nijhoff, pp. 157–78.

Drobnig, Ulrich and Sjef van Erp (eds) (1999). *The Use of Comparative Law by Courts.* The Hague, London, and Boston: Kluwer Law International.

Edge, Ian (ed.) (2000). *Comparative Law in Global Perspective.* Ardsley, NY: Transnational Publishers.

Ehrlich, Eugen (1913). *Grundlegung der Soziologie des Rechts.* München und Leipzig: Duncker & Humblot.

Engels, Dagmar (1983). 'The Age of Consent Act of 1891: Colonial ideology in Bengal'. *South Asia Research*, Vol. 3, no. 2, November, pp. 107–34.

Fawcett, Charles (1979). *The First Century of British Justice in India.* Reprint. Aalen: Scientia.

Firth, Shirley (1997). *Dying, Death and Bereavement in a British Hindu Community.* Leuven: Peeters.

Fisch, Jörg (1983). *Cheap Lives and Dear Limbs: The British Transformation of the Bengal Criminal Law 1769–1817.* Wiesbaden: Franz Steiner Verlag.

Foster, H. (1985). *Postmodern Culture.* London: Pluto Press.

Foucault, Michel (1970). *The Order of Things: An Archaeology of the Human Sciences.* New York: Random House.

——— (1980). *Power/Knowledge: Selected Interviews and Other Writings 1972–1977.* New York: Pantheon Books.

Frankel, Francine R. and M.S.A. Rao (eds) (1989). *Dominance and State Power in Modern India: Decline of a Social Order.* Vol. I. Delhi: Oxford University Press.

Freed, Roy N. (1998). 'A task for comparative law teachers in the age of globalization: To harmonize laws through international cross fertilization'. In: *Toward Comparative Law in the 21st Century.* Tokyo: Chuo University Press, pp. 1057–73.

Friedman, Lawrence M. (1998). 'Some thoughts on the rule of law, legal culture, and modernity in comparative perspective'. In: *Toward Comparative Law in the 21st Century.* Tokyo: Chuo University Press, pp. 1075–90.

Friedrich, Elvira (1993). *Das Āpastamba-Dharmasūtra—Aufbau und Aussage.* Frankfurt: Peter Lang.

Fruzzetti, Lina M. (1990). *The Gift of a Virgin: Women, Marriage and Ritual in a Bengali Society.* Delhi: Oxford University Press.

Fry, Greg and Jacinta O'Hagan (eds) (2000). *Contending Images of World Politics.* Basingstoke and London: Macmillan.

Fuller, Chris J. (1992). *The Camphor Flame: Popular Hinduism and Society in India.* Princeton: Princeton University Press.

Gajendragadkar, P.B. (1963). 'The historical background and theoretical basis of Hindu law'. *AIR* 1963, Journal section, pp. 18–26.

Galanter, Marc (1972). 'The aborted restoration of "indigenous" law in India'. *Comparative Studies in Society and History*, Vol. 14, no. 1, pp. 53–70.

——— (1981). 'Justice in many rooms: Courts, private ordering and indigenous law'. *Journal of Legal Pluralism and Unofficial Law*, Vol. 19, pp. 1–25.

____ (1984). *Competing Equalities: Law and the Backward Classes in India.* Berkeley: University of California Press.

____ (1989). *Law and Society in Modern India.* Delhi: Oxford University Press.

Galanter, Marc and Jayanth Krishnan (2001). 'Personal law systems and religious conflict: A comparison of India and Israel'. In: Gerald James Larson (ed.): *Religion and Personal Law in Secular India: A Call to Judgment.* Bloomington and Indianapolis: Indiana University Press, pp. 270–300.

Ganai, Nisar Ahmed (1990). 'Judicial contribution to Muslim matrimonial law in a changing society in India: some policy perspectives'. In: 1990(2) *KLT*, Journal section, pp. 14–18.

Gandhi, Indira (1992). *Safeguarding Environment.* New Delhi: Wiley Eastern Limited.

Ghai, Yash, Robin Luckham, and Francis Snyder (eds) (1987). *The Political Economy of Law: A Third World Reader.* Delhi: Oxford University Press.

Ghosh, Rupak (2001). 'The Indian Divorce (Amendment) Bill 2000: An enigma'. *Lawyers Collective*, September, pp. 23–5.

Ghouse, Mohammad (1973). *Security, Society and Law in India.* New Delhi: Vikas.

Ghurye, G.S. (1979). *Vedic India.* Bombay: Popular Prakashan.

Giddens, Anthony (2000). *The Third Way and Its Critics.* Cambridge: Polity Press.

Glenn, H. Patrick (2000). *Legal Traditions of the World.* Oxford: Oxford University Press.

Gonda, Jan (1960). *Die Religionen Indiens. I: Veda und älterer Hinduismus. II: Der jüngere Hinduismus.* Stuttgart: W. Kohlhammer Verlag 1960–1963.

____ (ed.) (1975). *A History of Indian Literature. Vol. I Fasc. 1: Vedic literature.* Wiesbaden: Harrassowitz.

Griffiths, John (1986). 'What is legal pluralism?'. *Journal of Legal Pluralism and Unofficial Law*, Vol. 24, pp. 1–56.

Guha, Ranajit (ed.) (1982). *Subaltern Studies I: Writings on South Asian History and Society.* Delhi: Oxford University Press.

____ (1997). *Dominance Without Hegemony: History and Power in Colonial India.* Cambridge, MA and London: Harvard University Press.

Gulati, Leela (1981). *Profiles of Female Poverty.* Delhi: Hindustan Publishing.

Gupta, R.L. (1979). *The Medico-legal Aspects of Sexual Offences.* 2nd ed. Lucknow: Eastern Book Co.

Gupte, N.Y. (2001). *Law Relating to Family Courts Act, 1984.* 3rd ed. Mumbai: Ravindra.

Hai, Maulana Hakim Syed Abdul (1977). *India during Muslim Rule.* Lucknow: Academy of Islamic Research and Publications.

Haksar, Nandita (1994). 'Dominance, suppression and the law'. In: Lotika Sarkar and B. Sivaramayya (eds): *Women and Law: Contemporary Problems.* New Delhi: Vikas, pp. 29–40.

Hamilton, Charles (1891). *The Hedaya, or Guide: A Commentary on the Mussulman Laws.* Vols I–IV. London: T. Bensley.

Hardgrave, Robert L. Jr. and Stanley A. Kochanek (2000). *Indian: Government and Politics in a Developing Nation.* 6th ed. Fort Worth, TX: Harcourt College Publishers.

Harding, Andrew (2001). 'Comparative law and legal transplantation in South East Asia: Making sense of the "nomic din"'. In: David Nelken and Johannes Feest (eds): *Adapting Legal Cultures.* Oxford and Portland, OR: Hart Publishing, pp. 199–222.

—— (2002). 'Global doctrine and local knowledge: Law in South East Asia'. *International and Comparative Law Quarterly,* Vol. 51, no. 1, pp. 35–53.

Hart, H.L.A. (1994). *The Concept of Law.* 2nd ed. Oxford: Clarendon Press.

Heimsath, C.H. (1962). 'Origin and enactment of the Indian Age of Consent Bill, 1891'. *Journal of Asian Studies,* Vol. 21, no. 4, pp. 491–504.

—— (1964). *Indian Nationalism and Hindu Social Reforms.* Princeton: Princeton University Press.

Hershman, Paul (1981). *Punjabi Kinship and Marriage.* Delhi: Hindustan Publishing Corporation.

Hoadley, M.C. and M.B. Hooker (1981). *An Introduction to Javanese Law.* Tucson, Arizona: University of Arizona Press.

Holden, Livia Sorrentino (2003). *Seeking Equity through Custom: Divorce and Remarriage on the Woman's Initiative in Hindu Law.* London: SOAS (PhD thesis in preparation).

Hooker, M.B. (1975). *Legal Pluralism: An Introduction to Colonial and Neo-colonial Laws.* Oxford: Clarendon Press.

Horstmann, Alexander Klaus (2002). 'Incorporation and resistance: Border-crossing and social transformation in Southeast Asia. Review article'. *Antropologi Indonesia: Indonesian Journal of Social and Cultural Anthropology,* Vol. XXVI, no. 67, January–April, pp. 12–29.

Hossain, Sara, Shahdeen Malik, and Bushra Musa (eds) (1997). *Public Interest Litigation in South Asia: Rights in Search of Remedies.* Dhaka: University Press.

Hunt, A. and G. Wickham (1998). *Foucault and Law: Towards a Sociology of Law as Governance.* London: Pluto Press.

Hurra, Sonia (1993). *Public Interest Litigation: In Quest of Justice.* Ahmedabad: Mishra & Co.

Huxley, Andrew (ed.) (1996). *Thai Law: Buddhist Law: Essays on the Legal History of Thailand, Laos and Burma.* Bangkok: White Orchid Press.

—— (ed.) (2002). *Religion, Law and Tradition.* London: RoutledgeCurzon.

Ikari, Yasuke and Nobuyuki Watase (2002). *Yājñavalkya hoten.* (*The code of Yājñavalkya*). Tokyo: Heibon Sha. (In Japanese).

Ilaiah, Kancha (1996). *Why I Am Not a Hindu.* Calcutta: Samya.

Inden, Ronald (1990). *Imagining India.* London: Hurst & Company.

Ingalls, D.H.H. (1954). 'Authority and law in ancient India'. *Journal of the American Oriental Society*, Vol. 17, pp. 34–45.

Iyer, Venkat (ed.) (2001). *Constitutional Perspectives: Essays in Honour and Memory of H.M. Seervai.* Delhi: Universal.

Iyer, V.R. Krishna (1979). *Of Law and Life.* Sahibabad: Vikas.

____ (1985). *Judicial Justice: A New Focus Towards Social Justice.* Delhi and Bombay: Campus Law Centre and N.M. Tripathi.

____ (1990). *Human Rights and Inhuman Wrongs.* Delhi: B.R. Publishing.

____ (1993). 'Human right to be woman'. In: Kusum (ed.): *Women—March towards Dignity: Social and Legal Perspectives.* New Delhi: Regency, pp. 1–21.

Jahagirdar, R.A. (2001). 'Secularism in India: The inconclusive debate'. In: Venkat Iyer (ed.): *Constitutional Perspectives: Essays in Honour and Memory of H.M. Seervai.* Delhi: Universal, pp. 53–73.

Jain, B.S. (1970). *Administration of Justice in Seventeenth Century India.* Delhi: Metropolitan.

Jain, Madhu (1986). 'Divorce getting common'. *India Today*, 31 December, pp. 44–51.

Jain, M.L. (1961). 'Validity of Hindu marriages solemnised without performing any customary ritual or ceremony'. *AIR* 1961, Journal section, pp. 84–6.

Jain, M.P. (1966). *Outlines of Indian Legal History.* 2nd ed. Bombay: N.M. Tripathi.

____ (1990). *Outlines of Indian Legal History.* 5th ed. Bombay: N.M. Tripathi.

Jain, Sagar Chand (1983). *The Law Relating to Marriage and Divorce.* Delhi: Surjeet Book Depot.

Jaising, Indira (ed.) (2001). *Law of Domestic Violence. A User's Manual for Women.* Delhi: Universal Law Publishing.

Jalal, Ayesha (1995). *Democracy and Authoritarianism in South Asia.* Lahore: Sang e-Meel.

Jameson, F. (1991). *Postmodernism, or, the Cultural Logic of Late Capitalism.* London: Verso.

Jencks, C. (1996). *What is Postmodernism?* 4th ed. Chichester: Academy Editions.

Jenkins, Laura Dudley (2001). 'Personal law and reservations: Volition and religion in contemporary India'. In: Gerald James Larson (ed.): *Religion and Personal Law in Secular India: A Call to Judgment.* Bloomington and Indianapolis: Indiana University Press, pp. 104–123.

Jethmalani, Rani (ed.) (1995). *Kali's Yug: Empowerment, Law and Dowry Deaths.* New Delhi: Har Anand.

John, Mary E. and Janaki Nair (2000a). 'Introduction: A question of silence? The sexual economies of modern India'. In: Mary E. John and Janaki Nair (eds): *A Question of Silence? The Sexual Economies of Modern India.* London and New York: Zed Books, pp. 1–51.

—— (eds) (2000b). *A Question of Silence? The Sexual Economies of Modern India.* London and New York: Zed Books.

Jois, Rama M. (1990a). *Legal and Constitutional History of India.* Vol. I: Ancient Legal, Judicial and Constitutional System. Bombay: N.M. Tripathi.

—— (1990b). *Seeds of Modern Public Law in Ancient Indian Jurisprudence.* Lucknow: Eastern Book Company.

—— (2000). *Seeds of Modern Public Law in Ancient Indian Jurisprudence.* 2nd ed. Lucknow: Eastern Book Company.

Jolly, Julius (1892). 'Beiträge zur indischen Rechtsgeschichte. 5. Zur Geschichte der Kinderehen'. *ZDMG,* Vol. 46, pp. 413–26.

—— (1975). *Hindu Law and Custom.* Varanasi and Delhi: Bhartiya Publishing House.

—— (1977). *The Minor Law Books.* Reprint. Delhi: Motilal Banarsidass.

Jones, Richard and Gnanapala Welhengama (2000). *Ethnic Minorities in English Law.* Stoke-on-Trent: Trentham Books.

Kane, P.V. (1968–77). *History of Dharmaśāstra.* Vols 1–5. Poona: Bhandarkar Oriental Research Institute.

Kangle, R.P. (1972). *The Kautilīya Arthaśāstra.* Part II. Bombay: University of Bombay.

Kapadia, K.M. (1972). *Marriage and Family in India.* 3rd ed. Calcutta: Oxford University Press.

Kapur, Ratna and Brenda Cossman (1995). 'Communalising gender: Engendering community. Women, legal discourse and the saffron agenda'. In: Tanika Sarkar and Urvashi Butalia (eds): *Women and the Hindu Right: A Collection of Essays.* New Delhi: Kali for Women, pp. 82–120.

Kapur, Ratna and Brenda Cossman (1996). *Subversive Sites: Feminist Engagements with Law in India.* New Delhi: Sage.

Karve, Irawati (1994). 'The kinship map of India'. In: Patricia Uberoi (ed.): *Family, Kinship and Marriage in India.* Delhi: Oxford University Press, pp. 50–73.

Kaviraj, Sudipta (ed.) (1999). *Politics in India.* Delhi: Oxford University Press.

Keith, Arthur Berriedale (1993). *A History of Sanskrit Literature.* Indian edition. Delhi: Motilal Banarsidass.

Kelly, J.M. (1992). *A Short History of Western Legal Theory.* Oxford: Clarendon Press.

Kelsen, Hans (1945). *General Theory of Law and the State.* New York: Russell & Russell.

Kesari, U.P.D. (1998). *Modern Hindu Law.* 2nd ed. Allahabad: Central Law Publications.

Khanam, Firdous (1960). *Attitudes of Men and Women Towards Polygyny.* Lahore: Alnaseem.

Khilnani, Sunil (1997). *The Idea of India.* London: Penguin Books.

Khodie, Narmada (ed.) (1975). *Readings in the Uniform Civil Code.* Bombay: Thacker.

King, A. (1995). 'The times and spaces of modernity (or who needs postmodernism?)'. In: M. Featherstone, S. Lash, and R. Robertson (eds): *Global Modernities.* London: Sage, pp. 108–23.

King, Michael (ed.) (1995). *God's Law versus State Law.* London: Grey Seal.

Kishwar, Madhu (1990). 'Women's organisations. The pressure of unrealistic expectations'. *Manushi*, Vol. 59, pp. 11–14.

____ (2000). 'Flagellating the mythical enemy'. Internet article. (http://www.freespeech.org/manushi/117/manusmriti.html).

Kishwar, Madhu and Ruth Vanita (eds) (1991). *In Search of Answers: Indian Women's Voices from Manushi.* New Delhi: Horizon India Books.

Kosambi, D.D. (1992). *The Culture and Civilisation of Ancient India in Historical Outline.* Reprint. New Delhi: Vikas.

Krishnaswamy, P. (2000). *Justice V.R. Krishna Iyer. A Living Legend.* New Delhi: Universal Law Publishing.

Kulke, Hermann (ed.) (1997). *The State in India 1000–1700.* Delhi: Oxford University Press.

Kulke, Hermann and Dietmar Rothermund (1998). *History of India.* 3rd ed. London and New York: Routledge.

Kuppuswami, Alladi (ed.) (1986). *Mayne's Treatise on Hindu Law and Usage.* 12th ed. New Delhi: Bharat Law House.

Kusum (1990). 'Maintenance for husbands'. *JILI*, Vol. 32, no. 3, July–September, pp. 403–04.

____ (1991). 'Women's shelter after divorce or separation'. In: Shamsuddin Shams (ed.): *Women, Law and Social Change.* New Delhi: Ashish, pp. 55–60.

____ (1993a). *Harassed Husbands.* New Delhi: Regency.

____ (ed.) (1993b). *Women—March Towards Dignity: Social and Legal Perspectives.* New Delhi: Regency.

____ (2000). 'Matrimonial adjudication under Hindu law'. In: S.K. Verma and Kusum (eds): *Fifty Years of the Supreme Court of India: Its Grasp and Reach.* New Delhi: Indian Law Institute and Oxford University Press, pp. 231–68.

Kusum and P.M. Bakshi (1982). *Customary Law and Justice in the Tribal Areas of Meghalaya.* Bombay: N.M. Tripathi and Indian Law Institute.

Larivière, Richard W. (1976). 'Dharmaśāstra, custom, 'real law' and 'apocryphal' smṛtis'. In: Bernhard Kölver (ed.): *Recht, Staat und Verwaltung im klassischen Indien*. München: R. Oldenbourg Verlag, pp. 97–110.

____ (ed.) (1984). *Studies in dharmaśāstra*. Calcutta: Firma KLM.

____ (1989). *The Nāradasmṛti*. Vols I–II. Philadelphia: University of Pennsylvania.

____ (1991). 'Matrimonial remedies for women in classical Hindu law: Alternatives to divorce'. In: Julia Leslie (ed.): *Rules and Remedies in Classical Hindu Law*. Leiden: Brill, pp. 37–45.

____ (1993). 'A persistent disjunction: Parallel realms of law in India'. In: Robert D. Baird (ed.): *Religion and Law in Independent India*. New Delhi: Manohar, pp. 351–60.

Larson, Gerald James (ed.) (2001). *Religion and Personal Law in Secular India. A Call to Judgment*. Bloomington and Indianapolis: Indiana University Press.

Lawyers Collective. Women's Rights Initiative (ed.) (2000). *Domestic Violence and Law: Report of Colloquium on Justice for Women: Empowerment Through Law*. New Delhi: Butterworths India.

Legrand, Pierre (1996). 'How to compare now'. *Legal Studies*, Vol. 16, no. 2, July, pp. 232–42.

Lingat, Robert (1973). *The Classical Law of India*. Berkeley: University of California Press.

Lüders, Heinrich (1959). *Varuna. Vol. II: Varuna und das Ṛta*. Göttingen: Vandenhoeck & Ruprecht.

Lyotard, J.F. (1984). *The Postmodern Condition: A Report on Knowledge*. (tr. Geoff Bennington and Brian Massumi). Manchester: Manchester University Press.

Macnaghten, W.H. (1894). *Principles and Precedents of Hindu Law*. 4th ed. Madras: Higginbotham & Co.

Madan, T.N. (1987). 'Secularism in its place'. *Journal of Asian Studies*, Vol. 46, no. 4, pp. 747–59.

____ (1996). 'Anthropology as critical self-awareness'. In: D.L. Sheth and Ashis Nandy (eds): *The Multiverse of Democracy: Essays in Honour of Rajni Kothari*. New Delhi: Sage, pp. 242–65.

____ (1998). *Modern Myths, Locked Minds: Secularism and Fundamentalism in India*. Delhi: Oxford University Press.

Mahmood, Tahir (1976). *An Indian Civil Code and Islamic Law*. Bombay: N.M. Tripathi.

____ (1978). *Civil Marriage Law: Perspectives and Prospects*. New Delhi: Indian Law Institute.

____ (1980). 'Marriage-age in India and abroad—A comparative conspectus'. *JILI*, Vol. 22, no. 1, pp. 38–80.

____ (1981). *Hindu Law*. Allahabad: Law Book Company.

____ (1986). *Personal Law in Crisis.* New Delhi: Metropolitan.

____ (1991). 'Freedom of conscience and conversion to a minority religion: Legal parameters and social realities'. In: Tahir Mahmood (ed.): *Minorities and State at the Indian Law: An Anthology.* New Delhi: Institute of Objective Studies, pp. 56–81.

Maine, Henry Sumner (1861). *Ancient Law.* London: John Murray.

Majumdar, M.B. (1966). 'Bhaurao Shankar v. State vis à vis S.17 Hindu Marriage Act, 1955'. In: (1966) 68 *BomLR*, Journal section, pp. 57–60.

Malik, Shahdeen (1994). *The Transformation of Colonial Perceptions into Legal Norms: Legislating for Crime and Punishment in Bengal 1790–1820.* London: SOAS (Unpublished PhD thesis).

Manooja, Dalip Chand (1993). *Adoption Law and Practice.* New Delhi: Deep & Deep.

Mansfield, John H. (1993). 'The personal laws or a Uniform Civil Code'. In: Robert D. Baird (ed.): *Religion and Law in Independent India.* Delhi: Manohar, pp. 139–77.

Marcus, G.E. and M.M.J. Fischer (1986). *Anthropology as Cultural Critique: An Experimental Moment in the Human Sciences.* Chicago: Chicago University Press.

Master, M.K. (1968). 'Section 5(iii) of the Hindu Marriage Act, 1955: Effect of its contravention'. In: (1968) 70 *BomLR*, Journal section, pp. 79–83.

Mathur, K.S. (1962). 'Validity of Hindu marriages solemnised without any customary ritual or ceremony'. *AIR* 1962, Journal section, pp. 27–8.

Mattei, Ugo (2001). 'The comparative jurisprudence of Schlesinger and Sacco: A study in legal influence'. In: Annelise Riles (ed.): *Rethinking the Masters of Comparative Law.* Oxford and Portland, Oregon: Hart Publishing, pp. 238–56.

May, Reinhard (1985). *Law & Society East and West. Dharma, li and nomos, Their Contribution to Thought and to Life.* Stuttgart: Franz Steiner Verlag.

____ (2001). 'Über "Law in a changing world: Asian alternatives"'. *Archiv für Rechts-und Sozialphilosophie*, Vol. 87, no. 2, pp. 270–86.

Mayo, Katherine (1927). *Mother India.* London: Jonathan Cape.

Mehta, Rama (1975). *Divorced Hindu Woman.* Delhi: Vikas.

____ (1987). *Socio-legal Status of Women in India.* New Delhi: Mittal.

Mehta, Ved (1977). *Mahatma Gandhi and His Apostles.* London: Andre Deutsch.

Menon, Nivedita (2000). 'Embodying the self: Feminism, sexual violence and law'. In: Partha Chatterjee and Pradeep Jeganathan (eds): *Community, Gender and Violence: Subaltern Studies XI.* London: Hurst & Co, pp. 66–105.

Menski, Werner F. (1983). 'Is there a customary form of widow-remarriage for Hindus?'. In: 1983 *KLT,* Journal section, pp. 69–72. (Reprinted in Menski 2001, pp. 20–4).

_____ (1984). *Role and Ritual in the Hindu Marriage.* London: SOAS. (Unpublished PhD thesis).

_____ (1985). 'Solemnisation of Hindu marriages: The law and reality'. In: 1985 *KLT,* Journal section, pp. 1–10. (Reprinted in Menski 2001: 24–33).

_____ (1986a). 'Legislative overkill and the Kerala Joint Hindu Family System (Abolition) Act, 1975'. In: 1986 *KLT,* Journal section, pp. 17–20. (Reprinted in Menski 2001: 305–10).

_____ (1986b). 'Legislative overkill—A rejoinder'. In: 1986 *KLT,* Journal section, pp. 63–5. (Reprinted in Menski 2001: 311–14).

_____ (1987). 'Legal pluralism in the Hindu marriage'. In: Richard Burghart (ed.): *Hinduism in Great Britain.* London and New York: Tavistock, pp. 180–200.

_____ (1988). 'English family law and ethnic laws in Britain'. In: 1988 (1) *KLT,* Journal section, pp. 56–66.

_____ (1991a). 'Change and continuity in Hindu marriage rituals'. In: S.Y. Killingley (ed.): *Hindu Ritual and Society.* Newcastle: Grevatt and Grevatt, pp. 32–51. (The Sanskrit Tradition in the Modern World, no. 2).

_____ (1991b). 'Marital expectations as dramatized in the Hindu marriage rituals of ancient India'. In: I. Julia Leslie (ed.): *Roles and Rituals for Hindu Women.* London: Pinter, pp. 47–67.

_____ (1992a). 'Crime and punishment in Hindu law and under modern Indian law'. *Recueils de la Société Jean Bodin,* Vol. LVIII, pt. 4, Bruxelles: De Boeck Université, pp. 295–334.

_____ (1992b). 'The role of custom in Hindu law'. *Recueils de la Société Jean Bodin.* Vol. LIII, pt. 3, Bruxelles: De Boeck Université, pp. 311–47.

_____ (1992c). 'The Indian experience and its lessons for Britain'. In: Bob Hepple and Erika M. Szyszczak (eds): *Discrimination: The Limits of Law.* London: Mansell, pp. 300–43.

_____ (1993a). 'Asians in Britain and the question of adaptation to a new legal order: Asian laws in Britain?'. In: Milton Israel and N.K. Wagle (eds): *Ethnicity, Identity, Migration: The South Asian Context.* Toronto: University of Toronto, Centre for South Asian Studies, pp. 238–68.

_____ (1993b). 'Law and religion: The Hindu and Jain approach'. In: N.N. Bhattacharya (ed.): *Jainism and Prakrit in Ancient and Medieval India: Essays for Prof. Jagdish Chandra Jain.* New Delhi: Manohar, pp. 361–74.

_____ (1994). 'Maintenance for divorced Muslim wives'. In 1994(1) *KLT,* Journal section, pp. 45–52. (Reprinted in Menski 2001, pp. 238–46).

_____ (1995a). 'Hinduism'. In Seymour Martin Lipset (ed.): *The Encyclopedia of Democracy.* Washington DC: Congressional Quarterly Books, pp. 561–5.

——(1995b). 'Widow's right to property: Prejudices against remarried women'. *Manushi*, no. 89, July–August, pp. 15–16. (Reprinted in Menski 2001: 33–5).

——(1996a). 'Hinduism'. In: Peggy Morgan and Clive Lawton (eds): *Ethical Issues in Six Religious Traditions*. Edinburgh: Edinburgh University Press, pp. 1–54.

——(1996b). 'Introduction: The democratisation of justice in India'. In: Gurjeet Singh (ed.): *Law of Consumer Protection in India: Justice Within Reach*. New Delhi: Deep & Deep, pp. xxv–liv.

——(1998a). 'Sati: A review article'. *B.S.O.A.S.*, Vol. 61, no. 1, pp. 74–81.

—— (ed.) (1998b). *South Asians and the Dowry Problem*. Stoke-on-Trent: Trentham Books.

——(2000a). *Comparative Law in a Global Context: The Legal Systems of Asia and Africa*. London: Platinium.

——(2000b). 'From imperial domination to bhaji on the beach: Fifty years of South Asian laws at SOAS'. In: Ian Edge (ed.): *Comparative Law in Global Perspective*. Ardsley, NY: Transnational Publishers, pp. 121–44.

——(2001). *Modern Indian Family Law*. Richmond: Curzon.

—— (2002). 'Hindu law as a religious system'. In: Andrew Huxley (ed.): *Religion, Law and Tradition*. London: RoutledgeCurzon, pp. 108–26.

Menski, Werner F., Ahmad Rafay Alam, and Mehreen Kasuri Raza (2000). *Public Interest Litigation in Pakistan*. London and Karachi: Platinium and Pakistan Law House.

Menski, Werner F. and Tahmina Rahman (1988). 'Hindus and the law in Bangladesh'. *South Asia Research*, Vol. 8, no. 2, pp. 111–31.

Meyer, Johann Jakob (1952). *Sexual Life in Ancient India*. Calcutta: The Standard Literature Co.

Michaels, Axel (2001a). 'The pandit as a legal adviser: *rājaguru, rājapurohita* and *dharmādhikārin*'. In: Axel Michaels (ed.): *The Pandit: Traditional Scholarship in India*. New Delhi: Manohar, pp. 61–77.

——(ed.) (2001b). *The Pandit: Traditional Scholarship in India*. New Delhi: Manohar. (South Asia Institute, New Delhi Branch. Heidelberg University South Asian Studies No. XXXVIII. Festschrift Parameswara Aithal).

Midha, Seema (1990). 'Women, law and social justice'. In: Leelamma Devasia (ed.): *Women in India: Equality, Social Justice and Development*. New Delhi: Indian Social Institute, pp. 69–78.

Miller, Jeanine (1985). *The Vision of Cosmic Order in the Vedas*. London: Routledge & Kegan Paul.

Minattur, Joseph (1980). 'Women and the law: Constitutional rights and continuing inequalities'. In: Alfred de Souza (ed.): *Women in Contemporary India and South Asia*. New Delhi: Manohar, pp. 165–78.

Mishra, Srikanta (1994). *Ancient Hindu Marriage Law and Practice*. New Delhi: Deep & Deep.

Mitra, Veda (1965). *Happy Married Life in Ancient India.* New Delhi: Arya Book Depot.

Mitter, Sara S. (1992). *Dharma's Daughters: Contemporary Indian Women and Hindu Culture.* New Delhi: Penguin.

Monier-Williams, Monier (1976). *Sanskrit-English Dictionary.* Indian edition. New Delhi: Munshiram Manoharlal.

Monsoor, Taslima (1998). *From Patriarchy to Gender Equity: Family Law and Its Impact on Women in Bangladesh.* Dhaka: UBL.

Moore, Sally Falk (1978). *Law as Process: An Anthropological Approach.* London: Routledge & Kegan Paul.

_____ (1986). *Social Facts and Fabrications: "Customary" Law on Kilimanjaro 1880–1980.* Cambridge: Cambridge University Press.

Moore-Gilbert, B. (2000). *Postcolonial Theory: Contexts, Practices, Politics.* London: Verso.

Morigiwa, Yasutomo (ed.) (1998). *Law in a Changing World: Asian Alternatives.* Stuttgart: Franz Steiner Verlag.

Morley, D. (1996). 'EurAm, modernity, reason and alterity: Or, postmodernism, the highest stage of cultural imperialism?'. In: D. Morley and K.H. Chen (eds): *Stuart Hall: Critical Dialogues in Cultural Studies.* London: Routledge, pp. 326–60.

Mukhopadhyay, M. (1985). *Silver Shackles: Women and Development in India.* Oxford: Oxfam.

Murthy, K.S.N. (1969). 'Marriages of Hindu minors'. *AIR* 1969, Journal section, pp. 72–5.

Nair, Janaki (1996). *Women and Law in Colonial India: A Social History.* New Delhi: Kali for Women.

Nair, P.T. (1978). *Marriage and Dowry in India.* Calcutta: Minerva.

Nakano, Gisho (1935). *Indo shiso: Hosei shiso.* (Indian thought: Legal system and thought). Tokyo: Iwanami Shoten. (In Japanese).

_____ (1974). *Indo ho no kenkyu.* (Research on Indian law). Wakayama: Nihon Indo Gakkei. (In Japanese).

Nanda, Ved P. and Surya Prakash Sinha (eds) (1996). *Hindu Law and Legal Theory.* New York: New York University Press.

Nandy, Ashis (1980). *At the Edge of Psychology: Essays in Politics and Culture.* Delhi: Oxford University Press.

_____ (1983). *The Intimate Enemy: Loss and Recovery of Self Under Colonialism.* New Delhi: Oxford University Press.

_____ (1990). 'The politics of secularism and the recovery of religious tolerance'. In: Veena Das (ed.): *Mirrors of Violence: Communities, Riots and Survivors in South Asia.* Delhi: Oxford University Press, pp. 69–93.

——— (1999). 'The twilight of certitudes: Secularism, Hindu nationalism and other masks of deculturation'. In: Veena Das, Dipankar Gupta, and Patricia Uberoi (eds): *Tradition, Pluralism and Identity: In honour of T.N. Madan.* New Delhi: Sage Publications, pp. 401–19.

——— (2001). *An Ambiguous Journey to the City. The Village and Other Odd Ruins of the Self in the Indian Imagination.* New Delhi: Oxford University Press.

——— (2002). *Time Warps: Silent and Evasive Pasts in Indian Politics and Religion.* London: Hurst & Co.

Nankani, Sandhya (ed.) (2000). *Breaking the Silence: Domestic Violence in the South Asian-American Community.* Boston: Xlibris.

Nanavati, R.I. (ed.) (1998). *All-India Oriental Conference: Thirty-ninth Session (13–15 October 1998): Vadodara: Summary of Papers.* Vadodara: Oriental Institute, M.S. University of Baroda.

Narang, Sudesh (ed.) (1988). *Dharmasastra in Contemporary Times.* Delhi: Nag Publishers.

Nelken, David and Johannes Feest (eds) (2001). *Adapting Legal Cultures.* Oxford and Portland, Oregon: Hart Publishing.

Nijjar, Manjit Singh (1994). *Nullity of Marriage Under Hindu Law.* New Delhi: Deep & Deep.

Nikam, N.A. and R. McKeon (1962). *The Edicts of Aśoka.* Bombay: Asia Publishing House.

Örücü, Esin (1999a). 'Comparative law in British courts'. In: Ulrich Drobnig and Sjef van Erp (eds): *The Use of Comparative Law by Courts.* The Hague, London, and Boston: Kluwer Law International, pp. 253–95.

——— (1999b). *Critical Comparative Law: Considering Paradoxes for Legal Systems in Transition.* Dewenter: Kluwer.

O'Flaherty, Wendy Doniger and J.D.M. Derrett (eds) (1978). *The Concept of Duty in South Asia.* New Delhi and London: Vikas and SOAS.

Ojha, P.N. (1978). *Aspects of Medieval Indian Society and Culture.* Delhi: B.R. Publishing.

Olivelle, Patrick (1993). *The āśrama System: The History and Hermeneutics of a Religious Institution.* New York and Oxford: Oxford University Press.

——— (2000). *Dharmaśāstras: The Law Codes of Āpastamba, Gautama, Baudhāyana and Vasishtha. Annotated Text and Translation.* Delhi: Motilal Banarsidass.

Omvedt, Gail (1993). *Reinventing Revolution: New Social Movements and the Socialist Tradition in India.* Armonk and London: East Gate and M.E. Sharpe.

Oommen, T.K. (1990). *State and Society in India: Studies in Nation-building.* New Delhi: Sage.

Panchamukhi, V.R. (1999). 'Vedic research and studies: Past, present and future'. *Bhavan's Journal*, Vol. 46, no. 1, 15 August, pp. 205–21.

Pandey, R.B. (1969). *Hindu saṃskāras.* Delhi: Motilal Banarsidass.

Pandey, Vikash N. and Akhileshwar Pathak (1995). 'Sociology of law in India: Postscripts and prospects. *Economic and Political Weekly,* Vol. 30, 5–12 August, pp. 1974–7.

Panikkar, Kavalam Madhava (1960). *The State and the Citizen.* 2nd edition. London: Asia Publishing House.

Pant, Prafulla C. (2000). *The Law of Marriage, Divorce and Other Matrimonial Disputes.* 2nd ed. New Delhi: Orient.

Parashar, Archana (1992). *Women and Family Law Reform in India: Uniform Civil Code and Gender Equality.* New Delhi: Sage.

_____ (1999). 'Feminism in Indian legal education'. In: Amita Dhanda and Archana Parashar (eds): *Engendering Law: Essays in Honour of Lotika Sarkar.* Lucknow: Eastern Book Co., pp. 89–116.

Parekh, Bhikhu (1996). 'The nature of the modern state'. In: D.L. Sheth and Ashis Nandy (eds): *The Multiverse of Democracy: Essays in Honour of Rajni Kothari.* New Delhi: Sage, pp. 27–49.

Parekh, Bhikhu (1997). *Gandhi.* Oxford and New York: Oxford University Press.

Parekh, Bhikhu (2000). *Report of the Commission on the Future of Multi-ethnic Britain.* London: Profile Books.

Parker, Kunal M. (2001). 'Observations on the historical destruction of separate legal regimes'. In: Gerald James Larson (ed.): *Religion and Personal Law in Secular India: A Call to Judgment.* Bloomington and Indianapolis: Indiana University Press, pp. 184–99.

Pathak, D. (1986). *Hindu Law and its Constitutional Aspects.* New Delhi: Capital Law House.

Pawate, I.S. (1975). *Dāya-Vibhāga or the Individualization of Communal Property and the Communalization of Individual Property in the Mitakshara law.* 2nd ed. Dharwar: Karnatak University.

Pearl, David (1986). *Family Law and the Immigrant Communities.* Bristol: Jordan & Sons.

Pearl, David and Werner Menski (1998). *Muslim Family Law.* 3rd ed. London: Sweet & Maxwell.

Peters, Anne and Heiner Schwenke (2000). 'Comparative law beyond post-modernism'. *International and Comparative Law Quarterly,* Vol. 49, October, pp. 800–34.

Phillips, D.Z. (ed.) (1996). *Can Religion Be Explained Away?* Basingstoke, London and New York: Macmillan Press and St. Martin's Press.

Popkin, William D. (2001). 'Some continuing issues'. In: Gerald James Larson (ed.): *Religion and Personal Law in Secular India: A Call to Judgment.* Bloomington and Indianapolis: Indiana University Press, pp. 330–47.

Poulter, Sebastian (1986). *English Law and Ethnic Minority Customs.* London: Butterworths.

____ (1995). 'Multiculturalism and human rights for Muslim families in English law'. In: Michael King (ed.): *God's Law Versus State Law.* London: Grey Seal, pp. 81–7.

Price, Pamela (1979). 'Rajadharma in Ramnad, land litigation and largess'. *Contributions to Indian Sociology,* Vol. 13, no. 2, new series, pp. 207–40.

____ (1989). 'Ideology and ethnicity under British Imperial rule: 'Brahmans', lawyers and kin-caste rules in Madras Presidency'. *Modern Asian Studies,* Vol. 23, no. 1, pp. 151–77.

Pujari, Premlata and Vijay Kumari Kaushik (1994). *Women Power in India.* Vols I–III. Delhi: Kanishka.

Punj, Amita (2001). *L.S. Shastri Hindu law digest, 1837–2000.* 5th ed. New Delhi: Butterworths India.

Purohit, S.K. (1994). *Ancient Indian Legal Philosophy: Its Relevance to Contemporary Jurisprudential Thought.* New Delhi: Deep & Deep.

Pylee, M.V. (2000). *Our Constitution, Government and Politics.* Delhi: Universal.

Qureshi, Mohammed (1978). *Marriage and Matrimonial Remedies: A Uniform Civil Code for India.* Delhi: Concept.

Rai, Raghu and Inderjit Badhwar (1986). 'Child marriage: Wedding of the dolls'. *India Today,* 15 June, pp. 34–43.

Rajan, Nalini (1998). *Secularism, Democracy, Justice: Implications of Rawlsian Principles in India.* New Delhi: Sage.

Rajan, Rajeswari Sunder (ed.) (1999). *Signposts: Gender Issues in Post-independence India.* New Delhi: Kali for Women.

Rambilass, Bisram (2001). *Vaidik vivah vidhi (Vaidik wedding ceremony).* Durban: Veda Niketan.

Ramesam, Vepa (1946). *Principles of Hindu Law by the Right Honourable Sir Dinshah Fardunji Mulla.* 10th ed. Calcutta: Eastern Law House.

Rao, R. Jaganmohana (1975). 'P. Appalasuramma v. G. Ganpatlu (A critique)'. In: 1975 (II) *An WR,* Journal section, pp. 1–7.

Rau, Wilhelm (1957). *Staat und Gesellschaft im alten Indien. Nach den Brāhmaṇa Texten dargestellt.* Wiesbaden: Harrassowitz.

Reddy, G.B. (1999). *Women and the Law.* 2nd ed. Hyderabad: Gogia Law Agency.

Renteln, Alison Dundes (1990). *International Human Rights: Universalism Versus Relativism.* Newbury Park: Sage.

Riles, Annelise (ed.) (2001). *Rethinking the Masters of Comparative Law.* Oxford and Portland, Oregon: Hart Publishing.

Robb, Peter (ed.) (1993). *Society and Ideology: Essays in South Asian History Presented to Professor K. A. Ballhatchet.* Delhi: Oxford University Press.

____ (1997). *The Concept of Race in South Asia.* Delhi: Oxford University Press.

Roberts, Simon (1979). *Order and Dispute: An Introduction to Legal Anthropology.* New York: St. Martin's Press.

Rocher, Ludo (2002). *Jīmūtavāhana's Dāyabhāga. The Hindu Law of Inheritance in Bengal: Edited and Translated with an Introduction and Notes.* Oxford: Oxford University Press.

Rosen, Lawrence (1989). *The Anthropology of Justice: Law as Culture in Islamic Society.* Cambridge: Cambridge University Press.

Ross, Aileen D. (1961). *The Hindu Family in its Urban Setting.* Delhi: Oxford University Press.

Rothermund, Dietmar (ed.) (2000). *The Role of the State in South Asia and Other Essays.* New Delhi: Manohar.

Roy, Kumkum (1995). '"Where women are worshipped, there the gods rejoice". The mirage of the ancestress of the Hindu woman'. In: Tanika Sarkar and Urvashi Butalia (eds): *Women and the Hindu Right: A Collection of Essays.* New Delhi: Kali for Women, pp. 10–28.

Roy, Sripati (1911). *Customs and Customary Law in British India.* Calcutta: Thacker, Spinks & Co.

Rudolph, Lloyd I. and Susanne Hoeber Rudolph (1987). *In Pursuit of Lakshmi: The Political Economy of the Indian State.* Chicago and London: University of Chicago Press.

_____ (2001). 'Living with difference in India: Legal pluralism and legal universalism in historical context'. In: Gerald James Larson (ed.) (2001). *Religion and Personal Law in Secular India: A Call to Judgment.* Bloomington and Indianapolis: Indiana University Press, pp. 36–65.

Rushdie, S. (1992). *The Satanic Verses.* New York: The Consortium.

Sagade, Jaya (1981). 'Law and social reforms in rural India with special reference to child marriages'. In: (1981) 1 *SCJ*, Journal section, pp. 27–35.

_____ (1989). 'Polygamy and women's right of maintenance: Survey of judicial decisions'. *JILI*, Vol. 31, no. 3, July–September, pp. 336–45.

Said, Edward W. (1978). *Orientalism.* New York: Pantheon.

Sampath, B.N. (1969). 'Marriageable age, consent and soundness of mind in Indian matrimonial law: A plea for rationalization'. *Banaras Law Journal*, Vol. 5, pp. 28–52.

_____ (1972a). 'Can a civil court issue an injunction restraining a husband from entering into a bigamous marriage?'. In: 1972(I) *MLJ*, Journal section, pp. 2–6.

_____ (1972b). 'Child marriage: Revision of marriageable age and its effective implementation'. *Lawasia*, Vol. 3, pp. 386–402.

Sangari, Kumkum (1995). 'Politics of diversity: Religious communities and multiple patriarchies'. *Economic and Political Weekly*, Vol. XXX, no. 51, 23 and 30 December, pp. 3287–310 and 3381–9.

Sarkar, G. (1940). *Hindu Law.* 8th ed. Calcutta: Sarkar & Sons.

Sarkar, Lotika (1992). 'Gender justice in legislation—Nehru era: One step forward, one step backward'. In: Upendra Baxi (ed.): *Dimensions of Law: Festschrift in Honour of Prof. S.P. Sathe*. Pune: Indian Law Society, pp. 186–202.

Sarkar, Lotika and B. Sivaramayya (eds) (1994). *Women and Law: Contemporary Problems*. New Delhi: Vikas.

Sarkar, Tanika (1993). 'Rhetoric against age of consent: Resisting colonial reason and death of a child-wife'. *Economic and Political Weekly*, Vol. XXVIII, no. 36, 4 September, pp. 1869–78.

Sarkar, Tanika and Urvashi Butalia (eds) (1995). *Women and the Hindu Right: A Collection of Essays*. New Delhi: Kali for Women.

Sarup, M. (1993). *An Introductory Guide to Post-structuralism and Postmodernism*. 2nd ed. Athens: University of Georgia Press.

Sastri, A. Mahadeva (1988). *The Vedic Law of Marriage or the Emancipation of Woman*. Reprint. New Delhi and Madras: Asian Educational Services.

Sathe, S.P. (1995). 'Uniform civil code: Implications of Supreme Court intervention'. *Economic and Political Weekly*, Vol. 30, 2 September, pp. 2165–6.

——— (2001). 'Seervai, legal positivism and Indian democracy'. In: Venkat Iyer (ed.): *Constitutional Perspectives: Essays in Honour and Memory of H.M. Seervai*. Delhi: Universal, pp. 38–52.

——— (2002). *Judicial Activism in India. Transgressing Borders and Enforcing Limits*. New Delhi: Oxford University Press.

Saxena, Poonam Pradhan (1993). 'Concept of matrimonial property'. In: Kusum (ed.): *Women—March Towards Dignity: Social and Legal Perspectives*. New Delhi: Regency, pp. 74–86.

Saxena, Sarojini (1993). *Femi Juris: Law Relating to Woman in India*. Indore: India Publishing House.

Sayyid, Bobby S. (1997). *A Fundamental Fear: Eurocentrism and the Emergence of Islamism*. London and New York: Zed Books.

Seervai, H.M. (1991). *Constitutional Law of India*. Vols I–III. 4th ed. Bombay: N.M. Tripathi.

Sehgal, B.P. Singh (1989). *Population Control and the Law: Problems, Policies, Remedial Measures*. New Delhi: Deep & Deep.

Sen, Bisakha (1998). 'Why does dowry still persist in India? An economic analysis using human capital'. In: Werner Menski (ed.): *South Asians and the Dowry Problem*. Stoke-on-Trent: Trentham Books, pp. 75–95.

Sen, Samita (2000). 'Offences against marriage. Negotiating custom in colonial Bengal'. In: Mary E. John and Janaki Nair (eds): *A Question of Silence? The Sexual Economies of Modern India*. London and New York: Zed Books, pp. 77–110.

Settar, S. (1989). *Inviting Death. Indian Attitudes Towards the Ritual Death*. Leiden et al.: E.J. Brill.

Shams, Shamsuddin (ed.) (1991). *Women, Law and Social Change.* New Delhi: Ashish.

Sharan, B.R. (1992). *Status of Indian Women: A Historical Perspective.* New Delhi: Uppal.

Sharda, Neel K. (1988). *The Legal, Economic and Social Status of the Indian Child.* New Delhi: National Book.

Sharma, B.K. (1989). *Inter-spousal Conflicts in Relation to Maintenance, Property and Custody of Children.* New Delhi: Deep & Deep.

Sharma, B.K. and Vijay Nagpal (1992). 'Let them bury the marriage breakdown theory: Its Indian perspective'. *Panjab University Law Review,* Vol. 39, no. 1, pp. 83–97.

Sharma, Mani Ram (1993). *Marriage in Ancient India.* Delhi: Agam Kala Prakashan.

Sharma, Narendra Nath (1976). *Āśvalāyana Gṛhyasūtram.* Delhi: Eastern Book Linkers.

Sharma, Preeti (1990). *Hindu Women's Right to Maintenance.* New Delhi: Deep & Deep.

Sharma, Vijay (1994). *Protection to Women in Matrimonial Home.* New Delhi: Deep & Deep.

Shastri, Madhu (1990). *Status of Hindu Women. A Study of Legislative Trends and Judicial Behaviour.* Jaipur: RBSA.

Sheth, D.L. and Ashis Nandy (eds) (1996). *The Multiverse of Democracy: Essays in Honour of Rajni Kothari.* New Delhi: Sage.

Shourie, Arun (1993). *A Secular Agenda: For Strengthening our Country, for Welding it.* New Delhi: HarperCollins.

—— (2001). *Courts and their Judgments: Promises, Prerequisites, Consequences.* New Delhi: Rupa & Co.

Shrivastava, Ashok Kumar (1981). *Hindu Society in the Sixteenth Century.* New Delhi: Milind.

Singh, Andrea Menefee (1980). 'The study of women in South Asia: Some current methodological and research issues'. In: Alfred de Souza (ed.): *Women in Contemporary India and South Asia.* New Delhi: Manohar, pp. 61–93.

Singh, Chhatrapati (1990). 'Dharmasastras and contemporary jurisprudence'. *JILI,* Vol. 32, no. 2, pp. 179–88.

Singh, Gurjeet (1996). *Law of Consumer Protection in India: Justice Within Reach.* New Delhi: Deep & Deep.

Singh, Indu Prakash (1989). *Women, Law and Social Change in India.* London: Sangam.

—— (1990). *Indian Women: The Captured Beings.* New Delhi: Intellectual.

Singh, Ranbir (1991). 'Women and compulsory registration of Hindu marriage: Need for uniform legislation'. In: Shamsuddin Shams (ed.): *Women, Law and Social Change.* New Delhi: Ashish, pp. 39–54.

Singh, Shiv Sahai (1993). *Unification of Divorce Laws in India.* New Delhi: Deep & Deep.

Singh, Shyam (1990). 'Bigamy—An impediment to matrimonial relief under Hindu law'. In: K.L. Bhatia (ed.): *Judicial Activism and Social Change.* New Delhi: Deep & Deep, pp. 428–35.

Sinha, Raghuvir (1993). *Dynamics of Change in the Modern Hindu Family.* New Delhi: Concept.

Sinha, S.N. and N.K. Basu (1992). *The History of Marriage and Prostitution: (Vedas to Vatsyayana).* New Delhi: Khama.

Sivaramayya, B. (1988). 'Dharmaśāstra and contemporary Hindu law'. In Sudesh Narang (ed.): *Dharmasastra in Contemporary Times.* Delhi: Nag Publishers, pp. 67–76.

Sivaramayya, B. (1993). 'Irretrievable breakdown of marriage as a ground for divorce'. In: Kusum (ed.): *Women - March Towards Dignity: Social and Legal Perspectives.* New Delhi: Regency, pp. 56–62.

Smith, Graham and J.D.M. Derrett (1975). 'Hindu judicial administration in pre-British times and its lesson for today'. *Journal of the American Oriental Society,* Vol. 95, no. 3, July–September, pp. 417–23.

Sontheimer, Günther-Dietz (1977). *The Joint Hindu Family. Its Evolution as a Legal Institution.* New Delhi: Munshiram Manoharlal.

Sontheimer, Günther-Dietz and Parameswara Kota Aithal (eds) (1982). *Indology and Law. Studies in Honour of Professor J. Duncan M. Derrett.* Wiesbaden: Franz Steiner Verlag.

Sontheimer, Günther-Dietz and Hermann Kulke (eds) (1989). *Hinduism Reconsidered.* New Delhi: Manohar.

Sorabjee, Soli (1991). 'Women, Constitution and the courts.' In: Shamsuddin Shams (ed.): *Women, Law and Social Change.* New Delhi: Ashish, pp. 259–66.

Spivak, Gayatri (1988). 'Can the subaltern speak?'. In: C. Nelson and L. Grossberg (eds): *Marxism and the Interpretation of Culture.* London: Macmillan Press, pp. 271–313.

____ (1990). *The Postcolonial Critic.* London: Routledge.

____ (2000). 'Discussion: An afterword on the New Subaltern'. In: Partha Chatterjee and Pradeep Jeganathan (eds): *Community, Gender and Violence: Subaltern Studies XI.* London: Hurst & Co., pp. 305–34.

Sprockhoff, Joachim Friedrich (1976). *Saṃnyāsa. Quellenstudien zur Askese im Hinduismus. I. Untersuchungen über die Saṃnyāsa-Upaniṣads.* Wiesbaden: Franz Steiner GmbH.

Srivastava, K.C. (1978). 'The Hindu Marriage Act, 1955'. In: V. Bagga (ed.): *Studies in the Hindu Marriage and the Special Marriage Acts.* Bombay: N.M. Tripathi, pp. 98–109.

Stein, Burton (1997). 'The segmentary state: Interim reflections'. In: Hermann Kulke (ed.): *The State in India 1000–1700.* Delhi: Oxford University Press, pp. 134–61.

Stein, Burton (1998). *A History of India.* Oxford: Blackwell.

Subba Rao, G.C.V. (1994). *Family Law in India.* 6th ed. Hyderabad: S. Gogia & Co.

Subedi, Surya P. (1999). 'Are the principles of human rights "Western" ideas? An analysis of the claim of the "Asian" concept of human rights from the perspectives of Hinduism'. *California Western International Law Journal,* Vol. 30, no. 1, Fall, pp. 45–69.

Subramanian, Narendra (1999). *Ethnicity and Populist Mobilization: Political Parties, Citizens and Democracy in South India.* Oxford: Oxford University Press.

Swarup, Hem Lata (ed.) (1991). *Women, Politics and Religion.* Etawah: A.C. Brothers.

Talbot, Ian (2000). *India and Pakistan.* London and New York: Arnold and Oxford University Press.

Tamanaha, Brian Z. (1993). 'The folly of the "social scientific" concept of legal pluralism'. *Journal of Law and Society,* Vol. 20, no. 2, pp. 192–217.

—— (2001). *A General Jurisprudence of Law and Society.* Oxford: Oxford University Press.

Tanase, Takao (2001). 'The empty space of the modern in Japanese law discourse'. In: David Nelken and Johannes Feest (eds): *Adapting Legal Cultures.* Oxford and Portland, Oregon: Hart Publishing, pp. 187–98.

Tarachand, K.C. (1991). *Dēvadāsi Custom: Rural Social Structure and Flesh Markets.* New Delhi: Reliance.

Teja, Mohinderjit Kaur (1993). *Dowry: A Study in Attitudes and Practices.* New Delhi: Inter-India.

Thaplyal, Abha (1986). 'Proving bigamy: Unfair burden?'. In: 1986(4) *SCC,* Journal section, pp. 11–18.

Tharamangalam, Joseph (1995). 'Indian social scientists and critique of secularism'. *Economic and Political Weekly,* no. 30, 4 March, pp. 457–61.

Thomas, P. (2000). *Women Marriage and Customs in India.* New Delhi: Mohit.

Tiwari, Y.K. (1991). 'Status of Hindu woman and efficacy of protective legislations'. In: Shamsuddin Shams (ed.): *Women, Law and Social Change.* New Delhi: Ashish, pp. 21–38.

Toward Comparative Law in the 21st Century (1998). Edited by the Institute of Comparative Law in Japan. Tokyo: Chuo University Press.

Towards Equality. (1974). Report of the Committee on the Status of Women in India. New Delhi: Ministry of Education and Social Welfare, Government of India.

Upadhyay, H.C. (1991). *Status of Women in India.* Vols I–II. New Delhi: Anmol.

Vaid, Sudesh and Kumkum Sangari (1991). 'Institutions, beliefs, ideologies: Widow immolation in contemporary Rajasthan'. *Economic and Political Weekly,* Vol. 26, no. 17, 27 April, pp. 2–18.

van Creveld, Martin (1999). *The Rise and Decline of the State.* Cambridge: Cambridge University Press.

Variar, K. Sreedhara (1985). *Indian Family Law.* 6th ed. Trivandrum: Janatha.

Varma, Rameshwari (2000). *Girl Child and Family Development in Indian Society.* New Delhi: Anamika.

Vatuk, Sylvia (2001). '"Where will she go? What will she do?": Paternalism toward women in the administration of Muslim personal law in contemporary India'. In: Gerald James Larson (ed.) (2001). *Religion and Personal Law in Secular India. A Call to Judgment.* Bloomington and Indianapolis: Indiana University Press, pp. 226–48.

Venkataramiah, E.S. (1982). 'Certain aspects of adoption prevailing amongst the Hindus'. In: G.D. Sontheimer and P.K. Aithal (eds): *Indology and Law: Studies in Honour of Professor J. Duncan M. Derrett.* Wiesbaden: Franz Steiner Verlag, pp. 225–47.

Verma, Arvind (2001). 'The uniform civil code debate: Lessons from the criminal procedures'. In: Gerald James Larson (ed.): *Religion and Personal Law in Secular India. A Call to Judgment.* Bloomington and Indianapolis: Indiana University Press, pp. 124–41.

Verma, Binita (1993). *Exploitation of Women Labour in India.* New Delhi: Deep & Deep.

Verma, S.K. and Kusum (eds) (2000). *Fifty Years of the Supreme Court of India: Its Grasp and Reach.* New Delhi: Indian Law Institute and Oxford University Press.

Virdi, P.K. (1972). *The Grounds for Divorce in Hindu and English Law.* Delhi: Motilal Banarsidass.

von Stietencron, Heinrich (1989). 'Hinduism: on the proper use of a deceptive term'. In: Günther-Dietz Sontheimer and Hermann Kulke (eds): *Hinduism Reconsidered.* New Delhi: Manohar, pp. 11–27.

Vyas, Mohan K. (1993). *National Integration and the Law.* New Delhi: Deep & Deep.

Watase, Nobuyuki (1990). *Manu hoten. Hindukyo sekai no genkei.* (*The Code of Manu. The prototype for the world of Hinduism*). Tokyo: Chuo Koron Sha. (In Japanese).

Weinberger-Thomas, Catherine (1999). *Ashes of Immortality: Widow-burning in India.* Chicago and London: The University of Chicago Press.

White, Sarah C. (1992). *Arguing with the Crocodile. Gender and Class in Bangladesh.* Dhaka: University Press.

Winternitz, Maurice (1968). *Geschichte der indischen Literatur.* Vols 1–3. Reprint. Stuttgart: K.F. Koehler Verlag.

Winternitz, Maurice (1985). *History of Indian Literature.* Translated from German into English by Subhadra Jha. Reprint. Delhi: Motilal.

Yadav, R.R. (2001). 'Conceptualisation of justice'. In: *AIR* 2001, Journal section, pp. 267–70.

Yamazaki, Toshio (1982). 'Indo no ho seido'. (The Indian legal system). In: Toshio Yamazaki and Nobuyuki Yasuda (eds): *Ajia shokoku no ho seido.* (*Legal Systems in Asian Countries*). Tokyo: Institute for Developing Economies, pp. 265–312. (In Japanese).

Yamazaki, Toshio (1985). 'Hindu ho' (Hindu law). In: Shozaburo Kimura et al. (eds): *Chusei no ho to kenryoku* (*Medieval Law and Authority*). Tokyo: Gakusei Sha, pp. 385–99. (In Japanese).

Yamazaki, Toshio and Nobuyuki Yasuda (eds) (1982). *Ajia shokoku no ho seido.* (*Legal Systems in Asian Countries*). Tokyo: Institute for Developing Economies. (In Japanese).

Yang, Anand A. (1989). *The Limited Raj. Agrarian Relations in Colonial India, Saran District, 1793–1920.* Delhi: Oxford University Press.

Yilmaz, Ihsan (1999). *Dynamic Pluralism and the Reconstruction of Unofficial Muslim Laws in England, Turkey and Pakistan.* London: SOAS (Unpublished PhD thesis).

Young, Robert J.C. (2001). *Postcolonialism: An Historical Introduction.* Oxford: Blackwell.

Index

This includes a glossary of technical terms. Several entries may be found under 'Hindu law' or under the respective key word itself.